Administrative Justice *in* China

JCL Studies in Comparative Law: Second Series

Series Editors

Professor William E. Butler

Professor Michael Palmer

1. W. E. Butler and O. V. Kresin (eds.), *Discovering the Unexpected: Comparative Legal Studies in Eastern and Central Europe* (Clark, New Jersey, Talbot Publishing, 2021). ISBN 9781616196554

2. Simon Palmer and Zhai Xiaobo (eds.), *Bentham Around the World* (Clark, New Jersey, Talbot Publishing, 2021). ISBN 9781616196561

3. O. V. Kresin, *Comparative Law in Warsaw: 1800-1835*, transl. W. E. Butler (Clark, New Jersey, Talbot Publishing, 2022) ISBN 9781616196585

4. W. E. Butler and O. V. Kresin (eds.) *The Comparative Method in the Science of Law* by Lev Rebet (Clark, New Jersey, Talbot Publishing, 2022) ISBN 9781616196653

5. Horst Dippel, *Modern Constitutionalism*, 2 vols. (Clark, New Jersey, Talbot Publishing, 2022) ISBN 9781616196769

6. Stephan Meder, *Legal Machines* (Clark, New Jersey, Talbot Publishing, 2023) ISBN 9781616196813

7. Ama F. Hammond, Folashade Rose Adegbite, Maame Yaa A. Mensa-Bonsu, Prosper Batariwah (eds.), *Family Law in Africa: Perspectives on Selected Systems of Marriage* (Clark, New Jersey, Talbot Publishing, 2023) ISBN 9781616196844

8. William E. Butler and Oleksiy V. Kresin (eds.), *The World Picture of Comparative Law* (Clark, New Jersey, Talbot Publishing, 2024) ISBN 9781616196905

9. Carmelo Massimo De Iuliis (ed. & trans.), *Gottfried Wilhelm Leibniz: Model of Certainty or Demonstrations in Law, Expounded in the Doctrine of Conditions* (Clark, New Jersey, Talbot Publishing, 2025) ISBN 978-1-61619-693-6

10. Michael Palmer, Ling Zhou and Yang Lin (eds), *Administrative Justice in China: Institutional Conflicts and Governance Transformation* (Clark, New Jersey, Talbot Publishing, 2026) ISBN 978-1-61619-703-2

Administrative Justice *in* China

INSTITUTIONAL CONFLICTS AND GOVERNANCE TRANSFORMATION

EDITED BY Michael Palmer, Ling Zhou AND Yang Lin

TALBOT PUBLISHING
Clark, New Jersey

ISBN: 978-1-61619-703-2

TALBOT PUBLISHING
AN IMPRINT OF
The Lawbook Exchange, Ltd.
33 Terminal Avenue
Clark, New Jersey 07066-1321

Please see our website for a selection of our other publications and fine facsimile reprints of classic works of legal history www.lawbookexchange.com

Library of Congress Cataloging-in-Publication Data

Names: Palmer, Michael J. E., 1944- editor | Zhou, Ling, 1987- editor | Lin, Yang (Editor) editor
Title: Administrative justice in China : institutional conflicts and governance transformation / Michael Palmer, Ling Zhou, and Yang Lin, editors.
Description: First edition. | Clark, New Jersey : Talbot Publishing, an Imprint of The Lawbook Exchange, Ltd, 2026. | Series: JCL studies in comparative law, second series | Includes bibliographical references and index. | Summary: "This volume examines the evolution of administrative processes and institutional tensions in contemporary China, focusing on the balance between procedural innovation and the structural constraints of the party-state"-- Provided by publisher.
Identifiers: LCCN 2026023989 | ISBN 9781616197032 hardcover
Subjects: LCSH: Administrative procedure--China | Administrative law--China | Judicial review of administrative acts--China | Justice, Administration of--China
Classification: LCC KNQ2764 .A94 2026
LC record available at https://lccn.loc.gov/2026023989

Printed in the United States of America on acid-free paper

CONTENTS

Preface and Acknowledgments		vii
Contributors' Profiles xv		xi
Michael Palmer, Zhou Ling and Lin Yang	Introduction: Between Legal Form and Political Control	3

PART I: HISTORICAL FOUNDATIONS AND INSTITUTIONAL EVOLUTION

Mou Xiankui	Why Not American-Style Judicial Review? Judicial Power and the Constitutional Interpretation System in China's Northern Warlords Government Era (1912-1928)	17
Michael Palmer	Administrative Justice and the Transformation of China's Population Policies	38

PART II: JUDICIAL POWER AND REVIEW MECHANISMS

Björn Ahl	The Development of the Due Process Principle in post-2013 China	65
Xiao Shiling and	Judicial Review of Administrative Rules:	
Yang Lin	Incremental Expansion of Judicial Power	91
Yuhong Zhao	Adjudication of Environmental Administrative Disputes in China	117

PART III: INSTITUTIONAL CONFLICTS AND POWER REDISTRIBUTION

Ding Chunyan	Mandarins v. Mandarins: Procuratorate-initiated Administrative Public Interest Litigation in China	151
Yang Lin	Cross-Border Data Governance in the Greater Bay Area: Towards Integration and Administrative Justice in a Fragmented Landscape	183
Say Hak Goo	The Role of Party Committees in State Owned Enterprises and Stakeholder Representation in China	223

PART IV: IMPLEMENTATION CHALLENGES AND BUREAUCRATIC DYSFUNCTION

Sarah Biddulph	Lazy Officials and Administrative Justice: Governance and Ideology	259
Carlos Wing-Hung Lo, Jingwen Cai, Ning Liu, and Pansy Hon Ying Li	Tightening up the Regulatory Enforcement of Pollution Control Regulations: Local Environmental Officials under Stress in China	295
Jingwen Cai, Carlos Wing-Hung Lo, and Ning Liu	The Sword of Damocles: Enterprises' Strategies Under Campaign-Style Enforcement	324
Song Yuechan	The Authority Deficit: How does China's Pharmaceutical Administration Work?	345

PART V: ADMINISTRATIVE POWER AND CITIZEN RIGHTS

Hualing Fu	Pandemic Control in China's Gated Communities	383
Yan Mei Ning	Police Powers to Punish Law and Order Violations: Controversies and Recurring Issues	411
Ling Zhou	Administered Divorce in China: Reflecting on the 2020 Civil Code's Restrictive Turn	445
Faye Wang	A Comparative Study of Administrative Enforcement of Copyright Protection in China and Europe.	461

REFLECTIONS

Michael Palmer, Zhou Lin and Lin Yang	Reflections: Administrative Justice Between Innovation and Control	491

REFERENCES 509

INDEX 555

PREFACE

This volume is dedicated to the memory of Wu Tingfang (伍廷芳), whose late Qing legal reform efforts demonstrated both the possibilities and constraints of administrative development in China—themes that resonate throughout this volume.

The contributions within this edited volume address the complexities of administrative justice in contemporary China. This compilation arises from a conviction that examinations of administrative law in China are often excessively formal, predominantly focussing on legal texts and theoretical constructs while giving insufficient attention to the pragmatic realities of how something beyond mere 'law'—specifically 'administrative justice'—is perceived and enacted in ordinary life. Furthermore, it posits that the contemporary administrative justice system in China possesses a distinctive character that differentiates it from conventional interpretations prevalent in liberal democratic contexts. While Western scholarship has traditionally approached administrative justice through the lens of individual rights protection and judicial oversight, China's experience reveals alternative pathways—and persistent obstacles—in the pursuit of fair, accountable governance.

The chapters in this collection demonstrate that administrative justice in China operates through complex institutional conflicts and power redistributions that extend far beyond simple state-citizen relationships. From historical continuities dating back over a century to contemporary innovations in environmental enforcement and cross-border data governance, these studies reveal how administrative justice often emerges through negotiations between competing institutional logics rather than through linear legal modernization.

Administrative justice has been a long-standing central topic in legal and political philosophy, concerning the exercise of public power and its impact on people. Specific understandings of the phrase 'administrative justice' are not only often much debated but also may vary considerably according to context. Nevertheless, contributors were encouraged (but not required) to think of administrative justice as primarily comprising three dimensions as identified by a leading European scholar in the field, namely Marc Hertogh.[1]

First, the procedural dimension focuses on whether government agencies adhere to fair processes when making decisions that impact citizens. This includes questions like: Do they provide sufficient notice? Do they allow meaningful participation? Do they clearly explain their reasoning? Secondly, the substantive dimension examines the fairness of the decisions themselves. Are the outcomes reasonable, proportionate, and legally sound? It is not just about how decisions are made, but whether

[1] Hertogh, M (2022) 'Administrative Justice as a Field of Study' in Hertogh, M; Kirkham, R; Thomas, R and Tomlinson, J (eds) (2022) *The Oxford Handbook of Administrative Justice* Oxford University Press.

the results are justifiable. Third, the institutional dimension considers the mechanisms of accountability available when things go wrong. Can citizens effectively challenge unfair decisions through internal reviews, courts, ombudsmen, or other oversight bodies?

In practical terms, these dimensions boil down to fundamental questions of fairness: Did the government follow proper procedures before rejecting a business licence? Was the environmental fine imposed on a polluting company fair, given the actual harm caused? And if a complainant believes a decision to be unjust, do they have meaningful ways to contest it and seek redress?

Our contributors challenge binary thinking that positions authoritarian systems as simply antithetical to administrative justice. Instead, they document how China's system produces genuine procedural innovations—from specialized environmental courts to procuratorate-initiated litigation—while simultaneously maintaining structural constraints that limit individual rights protection. This paradox of "authoritarian administrative justice" may well offer important insights for understanding governance transformation in non-Western contexts.

The organisation of this volume reflects our view that in China, historical foundations shape contemporary challenges, that judicial power operates within distinct political constraints, that inter-institutional conflicts drive legal innovation, that implementation failures often stem from structural rather than individual problems, and that administrative power affects citizens across diverse policy domains through consistent and persisting patterns of state control.

These insights emerge from extensive empirical research conducted across China's legal and administrative institutions. Our contributors have analyzed many court case reports, conducted interviews with officials and citizens, and examined regulatory practices spanning environmental protection, pharmaceutical oversight, police conduct, copyright enforcement, and family governance. This evidence-based approach grounds theoretical insights in the lived experiences of those navigating China's administrative system.

We hope this volume contributes to broader comparative discussions about administrative justice, especially administrative justice in authoritarian regimes, while respecting the distinctive features of China's institutional landscape. Understanding how administrative justice functions in the world's second-largest economy and most populous authoritarian system has implications that extend far beyond China's borders.

ACKNOWLEDGMENTS

This volume represents the culmination of collaborative research and institutional support across multiple jurisdictions and academic communities. We are deeply grateful to the many individuals and organizations that made this work possible.

Our greatest debt is to the government officials, legal practitioners, business operators, and citizens who shared their experiences with the various research teams. Their willingness to discuss sensitive topics and provide candid assessments of institutional performance enabled the empirical depth that we believe is an important feature of this volume. While we cannot name many of them individually due to confidentiality requirements, their insights form the foundation of our analysis.

Institutional support has also been vital. Financial support came from multiple sources: the Research Grants Council of Hong Kong, the Australian Research Council, the Economic and Social Research Council (UK), the National Science Foundation of China, and the Chiang Ching-kuo Foundation. In some cases, internal university grants from contributors' respective institutions enabled conference presentations and collaborative workshops that refined the arguments. We also thank Professor Steve Tsang, Director of the China Institute, SOAS, for warm institutional support.

We are especially grateful to the Chinese Law Programme of the Hong Kong Institute for Asia-Pacific Studies (HKIAPS) at the Chinese University of Hong Kong (and especially Professor Xi Chao, Director of the Chinese Law Programme, and Ms. Tiffany Yu) for supporting and hosting a planning workshop for this project on November 8, 2019. A number of the contributors also presented their papers in nearly final form at the European China Law Studies Association's Annual Conference 2024 held at the Faculty of Law, The Chinese University of Hong Kong, September 19-21, and we thank the ECLSA and the CUHK for their interest in, and support for, the project.

Our contributing authors deserve recognition for their patience with editorial requests and their commitment to empirical rigour. Each chapter represents extensive original research conducted under challenging conditions, and we are honoured by their willingness to contribute to this collective enterprise.

Editorial support came from Dr Brian Hill, who understood the project's significance from the beginning and provided invaluable guidance for the publication process, and Peter Lo Ricco at Talbot Publishing. Anonymous reviewers offered constructive criticism that substantially improved the final manuscript. The Chapter contributed by FU Hualing was originally published in Christine Loh (ed) *How COVID-19 Took over the World: Lessons for the Future* (Hong Kong University Press, 2023). The *Journal of Comparative Law* thanks Hong Kong University Press for permission to reproduce the essay.

We also acknowledge family members and friends who supported long research trips, extended writing periods, and the intellectual concerns that sustain academic careers. Their understanding enabled the sustained focus necessary for comparative institutional analysis.

Any errors or omissions remain our responsibility. We hope this volume advances understanding of administrative justice in China while contributing to broader comparative discussions about governance, accountability and institutional change in diverse political contexts.

The Editors

CONTRIBUTORS

Björn AHL is Professor and Chair of Chinese Legal Culture at the University of Cologne. He is also President of the European China Law Studies Association. Professor Ahl has considerable experience in China law research. His research focuses on constitutional development, in particular on judicial reform and rights litigation, in China. Chinese administrative law and practice of public international law are further focal points in his research. Areas of research interest include comparative law, legal transfers, and legal culture, especially as related to Greater China and Chinese legal development. Professor Ahl is also a visiting professor at the University of Helsinki's Finnish China Law Center, where he works with colleagues on issues of comparative law, Chinese law, and Chinese understandings of international law. He is the editor of *Chinese Courts and Criminal Procedure: Post-2013 Reforms* (Cambridge University Press, 2021). Email: bjoern.ahl@uni-koeln.de.

Sarah BIDDULPH is Director of the Asian Law Centre, Melbourne Law School, at the University of Melbourne, and a Professor at the Law School. Sarah's research focuses on the Chinese legal system with a particular emphasis on legal and policy dimensions of the administration of justice and human rights in China. Her areas of research are contemporary Chinese administrative law, criminal procedure, labour, comparative law and the law regulating social and economic rights. Email: s.biddulph@unimelb.edu.au

Jingwen CAI is a postdoctoral fellow in the Department of Management and Marketing at the Hong Kong Polytechnic University: https://www.polyu.edu.hk/mm/people/research-staff. She was awarded her PhD at the Chinese University of Hong Kong in 2023. Her research interests include corporate compliance, government-business relations, and public policy. Email: mjingwen.cai@polyu.edu.hk

DING Chunyan is a Professor at the School of Law, City University of Hong Kong. She earned her LLB and LLM degrees from Peking University, followed by an LLM at University College London and a PhD from the University of Hong Kong. A qualified PRC lawyer since 2001, she joined CityU in 2010 after serving as a Fulbright research fellow at Harvard Law School, where she conducted research on comparative health law and on tort law in 2008-09. Her primary areas of expertise include tort law, medical law, and Chinese and comparative civil law. She is the author of *Medical Negligence Law in Transitional China* (2012) and has published forty journal articles and book chapters in her research fields. Email: chunding@cityu.edu.hk

FU Hualing is Professor of Law and the Warren Chan Professor in Human Rights and Responsibilities and Dean in the Faculty of Law at the University of Hong Kong. His research focuses on political and legal reform, anti-corruption enforcement, mediation processes, and the evolution of the rule of law in China. He also studies Hong Kong's constitutional status, central-local relationships, and national security legislation. Professor Fu is widely published, co-editing significant works such as *Socialist Law in Socialist East Asia* (2018), *Authoritarian Legality in Asia* (2020), *Hong Kong's National Security Law: Restoration and Transformation* (2022), and *Regime Type and Beyond: Asian Police in Transition* (2023). He serves as China Law Editor for the *Hong Kong Law Journal*, and Co-editor of the 'Routledge Rule of Law in China and Comparative Perspectives Series'. His work is widely published in leading journals, including the *China Quarterly*, the *China Journal*, and the *Journal of Contemporary China*. He has also served for many years on the Editorial Board of the *Journal of Comparative Law*. Email: hlfu@hku.hk

Professor Say Hak GOO is a distinguished scholar in the field of corporate law and governance, with extensive academic contributions and research. He has published widely, including books and journal articles cited by the English Law Commission and courts in England and in Hong Kong. His research focuses on corporate governance, financial law, and legal transplantation, with involvement in major research projects such as enhancing Hong Kong as an international financial centre and studying corporate governance in China, Hong Kong, and Taiwan. He has held academic positions at prestigious institutions, including Columbia University, Renmin University of China, and the East China University of Political Science and Law. His work has been recognized internationally, with invitations to speak at leading universities like Harvard, Yale, and Oxford, as well as global forums such as the UN, UNCITRAL, and APEC. Email: shgoo@hku.hk

Pansy Hon Ying LI was formerly a Teaching Fellow in the Department of Management and Marketing at the Polytechnic University of Hong Kong.

Dr. Yang LIN is Research Officer at the University of Hong Kong (HKU), where he also obtained his PhD in Law. He holds an LLB with distinction from Shantou University and an LLM from SOAS, University of London. His research interests include dispute resolution, internet governance, e-commerce law, and comparative legal studies. He has been actively involved in international moot court competitions as both a participant and a coach. His recent publications include 'From Safe Harbours to AI Harbours: Reimagining DMCA Immunity for the Generative AI Era' (*Journal of Intellectual Property Law & Practice*, 2025), 'Self-Regulatory Online Dispute Resolution in China's E-Commerce Market' (*Amicus Curiae*, 2025), 'E-Commerce and Online Dispute Resolution in Hong Kong: The Case of eBRAM' (*Amicus Curiae*, 2023) and 'China's Three Internet Courts' in *Amicus Curiae* (2021). Email: linyhku@hku.hk

Ning LIU is an associate professor in the Department of Public and International Affairs at the City University of Hong Kong. Her research focuses on government-business relations, environmental regulation, and smart government, https://scholars.cityu.edu.hk/en/persons/ning-liu(d81d8e3f-5be3-4301-8017-f5e1da8cf72c).html. She has published in top academic journals, including the Academy of Management Journal, Public Administration Review, Policy Studies Journal, Public Administration, Public Management Review, and the Journal of Environmental Policy and Planning, among others. Email: ninliu@cityu.edu.hk

Carlos Wing-Hung LO is a Professor in the School of Governance and Policy Science at The Chinese University of Hong Kong, https://sgps.cuhk.edu.hk/profile/prof-lo-wing-hung-carlos/. His main research interests are in the areas of law and government, environmental management, public sector management, and corporate social and environmental responsibility, within the contexts of China and Hong Kong. Email: carlos.lo@cuhk.edu.hk

Simon (Xiankui) MOU is a Professor at the College of Comparative Law, China University of Political Science and Law, appointed to his position in 2021. Prior to this, he was a Professor at the Law School of Shandong University, where he taught courses on constitutional law, administrative law, civil law, commercial law, and Japanese law. His research areas encompass comparative law, human rights, judicial review, corporate governance, AI regulation, environmental justice, and dispute resolution.

Michael PALMER was until recently a co-editor of the *Journal of Comparative Law*. At the University of London he is Professor Emeritus in Law, and Senior Research Fellow at the China Institute, SOAS, and at the IALS, School of Advanced Study. In Hong Kong he is Cheng Yu Tung Visiting Professor of Law, University of Hong Kong, and a Senior Research Fellow in the China Law Programme at the HKIAPS, Chinese University of Hong Kong. Email: mp@soas.ac.uk

Dr. SONG Yuechan is a practicing legal counsel. She holds a doctoral degree from the University of Hong Kong and an LLB and MPhil in Criminal Jurisprudence from Beijing Normal University. Her research focuses on pharmaceutical administration, medical insurance systems, and hospital management policies in China, using empirical methods like interviews to study the interaction between law and society. Her doctoral thesis examined regulatory compliance in Chinese retail pharmacies, highlighting the influence of institutional and cultural factors on corporate conduct. Dr. Song's current research interests include legal and ethical aspects of emerging health technologies. Email: yuechanyaaa@gmail.com

Dr. Faye Fangfei WANG is a Senior Lecturer in Law at Brunel Law School and an International Fellow at the Centre for Chinese Law at the University of Hong Kong. She served as convenor for the Society of Legal Scholars Cyberlaw Section in the UK from 2009 to 2016 and is currently a member of the UK's All-Party Parliamentary Group on Artificial Intelligence. A specialist in cyberlaw, her research spans private law topics such as contract, commercial law, online dispute resolution, data protection, and digital IP rights. Educated in both law and computer science, Dr. Wang has published five monographs, including the book Online Arbitration (2017). Email: fangfei.wang@gmail.com

Dr. Shiling XIAO is a lecturer at the University of Manchester. He holds a PhD in Law from HKU, an MPhil in International and Comparative Law from the University of Macau, and an LLB from Southwest University of Political Science and Law. A former practicing lawyer in Mainland China, he was called to the bar in 2018. His research interests include comparative public law, human rights law, and judicial review, with a focus on Greater China. Recent publications include the article "Proportionality,

Unreasonableness and a Unified Model" in the Hong Kong Law Journal (2021). Email: shiling.xiao@manchester.ac.uk

Dr. Mei Ning YAN specializes in media and information law, and human rights law. She was an Associate Research Fellow at the Institute of Advanced Legal Studies, University of London, 2024-5. She is also a visiting research associate at the Faculty of Law, The University of Hong Kong. Between October 2023 and October 2025, she was also a visiting scholar, School of Law, Queen's University Belfast. Email: yanmeining@gmail.com

Yuhong ZHAO is an Associate Professor in the Faculty of Law at The Chinese University of Hong Kong, where she is also a Fellow of United College and the Institute of Environment, Energy, and Sustainability. Her areas of expertise include Chinese environmental law, climate law and policy, and comparative environmental law, alongside teaching Chinese civil law. Her recent book *Chinese Environmental Law* (2021) highlights her work in this field. Email: yuhong.zhao@cuhk.edu.hk

Dr. Ling ZHOU is an Assistant Professor at Shenzhen Technology University, and a visiting lecturer at Shenzhen University. She was an Associate Research Fellow at the IALS, School of Advanced Study, University of London between 2020 and 2025. She obtained her DPhil in Law from Oxford University in 2018, having earlier graduated with distinction in her LLM from SOAS, London. Her research interests include civil justice, dispute resolution, socio-legal studies, and consumer protection. Her monograph, *Access to Justice for the Chinese Consumer*, was published in 2020. Email: zhouling@sztu.edu.cn

INTRODUCTION

Introduction: Between Legal Form and Political Control

MICHAEL PALMER
University of London;
ZHOU LING
Shenzhen Technology University;
YANG LIN
University of Hong Kong.

INTRODUCTION

China's political system poses a significant challenge to conventional scholarship on administrative justice. As the world's most populous authoritarian regime, the mainland People's Republic of China (hereafter, 'China' or the 'PRC') has established intricate legal frameworks, sophisticated bureaucratic institutions, and comprehensive dispute resolution mechanisms that superficially resemble the administrative justice systems found in democratic contexts. However, these institutions function within a party-state paradigm in which the Communist Party wields ultimate authority over all governance processes, courts remain politically subordinate to administrative agencies, and citizen rights are regarded as instrumental rather than as fundamental constraints. This engenders what appears to be a paradox: how does administrative justice function in the absence of the foundational elements that scholars typically associate with such justice?

Rather than dismissing China's experience as irrelevant to administrative justice scholarship, this volume argues that understanding how administrative justice functions in authoritarian contexts reveals important insights about the relationship between institutional design, political power, and governance outcomes. The Chinese case demonstrates that administrative justice is not simply present or absent, but operates along multiple dimensions that can improve or deteriorate independently of broader political transformation. Courts can expand procedural protections while remaining structurally subordinate to political authority. Legal frameworks can achieve comprehensive reform while preserving state control over fundamental choices. Bureaucratic reforms can reduce arbitrary enforcement while maintaining authoritarian governance structures. At its core, this volume examines the operational paradigms of administrative processes within the PRC's distinctive and evolving political, social, and legal landscapes, revealing the struggles and tensions that arise amid shifting policies, escalating public demands, and the Party-state's determined pursuit of control and stability. By offering a diverse array of case studies, this book not only investigates the operational dimensions of administrative law but also explores the broader implications of governance strategies, their societal impact, and the nascent tensions within authoritarian systems of control.

Administrative justice, as characterized by Marc Hertogh,[1] operates through three interconnected dimensions: the procedures for making administrative decisions regarding individuals and groups, the law under which such decisions are made, and the systems for resolving disputes and grievances arising from those decisions. This tripartite framework has considerable potential in analyzing how citizens experience justice through their interactions with state bureaucracies across diverse political systems. Yet this conceptual apparatus was developed primarily within liberal democratic contexts, where judicial independence, constitutional constraints on administrative power, and meaningful citizen participation in governance processes establish, at least in theory, the fundamental tenets for administrative accountability.

In China's administrative culture and practice, these relationships are arguably often reversed. Procedural fairness often fulfils instrumental functions rather than safeguarding intrinsic rights. Legal authority derives from party-state policy objectives rather than constitutional limitations on government power. Dispute resolution mechanisms operate to manage social tensions and promote political stability rather more than they do to provide meaningful redress against administrative harm. This creates what several chapters characterize as 'authoritarian administrative justice'—a framework capable of achieving substantial procedural enhancements while perpetuating fundamental power asymmetries between the state and its citizens. In order to fully grasp the nature of administrative justice in China, we also need to adopt a contextualizing perspective that transcends narrow legalistic or procedural definitions. Administrative justice is not a static or uniform concept—it operates across multiple dimensions, shaped by historical legacies, institutional dynamics, implementation realities, and the evolving relationship between state power and citizen rights. A broad view is important not only because in the Chinese socialist system understanding of what constitutes the 'public' is expansive, but also because it allows us to see how legal reforms, bureaucratic practices, and political imperatives interact in complex and sometimes contradictory ways. By examining administrative justice through diverse case studies and methodological approaches, we uncover how procedural innovations can coexist with authoritarian control, how institutional competition influences legal outcomes, and how citizen experiences vary across policy domains. This panoramic perspective reveals not only the tensions and transformations within China's governance system but may also offer comparative insights into how administrative justice functions in other hybrid or non-democratic regimes.

[1] Hertogh, M (2022) 'Administrative Justice as a Field of Study' in Hertogh, M; Kirkham, R; Thomas, R and Tomlinson, J (eds) (2022) *The Oxford Handbook of Administrative Justice* Oxford University Press.

The literature on 'authoritarian constitutionalism' and 'legal authoritarianism' has demonstrated that non-democratic systems can deploy legal forms for governance purposes without accepting liberal democratic constraints on state power.[2] This volume extends the analysis to administrative justice, showing how authoritarian systems can innovate within legal frameworks to address governance challenges while maintaining political control. The comparative significance extends beyond China itself. Many countries worldwide operate hybrid systems that combine democratic forms with authoritarian practices, or democratic systems under stress where administrative power expands at the expense of citizens' rights. Understanding the manner in which administrative justice functions in the PRC provides insights into these broader patterns of governance transformation. The analysis reveals how institutional conflicts, implementation gaps, and power redistribution shape administrative outcomes across different political contexts.[3]

HISTORICAL CONTINUITIES AND CONTEMPORARY CHALLENGES

Part I of the volume establishes that contemporary challenges in Chinese administrative justice have deep historical roots extending back over more than a century. Professor Mou Xiankui's analysis of the Northern Warlords period (1912-1928) (Chapter Two) demonstrates how conflicts between judicial independence and administrative supremacy have persisted across different political systems, while Palmer's longitudinal study of population policy since the early 1970s (Chapter Three) shows how dramatic policy reversals can occur without fundamental changes to underlying authoritarian governance structures. These chapters challenge linear narratives of legal development by showing how institutional continuities shape administrative justice outcomes regardless of surface-level reforms.

[2] See, for example, Ginsburg, T, and Simpser, A (2013) 'Introduction: Constitutions in Authoritarian Regimes', in Ginsburg, T and Simpser, A (eds) *Comparative Constitutional Law and Policy* Cambridge: Cambridge University Press, 2013, 1-18

[3] The reader's attention is also drawn to the insightful essay by Eric Ip in *The Oxford Handbook of Administrative Justice*. This provides a valuable foundation for understanding the paradoxical role of administrative justice in authoritarian states, including China. Ip highlights the manner oversight mechanisms like judicial review and administrative procedures are used to address governance challenges while remaining constrained by the imperative to maintain regime security. The essays contributed to his volume align with Ip's observation that administrative justice in China is deeply paradoxical, serving both as a tool for governance and as a mechanism for reinforcing state control. However, they diverge by emphasising the multidimensional nature of administrative justice, particularly the horizontal dynamics of inter-institutional relations, the very broad context in which 'administrative justice' should be understood in mainland China, and the experiential dimension of citizen interactions with the party-state. While Ip focuses on the principal-agent dynamics between the state and its bureaucracies, this volume offers a complementary exploration of how administrative justice operates across multiple dimensions, including historical continuities, implementation realities, and the evolving relationship between state power and citizen rights. Ip, Eric 'Administrative Justice in Authoritarian States' in Hertogh, Kirkham, Thomas, and Tomlinson *Handbook of Administrative Justice* supra note 1.

The historical analysis reveals that China's current administrative justice system represents a distinctive solution to enduring tensions between bureaucratic efficiency and political control. The late Qing dynasty reforms that separated judicial and administrative functions failed not because of technical inadequacies but because broader political realities undermined institutional autonomy. Somewhat similarly, contemporary reforms achieve procedural improvements while preserving political constraints that limit their transformative potential.

This historical perspective provides essential context for understanding why formal legal empowerment in contemporary China often fails to deliver the benefits of accountability typically associated with expanded judicial power. The persistence of administrative supremacy over judicial authority reflects structural features of Chinese governance that transcend particular policy regimes or leadership transitions. Understanding these continuities helps explain why procedural innovations, however sophisticated, remain vulnerable to reversal based on changing political priorities. Yet the volume also demonstrates that some contemporary governance challenges—particularly those involving technological transformation, cross-jurisdictional data governance, and AI-powered administrative decision-making—represent relatively novel problems that cannot be fully explained by historical patterns alone. The interplay between enduring structural constraints and emerging governance complexities creates distinctive challenges for administrative justice in contemporary China.

INSTITUTIONAL DYNAMICS AND POWER REDISTRIBUTION

Parts II and III of this book examine how Chinese institutions navigate tensions between legal development and political control through procedural innovation and inter-institutional competition. The chapters on courts present a dual portrait: institutions bound by constraints yet capable of strategic adaptation through incremental procedural reforms while avoiding direct challenges to political authority. Professor Ahl's (Chapter Four) analysis shows how courts strategically focus on procedural rather than substantive violations, while Drs Xiao and Lin (Chapter Five) reveal the limits of 'weak-form' judicial review that can identify but not remedy administrative illegality. Zhao's environmental cases (Chapter Six) illustrate how specialized courts and cross-jurisdictional arrangements represent creative institutional responses to local protectionism, even though judicial deference patterns persist.

However, the volume's empirical findings reveal systematic patterns that raise questions about the practical significance of these procedural innovations. Multiple chapters document strikingly similar judicial deference rates: Yan's research (Chapter 15) on police penalties shows courts dismiss approximately 93% of appeals, while Xiao and Lin's study of administrative rule review reveals courts rejected approximately 93% of petitions between 2015 and 2022. This remarkable parallel suggests not isolated implementation problems but systematic structural subordination of judicial to administrative authority. Courts frequently copy administrative submissions verbatim rather than conducting meaningful independent review, and even when procedural irregularities are identified, penalties are often upheld anyway. These patterns indicate that judicial review may function more as symbolic ritual than meaningful accountability mechanism, serving legitimating rather than constraining functions within China's political system.

These findings challenge assumptions about the relationship between judicial power and administrative accountability. Courts can achieve significant procedural innovations without gaining meaningful independence from political control. The expansion of judicial review can serve legitimating functions rather than providing effective constraints on administrative power. Specialized courts can address technical challenges while remaining embedded within political hierarchies that limit their transformative potential.

The inter-institutional analysis reveals even more complex dynamics that extend beyond conventional vertical state-citizen relationships. Professor Ding Chunyan's examination of procuratorate-initiated litigation (Chapter Seven) demonstrates how administrative justice in China may fundamentally involve horizontal conflicts between state institutions—what she characterizes as 'mandarins v. mandarins'—rather than merely vertical state-citizen disputes. This represents a distinctive feature of Chinese administrative law that challenges Western frameworks developed primarily around citizen-initiated challenges to government action. The procuratorate system has gained new oversight powers to compensate for lost anti-corruption functions, demonstrating how bureaucratic institutions adapt to maintain relevance and authority within ongoing jurisdictional struggles.

Dr. Yang Lin's study of cross-border data governance (Chapter Eight) shows how jurisdictional fragmentation creates accountability gaps that undermine administrative justice even when individual jurisdictions maintain robust internal procedures. The Greater Bay Area case reveals how three distinct legal systems attempt to coordinate data flows under China's "One Country, Two Systems" framework, but procedural safeguards within individual jurisdictions cannot extend across borders, creating enforcement voids that reflect deeper tensions about data sovereignty and regional integration. This fragmentation problem appears repeatedly across the volume's case studies, suggesting that coordination failures represent a systematic challenge rather than isolated implementation difficulties.

China's administrative justice landscape is of course not static but, rather, deeply influenced by broader social transformations, economic development, political reforms, and external pressures including globalization and environmental crises. Alongside these forces is an evolving tension between centralization and decentralization of power, which profoundly shapes the ways laws are crafted, interpreted, and enforced. The recent formalization of Party committee involvement in state-owned enterprises, as examined by Professor Goo in Chapter Nine, exemplifies this tension, demonstrating how administrative power is exercised, contested, and reconfigured within China's governance framework. Through the analysis offered in this volume, the aim is not only to document these changes but to consider their implications for governance, citizen rights, corporate responsibility, and the broader rule of law in the PRC.

These chapters illuminate how administrative justice in China depends not just on vertical state-citizen relationships but on horizontal power struggles between different state institutions. Legal innovation serves institutional survival strategies rather than rights protection. Administrative justice becomes more complex when operating across multiple legal systems with competing logics. Bureaucratic institutions compete for relevance and authority within the state apparatus, using legal mechanisms as tools in ongoing jurisdictional conflicts.

IMPLEMENTATION REALITIES AND SYSTEMIC CONSTRAINTS

Part IV examines the systematic implementation failures that undermine administrative justice despite comprehensive legal frameworks and policy reforms. The chapters document how street-level bureaucrats contend with impossible institutional constraints—from overwhelming workloads and inadequate authority to conflicting performance pressures and resource limitations. Professor Biddulph's analysis of bureaucratic inertia (Chapter Ten) reveals how campaigns against 'lazy officials' misdiagnose structural problems as individual failings, reflecting broader patterns of campaign-style governance that create temporary compliance pressure without generating sustainable institutional change. The environmental enforcement studies of Professor Lo and colleagues (Chapter Eleven) explain how officials lack legal tools to achieve their assigned responsibilities, trapped in institutional paradoxes where they bear full accountability for environmental outcomes they cannot directly control.

The enterprise research also carried out by Lo and colleagues (Chapter Twelve) demonstrates how campaign-style enforcement creates strategic uncertainty rather than consistent compliance. Their "Sword of Damocles" metaphor captures how sporadic yet intense enforcement periods, combined with continuous technological surveillance, maintain persistent compliance pressure that extends beyond active campaign periods. However, this enforcement model fundamentally differs from rule-based administration by transforming regulatory matters into political mobilization exercises. Campaign-style governance employs militaristic language and references to central leadership concepts, creating an enforcement system where enterprises must navigate not just legal requirements but broader political expectations that shift unpredictably.

Dr. Song's pharmaceutical regulation research (Chapter Thirteen) introduces the crucial concept of 'authority deficit'—a situation where local authorities issue more licences than their regulatory capacity allows them effectively to monitor. This concept captures dynamics that extend beyond simple implementation gaps or bureaucratic drift. Authority deficit represents a structural misalignment where administrative reforms paradoxically weaken governance by devolving licensing power to county levels susceptible to local protectionism while concentrating specialized expertise at provincial levels unable to conduct effective oversight. The result is systematic regulatory dysfunction that neither central reformers nor local officials intended, demonstrating how well-meaning recentralization efforts can create new forms of fragmentation and accountability failure.

These studies reveal that administrative justice fails not because of inadequate formal rules but because of fundamental misalignments between institutional design and implementation capacity. Song's pharmaceutical study reveals how frequent institutional restructuring creates regulatory uncertainty, with local implementers often unclear about which legal standards apply. The dilution of professional expertise through administrative consolidation undermines decision-making quality, as officials trained in industrial regulation now handle complex pharmaceutical oversight without adequate specialized knowledge. Most problematically, blocked joint implementation mechanisms create accountability gaps where no single agency has clear authority over complex regulatory challenges.

The implementation analysis provides crucial insights into why procedural reforms often fail to achieve their stated objectives. Administrative justice requires not merely formal procedures but institutional structures capable of implementing those procedures consistently and fairly. When authority is misaligned with capacity, when resources are an inadequate match to responsibilities, and when performance incentives conflict with procedural requirements, even well-designed systems will likely produce arbitrary outcomes.

These findings have broader relevance for understanding governance challenges in complex administrative systems worldwide. The concept of 'authority deficit' captures dynamics that extend beyond China's specific context. Many administrative systems struggle with similar misalignments between formal authority distribution and practical implementation capacity, suggesting that institutional design must address these structural challenges rather than focusing solely on procedural reform.

STATE POWER AND CITIZEN RIGHTS

Part V examines how administrative power directly impacts individual rights across diverse policy domains, revealing consistent patterns of state control despite varying regulatory contexts. Professor Fu's pandemic governance analysis (Chapter Fourteen) shows how emergency powers during the COVID pandemic amplified existing authoritarian control mechanisms, with gated communities becoming sites of intensive surveillance and enforcement that blurred boundaries between state power and everyday life. The mobilization of grassroots governance structures—neighbourhood committees, grid monitors, and property management companies—exemplified how China's centralized system enables rapid, decisive action through infrastructural power embedded within localized control mechanisms.

Dr. Yan's police powers study (Chapter Fifteen) exposes systematic violations of procedural rights that courts routinely ignore. Her analysis of 225 court cases combined with six notable incidents reveals that police simultaneously serve as investigators, prosecutors, and adjudicators for minor offences, with offenders denied legal representation throughout investigations that can last up to 24 hours. Courts dismiss approximately 93 per cent of appeals against police penalties, often copying police submissions verbatim and dismissing complaints of coercion or torture without investigation. Vague provisions like "picking quarrels and provoking trouble" function as catch-all offences enabling arbitrary punishment for trivial acts or political dissent, revealing how administrative penalties create a parallel justice system that bypasses constitutional protections while enabling "low-level, low-visibility police oppression" that affects millions annually.

Dr. Zhou's divorce regulation research (Chapter Sixteen) demonstrates how administrative procedures can restrict individual autonomy under the guise of social stability. The 2020 Civil Code's mandatory 30-day cooling-off period for consensual divorce represents what Zhou characterizes as indirect population control, using family law to address demographic concerns about declining birth rates and an ageing population. The policy's discriminatory impact on women is particularly significant given that over 70% of divorces are initiated by women, yet the cooling-off period enables unilateral withdrawal that allows controlling spouses to block previously agreed divorces. Zhou's analysis reveals how administrative justice failures in family law reflect broader instrumentalization of individual rights for collective social objectives.

Dr. Wang's copyright enforcement comparison (Chapter Seventeen) reveals how technological automation creates new forms of unaccountable administrative power that challenge traditional administrative justice frameworks. Her comparative study of approaches taken by China, the EU, UK, and US demonstrates how AI-powered content moderation systems make copyright infringement decisions without the transparency, reasoned explanation, or human oversight that characterize legitimate administrative action. Automated systems flag content based on technical similarity rather than legal criteria, leading to removal of legitimate parody, criticism, or educational content. Platform companies increasingly function as de facto administrative authorities without corresponding accountability mechanisms, representing a growing form of private governance that traditional state-centred administrative law frameworks struggle to address.

These chapters demonstrate that administrative justice failures in China are not confined to complex regulatory domains but permeate everyday interactions between citizens and state power. Administrative discretion consistently prioritizes collective state objectives over individual rights, whether in public health, public security, family relations, or intellectual property protection. The analysis reveals how different policy domains share common structural features that subordinate individual interests to state priorities.

The citizen rights analysis also illuminates the gendered dimensions of administrative justice in China that deserve systematic attention. Zhou's divorce study shows how cooling-off periods particularly burden women who initiate the majority of divorces, enabling gender-based control through seemingly neutral administrative procedures. Palmer's population policy analysis reveals how both restrictive and pronatalist policies place disproportionate pressures on women, with reproductive governance strategies—whether coercive restrictions or incentivized encouragement—fundamentally treating women's bodies and reproductive choices as legitimate subjects of state regulation for demographic objectives. These findings suggest that administrative justice scholarship must examine how seemingly neutral procedures affect different groups differently, with particular attention to how state power operates along gendered lines even when formal legal language appears neutral.

METHODOLOGICAL CONSIDERATIONS

This volume uses multi-method approaches to administrative justice research. The chapters employ historical analysis, comparative case studies, empirical surveys, statistical analysis, and theoretical modelling to examine different aspects of administrative justice operations. This methodological diversity enables comprehensive analysis that captures both institutional dynamics and individual experiences across multiple levels of governance.

The historical chapters show how archival research can illuminate the contingent development of administrative justice institutions and reveal continuities that contemporary analysis might miss. The empirical chapters demonstrate how survey research and case analysis can expose gaps between formal procedures and actual implementation. The comparative chapters reveal how institutional differences across jurisdictions create different administrative justice experiences even within the same political system.

The sixteen chapters in this collection examine the dynamics of administrative justice across diverse policy domains and institutional contexts, revealing patterns that are potentially useful for broader comparative analysis. The chapters span historical foundations dating to the Northern Warlords period (1912-1928), contemporary judicial innovations in due process and environmental law, inter-institutional conflicts between procuratorates and administrative agencies, implementation challenges faced by street-level bureaucrats, and direct interactions between administrative power and individual rights in domains ranging from pandemic control to family law. This comprehensive approach enables systematic analysis of how administrative justice operates when fundamental political constraints remain largely unchanged.

THEORETICAL AND COMPARATIVE IMPLICATIONS

This volume offers a range of possible insights for administrative justice scholarship. First, it suggests that administrative justice in authoritarian contexts may well involve not only vertical state-citizen relationships, but also horizontal state-state conflicts ('mandarins v. mandarins'), so that our focus should not only be around citizen-initiated challenges to government action. The procuratorate's role in administrative litigation, the coordination failures between different regulatory agencies, and the competition for institutional authority within the state apparatus reveal how legal mechanisms may come to serve inter-bureaucratic power struggles rather than primarily protecting citizens' rights.

Secondly, the volume introduces analytical concepts that may have broader applicability beyond China's specific context. The 'authority deficit' concept captures how administrative reforms can create systematic misalignments between formal authority distribution and practical implementation capacity—a dynamic that appears in many complex administrative systems worldwide. The analysis of campaign-style enforcement versus rule-based administration illuminates distinctive governance patterns that transform regulatory matters into political mobilization exercises, with implications for understanding administrative justice in other contexts where political campaigns shape regulatory implementation.

Thirdly, the research suggests that the liberal democratic model may not necessarily provide appropriate normative frameworks for evaluating administrative justice in authoritarian contexts. While several chapters suggest that stronger judicial review would likely improve administrative governance, the volume also documents alternative accountability mechanisms—including party discipline, administrative hierarchy, and performance evaluation—that may serve (however imperfectly) similar governance functions through different institutional channels. However, the analysis reveals critical limitations of these 'functional equivalents': party discipline prioritizes political loyalty over legal consistency, administrative hierarchy emphasizes results and compliance with superior directives rather than procedural fairness, and performance evaluation focuses on measurable outcomes that may not capture important qualitative aspects of good governance. While these mechanisms may achieve certain governance objectives, they cannot fully substitute for the rule-of-law values that judicial review is designed to protect, including predictability, impartiality, and protection of individual rights against arbitrary state action.

Fourthly, the volume may be said to demonstrate how technological transformation creates new administrative justice challenges that historical institutional analysis alone cannot fully address. AI-powered content moderation, cross-border data governance, and algorithmic decision-making represent emerging forms of administrative power that operate according to different logics than traditional bureaucratic action. The growing importance of private governance by platform companies challenges state-centered conceptions of administrative justice, requiring new theoretical frameworks to understand hybrid public-private governance arrangements and their implications for accountability and democratic oversight.

Finally, the empirical findings reveal a striking pattern of systematic judicial deference that extends across multiple policy domains. The independent discovery by multiple researchers that courts dismiss or reject approximately 93% of challenges—whether appeals against police penalties or petitions for administrative rule review—suggests not isolated implementation problems but fundamental structural subordination of judicial to administrative authority. This pattern indicates that procedural innovations, however sophisticated, may serve primarily legitimating rather than constraining functions when courts remain embedded within political hierarchies that prioritize stability and control over rights protection.

The comparative significance of these findings extends beyond authoritarian contexts. Many countries worldwide face challenges of regulatory fragmentation, implementation capacity deficits, and technological disruption of traditional administrative processes. Understanding how these dynamics operate in China's distinctive political system provides insights into broader patterns of governance transformation, while raising questions about the conditions under which administrative justice reforms can achieve meaningful accountability rather than merely symbolic change.

By 'administrative justice', then, we mean in the first instance the domain that Marc Hertogh's tripartite framework marks out: the procedures through which administrative decisions affecting individuals and groups are made, the body of law under which they are made, and the mechanisms through which the resulting disputes and grievances are resolved. We take this as our point of departure rather than our destination. Understood in this way, administrative justice names a domain of governance—the institutional space in which state power encounters the governed—and not, at the outset, a verdict upon it. The evaluative question, whether that power is in fact exercised justly, we hold separate; it is an issue pursued in some, though not all, of the specific findings of the chapters that follow.

The Chinese case obliges us to add two further layers to this domain conception. The first is functional: in the party-state the three Hertoghian dimensions frequently serve purposes other than those they are assumed to serve in liberal democratic settings—procedure to legitimize rather than to constrain, legal form to assert state authority rather than to limit it, dispute resolution to manage social stability rather than to check administrative power. The second is critical: once these inversions are taken seriously, the governing question ceases to be whether China's institutions conform to a template of legal design and becomes, instead, how administrative power renders itself legitimate—how it is justified, contested, and made to appear lawful. It is in this sense that we, with several of our contributors, speak of 'authoritarian administrative justice'—a configuration in which considerable procedural and institutional sophistication coexists with, and indeed helps to sustain, the fundamental asymmetry of power between the state and the citizen.

These three layers—the domain, its distinctive functions, and the work of self-justification it performs—are cumulative rather than competing, and the argument of this volume is precisely the passage from the first to the third. This is also why we resist a narrowly legalistic or remedial definition that would equate administrative justice with individual redress alone. In a system where the 'public' is expansively conceived and state objectives routinely take precedence, such a definition would render invisible the horizontal conflicts between state agencies, the 'authority deficits' that disable implementation, and the campaign-style enforcement that together constitute so much of how administrative power is actually experienced. Our conception is broad by design; its boundary is the exercise, justification, and contestation of administrative power, and its analytical payoff is the capacity to show how procedural advance and the erosion of rights can proceed together.

Ultimately, this collection seeks to advance a vision of administrative justice as a dynamic and contested field. It is shaped not only by laws on the books but by historical legacies, institutional rivalries, technological disruptions, and the ever-present tension between political control and effective governance. By exploring how these forces interact across a wide array of policy domains—from population control to pandemic response, from environmental protection to copyright enforcement—the following chapters illuminate the distinctive character of administrative justice in contemporary China. They collectively demonstrate that understanding this system requires us to look beyond the presence or absence of formal legal mechanisms. By doing so, this collection reframes administrative justice not as a matter of legal design but as a study of how power justifies itself under law in the Chinese party-state.

If this reframing holds, its significance reaches well beyond the Chinese case. Comparative scholarship on administrative justice has long taken the liberal democratic characterisation—independent courts, justiciable rights, procedural constraint upon the executive—as at once its descriptive baseline and its measure of success, so that systems departing from that arrangement appear chiefly as deficits, as administrative justice in some lesser or incomplete degree—a tendency that recent work on administrative justice in authoritarian states has begun to unsettle.[4] To define the field instead as a domain—the space in which administrative power is exercised, justified, and contested—and to hold that domain apart from any single normative template, is to convert administrative justice from a yardstick into a variable.[5] The same questions may then be put to very different polities: what work procedures, legal form, and dispute resolution actually perform; whose interests they secure; and through what channels, judicial or otherwise, power is held to account, and with what limits. Posed in these terms, the authoritarian case is not an absence to be measured against the democratic norm but a positive configuration to be set beside it—and beside the hybrid and stressed-democratic configurations that a growing number of states now display. A comparative administrative justice built on this footing would be concerned less with how closely a system approximates an ideal than with how, in each, power is clothed in legal form, and with what that clothing secures, conceals, or constrains. It is to that wider inquiry, as much as to the understanding of China itself, that the chapters below are offered as a contribution.

[4] See in particular Ip, *supra* note 3, who reads the authoritarian case not as a deficient approximation of the liberal model but as a paradoxical configuration in its own right; the present discussion seeks to extend that insight into a comparative frame.

[5] On the case for a general and comparative jurisprudence that travels across legal traditions rather than measuring them against a single template, see Twining, W (2009) *General Jurisprudence: Understanding Law from a Global Perspective* Cambridge: Cambridge University Press. For the comparative study of administrative law as an established field, see Rose-Ackerman, S and Lindseth, P L (eds) (2010) *Comparative Administrative Law* Cheltenham: Edward Elgar (2nd edn, with Emerson, B, 2019).

PART I
HISTORICAL FOUNDATIONS AND INSTITUTIONAL EVOLUTION

Why Not American-Style Judicial Review? Judicial Power and the Constitutional Interpretation System in China's Northern Warlords Government Era (1912-1928)

XIANKUI MOU

China University of Political Science and Law

INTRODUCTION

Alexander Hamilton, one of America's Founding Fathers, advised: 'The interpretation of the laws is the proper and peculiar province of the courts. A constitution is, in fact, and must be regarded by the judges as a fundamental law. It therefore belongs to them to ascertain its meaning as well as the meaning of any particular act proceeding from the legislative body.'[1] This idea was restated in Chief Justice Marshall's *Marbury* v *Madison* judgment in 1803, thereby laying the foundation of the American-style judicial review that empowers the judge in the United States to interpret the constitution and review the constitutionality of laws. This idea also had much influence in East Asia. For example, the Japanese Constitution has proclaimed that the Supreme Court has power to review the constitutionality of laws. China experienced the influence too. The Constitution of the Republic of China in 1946 also tried to transplant an American-style judicial review system, although this failed ultimately. This paper concerns earlier efforts at such a transplantation.

This Chapter mainly discusses the following issues: why was an American-style judicial review system not established in the early Republic of China? What unresolved problems did this history leave us? To answer these questions, it is necessary to trace the tortuous tracks by which initial efforts were made to introduce a judicial review system in the early Republic of China. This paper focuses on the Northern Warlords' Government period (1912-1928) as the subject of study, in order to analyse the core topics of judicial power and the constitution interpretation system. It investigates deep-layer causes blocking the possibilities of robust constitutional interpretation by courts by exploring the formulation and predicament of the Dali Yuan system, and dilemmas in constitutional thought during this period.

[1] Madison, J; Hamilton, A and Jay, J (1980) *The Federalist Papers* China Social Science Publishing House at 467. The author of this paper wishes to thank Dr. Amy Kellam for her kind editorial assistance in preparing the manuscript for this essay.

THE CREATION OF THE DALI YUAN SYSTEM

The Import of a 'Western' style Judicial System

The combination of fused judicial and administrative powers in the governmental system was the basic characteristic of China's imperial judicial system, where an administrator also acted as a judge.[2] Owing to this fusion, it was certainly impossible for the concept of 'judicial' or 'judicial power' in the modern constitutional sense to come into being.

Against this background, the reform promoting modernization of the judicial system, in which the independence of judicial organs was an unavoidable core issue, was launched by the late Qing Dynasty in the last years of the 19th century and the first decade of the 20th. Under domestic and international pressure,[3] the Qing Government issued an imperial edict to announce 'Preparation of Constitutional Politics' and carried out reform of the civil service system in 1906. According to the new civil service system, the Board of Punishments became the Legal Department (or, Ministry of Justice), exclusively in charge of judicial administration. The Dali Si (Chamber of Revision) was transformed into the Dali Yuan (provisional Supreme Court), placed exclusively in charge of trials, and was now the highest court in the state.[4] The Organic Law of the Dali Yuan, issued the same year, stipulated in Article 6 that 'the courts below and

[2] See Guan, Ou (1990) *Fayuan zuzhi fa* (The Organic Law of Courts) Sanmin Shuju, at 9; Shi, Qingpu (2001) *Fayuan zuzhifa xinlun* (New Theory of the Organic Law of Courts) Sanmin shuju, at 37.

[3] China was forced to enter into unequal treaties after the Opium War, acknowledging the consular jurisdiction of Britain and 17 other countries. In 1899, Japan, which was in the same circumstances as China, abolished consular jurisdiction by means of law revision and judicial system reform. Thereafter China also sought to implement such reforms, but its efforts were turned down by the Great Powers on the basis that it had a backward legal system. After 1902, Britain, Japan and America promised in succession to abrogate consular jurisdiction on the condition that China would change law and judicial procedure to meet their standards. The Qing Government then appointed Shen Jiaben and Wu Tingfang as Law Revision Chancellors, and ordered them to refer to the laws of other countries so as to revise China's existing law and moderize China's law so that it became more effective at home and internationally. See Huang Yuansheng (1998) 'Mingchu daliyuan' (Dali Yuan in the Early Republic of China) (1998, 60) *Zhengda falü pinglun* (Chengchi Law Review), at 94. Thereafter the Japanese victory over Russia in the Japan-Russia War came as a great shock for the Chinese people. This victory was seen as the triumph of a constitutional system over feudal absolutism and Japan's victories in the Sino-Japanese War of 1894-1895 and in the Japan-Russia War were considered as proof that constitutionalism would make a country strong. Constitutionalism became a national topic and an overwhelming public concern. See Yang Youjiong (1936) *Jindai zhongguo lifa shi* (Legislative History of Modern China) Shangwu yingshu guan, at 31; Pan Shufan (1935) *Zhonghua minguo xianfa shi* (Constitution History in Republic of China) Shangwu yingshu guan, at 3; Jing Zhiren (1984) *Zhongguo lixian shi* (China Constitutionalism History) Lianjin chuban shiye gongsi, at 27-36.

[4] Ming and Qing Archives Department of the Palace Museum (1979) *Qingmo choubei lixian dangan shiliao (shangce)* (Archival Documents Relating Late Qing Dynasty (I)) Zhonghua shuju, at 471; Guan *The Organic Law of Courts* supra note 2 at 9; Kajikawa Shunkichi (1943) *The Judicial System of the Republic of China: on Extraterritoriality* Institute of Justice, at 14.

under the direct jurisdiction of Dali Yuan definitely may not be interfered with by administrative agencies, in order to make clear the importance of independent judicial power for protecting people's person[al rights] and fortune'.[5] Thus, judicial independence and the legislative purpose of protecting human rights were declared.

In 1909, a Law of Court Organization was enacted,[6] replacing the Organic Law of the Dali Yuan. The new Law stipulated a four-instance and three-level system for introducing a 'Western' style judicial system, in a manner similar to the Organic Law of Judicatories in Japan. In the same year, the Leading Methods of Organizations for Courts in Provincial Capitals and Commercial Ports were issued, signifying the beginning of the separation between the judicial and administrative bodies. But soon after that, the Qing Dynasty collapsed, with the consequence that reformed courts were only established in the capital, provincial capitals and commercial ports at that time.[7]

It is worth noting that the Law of Courts Organization in the late Qing Dynasty stipulated in Article 35 that 'the President of the Dali Yuan has power to interpret law unified and dispose of related affairs, but it may not interfere in specific trials', which conferred a 'unified' power to interpret law on the President of the Dali Yuan. So a judicial interpretation system in which it was not the judges who interpreted the law appeared on the historical stage at the moment that the reform of the judicial system began.[8]

The Establishment of a Continental-style Judicial System

The Provisional Constitution of the Republic of China (1912), enacted soon after the founding of the Republic of China, adopted the principle of separation of powers. In Chapter Six, *Courts*, the Constitution stipulated many basic principles that were seen as originating from 'Western' judicial systems, including the organization and authority of the courts, the identification and appointment of judges, and the independence and

[5] Political Science Club (1972) *Daqing fagui daquan* (Qing Dynasty Statutes at Large) Kaozheng chubanshe, at 1-3.

[6] Xie, Zhenmin (2000) *Zhonghua minguo lifashi (xia)* (The Legislative History of the Republic of China (II)) Zhongguo zhengfa daxue chubanshe, at 987. As mentioned below, the Law of Courts Organization in late Qing dynasty experienced several revisions during the period of the Republic of China and was effective until 1930s.

[7] Guan *The Organic Law of Courts* supra note 2 at 9-10. At that time, Legal Department made a specific plan called Instalment Methods for Dealing with Judicial Administrative Business to establish modern judicial system step by step and submitted to Qing Government in February 1909. For details, See Kajikawa *The Judicial System of the Republic of China* supra note 4 at 15.

[8] In the following period of the Republic of China, supreme judicial bodies like the Dali Yuan, Supreme Court and Judicial Yuan were entrusted with the unified power of legal interpretation. Moreover, after new China was founded, the supreme judicial body of the People's Republic of China, the Supreme Court, often replies the questions on application of law from lower courts, sometimes making written law which is called 'judicial interpretation', eg The Supreme Court's Opinions on the Application of General Provisions of the Civil Law.

openness of trials. As to the construction of judicial power, the Constitution adopted the same framework as that of Japan, which had established an Administrative Appellate Court (Pingzheng Yuan) in addition to ordinary courts.[9] As to the organizational system of courts, the old laws such as the Law of Court Organization were still effective, in accordance with the provisional President's order,[10] so that the four-instance and three-level system, in which the Dali Yuan was the highest judicial body, continued. However, in reality, as the new judicial body had yet to be established, it was still the governmental administration that dealt with judicial business in many places. On June 20, 1915, the Northern Warlords Government issued a revised Law of Court Organization. In this new version, basic level grassroots courts were eliminated and the court system was restructured into three levels, including local courts, the high court and the Dali Yuan (The Supreme Court).[11] There was no revision of the provisions applicable to the Dali Yuan, meaning that the President of the Dali Yuan still held unified power and ultimate authority for legal interpretations.

Frustration in Congress—Constitution Making

Due to the dictatorial nature of government at that time, continuing political unrest, and other difficulties, Congress (Guohui) was not in the position to discuss official businesses in a sensible fashion after Yuan Shikai's inauguration as President. Hence, the drafting of Constitution was postponed several times. Here, this essay will take the Constitution of the Republic of China in 1914 and 1923 as subjects to study the stipulations relating to judicial power.

In 1914, Yuan Shikai dissolved Congress and abandoned the draft constitution (the Temple of Heaven Constitution Draft) worked out by Congress. Yuan then organized a Provisional Constitutional Conference in order to amend the Provisional Constitution of the Republic of China.

[9] As to administrative trial, the Provisional Constitution of the Republic of China stipulated that 'courts should hear and decide civil litigation and criminal suit according to law. But special law related to administrative litigation and other special suits should be made separately' (Article 49); People are entitled to complain before Pingzheng Yuan when their rights are harmed by government official's illegal activities' (Article 10). For the original text of Provisional Constitution, see Zhang, Yaohui and Cen, Dezhang (1981) *Zhonghua minguo xianfa shiliao shangbian* (Historical Documents on the Constitution of the Republic of China (I)) Wenhai chubanshe. The Pingzheng Yuan was established to hear administrative litigation after the Organic Law of Pingzheng Yuan was issued. In addition, a Higher Civil Service Disciplinary Committee was established and began to take charge of disciplinary action against senior civil servants according to the Organic Law of the Civil Service Disciplinary Committee, issued in the same year. See Shi *New Theory of the Organic Law of Courts* supra note 2 at 37-8.

[10] Xie, Zhenmin (2000) *Zhonghua minguo lifashi (shang)* (The Legislative History of the Republic of China ([II]) Zhongguo zhengfa daxue chubanshe, at 54-5.

[11] The original text of Law of Courts Organizations, see Commercial Press (1933) *Zhonghua minguo xianxing fagui daquan* (The Republic of China Statue at Large) Shangwu yingshu guan, at 1119-25. For the Japanese version, see Taiwan Governor's Official Investigation Section (1920) *Biantong zizai de zhonghua minguo sifa zhidu* (The Flexible Judicial System of the Republic of China) (No.42 in Investigation of South China and Araucaria), at 19-52.

He promulgated in 1914 the revised edition, called the Constitution of the Republic of China, (also known as the 'New Constitution', and 'Yuan's Constitution'). The Chapter on *Courts* in the new edition differed from its counterpart in the provisional version in the following respects. First, regarding independence of judicial power: the Provisional Constitution stipulated that 'the judge should adjudicate independently and be free from any interference by higher organs', while the New Constitution stipulated only that 'the courts should decide civil and criminal cases in accordance with law', emphasized the independence of the 'courts' and the need to decide cases 'in accordance with law'. Secondly, regarding the appointment of judges, the Provisional Constitution stipulated that the court should consist of judges appointed by the provisional President and the Chief Law Officer, while the New Constitution stipulated that the court should consist of judges appointed by the President which in practice meant that the power of appointment of the judges was centralized in the President. Thirdly, the Constitution granted the Legislative Yuan power to bring a suit to the Dali Yuan to impeach the President, by which the jurisdiction of impeachment cases fell within the authority of the Dali Yuan.[12] After the failure of Yuan Shikai's Restoration, an executive order was issued on 29 June 1916, announcing the restoration of the Provisional Constitution and the authority of Congress. The 1914 Constitution of the Republic of China was thereby abandoned.[13]

Congress began to deliberate a draft Constitution after it was revived. In 1917, an argument between the President and Prime Minister occurred as to whether to take part in the First World War, leading to the second dissolution of the Congress and the deliberation on the draft Constitution was therefore interrupted. Cao Kun, victorious in the struggles between various warlords, convened the senators of the prior congress of the early Republic of China in Beijing to convoke congress again by means of large-scale bribes. The third-time convoked congress elected Cao Kun as president, quickly deliberated and passed the draft constitution, and issued the Constitution of the Republic of China (also called the 'Cao Kun Constitution' or 'Vote Buying Constitution') on the day Cao Kun was inaugurated as president. In comparison with the Provisional Constitution and New Constitution, the section on judicial power in this constitutional code stipulated that 'the President's appointment of President of the Supreme Court must be approved by Senate' (Article 98, Clause 2). In addition, in response to the provisions related to legislative power and administrative power, it also stipulated that 'the judicial power of the Republic of China should be exercised by courts' (Article 97), making clear a political framework of separation of powers.

In particular, regarding the jurisdiction of judicial power, the Constitution stipulated that 'the court accepts and hears civil, criminal, administrative

12 For the original text of the Constitution of the People's Republic of China, see Zhang and Cen *Historical Documents on the Constitution of the Republic of China (I)* supra note 9.

13 Xie *The Legislative History of the People's Republic of China (II)* supra note 10 at 118-9.

and any other cases unless special provisions have been made in constitution and laws' (Article 99).[14] On this stipulation, the draft constitution specially emphasized that 'it should be noted that it is not advocated to establish the Pingzheng Yuan',[15] clearly expressing the framers' intention to change the dual court system (ie, separately established common courts and administrative courts) into a unified one. However, this Constitution did not actually bring revolutionary influence on the judicial system due to the quick downfall of the Cao Kun regime the next year.

THE ROLE OF THE DALI YUAN AND THE PRACTICAL PROBLEMS OF THE DALI YUAN SYSTEM

The role of the Dali Yuan

The Congress in the early Republic of China period had been in chaos and flux and experienced several dissolutions. However, the Dali Yuan did not stop working as the supreme judicial organ until 1927 and played a key role in the establishment of judicial authority at a time when there was political instability. It is therefore useful to observe the functioning role of the Dali Yuan when studying the judicial system in the early Republic of China.

First, in addition to trials, the Dali Yuan compiled case law summaries based on the judgments it had delivered. In the early Republic of China period, Congress was not in the position to perform its functions normally due to political instability, and therefore the drafts of civil law and commercial law were not fully put into force. Against this background, the Dali Yuan often decided cases according to the laws of the former Qing Dynasty,[16] and existing jurisprudence of law and custom. In addition, a form of case law with precedent effect emerged, the Dali Yuan omitted specific facts of cases and entered the universal normative part of the judgment into Dali Yuan Case Law Summaries.[17] The case law precedents of the Dali

[14] For the original text of the Constitution of the People's Republic of China (1923), see Zhang and Cen *Historical Documents on the Constitution of the Republic of China (I)* supra note 9.

[15] See the written indication on the *Courts* part in draft constitution from Liu Chongyou, member of Committee for Drafting the Constitution. Wu, Zongci (1973) *Zhonghua minguo xianfa shi (qianbian)* (The Constitutional History of the Republic of China (I)) Tailian guofeng chubanshe, at 123-4.

[16] In the early period of Republic of China, the formal resources of law for criminal justice included: the New Criminal Law of the Qing Dynasty in 1910, Provisional Criminal Law of the Qing Dynasty in 1912 and Supplementary Regulations to Provisional Criminal Law of the Qing Dynasty in 1914. And as to the civil justice, the statute law that could be applied only consisted of the civil part in New Criminal Law of the Qing Dynasty which was confirmed as still effective and a few special regulations promulgated after the establishment of the Republic of China, due to the fact that civil code had not been issued yet. Huang 'The Supreme Court of China' supra note 3 at 134-5.

[17] The civil part in the New Criminal Law of the Qing Dynasty could be applied only after the Dali Yuan confirmed it. The precedents of the Dali Yuan in this period became the most important source of civil law, which had a profound effect on the trials of the day. From 1913-1920, every time the Dali Yuan made a judgment, a precedent arose, especially from 1918 to

Yuan were actually binding on the lower courts, and therefore became sources of law for judges.[18] What is more, the principles established in these precedents were mostly assimilated by the Civil Code enacted later by the National Government.[19] So some scholars in the period of the Republic of China believe that we should conclude that an Anglo-American law styled legal precedent system was implemented in the early Republic of China.[20]

Secondly, the Dali Yuan had autonomy in its internal affairs. The Law of Court Organization stipulated that 'the Justice Minister supervises courts and procuracies all over the country' in the first paragraph of Article 158. But it also stipulated that 'the regulations of Dali Yuan and its branch Yuan [courts] were to be approved by the Dali Yuan, but needed only to be reported to Ministry of Justice before implementation'.[21] So the judicial administrative authority, the Ministry of Justice, was limited in its business, having no reference to the administrative affairs of the Dali Yuan. The Dali Yuan formulated the regulations about judicial administrative affairs and supervised their implementation, which meant autonomy, and its outward independence was thereby consolidated objectively.

In addition, the Dali Yuan had a 'unified power' to interpret laws (Tongyi Jieshi Falingquan). That is to say, a very important dimension of the functions of the Dali Yuan was to unify the interpretation of laws and

1920, when most precedents were created. Because there was no law to rely on, no established precedent to abide by, the situation was difficult. After 1921, owing to the existing precedents, there was no need to establish new precedents, and the number of precedents reduced obviously. As required by the *Dali Yuan Editing Rules*, civil precedents and interpretation precedents were to be edited according to the structure and framework of the Qing Dynasty Draft Civil law in the sequence of parts, chapters, and sections. The precedents complied with the requirement that the facts of specific cases be omitted and the more universal, normative part be entered, and were called Case Law Summaries and the interpretation precedents were also complied in general matters. Professor Huang Yuansheng believed that the results were the Dali Yuan's 'fruits' of its law-making efforts, 'Da Li Yuan' supra note 3, at 136-8.

[18] Article 35 in the Law of Courts Organizations stipulated that the President of the Dali Yuan had power to interpret law unified and dispose related affairs. Therefore the precedents of the President's interpretation of law, published with his permission, could be understood as the function of his interpreting power and had binding effect on lower courts. If the lower courts made decisions conflicting with the precedents of the Dali Yuan, the Dali Yuan could withdraw the decision for destroying unified interpretation system of laws. And the privies could also petition for the abrogation or amendment of the judgment for the reason of violating the precedent of the Dali Yuan. Ibid at 135, 137.

[19] The Dali Yuan edited the civil precedents and interpretation precedents according to the structure and frame of Civil Law of the Qing Dynasty and the civil law system was established actually. See Huang'Da Li Yuan' supra note 3, at 5.

[20] Hu, Changqing (1997) *Zhongguo minfa zonglun* (Genera Introduction to Chinese Civil Law) Zhongguo zhengfa daxue chubanshe, at 36. Hu served as the chief complier during the formulation of Civil Code Draft in the National Government period.

[21] Taiwan *The Flexible Judicial System of the Republic of China* supra note 11 at 28, 51. Rely on this, Dali Yuan formulated 1919 Dali Yuan Regulations, replacing 1913 Dali Yuan Rules. The Regulations provided details including the relation between Dali Yuan and its branch Yuans, the judicial administrative power the President of Dali Yuan had got, the organisation of Yuan, how to exercise the unified power to interpret law, editing affairs, meeting rules and so on, up to 230 clauses.

regulations. Congress was weak and limited in its effectiveness. But the Qing legal codes could not simply continue unchanged in a reforming Republic of China. The Dali Yuan thus not only handled cases, but also became a 'legislating' court, in particular by drawing up abstract reviews with the goal of unifying the various interpretations of laws and regulations. More specifically, the characteristics of the unified power of interpreting law are illustrated below.

Characteristics of Unified Interpretation of Laws

The most distinguishing characteristic of the Dali Yuan's work was its unified interpretation of laws. In the Dali Yuan Regulations formulated in 1919,[22] the following characteristics of the unified interpretation of laws were presented clearly.

About the Applicant seeking Interpretation

The Regulations specified that 'only public judicial persons and civil servants who are so permitted by virtue of [their] government office and laws, are entitled to make a request for interpretation of law related to his duties only' (Article 204). Therefore, private requests for interpretation would not be accepted. In practice, in addition to lower judicial organs, the list of appropriate applicants included the State Council, the War Department, the Justice Department, other central administrative departments and local governors in charge of military and administrative business. The unified interpretation made by the Dali Yuan, which had the highest status in the system of courts, had binding effect and enhanced the status of judicial authority within the legal and the political systems.[23]

The object of interpretation

In addition to consideration of doubtful points of law, 'a request for interpretation of items that laws fail to stipulate clearly may not be turned down'(Regulations, Article 205). Questions about specific cases, however, fell outside the scope of this provision.

Effect of interpretation

The Regulations also required that 'the interpretations made by Dali Yuan have binding effect on the same category of items except in the situation that was provided in the provision in Article 35 in the Law of Court Organizations' (Article 203).

[22] See Dali Yuan Clerks Room (1919) 'Tongyi jieshi falingquan zhi xingshi' (The Implementation of Unified Power to Interpret Law) in *Dali yuan banshi zhangcheng* (Dali Yuan Regulations) (Chapter 5) at 80.

[23] Huang 'The Supreme Court of China (1912-1928)' supra note 3 at 107.

Interpretation procedure

The Regulations further stipulated that 'the request should be handled by the President of Dali Yuan and sent to the heads of criminal chambers and civil chambers for drafting the replies'. The request and the reply should be considered by the heads and judges of criminal chambers and civil chambers. In the event that the interpretation might contradict with Dali Yuan decisions or interpretations or newly established precedents, the heads and judges were entitled to express their opinions on the conflict. However, if two different opinions emerged, then a plenary session of criminal or civil judges should be held in order to reach a decision on the matter (Article 206).

The contents of an interpretation

The Regulations stipulated that: 'The request and reply should be published by Government Notice' (Article 210). Unifying interpretations of the Dali Yuan were binding on lower courts, so that the judicial interpretations had the same force as statutory law, and therefore were sources of law provided for lower courts. However, the unified interpretations made by the Dali Yuan were not located in specific judgments but, rather, were opinions separated out from specific cases, and represented abstract interpretations of law. Hence, in terms of its legal nature, this kind of interpretation should be regarded as having more of a legislative function rather than a judicial task.

On the other hand, requests for unified interpretation of laws provided ways for judges to escape from independent judgment and this violated the principle of exercising functions independently. Furthermore, the opportunity to appeal provided by the trial level system was rendered meaningless, which essentially restrained people's procedural rights. In terms of practical consequences for issues such as the maturity of the judicial system, especially the state of the local trial system and the qualifications of judges serving in grass-roots courts, this 'request-reply' interpretation system should not be considered as having not any value. However, we can still see today some traces of this abstract judicial interpretation system in the current judicial systems of the Chinese mainland and Taiwan.[24]

Practical Problems of Judicial Independence

The reform of the judicial system in China remained persistently focused on the independence of judicial organs from the late Qing Dynasty onwards. However, striving for the independence of judicial organs was a process which bristled with difficulties. Local judicial organs were only set up in

[24] At present, when the Supreme People's Court of the mainland of China publishes the official reply to the lower court's request for instructions on the application of law, it actually provides the benchmark for the lower people's court's judicial work. However, in Taiwan, the 'judges of the judicial court' exercise the 'power of constitutional interpretation', and also exercise the 'power of uniform interpretation of laws'.

provincial capitals or commercial ports, while grass-roots courts could not be established due to a financial squeeze. Therefore, the situation in which county magistrates dealt with judicial business continued.[25] As a matter of fact, the political conference, which replaced the Congress dissolved by Yuan Shikai, decided to abolish grass-root courts, reduce some local judicial organs, and issue several judicial regulations in succession, including the Interim Regulations for County Magistrates Dealing with Judicial Business, Interim Regulations for Judicial Business of Counties in Jingzhao, and Interim Regulations for County Magistrates to Judge Cases.[26] Although the judicial system was seemingly established according to Provisional Constitution and the Law of Court Organization, its trunk had been hollowed out. The 'four-instance and three-level' system for examining a case had been practically abolished. And it was hard to imagine any genuine independence of judicial power considering the separatist warlord regimes, constant wars and the unguaranteed stability of national power. Under the warlords' regime, judicial organs sometimes indeed ignored people's rights at trial to serve political and military intentions.[27]

On the other hand, in the legal system's adoption of a new judiciary, the supervision from the Dali Yuan did have a large influence on judges' independent performance of their duties. As to the supervision over lower courts, it was stipulated clearly in the Law of Court Organization that 'lower courts may differ in the understanding of laws from Dali Yuan and its branches [...] when a case is handed over to the lower courts for their consideration' (Article 45).[28]

The Dali Yuan Regulations stipulated that if the President of the Dali Yuan found after trial that a judgment was not appropriate when reviewing the first draft of judgment or the trial procedure had not been in accordance with law, he or she was entitled to point the problem out immediately. And if necessary, the President of the Dali Yuan could ask for a report on specific cases (Articles 35, 36).[29] This kind of internal supervision

[25] Yang, Youjiong (1937) 'Jindai zhongguo sifa zhidu' (The Judiciary in Modern China) (1, 5 & 6) *Zhonghua faxue pinglun* (China Law Review) at 30.

[26] For the Japanese version of these regulations, see Taiwan *The Flexible Judicial System of the Republic of China* supra note 11 at 83. As a provisional solution, court and procuratorate offices were established in 1913 in counties where courts had not been set up, in which judicial officers adjudicated cases. This incurred many disputes, including conflicts of jurisdiction between judicial officers and County Magistrates, and caused impediment in practice. Therefore the Interim Regulations for County Magistrates dealing with Judicial Business issued in April 5th the next year changed the judicial officers to assistant of county magistrates while county magistrates held the power to deal with judicial business exclusively and the Shenjian Offices in the counties were abolished. Kajikawa *The Judicial System of the Republic of China* supra note 4 at 20.

[27] Li, Jun (2000) 'Lun beiyang zhengfu shiqi de sifa duli' (On Judicial Independence During Northern Warlords Government Period) (2000, 10) *Nanjing shehui kexue* (Social Sciences in Nanjing) at 39.

[28] See Taiwan *The Flexible Judicial System of the Republic of China* supra note 11 at 28.

[29] Dali Yuan *Dali Yuan Regulations* supra note 22 at 80.

within the court system may remind us of the reflections and criticism of the 'Otsu Event'(1891)[30] that was later expressed during 'the Hiraga Letter Event' of 1969.[31] The Otsu Event[32] was a very symbolic incident in

[30] Otsu Event: In May, 1891(Meiji 24), Nicholas II, the prince royal of tsarist Russia, passed through Japan when he went to Vladivostok to preside the ceremony for the opening of the construction of Siberian Railway. When Nicholas II arrived at Otsu, the southwest city in Shiga Prefecture, he was attacked by Tsuda Sanzo who served as a guard, his forehead being wounded by blade two times. Tsuda assassinated Nicholas because he thought that Nicholas actually intended to find out something about Japanese Military strength on this visit to assist in preparations for attacking Japan. Worried about the diplomatic relations with Russia, the Government of Japan forced the trial judges to apply the criminal rules about murdering royal family and sentenced Tsuda to death. But Kojima Iken, the president of the Japanese Supreme Court at that time, believed that strict implementation of a country's laws forms the correct basis governance. In addition the concept of 'royal princes' in Japanese criminal law did not include those of foreign countries, hence the rules about common murdering should be applied. He went to Otsu in person and persuaded the trial judges of his viewpoint. As a result, the court sentenced Tsuda to life imprisonment for the common offence of attempted murder. After the sentence, Japan's Foreign Minister, Justice Minister and Home Secretary resigned in succession while Tsuda died of illness in prison later. Surprisingly, Russia, who took a hard line before trial, accepted the sentence. They said that Nicholas was not badly hurt, Japan apologised immediately, and Russia was very pleased with Japan's response. Eleven years later, the Japan-Russia War broke out; Nicholas II appeared on the historical stage as the last tsar.

[31] Hiraga Letter Event: In 1969, the local residents in Naganuma of Hokkaido sued the Japan Government for violation of Article 9 of the Japanese Constitution, which forbids military power, because the Japanese Government had built a surface to air missile base in a protected forest area. The president of Sapporo Regional Court, Hiraga Kenta, wrote a letter to Fukushima Shigeo, the trial judge, expecting him to respect the Government's decision. However, Fukushima thought Hiraga's behaviour interfered with judicial independence, and published the letter in the press—which produced a huge reaction in Japanese society. Compelled by the pressure of public opinion, the Supreme Court warned Hiraga for causing national worries about the 'justness' of the adjudication process and transferred him to the Tokyo High Court. Conservative judges criticised Fukushima publicly and said that he was the leader of a 'Young Jurists Association'. The next year, the Supreme Court criticised Fukushima for 'joining a group with a political complexion' publicly, while Commission for Prosecution of Judges refused to prosecute Hiraga and withdrew the intended prosecution against Fukushima. The Hokkaido Court gave Fukushima a verbal warning, but four years later (1973), he declared the Japan's Self-Defense Forces unconstitutional in the above-mentioned case. The General Directorate for Affairs of the Supreme Court then transferred (demoted) him to the Tokyo Regional Court. After being transferred to the Fujii Family Court and having worked for 12 years there, he resigned as judge and became a lawyer.

[32] In the Otsu Event, Kojima persuaded the trial judges to resist interference from the Government. For this, Kojima was widely regarded as God for Protecting Law, and there was also the viewpoint that it was after Otsu Event that Japanese Courts established judicial independence. But an observer also pointed out critically that Kojima interfered with the trial judges' independence while he emphasised judicial independence. Miyazawa Toshiyoshi argued that 'the legitimacy of interference from other people besides the judge depended on the content of judgment being interfered with', 'if not, it was probably untenable for us to argue the legitimacy of Kojima's action in association with the principle of judicial independence.'(Miyazawa Toshiyosh (1967) 'The Significance of Otsu Event in Legal Philosophy' (62, 11) *Journal of the Law Association* in Miyazawa Toshiyoshi (1967) *Constitution and Judgment* Yuhikaku Publishing at 226.) Ienaga Saburo expressed different views towards Miyazawa Toshiyoshi's point, sating: 'All the interveners, no matter he or she is government or the judge from higher court, decide to interfere on basis of deep belief that their propositions are correct. Therefore the discussion of legitimacy of interference will turn to meaningless arguments that each side only expresses his own thought and the interference

Japanese judicial history in which Kojima Iken, President of the Japanese Supreme Court, persuaded the trial judges in a case to resist interference from the government, and was highly praised for having protected judicial independence. However, it could not be denied that in so doing he himself interfered with the trial judges' independence. Hence the question of how best to evaluate the behaviour of Kojima Iken remains a matter for legal philosophy.

CONSTITUTIONAL DESIGN OF JUDICIAL POWER

The 1912 Constitution experienced twists and turns in the early period of Republic of China, and came to a conclusion in the Cao Kun Government era (1922-1924). This section will focus on the historical materials concerned with the establishment of the 1923 Constitution and study the ideas and knowledge of the framers of that time.

How Far Should Judicial Power Extend?

During the drafting work, the Congress put great emphasis on the question of whether the power to interpret the constitution and to decide administrative cases should fall within the scope of judicial authority. There was indeed a relatively detailed illustration of constitutional design for judicial power in the interpretation of the constitution.

The power to interpret the Constitution

At the beginning of the moves towards constitutional reform and possible greater concern with 'constitutionalism', 'congressional centralism 'dominated the field, and congress asserted its power to interpret constitution by means of implementing legislative power (similarly, in Japan scholars within the 'school of constitutionalism' under the Meiji Constitution such as Minobe Tatsukichi also believed that 'the constitution should be protected by the legislature'). In contrast, other arguments were also put forward advocating the superiority of administrative power, and proposing that the duties to protect the constitution should be entrusted to the state president (and in a spirit that we might characterize as akin to Schmitt's *The Guardian*

still can not be ruled out', 'The interference with Fukushima's adjudication independence in 1969 by Hiraga, the president of Sapporo Court, was basically based on this logic'. Ienaga Sahuro believed that the reason why Kojima's persuasion pressure on the trial judge was legal lay in the fact that 'the behavior's character of urgent danger prevention and therefore the illegality was eliminated'(Ienaga Saburo (1971) 'Judicial Independence in Otsu Event' in Kojima Iken and Ienaga Saburo (eds) (1971) *The Interpretation of Otsu Event Booklog (II)* Heibonsha Publishing at 264-5). He further stated that the Supreme Court continues to interfere with the adjudication of lower courts and the evaluation of Kojima's action, if it was not based on strict logic, would lead to the legalisation of interference from supervising organs, which is a serious worry (Ienaga Saburo (1967) *A Historical Review of the independence of judicial power* Nippon Hyoronsha Publishing at 68-9). In addition, Taoka Ryoichi argued that Kojima's interference was illegal according to The Law of Courts Organizations, Article 14. But one thing is worthy of notice, that was, his comments on Ienaga Sahuro were based on the point of international politics. See Taoka Ryoichi (1983) *A Review of the Otsu Event* Yuhikaku Publishing at 162.

of the Constitution). That the United States Supreme Court exercises broad powers of judicial review in specific cases was considered an exceptional case rather than a model to be followed.[33]

But in the early period of the Republic of China, there were also some scholars—such as Wang Chonghui–who advocated entrusting the power to interpret the Constitution to the courts.[34] However, the 1923 Constitution drafted by the Congress entrusted the power to a 'Constitutional Conference' consisting of members of Congress (Articles 139, 140). Tang Yi, Chairman of Committee for Drafting the Constitution, explained the reasons as follows in *The Interpretation of Constitution*.[35]

First, regarding the function of the power to interpret constitution, orders which conflicted with laws were certainly invalid and that laws which conflicted with the Constitution were also certainly invalid, but in the latter case 'the reason must be proved' by means of constitutional interpretations.

Secondly, a survey of various constitutions of other countries exploring which organ enjoyed the power to interpret the constitution was inconclusive. Although Article 155 in Constitution of Republic of Chile, Article 170 in Turkish Constitution, and Article 76 in the Constitution of Commonwealth of Australia entrusted the power to interpret the constitution to their respective Congresses many countries did not have clear stipulations. It was also observed, however, that those which belonged to the Anglo-American common law tradition tended to entrust such power to courts while those that belonged to the Continental law tradition tended to deny courts such power.

Finally, regarding the process of drafting the constitution, the principle to be followed was that the power to interpret constitution should reside in the organs formulating the Constitution. Three reasons were provided for this. First, the constitution was wholly the work of the organ formulating it. Therefore, it should be the formulating organ who resolves conflicts with other laws after the Constitution had been established. If the views of other organs were incorporated into the interpretation process, the foundation of the Constitution might 'suffer, waive and falter'. It was therefore argued that it was better for the power to interpret the Constitution to reside in the organ that formulated it, rather than in the courts. Secondly, there was an important need to adhere to the original intentions of the framers. If the formulating organ and the interpreting organ were not the same then this need might not be met. Instead, interpretations would lack 'real

[33] Higuchi Yoichi (1998) *Constitutional Law* Sobunsha Publishing at 420-1. See also Vinx, Lars (2015) *The Guardian of the Constitution : Hans Kelsen and Carl Schmitt on the limits of constitutional law* Cambridge University Press.

[34] See Wang, Chunghui (1981) '*Zhonghua minguo xianfa chuyi*' (On the Constitution of the Republic of China) in Zhang Yaohui and Cen Dezhang (eds) (1981) *Zhonghua minguo xianfa shiliao xiabian* (Historical Documents on the Constitution of the Republic of China (I)) Wenhai chubanshe.

[35] Wu The Constitutional History(I) supra note 15 at 75-6.

understanding' of these intentions, or be reduced to erroneous conclusions by use of 'false analogy'. In these ways, 'the spirit of the Constitution' might be 'damaged.' Finally, it was observed that, '"constituent" and legislative power are two kinds of power' and the 'Constitutional Conference is a special constitution-formulating organ which while different from the Congress itself, is organized by representatives entrusted by the majority of the people. A court, however, consists of several judges appointed by the government.' Accordingly, it was reasoned that if the court was authorized to interpret the Constitution, then the opinions of representatives delegated by the majority of the people would, as a consequence, be open to challenge by the views of a few judges. Such a state of affairs would be contrary to the established principles for formulating the constitution.

The position—strongly taken—was that a case about constitutionality of Yuan Shikai's (President, 1912-1916) restoration was thrown out by the Dali Yuan also showed that the ability of courts to handle interpretation issues regarding the Constitution was limited by courts' subservience to the government.

The power to decide administrative cases

As mentioned above, the Provisional Constitution entrusted the jurisdiction of administrative cases to the Pingzheng Yuan, which meant that the power to decide administrative cases was taken out of judicial power, while in contrast, the draft constitution by the Congress included that power into the authority of court. Yuan Shikai (President, 1912-1916) took this as a reason for his opposition to the Congress' 1913 'Temple of Heaven Constitutional Draft' (Tantian Xianfa Cao'an) and other constitution-establishing activities.[36] So the stipulations of Pingzheng Yuan appeared in Yuan's New Constitution, differing from the draft constitution made by the Congress. The regulations about judicial power in the Temple of Heaven Constitutional Draft were continued after Yuan's death in 1916, however, resulting in the 1923 Constitution. Jiang Juqing, a Constitutional Draft Committee Member, after overviewing the administrative jurisdiction system of various countries at that time, explained that the principle of legal equality—people living in the same area should be governed by the same law—meant that it was inappropriate to introduce a separate system of administrative courts.[37]

More specifically, there were issues of, first, jurisdiction—in countries with an administrative court system, it was observed that courts could find themselves competing to hear a case, or refusing to hear a case, with another court: 'So a superior organ situated above the two systems to resolve such jurisdictional conflicts has to be established, as in the cases of Germany and France.' But these complicated formalities 'might well cost the parties significant time and costs. If the administrative cases fall within

[36] Xie *The Legislative History(I)* supra note 10 at 86.

[37] Wu *The Constitutional History(I)* supra note 15 at 76-8.

the jurisdiction of ordinary courts, such disadvantages would likely not arise'.

Secondly, there was the issue of trial levels:

> While there is a one level administrative court system in Japan, France and Germany have adopted a two-level administrative court system, and Prussia has adopted a three-level administrative court system. Considering the vast territory of China, a two-level administrative court system ought to be adopted at [the very] least. But it must also be kept in mind that if administrative courts are set up in provinces and special regions, annual salaries for judges and other expenditure ensue. This is truly superfluous and is not permitted by either theory or the practical situations of our period, with people poor and the country weak. That's why the Draft Committee dare not adopt the administrative court system already implemented in other countries even after a long, long consideration.[38]

Ideal of Judicial System

As noted above, the Constitutional draft prepared by Congress entrusted the power to decide administrative cases to court, which meant that civil cases, criminal cases and administrative cases all fell within the jurisdiction of courts. However, we cannot assert that the Constitution draft had explicitly accepted the ideas of the common law tradition. The principle of the 'rule of law' might be said to have at its heart the idea that the court has independence from the political power of the legislature and the administration, and in that sense has the final say on what is the law.[39] Based on this principle, the idea that administrative cases differ from civil cases is not pertinent. This is very different from the Continental legal system which holds that administrative and civil cases differ in nature. Therefore, in Great Britain and the United States , the idea that the power to decide administrative cases is a matter for the judicial power of ordinary courts is taken as standard.[40]

The Constitution as drafted by the Congress in the early period of the Republic of China intended to include the power to decide administrative cases within the courts' judicial power, similar to the common law tradition. But the draft also required judicial activities to take law as criteria. This was broadly similar to the principle of deciding cases in accordance with law under the provisions of the revised New Constitution, so that the situation which emerged was one of 'rule by law' rather than 'rule of law'. In addition, the interpretation of constitution was seen as a function of the framers, and the judicial interpretation of the Constitution was characterized

[38] Ibid at 78.

[39] Tanaka Kazuo (1967) *Introduction to Anglo-American Law* Yuhikaku Publishing at 72.

[40] Urabe Noriho (2000) *New Edition of Constitutional Law Classroom* Nippon Hyoronsha at 316-7.

as an 'invasion' of the territory of the framers. This standpoint neglected the judicial function of making law, which was an essential ingredient in the judicial process, reflecting the idea that takes the judicial process as execution of law. This idea of 'administration-style judicial process'[41] is clearly inconsistent with the ideas of 'rule of law' in common law tradition.

THE POSSIBILITIES OF JUDICIAL REVIEW

The Problems of the Judicial System behind the Constitutional Interpretation System

We can see the understanding and attitude of the constitutional framers in Congress towards a constitution interpretation system in the 1923 Constitution, and their awareness of the idea that constitutional interpretation consisted not only of the interpretation of words but also should have the function of 'reviewing' law based on public opinion. Three reasons for denying courts the judicial authority to interpret the constitution were offered. First, interpreting the constitution was the function of the framers of that constitution, and should not be carried out by judicial organs. Secondly, as long as the power to interpret the constitution resided in the framers, the consistency between interpretation and the constitution's original text was ensured. If courts intervened, then this guarantee was lost. Thirdly, judicial interpretation of the constitution lacked the foundation of public opinion and support. Of the three, the last point is the Achilles' heel of a judicial review system, founded as it is on unelected courts. Due to a perceived tension between judicial review and the democracy, disputes over the legitimacy of judicial review may, it was feared, become common. The third reason was seen as more persuasive. The first and second reasons did not allow organs other than the body of framers of the constitution to exercise the power to interpret the constitution. It also, however, said nothing about the unified power to interpret law performed by Dali Yuan in the then current system, which also played a role in making law.

In addition, *The Interpretation of Constitution* noted the court's inadequate function in a case of interpreting the Constitution, and pointed out that judicial power at that time still lacked independence from government. However, as far as the case mentioned above is concerned, the problem of whether a system of imperial rule should be restored was a political problem, and inappropriate for the Supreme Court to take a position on. On the other hand, the Congress did not wish to create possibilities for the exertion of the function of judicial review by means of reinforcing the independence of judges. Instead, it saw the prevention of despotism as its

[41] Ashibe Nobuyoshi had discussed the status of judicial power between the 18th and 19th centuries in Europe. He stated that the implementation of judicial power at that time was purely application of law while judicial systems that restricts other powers were excluded, and briefly named this feature 'administration-style'. See Ashibe Nobuyoshi (1994) *Human Rights and Judicial Review* Yuhikaku Publishing at 5-7.

duty, and in the interests of limiting governmental power, forbade judicial 'invasion' into the region of constitutional interpretation.

This understanding of constitutional interpretation is inseparable from the historical context of the early period of the Republic of China. Especially during the drafting of the Constitution, there were intense collisions between arguments such as whether to adopt a presidential system or a cabinet system, and whether centralized authority or local autonomy was better. Lurking just below the surface was the struggle between democracy and dictatorship, a legacy of the constitutional movement in the late Qing—that Yuan Shikai dismissed the Congress, interrupted the drafting of the Constitution, and restored imperialization were extreme manifestations of these problems. These developments came as a great shock to the members of the Congress, and Tang Yi, the chairman of the Constitution Drafting Committee, recalled:

> The argument about the constitution began in the first year of the Republic of China and was very heated on the day the draft came out in the second year of the Republic [1913]. The opponents [of Constitutionalism] went so far that they did not hesitate to overthrow the Congress to gain their ends [...] The opponents said that a Constitution could make a nation [...] either strong or weak and conquered. Their essential point was that centralizing power into the hands of one person made a nation strong, while separating powers to different organs made a nation weak and adoption of parliamentary system ruined a nation.

On this, Tang Yi further pointed that the spirit of the constitution was the same as the purpose of revolution, 'first, to prevent autocracy, and second, strive for the political freedom'. In his view, there are two kinds of autocracy namely, 'personal autocracy' and 'institutional autocracy'. Personal autocracy is not something that can be prevented by mere legislation, so the notion of making law against one person is to be absolutely rejected by the Constitution.[42] In the framers' eyes, a constitution adopting the principle of separation of the three powers was a modern ideal, and supportive of the authority of parliament. But they neglected the possibilities that a parliamentary body such as a congress might be dictatorial. Nevertheless, in that era of unrest, there was significant chaos and flux, so how could the courts, 'which had no financial and military power', resist the warlord regime just by interpreting the constitution? Therefore, for the Congress to keep the power to interpret Constitution in its own hands was an essential choice, especially given the lack of judicial independence.

Legal Characteristic of Constitutional Interpretation by the Dali Yuan

As discussed above, the unified law interpretation system was not one inherent in the judicial process but in essence a decision about what was the law, divorced from the judicial process of handling a specific case. So it

42 Wu *The Constitutional History(I)* supra note 15 at 69-70.

was not a form of case law, as found in common law systems. The Dali Yuan was, rather, providing advisory opinions.

It is worth noting that there were forms of interpretation for constitutional documents in the judicial interpretation precedents and applications of the Constitution in cases decided by the Dali Yuan. These could be seen as constitution interpretations. Thus, in replying to the telegram request from Hubei High Court, Interpretation 7 (March 10, 1913) the Dali Yuan replied: 'the current civil litigation process shall apply to such electoral law suits and it should be heard by the civil chamber'.[43] Similarly, the response to a request from Jiangxi High Court, Interpretation 779 (May 9, 1918) stated: 'according to the freedom of religious belief clause in Constitution, the husband may not stop the wife believing in some religion of her own choice'.[44] Case 46 (1914) said that: 'according to Article 10 of the Constitution of Republic of China, administrative litigation may not be heard by ordinary courts'.[45] In Case 176 (1915), meanwhile, Article 8 in the New Constitution was applied according to the Constitution and the Law of the Administrative Appellate Court (Pingzheng Yuan) organizations, ordinary courts can only hear civil and criminal cases. Administrative litigation and petitions should be submitted to higher administrative officers and the Administrative Appellate Court (Pingzheng Yuan), and may not be heard in ordinary courts.[46]

To give a final example, Case 1308 (1918) said that:

> The Constitution claims that the people have freedom to believe in religion or not. Thinking deeply about this clause, people—regardless of gender, no matter whether of full capacity or not, are free to believe in religion with no restrictions imposed. A woman's civil conduct is confined by the right of the husband, but her religious belief may not be restricted by that right.[47]

The constitutional interpretations noted above shared the same aspect in that they did not review the constitutionality of law according to constitutional norms in order to 'defend' the constitution, but rather merely invoked constitutional norms or made supplementary interpretations. The Dali Yuan on the whole took a rather negative attitude towards constitutional review.

As judicial interpretation from the Dali Yuan was not a judicial function in nature, it should not be characterized as a 'judicial interpretation of constitution'. Such interpretations, whether they operated to protect human rights or supplement so-called loopholes in the constitution, were all sources

[43] Guo Wei (1972) *Dali yuan jieshi li quanwen* (Complete Text of Interpretation Precedent by Dali Yuan) Chengwen chubanshe, at 3.

[44] Ibid at 429.

[45] Ibid at 1.

[46] Ibid at 2.

[47] Ibid at 1.

of law that the Dali Yuan provided to judges directly, and thereby replaced the independent judicial function of the judges in lower courts. This was also a reflection of the idea of 'administration-style' judicial system.

CONCLUSION

A constitution becomes the criterion for decision-making in trials only when it is interpreted concretely and clearly. Therefore, it is the organ holding the power to interpret the constitution who safeguards the constitution. In the Northern Warlords Government era (1912-1928), there were some scholars who claimed that the power to interpret the constitution should be entrusted to courts, expecting the courts to be the constitution's defenders. But this Hamilton-style understanding of the judicial role did not gain sufficient support from the framers and judges during that period.

The Congress in the early Republic of China experienced turbulence in the restless stratocracy of that time and was unable to function properly. The situation in which the logic of democracy conflicted with the reality of the warlord regime reinforced the framers' eagerness and longing for parliamentary democracy. In their eyes, the threat to constitutional government mainly came from the administrative forces, which were under the control and authority of the warlords. The way to protect private rights and restrict public power was perceived to be through congress issued legislation and the impartial judgement of the courts, rather than by a functional system of checks and balances between legislative, judicial and administrative power. Therefore the power to interpret constitution must be kept in the hands of the supreme organ, the Congress. This is to some extent reminiscent of the British idea of parliamentary sovereignty. In the famous Dr Bonham's case (1610), Sir Edward Coke, the court's Chief Justice declared an Act of Parliament 'against common right and reason' to be void, and ruled that 'in many cases, the common law will control Acts of Parliament, and sometimes adjudge them to be utterly void'.[48] After the Glorious Revolution, however, Britain established the principle of parliamentary sovereignty, by which the Court must comply with statute law and the review of legislation could only be carried out by Upper House, hence Coke's idea was not put into practice. However, the essence of his idea spread across the Atlantic and influenced the evolving common law system there. It bore fruit in the growth of an American-style judicial review and a system of checks and balances.

In the judicial area during the Northern Warlords Government era, the idea of independence of the courts had only just taken off. The weaknesses in the independence of judicial organs deepened distrust in the ability of the courts to deliver justice and fostered resistance to the idea of judicial interpretation of the Constitution. That is another reason why the framers denied the courts powers to interpret the Constitution. Legislative control over judges by means of laws, judicial interpretations and case law

[48] Stoner, JR (2005) *Common Law and Liberal Theory: Coke, Hobbes, and the Origins of American Constitutionalism* Peking University Press, at 81-2.

summaries, thereby gained legitimacy and led to a formation of ideal of continental judicial system in which judges were positioned as law executors, required to decide cases according to law. Judicial and administrative organs both performed the same role in enforcing laws, but the question of whether the law met the requirements of justice and constitutionality was taken out of the courts and their judicial decision-making. Under the restrictions of this ideal of a continental-style judicial system , the judges seemed like dancers in irons when deciding cases according to law, even though they were occupying the seats for judges in the courtroom.

It is worth noting that the judicial interpretation system, as it appeared on the historical stage in the late Qing Dynasty and the early years of the Republic of China under the Dali Yuan system, has continued right up until the present day and has become a unique feature of Chinese judicial system. Occasionally, we can find single words citing constitutional documents in the case law precedents and judicial interpretation precedents, but the courts do not review the constitutionality of legislation. It is fair to say the judicial organs of the early Republic were not equipped with the subjective and objective conditions for questioning parliamentary legislation and safeguarding constitutional order, whether from the viewpoint of the judges' position or the actual function of judicial interpretation system. In such a context, Hamilton's ideal of judicial interpretation of the constitution could only resonate with the ideas of a few elite scholars.

GLOSSARY OF CHINESE TERMS

Romanisation (Hanyu Pinyin)	**Chinese Characters**	**English Translation**
Beiyang Zhengfu	北洋政府	Northern Warlords Government
Dali Si	大理寺	Chamber of Revision
Dali Yuan	大理院	Dali Yuan (provisional Supreme Court)
Fabu	法部	Legal Department
faling tongyi jieshi quan	法令统一解释权	unified power for legal interpretation

gongshu	公署	government office
guanzhi gaige	官制改革	reform of civil service system
Guohui	国会	Congress
Pingzheng Yuan	平政院	Pingzheng Yuan (Administrative Court)
shenpan ting	审判厅	Appellate courts
siji sanshen zhi	四级三审制	four-instance and three-level system
Tiantan Xianfa Cao'an	天坛宪法草案	Draft Constitution of the Temple of Heaven
xian zhishi	县知事	county magistrate
Xianfa Huiyi	宪法会议	onstitutional Convention
Xingbu	刑部	Board of Punishments
xingzheng caipan suo	行政裁判所	administrative courts
Yubei Lixian	预备立宪	Preparatory Constitutionalism

Administrative Justice and the Transformation of China's Population Policies

MICHAEL PALMER

SOAS & IALS (University of London)

University of Hong Kong & Chinese University of Hong Kong

INTRODUCTION

Family planning policy and law in the People's Republic of China (hereafter 'PRC' or 'China') has for many years been primarily characterized as administrative in nature rather than—as might be considered more appropriate—matters of family and civil law.[1] The key legislation was and still is the 2001 Population and Birth Planning Law (Renkou yu Jihua Shengyu Fa), revised in 2015 and then again in 2021. This was initially a national level codification of existing rules restricting family size and promoting genetic selection policies—a consolidating statute. For a span of approximately four decades, from the late 1970s to the mid-2010s, the evolving framework of population control was implemented through administrative mechanisms and governmental agencies rather than through civil litigation between private entities. However, the 2001 Law, which was imbued with an ethos of control, has undergone substantial revisions over the past decade, introducing modifications that champion a novel pronatalist paradigm in population and birth planning. This paper examines several related issues: what are the legal and policy features of these revisions in law and policy in favour of a more pronatalist system, how has the transition from birth restriction to birth encouragement affected administrative justice in China, and what does the transformation reveal about administrative control and administrative justice in China today? The paper confirms the fundamental significance of the shift from birth limitation policies to pronatalist policies, and that among the most important consequences of the new approach has been a shift from administrative control, often experienced by Chinese

[1] As a result, Chinese family law textbooks have hitherto given limited attention to family planning and birth control regulations. These matters have historically been treated as administrative law and policy rather than as elements of family or civil law. This classification reflects the state's approach to population control as a matter of governmental administration and public policy implementation rather than as an aspect of private family relations governed by civil law. It is primarily enforced through administrative mechanisms, such as government agencies and local authorities, rather than criminal or civil legal frameworks, allowing for measures like registration systems, fines, and incentives to ensure compliance. As a result, discussions of these regulations tend to appear in administrative law materials rather than in family law educational resources. It should be noted that the primary purpose of marriage in traditional China was to produce a male heir. Therefore, in modern times, classifying family planning as a state administrative matter rather than a private family concern is particularly remarkable.

citizens as coercive in nature, to supportive civil justice and social welfare systems, and significantly less administrative injustice.

The first significant formal amendment to the law, following party-led initiatives, occurred in 2015. China officially ended its one-child policy and introduced a universal two-child policy. In 2021, the Law was revised again to implement the three-child policy, allowing married couples to have up to three children.[2] This revision was adopted on August 20, 2021, and offered formal revisions to family planning throughout the law. Additional revisions made in 2021 included abandonment of restrictive measures that had previously been in place to limit births, such as removing social maintenance fees (*shehui fuyang fei*–in effect, fines for excess births), and adding supportive measures for families. These revisions reflected China's shifting demographic priorities as the country began facing challenges related to an ageing population, declining birth rates, and changing economic conditions, especially a shrinking labour force. As China has transitioned from a policy of birth limitation to one of birth encouragement in response to these formidable challenges, so the underpinnings of birth planning have evolved from being governed by administrative law and policy to an increasing emphasis also on aspects of civil and social protection law. Whilst this transformation remains incomplete, studying it does provide valuable insights into legal development, the nature of administrative justice in China, and the nature of state-family relations in China. As proposed in this paper, this shift in policy and law could also be seen as enhancing 'administrative justice' by reducing the negative impact of administrative norms and their enforcement on the reproduction process.

HISTORICAL DEVELOPMENT OF CHINA'S BIRTH PLANNING SYSTEM (1970S-2010S)

From the late 1970s until the early 2010s, China's population control system operated through a mainly administrative framework, characterised by hierarchical control and comprehensive surveillance. The government's belief was that unless demographic pressure was restrained, China would not be able to secure meaningful economic development. Longitudinal analysis reveals how this system evolved through distinct phases while maintaining fundamental characteristics that created persistent administrative injustices during much of its implementation.

Administrative Framework and Enforcement Apparatus

The prevailing normative ethos during this period was essentially administrative, with policy generation and enforcement responsibilities vested in dedicated administrative bodies led by the National Population and Birth Planning Commission (Guojia Renkou he Jihua Shengyu Weiyuanhui) and its local branches operating through a hierarchical structure from

[2] Private sources in China advise that in practice, the cap of 'three children' is not applied and that some couples bear four or more children, apparently without any penalties being imposed on them.

national to local levels.[3] This ministerial agency reported directly to the State Council and orchestrated comprehensive population control through Local Birth Planning Commissions at provincial, municipal and county levels. These bodies conducted systematic household registration verifications, oversaw the issuance of birth permits (*zhunsheng zheng*) mandated for lawful procreation, and imposed social maintenance fees (*shehui fuyang fei*) upon policy violators. China's One-Child Policy violated fundamental reproductive rights under international human rights law. Through coercive measures that limited the number of children per couple, these policies infringed upon the right to freely determine family size and child spacing, as well as the right to health. These violations contravene obligations established under the Convention on the Elimination of All Forms of Discrimination against Women (CEDAW) and the International Covenant on Economic, Social and Cultural Rights (ICESCR).[4]

Local regulation relied heavily on ground-level officials and local community committees, specifically urban resident committees (Jumin Weiyuanhui) and rural village committees (Cunmin Weiyuanhui). These officials executed regular household inspections to oversee familial compliance with birth restrictions, communicated unauthorized pregnancies to superior authorities, and exerted pressure on non-compliant households through various tactics including workplace sanctions. Intimidation and coercion were common characteristics of the system in practice. Officials faced career repercussions for not meeting birth planning objectives. This created powerful motivations for stringent compliance as pressure cascaded downwards through all administrative strata. Despite this robust enforcement apparatus, a significant implementation challenge emerged from the tendency of local officials to collude with community counterparts to circumvent rigorous application of regulations, especially in rural areas.

Legal Development Through Three Phases

Until the early 2000s, China lacked a comprehensive national family planning law. It relied instead on constitutional provisions, marriage law requirements, and provincial regulations. Provincial regulations initially emphasised rewards for compliance. When these proved ineffective, authorities implemented increasingly strict penalties. From the mid-1980s onward, provincial regulations imposed fines on couples with unplanned births, with heavier penalties for subsequent violations.

The 1995 study highlighted multiple crucial tensions within this system. Rural economic reforms engendered conditions where farming families

[3] The Commission was merged with the Ministry of Health in 2013 to form the National Health and Family Planning Commission (Guojia Weisheng he Jihua Shengyu Weiyuanhui), reflecting a redefinition of policy priorities.

[4] See, for example,Wang, VX (2025) 'Reproductive Governance in China: National Policies Accountability under International Law' (23) *Northwestern Journal of Human Rights* 1, available at: https://scholarlycommons.law.northwestern.edu/njihr/vol23/iss2/2

would disregard birth quotas due to their reliance on familial labour and their capacity to forfeit single-child benefits. Women were pressed between the state and the family.[5] These pressures often meant that families hid excess births, creating the problem of unregistered 'black children' (*heihaizi*) born outside family planning policies that denied access to many kinds of public service.[6] The local implementation of these policies exhibited significant variation, with certain provinces permitting a second child if the firstborn was female or disabled. Officials confronted escalating challenges in enforcing restrictions in rural areas where entrenched preferences for male heirs remained prevalent. By the early 1990s, additional apprehensions arose regarding migrant workers circumventing birth planning policies, and the perceived 'low quality' of births in economically disadvantaged regions. This prompted an intensified focus on eugenic considerations, culminating in the contentious 1994 Mother and Infant Healthcare Law (Muying Baojian Fa), which incorporated eugenics-oriented provisions despite widespread international condemnation.[7]

The 2001 Population and Birth Planning Law represented China's first comprehensive national legislation, consolidating previously fragmented local regulations into a unified code. Unlike the Marriage Law revision of the same year, which generated very substantial public debate, the birth planning code was developed with minimal public consultation and deliberation, reflecting its politically sensitive nature.[8] My 2007 analysis in *The China Quarterly* traced how family planning was nevertheless gradually shifting from being primarily characterized as administrative law towards greater integration with family and civil law frameworks.[9] While maintaining birth limitation as central policy, the 2001 Law acknowledged

[5] Tang, L and Liu, Y (2024) 'Family Planning Policy in China and Gender Equality in Family and Labor Market' (4) *European Journal of Development Studies* 75, who conclude that while the One Child Policy improved some aspects of gender equality (especially education and career opportunities), it also maintained traditional dependencies on women in domestic spheres, creating complex pressures on Chinese women who gained economic opportunities but retained household burdens.

[6] The social psychological dimensions of this discrimination can be understood through Goffman's analysis of stigma, where children born outside policy limits carried a 'discrediting stigma' that had material consequences for access to education, healthcare, and legal recognition. Goffman, E (1963) *Stigma: Notes on the Management of Spoiled Identity* Prentice-Hall.

[7] The Law met with criticism for its eugenics-related provisions, including premarital medical exams and recommendations to delay marriage or terminate pregnancies in cases of hereditary diseases. Articles 10 and 16 specifically raised ethical concerns about reproductive rights and discrimination against people with disabilities. See Palmer, M (1997) 'Protecting the Health of Mothers and their Children? Developments in the Family Law of the People's Republic of China' in Bainham, A (ed.) *Annual Survey of Family Law: 1995*, Dordrecht: Kluwer (for The International Society on Family Law) 107 at 116.

[8] Palmer, M (1995) 'The Re-Emergence of Family Law in Post-Mao China: Marriage, Divorce and Reproduction' (141) *The China Quarterly* 110.

[9] Palmer, M (2007) 'Transforming Family Law in Post-Deng China: Marriage, Divorce and Reproduction' (191) *The China Quarterly* 675.

negative impacts on women and stipulated that population control work should be supplemented with efforts enhancing women's educational and employment opportunities. It also provided a right to reproduce.

Administrative Injustice

Comparative analysis of the 1995 and 2007 periods covered in the two papers revealed that, notwithstanding procedural advancements such as the formalization of birth limitation regulations within national legislation, the fundamental framework remained essentially unaltered. The 1995 study established a crucial understanding of administrative injustice within China's family planning system. It documented how policies were enforced through increasingly draconian administrative measures, such as large fines, disciplinary actions, and other sanctions against individuals exceeding birth quotas. This fostered an environment of administrative coercion rather than voluntary compliance. Enforcement mechanisms frequently lacked the procedural safeguards indispensable to administrative justice, with local officials wielding extensive discretionary authority in the imposition of penalties and demonstrating minimal accountability for their determinations.

The 2007 analysis revealed that citizens still faced limited legal routes to address complaints stemming from official misconduct or mistakes. The system offered inadequate remedies through administrative review (*xingzheng fuyi*) or litigation (*xingzheng susong*). This predicament left individuals with scant options to challenge unjust penalties or treatment. The 2001 Law perpetuated an administrative target management system wherein higher government tiers assigned demographic objectives to subordinate levels and assessed, rewarded, or penalized them based on adherence to the targets. This administrative structure created pressure that often led to abuses at the local level, as officials aimed to meet quotas rather than ensure fair implementation.

Significant disparities in policy enforcement emerged between urban and rural locales. This exposed inconsistencies in administrative application. Urban residents faced increased scrutiny within the administrative structure. Rural families frequently developed tactics to bypass regulations, exposing disparities in administrative control across different populations. Despite constitutional assurances of gender equality, these administrative policies placed significantly unequal burdens on women. The system ensnared women in a conflict between state mandates aimed at restricting reproduction and familial pressures to produce male heirs, ultimately reinforcing rather than alleviating social biases and gender discrimination.

Incorporating eugenic principles into family planning administration introduced further concerning aspects. Practices such as mandatory abortions for individuals with hereditary conditions revealed serious ethical oversight gaps in administrative implementation of population control. As noted above, those who breached population control policies faced imposition of social maintenance fees. These fees acted as administrative penalties for supposedly adding 'societal burdens' through births beyond the plan. Failure to pay these fees triggered further administrative and legal consequences, creating cycles of financial and legal strain with little consideration for individual circumstances.

Despite fundamental problems in the system, the 1995 analysis was also able to identify some limited signs of administrative learning and adaptation. Provincial regulations evolved over time in response to practical challenges, demonstrating some flexibility within the system. Provincial policies and regulations gradually incorporated exceptions for unique situations, such as families with disabled first children or allowances for additional births where men died without male heirs followed by close agnatic adoption.[10] These exceptions, though limited, represented small steps towards recognising individual circumstances within the administrative framework.

By the mid-2000s, authorities began acknowledging contradictions between population control and social welfare policies, emphasising the family's role as a care provider. As China increasingly faced challenges posed by in particular an ageing population,[11] birth planning fundamentally began transforming from administrative restriction towards a civil law and social security framework more focused on supporting families, though this transition remained in its infancy when the 2007 article was published.[12]

[10] This allowed, for example, continuation in part of a traditional form of marriage and adoption based on double ancestral hall marriage *(jiantiao)* in which the brother of an adult male who had failed to procreate could take a second wife, despite strict statutory rules against bigamy, and allow male children born to the second wife to belong to the ancestral descent line of the childless brother. Thus, Article 8 of the Sichuan Province Birth Planning Regulation (Sichuan Sheng Jihua Shengyu Tiaoli) provides that 'couples who can meet the following requirements may give birth to a second child: (vii) A person is the only one of several brothers in a rural area who can have children'. See Palmer, M (1988) 'The People's Republic of China: Problems of Marriage and Divorce' (27) *Journal of Family Law* 57.

[11] Various projections show over 400 million citizens above age 60 by 2040, with China's workforce decline beginning around 2012 and fertility rates estimated at approximately 1.3 children per woman in 2020, well below the replacement level of 2.1.In addition, in discussions of population issues, there was a growing preference for using the term *'shengyuquan'* or reproductive rights rather than *'jihua shengyu'* or birth planning. See, for example, Zhang, XJ (2010) *Shengyu quan ji qi jiuji zhidu yanjiu — yi "Deng Jun taoyao shengyu quan" deng sange anli wei li* (Research on Reproductive Rights and Their Relief System — Taking "Deng Jun Claiming Reproductive Rights" and Three Other Cases as Examples) Master of Law dissertation, Lanzhou University. For an example of how reproductive rights operate in practice within China's evolving legal framework, see Ding, Chunyan (2015) 'Surrogacy litigation in China and beyond' (2015) *Journal of Law and the Biosciences* 33, which examines judicial approaches to reproductive autonomy in surrogacy cases and the tension between administrative control and civil law principles. The author presents the family planning system as both a driver of surrogacy demand (through restricting family size and creating vulnerable populations when only children die) and a bureaucratic framework that complicates the legal status of surrogate children through permit and registration requirements.

[12] This allowed, for example, continuation in part of a traditional form of marriage and adoption based on double ancestral hall marriage *(jiantiao)* in which the brother of an adult male who had failed to procreate could take a second wife, despite strict statutory rules against bigamy, and allow male children born to the second wife to belong to the ancestral descent line of the childless brother. Thus, Article 8 of the Sichuan Province Birth Planning Regulation (Sichuan Sheng Jihua Shengyu Tiaoli) provides that 'couples who can meet the following requirements may give birth to a second child: (vii) A person is the only one of

The demographic challenges of ageing population, and also low fertility rates, reducing workforce, and gender imbalance created growing alarm that these developments challenged China's economic growth and social stability, setting the stage for the more fundamental policy transformations that would emerge in the following decade.[13]

LIMITS TO PROGRESS

Despite China's dramatic shift from restrictive birth policies to comprehensive pronatalist measures over the past decade, with the creation of a comprehensive legal and administrative architecture, which will be considered in some detail below, several significant hurdles continue to impede progress in raising fertility rates and enlarging family size. These challenges reflect changes in society in mainland China stemming largely from policies of economic reform and they help us understand why the transformed approach will likely struggle to achieve its demographic objectives.[14]

Economic pressures on households continue to pose significant challenges. The cost of raising children in urban China has now become prohibitively high. Housing expenses in major cities often exceed several times the average annual household income. Rising housing prices are viewed as a key factor contributing to these rising costs. Despite some reductions in recent years, they continue to place further strain on households. Excessive housing expenses have in general been recognized as a key deterrent to childbirth, contributing to lower fertility rates. In regions with higher housing costs, individuals tend to marry and have children later in life, delaying the timing of first childbirth and compounding the demographic issue. Social housing initiatives may offer a potential policy lever to address this barrier, as Jin and Chen's research indicates that housing inclusion programmes could positively influence fertility intentions. This suggests that comprehensive demographic policy requires coordination between family planning frameworks and broader economic policies addressing housing affordability and economic security. Social (public) housing initiatives could serve as an important policy tool to overcome this barrier. Jin and Chen's analysis concludes that housing inclusion programmes may positively impact fertility intentions. This highlights the necessity of a comprehensive demographic policy that combines family

several brothers in a rural area who can have children'. See Palmer, M (1988) 'The People's Republic of China: Problems of Marriage and Divorce' (27) *Journal of Family Law* 57.

[13] See. For example, Sarah Rodriguez (2023) *Reproductive Realities in Modern China: Birth Control and Abortion, 1911–2021* Cambridge University Press. See especially 'The Rise and Demise of the One Child Policy 1970-2015' at 167-203.

[14] Empirical research suggests that the removal of birth restrictions has had only a transient effect on the escalation of birth rates and the rates of natural population increase. Birth policy predicated solely on the elimination of such restrictions is unlikely to engender a sustained impact on population growth over the long term. See: Lin, YD; Zhang, BY; Hu, Meijing; Yao, Q; Jiang, M and Zhu, CR (2024) 'The effect of gradually lifting the two-child policy on demographic changes in China' (39) *Health Policy and Planning* 363.

planning strategies with broader economic measures centred on housing affordability and financial security.

In China's push towards pronatalist policies, education costs have also emerged as a significant barrier despite government efforts to ease the burden. The 2021 'double reduction' policy (*shuangjian zhengce*) sought to reduce education expenses by curbing for-profit tutoring in core subjects.[15] However, families continue to spend an estimated 20-30% of their household budgets per child on education. This financial strain stems from a range of interconnected factors: formal education costs, such as tuition, school supplies, and uniforms, persisting tutoring expenses, which have shifted to non-core subjects or underground markets, extracurricular activities considered essential for gaining a competitive edge, and indirect costs like inflated housing prices in desirable school districts. These various expenses make raising multiple children financially out of reach for most families. As a result, many parents are reluctant to reproduce, prioritising their ability to provide high-quality education in a small family over having more children. As noted above, compounding this issue is China's housing affordability crisis, which adds another layer of financial stress. Together, these pressures create a powerful disincentive to create larger families, effectively stalling the nation's pronatalist ambitions despite policy incentives designed to boost fertility. These economic realities undermine government efforts to encourage higher birth rates.[16]

In addition, decades of one-child policy enforcement have created deeply entrenched social norms that resist official policies intended to encourage reproduction. According to research by Liu and others, only two-fifths of women of childbearing age now prefer to bear two or more children, with less than 10 per cent contemplating three or more children. These now entrenched cultural preferences are not responsive to state policy interventions to encourage larger families.[17]

Furthermore, gender inequality remains a critical obstacle. Despite revisions in 2022 of the Law on the Protection of Women's Rights

[15] The 'double reduction policy' is an educational initiative in the People's Republic of China aimed at alleviating the burden of homework and after-school tutoring on primary and secondary school students. This policy aims to reduce the financial costs families face for tutoring services. It also aims to improve the quality of compulsory education.

[16] Hu, DZ; Li, HB; Li, T; Meng, LS and Nguyen, Binh Thai (2023) 'The Burden of Education Costs in China: A Struggle for All, but Heavier for Lower-Income Families' Available at: http://dx.doi.org/10.2139/ssrn.4558282. Also see Wei, Y (2023).'Household Expenditure on Education in China: Key Findings From the China Institute for Educational Finance Research-Household Surveys (CIEFR-HS)' (7, 3) *ECNU Review of Education* https://doi.org/10.1177/20965311241243389.

[17] Liu J, Liu M, Zhang S, Ma Q, Wang Q. (2019) "Intent to have a second child among Chinese women of childbearing age following China's new universal two-child policy: a cross-sectional study" (46,1) *BMJ Sex Reproductive Health* 59. Ren, Y., Cheng, X., Niu, C. et al. (2024). "Fertility intention of young people of childbearing age in China after the implementation of the two-child policy—A systematic review and meta-analysis" *BMC Public Health* 24, 3518., and Ni, S "Young People's Fertility Intentions and Concerns Under the Two-Child Policy Context" Chapter 5 in her *From One Child to Two Children*. Palgrave Macmillan.

and Interests[18] intended to counter workplace discrimination against women, there are many reports that such pregnancy-related workplace discrimination against females continues to be widespread.[19] Indeed, the continuing problems are to a significant extent a direct result of the multiple child policy. Limitations on the hiring of women, discrimination in the workplace, and unfair dismissal–including where companies make working conditions for pregnant women so harsh that they are pushed into stepping down–when in employment are problems that have been exacerbated because of the impact on women of pronatalist policies encouraging larger families. Many firms discriminate against women via job advertisements, interviews, and misconduct in the workplace itself such as being punished for taking maternity leave twice.[20] Although usually rather passive in such matters, some trade unions in China are advocating for stronger protections for women in the workplace to promote gender equality and prevent discrimination. The Hunan Federation of Trade Unions, for example, has recently issued guidelines urging employers to avoid gender-biased hiring practices, respect maternity rights, and ensure equal pay for equal work and other provinces have made similar calls[21]. Despite growing public concern, many women still face questions about marriage and childbirth during job interviews. Those who advocate change argue for legal reforms, financial incentives, and the equitable distribution of parenting responsibilities to mitigate discrimination and foster women's professional advancement.[22] But it is not at all clear that such measures will address the problem effectively. The population issue is impacted by city living and

[18] The revised Law came into force on January, 1 2023 and aims to provide stronger protection for women in various areas including political rights, personal rights, education, employment and social security, marriage and family rights, and to eliminate all forms of discrimination against women.

[19] Li, QX; Di, X (2025) 'Fertility discrimination in the Chinese labour market: Evidence from a correspondence study and an employer survey' (92) *Labour Economics* 102668. See also Yun Zhou's research findings in which she observes 'The women in my study worry that familial expectations, now uncurbed by state-imposed birth restrictions, will overtly or implicitly pressure them into having more than one child' Zhou, Y (2023) 'Toward a Feminist Re-problematization of China's Low Birth Rate' *Georgetown Journal of International Affairs* (January 6, 2023) available at https://gjia.georgetown.edu/2023/01/06/toward-a-feminist-re-problematization-of-chinas-low-birth-rate/

[20] Zhang, X., Lou, H., Tang, X. et al. (2021) 'Socio-demographic characteristics and outcomes of pregnant women who delivered prior to and after the termination of the one-child policy in China: a comparative study' (21) *BMC Pregnancy Childbirth* 318. Zhou, Yun (2023) 'Gender Inequality: A Key to Understanding China's Population Decline.' *Australian Institute of International Affairs*, March 8, 2023, available at https://www.internationalaffairs.org.au/australianoutlook/gender-inequality-a-key-to-understand-chinas-population-decline/ and (2025) 'How gendered lived experiences shape sex preference attitudes in contemporary urban China' (87, 1) *Journal of Marriage and Family* 365. See also Zhang, Y (2024) 'Discrimination against Women in the Workplace' (27) *Journal of Education, Humanities and Social Sciences* 135.

[21] Cheng, S (2025) 'Unions Call for Better Protection of Female Jobseekers, Employees: Employers Warned Against Biased Hiring and Unfair Treatment of Women' *China Daily*, March 14, 2025.

[22] Zhang, C., Tong, X., & Liu, A. (2025) 'Sociological studies on women/gender in China during the past 40 years' (11, 2) *Chinese Journal of Sociology*, 161

changing lifestyles. People are getting married much later now–numerous reports suggest women at almost 29 and men at about 30–compared to their early-to-mid 20s back in 2000.[23] This significantly reduces the time available for having children. Exacerbating the issue, other population trends pose a significant challenge to policy efforts. The number of women in their prime childbearing years is projected to continue to decline significantly in the next ten years. Insights from similar societies in East Asia reveal a serious reality: once birth rates fall to very low levels, they are exceptionally difficult to reverse, even with comprehensive government interventions.[24]

Economic and social barriers are not the only obstacles to effective policy implementation in China. Another issue is the significant gap that often exists between central directives and local execution. Local governments frequently face financial constraints and limited administrative capacity, making it difficult to fulfil their mandated responsibilities.[25] Moreover, these responsibilities are often fragmented across multiple ministries and agencies, hindering coordinated action despite the introduction of frameworks facilitating coordination across ministries. These implementation gaps pose a serious challenge to China's pronatalist policies. For example, one prominent issue is fiscal constraint coupled with regional disparities. Local governments are often underfunded for implementing centrally mandated childcare and family support initiatives. Research by Wang et al. (2023) in the *Journal of Chinese Governance* highlights this problem, noting that municipal and county-level governments are expected to cover approximately 70% of childcare expansion costs while receiving only about 40% of national tax revenues. This creates an 'unfunded mandate' scenario, leaving local authorities struggling to meet expectations. It should be added that this issue is deeply rooted and extends to other areas of public funding tied to government-mandated initiatives. A significant imbalance exists in fiscal responsibilities across different levels of government. In 2019, central government expenditures accounted for just 14.7% of total government spending, while local governments were responsible for a staggering 85.3%. This disproportion highlights a systemic distortion in China's fiscal framework, where unevenly distributed responsibilities have created an imbalance in government spending.[26] The western regions, often characterized by lower income levels, exhibited significantly lower compliance rates compared to the more prosperous eastern coastal provinces. Such findings highlight a crucial need for addressing funding

[23] Cang, W (2023) 'Provinces find couples are marrying later in life' *China Daily* (February 15, 2023) at https://global.chinadaily.com.cn/a/202302/15/WS63ebb6dea31057c47ebaec5f.html.

[24] Sobotka, T (2021) 'World's Highest Childlessness Levels in East Asia' (595) *Population et Sociétés* 1.

[25] Lin, SL. (2022) 'Fiscal Relationship between the Central and Local Governments' Chapter 11, in *China's Public Finance: Reforms, Challenges, and Options* Cambridge University Press, 350-390.

[26] Ibid at 190; see also Liu, Y. (2020). 'People's will or the central government's plan? The shape of contemporary Chinese local governance' *Journal of Contemporary East Asia Studies*, 9(2), 226-242. https://doi.org/10.1080/24761028.2020.1744290.

inequality and improving coordination in order to implement successfully China's pronatalist policy initiatives.

The challenges of implementing pronatalist policies highlight the difficulty of translating well-intentioned central directives into practical, local outcomes, potentially jeopardizing China's demographic goals. While the shift from restrictive to supportive population policies marks a significant reorientation, deeply rooted economic, social, and structural issues may hinder the success of even the most carefully designed approaches. The complex interaction between formal policy changes, informal social norms, economic pressures, and demographic trends creates an environment where rapid increases in fertility rates seem unlikely.[27]

POLICY AND REGULATORY CHANGES IN CHINA'S BIRTH PLANNING

Over the past decade, as we have emphasised, China's birth control policy and law have undergone a profound transformation, shifting from stringent restrictions to active promotion of childbirth. This policy shift has reshaped the legal and social landscapes of reproduction in the PRC, placing greater emphasis on civil normative structures, social welfare support, and reforms to administrative systems.

The Chinese leadership, as we have noted, formally ended the one-child policy in 2015 due to its unintended consequences, including a rapidly ageing population, a shrinking workforce, and a gender imbalance caused by a cultural preference for male children. These demographic challenges threatened economic growth and social stability, prompting the government to shift to a two-child policy to encourage population growth and address these long-term issues. A revised Population and Birth Planning Law 2015 introduced the universal two-child policy, allowing all married couples to have two children regardless of circumstances. This formally ended the one-child policy that had been in place since the late 1970s.The 2015 Law began introducing limited support measures, but nothing approaching the comprehensive infrastructure established later, in 2021. The focus remained primarily on managing the transition to two-child families rather than actively encouraging reproduction. Moreover, the 2015 amended law maintained the fundamental legal premise that reproductive decisions were subject to state administrative control for demographic management.

[27] China's demographic policies may also be said to illustrate Robert Merton's concept of "unanticipated consequences of purposive social action," where rational interventions lead to outcomes that counter their original goals. The one-child policy's unintended effects—gender imbalance, ageing population, and cultural resistance—were predictable results of large-scale social engineering. Merton's framework suggests that current pronatalist policies may face similar challenges, as complex social systems resist straightforward policy solutions, especially in areas like family formation. This perspective highlights why administrative approaches often fail to resolve deeply rooted social issues in reproductive decision-making. See Merton, Robert K 'The Unanticipated Consequences of Purposive Social Action' (1936) 1 (6) *American Sociological Review* 894; also (1968) *Social Theory and Social Structure* enlarged ed, Free Press at 475-490.

The law still treated family planning as primarily an administrative rather than a civil matter.

The 2021 CCP Central Committee and State Council Joint Decision

The policy transformation was formalized through the CCP Central Committee and State Council's comprehensive policy statement entitled 'Decision on Optimizing the Fertility Policy to Promote the Long-term Balanced Development of the Population', released in June 2021.[28] This statement laid the foundation for subsequent legislative changes, detailing comprehensive measures to implement the new pronatalist policy.

The Decision introduced an administrative framework that redefined the relationship between the state and individual reproductive rights. By transitioning from the restrictive two-child policy to a more permissive three-child policy, it signalled a significant shift in governmental strategy. The Decision explicitly mandated supportive measures including workplace protections, tax incentives, and social security benefits for families with children, establishing a robust administrative framework empowering individuals to seek redress if their reproductive or workplace rights are infringed.

The Decision also emphasized the need for enhancing 'population quality' (*renkou suzhi/suyang*) and eugenics considerations. By 2035, the goal is to significantly improve eugenic and child-rearing services, thereby enabling individuals to enjoy a better quality of life and strengthen family capacity for growth and prosperity.

Institutionally, the 2013 merger of the National Population and Family Planning Commission with the National Health Commission had marked a transformative shift from punitive enforcement to supportive service provision. The rigid enforcement framework began to disintegrate, with local birth control offices either repurposed or phased out. Officials who once focused on constraining births now actively advocate for them, reflecting a profound reorientation of administrative priorities.

The Revised Population and Birth Planning Law (2021)

On August 20, 2021, the Standing Committee of the National People's Congress approved amendments to the 2015 Population and Birth Planning Law.[29] Although the amended law saw more public discussion compared to its introduction in 2001, the policy change was ultimately framed as a top-down decision by the government, with only limited public consultation.

[28] Zhonggong Zhongyang, Guowuyuan (CCP Central Committee and State Council) (2021) 'Guanyu Youhua Shengyu Zhengce Cujin Renkou Changqi Junheng Fazhan de Jueding' (Decision on Optimizing Fertility Policies to Promote Long-Term Balanced Population Development) *Xinhua News Agency* July 20, 2021.

[29] NPC Observer (2021) 'Law of the People's Republic of China on Population and Family Planning' available at https://npcobserver.com/legislation/population-and-family-planning-law/

The 2021 amendment represents a multifarious approach to population management, providing evidence of both continuity and change in a pronatalist direction.

Key Legal Changes

One of the most significant formal changes was abolishing the decades-old birth permit system (*zhunsheng zheng*), which previously required couples to obtain official approval before having children. However, implementation varies significantly—some regions still require documentation resembling the former permit system as a precondition for securing household registration (*hukou*) for newborn children, while large urban areas may require no birth planning documentation at all.

The 2021 revised Law omitted provisions for the controversial 'social maintenance fee system—that is, as noted above, the punitive taxes imposed on families who exceeded birth quotas. These fines often amounted to several times a family's annual income, causing severe financial hardship and widespread perceptions of inequity.[30]

Just as importantly, the 2021 revisions implemented the new Three-Child Policy. Article 18, paragraph 1 now declares: 'A couple may give birth to three children' *(yidui fuqi keyi shengyu san ge zinü*), allowing for additional children if specific legal and regulatory conditions are met.

Legal Framework Structure

The Law, however, continues to reflect a state-centric governance model where the State Council plays the leading role in national population planning, with local governments implementing policies through administrative directives (Articles 5 and 10). The Law incorporates several key implementation mechanisms. Economic incentives (*jingji jili*) outlined in Articles 23-30 provide financial benefits for compliant families, extended maternity leave, and childcare service support. Social mobilization (*shehui dongyuan*) provisions in Articles 7 and 12 focus on engaging community organizations in implementation efforts. The educational dimensions covered in Article 13 require 'planned physiological hygiene education' (*shengli weisheng jiaoyu*)—a euphemistic term for basic sex education—in schools and promote voluntary compliance through education rather than punitive measures.

30 Xie, XW (2023) 'Shehui fuyang fei quxiao zhi hou' (After the Abolition of Social Maintenance Fees) (46) *Zhongguo xinwen zhoukan* (China News Weekly) 10 December 2023. See also Chen, GS (2020) *Shehui fuyang fei de falü shuxing yanjiu* (Research on the Legal Nature of Social Maintenance Fees) Master's dissertation. Shanghai Normal University. Chen argues that social administration fees should be classified as regulatory administrative charges rather than administrative penalties. This suggested re-classification aligned more closely with the developing birth policies and administrative fee management systems. Shortly afterwards, the fees were abolished.

Enforcement and Legal Protections

The Law establishes comprehensive enforcement and legal protection mechanisms. Articles 40-41 outline robust administrative approaches to regulatory compliance, granting health departments substantial punitive and corrective powers for violations including illegal abortions and sex-selective procedures. The enforcement framework combines immediate financial consequences with potential long-term professional repercussions. Article 46 provides legal recourse for citizens who believe their rights have been infringed during family planning management, allowing for administrative reconsideration (*xingzheng fuyi*) or administrative litigation (*xingzheng susong*).

Incentives and Social Security

Chapter IV outlines comprehensive state policies supporting birth planning and child welfare. Article 23 establishes state incentives for couples following family planning regulations, while Article 24 focuses on developing social security systems including medical and maternity insurance. Articles 25-26 provide parental leave incentives and employment protections for women during pregnancy, childbirth, and breastfeeding. The framework continues with Articles 27-28, which offer financial, educational, and housing support to reduce family fertility burdens. Articles 32-33 establish specific protections for vulnerable families and rural/impoverished families, and Article 34 allows local governments flexibility in developing tailored implementation measures suited to their particular circumstances.

Continued Eugenics Considerations

The 2021 Law maintains the focus on 'population quality' (*renkou suzhi*). Article 2 specifies that state functions include 'improving the quality of the population' (*tigao renkou suzhi*). Article 18 encourages age-appropriate marriage and eugenic childbearing (*yousheng youyu*). Articles 35 and 37 require establishing systems for premarital, prenatal, and postnatal healthcare to prevent birth defects and improve newborn health.

Related Normative Documents

Several documents supplement the 2021 Law. The Maternal and Infant Safety Action Enhancement Plans (2021-2025), issued by the National Health Commission, aim to reduce infant mortality through standardized screening, multidisciplinary assessments, and enhanced appointment systems using information technology.[31] The Birth Defects Prevention Capacity Enhancement Plans (2023-2027) focus on improving genetic screening, early detection of birth defects, and comprehensive genetic

[31] State Council (2021) 'China releases action plan to improve child health' Xinhua (November 5, 2021) available at https://english.www.gov.cn/statecouncil/ministries/202111/05/content_WS6185130bc6d0df57f98e4923.html

counselling services, emphasizing prevention through advanced medical technologies and specialized care.[32]

Employment Rights and Social Protection Women's Protection Law Amendments (2023)

The 2023 amendments to the Women's Protection Law[33] created a comprehensive framework addressing employment discrimination while supporting women's reproductive roles (Articles 41-48). In particular, Article 43 prohibits gender discrimination in recruitment, including inquiring about marital status or family planning intentions, while Article 44 mandates inclusion of gender equality principles in employment contracts and collective agreements. Article 45 guarantees equal pay for equal work and equal access to social benefits, and Article 46 prohibits gender discrimination in promotions and professional development. The framework extends to biological functions through Article 47, which establishes workplace protections during menstruation, pregnancy, childbirth, and breastfeeding, while Article 48 provides job security by prohibiting penalties due to marriage, pregnancy, or maternity leave.

Civil Law and Legal Framework Transformation

Civil Code Reforms (2020)

The Civil Code marked a decisive break with past restrictions, eliminating all language limiting family size and explicitly protecting reproductive rights without qualification. Marriage registration procedures no longer require birth planning certificates, and the process became free from reproductive scrutiny.

Property and Social Security Reforms

Other legal reforms have eliminated discriminatory practices against children born outside quotas through several key measures: universal household registration (*hukou*) regardless of birth order, equal inheritance rights and access to education, healthcare, and social services, expanded social insurance programmes supporting larger families, and new tax deductions for childcare expenses and increased education subsidies.[34]

[32] See An, Y; Shen, Y; Ma, Y and Wang, H (2024) 'Research needs for birth defect prevention and control in China in the genomic screening era' (386) *BMJ* e078637

[33] NPC Observer (2025) 'Law of the People's Republic of China on the Protection of Women's Rights and Interests', last updated August 9, 2025, available at: https://npcobserver.com/legislation/womens-rights-and-interests-protection-law/.https://npcobserver.com/legislation/womens-rights-and-interests-protection-law/

[34] See Wang, X (2020 'Permits, Points, and Permanent Household Registration: Recalibrating Hukou Policy under "Top-Level Design" '(49, 3) *Journal of Current Chinese Affairs* 269.

Anti-Divorce Policies

The mandatory 30-day 'cooling-off period' introduced in the Civil Code represents part of the broader pronatalist strategy, requiring couples to wait before finalizing divorce while either party can withdraw the application. China's anti-divorce policies, including the mandatory 30-day 'cooling-off period' introduced in the marriage and family section of the Civil Code 2020 (in force January 1 2021) represent part of the broader pronatalist strategy.[35] This policy requires couples seeking divorce to wait 30 days before finalising their separation, during which either party can withdraw the application. The cooling-off period was implemented amid growing concerns over declining birth rates and an ageing population. Chinese officials frequently stress the importance of family stability for raising children and have directly linked declining marriage rates to falling birth rates.[36]

Childcare Infrastructure

Policies emphasize expanding childcare infrastructure with explicit targets to increase public childcare facilities and achieve city-wide coverage. Government resources once devoted to enforcing birth limitations have been redirected towards enhancing maternal and child healthcare, including labour pain management and assisted reproductive technologies under medical insurance coverage.[37]

Implementation Challenges

While the legal framework is progressive, its social impact depends on local administration interpretation and implementation, judicial willingness to uphold principles, and prevailing social attitudes. Cultural norms play a critical role in either reinforcing or undermining the policy framework. Implementation varies significantly by region, with wealthier provinces typically offering more generous benefits while rural areas often lag in enforcement.

ADMINISTRATIVE JUSTICE IN CHINA'S BIRTH PLANNING TRANSFORMATION

The characterization of administrative justice offered by Marc Hertog encompasses three principal dimensions: the procedures for making administrative decisions regarding individuals, the law under which such

[35] See the Chapter in this book by Ling Zhou, entitled 'Administered Divorce in China: Reflecting on the 2020 Civil Code's Restrictive Turn'.

[36] Ibid.

[37] Sun, L (2025) 'China launches first national childcare subsidies in bid to tackle demographic crisis' (July 28 2025) *South China Morning Post*, https://www.scmp.com/economy/china-economy/article/3319872/china-launches-first-national-childcare-subsidies-bid-tackle-demographic-crisis

decisions are made, and the systems for resolving disputes and grievances arising from those decisions.[38] Administrative justice, in its ideal form, requires government decisions affecting individuals to be made through fair procedures, based on clear legal authority, and subject to meaningful review and redress mechanisms.[39]

Applying this framework to China's birth planning transformation reveals a complex picture of improvement and persistent limitations across these three dimensions.

Dimensional Analysis

Procedural Transformation: Significant but Incomplete Progress

The transformation of decision-making procedures signifies a profound enhancement in China's birth planning system. The eradication of invasive and coercive mechanisms—compulsory gynaecological examinations, menstrual cycle surveillance, and household inspections conducted by hierarchical bureaucratic networks—has been supplanted by more standardized processes characterized by heightened transparency. The abolition of the birth permit system and social maintenance fees has eliminated perhaps the most capricious elements of administrative control. Transitioning towards a civil and social welfare regulatory framework has fostered procedural equity through more uniform processes imbued with greater transparency. As family planning increasingly adopts a more rights-oriented approach, citizens may subsequently gain greater confidence more robustly to contest administrative decisions and seek redress for grievances. The relaxation of administrative oversight may have curtailed local officials' capacity to exploit discretionary power, thereby diminishing opportunities for malfeasance and facilitating a more nuanced consideration of individual circumstances rather than a rigid application of quotas and targets. Nevertheless, procedural enhancements remain geographically inconsistent. Certain regions still mandate documentation reminiscent of the former permit system, engendering uneven implementation across jurisdictions. This indicates that while the formal procedural framework has evolved, practical application continues to exhibit significant variability, undermining uniform administrative justice. Furthermore, it is suggested that the lingering collective memories of state-imposed reproductive controls from the initial three decades of the birth planning system continue to shape young women's scepticism towards state-driven pronatalist agendas. These 'counter-reproductive memories' as conceptualized by Zhang Jingxue serve as both a repository of past traumas and a critical lens through which these women negotiate and resist the state's coercive reproductive policies. Despite the enactment of ostensibly flexible approaches such as the Three-Child Policy, opposition

[38] Hertogh, M (2022) 'Administrative Justice as a Field of Study' in Hertogh, M; Kirkham, R; Thomas, R and Tomlinson, J (eds) (2022) *The Oxford Handbook of Administrative Justice* Oxford University Press, available at: https://doi.org/10.1093/oxfordhb/9780190903084.002.0016

[39] Ibid

from younger women persists, with their counter-reproductive narratives illuminating the contradictions and inconsistencies intrinsic to the party-state's biopolitical governance, as well as its perpetuation of reproductive trauma and controls stemming from earlier birth limitation policies.[40]

Legal Framework: Comprehensive Metamorphosis

The legal dimension shows the most complete transformation. The evolution from an absence of dedicated national legislation prior to 2001 to the comprehensive 2001 Population and Birth Planning Law, followed by significant amendments in 2015 and 2021, represents a fundamental shift from stringent administrative oversight to a supportive civil law paradigm. The 2020 Civil Code arguably serves as a pivotal inflection point, in effect rescinding all family size restrictions and the obligation of spouses to practice birth limitation.

This transformation symbolises a thorough legal redirecting from regulation to assistance, with birth planning now increasingly under civil and social protection law rather than administrative control.[41] However, the legislative process itself still poses challenges. Although there was more public discourse on the 2021 changes, it lacked true consultation where public feedback significantly influenced policy decisions, reflecting elite policymaking in response to demographic pressures rather than participatory democracy.

Dispute Resolution: Persistent Structural Deficiencies

The third dimension reveals the significant remaining problems. Despite procedural and legal enhancements, citizens encounter fundamental obstacles in contesting administrative rulings concerning reproductive policies. Article 46 of the 2021 revised law retains the same language as its predecessors (Article 44 in the 2001 and 2015 laws), meaning that the Law itself does not encourage civil litigation access for aggrieved individuals but, rather, continues to emphasize administrative tracks. But administrative review procedures are fundamentally compromised, taking place within the same bodies responsible for reproductive policies, leading to significant conflicts of interest. Both administrative review and administrative litigation heavily depend on mediation, which in the Chinese setting often involves evaluative rather than facilitative mediation, leading to enforced

[40] Zhang, JX. (2025). Counter-Reproductive Memory: Chinese Young Women Against State Pronatalism. (37, 1) *Feminist Formations*, available at https://dx.doi.org/10.1353/ff.2025.a962228.

[41] A further complication is that courts sometimes are uncertain whether to characterise villagers' infringement of local rules on reproduction as administrative or civil misdemeanours,resulting in inconsistency in the approaches taken and outcomes delivered by the courts. See Zhang, FG and Weng, CF (2021) ''Cungui minyue zhong jihua shengyu tiaokuan de sifa shencha—ji yu 70 jian sifa anli de fenxi' (Judicial Review of Family Planning Provisions in Village Regulations and Agreements: An Analysis Based on 70 Judicial Cases) (4) *Journal of Jiangxi Science and Technology Normal University* 39.

compromise rather than authentic resolution.[42] The state continues to maintain substantial authority over individual reproductive choices, undermining genuine legal protections.[43]

Limitations: Persistent Authoritarian Characteristics

Despite improvements in administrative justice, China's transition from birth limitation to pronatalist policies continues to reflect authoritarian characteristics. Whether restricting or encouraging births, the state treats population management as a centralized policy issue rather than a matter of personal choice. Both policy approaches treat citizens primarily as economic and demographic resources: current pronatalist policies view citizens as solutions to ageing population challenges, while previous restrictions aimed to prevent resource strain.

The underlying philosophy continues to limit—although less robustly than before—individual autonomy, with the state asserting its legitimate authority to guide reproductive choices for national objectives. This approach places disproportionate pressure on women under both policy regimes. Current pronatalist campaigns often emphasize traditional gender roles while maintaining social pressure through state media and official channels.[44]

Continuities in Administrative Justice

Examining the transition through Hertogh's framework reveals significant continuities despite the policy reversal. The bureaucratic mechanisms

[42] See Palmer, M. (2006). 'Controlling the State: Mediation in Administrative Litigation in the People's Republic of China' 16 *Transnational Law and Contemporary Problems* 165; Palmer, M. (2010) 'Compromising courts and harmonizing ideologies: mediation in the administrative chambers of the people's courts in the People's Republic of China' in A. Harding, & P. Nicholson (eds.), *New Courts in Asia* Routledge. Palmer, M (2014) 'Mediating state and society: social stability and administrative suits' in Trevaskes, S; Nesossi, E; Sapio, F; and Biddulph, S (eds) (2014) "*The Politics of Law and Stability in China* Edward Elgar Publishing.

[43] See, for example, Tian Yuan (2015) *Lun Woguo Gongmin Shengyuquan de Baohu: Yi "Renkou yu Jihua Shengyu Fa" wei Shi* (On the Protection of Citizens' Reproductive Rights in China with reference to the Population and Family Planning Law) Master's of Law Thesis, Dalian Maritime University. This essay highlights the importance of strengthening administrative remedies to address disputes and protect citizens' reproductive rights. It identifies various administrative actions, such as forced sterilizations, fines, or restrictions on childbirth, which often infringe on these rights. Such conduct sometimes exceeded the authority granted by law, and stems from a lack of proper oversight. To address this, the essay proposes creating a clearer legal framework that establishes transparent guidelines and procedures for managing disputes related to reproductive rights. It advocates for the establishment of independent review mechanisms. These mechanisms should consist of impartial decision-makers to ensure that complaints against administrative decisions are handled fairly.

[44] That is to say, the transformation from punitive birth restrictions to incentivized reproduction represents what Collins would characterize as a change in control mechanisms rather than a redistribution of power, with the state adapting its reproductive governance strategies to maintain demographic authority under changing economic conditions. See Collins, R (1975) *Conflict Sociology: Toward an Explanatory Science* 1st Ed Academic Press at 60-85.

previously used to monitor and limit births have been repurposed to track and incentivize childbearing, while the fundamental nature of state intervention in reproductive decision-making remains intact. The underlying legal principle that reproductive choices are legitimately subject to state policy and regulation for national interests remains unchanged.

The grievance mechanisms available to citizens remain largely unchanged. Both policy regimes lack robust, independent avenues for challenging the underlying premise of state reproductive control. Administrative review processes remain internal to implementing agencies, creating inherent conflicts of interest and limiting the independence of review. The extensive use of mediation in administrative disputes can act as a barrier to justice for aggrieved parties, particularly when power imbalances, lack of transparency, or undue pressure to settle are present.[45]

Observations

The overall assessment suggests incremental progress within an inherently flawed framework. While China's birth planning transformation has achieved improvements in administrative justice by reducing arbitrary enforcement and enhancing procedural fairness, it has not fundamentally altered the state-citizen relationship regarding reproductive autonomy. Genuine administrative justice in reproductive policy would require more fundamental restructuring, including independent review mechanisms and recognition of reproductive autonomy as a right that constrains, rather than is subject to, administrative authority. Hampshire's analysis of irreconcilable moral conflicts offers a theoretical foundation for understanding why China's policy reversals continue to reflect structural continuity. He contended that true moral dilemmas—such as the conflict between individual reproductive autonomy and state demographic control—cannot be resolved through mere policy adjustments but instead demand procedural fairness to achieve legitimacy. China's persisting procedural deficiencies, manifest in both its restrictive and pronatalist policies, seem to bear out Hampshire's assertion that substantial policy transformations fail to confront the more profound institutional challenges of reconciling competing values.[46]

REFLECTIONS. ADMINISTRATIVE JUSTICE IN CHINA. LESSONS FROM POPULATION POLICY TRANSFORMATION

Implementation Challenges and Persistent Inequalities

Despite comprehensive legal transformation, China's population policy reform reveals significant implementation challenges that illuminate broader patterns in Chinese administrative justice. In particular, regional

45 Ibid.

46 See, Hampshire, S (2000) *Justice is Conflict* Princeton University Press 21-47; and *Morality and Conflict (1983)* Harvard University Press 140-169.

variations remain pronounced, with wealthier provinces typically offering more generous benefits and stronger legal protections while rural areas lag in enforcement. These disparities reflect deeper structural inequalities, creating distinct experiences across social stratification lines where urban educated elites navigate different regulatory environments than rural agricultural communities, while ethnic minorities face particular tensions in the intersection between traditional cultural practices and state demographic objectives.

This uneven application suggests that administrative justice operates not as a uniform system but as a differentiated mechanism that reproduces existing social hierarchies through differential access to rights and protections. Economic pressures continue to constrain family size decisions in practice, with many young people choosing smaller families despite policy encouragement, while cultural attitudes shift more gradually than legal frameworks. This disconnect between legal transformation and social reality highlights the limitations of administrative reform in addressing deeply embedded social challenges.[47]

Structural Continuities Despite Policy Reversal

The analysis reveals that despite China's dramatic shift from restriction to encouragement, the approach to administrative justice in reproductive policy maintains fundamental structural continuities. The transformation represents primarily a shift in demographic objectives rather than a fundamental alteration of the state-citizen relationship regarding reproductive autonomy. The administrative justice framework continues to prioritize state objectives over individual rights or procedural fairness as primary values.

Comparative legal analysis illuminates how China's approach diverges significantly from what might be called 'liberal democratic models' of administrative justice. While 'Western' legal systems generally emphasize individual rights as constraints on state power, China's framework treats reproductive decisions as legitimate subjects of state regulation for collective objectives. This reflects broader differences between civil law systems that emphasize state authority and common law traditions that prioritize individual protections. Compared to states like Germany or France, which maintain strong constitutional protections for reproductive autonomy, China's system reveals how administrative justice can be subordinated to developmental state objectives.

[47] Arguably, Ritzer's concept of 'the irrationality of rationality' helps us to understand better how this highly rationalised system, designed to optimise population size, produced deeply irrational outcomes. These included demographic imbalances, social instability, unregistered children, and ultimately the crisis and moral panic that necessitated a complete policy reversal. See Ritzer, G (2021) *The McDonaldization of Society*, 10th ed. Sage Publications at 1-30.

Critical Deficiencies in the Administrative Justice Framework

From an administrative justice perspective, the legal framework suffers from several critical deficiencies: broad delegation of authority that permits inconsistent application, vague legal standards subject to frequent reinterpretation, insufficient protection of citizens' rights against arbitrary administrative action, and continued prioritization of state demographic goals over individual reproductive autonomy. While procedural improvements have been achieved, these structural problems remain largely unaddressed.

Such deficiencies create ongoing tensions between different social groups. Women bear disproportionate burdens under both restrictive and pronatalist regimes, facing workplace discrimination while navigating competing pressures from state policy and family expectations. Rural communities experience administrative justice differently from urban populations, with less access to formal grievance mechanisms and greater reliance on informal mediation processes that may not adequately protect individual rights.

Broader Patterns in Chinese Administrative Justice

The population policy case study reveals several persistent characteristics that likely extend across other policy domains. The system demonstrates remarkable capacity for elite-driven reform, achieving relatively rapid and comprehensive policy reversals that reflect top-down decision-making rather than bottom-up pressure for justice or genuine public consultation. This elite-driven approach operates within an instrumental rights framework where citizens are treated as resources for achieving state objectives rather than rights-bearers who constrain state power. Individual protections exist when they align with state objectives but remain subordinate to collective goals as defined by political leadership.

Perhaps more significantly, the case reveals inadequate dispute resolution mechanisms, with administrative review processes remaining internal to implementing agencies and creating inherent conflicts of interest. The heavy reliance on mediation often forces compromise rather than providing genuine redress for administrative harm. This reflects a broader administrative emphasis over judicial review, where the continued preference for administrative rather than judicial oversight mechanisms limits independent scrutiny of government decisions across policy domains.

The Paradox of Authoritarian Administrative Justice

China's population policy transformation represents a paradoxical case study in administrative justice. While the shift from restriction to encouragement has improved certain procedural aspects by reducing arbitrary enforcement and enhancing transparency, fundamental authoritarian characteristics persist unchanged. Administrative systems have evolved from imposing restrictions to providing support, and thereby reduced administrative injustice, yet the state maintains its assertion of legitimate authority over reproductive choices for national objectives. So. the transformation manages rather than resolves fundamental tensions between state control and individual autonomy. By transitioning from coercive restrictions to incentivized encouragement, the state has minimized overt conflict and mitigated bureaucratic inequities, all while preserving its overarching control over reproductive decisions. This strategy manages social tensions by providing material benefits, carefully sidestepping any challenge to the fundamental power dynamic between the state and its citizens.

Implications for Administrative Justice Reform

The persistence of administrative justice deficiencies under both restrictive and pronatalist policy regimes demonstrates that meaningful reform requires more than changing policy targets. Genuine administrative justice in reproductive policy—and by extension other domains—would require more fundamental restructuring: establishing independent review mechanisms, ensuring transparent decision-making processes, providing effective remedies for administrative harm, and recognizing individual rights as constraints rather than subjects of administrative authority.

Comparative legal studies suggest that without constitutional protection for individual autonomy and independent judicial review of administrative decisions, procedural improvements remain vulnerable to reversal based on changing state priorities. Reducing the scope of administrative control can strengthen administrative justice within the remaining framework by limiting arbitrary power and enhancing certain citizen rights, but this falls short of fundamental reform.

Final Musings

This analysis reveals that while China's demographic policy transformation has achieved certain procedural improvements in administrative justice, the deeper structural relationship between state authority and individual autonomy remains fundamentally unchanged. The transformation represents improvement within an inherently constrained framework rather than fundamental reform of how administrative power operates in relation to individual rights.

The population policy case suggests that Chinese administrative justice operates according to conditional rights that serve instrumental purposes, maintains implementation gaps that disproportionately affect marginalized populations, and provides limited meaningful citizen participation in policy-making processes. These patterns indicate that while China can achieve rapid administrative reforms and improve certain aspects of procedural fairness, the system remains structurally resistant to the kind of independent oversight and rights-based constraints that characterize administrative justice in liberal democratic contexts. True administrative justice in this domain—and likely others—remains constrained by the broader authoritarian governance structure, suggesting that fundamental rather than incremental reform would be necessary to establish genuine accountability and citizen redress mechanisms.

GLOSSARY OF CHINESE TERMS

Romanisation (Hanyu Pinyin)	Chinese Characters	English Translation
Cunmin Weiyuanhui committees	村民委员会	rural village
Jihua Shengyu Fuwu Zheng	计划生育服务证	Birth Planning Service Certificate
jingji jili	经济激励	economic incentives
Jumin Weiyuanhui	居民委员会	urban residents' committees
Guojia Renkou he Jihua Shengyu Weiyuanhui	国家人口和计划生育委员会	National Population and Birth Planning Commission
Guojia Weisheng he Jihua Shengyu Weiyuanhui	国家卫生和计划生育委员会	National Health and Family Planning Commission
heihaizi	黑孩子	'black children'—unregistered children born outside family planning policies
hukou	户口	household registration
Muying Baojian Fa	母婴保健法	Mother and Infant Healthcare Law
Renkou yu Jihua Shengyu Fa	人口与计划生育法:	Population and Birth Planning Law
renkou suzhi/suyang	人口素质/素养	population quality
shehui fuyang fei	社会抚养费	social maintenance fee'
shengli weisheng jiaoyu	生理卫生教育	physiological hygiene education (a term used

		for basic sex education)
shuangjian zhengce	双减政策	double reduction policy
tigao renkou suzhi	提高人口素质	enhance population quality
xingzheng fuyi:	行政复议	administrative reconsideration
xingzheng susong	行政诉讼	administrative litigation
yidui fuqi keyi	一对夫妻可以生	'A couple may give birth
shengyu san ge zinü	育三个子女,	to three children'
yousheng youyu	优生优育	eugenical childbearing
zhunsheng zheng	准生证	birth permit

PART II
JUDICIAL POWER AND REVIEW MECHANISMS

The Development of the Due Process Principle in post-2013 China

BJÖRN AHL*

University of Cologne

INTRODUCTION

Traditionally, continental legal systems have emphasised the ex-post control of administrative decisions by courts and largely ignored the ex-ante control through participation in the process of administrative decision making. Administrative agencies have wide discretion regarding their choices of decision-making procedures. The protection of rights and the limitation of state power were only effected through administrative reconsideration and litigation when the administrative decision violated substantive law.[1] Given that Chinese administrative law developed along the lines of the Soviet model and was later also influenced by the administrative law of other continental jurisdictions, a lack of attention in China to procedure in administrative decision-making comes at no surprise. Attempts to draft a uniform national law governing administrative processes have yet to succeed, and moves to define general processual standards for administrative decision-making have been slow. Moreover, as the protection of individual rights has only played a limited role in the development of Chinese administrative law, the development of due process rights and the introduction of legal restraints to administrative procedure appear rather exceptional.

The party-state's endorsement of socialist rule of law invigorated the Chinese academic debate about a general administrative procedure law in the 1990s. The debate provides some explanation of the functions of administrative procedure law in the context of instrumental legality in a Leninist constitutional system. Academic commentators regarded legal restraints of administrative procedure as improving transparency in the administration and preventing corruption, as facilitating 'democratic' participation of citizens and protecting the autonomy of enterprises in the evolving socialist market economy.[2] Further, they argued that an emphasis

* Professor and Chair of Chinese Legal Culture, University of Cologne. The author thanks Jingzi Cui, Shaoyu Liu, Cui Xu and Haixu Yu for invaluable research assistance. Research for this chapter was funded by the Fritz Thyssen Foundation (project no. 10.16.2.008RE).

1 Pünder, Hermann (2013) 'German Administrative Procedure in a Comparative Perspective: Observations on the Path to a Transnational Ius Commune Proceduralis in Administrative Law' 11 *International Journal of Constitutional Law* 940-961 at 942. It might be added here that as China's law on court review of administrative decisions (Xingzheng susong fa) is often referred to in English as the 'Administrative Procedure Law', the central concern of this paper is not with that law (referred to here as the 'Administrative Litigation Law') but rather with regulating the processes of administrative decision making. Draft laws in this area have been called 'Xingzheng chengxu fa' (Law on Administrative Procedures).

2 Jiang, Mingan (1995) 'Woguo xingzheng chengxu lifa moshi de xuanzi' (Choice of China's

of administrative procedure increases the societal acceptance of administrative decision making, guarantees sustainable social stability and safeguards the implementation of substantive administrative law.[3]

Over the years, administrative law scholarship and courts have been the main driving forces behind the development of due process requirements of administrative procedure in China. This appears remarkable in a socialist legal system where top-down dynamics of a Party-led legislature and supplementary legislation adopted by the Supreme People's Court (SPC) in the form of so called judicial interpretations have dominated legal reforms. Haibo He analysed the development of the due process principle against the backdrop of its role in common law legal systems.[4] On the basis of representative court decisions published in the Gazette of the SPC, the Selections from People's Court Cases[5] and interviews with judges involved in the adjudication of those cases, he concluded that it is difficult to create a system of administrative procedural law through court decisions and that the 'eventual establishment of the due process principle still relies on the completeness of statutory laws and the establishment of judicial authority'.[6]

Unlike previous studies, we focus on administrative cases that courts decided between 2014 and 2019. The central question addressed in this analysis is, have Chinese courts further expanded the application of the due process principle, even in the absence of any major legislative initiative? We argue that courts have continued their activist stance towards developing aspects of procedural justice during the post-2013 era, which is generally characterized as experiencing a regression of the rule of law and has become hostile to the very idea of protecting the fundamental rights of the individual through mechanisms that effectively limit state power.[7]

Administrative Procedure Legislation Mode) 1995(6) *Zhongguo Faxue* (Chinese Legal Science) 42-47 at 47.

[3] Zhang, Jiansheng (2001) 'Xiandai xingzheng chengxu de chengyin he gongneng fenxi' (Analysis of Origins and Functions of Modern Administrative Procedure) 2001(1) *Zhongguo faxue* (Chinese Legal Science) 79-88 at 80; Ji, Weidong (1993) 'Falü chengxu de yiyi – dui zhongguo fazhidu jianshe de yi zhong sikao' (The Significance of Legal Procedures - Another Thinking on the Construction of the Chinese Legal System) 1993(1) *Zhongguo shehui kexue* (China Social Science) 83-105 at 85.

[4] Chinese: *zhengdang chengxu yuanze*; He, Haibo (2008) 'The Dawn of the Due Process Principle in China' 22 *Columbia Journal of Asian Law* 57-118.

[5] *Zuigao fayuan gongbao* (Gazette of the SPC) is published monthly by the General Office of the SPC. It is the official platform for the SPC to publish judicial interpretations, judicial documents, judgment documents, typical cases and other relevant judicial information. *Renmin fayuan anlixuan* (Selections from People's Court Cases) is published monthly by the Zhongguo yingyong faxue yanjiusuo (China Institute of the Applied Jurisprudence) of the SPC.

[6] He, Haibo 'Dawn of Due Process' 2008 supra note 5 at 117.

[7] DeLisle, Jaques (2015) 'The Rule of Law with Xi-Era Characteristics: Law for Economic Reform, Anticorruption, and Illiberal Politics' 20 Asia Policy (July, 2015) 23-29; Cohen, Jerome (2019) 'Law's Relation to Political Power in China: A Backward Transition' 86 *Social Research: An International Quarterly* 231-251.

We located court decisions for a systematic doctrinal analysis in the *jufa anli* database, the data of which originated in the official open access court decision database of the SPC. The SPC database was established under a new transparency policy in 2013 and contained over 152 million full-text court decisions by the end of February 2025.[8] Although the court decision database's selectivity and the incomplete data therein pose difficult challenges for any quantitative research that is based on the available data, the database provides for an unprecedented access to court decisions.[9]

DUE PROCESS RIGHTS IN CHINESE ADMINISTRATIVE LEGISLATION

The Chinese Constitution lacks an express due process clause. Moreover, neither is there a national general administrative procedure law nor do national statutes provide for a general due process principle. However, certain national laws have stipulated specific due process rights such as the Administrative Penalty Law (1996), the Administrative Licensing Law (2003) or the Administrative Enforcement Law (2011).[10] All three laws require administrative agencies to observe the legally prescribed procedure when issuing administrative acts. The Administrative Penalty Law of 1996 was amended in January 2021. The amendment expanded the general provisions relating to due process under the chapter entitled decision-making on administrative penalties.[11]

Administrative penalties that lack a legal basis or which do not adhere to legally prescribed procedure are invalid.[12] Before an administrative agency issues an administrative penalty, it has to inform the addressee of the facts, reasons and the legal basis of the decision.[13] The written decision that denies an administrative license needs to explain the reasons for the

[8] Zuigao renmin fayuan guanyu renmin fayuan zai hulianwang gongbu caipan wenshu de guiding (2016 xiuding) (SPC Regulations of the Online Publication of Decision Documents of People's Courts (2016 version)) 29 August 2016; Ahl, Björn and Sprick, Daniel (2018) 'Towards Judicial Transparency in China: The New Public Access Database for Court Decisions' 32 *China Information* 3-22. For this study we used the *jufa anli* database (聚法案例at https://www.jufaanli.com) and not the official SPC database. The *jufa anli* database is widely used among practitioners and academics as it provides the most convenient and accurate search tools for locating Chinese court decisions.

[9] Ahl, Björn, Cai, Lidong and Xi, Chao (2019) 'Data-Driven Approaches to Studying Chinese Judicial Practice: Opportunities, Challenges, and Issues' 19(2) *The China Review* 1-14.

[10] Zhonghua renmin gongheguo xingzheng chufa fa (Administrative Penalty Law of the PRC) 17 March 1996, revised on 22 January 2021; Zhonghua renmin gongheguo xingzheng xuke fa (Administrative Licensing Law of the PRC) 27 August 2003, revised 23 April 2019; Zhonghua renmin gongheguo xingzheng qiangzhi fa (Administrative Enforcement Law of the PRC) 30 June 2011. Laws are cited with the date they (or relevant amendments) were adopted by the National People's Congress or its Standing Committee.

[11] Art. 39-50 Administrative Penalty Law.

[12] Art. 4 Administrative Penalty Law.

[13] Art. 44 Administrative Penalty Law.

denial.[14] In addition to the duty to inform and the duty to provide reasons for a decision, the Administrative Enforcement Law provides for the duty to hear the statements and defence of the addressee of the enforcement measure.[15]

The same rights are granted to the addressees of administrative penalties.[16] The Administrative Penalty Law further requires that the administrative agency that conducts the hearing must listen fully to the objections of the affected party and has to review the facts, reasons and evidence that is put forward in the hearing.[17] The Administrative Penalty Law provides for a duty to notify the addressee of an administrative act of the right to a hearing in case the penalty involves, inter alia, the suspending of production or business, the rescinding of a business permit or the imposing of a relatively large fine.[18] This provision is given a broad interpretation in practice. Courts apply it to all cases where the administrative penalty decision significantly affects the addressee of the penalty.[19] If an administrative agency does not inform the addressee of the administrative penalty of the facts, reasons and legal basis or if it objects to hear the addressee's statements or defence before issuing the decision, the penalty decision shall not be issued.[20]

The Administrative Licensing Law provides for the participation of interested third persons. Administrative agencies must inform third persons who have an important interest in the matter and give them, as well as the applicant of the administrative license, the opportunity to make

[14] Art. 38 (2) Administrative Licensing Law.

[15] Art. 18 No. 6 Administrative Enforcement Law.

[16] Art. 6 (1) Administrative Penalty Law.

[17] Art. 45 Administrative Penalty Law.

[18] Art. 63 Administrative Penalty Law.

[19] Zuigao renmin fayuan anli zhidao gongzuo bangongshi (Case Guidance Office of the Supreme People's Court) (2012) 'Zhidao anli 6 hao Huang Zefu, He Boqing he He Yi su Chengdu shi Jintang gongshang xingzheng guanli ju xingzheng chufa an de lijie yu canzhao' (The Understanding and Reference of the Guiding Case No. 6 [Huang Zefu, He Boqiong, and He Yi v. The Jintang Administration for Industry and Commerce of Chengdu Municipality]) 2012(15) *Renmin sifa* (People's Judicature) 51-54, at 53.

[20] Art. 62 Administrative Penalty Law. Before the amendment of the Law in 2021 the relevant provision stipulated that such a decision is invalid. The literal translation of *jueding bu neng chengli* ('invalid') reads 'the decision cannot be established'. The wording implies a distinction between the existence or effectiveness and the legality of an administrative act. Whereas the notification of the administrative act is a condition of its effectiveness (*shengxiao yaojian*), adhering to statutory procedural requirements is a condition of its legality (*hefaxing yaojian*). Luo, Haocai and Zhan, Zhongle (2015) *Xingzheng faxue* (Administrative Law) Beijing daxue chubanshe at 136; Ye, Bifeng (2014) *Xingzheng xingwei yuanli* (The Theory of the Administrative Act) Shangwu yinshuguan at 293; Jiang, Bixin and He Yiting (2021) 'Guanche Xingzheng Chufa Fa xu zhongdian bawo de ji ge wenti' (Key Issues to Focus on in Implementing the Administrative Penalty Law) 2021(5) *Falü kexue (Xibeizhengfadaxue xuebao)* (Science of Law (Journal of Northwest University of Political Science and Law)) 43-52, at 52.

statements and defend themselves.[21] Further, the Administrative Litigation Law stipulates that courts have the right to revoke administrative acts that violate statutory procedure.[22]

With regard to sub-national legislation the situation is quite different, as a number of provinces and cities have adopted general regulations on administrative procedure. Hunan Province adopted its Administrative Procedure Regulations in 2008.[23] In 2011 Shandong followed suit with similar regulations and Jiangsu adopted Administrative Procedure Rules in 2015, which were subsequently replaced by the Administrative Procedure Regulations in 2022.[24] The local regulations include due process provisions that stipulate the right to make statements and defend oneself,[25] hearing procedures,[26] rules on conflicts of interest,[27] the duty to explain the grounds of a decision,[28] participation rights of interested parties[29] as well as the duty to notify the addressees of administrative decisions of administrative and judicial remedies.[30] As the regulations do not distinguish between different administrative acts such as administrative penalties or administrative

[21] Art. 36 Administrative Licensing Law.

[22] Art. 70 (1) No. 3 Administrative Litigation Law.

[23] Administrative Procedure Rules of Hunan Province (Hubei sheng xingzheng chengxu guiding) 17 April 2008.

[24] Shandong sheng xingzheng chengxu guiding (Administrative Procedure Rules of Shandong Province) 22 June 2011; Jiangsu sheng xingzheng chengxu guiding (Administrative Procedure Rules of Jiangsu Province) 6 January 2015; Jiangsu sheng xingzheng chengxu tiaoli (Administrative Procedure Regulations of Jiangsu Province) 29 July 2022; similar regulations were enacted in Ningxia: Ningxia Huizu zizhiqu xingzheng chengxu guiding (Administrative Procedure Rules of Ningxia Hui Autonomous Region) 10 January 2015.

[25] Art. 73 (1) Administrative Procedure Rules of Hunan Province; Art. 9 Administrative Procedure Rules of Shandong Province; Art. 8 Administrative Procedure Rules of Ningxia Hui Autonomous Region; Art. 21, Art. 37 Administrative Procedure Regulations of Jiangsu Province.

[26] Art. 38, Art. 74 Administrative Procedure Rules of Hunan Province; Art. 32-35, Art. 47, Art. 75-83 Administrative Procedure Rules of Shandong Province; Art. 38, Art. 114 Administrative Procedure Regulations of Jiangsu Province.

[27] Art.18, Art. 62 Administrative Procedure Rules of Hunan Province; Art. 22 Administrative Procedure Rules of Shandong Province; Art. 23 Administrative Procedure Rules of Ningxia Hui Autonomous Region; Art. 30, Art. 31, Administrative Procedure Regulations of Jiangsu Province.

[28] Art. 62 (1), Art. 78 (1) Administrative Procedure Rules of Hunan Province; Art. 9 Administrative Procedure Rules of Shandong Province; Art. 8 Administrative Procedure Rules of Ningxia Hui Autonomous Region.

[29] Art. 24, Art. 62 (1) Administrative Procedure Rules of Hunan Province; Art. 74 Administrative Procedure Rules of Shandong Province; Art. 18, Art. 19, Art. 21, Art. 101 Administrative Procedure Regulations of Jiangsu Province.

[30] Art. 62 (2), Art. 77 (1) No. 6 Administrative Procedure Rules of Hunan Province; Art. 9 Administrative Procedure Rules of Shandong Province; Art. 8 Administrative Procedure Rules of Ningxia Hui Autonomous Region; Art. 36, Art. 46 (6), Art. 146 (6) Administrative Procedure Regulations of Jiangsu Province.

licenses, the procedural requirements apply to all administrative decisions that are based on laws, administrative regulations or administrative rules and affect the rights and obligations of citizens, legal persons and other organizations. The local administrative procedure regulations are experimental local legislation that is intended to provide the national legislator with experience for drafting a national administrative procedure law sometime in the future. Although scholars have criticised the local regulations' lack of system and their insignificance in court practice, they describe local administrative procedure legislation as providing valid models for drafting a national law on administrative procedure.[31] In fact, the 2021 amendment of the Administrative Penalty Law absorbed certain parts of local administrative procedure rules.[32]

In addition to national and local legislation, there are a number of policy documents that have been adopted by the State Council and which emphasize the importance of due process rights. Although those policy documents do not possess the legal binding force of administrative regulations of the State Council, they have a strong persuasive force as they have been adopted by the highest administrative state authority.[33] The 2004 State Council Outline of Comprehensive Promotion of Law-Based Governance mentions due process as one of the fundamental conditions of law-based administration.[34] The 2008 State Council Decision on Strengthening Administration according to Law of City and County Governments requires the extension of the application of hearing procedures in cases where laws, administrative regulations and rules provide for the possibility of a hearing and the matter of the decision affects important public interests or has a 'direct impact on the masses'.[35] The 2010 State Council Opinion on Strengthening the Construction of Administration according to Law required a strengthening of 'procedural consciousness' and strict law enforcement according to correct procedures.[36] Similar emphasis of procedural requirements are part

[31] Zhang, Jiansheng (2017) 'Cong difang dao zhongyang: woguo xingzheng chengxu lifa de xianshi yu weilai' (From Local to Central: The Reality and the Future of China's Administrative Procedure Legislation) 2017(2) *Xingzheng faxue yanjiu* (Adminsrative Law Review) 54-76; Yang, Dengfeng (2020) 'Xingzheng chengxu defang xianxing lifa de zhuti, moshi yu guifan' (Subject, Mode and Norms of Advancing Local Legislation on Administrative Procedures) 2020(3) *Zhengzhi yu falü* (Politics and Law) 64-76.

[32] For example, Art. 42, 43, and 46 of the new Administrative Penalty Law are nearly identical with Art. 66, 18 and 69 of the Administrative Procedure Rules of Hunan Province.

[33] Shen, Kui (2011) 'Xingzheng ziwo guizhi yu xingzheng fazhi: yige chushi kaocha' (Administrative Self-regulation and Rule of Administrative Law: A Preliminary Investigation) 2011(3) *Xingzheng faxue yanjiu* (Administrative Law Review) 12-17, at 14.

[34] Quanmian tuixing yifa xingzheng shishi gangyao (Outline of the Comprehensive Promotion of Administration according to Law) 22 March 2004; Art. 5 (3).

[35] Art. 8 Guowuyuan guanyu jiaqiang shixian zhengfu yifa xingzheng de guiding (Decision of the State Council on Promotion of Law-based Administration among City and County Governments) 12 May 2008.

[36] Art. 16 Guowuyuan guanyu jiaqiang fazhi zhengfu jianshe de yijian (State Council Opinion on Strengthening the Construction of a Rule-of-Law Government) 10 October 2010.

of the 2015 Implementation Outline for the Construction of a Rule-of-Law Government, the 2019 Regulations on the Construction of a Rule-of-Law Government, the Supervision of the Implementation of Responsibilities that were adopted by the State Council and the CPC Central Committee, as well as more recently, the 2024 CPC Central Committee Decision on Further Deepening Reform and Advancing Modernization with Chinese Characteristics.[37]

EARLY REPRESENTATIVE CASES AND LEGAL SCHOLARSHIP ON DUE PROCESS RIGHTS

The first court decision on due process rights was published in the SPC Gazette in 1991.[38] The court found that the decision of detaining the plaintiff for investigation was illegal on procedural grounds as the notice of detention for investigation was not shown to the plaintiff during the enforcement process. The court based its decision on Art. 54 (2) No. 3 of the Administrative Litigation Law, according to which the court can revoke an administrative act that violates legally prescribed procedure.[39] However, the administrative act was also found to be illegal on substantive grounds. Commentators have argued that it was difficult for courts to find administrative acts to be illegal just based on procedural grounds, as there were almost no legal provisions on administrative procedure at that time.[40]

In contrast, in a case of 1997 the court found that the defendant violated the legally prescribed procedure and revoked the administrative act only based on procedural grounds.[41] The defendant disregarded, inter alia, the duty to notify the plaintiff of the reasons of the decision and the duty to

[37] Art. 21 Fazhi zhengfu jianshe shishi gangyao (2015-2020 nian) (Implementation Outline for the Construction of a Rule-of-Law Government [2015-2010]) 23 December 2015; Art. 10 No. 3 Fazhi zhengfu jianshe yu zeren luoshi ducha gongzuo guiding (Regulations on the Construction of a Rule-of-Law Government and the Supervision of the Implementation of Responsibilities) 15 April 2019; Zhonggong zhongyang guanyu jinyibu quanmian shenhua gaige tuijin zhongguoshi xiandaihua de jueding (Decision of the CPC Central Committee on Further Deepening Reform and Advancing Modernization with Chinese Characteristics) 18 July 2024.

[38] People's Court of Lishi District of Luliang City (1992), *Chen Yingchun v. Lishi xian gonganju* (Chen Yingchun v. Lishi County Public Security Bureau), Administrative Dispute on Internment and Investigation, 16 June 1991. 1992(2) *Zuigao renmin fayuan gongbao* (Gazette of the Supreme People's Court) 62-63.

[39] Zhonghua renmin gongheguo xingzheng susong fa (Administrative Litigation Law of the PRC) 4 April 1989.

[40] Zhou, Youyong (2019) 'Sifa panjue dui zhengdang chengxu yuanze de fazhan' (The Development of the Due Process Principle in Court Decisions) 2019(3) *Zhongguo faxue* (China Legal Science) 26-45, 28-29.

[41] People's Court of Pingshan County of Hebei Province (1997), *Pingshan xian laodong jiuye guanliju v. tuiwu* (Pingshan County Labour Bureau v. Pingshan County Local Taxation Bureau), Administrative Dispute on Tax Administration,12 March 1997. 1997(2) *Zuigao renmin fayuan gongbao* (Gazette of the Supreme People's Court) 70-71.

hold a hearing according to the Administrative Penalty Law.[42] The court did not review the substantive legality of the administrative act because the court did not want to get involved in the merits of the dispute between two state organs.[43] In another case the court found that the decision of a ministry to revoke the administrative act of a lower administrative agency did not violate the legally prescribed procedure.[44] The court held that the procedure for revoking decisions of a lower-level administrative agency by a higher-level agency had not yet been regulated by statutes or administrative regulations and is conducted according to the 'principles of supervision work'. This decision reflects the conservative stance that violations of legally prescribed procedure can only be affirmed if there exist specific written procedural provisions.

In a 1999 case, the decision of a court of first instance found a violation of legally established procedure although the administrative entity did not disregard express procedural requirements written in statutory law or lower-ranking legislation.[45] The court held that a higher education institution that renders a decision which affects a student's fundamental rights has the duty to allow the student to defend herself or himself and has to deliver the decision in a timely manner. Further, the court found the administrative act violated substantive law. In 2014 the SPC elevated this case to a guiding case.[46] Courts at all levels are required to consult guiding cases issued by the SPC when hearing similar cases.[47] However, the guiding cases are only factually binding on lower courts. Due to their overall small number and relatively narrow scope of application, they have, so far, not become significant in practice.[48] The presiding judge admitted in an interview that the court decided the outcome pursuant to the 'legal spirit'. Although the provision on making statements and defending oneself in the Administrative Penalty Law may have guided the decision of the court, there is nothing in the decision that indicates an analogous

[42] Art. 45, 63 Administrative Penalty Law.

[43] He, Haibo 'Dawn of Due Process' (2008) supra note 5 at 130.

[44] Guangdong Higher People's Court, *Guangzhou sheng yaocai gongsi v. zhonghua renmin gongheguo caizhengbu* (Guangzhou Medicine Company v. Ministry of Finance of the People's Republic of China), Administrative Case of Second Instance Dispute on Administrative Decision, 20 October 2000.

[45] Beijing No. 1 Intermediate People's Court (1999), *Tian Yong v. Beijing kezhi daxue* (Tian Yong v. Beijing University of Science and Technology), Administrative Case of Second Instance, Dispute on the Denial of Awarding Diploma and Degree, 26 April 1999. 1999(4) *Zuigao renmin fayuan gongbao* (Gazette of the Supreme People's Court) 139-143.

[46] Ibid.

[47] Art. 7 Zuigao renmin fayuan guanyu anli zhidao gongzuo de guiding (SPC Provisions on Guiding Cases) 26 November 2010; Art. 9 Zuigao renmin fayuan guanyu tongyi falü shiyong jiaqiang lei'an jiansu de zhidao yijian (shixing) (SPC Guiding Opinions on the Unified Law Application and Fortifying the Retrieving of Similar Cases [Provisional]) 31 July 2020.

[48] Ahl, Björn (2014) 'Retaining Judicial Professionalism: The New Guiding Cases Mechanism of the Supreme People's Court' 217 *The China Quarterly* 121-139 at 129-130.

application of the due process rights of the Administrative Penalty Law to the case at hand.[49]

In a case where the court reviewed an administrative decision on compensation for demolishing a building, the court found that although the national and local regulations on demolishing buildings and relocating inhabitants did not include any procedural requirements, the involved parties had the right to make statements and defend themselves.[50] The court held that disregarding such hearing rights would constitute a lack of fairness and expanded the hearing requirement with regard to acts that are undertaken to prepare the final administrative act.[51]

In another case the court applied a broad interpretation to the preconditions for a hearing pursuant to Art. 42 (1) of the Administrative Penalty Law.[52] Although Art. 42 (1) does not explicitly specify that it applies to the confiscation of property, the court argued that the coverage of the article is a non-exhaustive list that includes administrative penalties requiring the confiscation of a relatively large amount of property. Later, the SPC elevated this decision to a guiding case.[53] Commentators argue that this decision has clarified the function of the due process principle to serve as a supplement to written procedural legislation.[54] In 2004 a court used the term of 'due process' for the first time.[55] The court confirmed that interested third persons must be notified in the administrative reconsideration procedure in order to be able to participate. The Administrative Reconsideration Law provides for the participation rights of interested parties but does not stipulate the duty of the administrative agency conducting the review

49 He, Haibo 'Dawn of Due Process' (2008) supra note 5 at 132.

50 Intermediate People's Court of Suqian City of Jiangsu Province (2004), *Song Lili v. Suqian shi jiansheju* (Song Lili v. Suqian City Development Bureau), Administrative Case of Second Instance, Dispute on Compensation for Demolishing Real Estate, 9 December 2003. 2004(8) *Zuigao renmin fayuan gongbao* (Gazette of the Supreme People's Court) 33-36.

51 Jiang, Hongzhen (2019) 'Zhengdang chengxu yuanze sifa shiyong de zhengdangxing: huigui guifan lichang' (Legitimacy of the Judicial Application of the Due Process Principle: Returning to the Normative Position) 2019(3) *Zhongguo faxue* (China Legal Science) 46-63 at 56.

52 Intermediate People's Court of Chengdu City of Sichuan Province (2006), *Huang Zefu, He Boqiong, He Yi v. Sichuan sheng Chengdu shi jintang gongshang xingzheng guanliju* (Huang Zefu, He Boqiong, and He Yi v. The Jintang Administration for Industry and Commerce of Chengdu Municipality), Administrative Case of Second Instance, Dispute on Administrative Penalty, 28 September 2006.

53 Guiding Case No. 6, 9 April 2012.

54 Yang, Dengfeng (2017) 'Zhidao anli 6 hao de weijing zhiye' (Unresolved Issues of the Guiding Case No. 6) 2017(3) *Fazhi xiandaihua yanjiu* (Research into Legal Modernisation) 124-137 at 126.

55 Jiangsu Higher People's Court (2005), *Zhang Chengyin v. Chengyin shi renmin zhengfu* (Zhang Chengyin v. People's Government of Xuzhou City), Administrative Case of Second Instance, Dispute on Administrative Reconsideration Decision on Real Estate Registration, 10 December 2004.

to make the relevant notification.[56] The court expressly said that such a notification duty arises from the requirement of due process.

The SPC held in 2006 that the defendant must, according to the due process requirement, revoke the monopoly right of the plaintiff first, before organizing new bids for a gas network.[57] Courts further found that on the basis of the due process principle and in order to protect the rights and interests of the owners and tenants of buildings that are about to be demolished, the owners and tenants should be served the valuation report of their property and that the issuing of an administrative act without ascertaining the underlying facts constitutes a violation of the due process principle.[58] Courts have further argued that although the Administrative Licensing Law did not provide for a specific procedure of revoking administrative licenses, this would not imply that no procedural requirements applied but, rather, that the administrative agency was bound by the principle of due process as the bottom line of a valid legal procedure.[59]

Legal Scholarship on the Justification of the Development of Due Process Rights by Courts

Chinese administrative law scholarship is another driving force behind developing due process rights. The first cases relating to university education were accompanied by academic discussions and many scholarly efforts to reach out and provide argumentative support to the plaintiffs in those cases.[60] The courts only rarely provided legal reasoning for invoking due process rights that do not have an express legal basis in statutory law. In contrast, legal scholarship has provided various legal arguments in favour of due process rights that go beyond the scope of the rights provided for in specific administrative legislation.

[56] Art. 10 (2) Zhonghua renmin gongheguo xingzheng fuyi fa (PRC Administrative Reconsideration Law) 29 April 1999.

[57] Supreme People's Court (2005), *Yimin gongsi v. Henan sheng Zhoukou shi zhengfu* (Yimin Corporation v. People's Government of Zhoukou City of Henan Province), Administrative Case of Second Instance, Dispute on Unlawful Administrative Act, 1 March 2005.

[58] Shanghai No. 2 Intermediate People's Court (2007), *Lu Tingzuo v. Shanghai shi Zhabei qu fangwu tudi guanliju* (Lu Tingzuo v. Housing and Land Administration of Zhabei District of Shanghai City), Administrative Case of Second Instance, Dispute on Administrative Adjudication on Demolishing Real Estates, 27 February 2006; Higher People's Court of Ningxia Hui Autonomous Region (2008), *Ningxia Pingluo xian huiyuan menggangchang v. Ningxia Pingluo xian renmin zhengfu* (Huiyuan Manganese Steel Factory of Luoping County v. People's Government of Luoping County of Ningxia Hui Autonomous Region), Administrative Case of Second Instance, Dispute on Administrative Adjudication on Land Ownership, 29 February 2008.

[59] Intermediate People's Court of Linyi City (2013), *Zhao Bo v. Pingyi xian renmin zhengfu* (Zhao Bo v. People's Government of Pingyi County of Shandong Province), Administrative Case of Second Instance, Dispute on Administrative Reconsideration on Land Use Licensing, 10 September 2010 Administrative Tribunal of the Supreme People's Court (2013) *Zhongguo xingzheng shenpan anli (di 3 juan)* (Administrative Cases in China [Vol. 3]), Zhongguo fazhi chubanshe at 118-121.

[60] He, Haibo 'Dawn of Due Process' (2008) supra note 5 at 85-88.

Scholars have acknowledged that due process is a general legal principle of administrative law.[61] Court practice can be regarded as being in support of this view as it refers to the due process principle without giving further justifications, implying that it is a broadly acknowledged unwritten principle of law.[62]

Further, scholars regard the basis of due process rights in a broad interpretation of certain provisions in the constitution and in administrative legislation. However, there is no consensus as to the provisions that should be broadly interpreted in order to include due process rights.

Although the Chinese Constitution of 1982 does not contain an express legal basis, Zhang argues that the term of the 'rule-of-law state' in Art. 5 (1) as well as the right of the people to 'administer state affairs' according to Art. 2 (3) provide the people with the right to participate in administrative affairs of the state.[63] Meng holds that 'respecting and protecting human rights' pursuant to Art. 33 (3) encompasses due process requirements'.[64]

The Administrative Litigation Law provides that courts can revoke administrative acts that violate legally prescribed procedure.[65] Commentators argue that 'legally prescribed procedure' does not only include written law but also aspects of the due process principle that have not been expressly included in legislation.[66] According to Art. 70 (1) No. 5 Administrative Litigation Law courts can also revoke administrative acts on the grounds of the abuse of authority. Xu argues that in the absence of a procedural legal basis, administrative agencies possess procedural discretion. A violation of the principle of due process in exercising procedural discretion constitutes an abuse of authority. Hence, the standard of due process is an inherent precondition of the abuse of authority in the sense of the Administrative

[61] Zhang, Zhiyuan (2014) *Xingzheng faxue zonglun* (General Introduction of Administrative Law) Beijing daxue chubanshe at 53-54; Li, Honglei (2014) *Xingzhengfa shiyixue: Xingzhengfa xueli de gengxin* (Administrative Law Hermeneutics: A Renewal of Administrative Law Doctrine) Zhongguo renmin daxue chubanshe at 48.

[62] For example, Shanghai No. 2 Intermediate People's Court (2006), *Lu Tingzuo v. Shanghai shi Zhabei qu fangwu tudi guanliju* (Lu Tingzuo v. Housing and Land Administration of Zhabei District of Shanghai City), Administrative Case of Second Instance, Dispute on Administrative Adjudication on Demolishing Real Estate, 27 February 2006.

[63] Zhang, Jiansheng (2005) 'Lun xingzheng chengxu zhengdangxing de xianfa guifan jichu: yi guifan shizheng fenxi wei shejiao' (The Normative Foundation of the Legitimacy of Administrative Procedure in the Constitution: From the Perspective of a Normative Empirical Analysis) 2005(4) *Faxue luntan* (Legal Forum) 95-98 at 98.

[64] Meng, Fanzhuang (2014) 'Lun zhengdang chengxu yuanze zai xingzheng shenpan zhong de shiyong – jiyu 75 fen yunyong zhengdang chengxu yuanze de xingzheng susong panjueshu de fenxi' (On the Application of the Due Process Principle in Administrative Trials - Based on an Analysis of 75 Administrative Law Court Decisions Applying the Due Process Principle) 2014(4) *Xingzheng faxue yanjiu* (Administrative Law Review) 139-144 at 142.

[65] Art. 70 (1) No. 3 Administrative Litigation Law.

[66] Yang, Dengfeng (2018) 'Fa wu guiding shi zhengdang chengxu yuanze zhi shiyong' (The Application of the Due Process Principle in the Absence of Law) 2018(1) *Falü kexue xibei zhengfa daxue xuebao* (Journal of Northwest University of Politics and Law) 191-200 at 191.

Litigation Law.[67] This view builds on the administrative law doctrine of abuse of discretion with regard to administrative procedure that is not confined to an abuse of discretion relating to substantive law.[68]

Chen argues that courts can apply provisions that stipulate due process rights analogously in order to realize the due process principle. He holds that in fact courts have done this in an implied manner in many cases.[69] A further legal basis of due process rights is seen in guiding cases issued by the SPC that possess factual binding force.[70] Courts do also take into account model cases that are published in the SPC Gazette and that guide courts in their judicial practice.[71]

ANALYSIS OF COURT DECISIONS IN THE POST-2013 ERA

Our study of court practice is based on the analysis of court cases that were decided between January 2014 and December 2019. We retrieved 321 administrative law cases from the *jufa anli* court decision database by using the keyword 'due process principle'.[72] We limited the search to court decisions of the High People's Courts (316 cases) and the SPC (5 cases) as in these courts the quality of judges' legal reasoning is higher than in lower courts. Cases relating to the due process principle appeared in all 26 provincial level high court districts of China. In 2018 there were 100 court decisions, in 2019 courts decided 65 cases, in 2017 and 2016 we counted about 50 decisions, and in 2015 and 2014 only a small number of due process cases was decided by high courts. The increase in the numbers of

[67] Xu, Chunhui (2019) '*Zhengdang chengxu: linyong chengxuquan de panduan biaozhun*' (Due Process Principle: Criteria for the Abuse of Administrative Discretionary Power) 2019(2) *Faxue Pinglun* (Law Review) 53-60 at 56-58.

[68] Zhu, Xinli (2012) 'Xingzheng lanyong zhiquan de xin dingyi' (New Definition of the Abuse of Administrative Discretionary Power) 2012(3) *Faxue yanjiu* (Studies on Law) 30-35 at 34-35; Jian, Bixin (2012) 'Xingzheng chengxu zhengdangxing de sifa shencha' (Judicial Review of the Administrative Due Process) 2012(7) *Zhongguo shehui kexue* (Social Sciences in China) 123-140 at 138-139.

[69] Chen, Qingliang (2008) 'Xingzhengfa jiben yuanze sifa shiyong de fazhan – yi zhengdang chengxu yuanze zai woguo de fazhan wei li' (The Development of the Administrative Principles in Judicial Application -Taking the Development of the Due Process Principle in China as an Example) 2008(3) *Fujian jingcha xueyuan xuebao* (Fujian Police College Journal) 93-97 at 95; Gansu Higher People's Court (1999), *Lanzhou Changde wuzi kaifabu v. Lanzhou renmin zhengfu* (Lanzhou Changde Material Development Department v. Lanzhou Municipal Government), Administrative Case of Second Instance, Dispute on Reply to Resumption of Land Use Rights, 9 August 1999; Jiangsu Higher People's Court (2004), *Zhang Chengyin v. Xuzhou renmin zhengfu* (Zhang Chengyin v. Xuzhou Municipal Government), Administrative Dispute, 10 December 2004.

[70] Zhou, Youyong 'Development Court Decisions' (2019) supra note 41 at 43.

[71] Meng, Fanzhuang 'Administrative Trials' (2014) supra note 65 at 143-144.

[72] Chinese: *Zhengdang chengxu yuanze*. Among the 321 court decisions, we identified 40 decisions that related to different parties but the same facts and applicable law.

due process cases reflects the overall increase of administrative law cases in the post-2013 era that rose from 151,000 in 2014 to 284,000 in 2019.[73]

Application of the Due Process Principle in Different Fields of Substantive Administrative Law

About 70 percent of court decisions dealt with rights relating to immovable property, including land use rights of state-owned land and the ownership of collectively owned land. Most cases related to compensation claims for the expropriation of land or buildings, the revocation of land use rights certificates or building ownership certificates, the demolition of unlawful buildings and other coercive measures, disputes over the ownership of land rights or the payment of land rights transfer fees. Some cases concerned the evaluation of work-related injuries by the bureaus of human resources and social security. Other claims related to the non-performance of legal duties by administrative agencies. Cases concerned the mandatory use of public facilities, coercive administrative measures ordering the stop of production or business, administrative penalties violating the Public Security Administration Punishment Law,[74] and other administrative permits relating to medical care and industry and commerce. Moreover, cases related to the publication of government information. However, cases concerning the conferral of academic degrees that triggered the academic debate about due process rights during the 1990s did not play a role in the adjudication practice of high courts any more. Only one case related to an administrative penalty for cheating in a public servant examination.

In most cases plaintiffs claimed the revocation of administrative acts that violated due process rights or the confirmation that the relevant administrative act is without legal effect. In some cases, plaintiffs claimed compensation for demolition and relocation. In addition, they claimed compensation for loss or damages. Although courts have referred to due process rights in various fields of substantive law, the main area of the application of this principle are disputes about the rights relating to immovable property. This focus is due to that such disputes make up a significant part of administrative cases that come before the courts.[75] As urban development led to growing social tension and violent disputes, the Central Government enacted the 2011 Regulations on Expropriation and Compensation relating to Real Estate on State-owned Land and the

[73] 2015 nian zuigao renmin fayuan gongzuobao (SPC 2015 Work Report) 12 March 2015; 2020 nian zuigao renmin fayuan gongzuobao (SPC 2020 Work Report) 25 May 2020.

[74] Zhonghua renmin gongheguo zhi'an guanli chufafa (PRC Public Security Administration Punishment Law) 25 August 2005.

[75] Disputes over land resources and urban construction usually make up a large proportion of administrative litigation cases. For example, pursuant to the Chongqing gaoji renmin fayuan 2019 nian xingzheng shenpan baipishu (2019 Chongqing Administrative Litigation White Book) disputes on resources and urban construction make up 35% of all administrative cases in Chongqing.

Implementation Measures of the Land Administration Law in 2014.[76] Consequently, courts have become important stability maintenance institutions that tried an increasing number of land-related administrative cases.

Application of the Due Process Principle to Different Forms of Administrative Action

Most court decisions apply the due process rights to individual administrative acts that are onerous to the addressee such as administrative penalty decisions.[77] Commentators are divided over the question whether due process rights only apply to onerous administrative acts or also to the repeal or change of administrative acts that are beneficial to the addressee such as administrative permits or decisions on granting subsidies.[78] According to our analysis, courts extend the application of the due process requirements to the repeal of beneficial administrative acts. For example, the High Court of Henan Province found that the administrative act of the Xingyang city government that repealed the plaintiff's land use right had violated the due process principle. In this case the government neither provided a prior notification of the legal basis and reasons for the decision nor did it hear statements or the defence of the plaintiff.[79] Courts also applied due process requirements to beneficial acts such as decisions on administrative compensation and administrative permits. The High Court of Chongqing held in a case where the Law on the Contracting of Rural Land did not apply that the due process principle applies to issuing a contract certificate.[80] Commentators see the reason of applying the due process

[76] Zhonghua renmin gongheguo tudi guanlifa shishi tiaolo (Implementation Regulations for PRC Law of Land Administration) 4 January 1991, revised 29 July 2014; Guoyou tudi fangwu zhengshou yu buchang tiaoli (Regulations on the Expropriation of Buildings on State-owned Land and Compensation) 21 January 2011.

[77] Chinese: *fudanxing xingzheng xingwei* or *qinyixing xingzheng xingwei.*

[78] Chinese: *shouyi xingzheng xingwei.* Tang, Wen (2013) 'Zhengdang chengxu yuanze zai xingzheng susong shiyong de kunhuo yu chulu – yi zuigao fayuan suo fabu de jiu ge quanwei anjian wei hexin de diaocha' (Problems and Solutions of the Application of the Due Process Principle in Administrative Litigation - Research Centered on Nine Authoritative Cases Issued by the Supreme People's Court). *Quanguo fayuan di 25 jie xueshu taolunhui huojianglun wenji: gongzheng sifa yu xingzhengfa shishi wenti yanjiu* (Award-winning Essays of the 25th National Court Academic Symposium: Research on the Issues of a Fair Judiciary and Administrative Law Implementation) 989-1002 at 994; Yang, Dengfeng 'Due Process Principle' (2018) supra note 67 at 196.

[79] Henan Higher People's Court (2016), *Zhengzhou dahe jingji fazhan gongsi v. Xingyang shi renmin zhengfu* (Zhengzhou Dahe Economic Development Ltd. v. Xingyang People's Municipal Government), Administrative Case of Second Instance, Dispute on Land Administration, 28 October 2016.

[80] Zhonghua remin gongheguo nongcun tudi chengbao fa (PRC Law on the Contracting of Rural Land) 29 August 2002; Chongqing Higher People's Court (2016), *Wu zhongshi v. Shizhu tujiazu zizhi xian renmin zhengfu* (Wu Zhongshi v. Shizhu Tujia Ethnic Autonomous County Government), Administrative Case of Second Instance, Dispute on Land Administration, 16 February 2016.

principle to the repealing or modifying of a beneficial administrative act in the fact that the applicant has formed a legitimate expectation with regard to the positive administrative decision.[81]

Courts have further extended the due process principle to abstract administrative acts such as a local governments' detailed land-use plans. The Guangdong High Court found that in general a suit against a detailed land-use plan cannot be brought by someone who is bound by such a plan if the plan affects rights and obligations that were only established by the land-use plan. However, if the affected interests already existed when the plan comes into existence and if the plan possesses specificity and generates legal effects with regard to a specific person, this person is entitled to bring an administrative suit against the plan. In this case a new land use plan changed the content of the plaintiff's land use right that was already established before the land use plan came into effect. The court held that such changes can only be affected according to the Administrative Licensing Law and in accordance with the relevant due process protections.[82] Other court decisions confirm the rule that the due process principle is applicable to abstract administrative acts if these acts directly affect the interests of the plaintiff.[83]

The due process principle is also applied to physical acts.[84] Such physical acts are enforcement measures without direct legal effects such as the demolition of buildings. Courts found that although laws, regulations and normative documents do not include express notification requirements for the physical demolition of buildings, such requirements derive from the due process principle.[85] It also constitutes a violation of the due process principle if during a coercive demolition of buildings no measures to preserve evidence with regard to the belongings within the buildings are conducted.[86]

Further, courts apply the principle to intermediate administrative acts.[87] Intermediate administrative acts are characterised as those acts that are

[81] Yang, Dengfeng 'Due Process Principle' (2018) supra note 67 at 196.

[82] Zhonghua renmin gongheguo xingzheng xuke fa (PRC Administrative Licensing Law) 1 July 2004; *Zhongshan shi renmin zhengfu v. Tang Fengyun* (Zhongshan Municipal Government v. Tang Fengyun), Administrative Case of Second Instance, 5 March 2018.

[83] Guangdong Higher People's Court (2019), *Zhongshan shi renmin zhengfu v. Li Yuqiao* (Zhongshan Municipal Government v. Li Yuqiao), Administrative Appeal Decision, 21 August 2019.

[84] Chinese: *Shishi xingwei.*

[85] Guizhou Higher People's Court (2018), *Sun Liangyan v. Zunyi shi Huichuan qu renmin zhengfu* (Sun Liangyan v. Zunyi Huichuan District Government), Administrative Case of Second Instance, Dispute on Administration of Demolishing Real Estate, 30 March 2018.

[86] Jiangsu Higher People's Court (2016), *Hu Mingjing v. Nanjing shi Xuanwu qu renmin zhengfu* (Hu Mingjing v. Nanjing Xuanwu District Government), Administrative Case of Second Instance, Dispute on Administrative Enforcement, 27 December 2016.

[87] Chinese: *Zhongjianxing xingzheng xingwei.*

preparatory or only constitute part of an administrative act and are not identical with the final administrative decision as such.[88] The Guangdong High Court held that the due process principle included the duty of the reconsideration authority to organize an adequate examination of the authenticity, legality and relevance of evidence that emerged during the reconsideration period and might significantly affect the interests of the applicant of the administrative reconsideration but that are not part of the final reconsideration decision. The reconsideration authority neither notified the applicant to exercise his rights regarding the examination of evidence nor did it hear his statements or defence, which the court found to be a violation of the due process principle.[89] The preparatory measure to which the due process principle applies is the organisation of the examination of new evidence by the administrative agency that conducts the reconsideration. The examination of evidence only prepares the reconsideration decision, which follows the examination and constitutes an administrative act.[90]

Moreover, the Heilongjiang High Court held that when a building is investigated as to whether it needs to be demolished because it poses an imminent danger, the due process principle requires that the addressee of the demolition order participates in the evaluation of the building and that he is served the evaluation report. The court argued that the evaluation of the building as a preparatory measure has the greatest impact on the final administrative act.[91] The High Court of Hainan province found that the due process principle also applied to the investigation of ownership of certain things attached to land when the final administrative act concerned the compensation for the administrative expropriation of land.[92]

There is no consistent court practice with regard to the application of the due process principle to internal measures without external legal binding force that higher administrative agencies take in relation to lower administrative agencies. The High Court of Jiangxi Province had to decide whether the due process principle required that the appellant was notified of the internal reply of the higher district government that approved an

[88] Liu, Xing (2018) 'Xingzheng chengxu zhongjian xingwei kesuxing biaozhun tantao – jiehe zuigao fayuan di 69 hao zhidao anli de fenxi' (Discussing the Standards of Justiciability of Intermediate Acts in Administrative Procedure: In Combination with an Analysis of Supreme Court Guiding Case No. 69) 2018(2) *Xingzheng faxue yanjiu* (Administrative Law Review) 81-89 at 83.

[89] Guangdong Higher People's Court (2014), *Li Zhaoqin v. Zhanjiang shi renmin zhengfu* (Li Zhaoqin v. Zhanjiang Municipal Government), Administrative Case of Second Instance, Dispute on Administrative Consideration, 8 July 2014.

[90] Luo, Haocai and Zhan, Zhongle 'Administrative Law' (2015) supra note 21 at 484.

[91] Heilongjiang Higher People's Court (2018), *Hu Nanhai v. Harbin shi Pingfang qu renmin zhengfu* (Hu Nanhai v. Harbin Pingfang District Government), Administrative Case of Second Instance, Dispute on the Administration of Demolishing Real Estate, 23 April 2018.

[92] Hainan Higher People's Court (2018), *Wu Duoli v. Wenchang shi renmin zhengfu* (Wu Duoli v. Wenchang Municipal Government), Administrative Dispute on Administrative Compensation, 12 September 2018.

accident investigation report by a lower administrative agency.[93] The court found that the reply regarding the accident investigation report was formally an internal approval document without direct external effect and not subject to the due process principle. In contrast, the Tianjin High Court held that the due process principle applied to the internal examination and approval process to revoke a land use right where this process is not regulated by law.[94]

Contents of the Due Process Principle as Applied in Court Decisions

When courts apply the general due process rights that enable addressees of administrative acts to participate in the relevant administrative procedure the courts do normally not elaborate on the specific contents of those due process rights.[95] Courts just determine whether the affected parties were heard by the administrative agency without defining the preconditions for fulfilling the requirements of the right to make statements and to defend themselves.[96]

However, in a small number of cases, the courts have developed more detailed requirements of due process rights. For instance, courts have ruled that the due process principle includes the requirement that the addressee of the administrative act has to be notified of the basic facts, the legal basis and the reasoning.[97] Further, courts have stated that the due process principle guarantees the adequate participation of interested third parties

93 Jiangxi Higher People's Court (2019), *Qianshan xian litong shiye youxian gongsi v. Shangrao shi Xinzhou qu renmin zhengfu* (Qianshan County Litong Co., Ltd. v. Shangrao Xinzhou District Government), Administrative Dispute, 3 July 2019.

94 Tianjin Higher People's Court (2018), *Ma Fengsheng v. Tianjin shi Xiqing qu renmin zhengfu* (Ma Fengsheng v. Tianjin Xiqing District Government), Administrative Case of Second Instance, Dispute on Land Administration, 30 May 2018.

95 Henan Higher People's Court (2018), *Zhengzhou shi Erqi qu renmin zhengfu v. Shi Mingqiang* (Zhengzhou Erqi District government v. Shi Mingqiang), Administrative Case of Second Instance, Dispute on Administrative Agreement, 14 December 2018; Anhui Higher People's Court (2017), *Sha Mingbao, Sha Minghu, Sha Mingli, Gu Hongying v. Maanshan shi Huashan qu renmin zhengfu* (Sha Mingbao, Sha Minghu, Sha Mingli, Gu Hongying v. Maanshan Huashan District Government), Administrative Dispute, 18 December 2017.

96 Hainan Higher People's Court (2016), *Hainan Dongfang haiyang yuye kaifa youxian gongsi v. Dongfang shi renmin zhengfu, Dongfang shi guotu ziyuanju* (Hainan Dongfang Marine Fisheries Development Ltd. v. Dongfang Municipal Government and Dongfang Municipal Land and Resources Administration), Administrative Case of Second Instance, Dispute on Land Administration, 17 October 2016; Supreme People's Court (2014), *Dingan chengdong jianzhu zhuangxiu gongcheng gongsi v. Hainan sheng Dingan xian renmin zhengfu* (Dingan Chengdong Construction and Decoration Engineering Company v. Dingan County Government), Administrative Case of Second Instance, Dispute on Resumption of Land Use Rights, 10 March 2014.

97 Henan Higher People's Court (2019), *Huang Fusheng v. Huaiyang xian renmin zhengfu* (Huang Fusheng v. Huaiyang County Government), Administrative Case of Second Instance, Dispute on Real Estate Registration, 3 September 2019; Guizhou Higher People's Court (2017), *Zhonghua renmin gongheguo Guiyang haiguan v. Wu Xiaosong* (Guiyang Customs v. Wu Xiaosong), Administrative Case of Second Instance, Dispute on Customs Administration, 1 December 2017.

and conferred on them hearing rights in the administrative procedure.[98] The requirements of 'adequate participation' were laid out in a case relating to a work-related injuries investigation report. The court held that the employer as an interested party must be notified and the employer's statements and defence must be heard.[99]

In some cases, courts have interpreted the due process principle in a very broad manner so that it has appeared to function as a catch-all clause for administrative injustices. We observed this approach in particular with coercive measures directed at the demolition of illegal buildings. In such cases courts held that the due process principle included the requirement that after the demolition decision is taken, the addressee of the administrative act should be allowed sufficient time to remove the private belongings inside the illegal building. Further, on the day of the demolition, the due process principle requires that an inventory of the remaining belongings within the building is completed and that the belongings are appropriately stored.[100] In cases of building expropriations, demolition and relocation, courts have concluded that the requirement of 'compensation first and demolition and relocation second' derives from the due process principle.[101]

The due process principle was even invoked in a case where the calculation of the processing time of an administrative reconsideration decision was at issue. The Anhui High Court decided that the time that documents need to be circulated among different administrative agencies also count towards the processing time. Otherwise the time limits for the processing time would lose their meaning and could be arbitrarily extended, which would be a violation of the due process requirement.[102]

[98] Liaoning Higher People's Court (2018), *Wang Chunfu v. Fuxin shi renmin zhengfu* (Wang Chunfu v. Fuxin Municipal Government), Administrative Case of Second Instance, Dispute on Administrative Reconsideration, 2 January 2018; Shandong Higher People's Court (2018), *Shi Binli v. Liu Maoju* (Shi Binli v. Liu Maoju), Administrative Dispute on Real Estate Registration, 29 January 2018.

[99] Hunan Higher People's Court (2019), *Duan Yuezhong v. Xinhua xian shichong kouzhen* (Duan Yuezhong v. Xinhua County Shizhongkou Town Shengli Colliery), Administrative Case of Second Instance, Dispute on Administrative Reconsideration, 17 October 2019.

[100] Liaoning Higher People's Court (2018), *Changjiang zuqiu juyebu v. Shenyang shi Huanggu qu renmin zhengfu* (Dachangjiang Football Club v. Shenyang Huanggu District Government), Administrative Case of Second Instance, Dispute on Forced Demolition and Compensation, 27 December 2018; Anhui Higher People's Court (2019), *Fan Chengke, Fan Tongming v. Shou xian renmin zhengfu, Shou xian chengshi guanli xingzheng zhifa ju, Shou xian fangchan guanli fuwu zhongxin* (Fan Chengke, Fan Tongming v. Shou County Government, Shou County Urban Management Bureau and Shou County Real Estate Management Centre), Administrative Case of Second Instance, Dispute on Forced Demolition, 18 December 2019.

[101] Henan Higher People's Court (2018), *Pingdingshan renmin zhengfu v. Liu Jianjun* (Pingdingshan Municipal Government v. Liu Jianjun), Administrative Case of Second Instance, Dispute on Real Estate Demolition, 6 July 2018; Heilongjiang Higher People's Court (2018), *Qiqihaer shi Longsha qu renmin zhengfu v. Zhao Chenyou* (Qiqihaer Longsha District Government v. Zhao Chenyou), Administrative Case of Second Instance, Dispute on Compensation of House Expropriation, 26 October 2018.

[102] Anhui Higher People's Court (2016), *Qi Xi, Lu Huaishan, Jiang Fang v. Fuyang shi renmin*

Relationship between the Unwritten Due Process Principle and Administrative Procedure Legislation

Whereas academic commentators have anchored due process rights in a general legal principle, in the broad interpretation of constitutional or ordinary legal provisions or in the analogous application of specific due process provisions, courts have not been very active in providing such justifications. We can interpret this practice in the sense that judges assume that there exists an unwritten due process principle and they take it for granted that this unwritten principle has been recognized as binding law. Hence, it does not need any further justification to base a decision on that principle. In general, courts just determine a violation of procedure based on the finding that an administrative act has violated the due process principle.[103]

Courts use the due process principle as guidance for the interpretation of ordinary legislation. When courts relate the due process principle to effective administrative legislation, the starting point of their argumentation is not a written due process right the application of which is then extended beyond its wording to comparable cases through conclusion by analogy. Courts rather start by assuming the existence of an unwritten due process principle in order to give due process provisions in effective legislation a broader scope of application. For example, Art. 22 of the Administrative Reconsideration Law stipulates that the reconsideration agency may hear the opinion of the applicant, the respondent or a third party. Courts have limited the discretion of the reconsideration agency with regard to the hearing rights of third parties as they noted that the reconsideration agency has to notify and hear third parties in accordance with the principle of due process.[104] The Jiangsu High Court stated that although the Administrative Reconsideration Law does not expressly require the administrative reconsideration agency to notify third parties to participate in the reconsideration, it must , according to the due process principle, notify and hear the opinion of the interested third party, if the administrative decision is not beneficial to that third party.[105]

zhengfu (Qi Xi, Lu Huaishan, Jiang Fang v. Fuyang Municipal Government), Administrative Case of Second Instance, Dispute on Administrative Reconsideration, 14 December 2016.

[103] See, for example: Guangxi Higher People's Court (2019), *Wu Yihai v. Qinzhou shi Qinnan qu renmin zhengfu* (Wu Yihai v. Qinzhou Qinnan District Government), Administrative Case of Second Instance, Dispute on Administrative Decision and Reconsideration, 28 January 2019. Meng, Fanzhuang 'Administrative Trials' (2014) supra note 65 at 142.

[104] Liaoning Higher People's Court (2019), *Zhang Qingqu v. Shenyang shi renmin zhengfu* (Zhang Qingyu v. Shenyang Municipal Government), Administrative Case of Second Instance, Dispute on Administrative Reconsideration, 29 March 2019; Zhenjiang Higher People's Court (2018), *Wenling shi renmin zhengfu v. Chen Xingeng* (Wenling Municipal Government v. Chen Xingeng), Administrative Case of Second Instance, Dispute on Administrative Reconsideration, 26 September 2018.

[105] Jiangsu Higher People's Court (2005), *Zhang Chengyin v. Xuzhou shi renmin zhengfu* (Zhang Chengyin v. People's Government of Xuzhou City), Administrative Case of Second Instance, Dispute on Administrative Reconsideration, 10 December 2004. 2005(3) *Zuigao renmin fayuan*

Moreover, courts have interpreted Art. 8 (1) of the Administrative Licensing Law in light of the due process principle. Art. 8 (1) states that issued licenses are protected by law. The Guangdong High Court held that according to the requirements of the due process principle the addressee of the license has to be notified of negative effects on the license and statements and defence of the addressee must be heard before taking a decision that has negative effects on the license.[106]

Some courts have even given the due process principle the status of an unwritten fundamental right. Although fundamental rights are not applied by Chinese courts, the Henan High Court has argued in 2015 that 'due process is a fundamental requirement of administrative acts that has already become a fundamental right of citizens in a rule-of-law society'.[107] An earlier court decision of 1999 has related the applicability of due process requirements to the question of whether the relevant administrative act encroaches on fundamental rights. In 2014 the SPC elevated this decision to a guiding case that has factual binding force when courts decide similar cases. Hence, arguments that relate the due process principle to fundamental rights have found some endorsement in judicial practice.[108]

In a number of cases, courts referred to the 2004 State Council Outline of Comprehensive Promotion of Law-based Governance, according to which administrative organs have to exercise their competences strictly according to the legally prescribed procedure.[109] For instance, courts held on the basis of the 2004 State Council Outline that before issuing an onerous administrative act the relevant addressee or interested parties have to be notified and given a chance to make statements and defend themselves.[110]

gongbao (Gazette of the Supreme People's Court) 43-46.

106 Guangdong Higher People's Court (2019), *Zhongshan shi renmin zhengfu v. Li Yuqiao* (Zhongshan Municipal Government v. Li Yuqiao), Administrative Case of Second Instance, Dispute on Administration of City Planning, 21 August 2019.

107 Higher People's Court of Henan Province (2015), *Xue Yangeng v. Neixiang xian renmin zhengfu* (Xue Yangeng and Xue Yangun v. People's Government of Neixiang County), Administrative Case of Second Instance, Dispute on an Administrative Decision, 29 June 2015.

108 Beijing No.1 Intermediate People's Court (2014), *Tian Yong v. Beijing kezhi daxue* (Tian Yong v. Beijing University of Science and Technology), Administrative Dispute of 26 April 1999; Guiding Case No. 38, 25 November 2014.

109 Quanmian tuixing yifa xingzheng shishi gangyao (Outline of the Comprehensive Promotion of Administration According to Law), 22 March 2004; Art. 5 (3) reads: 'Due Process. Administrative organs shall act in a transparent manner, except when state secrets, business secrets and personal privacy protected by law are involved. The opinions of citizens, legal persons and other organizations shall be listened to and legal procedures shall be strictly followed. The right to know, the right to participate and the right to legal remedies of the addressees of administrative measures and interested third persons shall be guaranteed. When performing their duties, the staff of administrative organs shall recuse themselves when they have a conflict of interest relating to the addressee of the administrative measure.'

110 Inner Mongolia Higher People's Court (2018), *Li De v. Neimenggu zizhiqu Chifeng shi Wengniuteqi renmin zhengfu* (Li De v. Inner Mongolia Autonomous Region Chifeng Wengniuteqi Government), Administrative Case of Second Instance, Dispute on

Legal Consequences of Due Process Violations

What kind of consequences the courts attach to procedural errors reveals how the conflicting aims of binding administrative agencies to strict procedural requirements and the cost-effective and expeditious processing of administrative decisions are balanced in practice. Depending on the nature of the violation and the nature of the relevant administrative act, courts attach different legal consequences to violations of the due process principle.

Pursuant to Art. 70 of the Administrative Litigation Law, courts will either fully or partly repeal the administrative act and may, in addition, order the defendant to issue the administrative act again. For example, the Hunan High Court decided to repeal the reconsideration decision in a case where the third party was not notified of its hearing rights during the reconsideration procedure.[111] In a case where the Jiangxi High Court reviewed the repeal of an administrative license, the court held that revoking the license without prior notice violated the due process principle and repealed the decision that revoked the license.[112] Most courts based their decision to repeal the administrative act on Art. 70 (3), the violation of legally stipulated procedure.[113] Only certain courts cite as grounds for repealing an administrative act Art. 70 (2), the flawed application of the law, or Art. 70 (6), the obvious inappropriateness of the administrative act.[114]

According to Art. 76 of the Administrative Litigation Law, courts confirming that an administrative act is unlawful or invalid, may order the defendant to adopt remedial measures or if harm was caused to the plaintiff decide that the defendant bears responsibility to pay compensation for loss and damages. Further, Art. 4 of the State Compensation Law provides for compensation for loss and damages, when actions infringe

Administrative Reconsideration, 13 August 2018; Hainan Higher People's Court (2019), *Dong Lanxiang v. Sanya shi Jiyang qu renmin zhengfu* (Dong Lanxiang v. Sanya Jiyang District Government), Administrative Dispute on Administrative Confirmation, 22 February 2019.

[111] Hunan Higher People's Court (2019), *Duan Yuezhong v. Xinhua xian shichong kouzhen* (Duan Yuezhong v. Xinhua County Shizhongkou Town Shengli Colliery), Administrative Case of Second Instance, Dispute on Administrative Reconsideration, 17 October 2019.

[112] Jiangxi Higher People's Court (2018), *Zhong Shuisheng v. Fenyi xian renmin zhengfu* (Zhong Shuisheng v. Fenyi County Government), Administrative Case of Second Instance, Dispute on Forestry Administration, 9 March 2018.

[113] Zhejiang Higher People's Court (2018), *Cangan xian renmin zhengfu v. Zhang Shuliao* (Cangnan County Government v. Zhang Shuliao), Administrative Case of Second Instance, Dispute on Administrative Compensation, 7 February 2018; Guangxi Higher People's Court (2017), *Dahua Yaozu zizhixian renmin zhengfu v. Li Shimin* (Dahua Yao Ethnic Autonomous County Government v. Li Shimin), Administrative Dispute on Land Administration, 28 December 2017.

[114] Henan Higher People's Court (2018), *Pingdingshan shi renmin zhengfu v. Ma Liren* (Pingdingshan Municipal Government v. Ma Liren), Administrative Case of Second Instance, Dispute on Real Estate Demolition, 18 July 2018.

on the property of the plaintiff.[115] Such decisions are normally taken in cases of the expropriation of land or the demolition of buildings, where the administrative act is irreversible.[116] Some courts rely on Art. 74 (1) No. 1 for confirming that an administrative act is unlawful without repealing it, if revoking the administrative act would cause significant harm to national or societal public interest. For example, the Zhejiang High Court confirmed the decision by the first instance court in a dispute on the withdrawal of a land use right that was conducted without the required hearing. As the use of the land was in the public interest, the court did not revoke the withdrawal.[117] In other cases courts have relied on Art. 74 (2) No. 1 as the legal basis, according to which the administrative act is unlawful but has no revocable content such as in a case where the building of the plaintiff was already demolished.[118]

Pursuant to Art. 74 (1) No. 2 of the Administrative Litigation Law courts confirm that an administrative act is unlawful without revoking it, if the violation of procedure is minor and does not actually affect the rights of the plaintiff. For instance, the Jiangsu High Court confirmed that demolishing a building was unlawful as the owner of the belongings within the building was not notified of the place where the belongings were stored and was not given in a timely fashion the stored belongings.[119]

In some cases courts held that administrative acts that are unlawful due to a violation of the due process principle can be cured during the administrative reconsideration or litigation, if the rights of the addressee of the administrative act are in general not affected, and issuing a new administrative act after revoking the original act would not change the outcome of the administrative decision. For example, the Gansu High Court found there had been a violation of hearing rights of the employer in a case of the evaluation of work-related injuries. Yet the court stated that during the administrative reconsideration procedure and the administrative litigation the hearing rights were sufficiently guaranteed.[120] It is important to note

[115] Art. 4 Zhonghua renmin gongheguo guojia peichang fa (PRC State Compensation Law) 1 January 2013.

[116] Liaoning Higher People's Court (2019), *Xinmin shi renmin zhengfu v. Cai Lei* (Xinmin Municipal Government v. Cai Lei), Administrative Case of Second Instance, Dispute on Administrative Compensation, 28 August 2019.

[117] Zhejiang Higher People's Court (2017), *Hangzhou shi renmin zhengfu v. Dongxinyuan yezhu weiyuanhui* (Hangzhou Municipal Government v. Dongxinyuan Owners Committee), Administrative Case of Second Instance, Dispute on Administrative Licensing, 24 July 2017.

[118] Shandong Higher People's Court (2019), *Linyi shi Lanshan qu renmin zhengfu v. Zhu Zhide* (Linyi Lanshan District Government v. Zhu Zhide), Administrative Case of Second Instance, Dispute on Real Estate Demolition, 17 January 2019.

[119] Jiangsu Higher People's Court (2018), *Chen Zhiming v. Nanjing shi Qixia qu renmin zhengfu* (Chen Zhiming v. Nanjing Qixia District Government), Administrative Case of Second Instance, Dispute on Administrative Enforcement, 15 October 2018.

[120] Gansu Higher People's Court (2018), *Gansu Jiantou tumu gongcheng jianshe youxian gongsi v. Baiyin shi renli ziyuan he shehui baozhang ju* (Gansu Jiantou Civil Engineering Construction

that the Administrative Litigation Law or other legislation does not provide for the curing of procedural errors during reconsideration or litigation.

Finally, the violation of the due process principle can make the administrative decision flawed but not unlawful. In the review of a reconsideration decision, the Hubei High Court held that the defendant violated the due process principle by not notifying the plaintiff. The omission of the notification constituted a procedural flaw. However, the court argued that this procedural flaw had no impact on the issue that the defendant has exercised its administrative supervision duty. Further, the omission of the notification obligation did not affect the protection of the legal interests of the plaintiff.[121]

CONCLUSION

In the post-2013 era, courts have further developed and expanded the application of the due process principle in administrative procedure. For example, courts extended the application of the due process requirements to the repeal of beneficial administrative acts, to mere physical acts and to abstract administrative acts such as land-use plans. Courts even granted due process protections with regard to the preparatory measures of administrative acts.

However, it is questionable whether courts apply the due process principle in a way that is in line with its purpose of strengthening administrative procedure in order to providing effective pre-judicial remedies, contributing to the legitimacy of administrative decisions and facilitating information gathering of the administration. We noticed two opposite developments. Some courts have extended the principle of due process in a way that turned it into a catch-all clause for administrative injustices. Other courts have restricted the due process principle as they either do not attach remedying legal consequences to a violation of the principle or the violation is no longer regarded as relevant if the aggrieved party exercises hearing rights subsequently during the reconsideration procedure or the administrative litigation. Mainland Chinese scholarship has discussed these different tendencies of court practice. Academic commentators have expressed concerns that courts deviate from statutory procedural requirements when they too easily rely on a wide due process principle.[122] Others have indicated that courts have applied the due process principle in a way that deviates from its original purpose.[123] More positive

Co., Ltd. v. Baiyin City Human Resources and Social Security Bureau, Gansu Provincial Human Resources and Social Security Bureau), Administrative Case of Second Instance, Dispute on Administrative Confirmation and Reconsideration, 8 April 2018.

121 Hubei Higher People's Court (2016), *Ming Tian v. Yichang shi renmin zhengfu, Hubei sheng renmin zhengfu* (Ming Tian v. Yichang Municipal Government, Hubei Provincial Government), Administrative Case of Second Instance, Dispute on Administrative Supervision, 7 June 2016.

122 Jiang, Hongzhen 'Legitimacy' (2019) supra note 52 at 62

123 Zhou, Youyong. 'Development Court Decisions' (2019) supra note 41 at 44.

accounts of court practice argue that the courts have successfully used the due process principle in order to interpret administrative law and clarify vague legal concepts.[124]

An important motivation of courts to apply the due process principle appears to be that it allows courts to repeal administrative acts or declare them unlawful on the grounds of procedural errors and avoid taking a decision on the substantive legality of the administrative acts. In particular when courts lack the authority to reign in more powerful administrative agencies or are hesitant to interfere in the conflict between different administrative agencies, they draw on the due process principle to identify procedural errors. Hence, the lack of authority with regard to other actors of the party state appears to explain at least in part why courts have taken a more activist approach to extend the application of the principle. Further, the nature of cases may also explain the more activist approach of courts. The majority of court decisions concerned compensation claims for the expropriation of buildings, the demolition of unlawful buildings and other land-related disputes. As urban development resulted in growing social tension and violent disputes, courts have become important stability maintenance institutions that were encouraged by the party-state to protect the weaker parties in those disputes in order to resolve social tensions.

Chinese scholarship has become more critical towards the judicial expansion of the due process principle compared to when the courts started to develop the principle in a number of university degree cases. But so far, the national legislator has not limited the discretion of courts through the adoption of a national administrative procedure law that defines the scope of due process rights and the legal consequences of procedural errors. The SPC has encouraged the extension of the due process principle by lower courts through issuing relevant guiding cases rather than limited the application of the principle by lower courts. Further, courts have so far been very hesitant to apply the local regulations of administrative procedure, although litigants have referred to them in numerous cases.[125]

What is the significance of courts innovating due process requirements for administrative justice in China? Taking a closer look at the status of the courts in relation to other actors within the party-state is illuminating. Despite the implementation of several judicial reform measures in the post-2013 period, which have served to enhance the status of courts in relation to local-level administrative agencies, the extent of their authority within the prevailing political hierarchy remains constrained.[126] In view of their weak status, courts in administrative litigation primarily focus on their own

124 Xu, Chunhui 'Due Process Principle' (2020) supra note 68 at 63-64.

125 Zhang, Jiansheng 'Administrative Procedure Legislation' (2017) supra note 32 at 70.

126 Ahl, Björn (2021) 'Post-2013 Reforms of the Chinese Courts and Criminal Procedure: An Introduction' Ahl, Björn (ed) *Chinese Courts and Criminal Procedure: Post-2013 Reforms*, Cambridge University Press, 1-28.

preservation and the avoidance of overt conflict with other state organs.[127] Another relevant aspect for contextualizing the due process innovations of Chinese courts is that, in an authoritarian context, the main function of administrative justice is the efficient control of bureaucrats rather than the protection of citizens' rights.[128] These two aspects appear to be driving the courts' due process innovations in the post-2013 period. In the early 1990s, when the courts were dealing with cases involving students who had been denied their university degrees, they seemed to be primarily concerned with protecting the individual rights of citizens, particularly the constitutional right to education enshrined in Art. 46 of the 1982 Constitution. In that earlier period, academic discourses that stressed the development of the rule of law and fundamental rights, as well as lawyers and legal academics who actively promoted rights litigation, may have been conducive to this, as well as a more open political atmosphere. Yet, since 2013, two seemingly contradictory dynamics have come to the fore: the empowerment of courts as policy-implementing institutions of the party state, and the necessity of self-preservation due to the courts' weak political status. This means that the innovations introduced by the courts in the area of due process are not primarily driven by a concern for the protection of individual rights, but rather by the need to implement important policies of the party state, such as maintaining stability in legal disputes relating to compensation for the expropriation of buildings. To avoid confrontation with more powerful party-state actors, courts focus on procedural issues, which are generally considered less sensitive than holding administrative agencies accountable for violating substantive laws. This explains why, in a number of disputes, the due process principle was extended beyond its original meaning and turned into a catch-all clause addressing administrative injustices.

GLOSSARY OF CHINESE TERMS

Romanisation (Hanyu Pinyin)	**Chinese Characters**	**English Translation**
Dianxing anli	典型案例	Model case
Falü	法律	Law (adopted by the National People's
Congress		or its Standing
Committee)		

[127] He. Xin (2024) *The Judicial System of China*, Oxford University Press, at 200.

[128] Ip, Eric (2022) 'Administrative Justice in Authoritarian States', Hertogh, Marc (ed) et al *The Oxford Handbook of Administrative Justice*, Oxford University Press, 263-284 at 265.

Fudanxing act xingzheng xingwei	负担性行政行为	Onerous administrative
Shehuizhuyi fazhi	社会主义法治	Socialist rule of law
shishi xingwei	事实行为	Physical act
shouyi xingzheng administrative *xingwei*	授益行政行为	Beneficial act
Xingzheng chengxu fa	行政程序法	Law on Administrative Procedure
Xingzheng fagui	行政法规	Administrative Regulations (adopted by the State Council)
Xingzheng susong fa	行政诉讼法	Administrative Litigation Law
zhengdang chengxu yuanze	正当程序原则	Due process principle
Zhidaoxing anli	指导性案例	Guiding cases
Zhongjianxing xingzheng xingwei	中间性行政行为	Intermediate administrative act
Zuigao Renmin Fayuan	最高人民法院	Supreme People's Court

Judicial Review of Administrative Rules in China: Incremental Expansion of Judicial Power

XIAO SHILING
University of Manchester

YANG LIN
University of Hong Kong

INTRODUCTION

The term 'judicial review' refers to the review of governmental acts by a judicial authority for their consistency with law.[1] The term may generally be separated into two categories: constitutional review and administrative review. Constitutional review is a proceeding that determines the compatibility of legislative or executive actions with the constitution.[2] Administrative review is a proceeding that examines the conformity of decisions made by executive authorities with laws other than the constitution.[3] When applying the concept of judicial review to China, it often refers to administrative review or administrative litigation (*xingzheng susong*), since the power of constitutional review is exclusively vested in the legislature of China–the National People's Congress (NPC) and its Standing Committee (NPCSC), while the Chinese courts are incapable of reviewing the constitutionality of any legislation and administrative actions.[4] There is only legislative constitutional review and no judicial constitutional review in China.

The constitutionalism movement after World War II (WWII) has led to a notable expansion of judicial power and considerable public confidence in judicial review. The phenomenon of the expansion of judicial review and particularly judicial influence over legislative and executive acts has

[1] There is no universally accepted definition of "judicial review". Judicial review, constitutional review, administrative review, and constitutional appeal are used interchangeably when comparing different legal systems. Grote, Rainer (2018) 'Judicial Review', *Max Planck Encyclopaedia of Comparative Constitutional Law*, available at <https://oxcon.ouplaw.com/view/10.1093/law-mpeccol/law-mpeccol-e334?rskey=LpB90t&result=1&prd=MPECCOL> (accessed 12 October 2021); Goldstein, Leslie Friedman (2011) 'Judicial Review' in Bertrand Badie and others (eds), *International Encyclopaedia of Political Science* SAGE Press 1372.

[2] See Grote ibid para 1.

[3] Woolf, Harry and others (2013), *De Smith's Judicial Review* (7th ed) Sweet and Maxwell 4.

[4] Zhu, Guobin (2010) 'Constitutional Review in China: An Unaccomplished Project or a Mirage' (43) *Suffolk University Law Review* 625.

drawn increasing academic attention.[5] Alec Stone Sweet first used the term ''judicialization of politics'' to refer to ''the general process in which legal discourse–norms of behaviour and language–penetrate and are absorbed by political discourse'.[6] This concept has been widely employed in scholarship to highlight a significant aspect of the expansion of judicial power since then.[7]

Ran Hirschl has suggested that the judicialization of politics consisted of three interrelated processes. In the first stage, legal discourse, jargon, rules, and procedures spread to the political sphere and policy-making fora and processes. At the second stage, the competences and province of courts and judges expand and their influence over public policy outcome increases mainly through judicial review of administrative acts and adjudicating fundamental rights disputes. Lastly, courts and judges decide core political questions.[8]

One can track the expansion of judicial power of Chinese courts against Hirschl's three-stage process.[9] China has gone through the first stage and entered into the second stage but is still far away from the final stage. China has been establishing for more than four decades a socialist legal system with Chinese characteristics,[10] which is still undergoing continuous reform. The Constitution of the People's Republic of China (PRC), the Law on Legislation, the Criminal Procedure Law and many administrative laws, such as the Administrative Coercion Law and the Administrative Penalty Law, provide essential legal frameworks, rules and procedures for legislative and administrative activities. As Hualing Fu has observed, "Under Xi Jinping's leadership, the authoritarian system has increasingly

[5] Sweet, Alec Stone (2000) *Governing with Judges: Constitutional Politics in Europe* Oxford University Press 37; Hirschl, Ran (2018) 'Opting Out of "Global Constitutionalism"' (12) *Law & Ethics of Human Rights* 3.

[6] Sweet, Alec Stone (1994) 'Judging Socialist Reform: The Politics of Coordinate Construction in France and Germany' (4) *Comparative Political Studies* 446.

[7] Neal, Tate C. and Torbjörn, Vallinder (eds) (1995) *The Global Expansion of Judicial Power* NYU Press; Hirschl, Ran (2008) 'The Judicialisation of Politics' in Whittington, Keith E., Kelemen, R. Daniel and Caldeira, Gregory A. (eds) *The Oxford Handbook of Law and Politics* Oxford University Press; Ginsburg, Tom (2009) 'The Judicialisation of Administrative Governance: Causes, Consequence and limits' in Ginsburg, Tom and Chen, Albert H. Y. (eds) *Administrative Law and Governance in Asia* Routledge Press.

[8] Hirschl ibid at 121-123.

[9] This chapter particularly tracks the expansion of judicial power from a public law perspective. We admit that the judicial power of Chinese courts is broader than judicial review power against government action. It also includes the power to adjudicate other types of cases and issue judicial interpretations, etc.

[10] Xi Focus: Xi stresses adherence to socialist rule of law with Chinese characteristics, 7 December 2021, *xinhuanet*, available at <http://www.xinhuanet.com/english/20211015/C9A-3F7AEA8800001CC1942E01396169A/c.html>, (accessed 29 March 2022).

become legalistic and characterised by reference and adherence to formal rules and procedures."[11]

China entered into the second stage of judicialization of politics by establishing a system of administrative litigation. The NPC enacted the first Administrative Litigation Law (ALL) in 1989. It is one of the milestones of the developmental trajectory of Chinese judicial review. Since then, administrative litigation has been governed by administrative litigation procedural rules, replacing the rules of the 1982 Provisional Civil Procedure Law. Subsequently, administrative divisions were established within many courts, at all levels, and thousands of complaints against executive actions were petitioned to the administrative divisions every year.[12]

Administrative litigation is an important tool which the Chinese courts may employ to examine executive actions (*xingzheng xingwei*). Initially, however, the jurisdiction of the courts in administrative litigation was limited to concrete administrative actions (as opposed to abstract executive acts or administrative rulemaking).[13] Legislation and administrative rules have long been excluded from the purview of courts, which completely stops Chinese courts from examining and influencing any policies through adjudicative activities, let alone deciding core political questions.

The NPCSC amended the ALL for the first time in 2014, a quarter-century after the ALL was originally enacted. This amendment came into force on 1 May 2015. Article 53 of the new ALL expressly entitles people to challenge and empowers the courts to review the lawfulness of normative documents (*guifanxing wenjian*) promulgated by certain administrative authorities.[14] This chapter will refer to those documents as administrative normative documents (hereafter, 'ANDs'), which are the most numerous administrative rules in China. This empowerment marks a step towards expanding judicial power, enhancing judicial supervision over administrative rulemaking, and improving public accountability and the rule of law.[15]

Judicial review of administrative rules in China has attracted some attention of scholarship.[16] Nonetheless, there is as yet no study, particularly in English, thoroughly examining this process. This chapter seeks to fill this gap by investigating the evolution, rules and practice of judicial review of

[11] Fu, Hualing (2019) 'Duality and China's Struggle for Legal Autonomy' (1) *China Perspectives* 5.

[12] The first administrative division was set up within the Basic Court of Miluo County, Hunan Province in 1986. The SPC established its administrative division in 1988.

[13] Cui, Wei, Cheng, Jie and Wiesner, Dominika (2019) 'Judicial Review of Government Actions in China' (1) *China Perspectives* 39.

[14] ALL, article 53. The ALL was amended in 2014 and again in 2017. References to the ALL in this chapter will be to the ALL of 2017, unless otherwise indicated.

[15] Ahl, Björn (2019) 'Judicialization in Authoritarian Regimes: The Expansion of Powers of the Chinese Supreme People's Court' (17) *International Journal of Constitutional Law* 255-256.

[16] Cui, Cheng, and Wiesner 'Government Actions' supra note 13.

administrative rules in China, especially the review of ANDs after 2014. It argues that whereas expanding the court's jurisdiction over ANDs is a landmark in judicial empowerment, China has merely established a weak-form judicial review of administrative rules; additionally, the timid and deferential approach of the courts to this new empowerment seriously limits the function of this mechanism for supervising government's policy-making.

This Chapter proceeds in four main parts. The next recalls the evolution of the Chinese judicial review of administrative rulemaking, which comprises three stages. The following part focuses on the newest judicial review mechanism against ANDs established by the Amendment of ALL in 2014. It emphasises that this is designed to be weak-from of judicial review with regards to the scope, intensity and effect of the review. Only ANDs that are at the bottom of the hierarchy of the Chinese legal system and have the lowest legal force are subject to judicial review. The courts are expected not to scrutinise the reasonableness and proportionality of ANDs and cannot strike down invalid ANDs. They use the report and record procedure to transfer the decision power to high courts.

The part which follows examines judicial review cases against administrative rules decided between 2014 and 2021, in particular those of the SPC, and reveals the timid and deferential attitude of courts towards reviewing administrative rules. They dismiss requests for reviewing administrative rules in a large majority of cases. Even when they accept the requests, they seldom closely and effectively scrutinized the substantive content and merits of ANDs. Moreover, they consult with the executive authorities and defer to their opinion during administrative litigation. The last part is a conclusion of the finding of this chapter and considers the prospects of Chinese judicial review of administrative rules.

EVOLUTION OF JUDICIAL REVIEW OF ADMINISTRATIVE RULES IN CHINA

The ALL of 1989, China's first law on administrative litigation, came into force on 1 October 1990. Before that, people's right of appeal against executive acts was extremely limited,[17] although civil divisions of the people's courts, following civil procedural rules, could adjudicate certain cases against very few executive acts.[18] According to the ALL, any individuals, legal persons and organizations may file a lawsuit if they believe an administrative action violates their legal rights and interests.[19]

[17] Ginsburg, Tom (2008) 'Administrative Law and the Judicial Control of Agents in Authoritarian Regimes' in Ginsburg, Tom and Moustafa, Tamir (eds) *Rule by Law: The Politics of Courts in Authoritarian Regimes* Cambridge University Press 67.

[18] Chen, Albert H. Y. (2011), *An Introduction to the Legal System of the People's Republic of China* (4th edn) LexisNexis 293.

[19] ALL, article 2.

In Chinese administrative law, the concept of administrative action embraces all executive authorities' acts backed up by the state's coercive power.[20] The ALL divides such actions into two categories: 'abstract acts' and 'specific acts'.[21] An abstract administrative act, which is also called a general administrative act, refers to executive authorities' activities of making rules of general application, such as administrative regulations and ANDs.[22] A specific administrative act is performed in relation to a particular person in a particular circumstance and may take the form of a grant, a confirmation, permission, a certification, an exemption, or a punishment.[23] Since the ALL of 1989, most concrete administrative actions have been included in the jurisdiction of courts, except for those explicitly excluded by the ALL, such as defense and foreign affairs.[24]

Not until 2014 did the ALL expand the jurisdiction of courts to cover ANDs. Before unfolding the evolution of judicial review of administrative rules in China, it is helpful to briefly examine the scope of administrative rules and their legal force rank in the Chinese legal system (Figure 1).

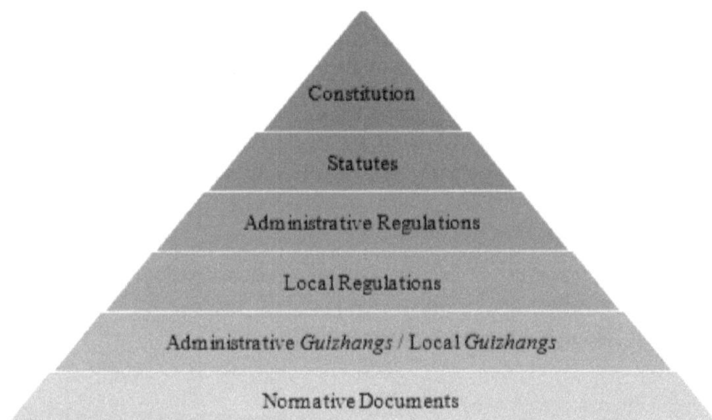

Figure 1: The hierarchy of legal authority in Chinese legal system

Source: the author draws up this figure based on the Law on Legislation

The Chinese legal system includes formal and informal legal sources.[25] Formal legal sources comprise the constitution, statutes (*falü*), regulations

20 Chen 'Introduction' supra note 18 at 334.

21 Ibid.

22 Ibid.

23 Ibid.

24 ALL, articles 12-13, 53. Chen 'Legal System' supra note 18 at 334.

25 'Guanyu shenli xingzheng anjian shiyong falü guifan wenti de zuotan jiyao' (Minutes of the Symposiums of the Supreme People's Court concerning Application of Laws in

(*fagui*) and rules (*guizhang*).[26] In administrative litigation proceedings, informal legal sources mainly include ANDs promulgated by executive authorities for guiding law enforcement and carrying out administrative measures. The force ranking of these legal sources is constructed as follows:

1. The Constitution is at the apex of the pyramid of the Chinese legal system. It is the fundamental law of the country and has supreme legal authority.[27] All statutes, regulations, and *guizhang* must be consistent with the Constitution;[28]
2. Statutes are the primary legislation enacted by the NPC or the NPCSC. They are usually titled as an 'act' or 'law' and have higher legal authority than regulations and *guizhang*;[29]
3. Administrative regulations, promulgated by the State Council, have higher legal authority than local regulations and all *guizhangs*;[30]
4. Local regulations are made by local people's congresses and their standing committees. They have higher legal authority than local *guizhang*;[31]
5. There are two kinds of *guizhang*: local *guizhang* promulgated by local governments and administrative *guizhang* issued by the departments of the State Council. They have equal legal force;[32]
6. Administrative normative documents are promulgated by executive authorities and repeatedly applicable with generally binding force.[33] They are usually titled as an 'announcement', 'plan', 'instruction', 'order', 'opinion', and 'notice'.[34]

Administrative rules in China comprise administrative regulations, *guizhang*, and ANDs. In relation to judicial review of administrative rulemaking, it has gone through three stages.

Adjudicating Administrative Cases) (2004), section 1.

[26] Law on Legislation, article 2. *Guizhang* is often referred to as rule in English literature. In order to distinguish them from administrative rules, this chapter uses *guizhang* in the following sections.

[27] Constitution of the PRC, preamble.

[28] Law on Legislation, article 87.

[29] Ibid article 88(1).

[30] Ibid article 88(2).

[31] Ibid article 89(1).

[32] Ibid article 91.

[33] 'Guowuyuan bangongting guanyu jiaqiang xingzheng guifanxing wenjian zhiding he jiandu guanli gongzuo de tongzhi' (Notice of the State Council General Office on Strengthening the Formulation, Supervision and Management of Administrative Normative Documents) (2018), para 1.

[34] 'Dangzheng jiguan gongwen chuli gongzuo tiaoli' (Regulations on Handling of Official Documents by Party and Governmental Organs) (2012), article 8.

In the first stage, between 1989 and 2000, China completely prohibited the courts from reviewing any abstract executive act. Article 5 of the ALL of 1989 provided that 'People's courts examine whether concrete administrative actions are lawful when hearing administrative cases.' Further, Article 12(2) expressly required the courts to dismiss any petitions against administrative regulations, *guizhang*, as well as decisions and orders of general application made by the administrative. During this period, the courts might check the legality of concrete administrative decisions in accordance with laws but could not review the laws, including statutes, regulations, *guizhang* or ANDs.

However, some courts reviewed ANDs and even declared them inconsistent with laws of superior rank in this period. For example, in 1999, Haidian District People's Court of Beijing Municipality declared that No 68 Emergency Notice on Strict Administration of Examinations promulgated by the University of Science and Technology Beijing was invalid on the grounds that this Notice contradicted Article 29 of the Provisions on the Administration of Students in Regular Higher Education Institutions, a *guizhang* of superior rank. The SPC later published this case in its Gazette, which indicated its supportive attitude towards judicial scrutiny of ANDs in administrative litigation.[35]

Next year the SPC promulgated the Interpretation on Several Issues Concerning the Implementation of Administrative Litigation Law. Article 62(2) of this interpretation provided that 'When people's courts hear administrative litigation cases, they may cite legitimate and valid *guizhang* and ANDs in their judgments.'[36] Some scholars asserted that the SPC empowered the courts to review *guizhang* and ANDs through this provision, as the courts have to confirm the legality of the rules they are applying.[37] This marks the second stage of judicial review of administrative rules in China, although the empowerment was veiled and ambiguous. The SPC reaffirmed the court's power of reviewing *guizhang* and ANDs in explicit words in 2004 after a controversial case – the *Luoyang Seed* case.

The *Luoyang Seed* case is as influential as *Qi Yuling v Chen Xiaoqi et al*, which is often cited as China's first constitutional case.[38] The facts of the case are simple enough: the plaintiff entered into a contract with the defendant, a seed retailer. The defendant breached the contract by selling the seeds to others. The case came to the Intermediate Court of Luoyang City in 2003. The core dispute of the case concerned determining the amount of compensation due to the plaintiff. The plaintiff argued that the damages

[35] SPC Gazette 1999(4).

[36] The SPC Interpretation on the Administrative Litigation Law of 2000, article 62(2).

[37] Yu, Jun and Zhang, Wen (2016) 'Xingzheng guifanxing wenjian sifa shenzhaquan de shixiaoxing fenxi' (A Survey of the Effectiveness of Power of Judicial Review of Administrative Normative Documents) (2) *Faxue yanjiu* (*Chinese Journal of Law*) 44.

[38] Morris, Robert J (2010) China's Marbury: Qi Yuling v. Chen Xiaoqi - The Once and Future Trial of Both Education & Constitutionalization (2) *Tsinghua China Law Review* 275.

should be calculated based on the market price of the seeds in question in accordance with the Seed Law of the PRC enacted by the NPCSC. But the defendant claimed that the damages should instead be calculated based on a government guidance price, according to Article 26 of the Regulations on Crop Seeds of Henan Province promulgated by the Standing Committee of People's Congress of Henan Province. Li Huijuan, the presiding judge, decided the case in favour of the plaintiff and applied the Seed Law. She took one more step and declared that the provisions in the Regulations on Crop Seeds of Henan Province were invalid as they contradicted the Seed Law. The leaders of the People's Congress of Henan Province reacted furiously to this declaration, claiming that the court had unlawfully reviewed the local regulation, which undermined China's people's congress system and encroached on the authority of local people's congresses.[39] The Intermediate Court of Luoyang City removed Judge Li Huijuan and the vice-head of the civil division from their posts, as demanded by the People's Congress of Henan Province.[40] This event sparked a national controversy. The SPC, on the request from the High Court of Henan Province, made a Reply and stated that when a law of inferior rank conflicted with a law of superior rank, the court should apply the law of superior rank and decide their cases accordingly.[41] This Reply indicated that Judge Li should not have declared the invalidity of the Regulations on Crop Seeds of Henan Province.

Because of the *Luoyang Seed* case, the debate on the courts' judicial review power was revived. The issues of whether the courts have power to review statutes, regulations and other laws, and which should be applied when they find inconsistency between laws, gave rise to heated discussion.[42] To respond to the court's concerns, the SPC organized a symposium on administrative litigation in October 2003 in Shanghai. It later issued the Minutes of the Symposium of the Supreme People's Court concerning Application of Laws in Adjudicating Administrative Cases (Minutes 2004).

In these Minutes, the SPC required the courts to suspend hearings and seek opinions from rulemaking agencies when they are confronted with conflicts between laws and are unable to decide which one should apply.[43] More importantly, the SPC expressly confirmed that the courts could review *guizhang* and ANDs before applying them. It stated: 'When referring to *guizhang* [to adjudicate administrative litigation cases], [the courts] should judge the legality of the provisions of *guizhang* and apply

[39] Hand, Keith (2011) 'Resolving Constitutional Disputes in Contemporary China' (7) *University of Pennsylvania East Asia Law Review* 109-110.

[40] Ibid at 110.

[41] Ibid.

[42] Jiang, Bixin (2009) 'Xingzheng susongfa he chouxiang xingzheng xingwei' (Administrative Procedure Law and Abstract Administrative Act) (3) *Xingzheng faxue yanjiu (Administrative Law Review)* 23.

[43] 'Guanyu shenli xingzheng anjian shiyong falv guifan wenti de zuotan jiyao' (Minutes of the Symposiums of the Supreme People's Court concerning Application of Laws in Adjudicating Administrative Cases) (2004), section 2.

legal and valid ones.'[44] It continued by saying that administrative normative documents 'are not formal sources of law. They are not legally binding on the people's courts. However, if the people's courts, after examination, consider that an AND is lawful, valid, reasonable, and proportionate and constitute the legal basis of the impugned concrete administrative decision, they should confirm its validity.'[45] Otherwise, the courts should apply the laws of superior rank, instead of the AND.[46]

The Minutes 2004 are important and revealing in two respects. First, the SPC explicitly affirmed that the courts may scrutinize *guizhang* and ANDs when adjudicating administrative cases. They may check the legality, reasonableness and proportionality of ANDs, as well as the legality of *guizhang*. Second, the Minutes 2004 did not give people the right to question *guizhang* and ANDs. Whether or not to review *guizhang* and ANDs is an issue entirely at the discretion of courts. Nonetheless, the Minutes 2004 did not spell out the details about the circumstances under which the courts may review *guizhang* and ANDs, and the standard the courts could use.

One might notice that the Minutes 2004 is an opinion of courts and the confirmation of the court's power of judicial review, and therefore it is no more than a judicial self-empowerment.

Nonetheless, this situation changed when the NPCSC's amendment to the ALL in 2014, marking the third stage of judicial review of administrative rules. The ALL amendment in 2014 expanded the scope of judicial review by removing the word 'concrete' from Article 5 of the ALL of 1989. The court now can 'scrutinize the legality of executive acts in administrative litigation', including abstract executive acts.[47] Additionally, Article 53(1) expressly enables people to question the legality of ANDs before the courts.[48] It states that:

> If citizens, legal person, and other organizations consider a normative document promulgated by the departments of the State Council, local people's governments and their departments, they may request the courts to review such normative document when they petition against [concrete] administrative actions.

The Chinese law for the first time rendered challenging the legality of ANDs in administrative litigation a right.[49] The SPC published a lengthy judicial interpretation on the enforcement of the ALL in 2018 (SPC Interpretation of

44 Ibid section 1.

45 Ibid section 1.

46 Ibid section 2 (1).

47 ALL of 2014, article 6.

48 Ibid article 53(1).

49 Cui, Cheng, and Wiesner supra note 13 at 41.

the ALL 2018), which gives detailed rules about procedure for reviewing ANDs and standards of review.[50]

WEAK-FORM JUDICIAL REVIEW OF ADMINISTRATIVE RULES

The 2014 amendment to ALL, for the first time, conferred the power on courts to review administrative rules. This has been a landmark in judicial empowerment since 1989 when China constructed the system of administrative litigation. Nonetheless, the judicial review of administrative rules that China has established is a weak-form judicial review and the ALL sets out strict limitations in terms of the scope, procedure, intensity and effect of review.

The first limitation relates to the scope of administrative rules that are subject to judicial review. The scope is narrow. In the Chinese legal system, as demonstrated in the preceding part, administrative rules include regulations, *guizhang* and ANDs. One may notice that Article 53(1) of the ALL merely entitles people to the right to challenge ANDs. Moreover, Article 53(2) particularly states that normative documents provided in Article 53(1) do not include *guizhang*. This seems to exclude *guizhang* from the jurisdiction of courts.

However, according to the Minutes 2004—still in force— the courts have the discretion to review *guizhang*. Therefore, there may be two contradictory opinions on the judicial review jurisdiction of courts over *guizhang*. One is to exclude *guizhang* from the courts' purview. The other is to keep them within it. But nonetheless, citizens are not entitled to request courts to scrutinize *guizhang*; instead, it is the courts that have entire discretion to initiate a review of *guizhang*. In practice, some courts take the first opinion,[51] and refuse petitions against *guizhang* on the ground of Article 53(2).[52] The ambiguity of court's jurisdiction and the subsequent judicial slackness seriously constrain

[50] SPC Interpretation of the ALL 2018, chapter 11.

[51] Chen, Yunsheng (2019) 'Guifan xing wenjian fudai shencha de qidong yaojian jiyu 1738 fen caipan wenshu yangben de shizheng kaocha' (The Initiation Requirements of Incidental Review of Normative Documents – An Empirical Examination Based on 1738 Judicial Decisions) (11) *Faxue (Legal Science)* 169.

[52] See examples including *Yu Xiongjie v The People's Government of Luqiao District, Taizhou City, Zhejiang Province* (2020) Zuigaofa xingshen No. 3551, trial Judgment handed down by the SPC in Beijing on 29 May 2020.

Cui Yong v The People's Government of Nankai District, Tianjin City (2017) Zuigaofa xingshen No. 4218, trial Judgment handed down by the SPC in Beijing on 26 September 2017.

Cai Yanwen v Lonshan Street Office, Zhangqiu District, Jinan City (2018) Zuigaofa xingshen No. 5714, trial Judgment handed down by the SPC in Beijing on 29 August 2018.

Houying Guo v The Management Committee of Jindong Management Zone of Yongzhou City, Hunan Province (2016) Zuigaofa xingshen No. 1792, trial Judgment handed down by the SPC in Beijing on 10 August 2016.

the effectiveness of judicial supervision over administrative rulemaking. Retaining the jurisdiction of courts over *guizhang* might be a better option than excluding them from the perspectives of maintaining the consistency of legal system, safeguarding individual rights and interests and enhancing government accountability. As for the judicial review of regulations, the ALL does not mention it. It is reasonable to believe that the legislature of China excludes regulations with relatively superior rank from the court's purview.

Second, the right to challenge ANDs is limited by procedural obstacles. A request for reviewing an AND cannot be filed independently. Instead, it must be filed concurrently with a lawsuit against a concrete administrative action.[53] Furthermore, the impugned ANDs must be the legal basis of the impugned administrative action.[54] Otherwise, the courts can dismiss review requests. The SPC Interpretation of the ALL 2018 requires the petition against an AND to be raised before the court's hearing in the first instance, and in the investigation stage of court's hearing at the latest.[55] Any delayed petitions will be rejected by courts.

Third, the courts are expected not to review the reasonableness and proportionality of ANDs, but primarily the legality. In contrast to the Minutes 2004, which explicitly allowed the courts to review the legality, validity, reasonableness and proportionality of ANDs, neither the ALL nor the SPC Interpretation of the ALL 2018 mention reasonableness and proportionality. This omission may not be unintended. In the press conference where the SPC published the first batch of typical cases concerning the review of ANDs, Yongwei Huang, the Chief Judge of the SPC Administrative Division, reiterated and emphasized that the review of administrative rules is, in principle, a legality review.[56] Zhenyu Wang, the Deputy Chief Judge of the SPC Administrative Division, stated:

> Reviewing administrative normative documents is a new mechanism created by the ALL. The legality of normative documents is the essence [of judicial review]. According to the current rules, the courts should focus on reviewing whether the rule-makers have the authority to promulgate the rule; whether they promulgate the rules according to the statutory procedure; whether the content of

[53] ALL, article 53(1).

[54] Wang, Guohua and Yi, Qingqing (2019) 'Xingzheng guifanxing wenjian fudai shencha de shizheng fenxi yi 947 fen caipan wenshu wei yangben' (Empirical Study of Judicial Review Administrative Normative Instrument: A Study based on 947 Judgments) (5) *fazhi xiandaihua yanjiu (Law and Modernisation)* 40-42.

[55] SPC Interpretation of the ALL 2018, article 137.

[56] 'Zuigao renmin fayuan fabu xingzheng susongfudai shen zha guifanxingwenjian dianxing anli' (The SPC Announced Typical Cases of Review of Normative Documents in Administrative Litigation) *Renmin fayuan bao* (People's Court Daily) (31 October 2018).

normative documents is valid, whether it is inconsistent with laws of superior rank or conflicts with the law of the same rank.[57]

Although Judge Wang mentioned reviewing the content of ANDs and examining the consistency with other laws, there are often only comparisons between the text of ANDs under review and that of other laws. *Faguo Yan v Yincheng District of Ningbao City, Zhejiang Province* is an illustrative case. The applicant challenged a property expropriation and compensation decision and No. 5 Notice about house price jointly issued by four local government departments. The SPC concluded the case with the statement: 'After examination, [it finds] No 5 Notice does not violate superior laws and other normative documents'.[58] But it did not articulate how this notice complies with the superior laws it has examined.

Last but not least, even if the courts consider an AND illegal, they cannot strike down that AND. They may only refuse to apply it.[59] Disapplying ANDs does not affect the effectiveness and validity of ANDs. The ANDs remain valid unless administrative authorities amend or repeal them. The power to amend and repeal illegal ANDs is fully vested in the administrative rule-makers and their superiors. According to Article 149 of the SPC Interpretation of the ALL 2018, if the courts consider an AND unlawful, they should provide AND-makers with a 'disposition proposal (*chuli jianyi*)' and may issue a 'judicial proposal (*sifa jianyi*)' for an amendment or repeal of the AND. A judicial proposal is more formal and solemn than a disposition proposal. The rule-makers must make written responses within 60 days after receiving a judicial proposal. Nonetheless, both disposition proposals and judicial proposals are no more than suggestions and recommendations of the courts and have no binding effect on administrative authorities. In an emergency, the courts can suggest AND-makers or their superiors suspend the enforcement of an AND.[60]

In addition to suggesting the AND-makers amend and repeal ANDs, the courts have to report their decision to the superior court for the record.[61] According to Article 150 of the SPC Interpretation of the ALL 2018, the report and record should proceed after the cases are decided (post-adjudication). But in practice, some courts send the disposition or judicial

[57] Ibid.

[58] *Faguo Yan v the People's Government of Yinzhou Disctrcit, Ningbo City, Zhejiang Province* (2019) Zuigaofa xingshen No. 132, trial Judgment handed down by the SPC in Beijing on 31 January 2019.

[59] Article 64 of the ALL provides that "The people's court in the hearing of administrative cases, after determining that a normative document is not legal, in accordance with article 53 of this Law, they cannot apply the normative document as the basis for determining the legality of administrative actions."

[60] SPC Interpretation of the ALL 2018, article 149(4).

[61] If the ANDs are enacted by the State Council or the provincial governments, the decisions must be sent to the State Council and the SPC for the record. SPC Interpretation of the ALL 2018, article 150.

proposals to their superior courts before making decisions.[62] By doing so, they seek informal endorsements from superior courts so as to prevent their decisions from being overturned by superior courts on appeal or at retrial. Despite the fact that this practice may help improve the consistency in judicial review of ANDs, it undermines the judge's independence and seems contrary to the rule of law.[63]

Why is the judicial review of administrative rules seriously restricted in terms of the scope, procedure, intensity and effect when the NPCSC has granted them such power? The NPCSC's Explanation of the Amendment to the ALL (Draft) provides an essential account for the weak-form review. It stated that 'This (arrangement) is in line with the basic principles of the Constitution and laws of PRC that the people's congresses supervise the governments, and the governments supervise their departments and lower levels of governments.'[64] This statement indicates that the courts are not the primary supervisory institutions of administration and administrative rulemaking. Conferring the power of reviewing administrative rules on courts is no more than letting them check and identify illegal rules and urge correction.[65] Judicial review of administrative rules is a fire alarm to bring violations to congresses and governments.

As demonstrated above, China has a legal system that divides rules into higher laws and lower laws, resulting in an inherent need to ensure that the lower laws do not contradict the higher laws, particularly the Constitution of the PRC. China has established a unique system of reviewing the compliance of lower laws with higher laws. Relevant powers are lodged with the people's congresses and governments at both central and local levels. Chinese courts have long been excluded from reviewing any laws. The NPC and the NPCSC, China's highest legislature composed of the cadres of the Chinese Communist Party (CCP), are the only constitutional review providers. They are empowered to amend, interpret and supervise the enforcement of the Constitution,[66] and have the final authority on the meaning of the Constitution of the PRC.[67] Article 97 of the Law on

62 Lu, Chao (2020) 'Guifanxing wenjian fudai shencha de sifa kunjing jiqi shuniu gongneng' (Judicial Predicament and Cohesive Function of Normative Documents Incidental Review) (3) *Bijiaofa yanjiu (Journal of Comparative Law)* 133.

63 Ibid.

64 Available at <http://www.npc.gov.cn/zgrdw/npc/lfzt/2014/2013-12/31/content_1822189.htm> (accessed 24 April 2022).

65 He, Haibo (2021) 'Lun fayuan dui guifanxing wenjian de fudai shencha' (On the Court's Collateral Review of Regulatory Documents) (2021, 3) *Zhongguo faxue (China Legal Science)* 143.

66 Article 62 of the Constitution of the PRC provides that 'The NPC exercises the following functions and powers: (1) to amend the Constitution; (2) to supervise the enforcement of the Constitution." Article 67 of the Constitution of the PRC provides that "The NPCSC exercises the following functions and powers: (1) to interpret the Constitution and supervise its enforcement.'

67 Constitution of the PRC, article 62 and 67; Law on Legislation, article 97.

Legislation expressly provides that they have the power to strike down unconstitutional statutes and regulations. Their constitutional review of statutes takes place in the form of self-control and pre-empt scrutiny because they are statute-makers and reviewers.[68] The Law Committee (now the Constitution and Law Committee) of the NPC is to discharge the duty of reviewing the constitutionality of legislative bills before votes.[69] It scrutinises bills and submits review reports to the legislator before voting.[70] In contrast, the courts may not even make decisions on the basis of the provisions of the Constitution of the PRC because the Constitution of the PRC is not justiciable.[71]

As for the review of administrative rules, this is accomplished through a procedure called filings and checks, or *bei'an shencha* in Chinese. Bei'an means 'for filing' or 'for the record', and shencha means 'examination' and 'review'. The review body comprises central and local people's congresses and people's governments.[72] These institutions can change and revoke administrative rules they consider inconsistent with higher laws.

The courts are now vested with powers to scrutinize ANDs, but this does not change the long-run political structure and power distribution. Ming'an Jiang, a Peking University law professor, has asserted that this arrangement was consistent with China's current model of division of power and duties, and considers that administrative agencies have more expertise and experience than courts in reviewing administrative measures and policies.[73] Within the system led by the congresses and governments to maintain the consistency of the legal system, Chinese courts may hardly be vested with substantial and substantive power of reviewing administrative rules.

Additionally, it has been an underlying principle of Chinese administrative law since the ALL of 1989 that courts are expected to

[68] Ahl 'Judicialisation' supra note 15 at 257.

[69] The Constitution of the PRC created a new committee – Constitution and Law Committee – in place of the Law Committee in 2018. Constitution of the PRC, article 70(1).

[70] Law on Legislation, article 20 and 33.

[71] 'Zuigao renmin fayuan guanyu yinfa renmin fayuan minshi caipan wenshu zhizuo guifan minshi susong wenshu yangshi de tongzhi' (Notice of the Supreme People's Court on Specifications for Making Civil Judgments by People's Courts and the Sample of Civil Judgments) (28 June 2016).

[72] Law on Legislation, article 97-98; 'Guowuyuan bangongting guanyu jiaqiang xingzheng guifanxing wenjian zhiding he jiandu guanli gongzuo de tongzhi' (Notice of the General Office of the State Council on Strengthening Management in Promulgation and Supervision of Administrative Normative Documents) (16 May 2018), point 10; 'fagui , sifa jieshi bei'an shencha gongzuo banfa' (Work Measures for Filing and Check of Regulations and Judicial Interpretations) (16 December 2019).

[73] 'Fayuan kedui guizhang yixia zhengfu hongtou wenjian fudai shencha' (Courts can Collaterally Review Read Header Documents having Lower Legal Authority than Rules) *xinhuanet* (23 December 2013), available at < http://www.npc.gov.cn/zgrdw/npc/xinwen/lfgz/2013-12/24/content_1819770.htm>, (accessed 1 September 2022)

be concerned primarily with the legality of executive actions and to be cautious about reviewing the merits and reasonableness of executive acts.[74] By legality is meant that the courts could only scrutinise the formal legality of executive actions, such as whether decision-makers act within the four corners of the power conferred on them and whether the decision-making violates statutory procedures.[75] By reasonableness, the courts are concerned with the discretionary decision-making and substantive merits of administrative decisions. The NPCSC has pointed out in its Explanation of the Administrative Litigation Law of the PRC (Draft),

> To deal correctly with the relationship between judicial power and administrative power, the people's courts should hear administrative cases in accordance with the law, and should not interfere with the executive actions that are within the confines established by statutes and regulations, and should not exercise administrative power in place of the executive authorities.[76]

Even though the courts are now equipped with the power to review some administrative rules, this reform does not change the underlying administrative legal principle. Legality is still the focus of the judicial review, while the merits and reasonableness of administrative rules remain nearly immune from the court's scrutiny.

The accounts revealed above for the limited empowerment of judicial review of administrative rules are relatively direct reasons. China's political context where the courts are embedded can provide deeper and more fundamental insight into those limitations.[77]

China is a centralized party-state and the CCP is the only ruling party. To rule such a big country, the CCP has had to establish large and complex bureaucracies and delegate authority to them. Once there is a delegation of power, principal-agent problems arise,[78] as the choice of officials as agents on the implementation of laws, regulations and policies may deviate from the goals of the CCP as principals.[79] With the information advantage over

[74] Chen, Jianfu (2016) *Chinese Law: Context and Transformation* Brill 331-332.

[75] Yang, Dengfeng (2021) 'Heli chengxin yihuo bili yuanze mudi zhengdang xing guishu zhi bian' (Reasonableness, Good Faith or Principle of Proportionality: Whither Legitimate Aim Test to Go) (4) *Zhongwai faxue* (Peking University Law Journal) 945.

[76] 'Guanyu zhonghua renmin gongheguo xingzheng susongfa cao'an de shuoming' (Explanation of the Administrative Litigation Law of the People's Republic of China (Draft)), SPC Gazette 1989(2).

[77] Fu, Hualing (2016) 'Building Judicial Integrity in China' (39) *Hastings International and Comparative Law Review* 167-168.

[78] McCubbins, Mathew D., Noll, Roger G., & Weingast, Barry R. (1987) Administrative Procedures as Instruments of Political Control, (3) *Journal of Law, Economics, & Organization* 246-247.

[79] Ip, Eric C. (2012) Judicial Review in China: A Positive Political Economy Analysis, (8) *Review of Law & Economics* 334.

the CCP, local governments and their officials often make administrative rules to create and expand their powers, such as establishing new licensing requirements and increasing tax.

Courts and judicial review are tools available for the CCP to inspect and reveal unwanted rulemaking activities of subordinate governments.[80] Through administrative litigation, the courts identify and reveal illegal and unwanted administrative rules. However, it does not lead to a conclusion that the CPP should or would better give courts substantive power to supervise administrative actions. On the contrary, judicial review power is seriously contained for various reasons. First, giving the courts too much power results in excessive judicial intervention in administration. After all, the CCP still relies on local government officials to implement its commands and policies, especially those relating to economic development and social stability.[81] Second, the CCP does not want independent and powerful courts because judicial behavior might become unpredictable and costly to control.[82] The courts are expected to play the role of 'fire alarm' by reviewing administrative rules to identify and warn the CCP and the central government about the deviation of the local government from their commands.[83] Third, the CPP has been establishing many mechanisms to ensure compliance of officials' activities with its goals, such as ideological indoctrination, supervisory institutions, and control of cadre's career. Among these mechanisms, judicial review is not the most direct and active.

In sum, the judicial review of administrative rules in China is a weak-form judicial review and the power of courts is constrained. This arrangement is designed to be consistent with China's legal-political structure of governing administrative activities.

JUDICIAL TIMIDITY AND DEFERENCE IN REVIEWING ANDS

Based on analysis of Chinese judgments available online, this part aims to analyze the practice of courts in reviewing administrative rules, in particular those of the SPC. It finds that the SPC has supported the lower courts' dismissal of review requests in a large majority of cases. Even when it reviews the impugned ANDs, it is deferential and defers to the opinion of AND-makers about the legality of ANDs. As a consequence, ANDs easily pass the review. As for documents issued by the CCP organizations, the SPC has avoided reviewing them by various means.

[80] Mathew, McCubbins D. & Schwartz, Thomas (1984) *Congressional Oversight Overlooked: Police Patrol versus Fire Alarm*, (28) *American Journal of Political Science* 165.

[81] Peerenboom, Randall (2009) 'More Law, Less Courts: Legalized Governance, Judicialization, and Dejudicialisation in China' in Ginsburg, Tom & Chen, Albert HY (eds) *Administrative Law and Governance in Asia: Comparative Perspectives* Routledge 186.

[82] Ip, Eric C. (2011) ''The Supreme People's Court and the Political Economy of Judicial Empowerment in Contemporary China' (24) *Columbia Journal of Asian Law* 374.

[83] Ahl 'judicialisation' supra note 15 at 252, 254.

Through a keywords search in the database https://law.wkinfo.com.cn,[84] 8,212 cases were identified with judgments available online from 1 May 2015 until 30 June 2022 in which the courts dealt with petitions against administrative rules. The qualitative analysis of the chapter is based on the 216 cases decided by the SPC.[85] As the apex court in China, the SPC's decisions are more influential and representative than those of lower courts. All decisions in these sample cases are in the form of orders (*caiding*) and the vast majority of cases are retrial proceedings. The retrial proceeding aims at reviewing and correcting the lower court's decisions. Through these cases, one can observe both the SPC's and lower courts' opinions and attitudes towards the review of ANDs. The findings of this chapter based on the sample cases are consistent with other large-number-case studies in Chinese.[86]

Within these 216 sample cases, the SPC upheld the lower court's decisions refusing to review ANDs in 184 cases. It considered the courts should have accepted the review petitions and remitted the cases to lower courts in 16 cases. It reviewed ANDs in 16 cases and confirmed the legality of all impugned ANDs. The data shows that the SPC rejected a large portion of petitions against ANDs (approximately 93 per cent). This shows the reluctance of courts to review ANDs.

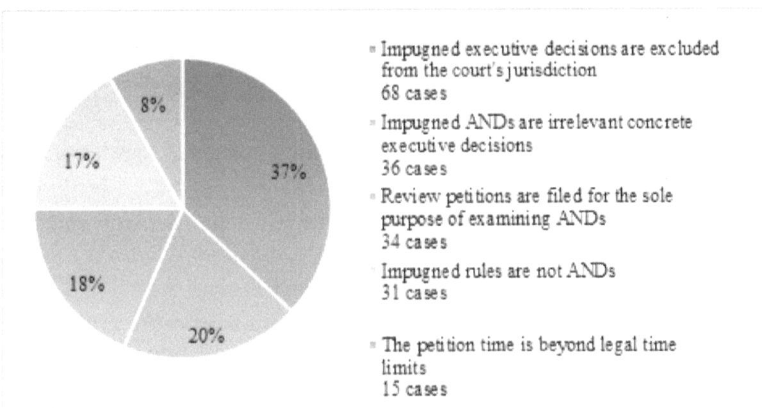

Figure 2: Reasons relied on the SPC for refusing review of ANDS

84 We used the keywords 'Administrative Litigation Law' and 'Article 53', in Chinese 'xingzheng susong fa' (行政诉讼法) and 'di 53 tiao' (第53条). The samples were collected on 16 July 2022.

85 This dataset does not include decisions based on Article 53 of the SPC Interpretation of the ALL 2018, rather it only includes decisions based on Article 53 of the ALL. It also does not include decisions in which petitioners did not challenge ANDs before the SPC, but only before the lower courts. Finally, it does not include decisions unrelated to the subject of the search, which are located due to database search character spacing.

86 For example, Wang and Yi supra note 54 at 28; Chen supra note 51 at 165.

The SPC relied on various grounds to refuse the review petitions against ANDs, including the limitations prescribed by the ALL in regard to the scope and procedure of reviewing ANDs. This proves that those limitations truly prevent people from exercising their rights effectively. To be precise, those limitations considered by the SPC include: (1) impugned concrete administrative decisions are excluded from the jurisdiction of courts in administrative litigation; (2) impugned ANDs are irrelevant concrete administrative decisions in dispute (that is to say, the impugned documents are not the legal basis of the administrative actions under review); (3) review petitions are filed for the sole purpose of examining ANDs (in other words, the petitioners did not challenge any concrete administrative actions); (4) impugned rules are not ANDs under Article 53 of the ALL; and (5) the petition time is beyond legal time limits. Nearly three-quarters of the 184 review requests denied by the SPC are in the first three situations. (Figure 2)

The SPC reviewed ANDs in some cases, but its decisions reveal that it did not scrutinize ANDs effectively. First, it did not review closely and substantively the impugned provisions. Second, it has no consistent and clear rules for the scrutiny of AND-making process. Lastly, it consults the executive authority and defers to their opinion about the legality of ANDs in administrative adjudication.

The SPC provided several grounds or standards of judicial review of ANDs in Article 148 of the Interpretation of the ALL 2018, including:

1. In excess of the authority or delegation from statutes, regulations and rules;
2. Contradicting superior laws, including statutes, regulations and rules;
3. Creating new obligations for individuals, legal persons and other organisations or sacrificing their rights and interests without grounds from statutes, regulations and rules;
4. Failing to follow the approval and publication procedures prescribed by law and seriously violating rule-making procedures; and
5. Other situations that ANDs are in breach of statutes, regulations and rules.

These standards of review are adequately broad so as to incorporate the various unlawfulness of ANDs, including AND-making authority, the substance of ANDs, and AND-making procedure. Article 148(4), in particular, protects people's rights from encroachments from executive authorities.

The standard, contradicting superior laws, is a substantive one, giving the courts discretion and enabling them to examine the substance of impugned ANDs and superior laws. It appeared in all cases in which the SPC claimed it reviewed the ANDs.[87] The SPC often concluded cases by stating that 'the impugned AND does not violate any provisions of statutes,

[87] A list of cases in which the SPC has reviewed the ANDs can be found in the Appendix.

regulations and rules'.[88] The SPC usually reached such conclusions after repeating impugned provisions of ANDs and relevant laws of higher rank. It is unknown from the decisions why the impugned ANDs contradict or comply with higher laws. In some cases, the SPC even did not indicate the superior laws it considered relevant.

In *Taixiang Wu and Rongqing Sun v The People's Government of Hunan Province*, two applicants requested the respondent to disclose several documents relevant to land expropriation. The respondent replied and asked them to resubmit their information disclosure applications to other government departments. The applicants considered that the respondent failed to discharge their duty. At the same time, they challenged three administrative documents, based on which the respondent denied their information disclosure application. The SPC dismissed their complaint on two grounds. First, one of the three documents, the Implementing Rules of Hunan Province on the Disclosure of Government Information, is a *guizhang*, which is not subject to judicial review according to Article 53 of the ALL. As for Notice No 25 and Letter No 125, which are ANDs, the SPC confirmed their legality and stated that 'they did not violate relevant provisions of statutes and regulations'. However, the SPC even did not tell what these relevant statutes and regulations were and did not explain why the impugned ANDs were consistent with them.

There are some cases where the SPC examined whether the AND-making process is legal. But the inquiry into the AND-making process is inconsistent and lax. In *Xiaozeng Zhang v The People's Government of Meijiang District of Meizhou City, Guangdong Province*, the applicant was unsatisfied with the respondent's land and property expropriation decision and challenged No. 26 Expropriation and Compensation Plan. The SPC considered the promulgation process of the No. 26 Plan legal as it has gone through drafting, circulating to the public for comments, hearing, voting, and reporting to the superior government. By contrast, in *Yongjian Kuang* v *The People's Government of Nanyue District of Hengyang City, Hunan Province*, the SPC upheld the lower court's opinion that the promulgation process of an eviction and relocation plan was lawful as it has been endorsed by the respondent and circulated.[89] It is apparent that the SPC has a lower AND-

[88] *Kefu Chu v the People's Government of Fuyang City, Anhui Province* (2017) Zuigaofa xingshen No. 8334, trial Judgment handed down by the SPC in Beijing on 28 December 2017.

Taixiang Wu v the People's Government of Hunan Province (2017) Zuigaofa xingshen No. 8310, trial Judgment handed down by the SPC in Beijing on 21 December 2017.

Yongjian Kuang v the People's Government of Nanyue District, Henghang City, Hunan Province (2017) Zuigaofa xingshen No. 6432, trial Judgment handed down by the SPC in Beijing on 11 November 2017.

Wei Guo v the People's Government of Nanzheng County, Shannxi Province (2018) Zuigaofa xingshen No. 723, trial Judgment handed down by the SPC in Beijing on 28 April 2018.

Faguo Yan v the People's Government of Yinzhou Disctrcit, Ningbo City, Zhejiang Province (2019) Zuigaofa xingshen No. 132, trial Judgment handed down by the SPC in Beijing on 31 January 2019.

[89] See *Yongjian Kuang v the People's Government of Nanyue district, Henghang city* (2016) Xiang

making procedural standard in this case. Or it might have no clear criteria for assessing the AND-making process.

The SPC sometimes consulted the executive authority about the legality of impugned AND in adjudication. It expressly stated that the courts should respect the executive authority's opinion on the legality of ANDs. Through this consultation, the courts accords remarkably broad deference to the administrative authorities. In *Xinbao Zhang v The People's Government of Guichi District of Chizhou City, Anhui Province* the applicant claimed that there was new evidence to overturn the original judgment on a dispute of compensation for land acquisition and requested a review of an AND, Gui Zheng [2010] No. 16 Document of Guichi District. The SPC held a hearing to consult the opinions of the AND-maker, namely the respondent, and the people's government at a higher level. The SPC emphasised in its decision that:

> When examining whether an AND contradicts provisions of superior laws, including statutes, regulations and *guizhang*, the courts should take into account the opinion of the authorities that enact the superior laws. They should respect the opinion of the authorities at a higher level where the legality of the ANDs is proved by them and there is no conflict between the ANDs and the provisions of laws, regulations, or rules of higher level.

This statement provides a revealing insight into the deferential attitude of the courts toward reviewing ANDs. The courts appear to relinquish their judgment on the legality of ANDs to the executive authorities, which is manifestly contrary to the purpose of judicial review of ANDs.

As for documents issued by the CCP organizations, there is no law stipulating whether the courts could review them or not. There have been petitions before the courts against documents jointly issued by local CCP committees and local governments. It is regretful to observe that the SPC has not been bold enough to review these documents. In three cases involving documents issued by party organizations, the SPC has chosen to avoid reviewing them. In *Houying Guo v The Management Committee of Jindong Management Zone of Yongzhou City, Hunan Province*, the applicant asserted the local government Jindong Management Committee and its party committee were in fact 'one institution with two names', and asked the SPC for a rehearing and a review of the AND, Chang Dang Fa (1987) No.3 Document, issued by Jindong Forest Farm Committee of the CCP, the predecessor of Jindong Management Committee. In response, the SPC held the position that the document had been issued by a party committee organization, which was not a competent defendant in the administrative proceedings. The dispute, therefore, did not fall within the competence of the courts in administrative litigation. This case shows that the SPC

xing zhong No. 595, trial Judgment handed down by the Hunan High Court in Changsha on 23 January 2017.

considers first and foremost whether the AND-maker is an administrative organization, regardless of whether the rule is eligible for review.

In *Changhai Liao v The People's Government of Dujiangyan City, Sichuan Province,* the plaintiff argued the jointly issued document by the local government and local CCP committee, the Notice on Further Stabilizing and Improving Rural Land Contracting Relationships, had not been promulgated following the prescribed procedures and was not an AND. In this disputed case of compensation for expropriation of land, the SPC reached the opposite conclusion to that of the local courts, holding that this Notice was a document of general application and was an AND. Nevertheless, the retrial application was still dismissed by the SPC on the basis that the applicant did not challenge concrete administrative actions. In other words, the SPC has still not reviewed the ANDs issued by party organizations. In the context of the reform of joint party and government offices that began in 2018, it is worth further discussing how the courts can safeguard the potentially growing number of administrative proceedings involving party organizations.[90]

In sum, the Chinese courts, including the SPC, have been reluctant to review ANDs, although the ALL has explicitly granted them judicial review power over ANDs. The SPC has rejected the petitions against ANDs in more than 90 per cent of cases. Even if it reviewed the ANDs, it accords broad leeway to the executive authorities. The judicial review power over administrative rulemaking appears to have not been effectively exercised because of judicial timidity and deference.

CONCLUSION

In the last four decades, the judicial review power in China experienced expansion, of which the enactment and amendment of the ALL could be considered landmarks. The ALL of 1989 first established Chinese administrative litigation and the jurisdiction of courts covered most concrete administrative action. The amendments to the ALL passed in 2014 empowered the courts to review administrative normative documents. The legislation is arguably significant and symbolic steps toward the rule of law and a higher level of judicialization.

This chapter demonstrates that the judicial review of administrative rules which China has established is a weak-form judicial review. The scope of administrative rules amenable to judicial review is limited to ANDs. Regulations and *guizhang* with higher legal force are still excluded from the court's purview. The procedural and substantive obstacles determine that judicial supervision cannot be powerful. The courts cannot invalidate illegal ANDs, but merely refuse to apply them and suggest rule-makers amend or repeal them. In practice, the courts acted timidly and rejected citizens' petitions in a large majority of cases. Even when they reviewed ANDs,

[90] Huang, Xianxiong (2020) '*Dangzheng heshe heshu yu xingzheng susong zhidu de huiying*' (The Response of Joint Office of Party Organs and Governmental Agencies and Administrative Litigation System') (11) *Zhongwai faxue* Peking University Law Journal 303.

the scrutiny was rather deferential. Björn Ahl observes that 'the transfer of power from other state organs to the courts in authoritarian system is not a continuous or irreversible process, as judicialization at this stage is not yet sustainable and judges have to act strategically in order to consolidate their power'.[91] The judicial deference shown by the courts since 2014 may be seen as a strategic choice of the courts, but it may also indicate that the courts are not aware of the new power they possess from the boundary between the judiciary and the executive that emerged as a result of the amendments to the ALL passed in 2014. How the judicial review of administrative rules in China will evolve and be practised in the future is an issue worthy of ongoing attention.

GLOSSARY OF CHINESE TERMS

Romanisation Hanyu Pinyin	**Chinese Characters**	**English Translation**
bei'an shencha	备案审查	'for filing' or 'for the record', and 'examination' and 'review'
fagui	法规	Regulation
falü	法律	Law(statute)
guifanxing wenjian	规范性文件	normative document
guizhang	规章	administrative rules
xingzheng xingwei	行政行为	executive action
xingzheng susong	行政诉讼	administrative litigation
chuli jianyi	处理建议	disposition proposal
sifa jianyi	司法建议	judicial proposal

[91] Ahl 'Judicialisation' supra note 15 at 254.

APPENDIX

Cases the SPC reviewed the ANDs

Case	Case Number	Decision Date	Document(s) in dispute	Documents legal or illegal
Yongjian Kuang v the People's Government of Nanyue District, Henghang City, Hunan Province	(2017) Zuigaofa xingshen No. 6432	11-Nov-17	Dongpianqu xiangmu chaiqian anzhi fang'an (East Area Project Demolition and Relocation Plan)	Legal
Yongnian Hou v the People's Govenment of Dali City, Yunnan Province	(2017) Zuigaofa xingshen No.6831	1-Dec-17	[2012] No.14 Document dalishi chengqu gaijian tisheng shishi banfa (shixing)'(Dali City urban reconstruction and upgrading implementation measures (for trial implementation));	Legal
Suining Tianlong Xinqiang Qicaichang and Bucheng Zhang v the People's Government of Suining County, Jiangsu Province	(2017) Zuigaofa xingshen No.5533	8-Dec-17	[2013] No.2 Document suiningxian renmin zhengfu guanyu guanbi feifa zhuanwa shengchan qiye de tonggao'（Notice of the People's Government of Suining County on the Closure of Illegal Brick and Tile Manufacturing Enterprises）	Legal

Taixiang Wu v the People's Government of Hunan Province	(2017) Zuigaofa xingshen No. 8310	21-Dec-17	Hunansheng shishi gongkai tiaoli banfa (Measures for the Implementation of Public Regulations in Hunan Province); [2013] No.3 Tongzhi guotu ziyuanbu bangongting guanyu zuohao zhengdi xinxi gongkai gongzuo de tongzhi (Notice of the General Office of the Ministry of Land and Resources on the Public Disclosure of Information on Land Acquisition); [2013] No.125 Hunansheng zhengfu bangongting guanyu weituo hunansheng guotu ziyuanting dafu hunansheng zhengfu pizhun jianshe yongdi pizhun wenjian xinxi gongkai shenqing de han (The General Office of Hunan Provincial Government on entrusting the Hunan Provincial Department of Land and Resources to respond to the Hunan Provincial Government's application for information disclosure on approved construction land use approval documents)	Legal
Yuan Gao v the People's Gorvenment of Liuzhou City, Guangxi	(2017) Zuigaofa xingshen No.6571	28-Dec-17	[2003] No. 18 Document Guanyu zaigu tingshan kaifaqu fanweinei zanting gongcheng baojian he gongcheng jianshe de tongzhi' (Notice on the Suspension of Project Submission and Construction within the Guting Hill Development Zone)	Legal
Kefu Chu v the People's Gorvenment of Fuyang City, Anhui Province	(2017) Zuigaofa xingshen No. 8334	28-Dec-17	[2011] No.7 Document guanyu yinfa fuyangshi chengshi guihua qunei jiti tudi zhengshou buchang anzhi zanxing banfa de tongzhi (Notice on the Issuance of Interim Measures for Compensation and Resettlement for Collective Land Acquisition within the Urban Planning Area of Fuyang City); [2013] No.53 Document fuyangshi renmin zhengfu guanyu yinfa fuyangshi zhengshou tudi qingmiao he fangwudeng fuzhuowu buchang biaozhun de tongzhi'(Notice of Fuyang Municipal People's Government on the Issuance of Compensation Standards for Land Acquisition of Greenery and Housing and Other Attachments in Fuyang City)	Legal
Wei Guo v the People's Government of Nanzheng County, Shannxi Province	(2018) Zuigaofa xingshen No. 723	28-Apr-18	[2014] No. 10 nanzhengxian 2011 nian he 2012 nian tuiyi shibing he zhuanye shiguan anzhi gongzuo fang'an (Nanzheng County 2011 and 2012 retired soldiers and transferred non-commissioned officers placement work program)	Legal

Xinbao Zhang v the People's Government of Guichi District, Chizhou City, Guizhou Province	(2018) Zuigaofa xingshen No.3312	27-Dec-18	[2010] No. 16 Document chizhoushi guichiqu nongcun jiti tudi zhengdi buchang anzhi ji beizhengdi nongmin ziyuan canjia bu chong yang ao baoxian shishi banfa (Chizhou City Guizhi District rural collective land requisition compensation and resettlement and land requisitioned farmers to voluntarily participate in supplementary pension insurance implementation measures)	Legal
Faguo Yan v the People's Government of Yinzhou Disctrcit, Ningbo City, Zhejiang Province	(2019) Zuigaofa xingshen No. 132	31-Jan-19	[2015] No.5 Document guanyu ceding gongbu 2014 nian 10, 11 yuefen yizhisilei diduan shangpin zhuzhai pingjun jiage de tongzhi（Notice on the Determination of Average Prices of Commodity Residences on Class I-IV Lots Announced for October and November 2014; [2014] No.51 Document guanyu ceding gongbu 2014 nian 10 yue shangpin zhuzhai pingjun jiage de tongzhi'Notice on the determination of the publication of the average price of commodity residential properties in October 2014; [2014] No.59 Document	Legal
			guanyu ceding gongbu 2014 nian 11 yue shangpin zhuzhai pingjun jiage de tongzhi'（Notice on the Determination of the Publication of the Average Price of Commodity Residences in November 2014)	
Rongqing Cao v the People's Government of Yinzhou District, Ningbo City, Zhejiang Province	(2019) Zuigaofa xingshen No.130	31-Jan-19	ibid	Legal
Junyue Cao v the People's Government of Yinzhou District, Ningbo City, Zhejiang Province	(2019) Zuigaofa xingshen No.129	31-Jan-19	ibid	Legal
Qiyou Lin v the People's Government of Yinzhou District, Ningbo City, Zhejiang Province	(2019) Zuigaofa xingshen No.134	31-Jan-19	ibid	Legal
Yiyuan Jin v the People's Government of Yinzhou District, Ningbo City, Zhejiang Province	(2019) Zuigaofa xingshen No.133	31-Jan-19	ibid	Legal

Jinqiu Cao v the People's Government of Yinzhou District, Ningbo City, Zhejiang Province	(2019) Zuigaofa xingshen No.131	31-Jan-19	ibid	Legal
Xiaozeng Zhang v the People's Government of Meijiang District, Meizhou City, Guangdong Province	(2019) Zuigaofa xingshen No.815	29-Mar-19	[2012] No.26 Document meijiangqu zhengshou jiti tudi buchang biaozhun he fangwu zhengshou buchang anzhi banfa (Meijiang District expropriation of collective land compensation standards and housing expropriation compensation and resettlement measures)	Legal
Rudong Hong Yu Chemical Co.v Jiangsu Provincial Market Supervision Administration	(2020) Zuigaofa xingshen No.3758	29-May-20	[2018] No.1033 Document Shengzhi jianju guanyu rudong hongyu huagong youxian gongsi ranmei guolu jianyan shixiang tousushu de fuhan'(Jiangsu Provincial Quality Supervision Administration on Rudong Hong Yu Chemical Co., Ltd. coal-fired boiler inspection matters complaint letter)	Legal

Adjudication of Environmental Administrative Disputes in China

YUHONG ZHAO*

Faculty of Law, Chinese University of Hong Kong

INTRODUCTION

Environmental governance in China is characterized by the government-led command-and-control regulation of pollution to protect the environment. The 2014 substantial revision of the Environmental Protection Law (EPL)[1] has on the one hand strengthened agency's enforcement powers from monitoring performance to imposing compulsory measures and administrative penalties and, on the other hand, empowered public participation in environmental decision making as well as improved access to environmental information and judicial redress. The environmental regime is further reinforced by the system of vertical administrative supervision and inspection from central to local levels, combined with the horizontal cross-departmental coordination in environmental enforcement and adjudication. In the same year, 2014, the Administrative Litigation Law (ALL) (1989) [2] was amended to strengthen the courts' power of judicial review by expanding the scope of review and revising standards of review and rules of jurisdiction. As a result, environmental administrative litigation has developed in terms of both the number of cases and diversity of plaintiffs, defendants, and the administrative actions in dispute. It is most legally intriguing to investigate and understand how Chinese courts review agency action or omission to settle the variety of disputes involving administrative penalty, administrative license, administrative omission, and more recently, administrative agreements.

A small but increasing body of Guiding Cases and Model Cases[3] on environmental administrative litigation promulgated by the Supreme

[1] The Environmental Protection Law (for trial implementation) was promulgated by the 5th National People's Congress Standing Committee (NPCSC) at its 11th meeting on 13 September 1979 for immediate implementation. It was repealed by EPL (1989) promulgated by the 7th NPCSC at its 11th meeting on 26 December 1989 for immediate implementation. EPL (1989) was substantially revised by the 12th NPCSC at its 8th meeting on 24 April 2014 for implementation on 1 January 2015.

[2] The Administrative Litigation Law (ALL) was adopted by the seventh National People's Congress (NPC) at its second meeting on 4 April 1989 for implementation on 1 October 1990. The Law was amended by the 12th NPCSC at its 11th and 28th meetings in 2014 and 2017. While the 2017 Amendment only concerned the standing of procuratorates in public interest administrative litigation, the 2014 Amendment was a substantial revision, which added 33 new articles, deleted five and revised 45 of the 75 articles of the ALL (1989).

[3] Guiding Cases and Model Cases are promulgated by the SPC to provide guidance over the adjudication work of courts so as to improve both quality and consistency for better delivery of justice. They typically address issues that have attracted widespread social

People's Court (SPC) provide critically important data for analyzing the role of courts in environmental governance in China. The SPC had issued a total of 22 Guiding Cases on environment and resources by the end of 2021, five of which are administrative cases including one public interest litigation (PIL) filed by procuratorate.[4] Guiding Cases are *de facto* binding. Courts at all levels 'should refer to' Guiding Cases when adjudicating similar cases.[5] Given the very small number of Guiding Cases, Model Cases function as important reference for court's adjudication and for education of the relevant parties and the public in general. The SPC promulgated 27 model environmental administrative cases (three of them also promulgated as Guiding Cases) from 2014 to 2021 to assist the adjudication work. The *Model Environment and Resources Cases of 2019* (2020) has ten cases each for civil, criminal, administrative and public interest litigation.[6] In other years, one or two administrative cases are found in each batch of Model Cases either generally on environment and resources or specifically on the protection of Yangtze River Basin or Yellow River Basin. Last but not the least, the SPC promulgated two batches of ten important environmental administrative cases in 2014 and 2016 respectively[7] to serve in practice similar functions to the Model Cases.

This article examines the issue: what are the patterns and trends of the fast-evolving environmental administrative litigation system in China? It focuses on how Chinese courts settle an array of environmental disputes over such matters as administrative penalties, administrative licenses, administrative omissions, and administrative agreements, among others by analyzing 48 impactful cases promulgated by the SPC from 2014 to 2021, including four Guiding Cases, 27 Model Cases (three of which selected

concern, apply legal rules that are too general for correct and consistent application, and often represent a significant number of cases or involve difficult, complicated, or new issues for judicial resolution. Guiding Cases that are similar 'shall be' referred to in adjudication while similar Model Cases 'may be' referred to in adjudication. See SPC Provisions on Case Guidance Work (2010), art.2; SPC Guiding Opinions on Unifying the Application of Laws to Strengthen the Retrieval of Similar Cases (for trial use) (2020), art.9. The case guidance system was launched by the SPC in 2010 under the Second Five-Year Plan on Judicial Reform (2005).

4 They are GC no.137 (procuratorial administrative EPIL), GC no.138 and GC no.139 of the 24th Batch of Guiding Cases promulgated by the SPC in 2019; GC no.177 and GC no.178 of the 31st Batch of Guiding Cases promulgated by the SPC in 2021.

5 SPC, Provisions on Case Guidance Word (2010), art.7. It was further clarified that the Provisions (2010) uses 'should refer to' instead of 'may refer to' to establish the authority of Guiding Cases. That is, judges 'must refer to' similar Guiding Cases in adjudication work. See Hu, Yunteng, 'Building the Reference System for Guiding Cases' (2018, no.14) *Journal of Law Application* 3-5. Judge Hu Yunteng was in charge of drafting judicial interpretations to establish the case guidance system.

6 SPC, Model Environment and Resources Cases of 2019 (2020), case no.21 to 30.

7 SPC, 10 Important Administrative Cases on Environmental Protection (2014); SPC, 10 Important Administrative Cases on Environmental Protection (second batch) (2016). While the SPC did not use 'Model Cases' in the title, they are treated as Model Cases by many. For instance, Liu, Changxing (2020) 'Judicial Review of Environmental Administrative Cases – A Study of Model Cases' 19 *Journal of Nanjing Tech University (Social Science Edition)* 1-13.

for promulgation as Guiding Cases), and twenty cases characterized as 'important'. Further included in this study are two landmark cases on judicial review and information disclosure published in the SPC Gazette. Upon a review of the changing landscape of plaintiffs in environmental administrative litigation and the diversity of defendants in the context of complicated environmental regulation that often requires cross-departmental collaboration and joint enforcement action, the article explores the expanding scope of review and scrutinizes the variety of administrative action or omission in disputes. It further addresses the problems as well as the prospects of environmental administrative litigation with legislative reform on standing, scope of review and standard of review as well as judicial innovation in designated jurisdiction and centralized jurisdiction that are pushing the boundary of judicial review and strengthening the role of courts in environmental governance.

THE CHANGING LANDSCAPE OF PLAINTIFFS IN ENVIRONMENTAL ADMINISTRATIVE LITIGATION

The ALL (1989) was hailed as ground-breaking in recognizing a person's right to sue the government and challenge administrative decisions that have infringed upon his rights or interests.[8] It expressly grants power to courts to uphold, revoke, compel or revise agency decisions.[9] While the Law has laid down the legal foundation for rights protection against unlawful agency actions, and the emergence of non-governmental organizations (NGOs) since the mid-1990s has made it possible for individuals to obtain professional legal assistance free of charge or at low cost in order to sue the government,[10] there were tremendous obstacles for private parties to gain access to courts and to secure judicial redress. There was a huge gap between the great expectations of the ALL (1989) and its implementation.[11] According to Professor He Haibo, the total number of administrative cases accepted by first-instance courts nationwide from 1990 to 2014 was 2.1 million while four to six million administrative disputes had reached

[8] Finder, Susan (1989) 'Like Throwing an Egg Against a Stone? Administrative Litigation in the People's Republic of China' 3 *Journal of Chinese Law* 1.

[9] ALL (1989), art.54.

[10] For example, the Centre of Legal Aid for Victims of Pollution (CLAPV) set up by Professor Wang Canfa at the Chinese University of Politics and Law offers legal assistance to victims of pollution to fight legal battles in courts. Zhao, Yuhong (2014) 'Environmental NGOs and Sustainable Development in China', in Percival, Robert et al eds. *Global Environmental Law at a Crossroads* Edward Elgar 63-80.

[11] He, Haibo (2011) 'Litigations without a Ruling: The Predicament of Administrative Law in China' 2011 (3) *Tsinghua China Law Review* 257; Pei, Minxin (1997) 'Citizens v. Mandarins: Administrative Litigation in China' 152 *The China Quarterly* 832; Wang, Xixin (1998) 'Administrative Procedure Reforms in China's Rule of Law Context' 12 *Columbia Journal of Asian Law* 251; Wang, Xixin (2007) 'Between Dreams and the Reality: Making of the Administrative Procedure Act in China' 7 *Journal of Korean Law* 157; O'Brien, Kevin J. and Li, Lianjiang (2004) 'Suing the Local State: Administrative Litigation in Rural China' 51 *The China Journal* 75.

the bureaus in charge of 'letters and visits' (*xinfang*)[12] each year during the period. Of the cases accepted by courts, roughly one-fourth of the plaintiffs had acquired some sort of relief.[13] Professor Lü Zhongmei's study on environmental disputes confirmed the small percentage of disputes being settled by courts.[14] Having a case accepted by court was the first obstacle to overcome by the parties suing the government.

The ALL (1989) stipulates that '[i]f a citizen, a legal person or any other organization considers that his or its lawful rights and interests have been infringed upon by concrete administrative actions of an administrative organ or its personnel, the infringed party shall have right to sue in court.'[15] In practice, most courts took a narrow approach to interpreting 'the infringed party' as a party 'directly subject to' agency decision. Others affected by the agency decision did not have standing. However, the impacts of an agency's environmental decision often go well beyond the parties directly subject to the administrative acts—for instance, administrative licenses and administrative omissions. An approval of the environmental impact assessment (EIA) document submitted by a project proponent often substantially affect those neighbours who endure the adverse environmental impacts generated by the construction and operation of the proposed project. Agency omissions in environmental enforcement leave ongoing pollution continue to harm the environment and the health and safety of victims of pollution. These potential victims of nuisance and pollution were in most cases denied judicial redress due to lack of standing under the ALL (1989).[16] There was no reported environmental administrative case where the plaintiffs were not directly subject to agency decisions.

The promulgation of the SPC's Interpretation of ALL (2000) had to certain extent broadened the narrow approach to standing by introducing the concept of 'parties ***with a legal interest*** (*falü shang lihai guanxi*) in the concrete administrative action'.[17] Shen Xixian and 181 residents belonged to this category in *Shen Xixian and Others v. Beijing Urban Planning Commission*

[12] The administrative system of 'letters and visits' was set up by the State to hear complaints and grievances by receiving 'letters and visits' from the people. It has become a mechanism heavily relied on by the aggrieved parties seeking resolution of disputes with local governments. See Regulation on the Work of Letters and Visits (2022) that replaced the Regulation on Letters and Visits (2005).

[13] He, Haibo (2018) 'How Much Progress Can Legislation Bring: The 2014 Amendment of the Administrative Litigation Law of the PRC' 13 *University of Pennsylvania Asian Law Review* 137, at 141-144.

[14] Lü, Zhongmei (2014) 'Environmental Administrative Adjudication: Problems and Responses – An Empirical Analysis', 2014 (4) *Journal of Law Application* 2.

[15] ALL (1989), art.2.

[16] For more, see Zhao, Yuhong (2021) *Chinese Environmental Law* Cambridge University Press at 338-339.

[17] SPC, Interpretation of ALL (2000), art.12.

(2003).[18] The plaintiffs were residents of building blocks less than 20 metres from the site of a proposed animal lab project. They sued the Beijing Urban Planning Commission that had issued the construction permit in violation of law and requested the court to revoke the permit. The fact that this case was published in the SPC Gazette (2004), and the established practice of judges and lawyers studying Gazette cases and treating them as important references in adjudication work and legal practice, have contributed to a surge of cases taking the liberal approach to standing. Examples are *Lu Hong and others v. Xiaoshan EPB (2013)*,[19] *Xia Chunguan and Others v. Dongtai EPB* (2014),[20] *Zhengwen Garden Homeowners' Committee and Another v. Shanghai EPB (2013)*,[21] and *Zhou Kun and Zhang Wenbo v. MEP (2014)*.[22] Plaintiffs, either residents potentially affected by the agency decisions or organization representing residents have challenged agencies' EIA approval to protect their rights and interests.[23]

The 2014 Amendment of the ALL (1989) confirmed the approach of the SPC's Interpretation (2000) on standing and clarified that 'any party ***subject to*** the administrative action, or any citizen, legal person or other organization ***with an interest in*** (*lihai guanxi*) the administrative action shall have the right to initiate the administrative litigation.'[24] The phrase 'with an interest' was explained to be even broader than 'with a legal interest'[25] and thus the Amendment has expressly expanded the standing to citizens, legal persons or other organizations not directly 'subject to' but affected by the administrative action. The law amendment has removed the obstacles that used to prevent potential victims of pollution or nuisance from challenging agency decisions in the early years following the implementation of the ALL in 1990. In fact, agency EIA approval decisions have become a major type of administrative action subject to judicial review and plaintiffs are predominantly potential victims affected the proposed projects.

The standing was further extended in the 2017 Amendment to procuratorates in four designated subject areas of administrative litigation: environment and resources, food and drug safety, state assets management,

18 SPC, (2004.3) The SPC Gazette, 40-43. For more, see Zhao *Chinese Environmental Law* supra note 16 at 340. Before the formal launch of the case guidance system, the SPC had already regularly published cases in its Gazettes to address new or difficult legal issues in adjudication. Both judges and lawyers treat such Gazette cases as important reference in practice.

19 Case no.4, SPC 10 Important Administrative Cases on Environmental Protection (2014).

20 Case no.9, SPC 10 Important Administrative Cases on Environmental Protection (2014).

21 Case no.10, SPC 10 Important Administrative Cases on Environmental Protection (2014).

22 Case no.8, SPC 10 Important Administrative Cases on Environmental Protection (2nd Batch) (2016).

23 For more, see Zhao *Chinese Environmental Law* supra note 16 at 341-343.

24 ALL (2014), art.25(1).

25 Tong, Weidong (2015) 'Progress and Compromise: Reflections on the Amendment of Administrative Litigation Law' 2015 *Administrative Law Review* 22, at 25.

and state land use rights.[26] Although procuratorial public interest litigation (PIL) also seeks judicial review of agency action or omission, procuratorates play the function of legal supervision over agencies' performance of their statutory duties. The litigation does not involve the traditional administrative disputes between private parties and state organs and is therefore not the subject of this study.

DIVERSITY OF DEFENDANTS IN ENVIRONMENTAL ADMINISTRATIVE DISPUTES

The considerable diversity of defendants in environmental administrative litigation reflects the very complicated nature of environmental regulation and institutional design in China. While environmental agencies from the Ministry of Ecology and Environment (MEE) to provincial and local Ecology and Environment Bureaus (EEB) play a leading role in pollution control and environmental protection, others in charge of natural resources, water resources, forestry and grassland, fishery also play indispensable regulatory functions in managing resources and protecting the environment.[27] All of these agencies are potential defendants in environmental administrative litigation. Such diversity is seen in these cases: *Beihai Naizhi Ocean Tech Co. Ltd v. Beihai Ocean and Fishery Bureau,*[28] *Haili Golf Course Co. Ltd v. State Oceanic Administration,*[29] *Jinhai Home Ware (Shanghai) Co. Ltd. V. Shanghai Fengxian District Urban Control Bureau,*[30] *Luo Jianlan and Others v. Fengdu County Water Bureau,*[31] *Yang Guoxian v. Sangzhi County Water Bureau,*[32] and *Fengdu County Dongyang State Power Station v. Pengshui Autonomous County Water Bureau.*[33]

Sometimes it is not clear which agency should be the defendant. While it is stipulated that the agency taking the administrative action in dispute is to be the defendant under article 26(1) of the ALL (2017), in practice this may not be that straightforward. In *Sun Guihua v. Zhejiang EPB* (Xihu District Court 2016),[34] the plaintiff was issued a 'yellow label' in March 2015 for

26 ALL (2017), art.25(4).

27 For a detailed account of environmental and relevant agencies, see Zhao *Chinese Environmental Law* supra note 16 at 39-53.

28 Guiding Case no.178, also case no.25, SPC Model Environment and Resources Cases of 2019 (2020).

29 Case no.3, SPC 10 Important Administrative Cases on Environmental Protection (2014).

30 Case no.6, SPC 10 Important Administrative Cases on Environmental Protection (2nd Batch) (2016).

31 Case no.10, SPC 10 Model Cases on the Environment and Resources Adjudication at the Yangtze River Basin (2017)

32 Case no.6, SPC 10 Model Cases on the Protection of the Ecological Environment (2019).

33 Case no.3, SPC 10 Model Environment and Resources Cases of 2020 (2021).

34 Case no.7, SPC Model Cases of Administrative Litigation Concurrently Reviewing Normative Documents (2018).

her vehicle registered in 1995 by Hangzhou City EPB. However, the label showed a chop of the Zhejiang Provincial EPB. The use of green and yellow labels on vehicles was to phase out high-emission vehicles from road use so as to better control air pollution by mobile sources. Vehicles issued yellow labels are subject to more restrictions on their road use and Sun Guihua sued the Zhejiang Provincial EPB, seeking the court's revocation of the yellow label. The defendant argued that it was not the agency making the decision and the label was issued by the Hangzhou City EPB. But the Court disagreed and decided that since its chop was on the yellow label so to the regulated party or to the general public, it was the Zhejiang Provincial EPB that was the agency taking the administrative action. But the court did not address the fact that the yellow label was issued by Hangzhou City EPB, which was the agency in reality taking the administrative action in dispute. According to article 26(4) on administrative actions jointly taken by multiple agencies, all agencies shall be joint defendants.

The mechanism of administrative reconsideration (or review) (*xingzheng fuyi*)[35] further complicates the matter. Previously under the ALL (1989), the supervisory body became defendant in administrative litigation if it had changed the original agency decision by administrative reconsideration.[36] In practice, agency decisions had been overwhelmingly upheld in administrative reconsideration and the aggrieved parties had to resort to the courts for resolution of the problem, which had in reality little to do with the administrative review body. The 2014 Amendment makes the review agency co-defendant with the agency making the original decision in administrative litigation if the former upholds the decision of the latter,[37] aiming to put pressure and impose responsibility on administrative review bodies in scrutinizing the original agency decision, and to enable the mechanism of administrative reconsideration function more effectively in settling administrative disputes.

In addition to agencies, local governments are increasingly sued for their decisions to shut down or relocate industrial or agricultural operations in the implementation of environmental laws that impose special protection of designated zones to ensure public health and ecological safety. Many disputes involve the designation of drinking water source reserves (DWSR) and restrictions imposed on land use including a ban of industrial or agricultural activities to ensure drinking water safety. Existing operations within the designated zones are shut down and relocated elsewhere by government orders. Affected operators, both individual operators and enterprises, have sued local governments to protect their lawful rights and interests. Examples are *Su Yaohua v. Guangdong Boluo County Government*

[35] Administrative reconsideration is conducted by a supervising government authority of a specific administrative act carried out by its subordinate that is complained by a citizen, legal person or any other organization as infringement of their lawful rights and interests. See Administrative Reconsideration Law (1999, amended 2009 and 2017).

[36] ALL (1989), art.25(2).

[37] ALL (2014), art.26(2).

(Guangdong High Court 2013),[38] *Shanghai Qinhui Concrete Co. v. Shanghai Fengxian District Government* (Shanghai No.1 Intermediate Court 2015),[39] *Yunnan Dexiang Mining Co. v. Yunnan Zhenkang County Government* (Yunnan High Court 2019),[40] *Ou Zuming v. Chongqing Tongliang District Government* (Chongqing High Court 2017),[41] and *Hexie Poultry Farming Co. v. Wuhe County Government* (Anhui High Court 2020).[42] Local governments make similar decisions to protect nature reserves such as in *Xuancheng Hengtai Metal Casting Co. v. Xuancheng Xuanzhou District Government* (Xuancheng Intermediate Court 2019)[43] and in *Lingbao Yuxiang Aquaculture Co. v. Management Committee of Demonstration District in SanMenXia and Lingbao Dawang Township Government* (Henan High Court 2020).[44] The former protects the natural habitats of Yangtze alligator and the latter special wetland by the Yellow River.

INCREASING TYPES OF ADMINISTRATIVE ACTION OR OMISSION UNDER JUDICIAL REVIEW

The 2014 amended ALL replaced 'concrete administrative action'[45] with 'administrative action'[46] and expanded the list of administrative action subject to judicial review from eight categories under ALL (1989)[47] to twelve, ranging from administrative penalties, administrative compulsory measures, administrative licenses to administrative agreements.[48] The following are especially relevant to environmental decision making:

(i) administrative penalty decision including administrative detention, suspension or revocation of permit or license, order to suspend production or business, confiscation of illegal gains, confiscation of unlawful property, fines and warning;

(ii) administrative compulsory measures such as restriction of freedom of the person, seal-up, seizing or freezing of property;

38 Case no.6, SPC 10 Important Administrative Cases on Environmental Protection (2014).

39 Case no.7, SPC 10 Important Administrative Cases on Environmental Protection (2nd Batch) (2016).

40 Case no.30, SPC Environment and Resources Model Cases of 2019 (2020).

41 Case no.4, SPC 10 Model Cases on the Protection of the Yangtze River Basin (2021).

42 Case no.2, SPC 14 Model Cases of Judicial Service to Yangtze River Delta (2021).

43 Case no.5, SPC 10 Model Cases on the Protection of the Yangtze River Basin (2021). The case was later appealed to Anhui Provincial High Court and petitioned to the SPC for retrial.

44 Case no.9, SPC 10 Model Cases on the Protection of the Yellow River Basin (2021). The case was later petitioned to the SPC for retrial.

45 ALL (1989), art.2.

46 ALL (2014), art.2.

47 ALL (1989), art.11.

48 ALL (2014), art.12.

(iii) agency decision relating to application for permit and its failure to make decision within the time limit;

(iv) agency decision on the ownership of or right to use natural resources including land, minerals, water, forests, mountains, grassland, uncultivated land, tidal flat and sea areas;

(v) agency decision on government taking or relevant compensation;

(vi) agency's refusal to perform its statutory duty to protect one's right of the person or property right or failure to respond to one's request of such performance;

......

(xi) agency's failure to perform agreement in accordance with law or as agreed upon, or illegal modification or rescission of an agreement, such as government franchise agreement or land and housing compensation agreement;

(xii) other agency acts that infringe upon one's legal rights and interests.

It should be noted that while administrative regulations, rules, or agency decisions or orders of general binding power are excluded from judicial review,[49] a normative document of general application that had served as the basis for the agency decision in dispute may be considered by the court concurrently in its review of the administrative action.[50] Judicial review is no longer strictly confined to 'concrete' agency action. In practice, administrative penalties are on top of the list of all administrative actions under judicial review, both in general and in regard to environmental cases.[51] The administrative license, especially EIA approval, is regularly challenged by parties with an interest in the agency decision. Revocation of license and local governments' decisions to shut down operation and relocate business, and their use of compulsory measures, are increasingly challenged in courts by existing operators and license holders. Disputes over administrative agreements are on the increase and it was the 2014 Amendment that included administrative agreement as a new category of administrative action subject to judicial review.

Administrative Penalties

Administrative penalty decisions have been on top of all types of agency action subject to judicial review since 1990. Chinese environmental law grants agencies a wide range of regulatory and enforcement powers

[49] ALL (2017), art.13.

[50] ALL (2017), art.53. For comments on the expansion of judicial power and institutional reform, see He 'Progress' supra note 13; Cui, Wei, et al. (2019) 'Judicial Review of Government Actions in China' (2019.1) *China Perspectives* 35.

[51] Wu, Weixing and Zhou, Jiamin (2021) 'Examination of Cases Lost by Defendants in Judicial Review of Administrative Penalties – An Empirical Analysis of 122 Cases' 20 *Journal of Nanjing Tech University* (Social Science Edition) 16, at 16; Liu 'Judicial Review' supra note 7.

by which to impose sanctions on parties in violation. Those subject to administrative penalties may seek judicial review to revoke the administrative penalty decisions. Of the four environmental administrative Guiding Cases (excluding procuratorial administrative EPIL), all involve review of administrative penalty decisions.[52] One half of the 20 important environmental administrative cases concern administrative penalty decisions.[53] Four of the 10 environmental administrative Model Cases issued by SPC in 2020 involve disputes over administrative penalty decisions.[54] An empirical study of 107 administrative cases involving EIA found that 53 challenged agency administrative penalty decisions.[55]

The exercise of the power by agencies' in imposing administrative penalty and punish environmental wrongdoing is subject to regulation by both the Administrative Penalty Law (APL)[56] and relevant environmental statutes. Any citizen, legal person or other organization subject to administrative penalty may apply for judicial review of the decision,[57] and seek compensation if they suffer loss caused by an unlawful administrative penalty imposed by agencies.[58] Administrative penalties in general include: (i) warning and criticism by circulation; (ii) fines, confiscation of illegal gains, and confiscation of unlawful property; (iii) suspension of permit, downgrading of qualification, and revocation of permits; (iv) restrictions on production or operation, suspension of production or operation, close down business, and restriction on employment; and (v) administrative detention.[59] Each environmental statute stipulates specific administrative penalties for different violations. In practice, courts would fully or partially revoke an administrative penalty decision upon a finding of lack of key evidence, violation of legal procedure or error in application of law in the agency's decision making. An empirical study of 122 administrative cases lost by the agencies found that among the 93 administrative penalty

52 SPC Guiding Case batch no. 24 (2019): GC no.138 *Chen Delong* v. *Chengdu Chenghua District EPB*; GC no.139 *Shanghai Xinjingshan Construction Materials Co.* v. *Shanghai Jinshan District EPB*; SPC Guiding Case batch no.31 (2021): GC no.177 *Hainan Lingao Yinghai Shipping Co.* v. *Sansha Fishery Branch*; GC no.178 Beihai *Naizhi Oceanic Technology Co.* v. *Beihai Ocean and Fishery Bureau*.

53 Five of each batch of the SPC 10 Important Administrative Cases on Environmental Protection (2014) and SPC 10 Important Administrative Cases on Environmental Protection (second batch) (2016) involve administrative penalty decisions.

54 SPC Environmental and Resources Model Cases of 2019 (2020).

55 Jin, Zining (2015) 'Environmental Impact Assessment Law in China's Courts: A Study of 107 Judicial Decisions' 55 *Environmental Impact Assessment Review* 35, at 37.

56 The Administrative Penalty Law (APL) was first enacted by the eighth National People's Congress (NPC) at its fourth meeting on 17 March 1996 for implementation on 1 October 1996. It was amended in 2009 and 2017, and substantially revised by the 13th NPCSC at its 25th meeting on 22 January 2021.

57 APL (2021), art.7(1).

58 APL (2021), art.7(2).

59 APL (2021), art.9.

decisions fully or partially revoked, 43 lacked key evidence, 38 involved violation of legal procedure, 20 erred in application of law and regulation, 21 were obviously improper.[60]

In *Sound Water Co v. Hainan Danzhou EPB* (Hainan No.2 Intermediate Court 2016),[61] the Intermediate Court upheld the first-instance decision of the Danzhou City Court that revoked an administrative penalty decision due to lack of key evidence.[62] The judgment emphasizes that an administrative penalty decision must be based on evidence of violation that has been legally collected. The environmental monitoring process including sample collection has to be done in strict compliance with legal requirements and appropriate technical guidance.[63] The Danzhou EPB's administrative penalty decision was based on flawed monitoring report that had failed to record the sample collection process as required, and there was no evidence other than the monitoring report. The court's decision in this case has far-reaching impact on environmental agencies in performing their routine duties of environmental enforcement. That is, the process of monitoring and data collection must be carried out in full compliance with the legal and technical procedural requirements so that the testing results and monitoring reports can serve as sound and sufficient evidence for the administrative penalty decision. In administrative litigation, agencies bear the burden of proof, and so must present evidence and convince the courts that the decision was made on the basis of solid evidence and in accordance with law.[64] Environmental agencies are thus alerted that they have a duty to record properly the sample collection process and to include that record in their monitoring reports.

The application of law is often subject to dispute, and agencies may be challenged for erroneous application of law when making administrative penalty decisions. In *Shanghai Xinjingshan Building Materials Co. v. Jinshan EPB* (Jinshan District Court 2017),[65] the plaintiff disagreed with Jinshan EPB in its application of the law in imposing an administrative penalty. The Xinjingshan Co. makes bricks from sludge and this process generates obnoxious odours. Following public complaints, the EPB conducted on-site inspection and found the odour emission to be in excess of state standards. The Xinjingshan Co. was fined 250,000 yuan and ordered to rectify under the Air Pollution Prevention and Control Law (APPCL) (2015). Article 18

[60] Wu and Zhou 'Examination of Cases' supra note 51, at 17.

[61] Case no.9, SPC 10 Model Criminal, Civil and Administrative Cases on Environment and Resources (2017).

[62] For more, see Zhao *Chinese Environmental Law* supra note 16, at 346.

[63] MEP Measures on Environmental Administrative Sanction (2010), art.34. It stipulates procedures for on-site inspection, which is to record sample-collection process or to include sample-collection process in the on-site inspection record. Such record maybe by photos, video-recording or any other means.

[64] ALL (2017), art.34.

[65] GC no.139.

requires units and production operators to comply with emission standards. In the event of violation, an EPB is required to issue an order of rectification or restriction/suspension of production and a fine of 100,000 to one million yuan under article 99(2). The plaintiff claimed that the agency erred in its application of the law. The applicable law should be the Law on the Prevention and Control of Pollution by Solid Waste (SWL) (2016) instead of APPCL (2015) because its operation was to turn waste (sludge) into resources (bricks) and the odour was generated by the sludge. Article 68 of the SWL (2016) stipulates that failure to take measures to prevent scattering, run-off, or leakage of industrial solid waste and cause pollution is liable to a fine of 10,000 to 100,000 yuan.[66] The Jinshan District Court (2017) dismissed the case upon review of the administrative penalty decision and its application of the law. It made clear that the APPCL (2015) controls emission of air pollutants, throughout the whole industrial process, including obnoxious odour generated by raw materials and end-of-pipe emissions. The fine imposed was within the range provided in article 99 of APPCL (2015) and appropriate taking into account all relevant factors such as adverse impacts, public complaints, and repeated previous violations.

Administrative Compulsory Action

Administrative compulsory action is regulated by the Administrative Compulsion Law (ACL) (2011),[67] which provides for administrative compulsory measures and administrative compulsory enforcement.[68] Administrative compulsory measures involve temporary restrictions imposed on one's personal freedom or property to stop ongoing violations from causing harm or danger. They include detention, seal of sites, facility or property, seizure of property, and freezing of bank accounts, which must be expressly stipulated by law.[69] The EPL (2014) for the first time adopted administrative compulsory measures of seizure and seal off in order to stop on-going pollution that poses a serious threat to the environment.[70] Administrative compulsory enforcement refers to agency enforcement against the regulated party who fails to take action as ordered by the agency.[71] For instance, this might involve removal of obstacles or restoration by an agency itself or by a third party to protect public

[66] The SWL was subsequently revised and under article 102 of the SWL (2020), failure to prevent scattering, run-off or leakage of industrial solid waste and causing pollution is liable to a fine of 1 to 3 times of the waste disposal cost. Where actual disposal fee is below 100,000 yuan, the amount of 100,000 yuan is used for calculation of the fine.

[67] The Administrative Compulsion Law (ACL) was adopted by the 11th NPCSC at its 21st meeting on 30 June 2011.

[68] ACL (2011), art.2.

[69] ACL (2011), arts.2, 9 and 10 (1).

[70] EPL (2014), art.25. Specialized environmental statutes have followed suits.

[71] ACL (2011), art.2.

health and environmental safety.[72] As for illegally constructed buildings, structures or facilities that should be dismantled, the agency is required to make a public announcement and notify the parties concerned to dismantle the offending construction within a reasonable time. In the absence of any action by the parties concerned—including dismantling and any application for administrative reconsideration or judicial review during the time given—the agency may proceed with dismantling action.[73] Disputes over administrative compulsory enforcement are on the increase as local governments are made accountable for the protection of nature reserves and drinking water safety.

In *Lingbao Yuxiang Aquaculture Co. v. Sanmenxia Management Committee of Urban-Rural Integration Demonstration Area and Dawang Township Government* (Henan High Court 2020),[74] the Yuxiang Aquaculture Co. sued the two defendants for taking dismantling action which destroyed its fishponds, seeking the court's declaration that the defendants' administrative compulsory action was unlawful. At the trial of first instance, the San Men Xia Intermediate Court found that Yuxiang Co., an aquaculture operation permit holder, had built extra fishponds covering 100 *mu* (approximately 6.67 hectares) beyond the area designated by the permit, and well into the State Nature Reserve of the Yellow River Wetland. Upon expiry of the operation permit in 2017, the two defendants had issued three notices to the Yuxiang Co. requesting dismantling of the fishponds and structures in the Nature Reserve by December 2018 as they violated both the State Regulation on the Protection of Nature Reserves and Henan Provincial Regulation on the Protection of Wetland. The Yuxiang Co. did not seek administrative reconsideration nor judicial review of these administrative decisions. Instead, it cleared six fishponds in December 2018 and applied for extension of the deadline for completion of the dismantling until the end of May 2019. On 29 May 2019, in the presence of the first defendant and staff of Yuxiang Co., the second defendant engaged a third party to dismantle the fishponds in the Nature Reserve, remove the illegal structures and restore the wetland. Yuxiang lost the case at the first-instance court and appealed. Henan High Court restated that the operation of fishponds in a State Nature Reserve was in violation of both national and local regulations and operators must be ordered to dismantle the illegal structures. It held that defendants' order of rectification and execution of the dismantling action were lawful as they had a sound legal basis and were in compliance with applicable legal procedure.

[72] ACL (2011), art.50.

[73] ACL (2011), art.44.

[74] Case no.9, SPC 10 Model Cases on the Protection of the Yellow River Basin (2021). Yuxiang Aquaculture petitioned further. The case was subsequently retried by the SPC, which affirmed the judgments of low courts in 2021.

Administrative License

Permits and approval are important command-and-control regulatory tools commonly used in China. The issuance, renewal or revocation of pollution discharge permits, hazardous waste operation license, and vehicle's environmental protection labelling among others and grant of EIA approval are subject to the Administrative License Law (2019)[75] and environmental statutes on pollution control, EIA, and waste management.

It should be noted that judicial review of EIA approval decisions is more often sought by parties 'with an interest in' (*lihai guanxi*) the decision. Of the 20 important environmental administrative cases, five involve judicial review of EIA decisions and all were sued by parties potentially affected by the agency decisions instead of applicants for EIA approval. They are *Lu Hong and others v. Xiaoshan EPB* (Xiaoshan District Court 2013),[76] *Xia Chunguan and Others v. Dongtai EPB* (Yancheng Intermediate Court 2014),[77] *Zhengwen Garden Homeowners' Committee and Another v. Shanghai EPB* (Shanghai No.2 Intermediate Court 2014),[78] *Zhou Kun and Zhang Wenbo v. MEP* (Beijing No.1 Intermediate Court 2014),[79] and *Zhang Xiaoyan and Others v. Jiangsu EPB* (Jiangsu Provincial High Court 2015).[80] Two more Model Cases involving EIA approval were promulgated by the SPC in 2019 and 2020 respectively, and both were filed by parties with an interest in the agency decisions. One by an enterprise in *Changzhou Deke Chemical Co. v. Jiangsu EPB, MEP and Guangda Co.* (SPC retrial 2018),[81] and the other by 51 residents in *Lin Hai and 50 Others v. Longyan Xinluo EEB* (Fujian High Court 2019).[82]

Judicial review of the EIA approvals has offered a valuable channel for public participation in environmental decision-making. The potentially affected individuals and enterprises have strong motivation to participate in the EIA process and their involvement will hopefully assist agencies to make well-informed decisions by considering both professional conclusions of the EIA documents and public comments and concerns. Where their rights of participation have been infringed, administrative litigation offers judicial redress to revoke the approval. Without doubt, judicial review of the EIA approval decisions provides a legal check over agency action to improve

[75] The Administrative license Law was adopted by the 10th NPCSC at its fourth meeting on 27 August 2003. It was amended by the 13th NPCSC at its 10th meeting on 23 April 2019.

[76] Case no.4, SPC 10 Important Administrative Cases on Environmental Protection (2014).

[77] Case no.9, SPC 10 Important Administrative Cases on Environmental Protection (2014).

[78] Case no.10, SPC 10 Important Administrative Cases on Environmental Protection *(2014).*

[79] Case no.8, SPC 10 Important Administrative Cases on Environmental Protection (2nd Batch) (2016).

[80] Case no.4, SPC 10 Important Administrative Cases on Environmental Protection (2nd Batch) (2016).

[81] Case no.5, SPC 10 Model Cases on Protection of Ecological Environment (2019).

[82] Case no.27, SPC Model Environment and Resources Cases of 2019 (2020).

the quality of the EIA process. It makes agencies to fully comply with the statutory procedural requirement including that of public participation and to decide on the EIA application by correct application of law and based on all relevant evidence. This will strengthen the function of EIA as an effective regulatory tool to project and prevent potential environmental harm and risks.

Disputes over administrative licenses further involve revocation of or refusal to renew license or permit and consequent government compensation under article 8 of the Administrative License Law.[83] Local governments are accountable for the local environmental quality under the EPL (2014) and they may order shutdown or relocation of existing projects that cause pollution and endanger public health and environmental safety. Disputes between lawful permit holders and local governments have been on the increase, and operators seek courts' review of governments' revocation of license or refusal to renew permit as well as the amount of compensation.

In *Su Yaohua v. Guangdong Boluo County Government* (Guangdong High Court 2014),[84] Su sued Boluo County Government to seek court's revocation of the decision that designated an area banned for livestock farming and ordered existing operators to relocate and clean up the sites. Su's pig farm was located in the designated area, but he had been a lawful operator holding relevant permits. The first instance Huizhou Intermediate Court (2013) dismissed Su's claim and held that Boluo County Government had the power to designate an area banned for livestock farming under the Guangdong Provincial Environmental Protection Regulation. Su appealed to Guangdong High Court, which dismissed the appeal and elaborated on the purpose of designating the area very near the river and the DWSR for special protection from pollution. The ban on livestock farming was necessary to ensure drinking water safety for the protection of public health. The High Court further confirmed Su's lawful rights and interest in operating the pig farm and advised Su to seek fair compensation from the county government.[85] It is worth noting that, for the purpose of settling the dispute, Guangdong High Court did not stop at dismissing Su's appeal. It took one extra step to address the grievances and concerns of Su Yaohua, balancing the public interest in environmental protection and Su's private lawful rights and interest in the business operation and advised Su of his entitlement to fair compensation from the government.

Similar disputes often involve the amount of compensation as well. In *Yunnan Dexiang Mining Co. v. Zhenkang County Government* (Yunnan High

[83] For an empirical analysis of how Chinese courts compensate operators for losses caused by enhanced environmental regulation, see Zeng, Si James (2022) 'Environmental Policy and Compensation in China: An Empirical Analysis of Article Eight of the Chinese Administrative License Law' 34 *Journal of Environmental Law* 287.

[84] Case no.6, SPC 10 Important Administrative Cases (2014).

[85] If government decides to revoke his permit or license for the protection of public interest, the government shall pay fair compensation. Administrative License Law (2003), art.8; SPC Provisions on the Adjudication of Administrative License Cases (2009), art.14.

Court 2019),[86] the defendant decided not to renew the permit for lead and zinc exploration as the relevant mining site was in a designated DWSR next to a reservoir. The Dexiang Mining Co. sued for compensation of its economic losses including 30.53 million yuan of expected profits from lead and zinc mining and 13.63 million yuan for expenses already incurred. The Lincang Intermediate Court (2019) held that Zhenkang County Government had cancelled all mining rights in the designated DWSR in accordance with articles 58 and 69 of WPPCL (2017). As the rights and interests of Dexiang Mining Co. had been adversely affected by the decision, it was entitled to claim compensation under the Administrative License Law. The amount of compensation is however limited to actual loss in the absence of express provisions to the contrary in the relevant laws, regulations or administrative rules.[87] That is, the loss of expected economic gains claimed by Dexiang Mining Co. was not an actual loss and it was reasonable for the Zhenkang County Government to compensate Dexiang's actual loss in the amount of 2.146 million yuan. Dexiang's appeal against this outcome to the Yunnan High Court was dismissed.

Administrative Omission

Agency enforcement is crucial for effective environmental regulation of pollution. Failure by an agency to monitor and sanction violations has incentivized non-compliance by polluters and even encouraged continuing and repeated violations in order to maximize their financial gains. Administrative omission is also a common cause of environmental administrative disputes and judicial review offers a tool to compel agency action. Where agencies are sued for failure to perform statutory duty, courts may order defendant to perform the relevant duty before a specified deadline.[88] Environmental agencies' omission often involve failure to disclose environmental information or failure to regulate, supervise and monitor pollution, or both.

Access to environmental information is essential for public participation and supervision in modern environmental governance. Agencies have statutory duties to disclose information under the *Regulation on Government Information Disclosure* (2007, revised 2019)[89] and the EPL (2014).[90] In *ACEF v. Xiuwen EPB* (Guiyang Intermediate Court 2012),[91] ACEF requested the

86 Case no.30, SPC Model Environment and Resources Cases of 2019 (2020). Dexiang Mining's petition to the SPC for retrial was dismissed.

87 SPC, Provisions on the Adjudication of Administrative License Cases (2009), art.15.

88 ALL (2017), art.72.

89 The Regulation on Government Information Disclosure was first promulgated by the State Council on 5 April 2007 and revised on 3 April 2019. For more, see Keith, Ronald C, Lin, Zhiqiu and Hou, Shumei (2014) *China's Supreme Court* Routledge, at 165-170.

90 EPL (2014), art.53.

91 SPC Gazette (2013), issue no.1.

Xiuwen EPB to disclose information with regard to Guizhou HaoYiDuo Diary Co. including its EIA report, record of inspection and approval of pollution control facilities, pollution discharge permit, discharge fees collected, number and locations of wastewater discharge outlets, types and volume of effluent discharge, monitoring data and sanction records. As the EPB failed to reply the ACEF sued to compel agency action. The Qingzhen City Court (2012) found that ACEF had applied for information disclosure in accordance with law and the information requested was clearly specified. It ordered the Xiuwen EPB to reply within 10 days and to disclose the environmental information requested by ACEF. The Xiuwen EPB appealed to Guiyang Intermediate Court (2012), but then changed its mind and applied to withdraw its appeal. This was a landmark environmental information disclosure case filed and won by an environmental NGO. Its publication in the SPC Gazette has generated profound impact on both adjudication and agency behaviour.

Judicial review also offers redress to individuals who suffer the pain of pollution as a result of agency's failure in environmental supervision and pollution control. In *Wu Yi v. Jiangsu EPB* (Nanjing Intermediate Court 2015),[92] Wu complained of excessive noise nuisance generated by road traffic on the highway only 18 meters from his home. While he launched a tort claim against the Highway company separately, Wu sued Jiangsu EPB for its failure to perform its statutory duty of noise pollution control. The section of Yanjiang Highway affecting Wu had its EIA approval and environmental inspection by Jiangsu EPB, which was aware of the noise levels over the State limits. Wu made complaint at defendant's online platform and requested agency action to control the excessive noise adversely affecting his life, health, and well-being. Upon receiving the complaint, the Jiangsu EPB (provincial level) passed it to Wuxi EPB (municipal level) which then passed it to Jiangyin EPB (county level). Wu was then informed by Jiangyin EPB that his complaint was not to be handled by the agency as the matter was pending at Jiangyin Court. That is, the tort litigation against the Highway Co. Nanjing Intermediate Court found that Jiangsu EPB, the EIA approval authority of the relevant highway section, had the statutory duty to supervise and ensure environmental compliance by the project proponent and ordered the agency to perform its duty within 30 days. The judgment has clarified the statutory duty of the Jiangsu EPB as the EIA approval authority and its duty to ensure compliance by project proponent may not be passed down to its subordinate bodies (where typically it would be dealt with as a matter of 'letters and visits', the system of administrative complaint noted earlier).

The enhanced guarantee of public participation by the EPL (2014) requires judicial implementation. In *Zhu Xiaochen v. Anyang County EPB* (Linzhou City Court 2019),[93] Zhu resorted to judicial review to compel

[92] Case no.1, SPC 10 Important Administrative Cases on Environmental Protection (2nd Batch) (2016).

[93] Case no.22, SPC Model Environment and Resources Cases of 2019 (2020).

agency action in both environmental enforcement and information disclosure. Zhu made a public complaint at MEE's online platform and reported a case of environmental violation by a pharmaceutical company in July 2018. Anyang County EPB's online response in August 2018 was that no violation found upon site inspection. Zhu then applied for disclosure of all information relating to the environmental enforcement against the complained company including data on its handling of solid wastes. Anyang EPB refused to disclose the requested information. Zhu applied for judicial review of the agency's conclusion of 'no violation' and of its decision not to disclose information and requested the court to revoke the agency decisions and compel agency action by re-investigation of the complained case and disclosing all relevant information. The Linzhou City Court confirmed Zhu's right to report cases of pollution and violation to agencies by public complaint under article 57(1) of the EPL (2014) and right of access to environmental information under article 53. It revoked the agency's conclusion of no violation for its lack of key evidence, ordered the agency to re-investigate and inspect the operation of the polluter concerned and follow up Zhu's complaint. The court further ordered the agency to disclose the environmental information requested by Zhu. It is an important case of judicial guarantee of public rights of access to environmental information and rights of supervision over polluters and governments by way of public complaints.

Administrative Agreement

Administrative agreements differ from civil contracts in nature and purpose. They are concluded between an agency and a citizen, legal person or any other organization on the basis of consultation, stipulating rights and duties of parties to achieve the goals of government administration or public service provision.[94] An aggrieved party may sue an agency for its failure to perform its obligations under an administrative agreement or for its illegal modification or rescission of an agreement, including government franchise agreement and compensation agreement for government taking of land and building.[95] Examples of administrative agreements most relevant to environment and resources are agreements on mining rights or other rights to use state-owned natural resources, and public-private partnership agreements.[96] Where an administrative agreement is modified or rescinded by an agency thereby causing economic loss to the private party, the injured party is entitled to claim government compensation known as *peichang* (where agency is at fault)[97] or *buchang* (where agency action is lawful and carried out for the protection of State interest or public

[94] SPC, Provisions on the Trial of Administrative Agreement Cases (2019), art.1.

[95] ALL (2014), art.12; ALL (2017), art.12.

[96] SPC, Provisions on the Trial of Administrative Agreement Cases (2019), art.2.

[97] SPC, Provisions on the Trial of Administrative Agreement Cases (2019), art.16(3).

interest).[98] If an agency's modification or rescission of the agreement is found to be unlawful, a court may also order continuing performance or remedial measures taken by the agency.[99]

In *Yang Guoxian v. Sangzhi County Water Affairs Bureau* (ZhangJiaJie Intermediate Court 2018),[100] Yang sued the bureau for compensation for signing a void agreement that cannot be performed. Yang obtained the right to mine sand and gravel through public auction for one million yuan and signed an agreement with the defendant Bureau. The agreement stipulated that Yang would pay one million yuan to acquire the mining permit issued by the defendant. Yang however was unable to obtain the mining permit. The section of the river for mining sand and gravel was located within the State Nature Reserve for the Giant Salamander in ZhangJiaJie (Hunan Province) where mining is expressly prohibited by State laws and regulations. In fact, the Nature Reserve Management Office had reminded the defendant that the mining of sand and gravel was prohibited in the nature reserve and requested suspension of the auction. The first-instance Sangzhi County Court (2018) found that the defendant had auctioned the mining rights in violation of State laws and regulations and that the agreement signed with Yang was void. The Court rescinded the mining rights and ordered full refund to Yang of the one million yuan paid. It further ordered the defendant to pay compensation to Yang for reasonably incurred actual expenses of 1.12 million yuan. The county bureau appealed. ZhangJiaJie Intermediate Court, however, upheld the lower court's judgment and reiterated the unlawful nature of the bureau's auction and transfer of mining rights in the nature reserves as well as its legal liability for compensation of the losses suffered by Yang.

Local governments routinely sign public-private partnership agreements with enterprises, hoping to attract investment for the development of local economy. Many such agreements have been repudiated as the State tightens environmental enforcement from central to local levels. In contrast to the *Yang Guoxian* case where the plaintiff was entitled to *peichang* (compensation) as the agency was in violation of the law, many disputes have involved governmental lawful repudiation of agreements, rendering the injured party entitled to *buchang*, that is, to some monetary payment to help cover its expenses already incurred. In *Yanjin Baishui River Wenyun Aquaculture Coop v. Yanjin County Government* (Zhaotong Intermediate Court 2019),[101] Wenyun Aquaculture signed an agreement with Yanjin county government to develop aquaculture in 2014. According to the Agreement, Wenyun

98 SPC, Provisions on the Trial of Administrative Agreement Cases (2019), art.16(1).

99 SPC, Provisions on the Trial of Administrative Agreement Cases (2019), art.16(3).

100 Case no.6, SPC 10 Model Cases on the Protection of Ecological Environment (2019). Sangzhi County Water Affairs Bureau petitioned to Hunan Provincial High Court for retrial in 2019. The parties then reached conciliation agreement and the case was withdrawn by the bureau.

101 Case no.29, SPC Model Environment and Resources Cases of 2019 (2020). The case was later appealed to Yunnan High Court, which upheld the first-instance judgment.

Aquaculture acquired the right to use water resources of Baishui River and was required to invest in the aquaculture project. In 2018, the defendant informed Wenyun in writing that it repudiates the agreement because the aquaculture project contravened environmental protection policy and the duties of Yanjin county for ecological conservation. Wenyun sued to claim compensation for its economic losses caused by repudiation of the agreement. The Zhaotong Intermediate Court held that while the defendant may unilaterally repudiate the agreement for protection of public interest or as a result of significant change in state law and policy, it must reimburse the expenses incurred by the injured party. Accordingly, the Yanjin County Government was ordered to pay 707,200 yuan to Wenyun Aquaculture to cover its loss of investment (657,200 yuan) and expenditure on appraisal fees (50,000 yuan).

Disputes between investor company and local government involving significant sums of money often see high rates of petition. In *Gansu Xingguo Hydropower Co. v. Gansu Xiahe County Government* (Gansu High Court 2019),[102] Xingguo Co. sued Xiahe County Government, asking the court to declare that the government's repudiation of the hydropower development agreement signed in 2007 was unlawful. Under the agreement, the Xingguo Co. had acquired the right to build a hydropower station on Daxia River (a tributary of the Yellow River) with installed capacity of 13,500 kw. In 2013 and before construction started, a local environmental regulation was promulgated by Gannan Tibetan Autonomous Prefecture (Gannan Regulation) to prohibit the construction of small-scale hydropower stations with installed capacity below 50,000 kw. In 2017, the defendant informed Xingguo Co. in writing that it was terminating the agreement and cancelling the hydropower development project. Both the Gansu High Court and Gansu Mining Zone Court held that Xiahe County Government's repudiation of the agreement was lawful as continuing performance of the administrative agreement would be in violation of the Gannan Regulation (2013). To protect public interest in a sound ecosystem of the Yellow River basin, hydropower development must be carried out in an orderly and regulated manner. The Xingguo Co. then petitioned to the SPC for retrial and requested the SPC to revoke the judgments of lower courts and to order payment to itself of government compensation of 49.7 million yuan for unlawful repudiation of the agreement. The SPC reviewed the case and dismissed the petition for retrial in 2020.[103] It upheld the judgment of Gansu High Court. As the Xiahe County Government's repudiation of the agreement was lawful, it was not liable to pay government compensation (*peichang*) claimed by Xingguo Co. The SPC elaborates the distinction between *peichang* and *buchang* and emphasizes that a government is not liable for *peichang* in the absence of a violation of law.

[102] Case no.5, SPC 10 Model Cases on the Environmental Protection of the Yellow River Basin (2020).

[103] SPC Administrative Petition no.9900 (2020).

THE PROSPECTS FOR MORE EFFECTIVE ADJUDICATION OF ENVIRONMENTAL ADMINISTRATIVE DISPUTES

Judicial review by a weak judiciary had resulted in low winning rates for the plaintiffs, high appeal and petition rates and high withdrawal rates.[104] Various studies of environmental administrative litigation found around 20 percent of winning rates by plaintiffs. One empirical study of 473 environmental administrative cases from 1993 to 2017 revealed that agencies lost in 19.45 percent of the cases.[105] Another study of 107 EIA related administrative cases found that plaintiffs won in 21.5 percent of the cases.[106] A focused study of 81 first-instance judgments in a province in central China from 2009 to 2013 found that plaintiffs won in 26.53 percent of the cases.[107] Study of administrative cases as a whole suggests even lower winning rates by the plaintiffs.[108] The direct result was high appeal rates and high petition rates.[109] Dissatisfied and frustrated with the outcomes of administrative litigation, a large number of aggrieved parties lost trust in local courts as fair adjudicators of disputes with local governments or agencies and would bring their complaints to higher-level authorities in Beijing through 'letters and visits'.[110] The SPC admitted that the failure of administrative litigation has resulted in increased number of petitions and irrational behaviours that severely undermined social stability.[111] Will the legislative reform and judicial innovation alleviate some of the concerns over local courts' capacity to settle administrative disputes and deliver justice to the aggrieved parties?

Innovation in Jurisdiction to Reduce Government Interference

It is no secret that interference in court's adjudication of administrative cases by local party committees or local governments has contributed to

104 One study found 15 to 21 percent chances for plaintiffs to obtain favourable ruling by revocation or modification of agency decisions at first-instance courts from 1990 to 1995. Pei 'Citizens v Mandarins' supra note 11, at 841-842.

105 Jin, Hai, et al. (2020) 'Empirical Study of the Cases Lost by Environmental Agencies' 46 *Environmental Protection Science* 7.

106 Jin 'Environmental Impact Assessment', supra note 55, at 37.

107 Lü 'Adjudication' supra note 14 at 4.

108 From 2009 to 2012, first-instance courts delivered judgments against defendants in only 12.07 percent, 11.18 percent, 9.89 percent and 9.87 percent of the cases. Jiang, Bixin (2013) 'Reform of China's Administrative Adjudication' (2013.4) *Administrative Law Studies* 3, at 4.

109 In 2012, the appeal rate of administrative cases was 70 percent, in contrast to 11 percent for criminal cases and 28 percent for civil cases. In the same year, the petition rate of administrative cases was 8 percent while civil and criminal cases only had 1 percent. Ibid , at 4-5.

110 Ibid, at 3-4.

111 SPC, Opinion on the Legal Protection of Parties' Rights to Sue in Administrative Litigation (2009).

the high losing rates of the plaintiffs.[112] Higher level courts, however, are more likely to render judgments favourable to applicants for judicial review because they are less controlled or influenced by the local governments and judges with better professional qualifications are more capable of taking less-biased approach.[113]

The 2014 ALL amendment has institutionalized many judicial innovations in jurisdiction to address local protectionism and reduce interference by local governments, These included 'centralized jurisdiction',[114] 'designated jurisdiction'[115] and 'upgraded jurisdiction'[116]. They aim to enhance prospects of a fair trial and of access to justice. First of all, provincial high courts may, subject to approval of the SPC, designate a few courts to adjudicate administrative disputes across different geographical jurisdictions within the province.[117] Secondly, where a court with jurisdiction cannot exercise that jurisdiction for a special reason, the higher court may designate another court to exercise jurisdiction. Thirdly, higher courts have power to hear, as first-instance courts, of administrative cases over which the lower courts have jurisdiction.[118] If a first-instance court deems it necessary to let a higher court or another court exercise jurisdiction, it may report to the higher court for a decision.[119] Last but not least, administrative disputes involving local governments of county level and above are tried first-instance by intermediate courts rather than basic-level courts.[120] As to disputes over administrative agreements, parties may by agreement determine which court shall have jurisdiction among those relevant to the dispute where defendant or plaintiff resides, where the agreement is made or performed,

[112] Jiang, Bixin (2014) 'Improvement of the Administrative Litigation System from a Macroscopic Perspective' 9 *Frontiers of Law in China* 1, at 6.

[113] O'Brien and Li 'Suing the Local State' supra note 11 at 86; Pei 'Citizens v Mandarins' supra note 11, at 847.

[114] SPC decided in 2012 that each provincial high court shall designate 1-2 intermediate courts and 2-3 basic-level courts to exercise jurisdiction over all administrative cases as pilot exercises. See SPC Notice on Pilot Exercise of Centralized Jurisdiction over Administrative Cases (2013).

[115] 'Designated jurisdiction' allows a higher court to designate a different court in another geographical region to exercise jurisdiction. The purpose is for the designated courts to remain geographically far from the influence of the defendants to offer better chance of a fair trial and ensures access to judicial redress to parties suing the governments. SPC Provisions on Jurisdictions over Administrative Cases (2008). ALL (2017), art.23(1).

[116] 'Upgraded jurisdiction' strengthens the power of higher courts to hear first-instance administrative cases of lower courts to eliminate local governments' intervention.

[117] ALL (2017), art.18(2).

[118] ALL (2017), art.24(1).

[119] ALL (2017), art.24(2).

[120] ALL (2017), art.15. Previously under article 14 of ALL (1989), intermediate courts exercise first-instance jurisdiction over administrative disputes involving state departments and provincial governments.

or where the subject matter of the agreement is located.[121] These newly developed rules of jurisdiction aim to adjudicate an administrative dispute in a first-instance court that is not directly subject to the control or influence of the local government involved in the dispute to ensure a better chance of a fair trial for the aggrieved party.

These innovations in jurisdiction for administrative litigation coincided with the judicial reform on specialization of environmental adjudication by environmental courts and tribunals (ECTs).[122] The specialized ECTs have been established all over China, from basic-level courts right up to the SPC, exercising environmental civil, criminal, administrative and even enforcement jurisdictions. An eye-catching feature of the ECTs is the 'nature-oriented approach' to geographic jurisdiction that not only tackles the problem of local protectionism but also facilitates integrated protection and conservation of the ecosystem. For instance, the Jiangsu Provincial High Court, with the approval of the SPC, set up a specialized division on environment and resources at Nanjing Intermediate Court to exercise first and second-instance jurisdiction of environment and resources cases for all intermediate courts in the province.[123] It further designated nine specialized ECTs to exercise centralized jurisdiction of all first-instance cases of environment and resources in the province. The geographic jurisdiction covered by each court is based on river basin or ecological function zone, instead of the conventional county or district. For instance, Yangtze River Basin ECT No.1 at Jiangyin Court, Yangtze River Basin ECT No.2 at Rugao Court, Lake Tai ECT at Suzhou Gusu District Court, and Yellow Sea Wetland ECT at Dongtai Court.[124] Since 1 July 2019, the '9+1' model of specialized environmental adjudication started operation[125] and set an example of centralized jurisdiction and cross-regional jurisdiction within a province.

A further step was taken by the SPC in 2017 to explore cross-provincial jurisdiction. It designated the Beijing No.4 Intermediate Court to exercise second-instance jurisdiction of environment and resources administrative cases appealed from Tianjin.[126] The court heard its first environmental appeal case from Tianjin Railway Transportation Court in 2018. In this case, the Tianjin Huwei Chemical Paint Co appealed to revoke the first-instance court's judgment that upheld the administrative penalty decision imposed

121 SPC, Provisions on the Adjudication of Administrative Agreement Cases (2019), art.7.

122 For more on ECTs, see Zhao *Chinese Environmental Law* supra note 16, at 56-64.

123 SPC, Reply on the Approval of Setting Up Specialized Environment and Resources Division at Nanjing Intermediate Court (2 January 2019); SPC, Reply on Cross-regional Jurisdiction over Environment and Resources Cases Exercised by Nanjing Intermediate Court (2019).

124 Jiangsu Provincial High Court, Notice on the Establishment of ECTs and Cross-regional Jurisdiction (2019).

125 Jiangsu Provincial High Court, Notice on the Launch of the Environment and Resources '9+1' Adjudication System (2019).

126 SPC, Environment and Resources Adjudication in China 2017-18 (2019), Part III.

by the Beichen District EPB in Tianjin.[127] Although the annual case load of environmental appeals from Tianjin remains small with 10 in 2019, 20 in 2020 and seven in 2021,[128] cross-provincial jurisdiction exercised by the Beijing No.4 Intermediate Court is groundbreaking in confronting the problem of undue influence by local governments in administrative litigation and will make a profound impact in establishing judicial authority and building public confidence in the judiciary.

Mediation Allowed to Effectively Settle Administrative Disputes

The ALL (1989) prohibited mediation[129] and thus no mediation report shall be prepared and delivered. However, the practice of judicial mediation in the name of 'coordination' (*xietiao*) had always existed.[130] There have been different views among scholars and judges over the role of mediation in judicial review since the drafting of the ALL (1989) and throughout its lifetime.[131] Traditional theory has it that agencies enforce the law to protect public interest and shall not bargain with the regulated at the cost of public interest and there are valid concerns that the aggrieved parties may be coerced to settle disputes in mediation. However, contemporary studies provide evidence that mediation mitigates conflicts and reduces administrative costs,[132] and the statutory ban of mediation had not prevented the practice of coercion over the years.[133]

Both defendants and courts are motivated to settle the disputes. Despite the low risk of losing a case, defendants still prefer to avoid the potential of negative media exposure or public outcry that may undermine agency authority and damage career of the persons in charge. Courts prefer disputes settled when case closed and prevent the escalation of dispute complaints via extra-judicial channels to higher authorities.[134] Caught in the

[127] 'Ten Impactful Cases of Beijing No.4 Intermediate Court', case no.8, People's Net, 2 January 2020. Accessible at: http://legal.people.com.cn/n1/2020/0102/c42510-31532385.html.

[128] Data released by Beijing No.4 Intermediate Court in its annual white paper on administrative adjudication entitled 'Judicial Review of Administrative Cases'. Reported by 21st Century Economic Report, 25 May 2022; *Economic Daily*, 10 August 2021.

[129] ALL (1989), art.50.

[130] He 'Litigations' supra note 11, at 257-281; He 'Progress' supra note 13, at 137-190.

[131] Michael Palmer (2006) 'Controlling the State?: Mediation in Administrative Litigation in the People's Republic of China' 16 *Transnational Law and Contemporary Problems* 165; Jiang, 'Improvement' supra note 112.

[132] Hu, Jianmiao and Tang, Zhen (2011) 'Mediation, Conciliation, or Coordinated Conciliation in Administrative Litigation: Assessment of Empirical Data and Regulatory Documents' 29 *Journal of Political Science and Law* 52.

[133] Palmer 'Controlling the State' supra note 131 at 184. An empirical study of nearly 200 cases found that only one fifth of the cases resulted from plaintiff's voluntary withdrawal while the rest under the pressure of either the defendant or the court or both.

[134] Pei 'Citizens v Mandarins' supra note 11, at 844-845.

dilemma of pressure from local governments and the potential aggravation of unsettled disputes, the courts resort to the strategy of coordination among the parties to settle the dispute and end the adjudication without a ruling.[135] While it is understandable for an aggrieved party to withdraw a case upon defendant's rectification of the administrative action or omission, less than half of withdrawal cases belong to this category.[136] The percentage of cases withdrawn by the plaintiffs without judgments in administrative litigation is abnormally high compared to civil and commercial cases.[137] Case withdrawal is an awkward but the only possible way to close an administrative case where the dispute is settled by the parties.

But mediation is just a tool for dispute resolution and what matters is how mediation is conducted. As pointed out by Professor He Haibo, mediation 'does not necessarily harm the plaintiffs' interests or the public interests, and thus the prohibition of mediation does not necessarily protect the plaintiffs' interests or the public interests.'[138] There is need for a more sophisticated and nuanced approach to mediation than a simple and complete ban of its use. The 2014 Amendment expressly allows courts to conduct mediation in cases involving administrative compensation or administrative discretion.[139] This legislative revision will hopefully allow the court to facilitate effective settlement of certain administrative disputes so that the aggrieved parties do not have to resort to further appeal or petition, or the extra-judicial means of complaints.

In *Hexie Poultry Farming Co. v. Wuhe County Government* (Anhui High Court 2020),[140] the second-instance court took the initiative to facilitate communication and dispute settlement between the poultry farm operator and local government to address the practical difficulties of the aggrieved party. At the first-instance Bengbu City Court, the Hexie Co. applied for the court to review a decision made by the Wuhe County Government to turn off the power supply so as to force suspension of operation, arguing that such action was unlawful. Hexie Co. had been in lawful operation with all the relevant permits and licences until its operation site was decided to be included in the designated Grade II DWSR. In this reserve, poultry and livestock farming was banned. To force relocation of those farm operators, the county government ordered power to be cut off. The Bengbu Court dismissed Hexie's application, holding that the government decision was lawfully made and in compliance with relevant procedural requirements. Upon appeal by the Hexie Co., the Anhui Provincial High Court aimed to settle the dispute by engaging the two parties in the search for a compromise

135 He 'Litigations' supra note 11, at 257-281.

136 Pei 'Citizens v Mandarins' supra note 11, at 843.

137 Palmer 'Controlling the State' supra note 131, at 182.

138 He 'Litigations' supra note 11, at 279.

139 ALL (2014), art.60.

140 SPC 14 Model Cases of Judicial Service to Safeguard Integrated Development of the Yangtze River Delta (2021), case no.2.

outcome acceptable to both. The Wuhe County Government agreed to offer logistic and financial assistance to Hexie Co. for relocation of the poultry farm so that it could continue its operation. For its part, the Hexie Co. withdrew the case once these practical difficulties were properly addressed by the government. The Anhui High Court thus successfully settled the dispute by balancing the legal protection of both public interest in drinking water safety and private rights of a lawful operator. Settlement of disputes to the satisfaction of both parties has positive social consequences, especially if compared to many other cases where the aggrieved parties continued to petition or make complaints via extra-judicial 'letters and visits' channels.

Beyond Legality Review

In principle, courts review the legality of agency acts in administrative litigation.[141] In adjudicating environmental administrative disputes, courts have primarily focused on legality review by examining whether the defendants' action is supported by evidence and in compliance with law, showing deference to agency's exercise of discretion. Of the 10 important environmental administrative cases involving administrative penalty decisions, courts have upheld agency decisions on the fines and other sanctions in all of them[142] upon finding that agency decisions had been made correctly in accordance with legal procedure and fines within the range stipulated by laws and regulations.

In *Chen Delong v. Chengdu Chenghua District EPB* (Chengdu Intermediate Court 2014),[143] Chen, owner of the Delong Factory, which processes glass, was found by Chenghua EPB to have discharged wastewater via hidden pipes and ordered to immediately dismantle the hidden pipes. The EPB also imposed a fine of 100,000 yuan. Chen sued to overturn the agency's administrative penalty decision and claimed that its discharge was in compliance with state standards and the fine of maximum 100,000 yuan was 'obviously' unfair. The Chengdu Intermediate Court upheld the first-instance judgment of Chenghua District Court (2014) that addressed both issues: the application of law and the appropriateness of the fine. It reiterated that the Water Pollution Prevention and Control Law (WPPCL) (2008) prohibits secret discharge by hidden pipes by article 22(2) and stipulates dismantling of the hidden pipes and a fine of 20,000 to 100,000 yuan under article 75(2). Whether the effluent discharge is in compliance with state standards is irrelevant as the provisions punish and deter the use of hidden pipes to evade environmental monitoring. On the appropriateness of the administrative penalty decision, the court confirmed agency discretion in determining the size of fines but emphasized that the

141 ALL (2017), art.6.

142 See SPC's 10 Important Administrative Cases on Environmental Protection (2014), case no.1, no.3, no.5, no.7 and no.8; SPC's 10 Important Administrative Cases on Environmental Protection (2nd Batch) (2016), case no.2, no.3, no.5, no.6 and no.9.

143 GC no.138; Case no.10, SPC 10 Model Environmental Criminal, Civil and Administrative Cases (2017).

exercise of discretion must have a basis and reasons. As the Chenghua District EPB had considered all relevant factors in the situation, including repeated violations by Chen, in making its administrative penalty decision within the range stipulated by law, Chen's request to revoke the 'obviously' unfair administrative penalty decision was dismissed.

Prior to the 2014 amended ALL, courts could entirely or in part revoke an agency action on one of the grounds: (i) lack of key evidence; (ii) erroneous application of law or regulation; (iii) violation of legal procedures; (iv) ultra vires; and (v) abuse of power.[144] This generally restrictive approach, limiting the court's review to the legality of the agency decision in dispute and excluding appropriateness or reasonableness of administrative action, was considered problematic by many legal commentators, given the wide degree of administrative discretion provided for in China.[145] The concern has been addressed by the 2014 ALL amendment in that it has included one more ground, i.e. 'obvious inappropriateness', for revocation of agency decision.[146] This legislative development has in theory strengthened judicial authority in reviewing agency's exercise of its discretion within the boundary of the law. Using the Chen Delong case as an example, court has the power to further scrutinize whether the amount of fine is reasonable and appropriate considering all factors, even though the agency has discretion to impose fines ranging from 20,000 to 100,000 yuan. It should be noted that although a court may modify the amount of a fine imposed by agency if the administrative penalty decision is found to be patently inappropriate,[147] a court may not increase plaintiff's obligations nor adversely affect plaintiff's rights or interests.[148]

This reasonableness review is deemed an important progress in administrative litigation as courts are enabled to review agency's exercise of administrative discretion and may invalidate an agency decision that the court considers to be unreasonable.[149] Given the power relationship between courts and governments in China, this reasonableness review may pose a challenge in practice and will take time for courts to put law into action.

Review of Regulatory Documents

Judicial review had been restricted to 'concrete' or 'specific' agency action under the ALL (1989).[150] That is, courts did not have power to review and revoke regulations, rules and other agency decisions and orders of general

144 ALL (1989), art.54(2).

145 Palmer 'Controlling the State' supra note 131, at 179.

146 ALL (2014) and ALL (2017), art.70.

147 ALL (2017), art.77(1).

148 ALL (2017), art.77(2).

149 He 'Progress' supra note 13, at 159-160.

150 ALL (1989), art.2.

binding force. Those 'other decisions and orders' promulgated by State ministries and commissions, local governments and their departments are referred to as 'regulatory documents' or 'normative documents' (*guifanxing wenjian*), and are also known as 'red letter head' documents (*hongtou wenjian*). They are detailed rules for the implementation of State laws and policies and are heavily relied on by agencies in their routine work of issuing permits and licenses, imposing sanctions or taking compulsory actions, and making other decisions. These regulatory documents are enormous in quantity and have often been promulgated without much restriction or scrutiny, resulting inter alia in contradictions with higher ranking laws, regulations or rules.

The 2014 amended ALL expanded the scope of review to cover regulatory documents, a 'foremost innovation of the administrative litigation system and a milestone for supervision of administrative organs'.[151] If a person takes the view that a regulatory document serving as the legal basis for an agency decision in dispute is unlawful, he or she may request the court to review that regulatory document concurrently with the agency action.[152] It should be noted that 'regulatory documents' do not include 'administrative rules' (*guizhang*) promulgated by State ministries and local governments.[153] If, upon review, a court deems any regulatory document to be unlawful, it shall not apply its provisions as the legal basis in determining the legality of the disputed agency action and is expected to make recommendations to the issuing organ for follow-up action in respect of the deficient regulatory document.[154] Chinese courts do not have the power to directly revoke such regulatory documents, and regulatory documents are only subject to judicial review if they serve the basis of the agency action in disputes and requested by the aggrieved party for concurrent review. The cautious steps taken by the 2014 ALL amendment has strengthened courts' power of supervision over agency's decision making and at least opened the door for courts to exercise restricted and indirect supervision over regulatory documents and to draw governments' attention to the problematic regulatory documents for rectification.

In *Sun Guihua v. Zhejiang EPB* (Xihu District Court 2016),[155] the plaintiff was issued a yellow label in March 2015 to her vehicle registered in 1995. Sun sued to revoke the issuance of the yellow label and applied for court's concurrent review of the *MEP Provisions on Environmental Testing and Labelling of Vehicles* (2009) (Labelling Measures). The court sought MEP's

151 Wang, Jing (2021) 'Judicial Review of Regulatory Documents in Administrative Litigation in China' 16 *University of Pennsylvania Asian Law Review* 328, at 356.

152 ALL (2017), art.53(1).

153 ALL (2017), art.53(2).

154 ALL (2017), art.64. The SPC's Interpretation on ALL (2018) arts.146-151 further elaborate how the courts should review the normative documents, convey their recommendations to the governments for follow-up action and report to higher courts for the record.

155 SPC Nine Model Cases of Administrative Litigation Involving Concurrent Review of Regulatory Documents (2018), Case no.7.

detailed explanation of the Labelling Measures (2009) as to its purpose and legal basis and concluded that it was not in violation of any law or regulation. The Labelling Measures (2009) aims to unify national practice in phasing out high-emission vehicles by stipulating technical criteria for issuing green and yellow labels. Environmental labels are issued in accordance with the State Catalogue of Vehicles in Compliance with Environmental Protection Standards. Where a vehicle cannot be found in the Catalogue, labels are issued according to the year of vehicle registration or by technical appraisal if the vehicle owner disagrees with the issuance of a yellow label by the year of registration. Sun had not been informed of the option to acquire green label by technical appraisal. This was a violation of due process by the issuing agency. The court ruled that the defendant's issuance of the yellow label was unlawful, but since the yellow label had expired and Sun had been issued a green label upon conducting a technical appraisal, there was no need to revoke the original decision.

Although the number of Model Cases on judicial review of regulatory documents is very small, the impact goes far beyond the courtroom. The small number of cases have drawn significant attention to the long-existing problems of regulatory documents contradicting existing laws, regulations or rules and put tremendous pressure on local governments. The State Council took action to strengthen 'legality scrutiny' over regulatory documents by issuing the Notice on Strengthening the Making and Supervision of Regulatory Documents in May 2018 and the Guiding Opinions on Comprehensively Implementing the Legality Review Mechanism for Administrative Regulatory Documents in December 2018. In addition, it targets environmental regulations, rules and regulatory documents by mandating a thorough self-examination to sort out those in contradiction with law and party policy.[156] As a result of this 'sorting out' exercise, the MEE reviewed and repealed 47 regulatory documents and revised three in 2019[157] and further repealed 26 regulatory documents in 2021.[158] The Ministry of Natural Resources (MNR) decided to maintain 357 regulatory documents among the 717 subjected to review.[159] Regulation and supervision over regulatory documents have accordingly become an important component of the work in building rule-of-law governments.

Role of Courts in Environmental Governance

Courts are playing an indispensable role in environmental governance building. By judicial review, they not only protect private rights and

[156] State Council, Notice on Sorting Out Environmental Regulations, Rules and Regulatory Documents (2018).

[157] MEE, Announcement on Repealing and Revising Certain Regulatory Documents (2019).

[158] MEE, Announcement on Repealing and Revising Certain Rules and Regulatory Documents (2021).

[159] 'Ministry of Natural Resources to Maintain 357 Regulatory Documents in Its First Sorting-Out Exercise of 717', China News Net, 3 July 2019.

interests of the parties subject to administrative decision but also safeguard the environmental rights of those with an interest in agency action. The environmental rights of access to information, participation in decision making and public supervision are crucial components of modern environmental governance.

In *Lu Hong and Others v. Xiaoshan EPB* (Xiaoshan District Court 2012),[160] 204 residents potentially affected by a road extension project sued to revoke Xiaoshan EPB's EIA approval decision made in violation of law. That is, the EIA report submitted to Xiaoshan EPB on 28 June 2012 was approved by the agency on the same day. The agency argued that it posted a public notice at the EPB service centre inviting comments for a period of two weeks from 23 April to 7 May 2012 during the EIA process. This however did not meet the public consultation requirement imposed by the Zhejiang Provincial Measures on Environmental Protection Management of Construction Projects. Article 22 requires the EPB to inform the public upon receiving EIA reports for approval in an easily accessible manner and invite comments for a minimum of seven days. By revoking the agency decision in violation of legal procedural requirements, the Xiaoshan District Court had protected the rights and interests of plaintiffs whose rights of environmental participation had been infringed. Similarly, in *Xia Chunguan and Others v. Dongtai EPB* (Yancheng Intermediate Court 2014),[161] the appellate court upheld first-instance Dongtai City Court decision that had revoked the EIA approval decision due to Dongtai EPB's violation of the administrative license procedural requirement under *Administrative License Law* (2003). The agency had failed to inform Xia Chunguan and others with a significant interest in the licensing decision of their rights to a hearing before granting the EIA approval.

It should be noted that some courts are already taking extra steps beyond exercising judicial review to alleviate concerns of the aggrieved parties by guaranteeing their rights of access to information. In *Zhang Xiaoyan and Others v. Jiangsu EPB* (Jiangsu High Court 2015),[162] the appellate court did not stop at upholding the first-instance judgment of Nanjing Intermediate Court that dismissed plaintiffs' claims. Jiangsu High Court further made recommendation to the EPB in its judgment on improvement of effective communications with the public and environmental information disclosure during the administrative licensing process. To alleviate the valid concerns of plaintiffs over the adverse health impacts of magnetic radiation to be generated by the proposed electricity sub-station project and to prevent further disputes, the court requested the EPB to ensure real-time monitoring and disclosure of the magnetic radiation data by the project operator for easy access by the public.

160 Case no.4, SPC 10 Important Administrative Cases on Environmental Protection (2014).

161 Case no.9, SPC 10 Important Administrative Cases on Environmental Protection (2014).

162 Case no.4, SPC 10 Important Administrative Cases on Environmental Protection (2nd Batch) (2016).

CONCLUSION

The action or omission of agencies frequently cause disputes with those affected directly or indirectly, and courts have become important venues for settling such disputes. In so doing, they exercise checks to ensure that agencies perform their statutory duties in compliance with the law. Environmental administrative litigation not only settles disputes but also allows courts to exercise supervision over administrative bodies to ensure their lawful performance of the statutory duties in environmental enforcement. Timely and effective implementation and enforcement of environmental law determines the state of environmental quality and underpins China's long-term sustainable development. Good environmental governance hinges upon a functional and robust process of judicial review. Despite the progress noted in this essay, the process is still an aspiration rather than reality in China. The administrative litigation system has operated for over 30 years within the political-legal constraints of relatively weak judicial independence, lack of judicial authority and limited judicial capacity. The legislative reforms and judicial innovations of the past few years have offered hopes of more independent and impartial adjudication of environmental administrative disputes by professional judges who are less subject to local interference.

GLOSSARY OF CHINESE TERMS

Romanization (Hanyu Pinyin)	**Chinese Characters**	**English Translations**
buchang	补偿	indemnity
falü shang lihai guanxi	法律上利害关系	with a legal interest in
guifanxing wenjian	规范性文件	regulatory documents
hongtou wenjian	红头文件	red letter head documents
lihai guanxi	利害关系	with an interest in
peichang	赔偿	compensation
xietiao	协调	coordination
xinfang	信访	letters and visits
xingzheng fuyi	行政复议	administrative reconsideration

PART III

INSTITUTIONAL CONFLICTS AND POWER REDISTRIBUTION

Mandarins v. Mandarins: Procuratorate-initiated Administrative Public Interest Litigation in China

DING CHUNYAN*

The Law School of City University of Hong Kong

INTRODUCTION

'Administrative litigation (*xingzheng susong*)', the equivalent term of 'judicial review' in the Chinese legal system, is seen as a judicial proceeding that aims to enforce administrative accountability and enhance administrative governance. In the conventional form of administrative litigation, the court, upon the request of the private-party applicant, is invited to review and decide on the legality and reasonableness of an administrative decision made by the respondent government.[1] This is sometimes described as 'citizens v. mandarins'.[2] Although it is rare for a public authority to initiate administrative litigation against the government, in July 2017, the Standing Committee of the National People's Congress (i.e., the Chinese national legislature) formally established a new and unique type of administrative litigation called 'administrative public interest litigation' (*xingzheng gongyi susong*, hereinafter 'APIL') and authorized the procuratorates (*jianchayuan*) to file APIL against delinquent administrative agencies.[3] This new form of administrative litigation might be usefully characterized as 'mandarins v. mandarins'.

[1] Art. 70 of the Administrative Procedure Law (*xingzheng susongfa*), which was promulgated by the National People's Congress (NPC) on 4 April 1989, effective on 1 October 1990, amended by the Standing Committee of the National People's Congress (NPCSC) in November 2014 and June 2017. It is worth noting that the term of 'legality' is divided into two categories in Chinese administrative law: one is 'formal legality' (*xingshi hefaxing*) and the other is 'substantive legality' (*shizhi hefaxing*). The latter addresses whether the administrative activity in question involves 'abuse of power' (*lanyong quanli*) or 'evident improperness' (*mingxian budang*). Although the term of 'unreasonableness' is not used by Chinese law, 'substantive legality' essentially refers to 'unreasonableness', see Yu, Lingyun (2021) 'On Unreasonableness Review in Administrative Litigation' (Lun xingzheng susong shang de helixing shencha) 1 *Journal of Comparative Law* (*Bijiaofa yanjiu*) 145; He, Haibo (2018) 'How Much Progress Can Legislation Bring: The 2014 Amendment of the Administrative Procedure Law of PRC' 13 (1) *University of Pennsylvania Asian Law Review* 159. However, the Chinese administrative litigation is a limited form of judicial review (a term not preferred to be used in Chinese law) because the legality of regulatory documents enacted by the government cannot be reviewed as a separated major issue in administrative litigation in China (see infra note 7).

[2] Pei, Minxin (1997) 'Citizens v. Mandarins: Administrative Litigation in China' 152 *China Quarterly* 833.

[3] Art. 25(4) of the Administrative Procedure Law. This provision was added in the 2017 Amendments to the Administrative Procedure Law and it grants the procuratorates legal standing to file APIL suits.

Despite the little attention paid by English-language literature to the innovative system of procuratorate-initiated APIL and its implementation, the new system has raised a number of interesting and important issues regarding: (1) the procuratorate-administration relationship, (2) the special features of the APIL system, and (3) the influence of APIL in terms of judicialization of administrative governance. This Chapter thus aims to present a timely discussion of these three issues from a sociolegal perspective.

The Chapter consists of five parts. The Introduction is followed by an analysis of the impact of the procuratorate-initiated APIL system on the procuratorate-administration relationship and the sociopolitical reasons for its rise. There then follows an examination of the major features of the procuratorate-initiated APIL system operating in China, with comparison to 'citizens v. mandarins' private party-initiated administrative litigation. The next Part discusses the roles, limitations, trends and reforms of procuratorate-initiated APIL in terms of judicialization of administrative governance. A Conclusion then completes the Chapter.

RISE OF THE PROCURATORATE-INITIATED APIL SYSTEM AND ITS IMPACT ON THE PROCURATORATE-ADMINISTRATION RELATIONSHIP

The Evolution of the Procuratorate-Administration Relationship

Under China's Constitution (as revised in 2018),[4] the legislature, the administration, the court, the procuratorate, and the Supervision Commission (*jiancha weiyuanhui*)[5] are five major branches of the Chinese government at the central and local levels. Unlike 'western' notion of separation of powers, the latter four branches of the Chinese government are all created by the same-level legislature and should be responsible for and supervised by it,[6] although in practice the administration has the most powerful and broad power in regulating various aspects of the society and business activities because China is a heavily regulatory state. In recent years, the relationships between the administration, the court and the procuratorate have evolved in a dynamic way.

Before July 2017, the courts were the only state organ authorized to judicialize administrative governance and compel administrative accountability because they, as the state's judicial organs, have the power to review 'specific administrative activity' (*juti xingzheng xingwei*) in

[4] The Constitution (Xianfa) was promulgated by the NPC on 4 December 1982 and became effective on the same day. It was amended by the NPC for five times, respectively in 1988, 1993, 1999, 2004, and 2018.

[5] Section 7 (titled "the Supervision Committee") of Chapter 3 of the Constitution. This section was added by the NPC in the 2018 Amendments to the Constitution.

[6] Art. 3(3) of the Constitution (revised in 2018).

administrative litigation filed by private parties.[7] The procuratorates, as the state's organ for legal supervision (*falü jiandu*), had four major functions that had little relevance to administrative governance: (1) criminal investigation and prosecution; (2) protesting illegal or incorrect judgments or verdicts on civil and administrative cases that are made by the lower-level courts or requesting the same-level court to conduct a re-trial (i.e., legal supervision of judicial proceedings); (3) legal supervision over the enforcement of effective Judgments or verdicts made by the courts; and (4) legal supervision over the practices of prisons and detention centres. The idea of procuratorate-initiated APIL emerged in 2004 and has been occasionally discussed by legal scholars since then.[8] And the practice of procuratorate-initiated APIL originated as a legal innovation in local provinces of the country in 2008.[9] However, a legislative proposal for establishing the APIL system had encountered strong opposition from the Legal Affairs Office of the State Council. Because of this, the proposal that the procuratorates should be empowered to file APIL was disapproved when the Administrative Litigation Law was amended in 2014.[10]

A turning point of the procuratorate-administration relationship came when the Standing Committee of the National People's Congress launched a two-year legal experiment with the procuratorate-initiated public interest litigation in thirteen selected provincial areas in July 2015.[11] After the national legislature formally empowered the procuratorates to file civil and administrative public interest litigation in July 2017,[12] procuratorial organs

[7] Art. 2 of the Administrative Procedure Law (revised in 2017). Although in the 2014 Amendments to the Administrative Procedure Law, the NPCSC changed the wording from "specific administrative activities" to "administrative activities" thus opening a door to include 'abstract administrative activity' (*chouxiang xingzheng xingwei*) to be reviewed by the court, private parties' legal standing to file administrative litigation has not been changed so far. See Lu, Hang and Yang, Zhengrong (2020) 'The Overlap between Specific Administrative Activities and Abstract Administrative Activities and Thoughts from the Legal Perspective' (Juti xingzheng xingwei he chouxiang xingzheng xingwei de jiaocha didai ji qi falü sikao) 20(3) *Journal of Hebei University of Science and Technology (Social Science Edition)* (*Hebei keji daxue xuebao (shehui kexue ban)*) 66; He, Haibo (2021) 'On the Court's Incidental Review of Regulatory Documents' (Lun fayuan dui guifanxing wenjian de fudai shencha) 3 *China Legal Science* (*Zhongguo faxue*) 142-143.

[8] E.g., Jiang, Ming'an (2006) 'Procuratorial Supervision in Administrative Litigation and APIL' (Xingzheng susong zhong de jiancha jiandu yu xingzheng gongyi susong) 3 *Legal Science Magazine* (*Faxue zazhi*) 10; Ma, Mingsheng (2010) 'Study on the APIL System' (Jiancha jiguan tiqi xingzheng gongyi susong zhidu yanjiu) 6 *Journal of China University of Pollical Science and Law* (*Zhongguo zhengfa daxue xuebao*) 92.

[9] Wang, Alex and Gao, Jie (2010) 'Environmental Courts and the Development of Environmental Public Interest Litigation in China' 3 *Journal of Court Innovation* 42.

[10] Jiang, Tao (2015) 'The System of the Procuratorate-initiated APIL: Thought about a Chinese-characteristic Problem' (Jiancha jiguan tiqi xingzheng gongyi susong zhidu:Yige zhongguo wenti de sikao) 33(6) *Tribune of Political Science and Law* (*Zhengfa luntan*) 15; He 'The 2014 Amendment of the Administrative Procedure Law of PRC' supra note 1 at 173.

[11] See the Decision on Authorizing the SPP to Launch the Pilot Work of Public Interest Litigation in Certain Areas (Guanyu shouquan zuigao renmin Jianchayuan zai bufen diqu kaizhan gongyi susong gongzuo shidian de jueding) promulgated by the NPCSC on 1 July 2015 and effective on the same day.

[12] Supra note 3; also see Ding, Chunyan and Xiao, Huina (2021) 'A Paper Tiger? Prosecutorial

nationwide established a new division and deployed manpower for this purpose.[13]

Specifically, in terms of the procuratorate's legal standing to initiate civil public interest litigation, Article 58(2) of the Civil Procedure Law[14] was added when the law was amended in 2017. It provides that:

> Where the people's procuratorate finds in the performance of functions any conduct that undermines the protection of the ecological environment and resources, infringes upon consumers' lawful rights and interests in the field of food and drug safety or any other conduct that damages social interest, it may file a lawsuit with the people's court if there is no authority or organization prescribed in the preceding paragraph or the authority or organization prescribed in the preceding paragraph does not file a lawsuit. If the authority or organization prescribed in the preceding paragraph files a lawsuit, the people's procuratorate may support the filing of a lawsuit.

Because non-governmental organizations were granted legal standing to initiate civil public interest litigation in 2012,[15] a two-track civil public interest litigation system came into being in July 2017. In terms of the procuratorate's legal standing to file APIL suit, Article 25(4) of the Administrative Litigation Law was added in the 2017 Amendments as follows:

> Where the people's procuratorate finds in the performance of functions that any administrative agency assuming supervision and administration functions in such fields as the protection of the ecological environment and resources, food and drug safety, protection of state-owned property, and the assignment of the right to use state-owned land exercises functions in violation of any law or conducts nonfeasance, which infringes upon national interest or public interest, it shall offer procuratorial recommendations to the administrative agency, and urge it to perform functions in accordance with the law. If the administrative agency fails to perform its functions in accordance with the law, the people's procuratorate

Regulators in China's Civil Environment Public Interest Litigations' 32 (3) *Fordham Environmental Law Review* 326.

13 The SPP established a special division to handle public interest litigations in accordance with the Plan on the Establishment of the Division of Public Interest Litigation of the SPP (Guanyu sheli zuigao renmin Jianchayuan gongyi susong ting de fangan), which was promulgated in the Third Meeting of the Central Committee for Compressively Deepening Reform (Zhongyang quanmian shenhua gaige weiyuanhui) in July 2018, available at <https://www.spp.gov.cn/spp/zhuanlan/202112/t20211214_539172.shtml>. Then local procuratorates across the country followed this practice.

14 The Civil Procedure Law (Minshi susong fa) was promulgated by the NPC on 9 April 1991 and became effective on the same day. It was amended by the NPCSC in 2007, 2012, 2017, and 2021. Art. 58(2) was added by the 2017 Amendments of the Civil Procedure Law.

15 Art. 58(1) of the Civil Procedure Law, which was added by the 2012 Amendments of the Civil Procedure Law.

shall file a lawsuit with the people's court in accordance with the law.

The three-fold impact of the procuratorate-initiated APIL system on the procuratorate-administration relationship is observed. First, the procuratorates have been empowered to *regularly* check and examine the activities and performance of the same-level or lower-level administrative organs in a wide range of fields, regarding both violation and nonfeasance conduct of the government. Secondly, the procuratorates in regulating the administration prefer 'moderate' measures, offering *less confrontation* between the two public authorities, such as issuing a procuratorial suggestion (*jiancha jianyi*) to the violating or delinquent administrative agency and urging it to correct its actions within a certain period of time. Finally, related to the second point, the procuratorates see bringing a suit under the system of APIL *as a last resort* when the violating or delinquent administrative agency fails to take effective measures as suggested by the procuratorates.

Conventional wisdom about the procuratorate-administration relationship holds that the administration has a higher status than the procuratorate in the political structure of the Chinese government.[16] This is evidenced by the fact that the official rank of the Prime Minister of the State Council (as the head of the administration at the central level) is a half-grade higher than that of the Chief Procurator of the Supreme People's Procuratorate (hereinafter 'SPP'). Although the removal of its anti-corruption functions (as noted below) has greatly weakened the status and authority of the procuratorate vis-à-vis the administration, the procuratorate's legal-political position has substantially bounced back after it took on a new role as an external public authority to supervise and monitor the administration through APIL.

Sociopolitical Reasons for the Rise of the Procuratorate-initiated APIL System

China's procuratorate-initiated APIL system formally rose in 2017 for four major sociopolitical reasons. First, the procuratorate's legal standing to initiate public interest litigation theoretically falls within the scope of its procuratorial power. As widely defined by Article 2(2) of the Organic Law of the People's Procuratorates,[17] its power is to prosecute criminals and safeguard state security and social order, to protect the lawful rights and interests of individuals and organizations and the national interest and public interest, to guarantee the correct implementation of laws, to safeguard fairness and justice and protect the unity, dignity and authority of the legal system, as well as to ensure the smooth progress of construction of

[16] Jiang 'System of the Procuratorate-initiated APIL' supra note 10 at 20.

[17] The Organic Law of the People's Procuratorates (Jianchayuan zuzhi fa) was promulgated by the NPC on 5 July 1979 and took effect on 1 January 1980. It was amended by the NPCSC in 1983, 1986, and 2018. Art. 2(2) was added by the 2018 Amendments to the Organic Law of the People's Procuratorates.

socialism with Chinese characteristics. Because the procuratorate has both the power and obligation to protect the national interest and public interest, it is constitutional for the procuratorate to be granted legal standing to APIL as the institutional guardian of the national interest and public interest concerning matters such as environmental protection, consumer protection, and protection of state-owned property and state-owned land.

Second, the power of procuratorial organs was significantly reduced after a new state organ called the Supervision Commission took over its authority and functions of criminal investigation and prosecution regarding anti-corruption through the 2018 Amendments to the Constitution.[18] As early as in November 2016, the legal experiment of establishing the Supervision Commission as a new state organ, into which the Commission for Discipline Inspection of the Chinese Communist Party (hereinafter 'CCP') merged, was carried out in three selected areas (i.e., Beijing, Shanxi Province, and Zhejiang Province) by the CCP.[19] The practice then expanded across the country after the 19th National Congress of the CCP confirmed the launch of this institutional reform nationwide in October 2017. Against this backdrop, the new power of procuratorial organs to pursue civil and administrative public interest litigation provides them, at the right time, with an important platform where they are able to exert a new influential role and increase the institutional importance given the significant change to the Chinese government's institutional structure. This largely explains why the SPP has paid special attention and made considerable efforts to promote its work on public interest litigation since the legal experiment was launched in July 2015. According to official data released by the SPP, from July 2017 to June 2022, the procuratorial organs nationwide altogether registered 670,000 public interest litigation cases, among which 58,000 were civil public interest litigation cases and 614,000 were APIL cases. The annual number of public interest litigation cases registered with the procuratorates has continuously grown: 100,000 cases in 2018, 110,000 cases in 2019, 150,000 cases in 2020, 169,000 cases in 2021, and 101,000 cases during just the first half of 2022.[20]

Third, the Chinese party-state has been seriously troubled by the ineffective regulation and implementation of law by the administration in a number of areas with perceived implications for social stability, such as environmental pollution and destruction of the ecosystem, unsafe food and drugs, loss of state-owned property, and misuse of state-owned land and alike. Originally, there were two traditional mechanisms used to

[18] Supra note 5.

[19] The Plan on Launching the Tested Reform of the State Supervision Commission System in Beijing, Shanxi Province and Zhejiang Province (Guanyu zai beijing shanxisheng zhejiangsheng kaizhan guojia jiancha tizhi gaige shidian fangan), which was released by the Central Committee of the CCP in November 2016, available at <http://www.gov.cn/xinwen/2016-11/07/content_5129781.htm>.

[20] The SPP, 'About the Work of Public Interest Litigations Compressively Carried out by the Procuratorates in the Past Five Years' (Jiancha jiguan quanmian kaizhan gongyi susong wuzhounian gongzuo qingkuang), available at <https://www.spp.gov.cn/spp/xwfbh/wsfbt/202206/t20220630_561637.shtml#1>.

monitor administrative accountability and try to ensure that administrative activities are carried out legally, properly, and fairly. The first was an internal mechanism managed by the Office of Administrative Supervision (*xingzheng jiancha jiguan*), which was abolished in 2018.[21] The other is an external mechanism through private party-initiated administrative litigation—which, however, is subject to various restrictions, making it difficult to achieve this goal.[22] Hence, the Chinese government has introduced procuratorate-initiated APIL as the third mechanism, which is external but led by a public authority. Compared to the internal Office of Administrative Supervision, the procuratorate can monitor the government more independently. Moreover, the party-state can have much more control over and trust in procuratorial organs than private parties challenging the authority of the government through administrative litigation. Moreover, in the procuratorate-initiated APIL proceeding, the court (i.e., the judicial branch) plays an important role in neutrally deciding cases in accordance with the due process principle to ensure substantive and procedural justice for the two public parties of APIL—the procuratorate branch and the administration branch. Indeed, the rise of the procuratorate-initiated APIL system is in line with a general trend of using the court to address and solve social tensions in China.[23]

Finally, the recent institutional reform of local procuratorial organs has enhanced their resistance against local interference and protectionism from the same-level administration. In 2015, led by the SPP, local procuratorial organs below the provincial level carried out an institutional reform aimed at bringing about the centralized management of personnel, financial and material resources by the provincial procuratorate.[24] In other words, the same-level administrative government no longer provides financial and material resources and makes personnel decisions for procuratorial organs below the provincial level. Therefore, local procuratorial organs have been equipped with a minimum capacity and autonomy that the work of APIL requires.

[21] The Administrative Supervision Law (Xingzheng jiancha fa) was promulgated by the NPCSC on 9 May 1997 and amended by the same authority in 2010. However, it was replaced and invalidated by the Supervision Law (Jiancha fa) promulgated by the NPC on 20 March 2018 and effective on the same day. In other words, the Office of Administrative Supervision was abolished after the establishment of the Supervision Committees at the central and local levels, which are mainly responsible for anti-corruption investigation against public servants.

[22] O'Brien, Kevin and Li, Lianjiang (2004) 'Suing the Local State: Administrative Litigation in Rural China' 51 *China Quarterly* 93-94; Peerenboom, Randall (2009) 'More Law, Less Courts: Legalized Governance, Judicialization, and Dejudicialization in China' in Ginsburg, Tom and Chen, Albert H. Y. (eds.) *Administrative Law and Governance in Asia: Comparative Perspectives* Routledge, 194-195.

[23] Liebman, Benjamin (2007) 'China's Courts: Restricted Reform' 21 *Columbia Journal of Asian Law* 39.

[24] Xu, Wei (2015) 'De-localization Enhancing Judicial Justice: Focusing on the Institutional Reform on the Centralized Management of Personnel, Financial and Material Resources of Courts and Procuratorates below Provincial Level' (Qudifanghua wei sifa gongzheng baojia huhang: Juqiao shengyixai fayuan jianchayuan rencaiwu tongguan zhidu gaige), *Procuratorate Daily* (*Jiancha ribao*), 27 July 2015, available at <https://www.spp.gov.cn/spp/zdgz/201507/t20150727_102052.shtml>.

MAJOR FEATURES OF THE PROCURATORATE-INITIATED APIL SYSTEM

The procuratorate-initiated APIL system has experienced three stages of development. Before July 2015, there were only sporadic local APIL cases reported by the media, which can be labelled 'the local innovation stage'. Led by the SPP, the system had been tested and rapidly developed when the national legislature launched the legal experiment from July 2015 to June 2017, which can be called 'the legal experiment stage'. In July 2017, the national legislature formally established the procuratorate-initiated APIL system, which signifies the start of 'the nationwide establishment stage'. Subsequently, the practice of procuratorate-initiated APIL diffused across the whole country.

In terms of designing procedural rules of APIL, since the second stage, the SPP and the Supreme People's Court (hereinafter 'SPP') have worked together to develop specific rules through a series of judicial interpretations shown in Table 1 below. A number of controversial issues aroused heated debates and discussions in relation to the uniqueness of procuratorate-initiated APIL,[25] such as the proper title of the procuratorate in the court proceeding,[26] the jurisdiction, the judiciability, the burden of proof, the time limitation, and the nature of the second-instance trial.[27] Most of these issues were finally settled after the promulgation of the Interpretation of the SPP and SPC on Issues concerning the Application of Law in Procuratorate-initiated Public Interest Litigation (as revised in 2020) (hereinafter 'Joint Judicial Interpretation') and the Rules for Procuratorial Organs on Handling Public Interest Litigation Cases 2021 (hereinafter 'PIL Rules').[28] This part of the Chapter focuses on three major features of procuratorate-initiated APIL.

[25] Gao, Zongxiang (2016) 'Study on the Practical Difficulties in Implementing the APIL System' (Xingzheng gongyi susong zhidu shixing yinan tantao) 10 *People's Procuratorate* (*Renmin jiancha*) 6.

[26] See the relevant discussion on the title of the procuratorate in judicial proceedings in the section of 'Limitations of APILs in Judicialization of Administrative Governance' below.

[27] More discussions about the jurisdiction, the judiciability, the burden of proof, and the nature of the second-instance trial are presented below in this part of the Chapter.

[28] There remain debates about how to set the time limitation in APIL. Art. 46 of the Administrative Procedure Law (as revised 2017) generally provides a six-month 'short time limitation' from the day when the applicant knew or should have known that the administrative action was taken, and a five-year 'long time limitation' after the administrative action was taken. However, because the procuratorate is not a counterpart to which an administrative action is addressed, there are different judicial opinions about the starting point of running the short time limitation. Some courts held that it should be the date when the procuratorial suggestion had been issued for 15 days/one month/two months, or the expiration date of the two-month period by which the administrative agency was required to correct its action or perform its duty through procuratorial suggestion. Other courts held that it should be the date when the procuratorate found the illegal administrative activity or nonfeasance harming the national or public interest or the date when the procuratorate received the reply of the relevant administrative agency. The issue of time limitation for APIL has not been settled so far. See Zhang, Haotian (2021) 'Study on the Issue of Time Limitation in APIL' (Xingzheng gongyi susong qisu qixian wenti yanjiu) 15(3) *Tsinghua University Law Journal* (*Qinghua faxue*) 115-116.

Table 1: Judicial Interpretations concerning Procuratorate-initiated APIL (2015-present)

Judicial Interpretations	Issuing authority	Issuing date
Implementation Measures on the Tested Work of Public Interest Litigation Initiated by the People's Procuratorate *(Renmin jianchayuan tiqi gongyi susong shidian gongzuo shishi banfa)*	SPP	24/12/2015
Implementation Measures on the Tested Work of the People's Court on the Adjudication of Procuratorate-initiated Public Interest Litigation Cases *(Renmin fayuan shenli renmin jianchayuan tiqi gongyi susong anjian shidian gongzuo shishi banfa)*	SPC	25/02/2016
Working Provisions of the SPC on the Adjudication of Environmental Public Interest Litigation Cases (Interim) *(Zuigao renmin fayuan guanyu shenli huanjing gongyi susong anjian de gongzuo guifan (shixing))*	SPC	01/04/2017
Interpretation of the SPP and SPC on Issues concerning the Application of Law in Procuratorate-initiated Public Interest Litigation *(Zuigao renmin fayuan zuigao renmin jianchayuang guanyu jiancha gongyi susong anjian shiyong falü ruogan wenti de jieshi)*	SPC & SPP	01/03/2018 (amended 29/12/2020)
Guidance for Procuratorial Organs on Handling Administrative Public Interest Litigation Cases (Interim) *(Jiancha jiguan xingzheng gongyi susong anjian ban'an zhinan (shixing))*	SPP (Civil & Admin. Division)	12/03/2018
Rules for Procuratorial Organs on Handling Public Interest Litigation Cases *(Renmin jianchayuan gongyi susong ban'an guize)*	SPP	29/06/2021

Jurisdiction and Judiciability of Procuratorate-initiated APIL

The procuratorates are granted a power to pursue APIL for the purpose of safeguarding the national interest and public interest, which is practically transformed into a rule of jurisdiction set out in Article 67 of the PIL Rules: first, when national interest or public interest is harmed; and secondly, when an administrative agency charged with the duty to supervise and administer in protecting the national interest or public interest in ecological, environmental, and resource protection, food and drug safety, protection of state-owned property, granting of rights to use state-owned land, protection of minors, and so forth, performs its duty illegally or fails to perform its duty. Given the open-ended nature of the terms 'national interest' and 'public interest', the listed areas in Article 67 are not exhaustive. Indeed, the jurisdiction of procuratorate-initiated APIL has further expanded to other areas, such as the protection of disabled persons, the protection of personal information, the implementation of poverty reduction policy, and the protection of historical or cultural heritage.[29] Hence, the procuratorate has a wide and substantial power to check the performance of the government, ensure administrative accountability, and influence administrative governance through APIL.

As Article 67 of the PIL Rules shows, two types of administrative activity are judiciable through the procuratorate-initiated APIL: one is illegal administrative activity (*weifa xingzheng xingwei*); and the other is administrative nonfeasance (*xingzheng buzuowei*). In the former case, procuratorial organs apply to the court for a judicial confirmation of the illegality of the administrative activity in question and, if necessary, for a judicial order to withdraw or correct the illegal administrative activity. This is in alignment with the state's goal of 'administration according to law' (*yifa xingzheng*).[30] In the latter case, procuratorial organs apply to the court for a judicial order to force the delinquent administrative agency to actively perform its administrative duty within two months.[31] In most cases, national interest or public interest is at stake because the administration fails to take the necessary action to prevent, prohibit, or abate the third party's violation

[29] E.g., Ten Typical Cases of Procuratorate-initiated Public Interest Litigation on Protection of the Disabled Persons' Rights and Interests Jointly Released by the SPP and China Disabled Persons Federation (Zuigao renmin Jianchayuan zhongguo canjiren lianhehui fabu shi jian canjiren quanyi baozhang jiancha gongyi susong dianxing anli) in May 2022; Eleven Typical Cases of Procuratorate-initiated Public Interest Litigation on Protection of Personal Information Protection Released by the SPP (Zuigao renmin Jianchayuan fabu shiyi jian jiancha jiguan geren xinxi baohu gongyi susong dianxing anli) in April 2021; Fifteen Typical Cases of Procuratorate-initiated Public Interest Litigation on Serving Rural Development and Poverty Reduction Released by the SPP (Zuigao renmin Jianchayuan fabu shiwu jian gongyi susong jiancha fuwu xiangcun zhengxing zhuli tuopin gongjian dianxing anli) in Feburary 2021; Ten Typical Cases of Procuratorate-initiated Public Interest Litigation on Protection of Relics and Cultural Heritage Released by the SPP (Zuigao renmin Jianchayuan fabu shi qi jiancha jiguan wenwu he wenhua yichan baohu gongyi susong dianxing anli) in December 2020.

[30] E.g., the SPP's Guiding Case No.63: *The People's Procuratorate of Tianmen City of Hubei Province v. The People's Government of Tuoshi Township (An APIL of failure to legally perform duties)* (Hubeisheng tianmenshi renmin jianchayuan v. Tuoshizhen zhengfu bu yifa lüxing zhize xingzheng gongyi susong an). In this case, the respondent government violated the Land Administration Law and the Environmental Protection Law and illegally rented a farmland for constructing a landfill and backfilling domestic garbage. The People's Court of Tianmen City confirmed the illegality of the government's administrative activities and ordered it to take remedial measures and comprehensive rectification.

[31] Art. 21 of the Joint Judicial Interpretation.

of the law. This is even so when public officials have become risk-averse and demonstrated a phenomenon of 'bureaucratic shirking' (*lanzheng*) due to fear of making mistakes and being implicated in corruption investigations after the CCP launched and intensified the anti-corruption campaign in 2012.[32] Therefore, it is practically significant for the procuratorates to handle prevalent administrative nonfeasance through APIL.

In practice, on one hand, procuratorial organs may find a large number of APIL case clues from various sources in the Internet age.[33] They include: reports by individuals, legal persons, or unincorporated associations to the procuratorate; referrals by state organs, social associations, representatives of the people's congress or members of a committee of the Chinese People's Political Consultative Conference (*Zhongguo renmin zhengzhi xieshang huiyi*); information released in traditional media, social media and other online platforms; and any clues found during the procuratorate's performance of duties (e.g., criminal investigation and prosecution[34]). On the other hand, procuratorial organs, subject to their limited financial and personnel resources, must be selective when suing administrative agencies through APIL.

Pre-litigation Procedure: Negotiation and Procuratorial Suggestion

The PIL Rules set out a pro-litigation 'buffer area' through two legal mechanisms. One is negotiation with the relevant administrative agency in the course of an investigation. Article 70 of the PIL Rules provides that procuratorial organs should serve a written 'Decision to Register an APIL Case' on the involved administrative agency within seven days after such a decision is made. It may also negotiate with the latter about the existence of an illegal exercise of power or omission to perform the duty, the consequential harm to the national interest or the public interest concerned, a corrective action plan, and other matters. The negotiation may be held in the form of a negotiation symposium (*cuoshang zuotanhui*) and delivering a confirmation letter of the fact to the administrative agency, which should be recorded in meeting records, minutes or other written documents. If the administrative agency has admitted its misconduct, comprehensively taken corrective actions, and performed its duties in accordance with the law, procurators should report to the chief procurator for a decision to close the APIL case and then serve a written decision on the administrative agency.[35]

[32] Tu, Wenyan and Gong, Ting (2022) 'Bureaucratic Shirking in China: Is Sanction-based Accountability a Cure?' 249 *China Quarterly* 259.

[33] Art. 24 of the PIL Rules.

[34] An empirical study found that the case clue of about 65 percent of APIL cases were from the procuratorate's own criminal cases, see Li, Cheng and Zhao, Weigang (2018) 'Difficulties and Solutions: Study on the APIL Case Clue Discovery System' (Kunjing yu tupo: xingzheng gongyi susong xiansuo faxian jizhi yanjiu) 45(4) *Journal of Sichuan Normal University (Social Science Edition)* (*Sichuan shifan daxue xuebao (shehui kexue ban)*) 55.

[35] Art. 74 of the PIL Rules.

The second mechanism is the issuance of a procuratorial suggestion. When the procuratorate holds after investigation that an administrative agency has caused detriment to the national interest or the public interest by failing to perform its duties in accordance with the law, it should report to the chief procurator so that she or he might approve a procuratorial suggestion to be addressed to the administrative agency, serving the procuratorial suggestion on the latter within three days.[36] The gist of a procuratorial suggestion includes an explanation about the key facts and the legal basis for establishing the illegality of the administrative activity concerned or the failure to perform a duty of the administrative agency. It will also include specific suggestions for taking corrective actions within a specified period of time.[37] Moreover, after the procuratorial suggestion has been served, the procuratorate should conduct a follow-up investigation into and collect evidence about the subsequent performance of duties by the administrative agency and their impact on the national interest or the public interest concerned.[38] When the procuratorate is satisfied that the administrative agency has followed the procuratorial suggestion, comprehensively taken corrective actions, and performed its duties as required by law, it will close the case upon the approval of the chief procurator. Otherwise, it will bring the case to the next stage, that is, filing an APIL suit with the court.

The pre-litigation legal mechanisms were designed in line with ancient China's philosophy of 'Courtesy before Force' (*xian li hou bing*) when the procuratorate-administration relationship is involved. From 'negotiation' to 'procuratorial suggestion', the procuratorate provides two chances to the administration to take corrective actions before escalating to APIL. In other words, the pre-litigation legal mechanisms help to 'save the face' of the administrative agency and avoid head-on confrontation between the procuratorate and the administration in the courtroom. Moreover, it can save significant institutional resources if most APIL cases registered with the procuratorate can be resolved through such pre-litigation legal processes.

'Mandarins v. Mandarins' Form of Administrative Litigation

As noted above, compared to the 'citizens v. mandarins' form of administrative litigation brought by private parties, the procuratorate-initiated APIL represents a 'mandarins v. mandarins' form of administrative litigation. On one hand, the national legislation has not made a special law to provide the procedural rules of APIL, which implies that the court can, in principle, follow the procedural rules stipulated by the Administrative Procedure Law in dealing with APILs. On the other hand, special procedural rules provided by the SPC and the SPP in the Joint Judicial Interpretation and the PIL Rules demonstrate the distinctness of 'mandarins v. mandarins' administrative litigation in four aspects.

36 Arts. 75 and 76 of the PIL Rules.

37 Art. 75 of the PIL Rules.

38 Art. 77 of the PIL Rules.

First, the two parties to APIL are both public authorities and enjoy an equal legal status in the proceedings. A private party files administrative litigation against the government when its lawful right or interest has been infringed due to administrative malfeasance or nonfeasance. Hence, the 'citizens v. mandarins' form of administrative litigation concerns the state-society relationship. By contrast, APIL is intended to safeguard the national interest or the public interest harmed by illegal activities or the omission of an administrative agency to act.[39] It concerns the procuratorate-administration relationship. However, both forms of administrative litigation are practically important to enhance administrative accountability and governance.

Second, unlike a private party applicant for administrative litigation, a procuratorial organ has been given more investigation powers in APIL. Article 32 of the PIL Rules requires that procuratorial organs should conduct investigations and collect evidence in a lawful, objective and comprehensive manner. Moreover, Article 35 empowers them to (1) access legal documents, and collect documentary evidence, physical evidence, audio-visual recordings, electronic data, and other forms of evidence, (2) inspect local scenes for evidence, (3) interview the administrative agency, the person subject to an administrative decision, interested parties, witnesses, (4) seek expert opinions and authentication reports, and (5) take any necessary investigation steps. Although procuratorial organs cannot take compulsory measures (such as restricting personal freedom and placing under seal, seizing, or freezing property) in APIL, they enjoy far more power than private parties or their lawyers in terms of investigation and evidence collection.

A related procedural issue concerns which party should bear the burden of proof in administrative litigation. Article 34 of the Administrative Litigation Law (as revised 2017) imposes the burden of proof regarding the administrative decision or act on the respondent administrative agency, but not the applicant citizen. However, Article 52 of the PIL Rules provides that the procurators who appear in court should present evidence to the court objectively and comprehensively and the court may decide which party should bear the burden of proof according to the specific circumstances of the case. This implies that the procuratorial organ may not in specific APIL cases easily shift the burden of proof to the administrative agency. In effect, it is found that in most cases the procuratorate presented evidence in court on the illegality of the administrative activity or administrative nonfeasance concerned as well as the consequential harm to the relevant national interest or public interest.[40]

[39] Therefore, the procuratorate is exempted from paying litigation fees when filing APIL in the court, see Art. 107 of the PIL Rules.

[40] Wang, Chunye (2022) 'On the Rule of Burden of Proof in APIL' (Lun xingzheng gongyi susong juzheng zeren fenpei guize) 39(3) *Journal of Jianghan University (Social Science Edition)* (*Jianghan daxue xuebao (shehui kexue ban)*) 8.

Third, the court will accept an APIL case only when the procuratorate has undergone pre-litigation procedures and the administrative agency continues to fail to perform its duties according to the law or correct its illegal conduct or nonfeasance.[41] In other words, the compulsory pre-litigation procedure is a prerequisite for starting the APIL proceedings in court. The rationale underlying such a requirement is given earlier in this part of the Chapter. In contrast, the Administrative Litigation Law (as revised 2017) does not mandate a compulsory pre-litigation procedure (such as an administrative reconsideration procedure) where a private party files an administrative litigation case for the purpose of ensuring citizens' right of access to justice.

Finally, like a private party who files for administrative litigation, a procuratorial organ as the applicant in APIL is entitled to appeal when it thinks the first-instance decision is erroneous.[42] The procuratorial organ at the next higher level ordinarily joins in so as to participate in the appeal proceedings. Moreover, in the capacity of the state's organs for legal supervision, the procuratorial organ at the next higher level has a power to protest the second-instance APIL decision when it thinks it is erroneous and the court must re-try the case.[43] Although standing in different shoes, the procuratorate in effect can appeal the APIL decisions twice; while the administrative agency normally can only appeal the APIL decision once because there is a much slimmer chance that the court in practice will accept its request for a re-trial.

INFLUENCES OF PROCURATORATE-INITIATED APILS REGARDING THE JUDICIALIZATION OF ADMINISTRATIVE GOVERNANCE

The concept of 'judicialization of administrative governance' refers to judicial involvement in the formation and regulation of public policy by the administration. This judicial involvement is often carried out through administrative litigation—where the courts can conduct a powerful check on the exercise of administrative power and influence on administrative decision-making.[44] The enquiry may further be extended to a deeper question about a proper role of judges in relation to the judiciary-administration relationship—if not generally, then at least in a specific sociopolitical setting under discussion.

In relation to China, the existing literature on the judicialization of administrative governance looks exclusively at private party-initiated administrative litigation and focus on the role of the courts. For instance,

[41] Art. 22 of the Joint Judicial Interpretation.

[42] Art. 58 of the PIL Rules.

[43] Art. 64 of the PIL Rules.

[44] Ginsburg, Tom (2009) 'The Judicialization of Administrative Governance: Causes, Consequences and Limits' in Ginsburg, Tom and Chen, Albert H. Y. (eds.) *Administrative Law and Governance in Asia: Comparative Perspectives* Routledge, p3.

Randall Peerenboom comprehensively analysed the political, economic, and normative causes for judicialization of administrative governance in party-state China.[45] He pointed out forcefully that the judicial role through private party-initiated administrative litigation has significantly been limited when the courts handle 'politically sensitive cases that reflect the growing pains of developing countries',[46] such as land taking, labor suits, and environmental law violations. He Xin's case study of a local city of Nantong discovered that the courts strategically sought support from the CCP and devised tactics (such as putting the chief official in the spotlight, issuing judicial suggestions, and innovative application of the laws in cases) in handling private party-initiated administrative litigation in order to overcome the resistance of the government and advance judicial regulation of administrative conduct.[47]

Since July 2017, the procuratorates nationwide have embarked on and engaged in APIL against administrative agencies. This not only brings a new public actor but also diversifies and enriches the practice of China's judicialization of administrative governance. This part of the Chapter first examines the special roles that the procuratorate-initiated APIL system has played in regulating administrative conduct and enhancing administrative governance, then analyses the limitations, and finally discusses about the trends of the practice of procuratorate-initiated APIL in relation to judicialization of administrative governance.

Roles of APIL in Judicialization of Administrative Governance

In general, administrative litigation can impose substantial political pressure on administrative agencies because such agencies are forced to appear in publicity limelight and attract public attention and criticism. Moreover, their involvement in administrative litigation may affect both institutional and individual officials' performance appraisal.[48] Hence, administrative litigation works as a legal mechanism to incentivize administrative agencies to exercise public power according to law or to correct misfeasance or nonfeasance in a timely manner. Although this is also the situation in private party-initiated and procuratorate-initiated administrative litigation, compared to a private party who files 'citizens v. mandarins' administrative litigation, procuratorial organs are in an advantageous position when pursuing APIL. These advantages include accessing official documents and collecting evidence, receiving policy and political support of the CCP, and enjoying a good relationship with the court. Specifically, procuratorial organs have played their special roles in judicialization of administrative

[45] Peerenboom 'More Law, Less Courts' supra note 22 at 186-189.

[46] Ibid, at 191.

[47] He, Xin (2013) 'Judicial Innovation and Local Politics: Judicialization of Administrative Governance in East China' 69 *China Journal* 20.

[48] Huang, Jianqiu (2014) 'The Appraisal regarding Administration according to Law under the Regime of the State Council's Outline' (Guowuyuan gangyao kuangjia xia de yifa xingzheng kaoji) 4 *Journal of the CCP Party School of Nanjing* (*Zhonggong nanjing shiwei dangxiao xuebao*) 80.

governance mainly through five categories of APIL cases in China's unique legal-political setting.

First, the procuratorate files APIL suits against administrative agencies when national interest or public interest is harmed while private parties are neither involved as an interested party nor have legal standing to sue against illegal administrative activities or nonfeasance. When administrative agencies have a statutory obligation to prevent a certain national interest or public interest from being harmed but fail to discharge it, procuratorate-initiated APIL serves as a gap filler to urge them to act because citizens are only granted limited legal standing to file administrative litigation,[49] and non-governmental organizations are illegible to initiate APIL in China.[50] APIL cases that fall into this category are often concerned with matters of ecological, environmental, and resource protection, protection of state-owned property, granting of rights to use state-owned land and so on,[51] as the state owns all urban land and massive natural resources according to the Constitution. For instance, in the case *The People's Procuratorate of Sanya of Hainan Province v. The Ocean and Water Bureau of Haitang District ('the Water Bureau')*,[52] a local concrete factory, which drew underground water much more than the statutory limit of 1000 cubic metres per year from 2017 to 2019, neither applied for a licence nor paid any water resource fees. After receiving a procuratorial suggestion, the Water Bureau failed to reply in a timely manner and only finally stopped the factory drawing underground water after multiple requests by the procuratorate. Additionally, the Water Bureau insisted that the factory had drawn the water below the statutory volume limit. The People's Procuratorate of Sanya then filed an APIL suit against the Water Bureau, claiming that it must continue performing its obligations. This meant confirming the illegality of the actions of the factory, recovery of the unpaid water resource fees, and imposing administrative sanctions on the factory in accordance with the law. The Intermediate Court of Sanya supported its claims and ordered the respondent to discharge its obligations accordingly. Moreover, after the case was closed, the People's Procuratorate of Sanya reported to the municipal Water Bureau and Justice Bureau the conflicts between the local enactment (Measures of Sanya City on the Administration of Water Resources[53]) and the national law (Law of

49 Supra note 7.

50 Art. 25 of the Administrative Procedure Law (as revised 2017).

51 E.g., *The People's Procuratorate of Fuqing City of Fujian Province v. The Bureau of Land and Resources of Fuqing City (An APIL)* (Fujiansheng fuqingshi renmin jianchayuan su fuqingshi guotu ziyuan ju xingzheng gongyi susong an).

52 *The People's Procuratorate of Sanya City of Hainan Province v. The Ocean and Water Bureau of Haitang District (An APIL to protect underground water resources)* (Hainansheng sanyashi renmin Jianchayuan ducu baohu dixiashui ziyuan xingzheng gongyi susong an).

53 The Measures of Sanya City on the Administration of Water Resources (Sanyashi shuiziyuan guanli banfa) was promulgated by the Government of Sanya City on 21 April 2016 and took effect on the same day. It was amended on 13 August 2019.

Water[54]). The conflicting local enactment was then accordingly amended by the municipal government. This case illustrates 'procuratorial activism' through APIL. Such activism pushed the local government to correct its bureaucratic reluctance to act which thereby indirectly harmed national and/or public interest. Indeed, we can see in the case a significant enhancement of the procuratorate's institutional status, perhaps balancing the loss of their anti-corruption functions that were taken away by the Supervision Commission system in 2018.

Secondly, the procuratorate initiates APIL suits to press for carrying out administrative actions for the purpose of preventing serious harm to the national interest or public interest. Such APIL cases are sometimes called 'preventative public interest litigation' (*yufangxing gongyi susong*). They often involve administrative obligations to ensure public safety, occupational safety, food and drug safety, transportation safety and so on.[55] For instance, in the case *The People's Procuratorate of Lueyang Country of Shaanxi Province v. The Emergency Management Bureau of Lueyang County ('the Emergency Management Bureau')*,[56] a local mining company owned an iron mine located in the Jialing River valley. The mine was closed and deserted by the company in 2006. Because the tailing mine was not properly handled by the company, it was classified as the highest-level 'dangerous tailing' mine by the government in 2018. It potentially risked leakage of hazardous contaminants and collapse of mine dams, thus threatening the personal and property safety of the residents who lived in the area just 50 metres away from the mine. The Emergency Management Bureau argued that it did not issue administrative sanctions because the owner of the company had died in 2013, and the mine had not a contactable owner. The People's Procuratorate of Lueyang Country, for the purpose of preventing a disaster threatening public safety, sued the Emergency Management Bureau through APIL. The Basic Court of Lueyang County found that the respondent failed to discharge its administrative obligations and ordered it to effectively eliminate the potential danger to public safety. It is worth noting that the case succeeded largely because the People's Procuratorate of Lueyang Country received strong backing from the higher-level procuratorates and successfully mobilized the local CCP committee and local government to support the case, as well as taking various post-litigation actions.

[54] The Water Law (Shui Fa) was promulgated by the NPCSC on 21 January 1988 and became effective on 1 July 1988. It was amended by the same authority in 2002, 2009, and 2016.

[55] Another example is the SPP's Guiding Case No. 113 *The People's Rail Transportation Procuratorate of Zhengzhou City of Henan Province v. The People's Government of Sanmenxia City (An APIL to rectify the illegal construction of the dam threatening the safe operation of the high speed railway system)* (Henansheng renmin jianchayuan zhengzhou tielu yunshu fenyuan ducu zhengzhi weijian tangba weihai gaotie yunying anquan xingzheng gongyi susong an). However this case was not filed with the court but closed through procuratorial suggestion.

[56] *The People's Procuratorate of Lueyang Country of Shaanxi Province v. The Emergency Management Bureau of Lueyang County (An APIL to rectify an unsafe tailing mining)* (Shaanxisheng lueyangxiang renmin Jianchayuan ducu zhengzhi weikuangku anquan yinhuan xingzheng gongyi susong an).

Third, the procuratorate files APIL suits where the relevant illegal administrative activities or nonfeasance has significantly affected the interests of a large number of citizens while the state nevertheless has concern about private party-initiated administrative litigation or collective civil action for fear of sociopolitical instability.[57] For instance, in the case *The People's Procuratorate of Yongxing County of Hunan Province and the Market Supervision and Management Bureau of Yongxing County*,[58] from December 2017 to August 2019, when marketing a protein beverage for babies, the manufacturers and the sellers exaggerated the product's beneficial functions and puffed that it was also suitable for babies with allergic reactions to food. After receiving the complaints of 63 parent consumers, the People's Procuratorate of Yongxing investigated the case and issued a procuratorial suggestion to the Market Supervision and Management Bureau of Yongxing County, urging it to perform its supervisory obligation to prohibit the illegal marketing conduct of the relevant parties. Because the case had attracted the attention of the four-level procuratorates (that is, from the SPP down to the provincial, municipal, and county-level procuratorates), the administrative agency quickly acted upon the receipt of the procuratorial suggestion, including fining the sellers 2 million yuan, and further investigated the violation of the manufacturers in a separate case. Moreover, the People's Procuratorate of Yongxing acted as mediator to help 63 parent consumers obtain compensation for punitive damages three times the product price through settlement with the manufacturers and sellers.

It is true that the affected consumers are entitled to sue the infringing manufacturers and sellers for breach of contract or product liability through collective action. However, the state has a policy of discouraging private collective actions because they may arouse public discontent against the government and escalate social conflict and social instability. As in the Sanlu Milk Power Scandal case, the courts usually refused to accept collective actions that threaten social stability,[59] and lawyers must report collective actions to the local lawyers association (perhaps even further, to the local Bureau of Justice) and cautiously handle them under the latter's close supervision.[60] To avoid escalating conflicts, the lawyers are required to use

[57] E.g., *The People's Procuratorate of Yangquan City of Shanxi Province v. The People's Government of Yuxian (An APIL to Promote the Construction of the Longhuakou Reservoir)* (Shangxisheng yangquanshi renmin jianchayuan ducu tuidong yuxian longhuakou shuiku jianshe xingzheng gongyi susong an); *The People's Procuratorate of Songzi City of Hubei Province v. The Market Supervision and Management Bureau of Songzi City (An APIL to ensure the safety of retail medicines)* (Hubeisheng songzishi renmin Jianchayuan ducu baohu lingshou yaopin anquan xingzheng gongyi susong an).

[58] *The People's Procuratorate of Yongxing County of Hunan Province and the Market Supervision and Management Bureau of Yongxing County (An APIL to rectify the unsafe formula products and foods for infants and young children)* (Hunansheng yongxingxian renmin jianchayuan ducu zhengzhi yingyou'er peifang shipin anquan yinhuan xingzheng gongyi susong an).

[59] Yang, Zhenglian (2008) 'The Court Rejected to Accept the Compensation Cases against Sanlu, Who Will Compensate the Victims for Sanlu?' (Sanlu suopei zan bu li'an shui lai ti sanlu peichang shouhaizhe), *China News Weekly* (*Zhongguo xinwen zhoukan*), 11 November 2008, available at <http://news.cctv.com/china/20081111/107887.shtml>.

[60] See Art. 3(1) and 4(7) of the Guiding Opinions of All China Lawyers Association on the

mediation as a preferred form of dispute resolution in collective actions.[61] On the other hand, the party-state's policy of 'responsive authoritarianism'[62] cannot in all cases suppress private parties' legitimate claims and must respond to the public cry for critical civic requests, such as food safety. The procuratorate, as a trustworthy public actor, thus plays a significant role in handling this category of cases through APIL to push the administrative agencies in charge to act.

Fourth, the procuratorate sometimes uses APIL for the purpose of reining in local officers in the cases of conflicting policy goals between the central and the local government. Many of such cases are concerned with administrative nonfeasance in regulating and sanctioning a polluter's violation of the law of ecological, environmental and resource protection or the violation of the law of protection of state-owned property and land,[63] because the relevant policy of the central government may conflict with the local government policy of economic development. In private party-initiated administrative litigation, the applicant often faces great resistance and strong defence of the local administration which prioritizes economic development and tax revenues over the central government's policy, for example, of environmental protection. Compared to the private applicant in 'citizens v. mandarins' form of administrative litigation, the procuratorate is in a better position to sue the local government. This has been especially so after the local procuratorates underwent institutional reform aimed at achieving a centralized management of personnel, financial and material resources by the provincial procuratorate to mitigate local interference and protectionism by the administration. For instance, in the case *The People's Procuratorate of Fengxiang County of Baoji of Shaanxi Province v. The Fengxiang Division of the Baoji Environmental Protection Bureau ('the Fengxiang EPB')*,[64] Shaanxi Changqing Energy Chemical Co. Ltd. violated the statutory emission limit of coal-fired boiler particulates (especially methanol) since January 2015. Although in July 2015 the Fengxiang EPB, following the instruction of the People's Procuratorate of Baoji, issued an administrative decision to urge it to correct its violation, the company ignored the decision and the Fengxiang EPB neither supervised the company closely nor fined

Management of Mass Cases by Lawyers (Zhonghua quanguo lüshi xiehui guanyu lvshi banli quntixing anjian zhidao yijian), which was promulgated by the All China Lawyers Association on 20 March 2006 and in force on the same day.

61 Ibid, Art. 4(6).

62 Qianan, Runya and Teets, Jesscia (2020) 'Responsive Authoritarianism in China – a Review of Responsiveness in Xi and Hu Administrations' 25 *Journal of Chinese Political Science* 141.

63 E.g., *The People's Procuratorate of Yunyang County of Chongqing City v. The Planning Bureau of Yunyang County (An APIL to rectify the residential buildings exceeding the approved building areas)* (Chongqingshi yunyangxian renmin jianchayuan ducu zhengzhi chao guihua xuke mianji jianshe fangwu wenti de xingzheng gongyi susong an).

64 The SPP's Guiding Case No.49: *The People's Procuratorate of Fengxiang County of Baoji of Shaanxi Province v. The Fengxiang Division of the Baoji Environmental Protection Bureau (An APIL to urge comprehensively discharge the administrative agency's obligations)* (Shaanxisheng baojishi huanjing baohu ju fengxiang fenju bu quanmian lüzhi an).

it according to the law. Upon receiving the procuratorial suggestion of the People's Procuratorate of Fengxiang County, the Fengxiang EPB ordered the company to reduce production and to pay a fine of 50,000 yuan and additional emission charges. However, given the company's continuous violating conduct, in May 2016 the People's Procuratorate of Fengxiang County filed an APIL suit against the Fengxiang EPB, claiming that the latter had failed to ensure that the company adopted pollution reduction facilities. Also, the amount of the fine was too small and out of proportion with the degree of the violation. To avoid possible administrative interference, the case was tried by another basic court—located outside Fengxiang County. During the litigation, the Fengxiang EPB imposed a daily-based fine on the company, which thus was pressured into installing pollution reduction facilities to control the emission. In December 2016, the court ruled that the respondent failed to comprehensively discharge its supervisory obligations and confirmed the illegality of its administrative activities.

The violating company in this case was a state-owned enterprise with more than 1.5 billion RMB registered capital. Its majority shareholders are three powerful state-owned enterprises which enjoy a close relationship with the governments of Jiangsu Province and Shaanxi Province respectively. Given the local government's financial and political interests in the operation of the company, it would be extremely difficult, if not impossible, for citizens to file and win an administrative litigation against such powerful defendants. This case has been highly publicized as the first procuratorate-initiated APIL case in Shaanxi Province since the legal experimental work was launched in July 2015. The case illustrates that the procuratorate may occasionally mobilize APIL to judicially rein the local administration when there is a conflict of policy goals between the central and local governments.

Finally, the procuratorates are greatly interested in exploring landmark APIL cases in the emerging areas for public interest protection, such as the protection of minors, the protection of persons with disability,[65] and cultural heritage protection.[66] By doing so, the procuratorate can not only expand its legal standing in filing APIL suits but also influence the government in shaping its administrative policy and allocating its regulatory resources. This category of APIL cases can help the procuratorate gain more legal-political bargaining power vis-à-vis the powerful and strong administration within the China's political system. For instance, in the case *The People's Procuratorate of Beijing v. The Cyberspace Administration of Beijing*,[67] a famous IT company with its business place registered in Beijing, through its app,

[65] Supra note 29.

[66] E.g., The SPP's Guiding Case No.115: *The People's Procuratorate of Rongjiang County of Guizhou Province v. The Zaima Township Government of Rongjiang County (An APIL to protect traditional villages)* (Guizhousheng rongjiangxian renmin jianchayuan ducu baohu chuantong cunluo xingzheng gongyi susong an).

[67] The SPP's Guiding Case No. 141. *The People's Procuratorate of Beijing v. The Cyberspace Administration of Beijing (An APIL to protect children's personal information rights and interests)* (Beijingshi renmin jianchayuan ducu baohu ertong geren xinxi quanyi xingzheng gongyi susong an).

provided a platform for distributing and sharing short-length videos. However, it did so without obtaining the necessary consent of the guardians of children using its platform, illegally collected personal information of minor users, including their address, contact number, facial and vocal features. The app, moreover, pushed algorithm-generated notifications of videos that involved the personal information of the minor shown therein to the selected users. After the company was sued by the procuratorate in a separate civil public interest litigation, the People's Procuratorate of Beijing found that the Cyberspace Administration of Beijing failed to properly perform its duty to supervise the company's conduct, resulting in the illegal acts. In October 2020, it issued a procuratorial suggestion to the Cyberspace Administration of Beijing, suggesting that the latter should act to comprehensively examine and investigate any cyberspace violation of the law regarding protection of minors' personal information. This case was not escalated to the level of an APIL suit because the administrative agency followed the suggestion and effectively launched a special campaign to enhance minor-related cyberspace governance. Further, the case indirectly resulted in the promulgation of an administrative enactment of the 'Provisions on the Administration of Algorithm-generated Recommendations for Internet Information Services'[68] in December 2021.

To sum up, the procuratorate-initiated APIL system theoretically provides the procuratorates with wide authority to judicially monitor and regulate administrative conduct as well as shaping administrative policies and even administrative regulations concerning the national and public interest protection through the five categories of APIL cases. Although the administration remains powerful and superior in the Chinese political regime, the system has largely bounced back as a force to be reckoned with, despite the loss caused by the removal of its anti-corruption functions. To some extent, the procuratorate has strengthened the institutional status and roles in terms of the procuratorate-administration relationship.

Limitations of APILs in Judicialization of Administrative Governance

Despite the special roles in judicialization of administrative governance, procuratorate-initiated APIL cases have significantly decreased in number and percentage of the total civil and administrative public interest litigation cases filed by procuratorial organs in recent years. Although the SPP announced that the annual number of APIL cases registered with procuratorial organs reached 119,787 in 2019, and it has continuously increased in the subsequent years,[69] less than 0.5 percent of them were filed

[68] The Provisions on the Administration of Algorithm-generated Recommendations for Internet Information Services (Hulianwang xinxi fuwu suanfa tuijian guanli guiding) was jointly promulgated by the Cyberspace Administration of China, the Ministry of Industry and Information Technology, the Ministry of Public Security, and the State Administration for Market Regulation on 31 December 2021 and effective on 3 January 2022.

[69] The SPP, '*2019, 2020, and 2021 Data on the Cases Handled by Procuratorial Organs Nationwide*' (*2019, 2020, 2021 Quanguo jiancha jiguan ban'an shuju*), released respectively on 2 July 2020, 8 March 2021, and 8 March 2022. They are available at <https://www.spp.gov.cn/spp/xwfbh/wsfbt/202006/

with court every year.[70] The SPP reported that the number of APIL cases that were brought to a conclusion through judgment was 303 in 2019 and 475 in 2020; however, it has not publicized the relevant data since 2021.[71] Out of all procuratorate-initiated public interest litigation with the courts, the percentage of APIL suits has dropped from 15.1 per cent in 2018, 11.9 per cent in 2019, to 10.5 per cent in 2020.[72] In addition, according to the cases database of PKU Law,[73] as of 6 October 2022, the annual number of published APIL judgments was 11 in 2016, 590 in 2017, 256 in 2018, 249 in 2019, 211 in 2020, and 25 in 2021, which also shows a declining trend of APIL cases decided by the courts. Therefore, the roles of procuratorate-initiated APILs in judicialization of administrative governance should not be overemphasized. In effect, they are primarily subject to three-fold restrictions, that is capacity restriction, 'mentality' restriction, and autonomy restriction.

The capacity of procuratorial organs to file APIL suits refers to the available personnel, financial and professional resources of the special division in charge of public interest litigation within each procuratorate. In practice, the majority of APIL cases are handled by the procuratorates at the district level.[74] However, the public interest litigation divisions in almost all procuratorates have been transformed from the previous division of civil and administrative legal supervision.[75] This has two implications. First, the procurators who have experience in dealing with civil and administrative legal supervision cases may not necessarily be good at handling public interest litigation cases, due to the very different nature of these two types of litigation and court proceedings.[76] Second, the previous division of civil and administrative legal supervision had a long-lasting problem of 'insufficient manpower for handing a large number of cases' (*an duo ren shao*).[77] Given that the public interest litigation divisions are on average allocated only one

t20200602_463796.shtml>, <https://www.spp.gov.cn/spp/xwfbh/wsfbt/202103/t20210308_511343.shtml#1>, <https://www.spp.gov.cn/spp/xwfbh/wsfbt/202203/t20220308_547904.shtml#1>.

70 Ibid.

71 Ibid.

72 However, there were no such data released for the year of 2021.

73 PKU Law (Beida fabao) is an online database of Chinese laws and judicial cases, available at <https://www.pkulaw.com>.

74 Liu, Yi (2020) 'The Development Tendency and Improvements of the APIL system' (Woguo jiancha gongyi susong zhidu de fazhan taishi yu zhidu wanshan) 26(4) *Journal of Chongqing University (Social Science Edition)* (*Chongqing daxue xuebao (shehui kexue ban)*) 176.

75 Ibid, at 179.

76 The Research Group of the People's Procuratorate of Chaoyang District of Beijing City (2019) 'Preliminary Study on the Difficulties in the Exercise of the Procuratorate's Power of Investigation and Verification in APIL and Ways for Improvement' (Xingzheng gongyi susong jiancha diaocha heshi quan xingshi kunjing yu wanshan lujing chutan) 311 *The Chinese Procurators* (*Zhongguo jianchaguan*) 72-73.

77 Li and Zhao 'APIL Case Clue Discovery System' supra note 34 at 57.

or two 'quota procurators' (*yuan'e jianchaguan*)[78] and several procurator's assistants, the procurators in the current public interest litigation division are still facing heavy caseloads and work pressures. Since it is both time and effort-consuming for procurators to file civil and administrative public interest litigation suits and engage in the resulting judicial proceedings, it is understandable that, due to the procuratorate's capacity restriction, the number of procuratorate-initiated APIL cases filed with the courts has significantly dropped after a peak time in the early years of the nationwide establishment stage.

Moreover, another restriction is concerned with the procuratorate's mentality, both at the institutional and individual level. First, most procurators who engage in public interest litigation see themselves exerting a similar role to the one they play in prosecution of criminals on behalf of the state. For instance, at the legal experiment stage, the SPP strongly disagreed that a procuratorial organ that files civil and administrative public interest litigation should be called 'the plaintiff' or 'the applicant' because such an organ is safeguarding national and public interest as a public actor. That organ therefore should not be treated in a same way as the private actor who is the plaintiff in civil litigation and the applicant in administrative litigation.[79] Nevertheless, the SPC as well as some scholars tended to agree that a procuratorial organ has the same legal status and holds primarily the same procedural rights and obligations as the plaintiff in civil litigation and the applicant in administrative litigation. This is because civil and administrative public interest litigation is essentially civil litigation and administrative litigation respectively, despite the special legal standing rule applied to the procuratorate.[80] The debate ended with a compromise that the procuratorate should be given a special title 'public interest plaintiff' (*gongyi susong qisu ren*) in both civil and administrative public interest litigation .[81] Second, based on the same sort of thinking, most procuratorates see the courts as their allies when pursuing public interest

[78] Liu, Yi (2021) 'The Exploring Practice and Theoretical Reflection of the Jurisdiction Rules of APIL' (Xingzheng gongyi susong guanxia jizhi de shijian tansuo yu lilun fansi) 4 *Journal of National Procurators College* (*Guojia jianchaguan xueyuan xuebao*) 78; Wang, Yinxuan (2018) 'On Barriers of Procuratorate-initiated APIL and Solutions' (Jiancha jiguan tiqi xingzheng gongyi susong de zhang'ai ji qi kefu) 9 *People's Rule of Law* (*Renmin fazhi*) 51. 'Quota procurators' refer to the procurators after the recent personnel reform within procuratorate organs and those who are unable to get a quota to be procurator can only work as procurator's assistant or clerk.

[79] Jiang 'System of the Procuratorate-initiated APIL' supra note 10 at 23. Some even argued for the title of "administrative prosecutor" (*xingzheng gongsuren*), see Wang, Wanhua (2018) 'Several Issues on the Improvement of the Procuratorate-initiated APIL System' (Wanshan jiancha jiguan tiqi gongyi susong zhidu de ruogan wenti) 1 *Legal Science* (*Faxue*) 101.

[80] Art. 14 of the SPC's Implementation Measures on the Tested Work of the People's Court on the Adjudication of Procuratorate-initiated Public Interest Litigation Cases 2015; Tang, Zheng (2018) 'The Position and Trend of Procuratorial Supervision through APIL' (Xingzheng gongyi susong zhong jiancha jiandu de dingwei yu zouxiang) 236 *Academics* (*Xueshu jie*) 154; Shen, Kui (2017) 'The Procuratorate's Claim and Political Responsibility in APIL' (Jiancha jiguan zai xingzheng gongyi susong zhong de qingqiuquan he zhengzhi zeren) 5 *China Law Review* (*Zhongguo falü pinglun*) 77.

[81] Art. 4 of the Joint Judicial Interpretation.

litigation because both of them are public actors and they collaborate to safeguard national and public interests, even though some judges may not feel comfortable to this point of view.[82] According to a judge working in the Environment Division of a Higher People's Court, such a disagreement between the procuratorate and the court often leads to practical difficulties when the court rejects the arguments and claims of the procuratorate based on the merit of a case.[83] Third, it is well known that the conviction rate in criminal cases has reached 99.9 percent in China during the past decade;[84] likewise, procuratorial organs pay a great attention to its winning rate in civil and administrative public interest litigation and firmly hold a view that they must win in all cases to show their effectiveness. For instance, the SPP always highlights the data on the winning rate in its official reports on procuratorate-initiated public interest litigation: from 99.6 percent in 2019, 99.3 percent in 2020, 99.8 percent in 2021,[85] and 100 percent in the first half of 2022.[86] Although scholars have put forward the criticism that procuratorial organs should not blindly pursue a high winning rate in public interest litigation,[87] it is hard to change their mindset in this regard. Therefore, the procuratorate's 'mentality' restriction as noted above has influenced decisions about whether to deal with a detected illegal administrative activity or nonfeasance, through bringing an APIL suit.

Finally, the procuratorate may experience restrictions to autonomy in filing APIL suits. Either the government[88] or the party committee intervenes in some APIL cases which have serious sociopolitical implications. Despite the institutional reform of the procuratorial system that has aimed to reduce local interference by the administration, the personnel, financial and material resources of lower procuratorates still depend on the provincial government. The party committee, through the political and legal affairs committee, remains a de facto authority leading and supervising local

[82] Liu, Bei (2019) 'Theory and Practice: Analysis on the Solutions for Improving Procuratorate-initiated APIL' (Lilun yu shijian: jiancha jiguan canyu xingzheng gongyi susong youhua lujing tanxi) 14 *South China Legal Science* (*Nanhai faxue*) 56.

[83] This judge is the author's student. With over 20-year working experiences in the court, she had been working and in charge of the Environment Division for more than ten years.

[84] China Justice Observer (2020) '*What is the Conviction Rate in China? - China Law in One Minute*', 16 November 2020, available at <https://www.chinajusticeobserver.com/a/what-is-the-conviction-rate-in-china>.

[85] Supra note 69.

[86] The SPP, '*The SPP Released General Data on the Cases Handled by the Procuratorates Nationwide in the First Half of 2022*' (*Zuigaojian fabu shangbannian quanguo jiancha jiguan zhuyao ban'an shuju*), released on 20 July 2022, available at <https://www.spp.gov.cn/spp/xwfbh/wsfbt/202207/t20220720_565763.shtml#1>.

[87] Zhang, Jiajun (2021) 'On the Tendency of Treating Civil Public Interest Litigation as Criminal Litigation by the Procuratorates and Suggestions' (Lun jiancha mingshi gongyi susong de xingshihua ji qi xiaojie) 185 *Journal of Henan University of Economics and Law* 104.

[88] Yu, Lingyun and Gao, Liuyang (2017) 'The Practical Difficulties of the Procuratorate-initiated APIL and Solutions' (Jiancha jianguan tiqi xingzheng gongyi susong de xianshi kunjing yu chulu) 13 *People's Judiciary* (*Renmin sifa*) 9.

judicial work. The public security office, the procuratorate, and the court at the same level need to comply with its policies and instructions in practice.[89] In this sense, procuratorial organs do not fully enjoy institutional autonomy in pursuing APIL cases. At the legal experiment stage and during the early years of the nationwide establishment stage, under the SPP's top-down policy to promote the public interest litigation system,[90] the local procuratorates treated as their political tasks establishing the public interest litigation division and filing APIL suits with considerable social impact. In some cases, the procuratorate even collaborated with the local government to together meet the top-down policy of the central government.[91] However, the autonomy restriction is real when APIL cases involve an intense conflict of the national or public interest and the local policy or interest; and the local procuratorates are inclined to circumvent such cases,[92] which partially explains a decrease of APIL suits in number and in percentage in recent years.

Trends of APILs in the Judicialization of Administrative Governance

On one hand, public interest litigation work has become a new focus and highlight of the work of procuratorial organs after their anti-corruption functions were removed in 2018. Hence, the procuratorates nationwide will likely continue to engage in civil and administrative public interest litigation enthusiastically. On the other hand, given the three-fold restrictions analysed above, they must adjust working strategies and wisely allocate limited resources in carrying out the work. Two trends in the procuratorate-initiated APIL practice are identified.

The first trend is that procuratorial organs have shifted their work's focus to pre-litigation negotiation and procuratorial suggestion, instead of filing APIL cases in court, to save procuratorial resources and enhance judicial efficiency. The number of administrative public interest litigation cases solved through pre-litigation stage on average accounted for 85 per cent of the total number of administrative public interest litigation cases registered with the procuratorate from 2019 to 2021.[93] In contrast, less than 0.5 per cent of the total registered cases were solved through APIL in court during the same period. As the SPP commented on the guiding case No.31:

[89] Duan, Runqun (2019) 'How to Corrdinate Cases? The Development and Reformed Functions of the Party Political and Legal Affairs Committee's Power of Law Implementation and Supervision' (Ruhe xietiao anjian: Dangwei zhengfawei zhifa jiandu zhineng yange yu gongneng zaizao) 6 *Shenzhen Social Science* (*Shenzhen shehui kexue*) 144-145.

[90] Liang, Hongfei (2020) 'Preventative APIL' (Yufangxing xingzheng gongyi suong) 34(4) *Journal of Central China Unviersity of Science and Technology (Social Science Edition)* (*Huazhong keji daxue xuebao (shehui kexue ban)*) 86.

[91] Ibid.

[92] Li, Kunhui (2019) 'Study on the Pre-litigation Procedure of APIL' (Xingzheng gongyi susong suqian chengxu yanjiu) 5 *Theoretic Observation* (*Lilun guancha*) 111.

[93] Supra note 69.

> The main purpose of pre-litigation proceedings is to increase the incentive of administrative agencies to correct their illegal administrative activities and to save litigation costs and judicial resources to a maximum extent. Solving cases harming public interests through pre-litigation proceeding not only constitutes an important part of the procuratorate's work on public interest litigation, but also essentially reflects the value of the public interest litigation system. Only if administrative agencies refuse to correct their activity and insist not discharging their statutory obligation when they should, thus rendering the national and public interests being continuously harmed, the procuratorate should file APIL against them in court. Procuratorate-initiated APIL serves as the last resort when there is no alternative solution to remedy the severely harmed public interests and thus is of remedial nature and finality.[94]

Pragmatically, procuratorial organs have evidenced their achievements by showing the increasing annual number of administrative public interest litigation cases registered with the procuratorate.[95] However, at the same time, they have more selectively and cautiously filed APIL cases with the court. This is due to several factors—their limited resources, the goal of reaching 100 percent winning rate in APIL suits, and a preference for avoiding intense conflict with the critical interests that the provincial government or local party committee is concerned with. Because the information about the cases solved through pre-litigation negotiation and procuratorial suggestion has not been accessible to the public, it is unclear to what extent procuratorial organs have played a role in regulating administrative conduct and enhancing administrative governance through pre-litigation proceedings.

Sometimes, the SPP first seeks a consensus from the central-level administrative agencies on collaborating with each other, and then instructs the lower procuratorates to investigate and correct illegal administrative activities of the relevant local-level administrative agency.[96] Due to the central administration's pressure and the procuratorate's preference to resolution through pre-litigation proceedings, the relevant local administrative agencies are more likely to coordinate in pre-litigation negotiation and follow the procuratorial suggestions. This helps the procuratorates achieve their purpose of enhancing administrative governance at a low cost.

The second trend in the procuratorate-initiated APIL practice is that procuratorial organs strategically file APIL suits in a campaign style by

[94] The SPP's Guiding Case No.31: *The People's Procuratorate of Qingliu County of Fujian Province v. The Environmental Protection Bureau of Qingliu County (An APIL)* (Fujiansheng qingliuxian renmin jianchayuan su qingliuxian huanbaoju xingzheng gongyi susong an).

[95] Supra note 69.

[96] The SPP has often worked with various administrative authorities at the central level (such as the Ministry of Emergency Management, the Ministry of Water Resources, the State Administration of Market Regulation, the National Medical Products Administration, the Ministry of Veteran Affairs) to promote APILs in 2021 and 2022.

focusing on a specific area of administrative activities or one policy-oriented theme, such as the protection of personal information,[97] the ecological protection of Yellow River valley,[98] the protection of cultural relics and cultural heritage issues,[99] and the protection of consumer rights and interests.[100] When filing APIL cases which have a clear theme or message, procuratorial organs can more easily attract wide public and media attention, through effective propaganda[101] and publicizing theme-based APIL cases, thus maximizing the sociopolitical impact and implications of a limited number of APIL cases that they have made efforts to file, and win.

Reforming APILs for the Judicialization of Administrative Governance

It is encouraging to note that Chinese scholars have begun emphasizing that the quality and impact of APIL cases are paramount, surpassing the mere quantity of cases registered with the procuratorate.[102] It should not be merely a numbers game. As projected earlier, due to the three-fold restrictions (capacity restrictions, "mentality" restrictions, and autonomy restrictions), procuratorial organs will not be able to consistently file a large number of APIL cases in court. This is supported by the SPP reporting a total of approximately 1,200 APIL cases annually filed nationwide in 2023 and 2024.[103] To enhance its role in the judicialization of administrative governance in China, three aspects of the APIL system should be considered carefully.

97 Supra note 29.

98 E.g., Twelve Typical Cases about the Procuratorates Serving to Safeguard the Yellow River Valley's Ecology Protection and High-quality Development Released by the SPP (Zuigao renmin jianchayuan falü shi'er qi jiancha jiguan fuwu baozhang huanghe liuyu shengtai baohu he gaozhiliang fazhan dianxing anli) in January 2022.

99 Supra note 29.

100 E.g., Eight Typical Cases of Procuratorate-initiated Public Interest Litigation on '15 March' Food and Drug Safety and Consumer Rights and Interests Protection Released by the SPP (Zuogao renmin jianchayuan falü ba jian '3.15' shipin yaopin anquan xiaofeizhe quanyi baohu jiancha gongyi susong dianxing anli) in March 2021.

101 For instance, the procuratorate can organize a public hearing at the pre-litigation stage, see Art. 44 of the PIL Rules. In principle, public hearing is open to the public and can be live broadcasted via Internet, see Arts.5 and 18 of the Guidance on the Public Hearing Work in Handling Public Interest Litigations (Gongyi susong ban'an tingzheng gongzuo zhinan), which was promulgated by the SPP on 5 January 2022, and effective on the same day.

102 Chen, Xiaoqing and Zhang, Jingyue (2024) 'Prosecutorial Power in Administrative Public Interest Litigation: Power Dilemma, Concept Adjustment, and Correction Path' (xingzheng gongyi susong Zhong de jianchaquan: quanli kunjing, linian tiaoshi yu jiupian lujing) 25(6) *Journal of Yanshan University (Philosophy and Social Science)* (yanshan daxue xueuebiao zhexue shehui kexue ban) 63.

103 See *The SPP's White Paper on Procuratorial Work in Public Interest Litigation 2023* (Zuigao renmin Jianchayuan gongyi susong jiancha gongzuo baipishu 2023) (available at <https://www.spp.gov.cn/xwfbh/wsfbh/202403/t20240309_648329.shtml>) and *The SPP's White Paper on Procuratorial Work in Public Interest Litigation 2024* (Zuigao renmin Jianchayuan gongyi susong jiancha gongzuo baipishu 2024) (available at <https://www.spp.gov.cn/xwfbh/wsfbh/202503/t20250309_688675.shtml>).

First, the law should provide detailed procedural rules to regulate pre-litigation negotiation and the issuance of procuratorial suggestions at the pre-litigation stage. While some scholars have acknowledged the practical importance of pre-litigation negotiation and procuratorial suggestions, they have called for clear and consistent legal standards for the registration of APILs by procuratorial organs.[104] Given that Article 25(4) of the Administrative Litigation Law stipulates two conditions for initiating an APIL case in court—the illegality of administrative activities and the violation of public interests, it has been proposed that these same two requirements should also be applied during the registration of APILs by procuratorial organs.[105]

In essence, a consistent application of legal standards concerning the illegality of administrative activities and the infringement of public interests should be maintained throughout the entire process,[106] from registration to pre-litigation negotiation and procuratorial suggestions, and ultimately through the APIL procedure. In line with this, other scholars have argued for the integration of pre-litigation negotiation and the issuance of procuratorial suggestions into the entirety of the APIL proceedings.[107] As such, procuratorial suggestions at the pre-litigation stage should not supplant or wield administrative authority or administrative discretion, but rather offer clear legal reasoning within the legal boundary, ensuring that the content of procuratorial suggestions aligns with the eventual pleading submitted to the court in the event of an APIL case.[108]

Second, despite the three-fold restrictions faced by Chinese procuratorates, it is crucial for the APIL system to keep filing the 'mandarins v. mandarins' administrative litigation in court. Without the court's participation in dealing with APIL cases, the system can hardly achieve its originally designed role in the judicialization of administrative governance. Regarding the first trend in APILs mentioned earlier, some scholars have raised concerns about the potential downplaying of the litigious nature of the APIL system as initially intended. As they argued, rather than functioning as a litigation process, the system appears to have shifted

[104] Wang, Yan and Sun, Dongmei (2025) 'Optimization of the Determination of the Admissibility and Application Standards of Administrative Public Interest Litigation' (Xingzheng gongyi susong kesuxing panding ji shiyong biaozhun de youhua) 453 *The Chinese Procurators* (Zhongguo jiancha guan) 4.

[105] Ibid.

[106] Yu, Lingyun (2023), 'The Theoretical Framework of Administrative Public Interest Litigation by Procuratorates' (Jiancha xingzheng gongyi susong de lilun gouzao) 5 *Administrative Law Studies* (Xingzheng faxue yanjiu) 92.

[107] Zhou, Min (2024) 'Nature and Positioning of the Pre-litigation Procedure in Public Interest Litigation Initiated by Prosecutors' (Jiancha gongyi susong suqian chengxu de xingzhi ji dingwei) 6 *Administrative Law Studies* (Xingzheng faxue yanjiu) 84;

[108] Zhang, Min (2022) 'Judicial Restraint in Administrative Public Interest Litigation' (Lun xingzheng gongyi susong Zhong de sifa qianyixing) 44(4) *Journal of Kunming University* (Kunming xueyuan xuebao) 19-20; Zhou, ibid, at 81.

towards a non-litigious procedure due to the current emphasis on extensive pre-litigation negotiation and coordination between procuratorial organs and administrative agencies.[109] If procuratorial organs tended not to bring APIL cases to court, it would become difficult for the courts to judicially review high-profiled cases involving illegal administrative activities and administrative nonfeasance that significantly impact national or public interests.

Moreover, although APIL cases challenging illegal administrative activities may demand additional time and effort from procuratorial organs to achieve a successful ruling compared to cases involving administrative nonfeasance, the procuratorate should not shy away from such challenging APIL cases solely for the sake of convenience. This is particularly crucial in cases where illegal administrative activities, such as unauthorized government permissions, do not pertain to a specific citizen or private entity (thus lacking standing for 'citizens v. mandarins' administrative litigation) but significantly impact public health, safety, and other vital aspects of public interest.[110] In these circumstances, the APIL system should make up the inadequacies of the 'citizens v. mandarins' administrative litigation in advancing the judicialization of administrative governance.

Third, procuratorial organs can play an indispensable role in scrutinizing the legality of administrative rules or regulations through the APIL system. In general, the Administrative Litigation Law does not grant the court the authority to review abstract administrative activities, which involve administrative agencies formulating normative documents that have universal applicability to unspecified individuals and matters.[111] However, in cases where procuratorial organs identify abstract administrative actions as illegal or invalid during the pre-litigation phase of APIL cases, they can offer procuratorial suggestions urging modifications to the relevant administrative agency and its superior authority. *The People's Procuratorate of Beijing v. The Cyberspace Administration of Beijing*, as discussed in the preceding section,[112] serves as a good example illustrating the procuratorate's impact on abstract administrative activities and the enhancement of administrative governance.

CONCLUSION

Unlike 'citizens v. mandarins' administrative litigation filed by private parties, Chinese procuratorate-initiated APILs illustrate a unique 'mandarins v. mandarins' form of administrative litigation. This enables Chinese procuratorates to enhance their institutional legal-political strength

109 Wang, Chunye (2025) 'The Departure and Restoration of the Operation of the Administrative Public Interest Litigation System' (Lun xingzheng gongyi susong zhidu yunxing de pianli he huigui) 519(2) *Law Science* (Faxue) 5.

110 Supra note 90, at 86.

111 Art. 12 of the Administrative Procedure Law (revised in 2017).

112 Supra note 67.

by engaging in the judicialization of administrative governance as a new public actor, thus substantially changing the conventional procuratorate-administration relationship. This has occurred against the backdrop of the removal of the procuratorate's anti-corruption functions, and much criticism of the government for the long-standing problem of ineffective regulation and implementation of laws, as well as defensive 'bureaucratic shirking' in response to the CCP's anti-corruption campaign.

As the institutional guardian of the national interest and public interest, procuratorial organs are granted a wide legal standing in APIL and a broad power to investigate any illegal administrative activity and administrative nonfeasance that affects the national interest or public interest. As this Chapter has suggested, procuratorate-initiated APILs mainly play a gap-filling role in five categories of APIL cases, where the national interest or public interest is at stake due to administrative misfeasance or nonfeasance but private parties neither have legal standing nor are suitable to file administrative litigation in the current sociopolitical setting. Potentially, 'mandarins v. mandarins' procuratorate-initiated APILs can have a much larger influence on administrative decision-making and governance than 'citizens v. mandarins' administrative litigation.

However, due to the factors we have identified as capacity restriction, 'mentality' restriction, and autonomy restriction, the influence of the procuratorate-initiated APIL system on judicialization of administrative governance should not be overestimated. Although the procuratorates nationwide continue enthusiastically carrying out their work of civil and administrative public interest litigation because they see it as a spotlight of the procuratorial work, they have shifted the work's focus from filing APIL with the courts to pre-litigation negotiation and procuratorial suggestion and strategically initiate APIL suits in a campaign style by focusing on a specific area of administrative activities or one policy-oriented theme. This explains a significant reduction in the number and the percentage of procuratorate-initiated APIL suits after the first several years of the nationwide establishment stage.

To enhance the APIL system's role in the judicialization of administrative governance, the focus should shift from the quantity of APIL cases to the quality and impact of such cases in three key aspects. First, the law should establish detailed procedural rules to regulate pre-litigation negotiation and procuratorial suggestions, ensuring a seamless connection to the APIL proceedings. Second, the procuratorate should continue to initiate the significant 'mandarins v. mandarins' administrative litigation in court, particularly challenging illegal administrative activities that do not involve specific private parties but have a substantial impact on public interests. Finally, the procuratorate can strategically leverage its role in scrutinizing the legality of administrative rules or regulations through the APIL system and enhance administrative governance concerning abstract administrative activities by utilizing its legal tool of procuratorial suggestions.

GLOSSARY OF CHINESE TERMS

Romanisation (Hanyu Pinyin)	Chinese Characters	English Translations
an duo ren shao	案多人少	insufficient manpower for handling a large number of cases
cuoshang zuotanhui	磋商座谈会	negotiation symposium
chouxiang xingzheng xingwei	抽象行政行为	abstract administrative activity
falü jiandu	法律监督	legal supervision
gongyi susong qisu ren	公益诉讼起诉人	public interest plaintiff
jiancha jianyi	检察建议	procuratorial suggestion
jiancha weiyuanhui	监察委员会	Supervision Commission
jianchayuan	检察院	procuratorates
juti xingzheng xingwei	具体行政行为	specific administrative activities
lanyong zhiquan	滥用职权	abuse of power
lanzheng	懒政	bureaucratic shirking
mingxian budang	明显不当	evident improperness
minshi susongfa	民事诉讼法	Civil Procedure Law
shizhi hefaxing	实质合法性	substantive legality
weifa xingzheng xingwei	违法行政行为	illegal administrative activity
xian li hou bing	先礼后兵	courtesy before force
yifa xingzheng	依法行政	administration according to law
xingshi hefaxing	形式合法性	formal legality
xingzheng buzuowei	行政不作为	administrative nonfeasance
xingzheng gongsuren	行政公诉人	administrative prosecutor
xingzheng gongyi susong	行政公益诉讼	administrative public interest litigation
Xingzheng jiancha jiguan	行政监察机关	Office of Administrative Supervision
xingzheng susong	行政诉讼	administrative litigation

Xingzheng Susongfa	行政诉讼法	Administrative Litigation Law
yuan'e jianchaguan	员额检察官	quota procurators
yufangxing gongyi susong	预防性公益诉讼	preventative public interest litigation
Zhongguo Renmin Zhengzhi Xieshang Huiyi	中国人民政治协商会议	Chinese People's Political Consultative Conference

Cross-Border Data Governance in the Greater Bay Area: Towards Integration and Administrative Justice in a Fragmented Landscape

YANG LIN*

Research Officer at the University of Hong Kong

INTRODUCTION: THE STRATEGIC STAKES OF CROSS-BORDER DATA IN THE GBA

The digital economy depends on the free and secure flow of data across borders. In a world marked by escalating tensions between digital sovereignty and global digital trade, jurisdictions face pressure to reconcile security, privacy, and openness in their data governance frameworks. This tension is most evident in the Guangdong–Hong Kong–Macao Greater Bay Area (GBA)- a region of nearly 70 million people with three co-existing legal systems operating under the "One Country, Two Systems" principle.[1] The GBA's ambition is to become a globally competitive innovation hub, integrating financial, logistics, legal, and digital services across Mainland China, Hong Kong, and Macao.[2] Its success hinges not only on economic complementarities but also on the seamless flow of data between jurisdictions that differ profoundly in legal traditions and governance philosophies. Hong Kong does not recognize a general common law right to privacy. Instead, its privacy protection framework is largely statutory, centered on the Personal Data (Privacy) Ordinance (PDPO) and the Bill of Rights Ordinance, and only supplemented in limited ways by common law doctrines such as breach of confidence and contractual duties.[3] Macao adheres to a civil law system inspired by European data protection norms; and the Mainland operates under a centralized, security-driven model

* The author wishes to express sincere gratitude to Professor Michael Palmer, Professor Yun Zhao, and Dr. Meining Yan for their valuable comments and guidance on earlier drafts of this article, as well as to the anonymous reviewers for their insightful suggestions. All remaining errors or shortcomings are the author's own responsibility.

1 InvestHK (HKSAR), 'What is the GBA?' (*GBA InvestHK Portal*, updated 23 June 2025) available at: <https://gba.investhk.gov.hk/en/what-gba/#:~:text=of%202019%2C%20the%20total%20population,South%20Korea%2C%20Spain%20or%20Australia>

2 Xinhua News Agency, 'China unveils development plan for Guangdong-Hong Kong-Macao Greater Bay Area' (*English.gov.cn*, 18 February 2019) available at: <https://english.www.gov.cn/policies/latest_releases/2019/02/18/content_281476527605892.htm>.

3 Greenleaf, Graham (2014) *Asian Data Privacy Laws: Trade & Human Rights Perspectives*, Oxford University Press 79-122; See also Law Reform Commission of Hong Kong, *Report on Reform of the Law Relating to the Protection of Personal Data* (Aug 1994), available at https://www.hkreform.gov.hk/en/publications/rdata.htm.

typified by laws like the Cybersecurity Law and Personal Information Protection Law (PIPL). These differences have created institutional fragmentation in regulating data flows.

This Chapter offers a legal analysis of cross-border data governance within the Greater Bay Area's "One Country, Two Systems" framework. While there is growing literature on China's data sovereignty and international transfers, scholarship has largely overlooked the unique challenge of integrating three distinct legal regimes under a single national sovereignty. Methodologically, this article employs a comparative legal approach to analyse divergences among the three GBA regimes and draws lessons from EU and US models. It foregrounds administrative justice as a distinct dimension-often neglected in debates that focus solely on substantive rules-thereby situating the GBA as a living laboratory of 'data federalism' in a multi-level governance setting. In selecting the EU and the United States as comparative models, this article adopts a functional perspective. The EU represents the most comprehensive, high-standard regime for cross-border data protection, while the US reflects a market-oriented and sectoral model. These two jurisdictions thus exemplify divergent regulatory logics that have profoundly shaped global debates. Crucially, Hong Kong's PDPO and Macao's PDPA were originally influenced by OECD privacy guidelines and European principles, while Mainland China has drawn both from EU-style rights protection and US-style emphasis on innovation and national security. This shared intellectual heritage establishes a common comparative baseline across the GBA, the EU, and the US, making the comparison analytically meaningful and practically instructive.[4] By examining the GBA as a microcosm of these tensions, this article addresses a critical gap and foregrounds the role of administrative justice-a dimension often absent from debates that focus solely on substantive rules. The GBA thus offers a living laboratory for what may be termed data federalism-a form of multi-level governance where different legal systems must coordinate without losing their autonomy.[5] In this sense, the GBA also illustrates how multi-level governance[6] and administrative justice[7] can operate in a fragmented setting.

[4] Schwartz, Paul M. (2019) 'Global Data Privacy: The EU Way' 94(4) *New York University Law Review* 771.

[5] Fahey, Bridget A. (2022) 'Data Federalism' 135 *Harvard Law Review* 1007, at 1015-16.

[6] Hooghe, Liesbet and Marks, Gary, *Multi-Level Governance and European Integration*, (Rowman and Littlefield 2001); See also Zhang, Liang and Lin, Haoming (2024) 'On the Improvement Approach of the Legal System for Cross-border Data Flows in the Guangdong-Hong Kong-Macao Greater Bay Area' 5 *Practice and Theory of SEZS* 91.

[7] In this article, "administrative justice" refers not only to the fairness of substantive rules, but also to the procedural safeguards and remedies available when regulators exercise their powers. In the context of cross-border data governance, administrative justice requires that decision-making processes be transparent, that affected parties have opportunities to be heard, and that independent avenues of review or appeal exist. Without such safeguards, even well-designed substantive rules may lack legitimacy or predictability in practice. This is especially pertinent in the Greater Bay Area (GBA), where three distinct regulatory authorities—the Cyberspace Administration of China (CAC), Hong Kong's Office of the Privacy Commissioner for Personal Data (PCPD), and Macao's Office for Personal

This challenge mirrors a global dilemma: as states assert "data sovereignty" and enact localization measures, the digital economy increasingly demands cross-border connectivity. In such contexts, regulatory interoperability-developing shared mechanisms and norms without full legal uniformity-emerges as a pragmatic solution.[8]

The central policy tension is clear: How can China promote national data sovereignty and security while enabling intra-regional data mobility within the GBA, all while continuing to pursue external digital trade and innovation? The stakes for getting this balance right are high. The GBA comprises one of China's most economically dynamic regions (with a combined GDP that would rank it among the world's top economies) and is a test case for integrating disparate data regimes under the country's broader digital strategy. Seamless cross-boundary data sharing is essential for sectors like finance, healthcare, e-commerce, and smart-city initiatives. Yet such data flows raise concerns about national security, personal privacy, and regulatory oversight. These concerns are not unique to China. Empirically, (i) the number of countries enacting localization or export-restriction measures rose from 35 (2017) to 62 (2021);[9] (ii) by early 2023, the OECD identified 96 measures across 40 countries;[10] (iii) by early 2024, a CGD analysis counted over 60 countries with localization restrictions;[11] and (iv) by late 2024, 144 countries had adopted comprehensive data-privacy laws.[12] These trends illustrate a rapid expansion of sovereignty-inflected controls alongside the globalization of privacy frameworks. China's approach,

Data Protection (GPDP)—exercise overlapping competences. Embedding administrative justice into cross-border data frameworks is therefore essential to ensuring that regulatory integration is not only effective but also procedurally legitimate. See Mashaw, Jerry L.(1985) *Due Process in the Administrative State,* Yale University Press. See also Zhang, Linghan (2023) 'Research On the Legal Nature and Remedy Approach of Security Assessment of Outbound Data Transfers' 1 *Administrative Law Review* 45-61.

[8] Mishra, Neha (2024) 'Regulatory Interoperability in the Digital Economy' *SSRN Working Paper* available at: <https://papers.ssrn.com/sol3/papers.cfm?abstract_id=4990518>.

[9] Cory, Nigel and Dascoli, Luke, 'How Barriers to Cross-Border Data Flows Are Spreading Globally' (*ITIF Report,* July 2021) available at: <https://itif.org/publications/2021/07/19/how-barriers-cross-border-data-flows-are-spreading-globally-what-they-cost/>.

[10] Organisation for Economic Co-operation and Development (OECD), *The Nature, Evolution and Potential Implications of Data-Localisation Measures (OECD Trade Policy Paper* No. 278, November 2023) 13, Figure 2, available at: <https://www.oecd.org/content/dam/oecd/en/publications/reports/2023/11/the-nature-evolution-and-potential-implications-of-data-localisation-measures_249df37e/179f718a-en.pdf>.

[11] Kenny, Charles, 'The Inequitable Impacts of Data Localization' (*Center for Global Development*, 11 January 2024) available at: <https://www.cgdev.org/blog/inequitable-impacts-data-localization>.

[12] Apacible-Bernardo, Aly and Bushey, Kayla, 'Data Protection and Privacy Laws Now in Effect in 144 Countries' (*IAPP,* 28 January 2025) available at: <https://iapp.org/news/a/data-protection-and-privacy-laws-now-in-effect-in-144-countries>.

however, has been particularly security-centric, reflecting a governance philosophy that treats control over data as an aspect of state sovereignty.[13]

Recent developments suggest incremental, though cautious, steps toward reconciling these interests. Since the enactment of the first Cybersecurity Law in 2017, followed by the Data Security Law (2021) and the PIPL (2021), the Chinese government has built a comprehensive framework to control outbound data transfers. These laws were implemented amid a global trend toward data localization, and initially China's regime emphasized strict oversight in the name of national security and cyber-sovereignty. However, following feedback from industry and in service of economic goals, regulators have begun refining the system to facilitate "lawful, orderly, and free" data flows while maintaining security baselines.[14] Notably, in March 2024, the Cyberspace Administration of China (hereafter "CAC") issued the Provisions on Promoting and Regulating Cross-Border Data Flow (hereafter "2024 Cross-Border Data Flow Provisions"), introducing targeted volume-based exemptions and streamlined procedures for routine, low-risk transfers, while preserving strict scrutiny for "important data" and sensitive personal information. *De minimis* flows are thus facilitated without altering the baseline security logic.[15] In parallel, Hong Kong and Macao have explored bridging mechanisms-including inter-governmental Memoranda of Understanding (MoUs)[16] on data cooperation and a pilot GBA Standard Contract[17] for personal-data transfers within the region-signalling a move toward interoperability under 'One Country, Two Systems'. These efforts reflect a recognition that the GBA's unique context requires creative solutions that respect the One Country, Two Systems framework while advancing an integrated digital market. Macao has pursued a parallel path, introducing a standard contract mechanism for transfers between Macao and the Mainland, implemented through cooperation between its Personal Data Protection Office (GPDP) and the CAC.

[13] Greenleaf, Graham (2023) 'Personal Data Localization and Sovereignty Along Asia's New Silk Roads' in Chander, Anupam and Sun, Haochen (eds), *Data Sovereignty*, Oxford University Press, available at: <https://fdslive.oup.com/www.oup.com/academic/pdf/openaccess/9780197582794.pdf>.

[14] Cyberspace Administration of China (CAC), *Provisions on Promoting and Regulating Cross-Border Data Flow* (Order No.16, issued 22 March 2024, effective upon publication)

[15] Ibid.

[16] Digital Policy Office (HKSAR), 'Facilitating Cross-boundary Data Flow within the Greater Bay Area', available at: <https://www.digitalpolicy.gov.hk/en/our_work/digital_infrastructure/mainland/gbacbdf/>; Macao SAR, 'Memorandum of Understanding on Facilitating Cross-boundary Data Flow within the Guangdong-Hong Kong-Macao Greater Bay Area', available at: <https://www.dsedt.gov.mo/en_US/web/public/pg_tpd_gbadata_memo>.

[17] Digital Policy Office (HKSAR), 'Facilitation Measure of "Standard Contract for the Cross-boundary Flow of Personal Information within the Guangdong-Hong Kong-Macao Greater Bay Area (Mainland, Hong Kong)', available at: <https://www.digitalpolicy.gov.hk/en/our_work/digital_infrastructure/mainland/gbacbdf/cross-boundary_data_flow/index.html>.

This Chapter examines the GBA as a microcosm of China's broader data governance dilemmas. It argues that the GBA presents both a challenge and an opportunity: a challenge due to the clash of regulatory logics, and an opportunity to prototype new coordination mechanisms that balance digital sovereignty with economic integration and procedural legitimacy. Through doctrinal legal analysis with a comparative perspective, the discussion will illuminate how cross-border data governance can be enhanced in the GBA and what lessons it offers globally.

The analysis begins by mapping the evolution of China's national regulatory architecture, tracing its shift from a control-oriented stance to recent moves toward conditional openness. It then turns to the jurisdictional divergences within the "One Country, Three Systems" model, highlighting the frameworks of Hong Kong and Macao and the fragmentation they generate. Building on this, the discussion reviews institutional coordination initiatives in the GBA, including the 2023–24 MoUs and the new standard contract pilot, and asks whether these represent a coherent solution or merely a patchwork. Comparative lessons are subsequently drawn from the EU and US models for cross-border data transfers before the analysis considers issues of administrative justice and procedural fairness in the current regime. Drawing on these insights, the article proposes policy measures to advance an integrated GBA data governance architecture grounded in mutual recognition and fairness. The discussion concludes by positioning the GBA as a test case for reconciling China's quest for digital sovereignty with the demands of regional and global data flows, suggesting that calibrated mutual-recognition mechanisms rooted in procedural fairness can reconcile sovereignty with integration and offer a prototype of "data federalism" for other multi-jurisdictional contexts.

CHINA'S REGULATORY TRAJECTORY: FROM CONTROL TO CONDITIONAL OPENNESS

Cybersecurity Law, Data Security Law, and PIPL

Mainland China's legal regime governing data flows is anchored in three major statutes: the Cybersecurity Law (CSL) of 2017,[18] the Data Security Law (DSL) of 2021,[19] and the Personal Information Protection Law (PIPL) of 2021.[20] Together, these laws established a tripartite architecture of regulatory control.[21] First, they introduced a security-centric classification of data, distinguishing "important data" and other categories tied to national security or public interests. Second, they imposed *ex ante* state oversight for

[18] Cybersecurity Law of the PRC (adopted 7 Nov 2016, effective 1 June 2017).

[19] Data Security Law of the PRC (adopted 10 June 2021, effective 1 Sept 2021).

[20] Personal Information Protection Law of the PRC (adopted 20 Aug 2021, effective 1 Nov 2021).

[21] Li, Mengyuan (2023) 'Exploring the Rules of Cross-Border Data Flow in the Guangdong–Hong Kong–Macao Greater Bay Area' 5 *Open Journal of Legal Science* 4569.

certain outbound data transfers, such as mandatory government security assessments for high-risk exports. Third, they emphasized the primacy of public interest and national sovereignty over private autonomy in data governance.

The Cybersecurity Law was the cornerstone, creating tiered obligations for network operators and especially for "critical information infrastructure operators" (CIIOs). Notably, Article 37 of the CSL mandates that CIIOs must store personal information and important data within mainland China, and any transfer of such data abroad requires a government-administered security assessment. This was China's initial attempt to ring-fence sensitive data domestically in the name of national security.[22] The Data Security Law built on this by establishing a hierarchical classification system for data based on its importance to national security, economic development, and public interest. Under the DSL, authorities can formulate catalogues of "important data" for different regions and sectors, and data designated as important is subject to stricter controls (e.g. risk assessments and approval before export). The PIPL complemented these laws by focusing on personal information protection; it imposes GDPR-inspired principles of consent, data minimization, and security, and provides individual rights over personal data. Crucially, PIPL includes specific provisions (Articles 38–40) governing cross-border personal data transfers, which formalize the requirement that personal information handlers must utilize one of three transfer mechanisms before exporting data.[23]

Under the PIPL and its implementing measures, three lawful pathways exist for cross-border personal-data transfers:

1. passing a CAC-administered security assessment (mandatory for large-scale or sensitive transfers, such as those by CIIOs or involving "important data" or exceeding certain volumes of personal information);
2. obtaining a personal information protection certification from a qualified institution inside China (envisioned for transfers among corporate affiliates or within certain regulated sectors);
3. using standard contractual clauses (SCCs) issued by the CAC (a mechanism akin to the EU's SCCs, intended for routine transfers by non-critical entities under certain thresholds). [24]

[22] Deloitte China, 'Regulations on Promoting and Regulating Cross-border Data Flow - Key Takeaways' (25 March 2024) available at: <https://www.deloitte.com/cn/en/services/consulting-risk/perspectives/cross-border-data-flow-regulations.html>.

[23] Panek, Wojciech (2024) 'People's Republic of China and the Adequacy - Why Chinese Data Protection Law Is Not Adequate Within the Meaning of the GDPR' 18(2) *Masaryk University Journal of Law & Technology* 143 available at: <https://journals.muni.cz/mujlt/article/download/37354/33339/67661>.

[24] Cyberspace Administration of China, 'Measures on Security Assessment for Outbound Data Transfer (2022)'; Cyberspace Administration of China, 'Provisions on Standard Contracts for Outbound Transfer of Personal Information (2023)'.

In practice, the security assessment route is required for high-risk scenarios – for example, if a company transfers personal data of over 1 million individuals or sensitive personal data of over 100,000 individuals, or if the data falls into the "important" category. The CAC reviews such transfers to evaluate national security risks and can reject those it deems impermissible. The certification route and standard contract route provide alternatives for less sensitive transfers, but as of the early implementation of PIPL, these mechanisms have not been widely recognized outside the Mainland and certainly not formally integrated with Hong Kong or Macao's regimes.[25] Chinese legal commentators have examined these provisions as forming a "three-track" transfer model, each with distinct compliance burdens and risk profiles. Under this reading, the security assessment route is positioned as the highest-scrutiny channel for large-scale or sensitive transfers, certification serves as an intermediate mechanism for ongoing intra-group or sectoral transfers, and the standard contract offers a streamlined option for low-risk exports. This doctrinal analysis emphasizes that the model's design reflects a deliberate calibration between national security objectives and economic functionality, while also creating differential procedural obligations for data handlers depending on the transfer pathway selected.[26]

The 2024 Cross-Border Data Flow Provisions

After a period of strict enforcement and industry pushback, Chinese regulators moved to fine-tune the regime. In March 2024, the Cyberspace Administration of China promulgated the Provisions on Promoting and Regulating Cross-Border Data Flow (Guifan he Cujin Shuju Kuajing Liudong Guiding, effective 22 March 2024). The Provisions introduced targeted volume-based exemptions for routine, low-risk transfers. For instance, outbound transfers involving personal data of fewer than 100,000 individuals per year (excluding sensitive personal data) are exempt from prior security review. Data generated in international trade, academic cooperation, or e-commerce likewise benefit from streamlined procedures, unless officially designated as "important data". The 2024 Provisions thus represent a calibrated move toward *de minimis* openness, while retaining strict oversight of critical sectors.[27] Similarly, data generated in contexts like international trade, academic cooperation, or e-commerce can bypass lengthy security reviews unless the data is explicitly classified as "important." In short, routine and low-sensitivity cross-border data exchanges have been made easier, aligning China's practice closer to global norms for *de minimis* data transfers. As recent scholarship has observed, the 2024 Provisions align with a broader policy experiment in China's pilot

[25] Hong Kong SAR, *Personal Data (Privacy) Ordinance* (Cap 486), s 33 (enacted 1995); PCPD, 'Guidance on Cross-border Data Transfer' (Dec 2014) available at: <https://www.pcpd.org.hk/english/resources_centre/publications/files/GN_crossborder_e.pdf>.

[26] Ye, Chuanxing and Yan, Wenguang (2024) 'Current Situation, Problems, and Relief Path of China's Cross-Border Data System' 37(1) *Journal of Beijing University of Aeronautics and Astronautics Social Sciences Edition* 57.

[27] CAC *Provisions on Promoting and Regulating* supra note 14

free trade zones (FTZs), where regulators have tested special compliance arrangements such as "negative lists" of restricted datasets and relaxed volume thresholds for certain sectors. In this view, the GBA's facilitation measures form part of an emerging pattern in which selected regions are granted procedural flexibility under close administrative oversight, serving as laboratories for refining national-level rules on data exports.[28]

These changes reflect a dual-track strategy: relaxing burdens on routine, low-risk flows while maintaining strict control over transfers in sectors involving critical infrastructure, sensitive personal data, or data with national security implications. Commentators have noted that previous restrictions on cross-border data transfers were seen by foreign companies as disruptive to business operations, and that the new CAC provisions were aimed at easing such burdens to support more efficient data-driven commercial activity and integration into global markets.[29] The new Provisions respond to these concerns by introducing targeted exemptions. For example, transfers arising from international trade, academic cooperation, or cross-border logistics no longer require a prior security review, provided they do not involve 'important data' or sensitive personal information.[30] This adjustment substantially reduces compliance burdens for ordinary business operations, while preserving strict controls at the "bottom line" for important or sensitive datasets. Notably, the final text reorders its title from the draft's "Regulating and Promoting" to "Promoting and Regulating," a rhetorical shift signalling a more facilitative stance towards cross-border data openness.[31]

For stakeholders in the GBA, these regulatory tweaks were a welcome development, but questions arose about their scope and application. The 2024 Provisions, being national rules, ostensibly apply only within Mainland jurisdictions (including the nine Guangdong cities of the GBA). It remained unclear to what extent their facilitative provisions would extend to Hong Kong–based or Macao–based data activities. For instance, if a Hong Kong company sends a small dataset to Shenzhen, can it rely on the new volume-based exemption? Or must it still treat the transfer as an "international" outbound transfer under PIPL since Hong Kong is treated as outside the Mainland for data regulation purposes? Without formal mutual recognition

[28] Ma, Guang and Wu, Hong (2025) 'Cross-Border Data Flow Supervision in China's Free Trade Zones: Security and Compliance Rules' *Asia Pacific Law Review* 1.

[29] Reuters, 'China relaxes security review rules for some data exports' (22 March 2024) available at:<https://www.reuters.com/technology/cybersecurity/chinas-cyberspace-regulator-issues-rules-facilitate-cross-border-data-flow-2024-03-22/>; see also Bloomberg, 'China loosens cross-border data rules, easing business pressure' (22 March 2024) available at <https://www.bloomberg.com/news/articles/2024-03-22/china-loosens-cross-border-data-rules-to-ease-business-pressure>.

[30] Li,Bob, 'China Released New Regulations to Ease Requirements for Outbound Cross-Border Data Transfers' (*White & Case*, 2 April 2024) available at: <https://www.whitecase.com/insight-alert/china-released-new-regulations-ease-requirements-outbound-cross-border-data-transfers>.

[31] CAC *Provisions on Promoting and Regulating* supra note 14

between the Mainland and the Special Administrative Regions (SARs), such uncertainties persisted. In practice, the new rules signalled Beijing's willingness to accommodate business needs, but true interoperability in the GBA would require additional measures beyond unilateral Mainland regulations - a gap that GBA-specific pilot programmes aimed to address. In comparative perspective, this shift represents a calibrated departure from earlier absolutism toward a model closer to global norms on *de minimis* transfers. While still far from EU-style adequacy findings, the new thresholds and exemptions show Beijing's recognition that over-restriction of routine data flows risks economic costs. Studies have found that stringent localization rules can significantly depress trade and productivity,[32] a risk that may have informed these recent adjustments. Empirical trade research also supports this concern: cross-border data flows are now a key driver of global commerce, and restrictions that raise compliance costs or slow transfers can significantly reduce productivity, exports, and participation in digital trade. Economic modelling suggests that the welfare gains from liberalising data flows are especially pronounced for digitally intensive sectors, making calibrated openness a critical element of competitiveness.[33]

National Security vs. Economic Integration

At the heart of China's data-governance dilemma lies the balance between data sovereignty and economic integration. National-security imperatives lead to localization requirements and state-controlled assessments, reflecting the Party-state's emphasis on cyber-sovereignty and risk mitigation.[34] Yet these controls create frictions for companies operating across borders, particularly within the GBA, which is intended to function as an integrated economic zone. The competing imperative is to ensure that data – often called the lifeblood of the digital economy – can circulate freely enough to unlock innovation and efficiency across the GBA's jurisdictions.

Tensions between these aims have surfaced in concrete ways. For instance, a cross-border medical services platform linking Guangdong and Hong Kong hospitals has reportedly faced challenges in synchronizing patient data for AI-driven diagnostics, due to unresolved regulatory mismatches and uncertainty over permissible transfers.[35] Similarly, fintech companies that straddle Hong Kong and Shenzhen find it cumbersome to share customer or transaction data across the boundary; a Hong Kong-licensed firm may need to undergo a CAC security review to access Mainland-sourced data, even if the data originally pertains to its own clients operating on both sides. These frictions illustrate how stringent data

[32] Cory and Dascoli 'Barriers to Cross-Border Data Flows' supra note 9

[33] Meltzer, Joshua P. (2015) 'The Internet, Cross-Border Data Flows and International Trade' 2(1) *Asia & The Pacific Policy Studies*, 90.

[34] Chander, Anupam and Lê, Uyên P. (2015) 'Data Nationalism' 64 *Emory Law Journal* 686.

[35] Case C-311/18, Data Protection Commissioner v Facebook Ireland Ltd & Schrems (Schrems II) [2020] ECLI:EU:C:2020:559 available at: <https://eur-lex.europa.eu/legal-content/EN/TXT/PDF/?uri=CELEX:62018CJ0311>.

controls, though motivated by legitimate security concerns, can impede the very cross-border synergy that the GBA initiative seeks to foster.

In response, China has embraced a strategy of conditional openness within certain contexts like the GBA. This includes selective exemptions (as discussed above), pilot zones where rules are slightly relaxed, and bilateral cooperation instruments (like Hong Kong–Mainland MoUs) to manage data flows. This approach is flexible and pragmatic, but it often lacks the predictability and transparency that businesses crave. Companies in the GBA may still feel uncertainty about how far they can trust these pilot arrangements, especially if core national laws remain unchanged. The subsequent parts of this article delve into how Hong Kong and Macao have dealt with these issues, what cooperative steps have been taken specifically in the GBA, and what can be learned from other jurisdictions' models.

ONE COUNTRY, THREE SYSTEMS: DIVERGENT DATA REGIMES IN MAINLAND, HONG KONG, AND MACAO

Hong Kong: Incomplete Section 33 And Regulatory Lag

Hong Kong's Personal Data (Privacy) Ordinance (PDPO), enacted in 1995 and substantially amended in 2012 (with further tweaks in 2021), is the core law protecting personal data in the territory.[36] It is a comprehensive privacy regime grounded in OECD/FIPPs principles and enforced by an independent Privacy Commissioner (PCPD). However, a crucial gap exists in Hong Kong's framework when it comes to cross-border data transfers. This is because PDPO Section 33, a provision intended to regulate cross-border data flows, has never been brought into operation since the law's inception.[37] Section 33, if activated, would prohibit the transfer of personal data from Hong Kong to jurisdictions that have not been officially deemed to provide a comparable level of protection, unless certain exceptions or safeguards apply. In effect, it was designed to function similarly to the EU's "adequacy" regime, requiring either a whitelisted list of approved jurisdictions or alternative measures (such as contracts or consent) before data could be exported.[38]

Despite decades of discussions and calls for reform, Section 33 remains dormant. The government has repeatedly postponed its implementation, citing concerns about Hong Kong's position as an open international business hub. Indeed, the Privacy Commissioner's office underscored in 2020 that 'cross-jurisdiction data flow is the life-blood of our data driven economy,' reflecting Hong Kong's reluctance to impose strict export

[36] Hong Kong SAR, '*Personal Data (Privacy) Ordinance* (Cap 486)'.

[37] Privacy Commissioner for Personal Data (PCPD), '*Guidance on Personal Data Protection in Cross-border Data Transfer*', available at: <https://www.pcpd.org.hk/english/resources_centre/publications/files/GN_crossborder_e.pdf>.

[38] Kuner, Christopher (2015) 'Extraterritoriality and regulation of international data transfers in EU data protection law' 5(4) *International Data Privacy Law* 235.

controls that might stifle its open digital environment.[39] Over the years, the Law Reform Commission and the PCPD conducted consultations on this topic - including issuing a detailed Guidance Note in 2014 on how organizations might prepare for cross-border data rules[40] - but as of 2025 the government still has not commenced Section 33. In the interim, the PCPD issued Recommended Model Contractual Clauses in May 2022 to give data users an off-the-shelf contractual safeguard for cross-border transfers under the PDPO, pending any activation of Section 33.[41] One practical reason is that Hong Kong has leveraged the absence of Section 33 as part of its business friendly environment, assuring companies that data can move freely in and out of Hong Kong (subject only to general privacy principles) without regulatory friction. Indeed, Hong Kong's free-flow stance stands in contrast to the stricter approach in Mainland China and Macao. Despite geographic proximity, data sent from Hong Kong to Guangdong is still treated as a cross-jurisdictional transfer engaging separate compliance regimes.[42] At the same time, had Section 33 been in force, its model was somewhat less rigid than the Mainland's current rules and even more flexible than Macao's: Section 33's framework allowed exceptions such as the data subject's consent, contractual safeguards, or situations where the transfer would avoid adverse action to the data subject. Those features indicate that Hong Kong, even in contemplating cross-border rules, favoured a pragmatic approach balancing protection with free flow.[43]

Why then has Section 33 not been implemented? Observers point to both economic and political factors. Economically, mandating equivalence or contracts for all exports could impose compliance costs on businesses (potentially hampering data-driven commerce), which Hong Kong has been keen to avoid in order to stay competitive. Politically, activating Section 33 might require designating which jurisdictions are "acceptable"

[39] Privacy Commissioner for Personal Data (Hong Kong), 'Response to media enquiry on data localisation' (15 April 2020) available at: <https://www.pcpd.org.hk/english/news_events/media_enquiry/enquiry_20200415.html>.

[40] Innovation and Technology Bureau (Hong Kong) & Cyberspace Administration of China, 'MoU on Facilitating Cross-boundary Data Flow within the GBA' (29 June 2023) available at: <https://www.info.gov.hk/gia/general/202306/30/P2023063000219.htm>.

[41] Privacy Commissioner for Personal Data (Hong Kong), 'Guidance on Recommended Model Contractual Clauses for Cross-border Transfer of Personal Data' (May 2022) available at: <https://www.pcpd.org.hk/english/resources_centre/publications/files/guidance_model_contractual_clauses.pdf>; See also Kennedy, Gabriela, 'Hong Kong's 2022 Guidance on Cross-border Data Transfers' (*Mayer Brown*, 2 June 2022), available at: <https://www.mayerbrown.com/en/insights/publications/2022/06/hong-kongs-2022-guidance-on-cross-border-data-transfers-implications-for-data-users-and-processors >.

[42] Chen, Baoxin and Feng, Zehua (2024) 'Practical Difficulties and Strategies for Integrating Cross-Jurisdictional Data in the GBA' 37(2) *Xingzheng* (Administration [in Chinese]) 18-33 available at: <https://www.safp.gov.mo/static/2024/11/07/baffa357-3ee7-41a5-b217-2f5b55ce41b2.pdf>

[43] Macao SAR & Cyberspace Administration of China, 'MoU on Facilitating Cross-boundary Data Flow within the GBA' (9 Sept 2024) available at: <https://www.dsedt.gov.mo/en_US/web/public/pg_tpd_gbadata_memo>

for Hong Kong data - a diplomatically sensitive exercise, especially if an objective assessment might find Mainland China not equivalent to Hong Kong's standards. In the One Country, Two Systems context, it would be awkward for Hong Kong to officially pronounce the Mainland's data protection regime as inadequate.[44] Thus, inertia prevails. The result is a paradox where Hong Kong currently has arguably the most open regime (no blanket restrictions on data exports), Macao the most closed (explicit requirement of adequate protection or consent for transfers), and the Mainland somewhere in between (permissions needed, but gradations and exemptions emerging).

It should be noted that Hong Kong's posture could change. Privacy advocates and some lawmakers have periodically urged the government to implement Section 33 to bolster personal data protection in an age of increasing data misuse concerns. Moreover, Hong Kong's recent efforts to reform its privacy laws (including 2021 amendments addressing doxxing) show that the legal landscape can evolve when there is political will. For now, though, Hong Kong serves as the "free-flow" pole in the GBA's triangle of systems, which in a way makes it the linchpin for any regional data bridging: Hong Kong can receive data from Mainland or overseas without special barriers and could act as a conduit or intermediary – but that very openness also causes Mainland regulators to worry about data escaping China's jurisdiction via Hong Kong.[45]

Macao: Civil Law Formalism and Consent-Based Adequacy

Macao's data protection regime, embodied in the Personal Data Protection Act (PDPA) of 2005 (Law No. 8/2005), is closely modeled on the European Union's older data protection frameworks (essentially the EU Data Protection Directive 1995). It is a comprehensive law enforcing principles similar to the EU's, and Macao's Office for Personal Data Protection (GPDP) serves as the dedicated regulator. A key aspect is that the PDPA, much like the GDPR, restricts transfers of personal data out of Macao unless certain conditions are met. Specifically, Article 19 of Macao's PDPA stipulates that personal data may only be transferred to a destination outside Macao if an "adequate" level of protection is ensured in that destination's legal system, or if one of several exceptions applies (such as the data subject's consent, contractual safeguards, or important public interest).[46] Article 19 codifies

[44] Kennedy, Gabriela and Lai, Justin, 'Guangzhou Internet Court decision on cross-border data transfer under PIPL' (*Mayer Brown*, 19 Dec 2024) available at: <https://www.mayerbrown.com/en/insights/publications/2024/12/guangzhou-internet-court-issues-the-first-decision-on-cross-border-transfer-of-personal-data-under-pipl>

[45] Zhu, Lindsay, Xu, Haowen and Scott, Warren, 'Court Ruling in China on Personal Data Transfer' (*PrivacyWorld Blog*, 19 Nov 2024) available at: <https://www.privacyworld.blog/2024/11/court-ruling-in-china-on-personal-data-transfer-by-international-hotel-chain/>

[46] Macao SAR, *Personal Data Protection Act* (Law No 8/2005), art 19. For a recent example of an adequacy assessment under the GDPR, see European Commission Adequacy Decision (Republic of Korea, GDPR) 2021/1772, available at: <https://eur-lex.europa.eu/legal-content/EN/TXT/PDF/?uri=CELEX:32022D0254>.

the adequacy requirement and sets out narrow exceptions-such as consent, contractual necessity, or important public interest-while empowering the GPDP to authorise transfers case-by-case.[47] In practice, since Macao has not published any whitelist of adequate jurisdictions, most cross-border transfers require either obtaining explicit consent from the data subject or seeking authorization from the GPDP (which can grant exemptions on a case-by-case basis). GPDP opinions indicate that controllers frequently approach the GPDP for guidance where the adequacy of the destination jurisdiction is uncertain.[48] This makes Macao's regime quite strict: businesses operating there have to treat external transfers cautiously and often put contractual measures in place or simply localize data to avoid the hassle.

Notably, Macao's law does not differentiate between Mainland China and other foreign jurisdictions – under Macao law, sending data to Guangdong is as much an "international" transfer as sending it to Europe. This has contributed to a relatively siloed approach: Macao's data stays mostly siloed unless formal consent or approval is obtained. The upside is strong formal protection; the downside is friction in integration with the Mainland and Hong Kong. Macao's stance hews closely to EU-style formalism (reflecting Macao's Portuguese legal heritage), emphasizing individual consent and regulatory oversight for data exports. Indeed, the PDPA's adequacy provision on paper mirrors the EU concept, but without a functioning whitelist mechanism Macao relies heavily on *ad hoc* permissions and the default rule of consent.[49]

In terms of enforcement and practice, Macao has had limited high-profile cases or controversies in this area, likely due to the small market and the fact that many businesses simply avoid risky transfers. The GPDP has issued some guidance indicating willingness to streamline processes – for example, template clauses for contracts – but Macao has not engaged in the kind of experimental pilots that the Mainland has in the GBA. Thus, in the trio, Macao represents the "by the book" jurisdiction that ensures alignment with global data protection norms, but perhaps at the expense of agility. In the GBA context, Macao's participation in cross-border experiments (like the GBA contract) needed to accommodate its legal requirements, which we will discuss in the Part below entitled 'GBA Institutional Coordination: MOUs, Standard Contracts, and Pilot Projects'.

[47] ibid.

[48] Office for Personal Data Protection (Macao), 'Opinion 0002/P/2013 - School A transfers data outside the Macao SAR' (2013) available at: <https://www.dspdp.gov.mo/file/Opinion/0002-P-2013-GPDP-EN.PDF>.

[49] DLA Piper (2023) 'Data Protection Laws in Macau SAR' , available at: <https://www.dataguidance.com/sites/default/files/gdpr_v._pdpa_macau__1.pdf>; see also Asian Business Law Institute (FPF Asia), 'Transferring Personal Data in Asia: A Path to Legal Certainty and Regional Convergence' (2021) 25, 30.

Fragmentation and the Need for Coordination

The upshot of these divergent regimes is a fragmented regulatory landscape for data in the GBA. A company operating regionally faces three sets of rules: near-unfettered flow from Hong Kong's side (for now), strict consent/adequacy conditions from Macao's side, and a conditional, security-reviewed flow from the Mainland's side. Without special arrangements, the default is that data cannot seamlessly circulate among Guangdong, Hong Kong, and Macao. Every transfer might trigger a compliance question: Is it allowed? Which law governs it? Could an action lawful in one jurisdiction (say, analyzing personal data for a marketing purpose consented to under Hong Kong law) inadvertently violate another jurisdiction's law (say, Mainland's PIPL if the data got shared back to a server in Shenzhen without additional consent)?

Scholars warn that without mechanisms for regulatory interoperability, the GBA risks becoming a set of "data islands," where legal incompatibilities undermine regional integration.[50] Mutual recognition arrangements, akin to adequacy findings or joint certification, could bridge these divides without requiring full harmonization of legal regimes. This fragmentation undermines the premise of the GBA as an integrated economic area. Data is as crucial a factor of production as goods, capital, or people in today's digital economy. Analogous to its initiatives aimed at facilitating the cross-border movement of people (e.g., through talent visa schemes) and goods (e.g., through customs streamlining), the Greater Bay Area is now subject to mounting pressure to dismantle or recalibrate regulatory and institutional impediments to the transboundary circulation of data. The comparative ease or difficulty of data movement can tilt decisions on where businesses locate their data centers, how they architect their IT systems, and which jurisdiction takes the lead in certain innovations (for example, a fintech platform might choose to base certain analytics in Hong Kong to leverage its freer data environment, but that comes with latency in pulling data from Shenzhen).

Local scholars and policymakers have increasingly called for a coordinated framework. For example, a recent study by Au and Witzleb (2024) highlights the legal disparities between Mainland, Hong Kong, and Macao and explicitly calls for a harmonized GBA data regime to bridge these gaps.[51] Zhang and Lin propose establishing a "three-tier" governance structure that links Mainland provincial authorities, the GBA as a regional bloc, and external jurisdictions in order to progressively align cross-border data flow rules. They argue this staged architecture would allow the GBA to function as a pilot zone for mutual recognition and rule convergence without

[50] Au, Adam K. and Witzleb, Normann (2024) 'Data Flows and Data Protection in the Greater Bay Area: The Need for a Coordinated Legal Framework'12 *Chinese Journal of Comparative Law* cxae013, https://doi.org/10.1093/cjcl/cxae013

[51] Ibid.

forcing premature full harmonization.[52] The next part of this article turns to what has been done so far to answer that call – the initial coordination measures and pilots within the GBA – evaluating their achievements and limitations.

GBA INSTITUTIONAL COORDINATION: MOUS, STANDARD CONTRACTS, AND PILOT PROJECTS

By 2023, it had become increasingly clear that reliance on comprehensive legislative harmonization for enabling data sharing in the GBA was unrealistic in the short to medium term, as statutory convergence could take years, if achievable at all. In this context, bespoke institutional arrangements were introduced to provide interim solutions. Two principal instruments emerged: first, governmental MoUs signalling administrative cooperation between jurisdictions; and second, the pilot "Standard Contract" mechanism, designed as a contractual vehicle to facilitate cross-boundary personal data transfers within the GBA.[53]

The GBA "Standard Contract" for Personal Data Transfers

In December 2023, following the Hong Kong–Mainland MoU earlier that year, the Cyberspace Administration of China (CAC) and Hong Kong's Innovation, Technology and Industry Bureau (ITIB) jointly introduced the Standard Contract for the Cross-boundary Flow of Personal Information within the GBA (hereinafter the "GBA Standard Contract" or "GBA SCC").[54] This instrument comprises a set of model contractual clauses, which enterprises may voluntarily adopt when transferring personal data between Guangdong Province and Hong Kong. Although modelled on the CAC's national standard contractual clauses under the Personal Information Protection Law (PIPL), the GBA SCC is specifically adapted to the intra-GBA context.

The clauses incorporate dual legal references: terms such as "personal data" are defined with reference to both Mainland and Hong Kong law, ensuring recognition of each side's fundamental legal concepts and principles. Parties are required to observe combined data security practices derived from the PIPL, Hong Kong's Personal Data (Privacy) Ordinance (PDPO), as well as international standards. Notably, execution of the GBA SCC is subject to mandatory filing with both Hong Kong and Guangdong authorities, thereby introducing a layer of parallel administrative oversight.

52 Zhang, Liang and Lin, Haoming 'On the Improvement Approach' supra note 6.

53 General Office of Guangdong Province People's Government, 'Notice on Issuing the "Digital Bay Area" Construction Three-Year Action Plan' (21 November 2023) available at: <https://www.gd.gov.cn/zwgk/wjk/qbwj/ybh/content/post_4287596.html>

54 Office of the Privacy Commissioner for Personal Data (Hong Kong), Guidance on Cross-boundary Data Transfer: Standard Contract for Cross-boundary Flow of Personal Information within the Guangdong–Hong Kong–Macao Greater Bay Area (Mainland, Hong Kong) (Dec 2023) 5-6. available at: <https://www.pcpd.org.hk/english/resources_centre/publications/files/standard_contract_gba.pdf>

This dual-filing requirement reflects its hybrid nature: contractual in form, but regulatory in function.

The pilot scheme was initially confined to selected industries, including financial services, credit information, and healthcare, and was voluntary. The intention was to establish a regulatory sandbox in which compliant enterprises could benefit from simplified transfer procedures. Where a Hong Kong company and a Shenzhen company executed and duly filed a GBA SCC, their transfers would *de facto* be treated as compliant. On the Hong Kong side, this would serve as a safeguard obviating the need for future reliance on the long-unenforced Section 33 of the PDPO. On the Mainland side, it would serve as an alternative to the CAC's full security assessment, provided that the transfer did not involve "important data" or otherwise high-risk categories. While welcomed as a pragmatic mechanism by industry stakeholders, commentators also highlighted its complexity: companies were compelled to engage with both legal systems simultaneously within a single instrument.[55]

Macao subsequently joined the initiative. Following the Mainland–Macao MoU of September 2024, a corresponding GBA SCC mechanism was introduced by late 2024 to govern transfers between Guangdong and Macao. Reflecting Macao's comparatively stricter regime, the Mainland–Macao version included additional procedural safeguards: in certain cases, notification to or approval by Macao's Office for Personal Data Protection (GPDP) was required to ensure compliance with the Personal Data Protection Act (PDPA). Nevertheless, Macao's accession marked the extension of the GBA contractual model across all three jurisdictions.

It should be emphasized that the GBA SCC does not amount to a legislative amendment. Rather, it operates in the interstices of existing law. The PIPL authorizes the CAC to designate standard contractual clauses for data export, and the GBA SCC may be regarded as a localized variant of that authority. Hong Kong's PDPO does not prohibit contractual mechanisms, thereby accommodating the arrangement, while Macao law permits transfers based on contracts subject to GPDP approval. Accordingly, the GBA SCC is best understood as a form of "soft law" instrument: an administrative workaround that establishes trust through contract, without the formality of treaty-making or legislative reform.

One concern relates to efficacy and early use. Within months of its launch, several dozen enterprises had filed GBA SCCs with Hong Kong and Guangdong authorities. Regulators established dedicated contact points for inquiries, and by mid-2024, Hong Kong's Digital Economy Development Office (the successor to OGCIO in this field) had issued detailed FAQs to guide implementation. A central limitation of the regime, however, is its territorial scope: it applies exclusively to transfers between the Mainland

[55] Gong, James and Ng, Wilfred, 'Save the Best for Last - All You Need to Know about the Standard Contract for GBA Data Transfers (Part I)' (*Bird & Bird Insights*, 29 Dec 2023) available at: <https://www.twobirds.com/en/insights/2023/china/part-1-all-you-need-to-know-about-the-standard-contract-for-gba-data-transfers>

and Hong Kong/Macao. Crucially, the clauses prohibit onward transfers outside the GBA unless the transfer separately satisfies the applicable national requirements for cross-border exports. For instance, personal data received by a Hong Kong entity from Guangdong under the GBA SCC may not subsequently be transmitted to servers in Singapore or to a parent company in the United States without fulfilling the relevant PIPL conditions. This restriction effectively creates a "GBA data enclave": intra-GBA flows are liberalized, but the region's external data borders remain tightly regulated. While defensible from a risk-control perspective, this design has raised concerns among multinational corporations, which fear operational fragmentation of their global data management systems.[56]

Another concern relates to enforceability. In theory, the GBA SCC provides for dispute resolution mechanisms, enabling parties to pursue contractual remedies through litigation or arbitration in the event of breach. In practice, however, the arrangement is deeply regulatory in character, making private enforcement unlikely. Instead, compliance is expected to be ensured primarily through administrative supervision: the CAC may sanction Mainland entities for PIPL violations, while Hong Kong's Privacy Commissioner retains powers to address non-compliance under the PDPO. The contract does not establish joint adjudicatory structures. Thus, enforcement remains dependent on domestic authorities' willingness to act.

Overall, the GBA SCC represents a novel experiment in contractual coordination and mutual recognition. While provisional and administratively fragile, it provides an unprecedented precedent: the Mainland's co-creation of a cross-border transfer mechanism with Special Administrative Regions. It may serve as a foundation for more formalized solutions in the future, such as mutual adequacy findings or treaty-based arrangements. The section in the Part below entitled 'Limitations of the Current Patchwork' will examine the structural limitations of this and other interim mechanisms in greater detail.

Cross-Boundary MoUs and Cooperative Oversight

Preceding and underpinning the standard contract were high-level Memoranda of Understanding. On June 29, 2023, Hong Kong's ITIB and the CAC signed the Memorandum of Understanding on Facilitating Cross-Boundary Data Flow within the Guangdong–Hong Kong–Macao Greater Bay Area. This MoU is a political commitment between the central authorities and Hong Kong to collaborate on data flow initiatives in the GBA. It was quickly hailed as a "policy breakthrough,"[57] setting the stage for subsequent

[56] Bird, Richard and Li, Fan, 'New Mechanism for Facilitating Cross-border Transfers of Personal Data between Mainland China and Hong Kong within the GBA' (*Freshfields TQ*, 3 Jan 2024) available at: <https://technologyquotient.freshfields.com/post/102iw72/new-mechanism-for-facilitating-cross-border-transfers-of-personal-data-between-ma>

[57] Innovation, Technology and Industry Bureau (Hong Kong), 'Facilitating Cross-boundary Data Flow within the Greater Bay Area', available at: <https://www.itb.gov.hk/en/facilitating-cross-boundary-data-flow/index.html>

technical measures. Similarly, on September 9, 2024, the CAC and Macao's Secretary for Economy and Finance signed a corresponding MoU to extend the cooperation to Macao. These MoUs are not legally binding instruments enforceable in court, but they serve as frameworks of intent. They outline principles such as ensuring data flows are "secure and orderly," pledging to establish contact points between authorities, and exploring mutual assistance in areas like cross-border data security administration.

The MoUs were crucial in providing political cover for the more detailed work. For example, after the June 2023 MoU, Hong Kong quickly formed an inter-agency task force (Digital Economy officials, the PCPD, etc.) to liaise with Guangdong's counterparts on implementation. Guangdong's provincial CAC office likewise took the lead on the Mainland side. Without the MoU's high-level green light, such joint efforts might have been stymied by jurisdictional caution. The MoUs also signaled to businesses that the governments were aware of the data issue and intended to mitigate it, which had a positive effect on business sentiment in the region.

Beyond personal data transfer contracts, the GBA coordination has spurred legal convergence initiatives in related areas. For example, Hong Kong and Mainland authorities have been improving mutual legal assistance mechanisms. In 2019, an arrangement was reached for reciprocal recognition and enforcement of civil judgments (covering many commercial matters) between Mainland and Hong Kong courts, which took effect in 2022. This doesn't directly address data, but it builds trust in cross-border legal dealings. Specific to data, one can envision extending these judicial cooperation moves to cover data disputes: for instance, perhaps a Hong Kong court judgment ordering a company to provide data to an individual could be enforced in Shenzhen, or a Mainland court's order regarding data misuse could be recognized in Hong Kong. The MoUs don't explicitly create such channels, but they create an expectation that agencies will help each other within existing legal limits.

One interesting development in late 2024 was a case in the Guangzhou Internet Court involving cross-border data transfer, often cited as the first such case under PIPL.[58] In the Yue 0192 Min Chu No.6486 case (decided in September 2023, published August 2024), a Mainland Chinese individual sued a French-headquartered hotel group for exporting his personal data to overseas entities without proper consent. The court strictly applied PIPL, ruling that while transfers necessary for contract performance (to book a hotel room abroad) were permissible, other transfers (for marketing or global management purposes) required separate consent and were unlawful in its absence. The court found that "bundled" consent via a general privacy policy did not satisfy PIPL's requirement of specific, separate consent for cross-border data sharing.[59] While this case did not involve Hong Kong or Macao, it set a tone for how Chinese courts may view unauthorized data exports. It suggests that if a similar issue arose

[58] (2022) Yue 0192 Min Chu No. 6486.

[59] Kennedy and Lai 'Guangzhou Internet Court decision' supra note 44.

involving a GBA transfer (say a Shenzhen user's personal data ends up in a Hong Kong company's database and is misused there), a Mainland court might assert jurisdiction and enforce PIPL requirements even over the Hong Kong party. This underscores the importance of having pre-arranged frameworks like the GBA SCC to avoid such legal conflicts. Legal commentary highlights that this case reflects the judiciary's willingness to apply PIPL strictly, reinforcing the need for contractual and institutional safeguards in cross-border scenarios.[60] It also raises the value of possibly formal judicial agreements for data cases, something not yet realized, but conceivable as a next step (akin to a regional CLOUD Act-type arrangement for government data requests, or an extension of the judgment enforcement arrangement to privacy injunctions or orders).

There have also been discussions about professional convergence – for instance, enabling Hong Kong data privacy professionals or lawyers to be recognized in the Mainland and vice versa, to facilitate smoother compliance consulting across the GBA. Additionally, to support cross-border e-discovery and law enforcement data requests, stakeholders have proposed clearer protocols. The 2023 MoU nods generally to "strengthening cooperation," which can be interpreted to encourage such endeavours even if details are sparse.

Limitations of the Current Patchwork

Despite these promising steps, the GBA's current coordination mechanisms have significant limitations. First, as noted, the MoUs and the GBA Standard Contract are soft-law and pilot measures; they do not override or amend the underlying statutes in each jurisdiction. PIPL still, on its face, treats Hong Kong and Macao as outside of China (i.e. as foreign for data export purposes), and Hong Kong's PDPO still has dormant Section 33 on its books which could theoretically be activated. The GBA SCC arrangement is an administrative facilitation, not a binding international agreement or legislation. Their legal authority derives from administrative approval, not statutory mandate. This reliance on soft-law[61] mirrors patterns in other transnational data arrangements, where political or constitutional constraints preclude formal treaties. This means the entire arrangement could be revisited or withdrawn if authorities changed their approach or if a security incident prompted a clampdown. In contrast, a formal treaty or a national law (such as an NPC Standing Committee decision carving out the GBA) would provide more certainty and durability. Without a statutory or treaty-based framework, pilot arrangements risk reversal in the face of political or security incidents, as seen in other transnational data regimes.[62]

[60] Ibid.

[61] Abbott, Kenneth W. and Snidal, Duncan (2000) 'Hard and Soft Law in International Governance' 54(3) *International Organization* 421, 423.

[62] Au and Witzleb 'Data Flows and Data Protection' supra note 50.

Secondly, as mentioned, the GBA SCC initiative functions as a pilot arrangement: within the GBA, it provides companies with a contractual path to move data more freely, while the underlying laws of Mainland China, Hong Kong and Macao continue to treat such transfers as outbound. The arrangement is best understood as a policy experiment rather than a legal redefinition of 'cross-border'. For businesses that operate globally, this enclave approach solves one problem but creates another, because data might circulate within GBA but still face hurdles leaving China via Hong Kong. Some companies might decide it's simpler to keep certain data entirely outside the GBA to avoid these complexities, an outcome that could marginalize the GBA's role as a data hub.

Third, key systemic differences remain unresolved by these measures. China's national security laws (for example, the PRC National Security Law imposed on Hong Kong in 2020, and the Mainland's Counter-Espionage Law as amended in 2023) cast long shadows. A business considering consolidating its regional data in Hong Kong might worry that Mainland authorities could demand access under broad national security mandates; conversely, a Mainland entity might worry that data handed to a Hong Kong partner could be accessed by Hong Kong or even foreign authorities. These trust issues go beyond what a contract can solve – they touch on sovereignty and governance at the highest level. The MoUs did not create new legal protocols for government-to-government data sharing or for handling national security requests; they rely on cooperation "within legal limits." True integration in the long run might require deeper arrangements, such as a bespoke cross-border data request mechanism among GBA governments (imagine something akin to a regional Mutual Legal Assistance Treaty or a narrow CLOUD Act agreement for the GBA).

On the technical side, infrastructural and interoperability challenges persist. Mainland China's internet environment is separated by the Great Firewall, meaning cross-boundary network traffic may be subject to latency or filtering. Companies often resort to dedicated leased lines or approved VPN connections to ensure stable connectivity between, say, a server in Shenzhen and one in Hong Kong – solutions that work but add cost and require regulatory permission (unapproved VPNs are illegal in China). There are reports of telecom authorities working on better direct cross-border links for the GBA, but until those materialize, the physical layer of data exchange remains less seamless than the legal agreements would hope. Additionally, differences in technical standards (e.g. encryption protocols, data format standards) can impede integration of IT systems across the border; none of the legal arrangements directly address these issues.

Another limitation is that institutional fragmentation is still largely intact. Each jurisdiction's regulator operates under its own mandate and there is no unified or jointly empowered regulatory body. The MoUs set up contact points and the notion of cooperation, but we do not yet have anything like a GBA-wide data authority or a binding dispute resolution body. If a company feels aggrieved under the GBA scheme – for example, if a Hong Kong company believes a Mainland partner misused data or a

Mainland regulator unfairly blocked a transfer – there isn't a clear one-stop forum to resolve it. They might have to petition both the CAC and the PCPD and hope for a coordinated response. This gap is precisely why, in the penultimate part of this Chapter, we will propose creating a GBA Data Governance Board or similar mechanism.

Lastly, some observers view the GBA measures as a form of political experiment that could be recalibrated. By giving Hong Kong and Macao a slight privilege in data flows, Beijing may be testing the SARs' trustworthiness and capacity. If the SARs demonstrate robust enforcement and no major incidents, the experiment could be expanded; if problems occur, the central government could reverse course and tighten data controls again. Internationally, the GBA will be watched as a precedent: if China can trust Hong Kong and Macao with freer data exchange, might it one day extend similar openness to, say, jurisdictions that sign bilateral data accords with China? Or is this strictly a one-off within the One Country framework? There is speculation that China's ultimate aim might be to craft its own sphere of data partnerships (some speak of an "Asia data sphere" or building blocks for China's own adequacy arrangements with friendly nations).[63] The GBA, being unique, might not directly translate abroad, but it is indicative of China's direction.

In sum, the current GBA framework is a pioneering patchwork: it marks real progress and provides practical fixes within a constrained scope, but it is not a comprehensive or permanent solution. It buys time and provides a learning experience. The next parts turn to lessons from beyond and principles of governance that can inform how the GBA approach could evolve into a sturdier, more rule-based arrangement.

COMPARATIVE MODELS: LESSONS FROM THE EU AND THE US

The challenges China faces in the GBA are not entirely *sui generis*; other jurisdictions have long grappled with how to regulate cross-border data flows. The two predominant models in the world can be loosely represented by the European Union and the United States, each offering instructive lessons. The EU has developed a high-standard, comprehensive regime (the GDPR) that seeks to export its privacy values abroad through adequacy decisions and contractual clauses, underpinned by strong oversight. The US, by contrast, has a patchwork of sector-specific privacy laws and generally promotes free data flows, relying on market forces and post hoc measures (with national security exceptions often invoked to access data). The inclusion of the United States in this comparative inquiry is not meant to suggest that the GBA should emulate the US model wholesale. Rather, the US illustrates how a jurisdiction without a comprehensive privacy statute manages cross-border data flows through a combination of sectoral rules,[64] enforcement by

[63] Greenleaf, Graham (2021) China's Completed Personal Information Protection Law: Rights Plus Cyber-security 172 *Privacy Laws & Business International Report* 20.

[64] Paul M Schwartz and Karl-Nikolaus Peifer (2017) 'Transatlantic Data Privacy Law' 106

the Federal Trade Commission,[65] and voluntary certification frameworks such as the APEC CBPR system.[66] These mechanisms resonate with the GBA context: like the US, the GBA is a fragmented regulatory space that must find pragmatic, interoperable solutions without full legal harmonization. The comparison therefore highlights functional equivalence in regulatory challenges, rather than formal convergence in statutory design. The first section of this Part discusses the EU's approach, the second analyses the US approach, and the final distils lessons for procedural legitimacy and interoperability that the GBA initiative could adopt.

GDPR Adequacy and Standard Contractual Clauses (EU Model)

The European Union's General Data Protection Regulation (GDPR) is widely regarded as the gold standard for personal data protection. Crucially for cross-border data flows, the GDPR provides an established mechanism whereby the European Commission can determine that a non-EU country provides an "adequate" level of data protection, thereby allowing personal data to flow from the EU to that country freely (just as it would within the EU). To date, the EU has granted adequacy decisions to a number of countries (including, for example, Japan, New Zealand, Canada for commercial data, South Korea, and recently the UK post-Brexit, among others). The EU's approach also exemplifies the so-called "Brussels Effect" - the EU's ability to export its regulatory norms globally by leveraging the size and attractiveness of its internal market. Through GDPR, the EU has set a *de facto* global benchmark for personal data protection, prompting even non-EU jurisdictions to align with its standards to maintain trade and data flows.[67] China notably does not have such status – in fact, as scholars have pointed out, the Chinese data protection framework would currently fall short of EU adequacy on multiple counts, such as the broad powers of state authorities to access data and the lack of an independent overarching data protection authority.[68] This is one reason Hong Kong and Macao maintaining distinct systems is strategically important: Hong Kong's prospects of an EU adequacy finding may be stronger than those of Mainland China, owing to its statutory PDPO framework and its track record of aligning with international data-protection practices. However, no such finding has yet been granted. Any potential role as a 'gateway' for EU-GBA data flows therefore remains hypothetical rather than established.

Georgetown Law Journal 147.

[65] Daniel J Solove and Woodrow Hartzog (2014) 'The FTC and the New Common Law of Privacy' 114 *Columbia Law Review* 583.

[66] APEC, Cross-Border Privacy Rules (CBPR) System Policies, Rules and Guidelines (rev 2019) available at: https://cbprs.org/wp-content/uploads/2019/11/4.-CBPR-Policies-Rules-and-Guidelines-Revised-For-Posting-3-16-updated-1709-2019.pdf

[67] Bradford, Anu (2020) *The Brussels Effect*, Oxford University Press at 2-3.

[68] Panek 'Adequacy' supra note 23.

When adequacy is absent, the GDPR permits other transfer mechanisms, chiefly Standard Contractual Clauses (SCCs) - template clauses approved by the European Commission that companies can sign to provide contractual assurances of data protection when exporting data. SCCs have been widely used by companies around the world dealing with EU data. However, a major lesson from the EU is that contracts alone are not always sufficient. In the landmark Schrems II case (Court of Justice of the EU, 2020), the court invalidated the EU–US "Privacy Shield" (an executive agreement that had allowed freer EU–US data flows) and cast doubt on SCC-based transfers to the US, because US surveillance laws meant that the contractual promises could not overcome the fundamental mismatch in legal frameworks.[69] The CJEU insisted that data exporters and regulators must verify whether foreign law undermines the protection of the transferred data, and if so, transfers may have to stop or require supplementary measures. In short, contractual devices like SCCs cannot cure fundamental deficiencies in a recipient country's public-law safeguards; sustainable interoperability depends as much on credible limits to state access as on private undertakings by data exporters.[70] Schrems II underscores that if there is a serious gap in systemic trust – for example, if one jurisdiction's laws allow government agencies unfettered access to data – then even robust legal tools like SCCs may fail to legitimize transfers. The relevance to the GBA is apparent: the Mainland and Hong Kong/Macao have to build mutual trust and possibly converge on baseline standards if they want their "contractual" solution (the GBA SCC) to be durable. Otherwise, one might analogize, Hong Kong would fear that Mainland state access powers could undercut any contractual promises of privacy, much as the EU feared US surveillance powers undercutting Privacy Shield.[71]

Another key feature of the EU model is the presence of independent supervisory authorities in each member state and a consistency mechanism to resolve disputes (the European Data Protection Board).[72] This multilateral governance ensures that no single country can unilaterally lower standards without scrutiny, and that individuals have recourse to an authority if their data travels abroad. While China's governance structure is very different, the principle of having checks and balances and cooperative oversight mechanisms is instructive. The idea floated in next section's discussion of a GBA Data Governance Board in some ways borrows from the notion of a supra-national or inter-regional body that can coordinate and oversee cross-border issues, akin to how the EDPB oversees EU-wide issues.

69 Case C-311/18, Data Protection Commissioner v Facebook Ireland Ltd & Schrems (Schrems II) [2020] supra note 35, para 133.

70 European Data Protection Board, *Recommendations 01/2020 on Measures that Supplement Transfer Tools to Ensure Compliance with the EU Level of Protection of Personal Data* (final, 18 June 2021); Zalnieriute, Monika (2023) 'Data Transfers after Schrems II: The EU–US Disagreements over Data Privacy and National Security' 55 *Vanderbilt Journal of Transnational Law* 1.

71 Au and Witzleb 'Data Flows and Data Protection' supra note 50.

72 General Data Protection Regulation (EU) 2016/679 art 68, recital 139.

Finally, the EU's experience shows the value of clear definitions and scope. The GDPR unambiguously defines what constitutes an "international transfer" and applies its rules essentially to any personal data leaving the EU. China's laws have similarly broad theoretical scopes (PIPL covers any personal information leaving mainland China), but the One Country, Two Systems scenario muddles the concept of "international" transfer: Are Hong Kong and Macao "internal" or "external"? The GBA experiments are effectively saying: for GBA internal purposes, treat these as not foreign. Drawing inspiration from the EU, China could move toward formally declaring certain regions as having an adequate status – effectively treating Hong Kong and Macao as "domestic" or safe territories for data. In EU terms, that would resemble an adequacy finding by China for its own SARs. Foreign commentators have argued that China's data laws need such flexibility; for instance, Witzleb and Au (2024) advocate developing a coordinated legal framework for the GBA precisely to bridge the gap between the different systems.[73]

US Sectoral Pluralism and Security Exceptions (US Model)

Compared with the European Union, the United States adopts a markedly different-indeed almost inverse-approach to the regulation of cross-border data flows. Unlike the EU, which relies on a single comprehensive framework under the General Data Protection Regulation (GDPR), the United States has not enacted an omnibus federal privacy statute. Instead, the US regulatory landscape is characterized by a fragmented, sector-specific regime: federal legislation governs discrete areas such as health information (the Health Insurance Portability and Accountability Act, HIPAA),[74] financial data (the Gramm-Leach-Bliley Act, GLBA),[75] and children's online privacy (the Children's Online Privacy Protection Act, COPPA).[76] In recent years, certain states have supplemented this patchwork by adopting more general privacy statutes of their own, most prominently California's Consumer Privacy Act (CCPA)[77] and its subsequent amendment, the California Privacy Rights Act (CPRA).[78] Nevertheless, the United States continues to lack a single, comprehensive federal standard for personal data protection.[79] As a result, the US imposes no blanket restrictions on data exports - generally, companies in the US can send data abroad freely unless a specific law (or export control, or sanction) prohibits it. The prevailing philosophy has been

[73] Ibid.

[74] Health Insurance Portability and Accountability Act 1996, 42 USC ch 7 (2018).

[75] Gramm–Leach–Bliley Act 1999, 15 USC ch 94 (2018).

[76] Children's Online Privacy Protection Act 1998, 15 USC §§ 6501-6506 (2018).

[77] California Consumer Privacy Act 2018, Cal Civ Code §§ 1798.100-1798.199 (2018).

[78] California Privacy Rights Act 2020, Cal Civ Code §§ 1798.100-1798.199.100 (2020).

[79] Paul M Schwartz and Karl-Nikolaus Peifer supra note 64.

to champion the free flow of information as part of free trade and the open internet.

However, the US model is not one of pure laxity; rather, it handles issues through other mechanisms. For privacy concerns, it relies heavily on *post hoc* enforcement (the Federal Trade Commission can punish companies for privacy misrepresentations or security failures, for instance) and on industry self-regulation.[80] To bridge differences with stricter jurisdictions, there have been bilateral and multilateral arrangements. The most notable were the EU–US arrangements: the Safe Harbor (2000), then Privacy Shield (2016), which allowed certified US companies to receive EU data by pledging to follow EU-equivalent principles. Privacy Shield, however, was invalidated by the EU's Schrems II decision as noted (due to US government surveillance access).[81] In response, the US and EU negotiated a new "Data Privacy Framework" in 2023, attempting to cure the defects by introducing more safeguards on US government access and a redress mechanism via a special Data Protection Review Court in the US Whether the new framework will survive legal challenge remains to be seen, but it reflects the US approach of diplomatic and executive solutions rather than baseline legislation.[82]

The US is also a key player in the APEC Cross-Border Privacy Rules (CBPR) system, a voluntary certification scheme among Asia-Pacific economies to facilitate cross-border data transfers through commonly recognized privacy practices.[83] Hong Kong is a member of APEC and has endorsed the CBPR system (though not fully implemented it yet). Notably, China (Mainland) is an APEC member but has not joined CBPR. For the GBA, the APEC CBPR is interesting because Hong Kong's participation could potentially act as a bridge between Chinese companies and an international framework. If, for example, a Shenzhen company obtained CBPR certification via Hong Kong's system, it might ease doing business with other APEC economies. This is speculative at this stage, but it's an example of leveraging US-backed frameworks as part of a broader strategy.

Where the U.S. regime most closely converges with China's is in the domain of national security and law enforcement. The U.S. government claims robust powers to access data for security purposes, even extraterritorially. The Clarifying Lawful Overseas Use of Data (CLOUD) Act of 2018 requires U.S.-based service providers to comply with valid U.S. court orders for data, regardless of whether the data is stored domestically or

[80] Daniel J Solove and Woodrow Hartzog supra note 65.

[81] Case C-311/18, Data Protection Commissioner v Facebook Ireland Ltd & Schrems (Schrems II) [2020] supra note 35.

[82] Commission Implementing Decision (EU) 2023/1795 of 10 July 2023 pursuant to Regulation (EU) 2016/679 on the adequate level of protection of personal data under the EU–US Data Privacy Framework [2023] OJ L 231/1.

[83] APEC supra note 66.

abroad.[84] Additionally, Section 702 of the Foreign Intelligence Surveillance Act (FISA) authorizes surveillance programs that may incidentally capture data of non-U.S. persons located abroad.[85] These authorities were central to the CJEU's concerns in Schrems II. As Greenleaf observes, the U.S. thus asserts its security prerogatives within an otherwise open, market-oriented system, whereas China adopts a state-managed, approval-based approach where national security review is embedded in the data transfer mechanism itself.[86] In other words, the difference is that the US asserts security prerogatives within an otherwise open system, whereas China does so within a more state-managed framework. From a GBA perspective, this comparison is a reminder that no system is absolute: even the "free flow" US erects barriers when security is at stake.

Implications for the GBA: Interoperability and Trust

From the EU model, the GBA can learn the importance of mutual recognition founded on strong baseline guarantees. The EU's internal data federalism works because each member trusts that the others enforce the same high standards and that there are remedies if something goes wrong. Translating that to the GBA, it suggests aiming for a situation where Hong Kong, Macao, and Guangdong can trust each other's data safeguards. That might mean, in the long run, raising Hong Kong's and Macao's standards further (or at least making them transparently equivalent in effect to the Mainland's requirements, and vice versa). It might also mean formalizing the current pilot into law – e.g. a GBA Data Agreement that has status in each jurisdiction's legal system, not just an MoU.

From the US model, the lesson is to consider pragmatic tools for interoperability. The US did not overhaul its system to appease the EU; instead, it found workarounds (Privacy Shield, Data Privacy Framework, APEC CBPR). The GBA likewise might not unify laws overnight, but it can develop tools to bridge gaps – like the GBA Standard Contract itself, or future mutual certification schemes (as will be proposed). Experience from the EU and APEC suggests that such schemes work best when combined with clear baseline standards, mutual audits, and enforcement cooperation between regulators. Under the GDPR, certification works as a form of "monitored self-regulation" that only delivers interoperability when there are clear baseline criteria, accredited bodies, and supervisory oversight.[87] Also, the US experience cautions that executive agreements can be fragile

[84] Clarifying Lawful Overseas Use of Data (CLOUD) Act, 18 USC § 2713 (2018).

[85] Foreign Intelligence Surveillance Act 1978, 50 USC § 1881a (2018).

[86] Greenleaf, Graham (2021) 'China's Completed Personal Information Protection Law: Rights Plus Cyber-security' 172 *Privacy Laws & Business International Report* 20-23.

[87] Lachaud, Eric (2020) 'What GDPR Tells about Certification' 38 *Computer Law & Security Review* 105457; See also European Data Protection Board, 'Guidelines 1/2018 on certification and identifying certification criteria in accordance with Articles 42 and 43 of the Regulation' (Final version, 4 June 2019) available at: <https://www.edpb.europa.eu/our-work-tools/our-documents/guidelines/guidelines-12018-certification-and-identifying_en>.

(Privacy Shield's downfall is instructive); thus, whatever the GBA builds should be resilient to legal scrutiny and have buy-in from stakeholders to avoid collapse at the first test.

Finally, both models underscore the centrality of administrative and judicial redress mechanisms. The EU has them in abundance; the US is now creating some (like the Data Privacy Framework's redress court) to satisfy the EU's concerns. In the GBA context, providing channels for companies or individuals to raise concerns and have them addressed across borders will bolster legitimacy and trust. The next section's discussion delves into that aspect–the current state of administrative justice in the three jurisdictions – which will lay the groundwork for the reform proposals in the Part below entitled 'Policy Proposals: Toward an Integrated GBA Data Governance Architecture'.

ADMINISTRATIVE JUSTICE AND PROCEDURAL GAPS

Building on the conception of "administrative justice" introduced earlier, this Part examines how principles of fairness, transparency, and accountability are operationalized in practice within the GBA's multi-jurisdictional data governance framework. In the cross-border context, administrative justice entails not only the design of rules but also the procedures through which regulatory decisions—such as approving or denying a data export—are made, reviewed, and contested. The central concern here is whether affected stakeholders, including businesses, individuals, and government bodies, have access to clear, impartial, and effective channels of participation and redress. This Part assesses the current state of administrative and procedural fairness in each relevant jurisdiction (Mainland China, Hong Kong, Macao) and identifies gaps that become most acute in cross-boundary scenarios where ordinary domestic processes are insufficient. The analysis begins by examining Mainland China's mechanisms, followed by an assessment of those in the SARs, before exploring the cross-border dimension and its unique challenges.

Appeals, Transparency, and Review in Mainland China

Mainland China's data regulation enforcement is characterized by strong administrative discretion with limited external checks. Under laws like the CSL, DSL, and PIPL, the CAC and other regulators (such as industry-specific agencies for certain data categories) wield significant power to approve or deny data transfer requests, investigate violations, and impose penalties. On paper, there are provisions for administrative reconsideration and judicial review of agency decisions – for example, if the CAC denies a security assessment application for a data export, the data exporter can apply for a reconsideration by the CAC (essentially asking the agency to re-examine its own decision), and beyond that the company could theoretically file an administrative lawsuit in a People's Court arguing that the CAC's decision was unlawful or exceeded its authority. In practice, however, such challenges are exceedingly rare.[88] By contrast, under the EU model, individuals have explicit rights to lodge a complaint with a supervisory authority and to an effective judicial remedy.[89] Mainland legal scholars have argued that even where national security is implicated, the CAC's denial of a data export request is an administrative act that, in principle, should be open to judicial review or administrative reconsideration. They call for legislative clarification to ensure that procedural rights are not entirely eclipsed by security concerns.[90] To date, there is no public record of any company suing the CAC over a cross-border data transfer decision, or even any known case of a formal reconsideration request. This could indicate either that companies are generally complying (perhaps self-censoring their transfer requests to avoid rejection) or that there is a perceived futility in challenging the authority on sensitive matters like data exports (which tie into national security).

Chinese courts, while increasingly assertive in some civil and commercial areas, remain deferential to executive agencies on matters implicating national security or major state interests. The broad and vague language of the laws (e.g., what constitutes an effect on "national security or public interest" justifying a transfer denial) grants agencies like CAC wide latitude. Courts are unlikely to second-guess these determinations, especially given the political sensitivities. *De facto*, a CAC decision to bar a particular data transfer is final. An affected company's recourse is more likely through informal or political channels–for instance, lobbying through an industry association, or seeking intervention from a higher government authority—rather than through a judicial remedy.

Transparency in administrative decision-making by Mainland authorities has historically been limited, though incremental improvements can be observed. In April 2025, the Cyberspace Administration of China (CAC) for the first time released summary statistics on cross-border data export security assessments, indicating how many applications were approved or denied. According to the published figures, of 298 security assessment submissions, 44 involved "important data," of which 7 were rejected while the remainder were approved, often subject to conditions.[91] Such disclosure represents a welcome step toward greater transparency, enabling businesses to better understand the overall contours of regulatory practice and demonstrating that the process is not a mere formality. However,

[88] Administrative Reconsideration Law of the PRC (adopted 29 April 2023, effective 1 January 2024) arts 2,3; Administrative Litigation Law of the PRC (adopted 1 November 2014, amended 29 April 2023) arts 12, 13.

[89] Regulation (EU) 2016/679 (GDPR), arts 77-79; Charter of Fundamental Rights of the European Union, art 47; see also art 8(3).

[90] Zhang, Linghan (2023) 'Research On the Legal Nature and Remedy Approach of Security Assessment of Outbound Data Transfers' 1 *Administrative Law Review* 45-61.

[91] Cyberspace Administration of China, 'Q&A on data export security management policies (April 2025)' (9 April 2025) available at: <https://www.cac.gov.cn/2025-04/09/c_1745906286623776.htm>

the information currently released remains insufficient. Crucially, the CAC has not provided any reasoning for why the seven applications were denied. Without clarification—whether the grounds concerned excessive data volumes, transfers to jurisdictions deemed high-risk, or deficiencies in contractual safeguards—regulated entities face uncertainty in adjusting compliance strategies. Unlike the European Union, where transparency is reinforced through obligations to publish at least redacted reasoning (e.g. GDPR recital 129) and the practice of supervisory authorities such as the EDPB and CNIL in releasing binding decisions or sanction notices,[92] the CAC has not yet institutionalized the publication of anonymized case summaries or explanatory guidance. Establishing such a practice would significantly enhance both predictability for businesses and the perceived legitimacy of regulatory decisions, thereby embedding procedural fairness more firmly into China's data governance regime.

A major procedural challenge is the vagueness of key standards such as "national security" and "public interest." These catch-all concepts allow intervention in almost any scenario, leaving companies uncertain about compliance.[93] The CAC has issued guidelines listing factors for security assessments (for example, whether the transfer is necessary for the business purpose, the volume of data relative to that purpose, and the sensitivity of the data, etc.), which brings some *ex ante* structure.[94] Moreover, the 2024 Provisions on Promoting and Regulating Cross-Border Data Flows clarified that data will not be treated as "important" unless officially designated as such, meaning companies are no longer expected to pre-emptively categorize their data as important absent government notification.[95] These measures represent incremental improvements in clarity.

Still, from a due process perspective, once a decision is made, there is effectively no independent platform to contest it. CAC's internal re-assessment procedure is the only option, and its outcome is final; judicial review is not meaningfully available.[96] Thus, Mainland China's model continues to emphasize substantive security control over procedural fairness. Authorities expect trust that they will make balanced decisions, but affected parties are not institutionally empowered to participate in or challenge those decisions in any substantive way. For the Greater Bay Area (GBA), this raises concerns: if a Guangdong company's data transfer to Hong Kong is blocked by the CAC, it has little recourse, which may deter

[92] Regulation (EU) 2016/679 (GDPR), recital 129; See also European Data Protection Board, 'Binding Decisions' available at: https://www.edpb.europa.eu/our-work-tools/consistency-findings/binding-decisions_en; see also CNIL, 'The sanctions issued by the CNIL' (2 January 2025) available at: <https://cnil.fr/en/investigation-powers-cnil/sanctions-issued-cnil>

[93] Tsz Hin Tan (2024) 'National Security as the Trump Card: Assessing China's Legal Regime on Cross-Border Data Transfer' 33 *Information & Communications Technology Law* 368-383.

[94] Cyberspace Administration of China supra note 91.

[95] Cyberspace Administration of China supra note 14.

[96] Cyberspace Administration of China supra note 91.

firms from relying on the GBA transfer schemes unless other procedural assurances are introduced.[97]

The SARs: Participation Rights and Oversight Mechanisms

Hong Kong and Macao, each with their own legal systems, generally offer more in terms of formal appeal and oversight channels in data regulation – albeit within their jurisdictions only.

In Hong Kong, if the Privacy Commissioner (PCPD) issues an enforcement notice to a company (for example, directing it to stop transferring data to a certain place without proper safeguards), the affected company has a clear path to appeal: it can take the case to the Administrative Appeals Board (AAB). The AAB is an independent quasi-judicial body chaired by legally qualified individuals, which will hold a hearing, consider evidence, and has the power to confirm, vary, or cancel the PCPD's decision.[98] If either the company or the PCPD is unhappy with the AAB's ruling, they can further seek judicial review in the High Court on points of law. This multi-tiered review system ensures that regulatory decisions are not unchecked–companies have 'their day in court'. Likewise, individuals in Hong Kong who feel the PCPD mishandled their complaint (say, refused to investigate a claim of data misuse) can also appeal to the AAB. These mechanisms bolster accountability: the PCPD knows its actions can be scrutinized, which likely encourages thorough reasoning in its decisions.

Hong Kong's tradition of transparency also means that PCPD decisions and case notes are often published (with identities anonymized), and public consultations accompany significant changes (as seen in the discussions over introducing mandatory data breach notification, or the consultation exercises on whether to implement Section 33). Stakeholders–from business chambers to privacy advocacy groups–thus have avenues to voice their views in the policymaking process. This consultative culture, rooted in Hong Kong's broader administrative and legal traditions, fosters a sense of legitimacy even when the law remains static (as in the case of Section 33 deliberations).

In Macao, the system is somewhat different due to its civil law framework. The GPDP's decisions (for instance, denying an authorization for an overseas transfer, or imposing a fine on a company for violating the PDPA) can be appealed to the courts – specifically, to the Administrative Court which reviews administrative acts. Macao's courts are separate from Mainland courts and have shown independence; one could expect them to objectively assess if GPDP acted within the law. The volume of publicly known cases is low (Macao's small market and generally conservative

97 Xie, Taojun and Liu, Jingting and Sengstschmid, Ulrike and Ge, Yixuan (2023) "Navigating Cross-Border Data Transfer Policies: The Case of China", Asia Competitiveness Institute Research Paper, available at <http://dx.doi.org/10.2139/ssrn.4408947>

98 Privacy Commissioner for Personal Data (PCPD), 'Administrative Appeals Board's Decisions', available at: <https://www.pcpd.org.hk/english/enforcement/decisions/decisions_detail.html>

business environment mean few test cases), but the framework for appeal exists and is analogous to how one would challenge any other administrative decision in Macao.

Additionally, Macao's PDPA includes internal procedural requirements – for example, a data controller seeking to export data must file an application or notice with the GPDP, which implies the GPDP must formally respond or grant permission. In practice, the GPDP has issued opinions clarifying the documentation and contractual clauses expected for authorization, aligning them closely with EU-style safeguards.[99] These interactions generate a paper trail and implicitly allow the data controller to present justifications. If GPDP were to refuse, that refusal would be a written decision that can be taken to court. So, while Macao's law is stricter, it is also procedurally orderly in a classical rule-of-law sense.

Cross-border complication:

Neither Hong Kong's nor Macao's review mechanisms, however, can directly address a Mainland authority's action. If a Hong Kong company is aggrieved that the CAC in Guangdong stalled its data transfer, complaining to the PCPD or Hong Kong courts does nothing – Hong Kong bodies have no jurisdiction over Mainland officials. Likewise, Macao's court cannot review a decision of the CAC or a Guangdong agency. This fragmentation means that, in a cross-border context, the normal oversight each system provides internally doesn't extend to the joint space. The section below discusses this gap further.

Cross-Boundary Coordination and Gaps in Redress

At present, if a dispute or issue arises from a GBA data transfer, there is no formal joint dispute resolution or appeals process. Without a joint dispute resolution body, cross-border frameworks tend to rely on informal diplomacy, which can leave private parties without effective remedies.[100] The MoUs established points of contact but not a mechanism for jointly adjudicating disagreements. For example, imagine a scenario: A Shenzhen company transfers data to a Hong Kong partner under a GBA Standard Contract, but the Guangdong CAC later issues an order halting the transfer citing national security concerns. The Hong Kong partner believes this is unfounded and that it is complying with all terms. What can it do? It cannot appeal to the Hong Kong AAB about the CAC's action, nor obviously can it sue CAC in a Mainland court with any real prospect. The Mainland company also would find no luck challenging CAC, as noted. The MoU would perhaps allow Hong Kong officials to inquire or mediate informally, but that is not certain.

[99] For instance, see Office for Personal Data Protection (Macao), 'Opinion No.02/P/2013 - School A transfers data outside the Macao SAR' (2013) available at: <https://www.dspdp.gov.mo/file/Opinion/0002-P-2013-GPDP-EN.PDF>

[100] Greenleaf 'Personal Data Localization and Sovereignty supra note 50 at 17-18.

This example illustrates a procedural void: cross-border arrangements need cross-border oversight. The GBA initiatives so far have sidestepped this by hoping that such conflicts won't arise often or will be handled through good-faith coordination. But as data flows increase, the likelihood of disagreements grows. One potential remedy is to set up a bilateral or trilateral panel to handle GBA data disputes – perhaps an arbitral body or a joint committee that can hear complaints from companies. This is among the proposals to be explored in next Part entitled "Policy proposals: toward an integrated GBAdata governance architecture". It is admittedly sensitive, since any formal role for Hong Kong or Macao officials in reviewing Mainland decisions (or vice versa) bumps into sovereignty issues. However, one could frame it as an internal collaborative mechanism given the GBA's unique status.

Another cross-border issue is enforcement of rights for individuals. Suppose a Mainland individual wants to exercise data subject rights regarding data that went to Hong Kong. Under PIPL, they have rights, but PIPL technically doesn't run in Hong Kong. Under PDPO, if that Hong Kong company collected the data from Mainland via the GBA contract, PDPO rights apply (which are similar, but not identical, and enforcement differs). There is currently no one-stop way for that individual to complain or get relief without navigating two systems. A person could complain to the PCPD if it's about the Hong Kong company, or to CAC if they think the issue is the transfer itself – but CAC might say, 'we allowed the transfer via the contract, so no issue under our law,' while PCPD might say "the individual isn't a Hong Kong resident or didn't directly give data here, etc." This scenario has not been tested yet, but one can foresee confusion.

The Guangzhou court case discussed earlier (where a Mainland individual sued a foreign company for overseas transfers) suggests Mainland courts are willing to assert jurisdiction if Chinese individuals' data protection rights are violated by cross-border movement. If that approach were applied to Hong Kong (i.e., a Mainland court claiming authority over a Hong Kong data recipient on grounds of protecting a Mainland citizen's PIPL rights), it would spark a jurisdictional conflict. Hong Kong courts would certainly not concede that easily, and the One Country, Two Systems principle would be strained.

All this points to a critical theme: the need for inter-jurisdictional administrative justice frameworks. How can we ensure that a decision made in one part of the GBA that affects parties in another part can be contested or reviewed in a fair manner? Right now, the answer is unclear.

In practice so far, cooperation has relied on goodwill and case-by-case coordination. For example, if an issue arises, the expectation (per the MoU) is that the authorities will consult each other and try to resolve it amicably. This might work for minor hiccups, but as a governance model it lacks predictability and neutrality.[101]

[101] OECD, *Recommendation of the Council concerning Cross-Border Co-operation in the Enforcement of Laws Protecting Privacy* (12 June 2007); APEC, *Cross-Border Privacy Rules (CBPR)*

In summary, Mainland China exercises strong regulatory control but provides comparatively limited opportunities for external review, while Hong Kong and Macao maintain internal review mechanisms that cannot extend beyond their jurisdictions. As a result, the GBA as a whole lacks an integrated redress mechanism, undermining the procedural fairness of the current framework. This institutional gap generates risks for businesses - which may hesitate to rely on GBA arrangements in the face of uncertainty - and for individuals, whose privacy rights may be unevenly enforceable depending on where they lodge complaints.

These systemic deficiencies underline the urgent need to strengthen administrative justice in the GBA. The following proposals therefore focus on enhancing transparency, creating joint oversight bodies, and exploring innovative cross-jurisdictional appeals mechanisms to bridge the divide.

POLICY PROPOSALS: TOWARD AN INTEGRATED GBA DATA GOVERNANCE ARCHITECTURE

Drawing together the analysis above, this Part proposes a set of measures to enhance and solidify cross-border data governance in the GBA. The aim is to move from the current pilot and patchwork arrangements to a more integrated architecture that reconciles security imperatives with free flow and embeds principles of administrative justice. These proposals draw on comparative lessons and seek to future-proof the GBA framework. They range from institutional innovations to legal reforms and technical cooperation. As an ensemble, they chart a possible roadmap for the GBA to evolve into a model data governance zone. While the diagnosis in earlier Parts has underscored the risks of fragmentation, the objective here is constructive: to outline feasible, sovereignty-sensitive instruments that can deliver predictability for regulators and certainty for market participants.

At a high level, the proposals recognise a recurring policy dilemma: unilateral tightening in the name of public interest may generate spill-over frictions unless embedded in cooperative structures. The GBA's challenge is therefore not to displace sovereign regulatory authority but to organize it-through stable fora, common baselines, portable compliance tools, transparent enforcement, and eventually a sound legal footing. In this sense, the blueprint below is neither an EU-style supranational harmonization nor a laissez-faire deferral to private ordering; it is a calibrated middle path for a multi-jurisdictional setting under "One Country, Two/Three Systems".

Institutionalize a GBA Data Governance Board

Evolve the current ad-hoc coordination under MoUs into a formal Greater Bay Area Data Governance Board comprising representatives from the CAC, Hong Kong's PCPD (and/or Innovation and Technology Bureau officials), and Macao's GPDP (and related authorities). This Board would have a mandate to oversee implementation of cross-border data measures

System Policies, Rules and Guidelines (rev 2019) (sections on the Joint Oversight Panel).

in the GBA, serve as a standing forum to resolve regulatory conflicts, and issue joint guidelines or FAQs. It should meet on a regular schedule and publish an annual (or semi-annual) report summarizing operational experience-e.g., the number and types of transfers under the GBA Standard Contract, typical conditions attached, and recurring compliance gaps-while respecting State-secrets constraints.

Importantly, the Board should be a live platform for mutual updates: if the Mainland plans to amend a relevant rule (or publish a new catalogue/negative list), the Board would assess likely effects on Hong Kong/Macao operators and suggest complementary adjustments, and vice versa. While it need not be a supra-jurisdictional authority with binding power (each regulator retains legal competence), joint recommendations and interpretations issued with all three authorities' endorsement would carry practical weight and help align practices.[102] In design, the Board would resemble the European Data Protection Board in its coordinating role-without supranational authority. Comparative experience indicates that in federated or quasi-federal data systems, an institutionalized trust-building platform is essential to reconcile local autonomy with shared goals.[103]

Crucially, the Board can operationalize principle convergence. As Chen and Zhao argue in the adjacent domain of digital dispute resolution, institutionalized cooperation on shared baseline principles-rather than premature, top-down harmonization-provides the normative glue for interoperability across diverse legal systems.[104] Translating that insight to data governance, the Board should articulate non-exhaustive baseline principles (necessity, proportionality, transparency, security by design, redress channels), leaving detailed rules and sectoral nuances to each jurisdiction. Over time, the Board may be supported by a small secretariat to handle routine cross-border compliance queries, manage a repository of joint FAQs, and administer one-stop processes (e.g., the data-subject request portal proposed below). This idea borrows from the EU's experience with the European Data Protection Board as a consistency mechanism, adapted to the One Country, Three Systems context. Similar multi-jurisdictional bodies in other federated systems have demonstrated that regular joint decision-making can significantly reduce legal uncertainty and foster trust between regulators.[105]

To ensure legitimacy and effectiveness, the Board's practice should follow a graduated institutionalization path. In the first stage, it could operate primarily as a policy forum with published minutes and soft-law

[102] Schwartz, Paul M., 'Global Data Privacy: The EU Way' (2019) 94(4) *New York University Law Review* 771, 803-813.

[103] Fahey, Bridget A, 'Data Federalism' (2022) 135 *Harvard Law Review* 1007, 1033.

[104] Chen, Hui and Zhao, Yun, 'Enhancing Legal Convergence in the GBA through Harmonization of the Digital Dispute Resolution Legal Framework' (2024) 12 *The Chinese Journal of Comparative Law.* cxae007, https://doi.org/10.1093/cjcl/cxae007

[105] Schwartz, Paul M., 'Global Data Privacy: The EU Way' (2019) 94(4) *New York University Law Review* 771, 803-813.

outputs. Next, it should introduce a predictable calendar and a public docket of issues, accompanied by thematic working groups organized by sector (for example, finance, health, logistics, and smart city development), echoing the subgroup model under the GDPR coordination framework.[106] After two cycles of operation, the Board could evaluate outcomes against pre-specified metrics of compliance and trust-building, drawing on comparative frameworks developed by the OECD for cross-border governance.[107] This gradual, transparent approach would embed accountability while avoiding the perception of supra-jurisdictional overreach, thereby reinforcing trust among regulators, industry, and the public.

Expand and Refine GBA Facilitation Measures

Building on the early success of the GBA Standard Contract, progressively widen the programme's scope in depth and breadth. In depth, incorporate carefully delimited non-personal datasets under controlled conditions-for example, anonymized/aggregated big datasets or supply-chain information critical to cross-border operations-avoiding a blunt, blanket localization where risk can be mitigated through technical and organizational safeguards. Consider a negative list of particularly sensitive non-personal datasets that remain restricted, while enabling freer movement of others subject to encryption, logging, and audit requirements. In breadth, expand participation beyond private companies to government-to-government exchanges for public-interest projects (e.g., epidemic surveillance interfaces, port logistics/traffic optimization, meteorological collaboration), with clear legal bases and reciprocal safeguards.[108]

Comparative evidence suggests that cross-border data exchange between public authorities can be a strong driver of regional integration-provided the exchanges rest on clear mandates, auditable controls, and transparency about purpose limitation.[109] The GBA, as a politically trusted intra-national space, is a natural venue to trial limited, high-value public-sector exchanges with ring-fenced channels, fixed retention schedules, and joint oversight. If the model proves robust, China could consider scaling externally by negotiating similar facilitation arrangements with trusted partners (e.g., within RCEP or select ASEAN states). In such a pathway, the GBA Stand Contract can evolve into a template for an "Asia data bridge"

[106] Similar to the EDPB's plenary-subgroup working model under the GDPR coordination framework, the GBA Board can adopt regular thematic working groups and procedural harmonization mechanisms. See European Data Protection Board, *EDPB plenaries, subgroups and taskforces, available at: <https://www.edpb.europa.eu/about-edpb/who-we-are/edpb-plenaries-subgroups-and-taskforces_en>*

[107] OECD, *Building More Resilient Cross-border Regions: Considerations in Governance and Partnerships* (2024) *available at:* <https://www.oecd.org/en/publications/building-more-resilient-cross-border-regions_d5fd3e59-en.html>

[108] Greenleaf, Graham, 'Global Data Privacy Laws 2021: Despite COVID Delays, 145 Laws Show GDPR Dominance' (2021) 169 *Privacy Laws & Business International Report* 1, 3-5 available at: <https://www.privacylaws.com/reports-gateway/articles/int169/s_int169dplaws2021/>

[109] Ibid.

network, positioning Hong Kong/Shenzhen as a hub that connects Chinese sovereignty with global data corridors.

Mutual Recognition and Multi-Tier Certification

Advance toward mutual recognition of compliance across the GBA and develop a GBA-specific certification/trustmark programme. In the near term, establish pathways whereby (for example) a Shenzhen company that has passed a CAC security assessment or obtained a PIPL certification may rely on that status as prima facie evidence when transferring to Hong Kong; conversely, Hong Kong entities adhering to ISO/IEC 27701(the privacy extension to ISO 27001) or certified under APEC CBPR may receive streamlined consideration for transfers to the Mainland. Over time, consolidate these bilateral pathways into a unified "GBA Data Trustmark", jointly issued (or jointly accredited) by the three authorities, signalling that an organisation's controls meet a highest-common-denominator standard across the region.

Functionally, such a scheme would operate like mutual-recognition arrangements in international trade-reducing duplicative checks while preserving substantive standards.[110] Mainland scholarship has floated similar multi-level governance concepts-beginning with intra-Mainland coordination, then building a GBA-wide regime, and finally extending recognition to trusted external partners-closely mirroring a staged certification pathway.[111] What the GBA adds is a portable and graded assurance layer: e.g., Tier 1 for routine, non-sensitive flows; Tier 2 for sensitive or large-scale flows with enhanced controls (independent audits, breach simulation, rigorous key management).

Comparative lessons from the GDPR reinforce the design choice. As Lachaud emphasises, certification in the GDPR is not merely proof of compliance; it is a governance instrument that builds trust and facilitates interoperability across fragmented legal orders.[112] Properly designed, certification creates portable trust: once accredited by a recognised scheme, the assurance "travels" with the data handler. For the GBA-where regulatory philosophies remain distinct-this portability is precisely what lowers transaction costs while maintaining a credible baseline of protection.

Enhance Transparency and Joint Review of Enforcement

In order to bolster trust, regulators should increase transparency about enforcement and consider bilateral review for contentious cases. The CAC could periodically publish anonymised case summaries explaining typical reasons for approving or denying certain transfers (without sensitive

[110] World Trade Organization, *World Trade Report 2020: Government policies to promote innovation in the digital age,* 135-136.

[111] Zhang, Liang and Lin, Haoming 'On the Improvement Approach' supra note 6.

[112] Lachaud, Eric (2020) 'What GDPR Tells about Certification' 38 *Computer Law & Security Review* 105457.

particulars). Hong Kong and Macao authorities could publish statistics on GBA Standard Contract filings and recurring deficiencies. These low-risk disclosures advance accountability without compromising security.[113]

For cross-boundary disputes that raise interpretive uncertainty, create a narrowly scoped GBA appeals/review panel-comprising (for example) one Mainland official, one Hong Kong official, and one independent expert/arbitrator-to examine whether a challenged decision followed agreed criteria. While Mainland law does not ordinarily permit foreign officials to intervene in enforcement, this intra-national, advisory panel would operate under a standing cooperative instrument and address only procedural and criteria-compliance questions, leaving sovereign merits to domestic authorities. At minimum, enhanced liaison (designated points of contact) can facilitate timely, informal resolution.

Comparative work on judicial review in Greater China underscores why an accountability layer matters. As Xiao shows, apex courts across the region display divergent postures-ranging from deference to activism-yet each plays a role in mediating between administrative power and individual rights.[114] The GBA should echo that function by embedding elements of proportionality review or structured reason-giving in cross-border decisions, thus strengthening perceived legitimacy and reducing the risk of forum-driven outcomes.

Empower Individuals with Cross-Border Data Rights

The GBA should implement a user-friendly mechanism for individuals to exercise their data subject rights seamlessly across the region. A practical step would be the creation of a one-stop GBA data rights portal, through which individuals could submit access, correction, or deletion requests, regardless of where the recipient entity is located. For example, a Mainland resident seeking to delete data held by a Hong Kong company (obtained via a GBA transfer) could file the request through a unified online platform. The request would then be relayed to the Hong Kong company and the PCPD, and the response communicated back through the same portal. Under a Memorandum of Understanding, the parties could agree that any such request lodged in one jurisdiction would be recognized as valid across the region and handled under the applicable law.

This approach would mirror the functional logic of the GDPR's "one-stop-shop," where data subjects interact with their local supervisory authority even for cross-border issues.[115] The key is not to transplant EU institutional law, but to provide a single front door for rights invocation,

[113] OECD, *Guidelines on the Protection of Privacy and Transborder Flows of Personal Data* (2013 rev), Part III (Accountability Principle).

[114] Xiao, Shiling (2024) *Judicial Review in Greater China: Activism and Deference of Four Apex Courts*, Cambridge University Press at 1-2, 193-196.

[115] Case C-645/19 Facebook Ireland and others v Gegevensbeschermingsautoriteit [2021] ECLI:EU:C:2021:483 (CJEU).

thereby avoiding duplication and inefficiency.[116] For businesses, participation in GBA data transfers would carry the commitment to honour cross-border rights requests in a harmonized spirit–for instance, treating a PIPL erasure request routed via the portal as substantively valid even if the PDPO does not explicitly confer a deletion right. Regulators would coordinate to ensure that compliance with one system does not breach another (for example, where Hong Kong companies are bound by statutory retention obligations under PDPO, the PCPD would clarify such limits in the response).

By embedding such a mechanism, the GBA framework would significantly enhance interoperability: residents could exercise rights without needing to navigate three different legal systems, while regulators and companies would converge on mutually acceptable responses. Comparative scholarship emphasises that cross-border regimes succeed where baseline responsiveness is guaranteed despite divergent domestic rules.[117] A relevant Hong Kong precedent, EA/17/2018, illustrates that even local authorities must grapple with erasure in mixed datasets, showing the practical value of having a structured mechanism to handle such disputes.[118]

Ground the Framework in Law (Eventually)

While pilots and MoUs offer flexibility, the GBA framework ultimately requires a firmer legal foundation. In the medium to long term, the National People's Congress Standing Committee could issue a special decision recognizing GBA-internal data flows, effectively treating Hong Kong and Macao as "inside" for approved transfers under the PIPL. Complementary local adoption-such as bringing PDPO Section 33 into force with exemptions for GBA-compliant transfers-would transform soft law into hard law, offering clarity if legal disputes arise.

However, this codification should be sequenced methodically, grounded in empirical evidence and regulatory learning. The Board should first validate the real-world effects of facilitation measures-monitoring risk, cost impact, and security outcomes-before proposing legislative reforms. Future legal instruments should embed review clauses or time-limited authorisations (sunset-style mechanisms) with scheduled ex post evaluations, ensuring adaptability rather than ossification.[119] Comparative experience supports this incremental approach: OECD work has long

[116] European Data Protection Board, Guidelines 02/2022 on the application of Article 60 GDPR (14 March 2022) available at: <https://www.edpb.europa.eu/our-work-tools/our-documents/guidelines/guidelines-022022-application-article-60-gdpr_en>

[117] Moerel, Lokke (2011) 'Back to basics: when does EU data protection law apply?' 1(2) *International Data Privacy Law* 92-110.

[118] Hong Kong Administrative Appeals Board, EA/17/2018 (decision published 21 July 2021, hearing 6 May 2019), available at: <https://www.pcpd.org.hk/english/enforcement/decisions/files/AAB_17_2018.pdf>

[119] Gersen, Jacob E (2007) 'Temporary Legislation' 74(1) *University of Chicago Law Review* 247.

stressed that systematic ex post evaluation and programmed reviews are essential to sustaining regulatory quality and legitimacy.[120] Scholars also point out that sunset clauses offer a structured way to introduce temporary policy-balancing flexibility with legal certainty, as shown in comparative analyses.[121] Experimental studies further indicate that sunsets can influence political support dynamics, underscoring the need for evidence-based renewal or expiry mechanisms.[122] Finally, both OECD and the World Economic Forum affirm that agile, adaptive governance-incorporating piloting and iterative progression-is vital in rapidly evolving technological contexts.[123]

CONCLUSION

As the GBA experiments with cross-border data governance, it sits at the crossroads of China's domestic priorities and global norms. This article has traced how the region is navigating a path between fragmentation and integration–piloting contracts, forging cooperation agreements, and learning from external models–in an effort to reconcile China's quest for digital sovereignty with the practical need for regional data fluidity.

The progress so far in the GBA demonstrates a pragmatic recognition that data cannot be siloed if the region is to fulfill its economic ambitions. Incremental steps like the 2024 CAC Provisions, the GBA Standard Contract, and inter-governmental MoUs have begun to chip away at the barriers, creating a more permissive environment within the One Country, Two Systems framework. At the same time, these measures are just the first layer. The analysis revealed remaining tensions–legal uncertainties, procedural gaps, and trust deficits–that must be addressed to achieve a truly durable solution.

One overarching theme is that administrative and procedural fairness is not a mere add-on; it is central to the sustainability of any cross-border regime. The GBA's future depends on building not just technical mechanisms, but also institutional trust–among governments, businesses, and the public. That means establishing forums for coordination (a GBA Data Board), mechanisms for redress (appeal or review processes), and

[120] OECD, *Regulatory Policy in Perspective: A Reader's Companion to the OECD Regulatory Policy Outlook 2015* (OECD Publishing 2015) 122 available at: <https://www.oecd.org/en/publications/regulatory-policy-in-perspective_9789264241800-en.html> see also OECD, *Regulatory Policy Outlook 2021*(OECD Publishing 2021) 84-85 available at: <https://www.oecd.org/content/dam/oecd/en/publications/reports/2021/10/oecd-regulatory-policy-outlook-2021_c5274577/38b0fdb1-en.pdf>

[121] Ranchordás, Sofia, 'Sunset Clauses and Experimental Regulations: Blessing or Curse for Legal Certainty?' (2015) 36(1) *Statute Law Review* 28.

[122] Underhill, Kristen and Ayres, Ian, 'Sunsets Are for Suckers: An Experimental Test of Sunset Clauses' (2022) 59 *Harvard Journal on Legislation* 103.

[123] World Economic Forum & OECD, *Agile Governance for Emerging Technologies* (2020) available at: <https://www3.weforum.org/docs/WEF_Agile_Regulation_for_the_Fourth_Industrial_Revolution_2020.pdf>

clear, transparent rules that all sides acknowledge. Without these, even well-intended policies may falter due to misunderstandings or lack of buy-in.

Comparatively, the GBA can draw on ideas from both the EU and US experiences. The EU shows the value of common standards and mutual oversight, while the US highlights creative flexibility and the interplay of trade and security considerations. The GBA will likely forge its own hybrid approach: maintaining China's emphasis on national security yet infusing it with greater inter-jurisdictional coordination and procedural safeguards inspired by global best practices. If successful, this GBA model could become a prototype for other regions or for China's engagement in international data governance debates.

At a theoretical level, what the GBA is attempting could be described as a form of "data federalism"–multiple legal systems under one sovereignty cooperating to manage data flows. Unlike traditional federalism which is constitutional and rigid, this is emerging through policy innovation and administrative agreement. It is a delicate balance of top-down control and bottom-up consent. Achieving that in the GBA would not only cement the region's role as a pivotal tech and finance hub, but also demonstrate a model of reconciling data sovereignty with cross-border interoperability to the world. In an era when global rules for data are still in flux, the GBA's experiment is one to watch.

In conclusion, navigating cross-border data governance in the GBA is a multifaceted challenge, but one that is showing promising progress. Through legal innovation, comparative insight, and a commitment to fairness and cooperation, the GBA can become a leading example of bridging jurisdictions in the digital era–ensuring that the flow of data, much like the flow of capital, goods, and people, underpins rather than undermines regional prosperity and the rule of law. The GBA's evolution also resonates with global initiatives such as the G20's "Data Free Flow with Trust," which seek to balance sovereignty with interoperability. If successful, the GBA could demonstrate that data sovereignty and cross-border flow are not mutually exclusive, but can be reconciled through carefully designed cooperation and procedural safeguards.[124] The coming phase, as these proposals are debated and potentially implemented, will determine whether the GBA fulfills that promise. The direction is set: towards integration with security, and openness with justice. The task now is to stay the course.

[124] G20, *Osaka Leaders' Declaration* (29 June 2019), para 10; World Economic Forum, *Paths Towards Free and Trusted Data Flows* (2020).

The Role of the Party Committee in State Owned Enterprises and Stakeholder Representation in China

SAY HAK GOO
University of Hong Kong

THE BACKGROUND

State Owned Enterprises (SOEs) in China have long been struggling with, amongst other problems, the question of the efficiency of their governance structure and their corporate social responsibility (CSR). The recent introduction of party committees into China's SOEs and the imposition of a duty of corporate social responsibility on the SOEs was intended to deal with these issues, but have raised concerns in the West of political interference by the Chinese Communist Party (CCP) in the SOEs' operations, thereby affecting the objectives and efficiency of the SOEs, and how this duty is to be fulfilled by SOEs. This paper therefore examines the research question: how China can improve the corporate governance structure of SOEs to better fulfil CSR while maintaining efficiency, and specifically, whether implementing stakeholder representation within existing party committee structures or boards of directors would be able to address current governance shortcomings? This research question emerges from my observation that while party committee involvement in SOEs has shown some positive results, there remain significant issues around transparency, stakeholder protection, and the effective implementation of CSR duties that current governance structures do not adequately address. I propose in this paper a specific solution which is to modify SOE governance by introducing stakeholder representation either through:

1. Stakeholder representation within party committees (if party committees have final decision-making authority), or
2. Stakeholder representation within boards of directors (if boards retain final authority)

This paper examines the research question through several analytical lenses:

- The historical evolution and struggles of SOE governance reform in China.
- The recent introduction of party committees into SOE governance and empirical evidence of their effectiveness.

- The development of CSR requirements in Chinese law and their implementation gaps.
- How stakeholder representation could address the opacity and lack of individual accountability in current party committee systems and improve societal efficiency.[1]

This analysis of SOE governance reform illuminates broader patterns of administrative justice in contemporary China. The evolution of party committee systems in state enterprises exemplifies the institutional conflicts and governance transformations that characterize China's administrative system more broadly. Rather than representing a departure from administrative justice principles, SOE governance demonstrates how the party-state adapts institutional forms to maintain political control while addressing legitimacy challenges. The struggles between State-owned Assets Supervision and Administration Commission of the State Council (SASAC), regulatory agencies, corporate boards, and party committees reflect the wider competition for authority that defines China's fragmented administrative landscape. These governance experiments in the economic sphere reveal how administrative power is exercised, contested, and reconfigured within China's governance framework.

The persistent problems of insider control, rent-seeking, and stakeholder neglect in SOEs mirror implementation gaps found throughout China's administrative system. Just as formal legal frameworks often fail to constrain administrative behaviour in other domains, corporate governance rules have proven insufficient to ensure accountability in state enterprises. The party-state's response—formalizing party committee roles rather than strengthening independent oversight—exemplifies the Chinese adaptation strategies that characterize administrative reform across sectors. Understanding how administrative justice operates in SOEs thus provides insights into the broader mechanisms through which the party-state manages the tension between institutional modernization and political control.

Developments of CSR in China SOEs

China has experienced unprecedented economic growth and development since its opening up in 1978, soon to overtake the US, and the projection is that by 2030, it would be double the size of the US's economy, measuring

[1] Societal or social efficiency means the sum total of the benefits to all the different constituencies in a society including shareholders, workers, consumers, the environment, the community and society more generally. The concept includes economic profit (or economic surplus), which is the sum total of producer surplus and consumer surplus, and other intangible or unquantifiable benefits that may be enjoyed by all stakeholders, including shareholders. Producer surplus is the difference between the price consumers are willing to pay and the cost of production. Consumer surplus is the difference between the price consumers are willing to pay and the price at which the producer is willing to sell the product. Shareholders will enjoy the producer surplus, whereas consumers will enjoy the consumer surplus.

countries' GDP by primary purchasing power (indeed by this measure, China had already become the largest economy in the world since 2014).[2]

This impressive achievement was obtained at various environmental, labour and social costs. In the West, economists believe that market is the best place for allocating resources, and that corporations, being a dominant actor in the market, are efficient vehicles for conducting business in a market.[3] It is also believed that corporations should maximise profit for shareholders, so long as they do so within the law, and internalize costs, as this is the most efficient way to create social welfare, provided there is free competition in the market.[4] Rather than using corporate law and governance structure to internalize all costs of production, they leave this to be regulated by other laws, for example, environmental, labour, consumer laws etc. In the early days of the opening up of the economy, the Chinese government and companies largely adopted the western approach, focusing primarily on profit maximization.[5] But in reality, both in the West and, perhaps to a greater extent in China in the early days of its opening up, certain costs were externalized by companies due to dysfunctional boards and monitoring mechanisms, and ineffective law enforcement: Laws were not enough to internalize costs[6] and often there was no free competition as the market was dominated by a few giant corporations and SOEs. Dysfunctioning boards act to externalize cost because (a) they perceive their duty 'to act in the best interest of the company' to mean 'to act in the best interest of the shareholders', that is, their duty is profit maximization for shareholders; (b) in China, there was managerial abuse, and as in the West, executive compensations are often tied to firm performance, and (c) either there is no market competition or competition drives firm to conduct themselves badly.[7] This has prompted debate in the West about conflicting ideas of profit maximization and societal interest,[8] and the Chinese government to take CSR more seriously as environmental and social problems caused by profit maximization, largely because such problems would undermine the legitimacy of the ruling party.[9]

[2] Bird, M (2014) 'China Just Overtook The US As The World's Largest Economy' *Business Insider* (8 October 2014).

[3] Coase, RH (1960) 'The Problem of Social Cost' 3 *Journal of Law and Economics* 1.

[4] See Friedman, M (1962) *Capitalism and Freedom* University of Chicago Press; Friedman, M (1970) 'A Friedman Doctrine: The Social Responsibility of Business Is to Increase Its Profits' *New York Times Magazine* (13 September 1970).

[5] Lin, L-W (2010) 'Corporate Social Responsibility in China: Window Dressing or Structural Change' (28) *Berkeley Journal of International Law* 64 at 69.

[6] That is, companies to bear all the costs of production.

[7] See also Hart, O and Zingales, L (2017) 'Companies Should Maximize Shareholder Welfare Not Market Value' (2) *Journal of Law, Finance, and Accounting* 247.

[8] Ibid

[9] Lin Corporate Social Responsibility supra note 4 at 93

Although China has adopted the market economy since the opening up of the economy in 1978, embracing market mechanisms and profit maximization ideologies, China characterises its brand of market economy as a socialist market economy with Chinese characteristics, or what some scholars and others would call 'state capitalism'.[10] Thus, profit maximization is not the sole purpose of a corporation in China, especially for SOEs. To tackle environmental, labour and social issues, the law requires corporations to also bear CSR.

There is no dearth of legal frameworks,[11] CSR principles,[12] standards, and guidelines, as well as regulations governing the disclosure of social and environmental information,[13] capital market regulations,[14] responsible

[10] Liebman, BL and Milhaupt CJ (eds.), (2016) *Regulating the Visible Hand? The Institutional Implications of Chinese State Capitalism*, OUP at 15. Friedman *Capitalism and Freedom* supra note 3; Adams, HC (1886) *Relation of the State to Industrial Action and Economics and Jurisprudence* AMS Press at 16; Hart and Zingales supra note 5

[11] For example, article 5 of Company Law 2005 and article 20 of Company Law 2023 that require companies to 'undertake social responsibility' in the course of business; articles 52 and 118 of Company Law 2005 and article 76 and 130 of Company Law 2023 require that at least one third of the board of supervisors to be employee representatives; article 170 of Company Law 2023 says party organization in state-funded companies should play leading role in accordance with CCP's articles of association and researched and discussed company's major business management issues.

[12] For example, the Guiding Opinion on the Social Responsibility Implementation for the State-owned Enterprises Controlled by the Central Government issued by the State-Owned Assets Supervision and Administration Commission of the State Council (Jan 2008)

[13] For example, the Regulation on Environmental Information Disclosure (Trial Edition) issued by the State Environmental Protection Administration (now Ministry of Environmental Protection of China) (May 2008); the Guide on Listed Companies' Social Responsibility issued by the Shenzhen Stock Exchange (2006), and the Guide on Environmental Information Disclosure for Companies Listed on Shanghai Stock Exchange and Notice on Strengthening Social Responsibility of Listed Companies (May 2008)

[14] For example, the first SRI fund in China – the Sustainable Growth Equity Fund launched by the Bank of China (May 2006); the Xingye SRI Fund to domestic investor in China launched by the Industrial Management Company (March 2008); the first SRI Index - the TEDA Environmental Protection Index launched by Shenzhen Securities Information Company and Tianjin Teda Company (focusing on top 40 environmentally responsible companies listed on Shenzhen and Shanghai Stock Exchanges (2008); the Responsibility Index launched by the Shanghai Stock Exchange (August 2009) (selecting the top 100 socially responsible companies on the stock exchange; the Opinion on Enforcement of Environmental Law and Prevention of Credit Risks jointly issued by the State Environmental Protection Administration, the Peoples' Bank of China, and the China Banking Regulatory Commission (July 2007) directing Chinese banks to include corporate environmental performance in credit assessments; the agreement between SEPA and International Financial Corporation to develop guidelines for the green credit policy for a number of key polluting sectors, and to introduce the IFC performance Standards and Equator Principles (Jan 2008); the green securities initiated by SEPA and China Securities Regulatory Commission subjecting 13 high-pollution and high-energy-consumption industries to environmental performance review when applying for initial public offering or refinancing

production standards,[15] and private initiatives[16] pertaining to CSR in China.[17] There is an increasingly burgeoning number of corporations in China, referred to as social enterprises—predominantly private entities—that integrate corporate social responsibility into their business practices within the prevailing legal framework.[18]

CSR ideals fit in with Chinese traditional ideology, as influenced by Confucianism, Zhen Buddhism. These schools of thought characterised family enterprises as an extension of families or clans with inherent social responsibilities to family members, larger communities and even the state, in large part to gain legitimacy and recognition by the state.[19] It also fits well with the policy of developing the Chinese socialist market economy.[20] Whereas SOEs used to provide social security function in the old, pre-1978, economy but subsequently social service responsibilities were removed from the SOEs. After 1978, employees' interests need to be looked after in a different way. The notion of CSR provides a balancing tool between the employees' interests and other stakeholders in the SOEs.[21] It also ties in with China's sustainable development policy statements and various policy guidelines since 1992,[22] and the long term goal of 'building a harmonious society' declared in the Sixth General Meeting of the Sixteenth Central Committee of the CCP in October 2006,[23] and more recently the 'common prosperity' goal championed by President Xi.

15 For example, Sustainable Growth Equity Fund (Bank of China, May 2006); Xingye SRI Fund (Industrial Management Company, March 2008); TEDA Environmental Protection Index (Shenzhen Securities Information Company and Tianjin Teda Company 2008); Responsibility Index (Shanghai Stock Exchange, August 2009); Opinion on Enforcement of Environmental Law and Prevention of Credit Risks (State Environmental Protection Administration, People's Bank of China, and China Banking Regulatory Commission, July 2007); Agreement between SEPA and International Financial Corporation (January 2008); Green Securities Initiative (SEPA and China Securities Regulatory Commission).

16 Lin 'Corporate Social Responsibility' supra note 4 at 93.

17 For example, the Responsible Supply Chain Association's CSC9000T and the Chinese Industrial Associations' joint declaration of the CSR Industrial Principles.

18 Some cities have promulgated specific rules to help companies implement CSR, eg. Chengdu city government has special regulations on this. In terms of legal structure these social enterprises are the same as traditional companies. But the founders are firm believers of CSR and find like-minded private investors and social/public benefit foundations (公益基金, *gongyi jijin*) to assist them by providing finance. Some of these companies are listed on stock exchanges in China (see report from China Social Entrepreneur Foundation).

19 Lin' Corporate Social Responsibility' supra note 4 at 93.

20 Ibid at 88.

21 Ibid at 88.

22 For example, the Ten Policies on China's Environment and Development (1992); China's 21 Agenda – the White Paper on China's Population, Environment and Development (1994); the Ninth (1996), Tenth (2001) and Eleventh (2006) Five-Year Plans for National Economic and Social Development adopted by the National People's Congress of China.

23 Lin 'Corporate Social Responsibility' supra note 4 at 88.

There are now also economic pressures in the global market that drives Chinese enterprises to meet international CSR[24] and now also environmental, social, and governance (ESG) standards, as well as social, economic and political interests[25] within China that argue that social and environmental problems pose a serious challenge to the legitimacy of the ruling CCP.[26] Thus, China has consistent political and economic motivations to promote the labour and environmental aspects of CSR. Furthermore, the Chinese government has used CSR to raise the standards of multinational companies that have direct operations in China.[27]

CSR initiatives are predominantly spearheaded by governmental entities; however, numerous non-governmental stakeholders also play a significant role.[28] There are even CSR awards.[29] However, there are a number of problems. First, it is not clear whether the CSR required under the Company Law and the Code of Corporate Governance (Article 86) is mandatory or exhortatory as it does not specify the contents of CSR and shareholders have limited access to the legal system to enforce fiduciary duties[30] even if CSR is part of the fiduciary duties. Though this is supplemented by various CSR principles and guidelines mentioned above, some CSR initiatives are in the trial stage and others are largely unenforced.[31]

However, there is no clear definition of what CSR is in the legislation. In my view, CSR should mean (i) the duty to comply with the law, and (ii) the duty not to externalize costs beyond levels which the law requires. The first is legally enforceable by shareholders and regulator, the second is a moral obligation not enforceable legally. Furthermore, externalities are currently weakly regulated by law which is weakly enforced. As a result, it is possible for companies to externalize costs not required by law to be absorbed by the company, and this creates societal inefficiency. We need a stakeholder committee or stakeholder board (the details of which are discussed below) to internalize costs; stakeholder committee members or directors can implement CSR and help internalize costs for China. They will

[24] Ibid at 89.

[25] Ibid at 91.

[26] Ibid at 93.

[27] Ibid at 94.

[28] For example, organisations such as China CSR, SynTao, China CSR Map, the Chinese Business Council for Sustainable Development, media such as China Economic Weekly, China WTO Tribune, Nanfang Weekend; Environmental Magazine, the China Central Television; the Green Bonds in China is the largest in the world; AIIB is to be a green bank; Hainan Airway is very strong on CSR

[29] For example, the Top One Hundred Corporations in the Annual CSR Survey launched by Peking University in 2006.

[30] Lin 'Corporate Social Responsibility' supra note 4 at 96.

[31] Ibid at 97.

form the invisible hand in the committee or boardroom.[32] CSR standards are currently primarily implemented in export-oriented companies, not domestic market businesses as domestic consumers are less concerned about CSR issues due to their pragmatism and lack of bargaining and enforcement power.[33] The same is true with SRI as domestic investors are speculators, and foreign investors are a small minority. Although insurance companies and pension funds may now be the potential driver for change, this is likely to take a long time.[34]

It is clear that China has historical foundations and real incentives to develop CSR, but there are also many constraints. The Chinese government plays an important role in driving CSR forward and has political, social and economic motivations to encourage and control the development of CSR in China.[35] What is needed is a corporate governance structure that allows stakeholder interests to be looked after. One mechanism the government has recently mandated is the adoption of CCP party committees in corporations with varying degrees of success, perhaps not surprising in view of the various constraints mentioned above.[36] Larger firms (either SOE or privately-owned enterprises [POE]) have a higher hazard rate of party-building adoption than smaller and less significant firms or firms that are cross-listed in Hong Kong.[37] This paper explains that as the purpose of Chinese company law is to serve the interest of the state, even though there is empirical literature on the effectiveness of the recently introduced party committee (as discussed later in this paper) a stakeholder committee or board weaved into the current structure can improve the system further. As the state has enormous influence in the economy this can be implemented relatively easily.

China's Struggle to Improve SOEs

China's 'modernization' of the SOEs has been through many failed experiments, from the initial decision to corporatize SOEs[38] and to separate politics from enterprises[39]as many SOEs had experienced the insider

[32] See also Ayuso, S and Argandone, A (2007) 'Responsible Corporate Governance: Towards a Stakeholder Board of Directors' *IESE Business School Working Paper* No 701

[33] Lin 'Corporate Social Responsibility' supra note 4 at 97.

[34] Ibid, at 98.

[35] Ibid at 99

[36] For a survey on the extent to which SOEs and POEs have adopted charter provisions that allow party committees to have a role see Lin, LYH and Milhaupt, CJ (2021) 'Party Building or Noisy Signalling? The Contours of Political Conformity in Chinese Corporate Governance' 50 *Journal of Legal Studies* 187.

[37] Ibid.

[38] November 1992, the Third Plenary Session of the 14th CCP Central Committee (Zhonggong 14 jie sanzhongquanhu)

[39] September 1995, the Fifth Plenary Session (Wuzhong Dahui))

control problem—managers who had control of SOEs were engaged in opportunistic misconduct (a phenomenon known as tunnelling), resulting in the loss of efficiency and assets and privatization of valuable operation of the SOEs[40]—not only to the detriment of shareholders—primarily the state but also the societal efficiency,[41] and then to the adoption of the Singapore model, and more recently the use of the Party Committee in SOEs.

The People's Republic of China (PRC) has tried to adopt the UK and US approach to issues of corporate governance without much success, for example, subjecting managers to fiduciary obligations, increasing shareholder protection through derivative suits, or shareholder activism especially by institutional investors, and use of independent directors and board committees, and takeovers mechanisms.[42] Being the dominant shareholder in SOEs, the government has the biggest stake in the success of SOEs. As the CCP serves as the governing authority, it possesses a compelling incentive to mitigate the agency problem (that is, conflicts of interest between principals [owners] and agents [managers]). Although in theory the shareholder meeting in China has more power than the board of directors, such power is not enough to monitor the decision-making process of the board and the conduct of the managers—as the government's agency, the State-owned Assets Supervision and Administration Commission (SASAC, 国资委 *guoziwei)* established in 2003, has been unable to deliver effective monitoring.

Although China initially adopted the Singapore model,[43] its implementation was rather different from the Singapore model in that in the China version, because it is derived more closely from the German model, allocated all major power to shareholders,[44] not

[40] Qingmu Chang Yan (1994) Dui neibu ren kongzhi de kongzhi: zhuan gui jingji zhong gongsi zhili de ruogan wenti '(Control on internal control: several corporate governance problems in the ransitional economy',*Gaige* (Reform) (6) , 11-24; Zhang, CL (1995) 'Cong rongzi jiaodu fenxi guoyou qiye de zhili jigou gaige' (An analysis of the reform of governance structure of SOEs from the perspective of fund raising', *Gaige* (Reform), (3), 34-36.

[41] See Wu YC (1995) 'Guoyou qiye neibu ren kongzhi wenti de chengyin ji duice' (The causes and solutions to the problem of insider control in SOEs ' (1995) , *Gaige* (Reform) (4), 73-78.

[42] Studies show that the correlation between independent directors and firm performance in China varies with the background of the former: firms with academics or accountants as independent directors are associated with higher productivity, whereas firms with politicians or financial professionals as independent directors are associated with lower operating performance: Jiao, H; Dong, Y; Hou, W and Lee, E (2013) 'Independent Directors and Corporate Performance in China' in Cumming, D et al *Developing China's Capital Market* Palgrave Macmillan

[43] Where a holding company Temasek (a Singaporean state-owned multinational investment firm which is a subsidiary of the Ministry of Finance) is formed to manage the portfolio of SOEs under its control.

[44] Under the Company Law 1993, article 38 provided that the meeting of shareholders shall

the board of directors, and the board was in truth only an executive committee of the shareholder meetings.[45] State ownership was transferred from SOE's superior-unit-in-charge to a supposedly independent SASAC, but SASAC was seen to be incapable of performing its functions properly due to the lack of incentive and expertise.[46] As a resuilt, the Central Huijin Investment Company Limited, was established to replace SASAC as the representative of state assets in the banking industry and Huijin II, the State-owned Capital Management Corporation, to take over from SASAC as the state asset representative for central SOEs. In other sectors where SASAC still retains control, it continues to exercise control over SOEs sometimes in a counter-productive manner.

As discussed below, the failed Singapore model led China into adopting a more proactive approach by having party members on the board of directors, and party committee having greater role in the decision-making process, an approach often seen by the West as 'administrative interference' by the party-state.

exercise the following powers: (1) to decide upon the operation policies and investment plan of the company; (2) to elect and replace directors and decide on matters relating to remuneration to directors; (3) to elect and replace the supervisors who are the representatives of shareholders and decide on the payment to supervisors; (4) to examine and approve the reports by the board of directors; (5) to examine and approve the reports by the supervisory board or individual supervisors; (6) to examine and approve the annual financial and budget plan and financial accounting plan of the company; (7) to examine and approve the plans for company's profit distribution and loss recovery; (8) to pass resolutions on the increase or decrease of registered capital; (9) to pass resolutions on the issue of bonds; (10) to pass resolutions on the transfer of investment by shareholders to people other than shareholders; (11) to pass resolutions on merger, division, change in corporate form, dissolution and liquidation and other affairs of the company; (12) to revise the articles of association of the company. In the 2023 version of the Company Law, paras. (1), (3), (6) and (10) have been deleted.

[45] Under the Company Law 1993, article 38 provided that the meeting of shareholders shall exercise the following powers: (1) to decide upon the operation policies and investment plan of the company; (2) to elect and replace directors and decide on matters relating to remuneration to directors; (3) to elect and replace the supervisors who are the representatives of shareholders and decide on the payment to supervisors; (4) to examine and approve the reports by the board of directors; (5) to examine and approve the reports by the supervisory board or individual supervisors; (6) to examine and approve the annual financial and budget plan and financial accounting plan of the company; (7) to examine and approve the plans for company's profit distribution and loss recovery; (8) to pass resolutions on the increase or decrease of registered capital; (9) to pass resolutions on the issue of bonds; (10) to pass resolutions on the transfer of investment by shareholders to people other than shareholders; (11) to pass resolutions on merger, division, change in corporate form, dissolution and liquidation and other affairs of the company; (12) to revise the articles of association of the company. In the 2023 version of the Company Law, paras. (1), (3), (6) and (10) have been deleted.

[46] Deng, F (2016) 'Indigenous Evolution of SOE Regulation' in Liebman, BL and Milhaupt, CJ (eds) *Regulating the Visible Hand? The Institutional Implications of Chinese State Capitalism* Oxford University Press at 15.

China's past failed attempts do not show that it was unwilling to make improvements. On the contrary, it has been keen to reform. But in my view, it has gone about reform in the wrong way: it has tried to control too much. The government's wish to maintain control is understandable given that it has the highest stake in SOEs. But I take the view that it should control only the appointment of personnel and leave business matters to the professionals appointed. Whilst the Communist Party wants to maintain a strong grip on all enterprises,[47] especially state-owned enterprises, it has surprisingly allowed China Securities and Regulatory Commission (CSRC) to impose a series of mandatory, often self-enforcing, governance mechanisms designed to offer protection to minority shareholders against the Party-state controlling shareholders, in order to ensure the continued financing of China's state capitalism model.[48] By the same token, given the Communist Party's pragmatic approach and determination on reform, if the Party can see the benefit of my proposed stakeholder committee or board to ensure the continued success and financing of SOEs in global capital markets and Belt and Road Initiative (BRI) countries, it is possible that the Party will allow such a mechanism, so long as it maintains the ultimate control over the appointment and removal of stakeholder committee or board members. Such a mechanism is important not only for national champions, but also as checks and balances for many local government financing vehicles which are created to finance local infrastructure and public service projects by local government faced with limited financing channels.

Another problem of the SOEs has been that, like the Anglo-American corporate boards, the board of Chinese SOEs also suffered from groupthink as most SOE executives shared similar educational, political, and career backgrounds.[49] It has been argued that the insider bias in executive recruitment in SOEs both impedes efforts to address problems in corporate governance and limits the global

[47] For example, some regulations, including extensive disclosure requirements imposed on non-public companies, appear designed to facilitate state supervision over private entities, due to state distrust of the private sector: Clarke, D (2016) 'Blowback: How China's Efforts to Bring Private-Sector Standards into the Public Sector Backfired' in Liebman, BL and Milhaupt, CJ (eds) (2016) *Regulating the Visible Hand? The Institutional Implications of Chinese State Capitalism* Oxford University Press at 29.

[48] Howson, NC(2016) Protecting the State from Itself? Regulatory Interventions in Corporate Governance and the Financing of China's 'State Capitalism', in Liebman BL and Milhaupt CJ (ed) (2016) *Chinese State Capitalism and Institutional Change: Domestic and Global Implications* OUP at 49.

[49] Lin, LW (2015) 'Balancing Closure and Openness: The Challenge of Leadership Reform in China's State-Owned Enterprises' in Liebman and Milhaupt 'Regulating the Visible Hand?'' supra note 8

competitiveness of these firms.[50] The proposed stakeholder committee or board that I advocate below will go some way to address such problems if members appointed come from diverse backgrounds. It may also lessen the continued reliance on informality in both contracts and regulation which limits the incentives to develop the human capital China needs to confront a range of new economic and legal challenges and to shift toward a rule-based system of governance.[51] Milhaupt and Zheng point out that the problem in China is not so much state ownership of enterprises, but state capture of companies with a range of ownership forms, including traditional SOEs, privately owned enterprises, and those with mixtures of private and state ownership.[521] Successful enterprises pursue strategies that seek proximity to power, state largesse and privileged market access. Despite the shift away from a command and control economic model, SOEs continue to enjoy ideological and positional advantages in the political economy of China as compared to other actors in the legal system, and are able to get their way in litigation and have their interests met in the legal system, often at the expense of values associated with the rule of law, such as effective enforcement of legal rules.[53] 'Moving legal reform forward in China requires not just reforming the courts but reforming the *role of powerful economic actors* in the political-legal system.'[54] Reforming SOEs and reducing their role in the economy is not simply a question of adjusting laws in ways that balance the playing field between SOEs and private firms; institutional reform of the state sector may actually be a prerequisite to effective legal reform.[55] Stakeholder committee or board in these SOEs could be an institutional change that may counter-balance the power of SOEs and guide them to their proper role in society.

As pointed out by Gallagher, state capitalism has helped Communist Party to stay in power: China has sought to balance two apparently competing goals, namely the market competition and state control throughout the reform period; as the state shifted toward greater engagement with global markets and capitalism, it

[50] Ibid

[51] For the problem of informality see Chen, R (2016) 'Legal Informality and Human Capital Development in China' in Liebman and Milhaupt supra note 8 at 151

[52] Milhaupt, CJ and Zheng, WT (2016) 'Reforming China's State-Owned Enterprises: Institutions, Not Ownership' in Liebman and Milhaupt supra note 6 at 175

[53] Zheng, L; Liebman, BL and Milhaupt, CJ (2016) 'SOEs and State Governance: How State-Owned Enterprises Influence China's Legal System' in Liebman and Milhaupt 'Invisible Hand' 'supra note 8 at 203

[54] Ibid (emphasis added)

[55] Liebman and Milhaupt Invisible Hand' supra note 8 at xxiv.

felt the need to strengthen its role in managing social conflict and society more generally.[56] Stakeholder committee or board can be a way to enable the state to maintain control and manage social conflict by having stakeholder committee members or directors balancing various stakeholder interests without impeding market competition as SOEs continue to operate in market economy.

A further problem of SOEs has been that until recent decades they had been major contributors to China's environmental degradation in large part due to the low priority that the Chinese political system had attached to environmental protection. However, as central authorities increase priority on environmental goals and offer a range of subsidies for greener industrial development, SOEs may come to play a more constructive role in addressing China's environmental problems, as SOEs are so entwined with the state and react to political incentives.[57] This is why it is important to introduce stakeholder committee or board to SOEs and if central authorities can see the benefit of such a committee or board, its implementation in SOEs is likely to be forthcoming.

With the success of China's state capitalism, China has emerged as a major capital exporter through overseas investment by SOEs, and in order to ensure that SOEs receive protection as investors under international investment treaties with host countries, China has brought its position into line with those of major Western economic powers.[58] At the same time, if stakeholder committees or boards are successfully implemented in SOEs, this could also lead the Western economies to change in this direction.

However, going forward, questions have been asked as to whether China's model can maintain social stability and economic growth with a legal system that fails to address basic political economy problems such as local protectionism, contains built-in structures for rent-seeking and corruption on a massive scale, and under-incentivizes the formation of professional human capital and private innovation.[59] The challenges may exceed those of other developing economies that have had to navigate the transition from middle income to developed economy against the backdrop of an unreformed political system and weak legal institutions, as China now faces dual challenges in that on the one hand increased international integration and the social changes accompanying economic development mean that China must confront problems facing Western economies, namely global crises and problems of mature economies,

[56] Gallagher, ME 'The Social Relations of Chinese State Capitalism' in Liebman and Milhaupt 'Invisible Hand' supra note 8 at 225.

[57] Wang, AL'China State Capitalism and the Environment,' in Liebman and Milhaupt 'Invisible Hand' supra note 8 at 251.

[58] Sauvant and Nolan 'China's Rising Outward FDI' supra n 9 at 285.

[59] Liebman and Milhaupt 'Invisible Hand' supra note 8 at xxiv.

and on the other hand, the limitations of its own political-legal system.[60] Liebman and Milhaupt argue that 'reducing the influence of the state sector of the economy on Chinese law and legal institutions is an essential step towards the creation of a sound institutional framework for sustainable development. Doing so, of course, poses a monumental conundrum for Chinese political leadership. But disentangling the Communist Party from business enterprise, and Party-permeated corporations from the legal system, may be the leadership's best hope for the sustained growth and stability so essential to its legitimacy.'[61] Whilst this may be so in theory, it is, as they put it, 'a monumental conundrum for Chinese political leadership'. It is unlikely that the Chinese leadership would do this anytime soon. If anything, the trend appears to be going in the opposite direction with the party exerting more influence on SOEs and POEs through party committee. This trend is going to get stronger with the pressures from Trump 2.0 on various fronts to contain China's development. In the meantime, I argue that stakeholder committee or board with the participation of the party can play a positive role in addressing some of the challenges mentioned above.

ROLE OF CCP'S PARTY COMMITTEE IN SOES

It has been argued that corporations are neither private nor public, but hybrid, and not established by private contract (contrary to the neo-classical economic belief) but, rather, fostered by government, and should be regulated by distinct rules and norms.[62] Thus, corporations are not like private individuals that can be protected against government or political interference; they are distinct bodies that cut across private and public dichotomies, and therefore companies with political connections are to be expected across the world.[63] It is on this basis that in 2010, the General Office of the Central Committee and the General Office of the State Council issued 'Opinions on Further Promoting State-Owned Enterprises to Implement the Three Majors and One Big Decision-making System.' The 'three majors' have to be decided by the SOE leadership collectively—that is major decision-making, important personnel appointment and dismissal, and major project arrangements, as does the 'one big', that is a large-amount fund operation.[64] On 24 August 2015, the Central Committee of the CCP and the

[60] Ibid, at xxv.

[61] Liebman and Milhaupt 'Invisible Hand' supra note 8 at xxiv.

[62] Ciepley, D (2013) 'Beyond Public and Private: Towards a Political Theory' (107) *American Political Science Review* 139 at 158.

[63] Jiang, DX(2018) 'Zhengzhi Zhengdang Yu Qiye : Zhengzhi Quanli Canyu Ziyuan Fenpei De Wenming Jiegou (Party Politics and Enterprises: The Civilized Structure for the Political Power to Participate in Resource Allocation' 2018 *Dangdai Faxue* (Contemporary Legal Studies) 11-31 at 14

[64] See Chloe Wang, 'Party-led Corporate Governance: Embedded Party Organization in Chinese State-owned Enterprises' (unpublished SJD draft chapter at HKU being written under the author's supervision) at 25-26.

State Council jointly issued a Guiding Opinion on deepening SOE reform.[65] Apart from a number of measures aimed at improving the corporate governance structure of SOEs, developing mixed ownership reform, and preventing the loss of state assets, the most striking and controversial feature of the opinion is the emphasis on enhanced Party's leadership, requiring that SOEs should incorporate into their corporate charters the general requirements for Party building.[66] A pre-discussion procedure for these matters was introduced. This was followed a year later, on 10 October 2016, by President Xi's speech at a national meeting on enhancing the role of the Party within SOEs, stressing that the Party's leadership is 'the root and soul' of SOEs and that SOEs should become important forces implementing the Party's decisions.[67] Soon after this, on 3 January 2017, SASAC issued a notice with an elaborate template for the specific provisions to be adopted in non-financial SOEs' corporate charters, whilst the Ministry of Finance also issued a similar template for financial SOEs. The template contains three important directives. First, the Party Committee should assume the core leadership role in the SOE. Second, the board of directors should heed the opinions of the Party committee when making important decisions. Third, the amendment should devote a special chapter on the Party committee with details on the composition of the committee, its roles and rights and obligations.[68] These are more concrete steps to implement a similar requirement in the 2005 Company Law which, by article 19, required companies to establish a Party organization within a company to carry out the activities of the Party in accordance with the charter of the Party, and that companies should provide the necessary conditions for the activities of the Party organization but no further detail was provided. In 2019, a Party organization research and discussion mechanism was introduced as a pre-procedure for any pre-discussion. This was later formally incorporated into the Company Law in 2023 by article 170. So, China now has a dual party and corporate governance structure.[69] As will be explained below, there are problems with this dual structure but my idea of a stakeholder committee or board fits in with these initiatives and can improve the system by giving Party members specific responsibilities to look after their own stakeholders, with proper control by the Party on the appointment of such Party members.

As a result of the 2015 joint Opinion, according to a survey, 83% of all SOEs listed on the domestic stock exchanges amended their charters

[65] Central Committee of the Party and State Council, Guiding Opinions on Deepening State-Owned Enterprises Reform (Central Committee of CCP and State Council, 24 August 2015)

available at <http://www.gov.cn/zhengce/2015-09/13/content_2930440.htm>

[66] Liu, JZ and Zhang, AH (2019) 'Ownership and Political Control: Evidence from Charter Amendments' (60) *International Review of Law and Economics* 1 at 3.

[67] 'Xi Stresses CCP Leadership of State-Owned Enterprises' *Xinhua News Agency* (11 October 2016).

[68] Liu and Zhang 'Charter Amendments' supra note 66 at 3.

[69] Wang 'Party-led Corporate Governance' supra note 64

between 24 August 2015 and 30 September 2018.[70] Some SOEs underwent extensive amendment with specific mechanisms allowing the Party to exercise decisive control over the firm, whilst others are more reserved adopting fairly general language without much detail.[71] In addition, 84% of firms surveyed adopted provisions requiring the board of directors to consult the Party committee before making important decisions, and 88% of SOEs stipulated that the Party committee be closely involved in personnel decisions, whilst 57% specified the diffusion of leadership between the Party and the firm, and only 31% required that the Party Secretary be simultaneously the Chairman of the firm.[72]

Liu and Zhang found that ownership is indeed associated with the Party's intervention in the SOEs: the higher the level of state ownership, the more quickly an SOE amends its charter; the more concentrated the non-state owners, and the less likely it is for the SOEs to amend its charter. They also found that amendments by cross-listed SOEs are less extensive than those solely listed in China, as the former are bound by the tighter overseas regulatory environment.[73] Lin and Milhaupt have similar findings in another survey,[74] but they also found that both outside shareholders (minority and foreign[75]) and SOE managers resisted these adoptions

[70] Liu and Zhang 'Charter Amendments' supra note 66. For another survey see Lin and Milhaupt ('Party Building or Noisy Signaling? supra note 35), which found that a total of 1046 non-financial A-share listed firms (30.35% of the total) amended their corporate charters between January 1 2015 and December 31, 2018. Of the adopting firms, 300 are central SOEs, 603 are local SOEs, and 143 are POEs.

[71] Liu and Zhang 'Charter Amendments' supra note 66 at 2. In another survey, Lin and Milhaupt ('Party Building or Noisy Signaling? supra note 35), found that of the adopting firms, 96.3% of SOEs and 91.95% of POEs adopted symbolic provision, whereas the adoption rates of decision-making provisions (57.88% for SOEs and 25.17% for POEs) and personnel provisions (52.34% for SOEs and 15.72% for POEs) are much lower. Among decision-making provisions, only 74.36% of SOEs and 36.55% of POEs adopted provisions to allow board's prior consultation with party committee and 41.4% of SOEs and 13.79% of POEs adopted provisions to allow management's prior consultation with party committee.)

[72] Liu and Zhang 'Charter Amendments' supra note 66, at 4. In another survey, Lin and Milhaupt ('Party Building or Noisy Signalling? supra note 35) found that with regard to personnel provisions, only 34.3% of SOEs and 4.83% of POEs adopted provision to allow the chairman to serve simultaneously as party secretary, and 27.41% of SOEs and 3.45% of POEs appoint full-time deputy party secretary, but SOEs are more amenable to party cadre management (65.93%), having a discipline inspection committee (75.87%) and dual appointment of a person to be top executives and representatives in the party committee (58.27%), compared to POEs with 22.76% 22.07% and 25.52% respectively.

[73] Liu and Zhang 'Charter Amendments' supra note 66 at 2.

[74] Lin and Milhaupt 'Party Building or Noisy Signalling' supra note 35

[75] Interestingly, BlackRock, Fidelity and Schroders voted for amendments even though Institutional Shareholder Services Inc. ("ISS'), a leading independent proxy advisory body, recommends caution against such amendments: Lin and Milhaupt 'Party Building or Noisy Signaling' supra note 35.

ostensibly fearing party's interference in business, but for managers, the real reason for resistance is the fear of losing the insider control they enjoy.[76]

Lin and Milhaupt also found that even after multiple amendments to their charter, SOEs that resisted adoption of party-building provisions still adopted much fewer provisions than those adopting SOEs, and they resisted adopting interlocking party-personnel provisions the most. These SOEs are central SOEs as they have more resources and political power to resist political intrusion from the CCP than local SOEs, and they are central SOEs that do not cross-list on foreign stock exchanges and are less profitable, less efficient in business operations and potentially suffer from managerial tunneling.[77]

The trend of the Party's involvement continues as is required more recently by article 170 of the Company Law 2023 which provides that the Party organization in state-funded companies should play leading role in accordance with CCP's articles of association, the company's research and discussions on the company's major business management issues. Liu and Lin's research implies SOEs are more likely to change their charters to allow stakeholder committee and board if such a mechanism is mandated by the government.

Chinese SOEs now have ten million Party members and 800,000 party committees.[78] The Party controls SOEs through the decision-making personnel appointment processes. The board of directors needs to listen to the opinions of the Party committee before making important decisions, important personnel appointments, important project arrangements, and large scale use of capital. The other main mode of control is to appoint executives who act collectively to influence the decision-making process of the firm.[79] Corporations would not only install a party committee in every SOE, but the secretary of the committee and his deputy are also members of the board of directors of the SOEs, and as mentioned below, some serve as Chairman of the board. For example, the executives of the top 53 central SOEs are directly appointed by the Party's Central Organization Department.[80]

Politically connected firms enjoy many advantages—for example, higher leverage, lower taxation, stronger market power, and special treatment in enforcement by regulators.[81] Foreign regulators and academics have been

[76] Ibid.

[77] Ibid.

[78] Wu, W(2017),'How the Communist Party Controls China's State-Owned Industrial Titans,' *South China Morning Post*, 17 June 2017.

[79] Wang, JY (2014) 'The Political logic of corporate governance in China's state-owned enterprises' (43, 3) *Cornell Internataional Law Journal* 632.

[80] Lin, LW and Milhaupt, CJ (2013) 'We Are the (National) Champions: Understanding the Mechanism of State Capitalism in China' 65 *Stanford Law Review* 697

[81] Jiang DX 'Party politics and enterprises' supra note 63 at 19.

wondering about the extent of the Party's control over many giant SOEs, especially those among the Global Fortune 500.[82] Some argue that the Party has extensive control over the decision-making of Chinese SOEs,[83] but others conclude that Chinese SOEs enjoy greater managerial autonomy than is generally assumed.[84]

One study shows the number of Party members represented on the board of directors in 75 centrally controlled SOEs surveyed.[85] Only five SOEs do not disclose whether they have party committee members on the board in order to avoid any controversy due to local political and legal requirements, as their headquarters are in Hong Kong or Macau. But this does not mean that the board does not have party committee members. Nine SOEs' boards consist entirely of party members. In most SOEs, the secretary of the party committee who sits on the board also serves as the chairman of the board, so has legal and practical control over the board. In most SOEs' boards, party committee members are in the minority, outnumbered by outside directors. This, however, does not mean that the political linkage with the CCP is weak. This is because most of the outside directors are former government officials, SOEs' senior managers, party officials or party members. So there is a complicated direct or indirect party political linkage. Secondly, the chairman and the secretary of the board are often party committee members. They are able to control the agenda of the board meetings and often have de facto control over the board resolutions.[86] Furthermore, most important positions are also taken up by party committee members, for example, the general manager, chief accountant, chief engineer and general counsel. They check what proposals are made to the board for consideration. This has been the reality even before the recent requirement by the Joint Opinion and SASAC Notice to amend SOEs' articles to establish Party committees, and President Xi's speech about the role of the party committee in corporate governance. And there was a legal basis for such an organization within a company under article 19 of the 2005 Company Law (now article 170 of Company Law 2023). It has been suggested that recognizing the party's right to form party organizations in a corporation would enhance the rights of employees to form trade unions within the corporation, as they are both freedom of assembly and association guaranteed by the state Constitution.[87] It is further justified by the argument that political involvement by the

82 For example, Milhaupt, CJ, and Zheng, WT, (2015) "Beyond ownership: state capitalism and the Chinese firms", 103(3); *Georgetown Law Journal* 49 Zhang, AHY,'The antitrust paradox of China Inc,' (2017) 50 *New York University Journal of International Law and* Politics 9.

83 McGregor, Richard (2012) *The Party: The Secret World of China's Communist Rulers*, Harper Perennial.

84 Milhaupt and Zheng 'Institutions not Ownershp' supra note 52; Liu and Zhang 'Charter Amendments' supra note 66; Lin and Milhaupt 'Party Building or Noisy Signalling?' supra note 35.

85 See Jiang DX 'Party politics and enterprises' supra note 63 at 21-23.

86 Ibid, at 26.

87 Ibid, at 28.

Party in corporations is a necessary tool, and the most civilized way, for the government to be involved in the process of allocation of resources in order for the government to have adequate resources to defend and support the country. Not only will it ensure the protection of a country's resources, but also that corporations are run in line with the need of the country, and fulfill the purposes of industrial policy, prevent tax evasion by corporations, stop corporations from breaking the law and ensure the stability of state power.[88] In the same vein, Campbell points out that Party organization in an enterprise, as a systemic force, helps to enhance societal supervision of an enterprise's behaviour, restrain conduct that is not related to its social responsibility, effectively make up for the gap between market regulation and government regulation, promote coordinated social development, and facilitate benefit for the whole and assist in the harmonious development of the society.[89] The Party is an important stakeholder in a corporation, especially SOEs, representing the interests of both society and the state. Logically, therefore, it would seem that there should be no objection for corporations to allow other stakeholders including the Party, employees and others to be represented on the board, and be involved in the process of allocation of resources—stakeholder involvement in the allocation of resources would lead to better societal efficiency.

The directives by SASAC and the Minister of Finance indicate the seriousness of the Party in exerting effective control over the SOEs, as ownership alone had not enabled them to exert effective control in the past. It is claimed that the lack of effective control has led to performance and corruption issues.[90] The SASAC has established an assessment mechanism to ensure compliance linking assessment result with compensation from the management. The Central Commission and local commissions for Discipline Inspection carry out inspection on compliance with disciplinary action and sanction from the Party for non-compliance.

The details on how SOEs should comply with the requirement that party committee should play a role in a corporation's decision-making process—the process of allocation of resources, is still uncertain and remain negotiable. For example, what should be the weight of the committee's decision (whether the committee's decision is only a suggestion put to the board, or is it binding?), and whether the Committee should bear any legal responsibility for the decision they make? I suggest that it is possible to combine the role of the Party committee with stakeholder representation to allow the Party to be involved in the allocation of resources and to achieve societal efficiency at the same time by giving members of the stakeholder committee or board specific terms of reference to represent different stakeholders.

[88] Ibid, at 31.

[89] Campbell DE (2007) *A Matter of Faith: Religion in the 2004 Presidential Election* Brookings Institute Press. .

[90] Liu and Zhang 'Charter Amendments' supra note 66 at 4.

IMPLEMENTING STAKEHOLDER REPRESENTATION IN CHINA

Since China has recently instituted the Party committee within SOEs, as previously mentioned, and considering its beneficial influence on the performance of SOEs, as examined in the next section of this paper, I contend that the system could be enhanced in one of two ways, contingent upon whether the Party committee or the board of directors retains ultimate authority in the decision-making process.

If the Party committee's decision is to be followed by the Board of Directors, there should be stakeholder representation in the Party committee. Such a Party committee would constitute my proposed stakeholder committee. Under this option, Party committee members are assigned to represent different stakeholders with clear terms of reference and duties of care and fiduciary duties to the stakeholder represented and the SOE as a whole. Party committee members could be appointed by the Party according to the current practice.

If the board of directors has the final decision-making power, and the decision of the Party committee is merely advisory, then there should be stakeholder representation on board of directors. Such a board would constitute my proposed stakeholder board. Under this option, board members will be assigned to represent different stakeholders with clear terms of reference and duties of care and fiduciary duties to the stakeholder represented and the SOE as a whole. Members of the board will be appointed by the Party committee according to the current practice.

As in the stakeholder board proposed for the Anglo-American system,[91] stakeholders represented in the stakeholder committee or board should generally include the workers, consumers, environment and community and shareholders. Depending on the specific industry and sector in which the SOEs operate, if there are other stakeholders affected, they can be added later if necessary.

The clear terms of reference given to stakeholder representatives would include a detailed description of the functions, duties and responsibilities of the representatives. The details would obviously vary from firm to firm depending on the industry and sector involved.

As stakeholders' interests are not homogenous, there are bound to be conflicts between stakeholder interests. This would be resolved through majority votes at committee or board meeting which may involve negotiation and compromise between the representatives to maximize the interest of the stakeholders they represent. To ensure representatives actually advocate for their assigned stakeholders, they should owe (i) a duty of care and fiduciary duties to their stakeholders to maximize stakeholder interests

[91] See Goo, SH (2017) 'An Economic Efficiency Approach to Reforming Corporate Governance: the Case of Multiple Stakeholder Board' (4) *Asian Journal of Law and Society* 387.

subject to (ii) an overriding duty to the firm to act in the best interest of the firm. Where representatives fail in their duties, they would be subject to the existing legal enforcement mechanisms including legal actions by the firm or personal or derivative actions by stakeholders they represent. These two-fold duties are different from the existing legal duties of directors which are owed only to the company, which is interpreted to mean the shareholders.

How does my proposed stakeholder committee or board fit in with supervisory board and audit committee? It is well known that the supervisory board in China is not working well and is inefficient due mainly to its lack of real powers and incentives.[92] As the board of supervisors performs a different function—one similar to the audit committee—stakeholder committee or board can co-exist with board of supervisors. The stakeholder committee or board would operate by majority rule, and in the event of a deadlock, a people's court or an arbitration commission can be used to resolve the dispute.

The Company Law 2023 articles 69 and 121 now provide that Limited Liability Companies (LLCs) and joint-stock companies may establish an audit committee within the board of directors, without the need to establish a board of supervisors or to appoint supervisors. Directors may sit on the Audit Committee and the Committee may exercise the powers of the board of supervisors. Employee representatives who sit on the Board of Directors may sit on the Audit Committee. In the case of joint stock companies, audit committees must have at least three members, of which more than half must be independent (that is, do not hold any other positions within the company other than being directors, and must also not be in any relationship with the company that could affect their independent and objective judgment). Article 137 stipulates that for publicly listed companies, prior to the board of directors adopting a resolution pertaining to the appointment or dismissal of auditors or financial officers, the publication of financial audit reports, or matters governed by the China Securities Regulatory Commission (CSRC), such a resolution must receive the endorsement of the Audit Committee through a simple majority vote. As the Audit Committee's primary function revolves around auditing (as delineated in Article 137) and supervisory responsibilities (assuming the authority of the Board of

[92] See Goo, SH and Hong, Fidy XX (2011) 'The curious model of internal monitoring mechanisms of listed corporations in China: the Sinonization process' (12) *European Business Organization Law Review* 469. Article 126 of Company Law 1993 provided that the Supervisory Board or individual supervisor has the following powers: (1) to check on the financial affairs of the company; (2) to monitor the acts of directors and managers against any violation of laws, regulations or articles of association of the company by directors or managers while performing their duties; (3) to require directors or managers who have caused harm to the company to remedy the situation; (4) to propose the convening of interim meetings of the shareholders; (5) to exercise other powers provided for in the articles of association. Article 78 of the Company Law 2023 has added the following powers: (1) to propose the termination and removal of directors and managers who have violated laws, regulations, articles of association or resolution of shareholder meeting; (2) to convene and chair shareholder meeting where board of director has failed to do so; (3) to make proposals to shareholder meeting; (4) to commence legal proceedings against directors and managers in accordance with article 189.

Supervisors under Articles 78 and 131) to ensure that directors fulfil their obligations appropriately, while my proposed stakeholder committee or board is fundamentally centred on safeguarding stakeholder interests and preventing the externalization of costs by the company, a distinct division of labour emerges between the two committees. Thus, they can coexist, each executing a unique function, albeit there are certainly potential overlaps; for instance, a decision made by the board may entail irregularities or a breach of a director's duty while simultaneously externalizing the company's costs onto society.

The 2023 Company Law articles 75 and 128 allow a small limited liability company (LLC) or joint stock company, or LLC or joint stock company with few shareholders the option not to establish a board of directors. In such cases, a single director may be appointed to exercise the functions and powers of the board of directors and the director may also serve as a manager of the company. Similarly, articles 83 and 133 provide that small LLCs or joint stock company or LLCs or joint stock company with few shareholders may decide not to establish a board of supervisor(s), but to appoint a supervisor instead. In the case of an LLC, the company may choose not to appoint supervisor at all if such a proposal is approved by the unanimous consent of all shareholders. Where these provisions apply to SOEs, which is less likely given the usually large size of SOEs, and there are CSR abuses by these SOEs there will be a need for stakeholder committee to ensure that the sole director will not externalize the company's costs single-handedly.

WHY WOULD STAKEHOLDER BOARD BE GOOD FOR SOES?

Fits in with Purpose of Chinese Company Law: From State Ascendancy to Promoting Socialist Market Economy

Historically, China did not develop anything close to the 'company' that is known in the western world.[93] The concept of 'company' was introduced into China in the Qing Dynasty in late 19th century encouraged by the Chinese self-strengthening movement: a political course:[94] 'to create a better legal environment to encourage private investment, *which would ultimately lead to greater national prosperity*.'[95] This thinking was continued by the Company Law of 1929 by the Guomindang government which saw company as a 'vehicle in promoting state ascendancy over all private

[93] Zelin, M (2005) *The Merchants of Zigong: Industrial Enterprise in Early Modern China* Columbia University Press; see also Howson, NC (2017) 'China's 'corporatization without privatization' and the late 19th century roots of a stubborn path dependency", 50(4) *Vanderbilt Journal of Transnational Law*,961. (Also available at SSRN)

[94] See Goetzmann WN and Köl E (2005) 'The History of Corporate Ownership in *China: State Patronage, Company Legislation, and the Issue of Control' in* Morck RK (ed), *A History of Corporate Governance around the World: Family Business Groups to Professional Managers* University of Chicago Press 149-184, aavailable at http://www.nber.org/chapters/c10269.pdf

[95] Goetzmann and Köl 'Corporate Ownership' supra 93at 162 (emphasis added).

enterprise, Chinese and foreign' in line with Dr. Sun Yat-Sen's policy of 'restricting private capital' and promoting state control in the economy.[96] The Communist Party, when the first PRC Company Law was enacted in 1993, characterized the Law as necessary to 'meet the needs of establishing a modern enterprise system, to standardize the organization and activities of companies, to protect the legitimate rights and interests of companies, shareholders and creditors, *to maintain the socio-economic order and to promote the development of the socialist market economy*.'[97] This was repeated almost verbatim in the 2005 Company Law, the 2013 revision and the recent Company Law 2023.

Furthermore, articles 19-20[98] of Company Law 2023 and article 86[99] of the Code of Corporate Governance for listed companies all require companies to bear corporate social responsibilities. [100] So, it is clear that whilst subscribing to the western idea of profit maximization for shareholders (which in the case of SOES are the state), this is to be done with other stakeholders' interests in mind. The problem is that, apart from saying that[101] companies should protect employees' rights and should fully consider the interests of stakeholders, the law does not say how (that is, by what mechanisms) a company is to carry out its social responsibilities. It is my view that stakeholder committees or boards would provide such a mechanism.

[96] Kirby, WC (1995) 'China Unincorporated: Company Law and Business Enterprises in Twentieth-Century China' (54) *The Journal of Asian Studies* 43 at 51-52, cited in Wang, J (2014) *Company Law in China* Edward Elgar.

[97] Company Law 1993, article 1. (emphasis added)

[98] Company Law 2023, article 19 requires a company, when engaging in business activities, to abide by laws and administrative regulations, observe social morality and business ethics, act in good faith, accept supervision by the government and the public. Article 20 provides that'when conducting business operation, a company shall fully consider the interests of the company's employees, consumers, and other stakeholders, and ecological and environmental protection and other public interests, and assume social responsibilities. Under article 248 Company Law 2023, a foreign company's branch in China is required to comply with the law of China and not to harm China's social public interests.

[99] Under Article 86 of the Code of Corporate Governance for Listed Companies, a listed company is required to, while maintaining the listed company's development and maximizing the benefits of shareholders, be concerned with the *welfare, environmental protection and public interests of the community in which it resides, and shall pay attention to the company's social responsibilities*.' (emphasis added)

[100] There are other measures relating to Corporate Social Responsibility, Environmental Protection, and Social Impact.

[101] Company Law 2023, article 16 requires a company to protect the lawful rights and interests of its employees, and enter into labor contracts with its employees, contribute social insurance premiums, strengthen labor protection and ensure production safety according to the law. A company is required to use various methods to strengthen the vocational education and on-the-job training of its employees in order to improve their capabilities.

Further Enhances Efficiency of Party Committee's Involvement in Boards

The involvement of Party members in SOEs is seen by the Party as an effective way of reducing its agency problem,[102] and in fact is a type of stakeholder participation in decision-making process ideologically similar to the stakeholder committee or board which I have proposed. However, it has been much criticized and not understood by western commentators, citing the overlaps between politics and business and the difference in the objectives pursued by the party and the business as examples of political interference by the Party.[103] However, the business of corporations cannot be simply to maximize profits for the shareholders, but rather should be to maximize the interest of society by internalizing all costs of production whilst maximizing the shareholders' interests. Given the objectives of China's company law and the socialist market economy in which it is embedded, it is right for Party members to pursue party's political objectives in the interest of both society and the state, so long as in so doing they are only internalizing the costs of production and seeking to maximize the interest of society as a whole, rather than purely pursuing narrower political objectives to the detriment of shareholder and other stakeholder interests. Being the dominant shareholder (albeit through SASAC or Huijin), it is also unlikely that party members who represent the interests of the state will do so to the detriment of shareholder interest (the state). So the ostensible involvement of Party members in board decision-making process is not likely to lead to decisions that are purely political and detrimental to the business interests of the state. In fact, it will lead to more balanced decisions that are both good for business and are politically acceptable, a conclusion supported by empirical evidence analyzed in a recent study.[104] That study looked at the participation of party members in the board of supervisors, board of directors and senior management—a process referred to as 'dual-direction entry' or processes that allow membership in both directions—in 344 SOEs listed in the Shanghai and Shenzhen stock exchanges between the financial years 2008-2010 , and their effect on the standards of corporate governance and efficiency of the board of directors. It found that the involvement of party members in those boards has a reverse U shape correlation with the corporate governance standards of the firm, meaning that the corporate governance standards improve with the intensity of the party members' involvement with the boards up to an optimal point before they decline as the intensity increases. This suggests that whilst the party members' involvement is initially good for corporate governance, such involvement must not be overdone. Thus, the challenge is to find the optimal point. The

[102] Lin, Lauren Yu-Hsin (2021)'Institutionalizing Political Influence in Business: Party-Building and Insider Control in Chinese State-Owned Enterprises' (45) *Vermont Law Review* 441.

[103] Ma Lianfu , Wang Yuanfang and Shen Xiaoxiu (2012) 'Zhongguo Guoyou Qiye Dang Zuzhi de Zhili Xiaoying Yanjiu' (Research on the Governance Effects of Party Organizations in Chinese State-Owned Enterprises] 83 *Zhongguo Gongye Jingji* (China Industrial Economics 83.

[104] Ibid, at 82.

study argued that this means that before internal control system and external market mechanism are well developed, administrative intervention is still necessary, and that government should in the meantime develop market mechanisms and reduce administrative intervention once such mechanisms are in place and effective, and that administrative intervention should take the form of political guidance rather than political directives.[105] Whilst I agree with the general thrust of the argument, it would be some time before such market mechanisms can become fully effective, if at all. I would argue that the existing board of directors (with members of Party Committee) can be turned into a stakeholder board by making directors individually represent different stakeholders with specific terms of reference as mentioned above. Alternatively, members of the Party committee can be assigned to represent different stakeholders.

The study also found that when the chief secretary of the party committee in the SOE also serves as the chairman of the board of directors or board of supervisors or general manager there is a negative impact on the SOE's corporate governance standards, whereas if the deputy secretary serves in such position, there is a positive correlation.[106] The explanation offered is that in the former case, there is a concentration of political power and corporate power in one person, whereas in the latter case, there is a separation of powers.[107] But such a dual role by either does

[105] Ibid, at 92. For another analysis see Chloe Wang's SJD study ('Party-led Corporate Governance' supra note 64) which looks at how party committee participates in SOE corporate governance and its impact on central and local SOEs and the risk to their autonomy and competitiveness in good as well as less developed market environments respectively, and the feasibility of involving party committee in SOE corporate governance as a good political interference that provides sufficient oversight in SOE without obstructing development of market economy and rule of law in an authoritarian state (HKU SJD thesis: Party-led Corporate Governance: Formalized Party Organization in Chinese State-owned Enterprises (2 October 2025)). It also assesses the extent of party's involvement by looking at two proxy variables, namely (1) the ratio of party organization members who serve on board of directors, supervisory board and senior management to the total number of members across these boards, (2) ratio of major issues determined by the board of directors and management. To assess the impact on agency cost arising from conflict between shareholders and management, and impact of efficiency of SOE, it looks at the asset turnover ratio and ratio of administrative and selling expenses to the total assets. The hypothesis is that there is an inverted U-shaped relationship between party's involvement and firm performance. It also looks at impact on business performance by using ROA, ROE and Tobin's Q collectively as proxy variables to eliminate individual bias. It chooses company's size, leverage, growth, age, industry and year as control variables. To assess impact on ESG performance it uses a propensity score matching (PSM) design and difference in difference (DID) model to investigate the causal effect of the pre-discussion decision making mechanism on SOE's ESG performance, using firm-level panel data set of Chinese listed companies from 2012 to 2022. To evaluate ESG performance, ESG evaluation rating developed by Sino-Securities Index Information Services (Shanghai) Company as proxy variable, based on company's ESG reports, social responsibility reports, sustainable development reports, annual reports, information from official websites and third party data.

[106] Ma Lianfu & Ors 'Governance Effects' supra note 103 at 90-92.

[107] Ibid, at 90-91. In another study, it was found that boards with a politically connected chairperson hire fewer academics, accountants, legal and finance professionals and overseas returnees; instead,they hire substantially more politicians as independent directors: Jiao H

not significantly improve the efficiency of the board of directors.[108] The study proposed that there should be further regulation on the principles, content and mode of party committee's involvement in the SOE's major decision-making processes, clearer stipulation of the purpose and extent of such involvement in SOEs' corporate governance, further regulation on the procedures of such decision-making process, various mechanisms to allow such involvement, and effective execution of decisions monitored.[109] It is also proposed that Party members who serve in the Party committee and board of directors should follow the evaluation criteria for the cadre as a party member and the criteria for economic expertise when conducting the affairs of the SOEs, so that they can be both 'red and professional' (*yuu hong you zhuan*). The authors of the study further proposed that either the secretary of the Party committee be the deputy chairman of the board of directors, or the deputy secretary of the Party committee be the chairman of the board of directors. This would help to ensure an appropriate degree of separation of powers arrangement, avoiding the concentration of power in the hands of one person and providing some form of checks and balances. It is also proposed that the chairman of the board of supervisors assume the role of the secretary of the Party committee, thereby augmenting the authority of the board of supervisors and integrating the administrative oversight functions executed by the Party committee with the economic supervision responsibilities carried out by the board of supervisors. This strategic alignment aims to ensure the efficacy of decision-making, oversight, and execution by the boards of directors, supervisors, and senior management.[110] These are all very sensible proposals. But the proposed stakeholder committee or board, for which I have advocated, will furnish an enhanced mechanism for the Party's engagement in the decision-making process by incorporating Party members within the stakeholder committee or board. This structure will delineate comprehensive terms of reference outlining the responsibilities of the stakeholder committee members or directors, alongside regulations governing the appointment and removal of these individuals, as well as the objectives and procedural guidelines for meetings, among other pertinent matters. Whilst in theory a socialist government should represent the interests of all members of society, in practice different stakeholder committee members or directors would be able to better articulate the interests of different stakeholders in the society in the decision-making process, thereby helping the government and the SOEs to make decisions that would maximize the interests of all stakeholders and also society.

In another related study looking at the appointment of Party Committee members in the board of directors, board of supervisors and senior management of A share listed SOEs in the period between 2008-2010, it is

et al (2013). This may affect the effectiveness of the board.

108 Ma Lianfu & Ors 'Governance Effects' (2012) supra note 103 at 92.

109 Ibid, at 94.

110 Ibid, at 94.

found from their annual reports that the involvement of Party Committee in the corporate governance of the SOEs increased the scale of employee redundancy, lowered the salaries of the senior management team, and inhibited the behaviour of senior management obtaining excessive salaries, and reduced the gap in the salary between the senior management team and the ordinary employees.[111] This is because as the members of the boards are also party members, they are more interested in promotion in political sphere, rather than their salaries per se. Thus, they accept the state's "salaries cap order' more positively, exercise restraint over their own salaries, and act more like the steward in the Stewardship Theory.[112] The study also confirms the existence of interference by the State in SOEs through Party Committees but concludes that the interference contributes to the corporate governance theories with Chinese characteristics. However, the same paper also suggests that there should be detailed laws and regulations to set out the content and the ways in which party's participation in corporate governance should take place. How party organization should exercise its political core influence in enterprises, and how the relationship between its influence and economic decisions should be clarified has long been a major challenge. I suggest that my proposed stakeholder committee or board with detailed terms of reference on stakeholder directors' appointment and powers is one way to address the challenge.

The Practical Need to Manage Stakeholder Issues and to Increase Efficiency

As noted in the Introduction to this essay, China is now the second largest economy in the world, and will soon overtake US as the largest. Many of its giant corporations are now in the Fortune 500 and this trend is likely to increase. Like the US counterpart, their operations have had, are having and will continue to have, huge impact on the society and the environment. China has a great opportunity to become the world leader in sustainable development and corporate social responsibility and is moving rapidly in that direction. Stakeholder committees or boards if adopted and work in China, will become the model for the world to emulate. I believe there is a very good chance that such a mechanism would work in China. It fits in with Chinese traditional cultures and Communist Party's political ideology and philosophy.

Secondly, like many developed and developing countries, China has experienced environmental problems, worker abuse, consumer product safety issues etc. It is of practical necessity for China to have a more effective corporate governance structure to deal with these issues. I argue that stakeholder committee or board could be part of that structure.

111 Ma Lianfu, Wang Yuanfang and Shen Xiaoxiu (2013)'Guoyou Qiye Dang Zuzhi Zhili, Rongyü Guyuan yu Gaoguan Xinchóu Qiyue' (Party Organization Governance, Redundant Employees and Executive Compensation Contracts in State-Owned Enterprises) *Guanli Shijie* (Management World) 100.

112 Ibid, at 113.

Whilst it is true that CCP is in charge of the economy and key SOEs, and therefore can look after stakeholders quickly and quite efficiently as the surveys mentioned above show, if the party members only represent the narrow interests of the factions within the party, there is a risk that other stakeholder interests may be sacrificed. Stakeholder committee or board can minimize the risk and achieve a more balanced and efficient outcome.

Furthermore, as the private sector in the Chinese economy is now becoming increasingly important (superseding the public sector) and the small SOEs are not looked after by CCP, so there is also a need to foster stakeholder interest in these sectors. A successful implementation of the stakeholder committee or board in giant SOEs can present a role model for small SOEs and other private enterprises.

As Milhaupt and Zheng point out, what China needs is not ownership but institutional reform to the SOEs.[113] Because of the close relationship all large Chinese firms inherit and maintain or nurture with the state in order to survive in China's prevailing political economy and institutional environment,[114] the state's influence and dominance is prevalent. This is unlikely to change for the foreseeable future. Firms have to conform to this political reality in order to obtain special advantages (for example, access to low cost financing, stock listings or state-sanctioned monopolies or oligopolies) from the national or local governments by aligning themselves with the political leadership's interest, goals, and priorities.[115] Furthermore, as the Communist Party has the real law making power and broad discretion in setting administrative rules, the legal and regulatory system is vulnerable to political influence and Communist Party directives.[116] Communist Party, being a party that cares for the people, will make law and administrative rules that are in the best interest of the people. However, occasionally, there have been instances of abuse, leading to allegations or criticism of corruption and cronyism,[117] or over or under-regulation. Thus, to provide adequate checks and balances on how corporate power in state-owned firms are exercised on the one hand, and to enable firms to align with the Communist Party's political objectives and goals in the economy on the other hand, stakeholder committee or board would be an ideal mechanism that I believe would be acceptable to both the Communist Party[118] and the economists. This is because the Chinese model of economic decision-making is highly decentralized to the local governments, and local government officials are rewarded and punished based on their economic

[113] Milhaupt and Zheng 'Institutions not Ownership' supra note 52 at 177.

[114] Ibid, at 182.

[115] Ibid, at 182.

[116] Ibid, at 184.

[117] Ibid, at 184-5.

[118] As Milhaupt and Zheng acknowledge,'contrary to popular perceptions, China's model of economic decision-making is highly decentralized.' Milhaupt and Zheng 'Institutions not Ownership' supra note 52 at 186.

performance. As local government officials have to compete for better economic performance, successful large firms, whether state-owned or private, are likely to be those favoured by local governments.[119] Stakeholder committee or board will assist the firms to increase the societal economic efficiency and performance, and therefore likely to be acceptable to local government and the Communist Party. Similarly, it would be acceptable to the economists because of its increased societal efficiency.

The investment activities of Chinese firms abroad has raised concerns not adequately addressed by the current foreign investment regime,[120] which tension will have to be resolved in some way, either 'through changes to Chinese regulatory structures and firms or to the global trade and investment regimes'.[121] The principal actor of Chinese state capitalism is the SOE, which typically takes the form of a corporation, whose shares are wholly or significantly owned by a state agency or organ.[122] This places the state in dual and often conflicting capacities: as institutional designer and enforcer on the one hand and participant in the economy on the other.[123] Many of these SOEs are now in the Global Fortune 500,[124] and their investment abroad has been both welcomed and feared by host countries around the world. How should China address these concerns? As noted elsewhere,[125] the availability of finance and corporations as an institution have been critical to the explosive and unprecedented growth in the world GDP since 1800. China has quite rightly adopted 'corporatization' as a crucial early move in its reform process, with the standard corporate governance organs of board of directors and shareholder meetings familiar to the international investors, using the Chinese and global capital markets to raise finance, and corporate groups to foster the growth of national champions.[126] However, China's state capitalism is different from corporate capitalism in the West in both its internal corporate form and externally how they are treated as actors in the political economy.[127] Internally, the standard corporate structures and operations are supplemented or altered by Chinese Communist Party organs, whilst externally they enjoy

[119] Ibid, at 187.

[120] Sauvant and Nolan (2016), at 285.

[121] See Liebman and Milhaupt (2016), at xv (emphasis added).

[122] See ibid, at xv.

[123] See ibid, at xv.

[124] China now has the second largest number of Global Fortune 500 companies after the United States and two-thirds of them are SOEs: See Liebman and Milhaupt (2019), at xv. For the list of Fortune 500 see http://fortune.com/fortune500/.

[125] Goo, SH (2019) 'Corporate Governance Reform' in Institute of Comparative Law in Japan's 70th Anniversary Commemorative Book Series Editorial Committee (ed), *Beyond Globalization: Future of Comparative Law in Asia-Pacific*, Chuo University Press, 293-310.

[126] Clarke 'Blowback' .supra note 47.

[127] Liebman and Milhaupt 'Invisible Hand' supra note 8 at xvii.

comparatively limited degree of autonomy from the state (whether state-owned or privately owned),[128] and pursuing comparatively broad scope of objectives extending beyond the corporation's shareholders and employees to include executing state policies and advancing the soft power of the state itself.[129] China has adopted market economy without capitalism since Dang Xiaoping's open door policy: market economy is not equivalent to capitalism and socialism is not equivalent to state planning. China's formula for success has been to adopt market economy in its socialism. This has 'profound implications for China's institutional development and for the integration of Chinese corporations into the global trade and investment regime'.[130] How should China maintain the balance in such integration?

In its search for the proper approach to SOE reform and regulation, as mentioned earlier, China moved away from the traditional Soviet model adopted in the 1980s to the Singapore model in the 1990s, but away from the Singapore model by 2000s as a result of the legal and political environment and the role of the bureaucrats in managing SOEs, which involved no restraints on state power and little respect for corporate governance norms.[131] The lack of restraints has helped to support Communist Party's control which is not a problem in itself, but also resulted in 'beds of corruption and nepotism' that prevent market competition. SOEs were seen as inefficient and 'a burden to the free market in China'.[132] Unlike the Singapore model, Chinese SOEs, though corporatized and even listed, were not managed on commercial basis or in competitive markets. China's state-asset regulators continue to maintain absolute control of important sectors and strategic areas, and majority control of backbone industries, new technology sectors, and strategic emerging industries.[133] It may well be that the leadership will gradually open up the markets, but before that how should Communist Party's control on corporations be managed? It is argued that stakeholder committee or board would enable the Party to maintain control of SOEs but at the same time increase its efficiency.

[128] Milhaupt and Zheng 'Institutions not Ownership' supra note 53 at 175.

[129] Li, JR (2022) *Zhongguo Qiji Yu Zhongguo Zhidu* (The China Miracle and Chinese System) Kai Ming Bookstore. 2022) at 7.

[130] Liebman and Milhaupt 'Invisible Hand' supra note 8 at xvii.

[131] See ibid, at xvii.

[132] Feng, Deng (2016) 'Indigenous Evolution of SOE Regulation' in Benjamin L. Liebman and Curtis J. Milhaupt (eds) *Regulating the Visible Hand? The Institutional Implications of Chinese State Capitalism*, OUP at 15.

[133] Rutkowski, R (2014)'Reform: the Long Wait for a Chinese Temasek Continues ... ,' *Peterson Institute for International Economics* (PIIE), 23 January 2014, available at file:///Users/peterg/Documents/Documents%20from%20old%20mac%20pro/TOSHIBA/phd%20degree/sg%20columbia/JSD%20reading%20list/State-Owned%20Enterprise%20Reform:%20the%20Long%20Wait%20for%20a%20Chinese%20Temasek%20Continues...%20%7C%20PIIE.webarchive

Improves the Transparency of SOEs

It is not entirely clear how stakeholder interests are protected even in SOEs that have done an excellent job in this regard. For example, the China High-speed Railway promotes primarily consumer and society's interest sacrificing shareholder interest, but how decisions are made and priorities set remains a block box. The high-speed railway and its economic trickledown effect would not have been possible if it was to focus purely on profit maximization. Operated by China Railway Corporation (CRC), the high speed railway went into operation since 2007. It is the largest high-speed railway network in the world, covering a total mileage of 38,000 kilometers and is still expending, estimated to reach 70,000 km by 2035. The cost of construction is enormous. Yet the fare is the cheapest in the world.[134] The seats are spacious and comfortable, and it is fast, frequent and efficient. CRC is a centrally managed state-owned enterprise formally established in March 2013[135] wholly owned by the Ministry of Finance of China. Its mission, among others, is to undertake the public welfare transportation prescribed by the state, and ensure the key transport and special transportation, rescue and disaster relief transportation and other tasks related to national economy and people's livelihood.[136]

Its annual report only covers use of capital and financial report.[137] It is not clear how decisions in the interests of stakeholders are made and implemented, although the corporation is spending resources on its social responsibility in environmental and ecology issues, relief of poverty and scholarship, and customers and community welfare.[138] Obviously many of the corporate social responsibility issues are dealt with by various departments and offices. CCP through its Party Committee in the CRC obviously has real influence on the policies, decisions and operation of the corporation. There are also various communication channels for employees and members of the public, for whistle-blowing and survey.[139] My proposed stakeholder committee or board would increase transparency in this regard.

Enhances Belt and Road Initiatives

The BRI, like the New Deal in the US but only in much larger scale, is the next phase of China's economic development involving huge infrastructural developments in more than 80 countries along the belt and road routes. To ensure that all the costs are internalized, all stakeholder interests are

[134] 0.04 euro per km, compared to Spain (0.19 euro), France (0.22 euro), Germany (0.27 euro), Italy (0.25 euro) and Japan (0.22 euro).

[135] http://www.china-railway.com.cn/zgsgk/gsjj/200303/t20030323_41984.html

[136] Ibid.

[137] http://www.shclearing.com/xxpl/cwbg/nb/201604/t20160429_150527.html

[138] http://www.china-railway.com.cn/shzr_1/hjst/

[139] http://www.china-railway.com.cn/hdjl/wsjy/

properly considered and taken care of to increase allocative efficiency, and the state in which such developments are carried out receives a fair share of the benefits, stakeholder committee or board should be introduced in the companies involved. Currently, China is pursuing a 'maximized flexibility' approach of using soft law and voluntary form of cooperation, avoiding engaging through treaties, and is passive in sensitive areas such as governance, labour, environmental and social impact issues.[140] These informal arrangements set out principles but do not bring much normative development regarding these non-trade concerns.[141] This could imply negative consequences for the BRI, in its overall treatment of these issues in a consistent and coherent manner, and reduce predictability, transparency, and risk management for BRI-involved parties.[142] For example, Chinese firms in Pakistan, Myanmar and Kenya face tension and opposition from local communities. It has been argued that a BRI-wide treaty with a formal institutional arrangement could help build the legitimacy and trust in BRI and deal with specific concerns of BRI countries including social and environmental standards.[143] It is not clear how the BRI will strike a balance between market considerations, social values, and other considerations, and how these considerations would be turned into operational norms, and which factor shall prevail if there is a conflict between profits and social values.[144] A major challenge is to identify appropriately constrained flexibility mechanisms that strike the balance.[145] I would argue that stakeholder committee or board in the BRI-corporations could play the role of the formal mechanism that would strike the balance between profit and social values, as the investors' interest (for example, Chinese corporation in BRI host countries) and local social values will be represented on the board to negotiate for a balanced decision. It could reduce the tension between Chinese firms and local communities.

CONCLUSIONS

The current Chinese corporate governance structure in SOEs is another limited type of stakeholder board with employee representatives on the Board of Directors and Board of Supervisors or Audit Committee and Party members on the Party Committee playing a role in the decision-making process. But this is not the same as my proposed stakeholder committee or board as in the current structure directors (other than the employee representatives) and party members individually do not represent any specific stakeholders. Party committees are fundamentally distinct entities

140 Wang, H (2019)'China's approach to Belt and Road Initiative: Scope, Character and Sustainability,' 22 *Journal of International Economic Law*, 29.

141 Ibid.

142 Ibid.

143 Ibid, at 51.

144 Ibid, at 52.

145 Ibid, at 53.

from boards of directors, with Party members embodying the state (which, in theory, encompasses all other stakeholders within society, yet encounters analogous challenges to the enlightened shareholder approach prevalent in the UK, or the Jensenian model of enlightened value maximization, wherein directors are collectively tasked with considering the interests of all stakeholders). Moreover, these members may lack the requisite qualifications or motivation to effectively engage with the concerns of other stakeholders. But the involvement of party members provides evidence that stakeholder involvement can improve social efficiency. From the empirical literature, it is clear that the involvement of party committee in the governance of SOEs is, to a certain extent, a positive step forward. However, there is a risk that it may not represent stakeholders adequately. If members of the party committee are given specific terms of reference and duties, it can be a mechanism that implements CSR in China, and enhances the advantages of the structure, that is, corporate efficiency and sufficient oversight of SOEs.[146] If the Chinese government can see the benefit of a stakeholder committee or board and combine it with the Party committee as suggested above, its implementation should not be a difficult issue.

This analysis of SOE governance reform also reveals fundamental dynamics of administrative justice in contemporary China that extend far beyond the corporate sector. The institutional conflicts between party committees, corporate boards, and regulatory agencies mirror the competitive fragmentation found throughout China's administrative system. The persistent implementation gaps between formal governance rules and actual practice reflect broader challenges in translating central directives into effective local action. Most significantly, the party-state's response to governance failures—formalizing political oversight rather than strengthening independent accountability mechanisms—exemplifies the Chinese adaptation strategies that characterize administrative reform across domains.

The proposed stakeholder representation system addresses a core challenge in China's approach to administrative justice: how to protect citizen interests while maintaining party-state control. By embedding stakeholder advocates within existing power structures rather than creating independent oversight bodies, this proposal reflects the broader pattern of procedural innovation within institutional constraints that defines contemporary Chinese governance. The success or failure of such mechanisms in SOEs will likely influence how administrative justice evolves in other sectors where state power directly impacts citizen welfare. The SOE governance experience thus serves as a laboratory for understanding how administrative justice can be reconceptualized within China's distinctive institutional framework, offering insights relevant to governance transformation beyond the economic sphere.

[146] Wang 'Party-led Corporate Governance' supra note 64 at 35-36.

GLOSSARY OF CHINESE TERMS

Chinese (Hanyu Pinyin)	Characters	English
dangwei fushuji	党委副书记,	deputy Party secretary
dangwei shuji	党委书记	Party Secretary (in the SOE)
gongyi jijin	公益基金	social/public benefit foundations
Guowuyuan Guoziwei	国务院国资委	State Council Assets Supervision and Administration Commission [also known as 国资委 Guoziwei])
jiaocha renzhi	交叉任职	dual positions - Chief secretary of party committee also serves as the chairman of the board of directors or board of supervisors or general manager
shangji zhuguan danwei	上级主管单位	superior-unit-in-charge
Shiwu Jie Sizhong Quanhui	十五届四中全会	Fourth Plenary Session of the 15th CCP Committee Meeting
you hong you zhuan.	又紅又專	'red and professional'

Zhonggong Di Shiqi Ci Congress Quanguo Daibiao Dahui	中共第十七次全 国代表大会	17th National of the CCP
Zhongyang Huijin Touzi Youxian Zeren Gongsi Company	中央汇金投资 有限责任公司	Central Huijin Investment Limited

PART IV

IMPLEMENTATION CHALLENGES AND BUREAUCRATIC DYSFUNCTION

Lazy Officials and Administrative Justice: Governance and Ideology

SARAH BIDDULPH
University of Melbourne

INTRODUCTION

Scope of the Inquiry

The editors of these two special sections of the Journal focusing on administrative justice, note that administrative justice is generally understood to comprise two dimensions. The first is on 'provision of public services and the conduct of public officials'.[1] The second is the processes for seeking redress against official conduct. The concern of this paper lies in the realm of the first, which is the governance of public officials. This paper is concerned with the problem of alleged failure by Communist Party of China ('Party' or 'CCP') and government officials (together referred to as officials) to exercise their roles and responsibilities either properly or at all. My focus is on the problem of bureaucratic inertia (*lanzheng daizheng*),[2] and its most recent iteration in the campaign against the 'lying flat officials' (*tangping shi ganbu*). It considers causes, remedial actions taken and what these might reveal about characteristics of governance of the Chinese bureaucracy. A point worth noting is that in the PRC, governance is exercised by the Party-state - which increasingly fuses Party and state power. Bureaucracy, then, includes the work of both Party officials and government officials. Since 2018 this extends down to the level of local government.[3] Since Xi Jinping's leadership from 2012 the separation between Party and state actors has been further eroded in theory, law and practice.[4]

What type of a problem is omission? There are a range of dimensions that are relevant. From a rule of law perspective, we can view both (mis) conduct and omission as a species of arbitrary exercise of administrative

[1] Palmer, M; Xi, C and Zhou, L 'Special Section: Issues in Administrative Justice Part One' (17) *Journal of Comparative Law* 253.

[2] While l*anzheng daizheng* could be more accurately translated as lazy governance, negligent (or idle) governance, I have chosen to use bureaucratic inertia as a way to capture all the different ways in which bureaucrats fail actively and positively to exercise their powers in the service of citizens. Biddulph, S (2019) 'The Impact of Transparency and Accountability Mechanisms on Bureaucratic Inertia: A Case Study of Work Safety Regulations' in Biddulph, S and Biukovic, L (eds) (2019) *Good Governance in Economic Development: International Norms and Chinese Perspectives* UBC Press 291.

[3] Wang, J and Mou, Y (2021) 'The Paradigm Shift in the Disciplining of Village Cadres in China: From Mao to Xi' (248) *The China Quarterly* 181.

[4] Li, L (2015) '"Rule of Law" in a Party-State: A Conceptual Interpretive Framework of the Constitutional Reality of China' (2) *Asian Journal of Law and Society* 93.

power (described by Martin Krygier as uncontrolled, unpredictable and unrespectful)[5] just manifesting in different ways. From a political point of view, failures of administration have been clearly identified by the Party as a threat to Party legitimacy. This point is discussed in more detail below. From the perspective of bureaucratic governance, there is a question about what ideological and institutional factors motivate officials to do their job in a professional and efficient manner, which is also a question of concern in this paper.

From a practical point of view, we need to ask whether the problem of bureaucratic inertia is as widespread or serious as it is made out to be. While this paper is not centrally concerned with this question, the harms caused by failure to exercise administrative powers and responsibilities in certain sectors are well documented, longstanding and serious. In the areas such as environmental protection, food and drug safety, labour rights and work health and safety, and local policing the consequences of failures can be catastrophic.[6] Regulatory failures in these sectors have frequently led to serious social unrest and have been dealt with by a nearly constant stream of rectification campaigns.[7] So, while it is difficult to determine the extent and seriousness of the problem of bureaucratic inertia across the whole spectrum of administration, it is possible to conclude that the current scare is not entirely fabricated even if there are extraneous political reasons for the political focus on it.

[5] Krygier, M (2021) 'Illiberalism and the Rule of Law' in Sajo, A; Uitz, R and Holmes, S (eds) (2021) *Routledge Handbook of Illiberalism* Routledge 533.

[6] In relation to food safety, the Sanlu tainted milk scandal is just one of many. Chung, S and Wong, CK (2013) 'Regulatory and Policy Control on Food Safety in China' (67) *Journal of Epidemiology and Community Health* 476. In relation to labour inspections see Ho, V (2009) 'From Contracts to Compliance? An Early Look at Implementation under China's New Labor Legislation' (23) *Columbia Journal of Asian Law* 35. In relation to environmental law enforcement see van Rooij, B (2006) *Regulating Land and Pollution in China: Lawmaking, Compliance, and Enforcement; Theory and Cases* Leiden University Press; van Rooij, B (2002) 'Implementing Chinese Environmental Law through Enforcement' in Chen, J; Li, Y and Otto, JM (eds) (2002) *Implementation of Law in the People's Republic of China* Kluwer Law International 149; van Rooij, B (2014) 'Regulation by Escalation: Unrest, Lawmaking and Law Enforcement in China' in Trevaskes, S; Nesossi, E; Sapio, F and Biddulph, S (eds) (2014) *The Politics of Law and Stability in China* Edward Elgar Publishing 83. I have looked at the impact of failures on the administration of justice in relation to work health and safety in Biddulph 'The Impact of Transparency and Accountability Mechanisms on Bureaucratic Inertia: A Case Study of Work Safety Regulations' supra note 2; Cooney, S; Biddulph, S and Zhu, Y (2013) *Law and Fair Work in China* Routledge.

[7] For example the campaign to address wage arrears for migrant workers was conducted between 2004 and 2007 and has been the subject of a rectification campaign nearly annually since then. Biddulph, S; Cooney, S and Zhu, Y (2012) 'Rule of Law with Chinese Characteristics: The Role of Campaigns in Law-Making' (34) *Law & Policy* 373; Cooney et al *Law and Fair Work in China* supra note 6; Biddulph, S (2018) 'Democratic Centralism and Administration in China' in Fu, H; Gillespie, J; Nicholson, P and Partlett, W (eds) (2018) *Socialist Law in Socialist East Asia* Cambridge University Press 195. In relation to local policing Scoggins, S and O'Brien, K (2016) 'China's Unhappy Police' (56) *Asian Survey* 225; Scoggins, S (2018) 'Policing Modern China' (3) *China Law and Society Review* 79.

As this paper focuses on the legal, institutional and ideological dimensions of omission and its rectification, I have not focused analysis on any particular level of local government, which could encompass all levels from provincial down to village level. The focus of the current campaign whilst addressing inertia generally, is particularly on the local level of governance. That does not necessarily mean that bureaucratic inertia is the sole preserve of the lowest levels of government. But in understanding the emphasis on local government failures, it is worth noting that responsibility for delivery of basic services and stability maintenance has largely been delegated to local governments and particularly to the village level. It is also common practice for blame, for this as for other problems of administration, to be shifted downwards along the vertical lines of authority to the lowest level. Blame shifting is also apparent in discussions of failures of law and policy implementation at the level of local government.[8] To the limited extent that the Party has acknowledged overwork exacerbated by meaningless tasks as a factor in bureaucratic inertia, it has been at the village level.

Targeting omission: political and ideological dimensions

The political dimension of the problem of omission was again thrust into the spotlight when in June 2023, the campaign against lying flat officials burst into public view. This is the latest in a long series of measures taken by the Party to address the problem of officials who (allegedly) do not do their job, or do not do it efficiently and diligently. Labels such as 'lying flat officials' and 'mediocre officials and lazy governance' (*yongguan lanzheng*), all represent dimensions of bureaucratic inertia, where officials do not fulfil their roles and responsibilities, or do so partially, or with lack of care and are seen as having forgotten their 'original intention' and 'mission' of wholeheartedly serving the people.[9]

For the Party, bureaucratic inertia is a big deal. For a vanguard party like the CCP, Party members and government officials are the corporeal embodiment of the Party and enact the relationship between the people and the Party. Their conduct gives substance to the ideological commitment of

[8] Ran, R (2017) 'Understanding Blame Politics in China's Decentralized System of Environmental Governance: Actors, Strategy and Context' (231) *The China Quarterly* 634. Li, J; Ni, X and Wang, R (2021) 'Blame Avoidance in China's Cadre Responsibility System' (247) *The China Quarterly* 681 at 682-683.

[9] Xinhua News Agency 'The Central Leading Group for Education on the Theme of "Don't Forget the Original Aspiration and Remember the Mission" Issued the "Work Plan on Finding Gaps in the Theme Education of "Don't Forget the Original Aspiration and Remember the Mission" in Comparison with the Party Constitution and Party Regulations (*Zhongyang 'buwang chuxin, laoji shiming' zhuti jiaoyu lingdao xiaozu yinfa "Guanyu zai 'buwang chuxin, laoji shiming' zhuti jiaoyu zhong duizhao dangzhang danggui zhao chuju de gongzuo fang'an" wwww. gov.cn* 21 July 2019. Xi, J (2020) "Don't Forget Your Original Intention and Keep Your Mission in Mind" Speech at the Conclusion of the Education Conference on the Theme of "Don't Forget Your Original Intention, Keep Your Mission in Mind" (*'buwang chuxin, laoji shiming' Xi Jjinping "zai buwang chuxin, laoji shiming' juti jiaoyu zongjie dahui shang de jianghua)' cpcnews.cn* 8 January 2020 Available at: <http://cpc.people.com.cn/n1/2020/0630/c64094-31765104.html>.

the mass line: to wholeheartedly serve the people.[10] Failure in the exercise of powers and responsibilities of office thus risks alienating the Party from the people and so eroding Party legitimacy. Xi Jinping has framed the hazard of officials forgetting their original intent and mission and becoming disconnected from the masses in urgent terms: as an existential risk to the foundations of Party legitimacy.[11] It is also interpreted as a failure of fealty to the Party under Xi Jinping.

The Party wants officials to stand up. It wants them to be motivated to stand up, to remember their mission and responsibility, to take on their responsibilities and not dare to lie down on the job.[12] However, rectifying a problem of *inaction* is more complex than rectifying wrong *action*. This paper looks at how the Party has gone about getting Party and government officials back on their feet. To do that it considers how this problem has been characterised. It thinks about the existing disincentives to proactive decision-making. On this point it argues that incentives to inaction are largely attributable to institutional factors, bureaucratic and legal, rather than individual fault, and so differs from the Party's strong emphasis on individual turpitude as being at the heart of the problem. It then looks at the strategies adopted for getting officials back on their feet. If the problem of lying flat is sufficiently serious to warrant address by way of a campaign, that suggests the Party is anxious about the quality of governance both in impacting negatively on citizens and in reflecting issues with the motivation and morale of government and Party officials.

The risks from widespread bureaucratic inertia might also be understood as a barrier to achieving the Party's key priorities of strengthening governance capacity and efficiency and as an ideological failure; of both discipline and loyalty. The most recent iteration of the program of promoting comprehensive governance according to law; *Xi Jinping's Thoughts on the Rule of Law,* has reiterated a basic objective of modernisation of the system of governance and strengthening governance capacity as foundational to China's overall modernization program.[13] Administrative law scholars

[10] Ding, I and Thompson-Brusstar, M (2021) 'The Anti-Bureaucratic Ghost in China's Bureaucratic Machine' (248, S1) *The China Quarterly* 116. Biddulph 'Democratic Centralism and Administration in China' supra note 7 at 202-203. for a discussion of the mass line and democratic centralism.

[11] Xi Jinping: There is no greater danger than forgetting the original intention and mission and becoming disconnected from the masses. (*Xi Jinping: Meiyou bu wangji chuxin shiming, tuoli chunzhong geng da de weixian*) 6 October 2021 *QStheory.cn* http://www.qstheory.cn/zhuanqu/2021-10/06/c_1127932976.htm

[12] Mengla County Relocation and Resettlement Office (*Mengla xian banqian anzhi bangongshi*) (2023) 'Deployment Meeting to Comprehensively Launch the Special Mobilisation Against the "Lying Flat Style" Official (*quanmian jidong 'tangping shi' ganbu zhuanxiang dongyuan bushu hui*)' 14 August 2023 Available at: <https://www.ynml.gov.cn/93.news.detail.dhtml?news_id=1472493>. 'There Is Something to Be Said in the Picture: Hitting Hard Against the "Lying Flat Style Officials" (*huali you hua—dui 'tangping shi' ganbu dong zhen pengying*)' (2023) *Website of the Central Commission for Discipline Inspection and National Supervision Commission (Zhongyang Jiwei Guojia Jianwei zhan)* 9 August 2023 Available at: <http://www.hebcdi.gov.cn/2023-08/09/content_9052328.htm>.

[13] Chen, Y (2020) 'Xi Jinping's Thought on Rule of Law is the latest achievement of

such as Professor Xue Gangling agree and have advanced theoretical claims that China has a distinctive form of governance under the rubric: 'holistic administrative law'. Her argument is that public administration is an integral part of politics, is expansive and proactively seeks to achieve development and modernisation objectives, where protection of individual rights might better be understood as an outcome, rather than primary objective, of administration. A focus of administration is to protect stability and provide public goods for the purposes of achieving overall objectives of social and national governance.[14] Framed thus, bureaucratic inertia risks undermining the capacity of public administration to achieve these overarching goals of developing 'governance by law' and strengthening governance capacity and efficiency.

Questions for this article

This paper first looks at the problem of lying flat and bureaucratic inertia. It considers how it has been located in political discourse and the Party's diagnosis of the problem as primarily one of individual fault that is reluctant to acknowledge some role for institutional or structural problems, particularly overwork. As I indicated above, my argument here is that primary responsibility for the problem is structural and largely a response to increasing costs and risks of exercising administrative powers.

The individual fault lens directs attention to the ethics and ideological integrity of the individual with blame attributed to personal failings. The structural fault lens directs attention back onto the political and institutional structures of governance. It asks questions about the governance of officials, as well as the legal factors that might add cost and risk to the exercise of administrative powers. These questions include how the legal framing of powers and responsibilities, procedural rules and accountability mechanisms have contributed to unwillingness to exercise official functions. These questions are not embraced by the Party as they tend to direct blame upwards and invite uncomfortable questions about the overall institutional design of the program for modernisation of governance.

Moving beyond the specific study of bureaucratic inertia, in this paper I would like to think about how the problem of inertia and the remedies adopted to correct it help us explore two broader, interrelated, features of governance. The first is the perplexing relationship between the political slogans that underpin Xi Jinping's formulation for modernisation of the system of national governance: to modernise and strengthen 'governance capacity' (*zhili nengli*) by insisting on upholding and strengthening the Party's comprehensive leadership (*jianchi he jiaqiang dang de quanmian*

sinicization of Marxism (*Xi Jinping fazhi sixiang shi Makesi zhuyiZhongguohua zuixin chengguo*)' *People's Daily (Renmin Ribao)* 30 December 2020 Available at: <http://paper.people.com.cn/rmrb/html/2020-12/30/nw.D110000renmrb_20201230_1-10.htm>.

14 Xue Gangling and Xiao Songyang (2023) 'Holistic Administration Model with Chinese Characteristics: Practical Generation and Theoretical Construction (*Zhongguo tese de zhengti xing xingzheng moshi: shijian shengcheng yu lilun chenggou*)' (457) *Zhongguo xingzheng guanli (Chinese Public Administration)* 68.

lingdao). and 'upholding the combination of governance by law and governance by virtue' (*jianchi yi fa zhiguo he yi de zhiguo xiang jiehe*).[15] At the conceptual and practical level, scholars have had difficulty in explaining how these slogans interrelate or are given practical effect. The tools used by the Party in its attempt to rectify bureaucratic inertia (framed as problems of formalism (*xingshi zhuyi*) and bureaucratism (*guanliao zhuyi*)) provide a useful platform for examining how, in concrete terms, Party leadership and the combination of governance by law and governance by virtue manifest in a specific problem of day to day governance. I trace how the ideologically framed concepts of formalism and bureaucratism are translated into bureaucratic and legal systems, shape how bureaucrats are managed and evaluated and how they are sanctioned.

The attack on bureaucratic inertia is also unavoidably bound up with increasingly personalistic dimensions of governance according to law. In the context of the rectification of bureaucratic inertia it has taken the form of the latest education campaign requiring all Party members to study and implement *Xi Jinping Thought on Socialism with Chinese Characteristics for a New Era* launched in April 2023.[16] Susan Shirk has observed that institutionalisation of leadership politics has been inadequate to protect against personalistic rule.[17] This case study also provides an opportunity to think about the ways in which personalistic rule manifests in the day to day of governance of officials.

My second point, illustrated by the treatment of bureaucratic inertia and omission in administration, is to suggest that Chinese governance is comprised of both bureaucratisation and campaigns. Michael Schoenhals conceives of movements or campaigns (*yundong*), as periodically punctuating, and essentially antithetical to, governance by rules.[18] In her examination of state building in Taiwan and the Sunan (PRC) in the 1940s and 1950s, Julia Strauss argues that China's style of governance comprises 'two overlapping modalities of state-building and policy implementation [....] the bureaucratic and the campaign.'[19] I argue that this continues to be the case today. But, unlike the campaigns of the Maoist era of interest to Schoenhals which were designed to transform society, the campaigns of the

[15] Xinhua News Agency (2016) 'Xi Jinping: Adhere to the Combination of Governing the Country by Law and Governing the Country by Virtue (*Xi Jinping: Jianchi yifa zhiguo he yide zhiguo xiangjiehe*)' *Xinhua* 10 December 2016 Available at: <http://www.xinhuanet.com//politics/2016-12/10/c_1120093133.htm>.

[16] 'Practical Exploration of Managing "Lying Flat Style Officials" (zhili 'tangping shi ganbu' de shijian tansuo)' (2023) *China Discipline Inspection and Supervision News (Zhongguo Jijian Jiancha bao)* Available at: <http://fanfu.people.com.cn/n1/2023/0303/c64371-32635521.html>.

[17] Shirk, S (2018) 'China in Xi's "New Era": The Return to Personalistic Rule' (29) *Journal of Democracy* 22 at 22-36.

[18] Schoenhals, M (1999) 'Political Movements, Change and Stability: The Chinese Communist Party in Power' (159) *The China Quarterly* 595.

[19] Strauss, J (2020) *State Formation in China and Taiwan: Bureaucracy, Campaign and Performance* Cambridge University Press at 16.

reform era are technical and pragmatic.[20] They depend upon a competent bureaucracy for implementation. They are designed to spur officials on to heightened performance and greater achievements despite the absence of additional resources.

So rather than conceive of campaigns as both antithetical and the exception to the decades long reform era project of bureaucratisation through legalisation, institutionalisation and professionalization of everyday administration, my argument is that both are well established mechanisms of governance that coexist and, together, constitute an established mode of government. In the governance of bureaucratic inertia, we see legalised and regularised modes of governance and mobilizational modes of administration operating side by side.[21] I argue both are interdependent and in tension. This tension increases the risk of maladministration and the arbitrary exercise of power.

In the case of the campaign against bureaucratic inertia, the great irony is that using a campaign to rectify the problems of omission caused in part by overwork and meaningless work demands precisely the types of meaningless work and overwork the campaign is designed to address. That is, the campaign itself, paradoxically, contributes to both bureaucratic inertia and maladministration, the very pathologies the Party is seeking to address.

LYING FLAT, FORMALISM AND BUREAUCRATISM

The 'lying flat style official' is the latest iteration of an old problem of lazy governance targeted during Xi Jinping's regime. Lying flat took on significance in an entirely different context near the end of the severe pandemic restrictions mandated by the Zero Covid policy. The story of Li Chuang giving up his high profile and demanding job because it had become meaningless and retreating in favour of a low stress, low consumption lifestyle went viral amongst Chinese youth in April 2021. Lying flat was seen as a rejection of the high striving, high consumption lifestyle that underpins China's economic development. Responding to disillusionment with the lack of opportunities for advancement, exhaustion from the long work hours expected in many sectors and despair of those unable to find employment, lying flat represents rejection of the Party's economic development model and nationalist ideology.[22]

[20] Dutton, M (1992) 'A Mass Line without Politics, Community Policing and Economic Reform' in Watson, A (ed) (1992) *Economic Reform and Social Change in China* Routledge 200 at 218-219; Biddulph, S (2007) *Legal Reform and Administrative Detention Powers in China* Cambridge University Press; Dutton, M (1995) 'Dreaming of Better Times: "Repetition with a Difference" and Community Policing in China' (3) *positions east asia cultures critique* 418.

[21] Biddulph 'Democratic Centralism and Administration in China' supra note 7.

[22] Lydia Feng 'Lying flat': The millennials quitting China's '996' work culture to live 'free of anxiety' 23 September 2021 ABC News https://www.abc.net.au/news/2021-09-23/tang-ping-lying-flat-generation-rejecting-chinas-work-culture/100477716 . '996' work culture is a shorthand reference to working 9am to 9pm 6 days per week.

Appropriating the terminology of 'lying flat' and applying it to public officials, the Party has sought to reframe this popular movement by transposing it to the world of officialdom, and re-characterising it in the negative terms of refusing to take responsibility, abusing a position of responsibility and harming the interests of the masses.

The Party has also tied its own iteration of lying flat to its long history of struggle against formalism and bureaucratism. As Martin King Whyte noted in 1986, despite having one of the 'world's oldest traditions of bureaucratic rule, 'bureaucracy is often seen as "a problem"'.[23] Liu Shaoqi, Mao Zedong, Zhou Enlai and Deng Xiaoping each, in their particular times (1957, 1966, 1963 and 1980), have criticized bureaucrats for arrogance, abuse of power, inefficiency and irresponsibility, failing to resolve problems, shifting responsibility onto others and being idle, amongst other egregious failures to serve the people. At the same time, each was responsible, in their own way, for increasing bureaucratisation of social, economic and political life.[24]

There are many differences between anti-bureaucratism of the Mao era (for convenience drawn as pre-1979) and that of today. Of importance is the contrast between the weak institutionalisation of governance then and its strong institutionalism today. Governance structures now feature the bureaucratic attributes of professionalization; institutionalisation, legalisation and standardisation. But still, failure to perform administrative functions well, or at all, undermines political objectives of ensuring Party leadership and legitimacy and so is significant not just in its social consequences, but in its capacity to confound the Party's governance and political agenda.

While high level concern about cognate problems of bureaucratism, hedonism, arrogance, and self-centeredness predate Xi Jinping's leadership,[25] from 2012, Xi Jinping has paid particular attention to formalism and bureaucratism as evils to be rectified.[26] Formalism has been described as form disconnected from content and taking the form as the goal rather than form as serving the content. Formalism occurs when the form is not deployed in aid of practical results.[27] Formalism is commonly identified as associated with local levels of government, though can appear at higher levels of government as well. At the local levels it has been associated with

[23] Martin King Whyte 'Who Hates Bureaucracy' accessed at https://deepblue.lib.umich.edu/bitstream/handle/2027.42/51105/337.pdf?sequence=1

[24] Harding, H (1981) *Organizing China: The Problem of Bureaucracy 1949-1976* Stanford University Press. Ding and Thompson-Brusstar 'The Anti-Bureaucratic Ghost in China's Bureaucratic Machine' supra note 10.

[25] Hu Jintao's speech identifying these issues is discussed in Yang, P (2011) 'Competitions Must Be Real, and Monitoring Must Be Substantial' (Vol 10 Issue 1) *Contemporary Labor Magazine* 10-11. And Biddulph 'The Impact of Transparency and Accountability Mechanisms on Bureaucratic Inertia: A Case Study of Work Safety Regulations' supra note 2 at 268.

[26] Ding and Thompson-Brusstar 'The Anti-Bureaucratic Ghost in China's Bureaucratic Machine' supra note 10.

[27] Zhao, F and Dong, M 'How to Overcome Formalism (*Zenyang kefu xingshi zhuyi*)' (2021 Issue 1) *Qianxian Luntan* 54-55.

the problems of privileging upward facing accountability that is divorced from accountability to the masses.[28] Historically as well, formalism has been closely associated with the broader concept of bureaucratism. Zhou Enlai for example identified formalism and inertia as a species of bureaucratic inefficiency.[29] Bureaucratism is largely associated with higher levels of government and captures hierarchical working style, and disconnection from the needs of the people. Bureaucratism has been framed as being divorced from reality and the masses, standing high above the masses, ignoring reality, being self-respecting and self aggrandizing.[30] It is closely associated with moral failings of individual officials.[31]

Under Xi Jinping's leadership (from 2012) the Party has targeted formalism and bureaucratism (as the root cause of inertia) under a series of policies, education campaigns and campaigns to rectify and punish inertia. The struggle against formalism and bureaucratism was announced as part of the Central Committee *8 Point Regulations* (*ba xiang guiding*) issued by the Politburo of the 18th Central Committee on 4 December 2012.[32] Xi Jinping is quoted as saying 'Cadres daring to take on their responsibilities, is both a political character and a political duty.'[33] It has also been identified as a problem to construction of governance according to law.

Bureaucratic inertia was targeted in 2014 at the 4th Plenary Session of the 8th Central Committee *Decision on Some Major Questions in Comprehensively Moving Forward Governing the Country According to Law* (the Fourth Plenum Decision) in Part 3 (*Deeply Move Administration According to the Law Forward, Accelerate the Construction of a Rule of Law Government*) providing:

28 Ibid.

29 Ding and Thompson-Brusstar 'The Anti-Bureaucratic Ghost in China's Bureaucratic Machine' supra note 10 at 122.

30 Zhao and Dong 'How to Overcome Formalism (*zhenyang kefu xingshi zhuyi*)' supra note 27.

31 Ding and Thompson-Brusstar 'The Anti-Bureaucratic Ghost in China's Bureaucratic Machine' supra note 10 at 125, 128.

32 Eight Provisions of the Political Bureau of the 18th CPC Central Committee on Improving Work Style and Closely Contacting to the Masses (*Shiba Jie Zhongyang Zhengzhi Ju guanyu gaijin gongzuo zuofeng, miqie lianxi qunzhong de ba xiang guiding*). They require that leaders maintain close contact with the grassroots, understand the real situation facing society through visits to the grassroots, pay greater attention to places where social problems are more acute, carry out inspection tours more thoroughly. They strictly prohibit inspection tours that are a mere formality, require leaders to work and listen to the public and lower level officials and tackle the most pressing problems facing ordinary people. For official visits, they prohibit welcome banners, red carpets, floral arrangements, and grand receptions. Editor (2023) 'Nine Keywords to Look at Ten Years after the Centre Introduced the Eight Point Regulations (*jiu ge guanjian ci fan Zhongyang ba xiang guiding ding chutai zhe shi nian*) *cpcnews.cn* Available at: <http://cpc.people.com.cn/n1/2023/0103/c164113-32598816.html>.

33 'Let the Willingness to Take Action, the Courage to Take Responsibilities Become Common Practice (Thoughts Going up and across (*rang yuan dandang gan dangdang shang dangdang weiran chengfeng (sixiang zongheng)*' (2023) *People's Daily (renmin ribao)* Available at: <http://paper.people.com.cn/rmrb/html/2023-07/20/nw.D110000renmrb_20230720_2-09.htm>.

> (1) Comprehensively carry out administrative functions according to the law. Perfect legal structures for administrative organization and administrative procedure, move forward with the creation of statutes for bodies, functions, powers, procedures and responsibilities. Administrative bodies must persist in their obligation to carry out their statutory rules and not do what is not authorized by law, *they must have the courage to be responsible, dare to shoulder burdens, firmly correct a lack of action or chaotic actions, firmly overcome laziness and indolence in government, and firmly punish neglect and dereliction of duties* (my emphasis).[34]

More recently the attack on formalism and bureaucratism has been framed under the political umbrella of *Xi Jinping Thought on Socialism with Chinese Characteristics for a New Era*[35] with its aim to strengthen governance capacity and build a modern, relatively prosperous society. The evils of formalism and bureaucratism,[36] are now also included in the rubric of rectifying the 'Four Winds' (*sifeng*) of formalism, bureaucratism, extravagance and hedonism.[37] In a speech at the 6th Plenary Session of the Central Commission for Discipline Inspection in January 2022, Xi Jinping again exhorted 'persevering in rectifying the Four Winds and establishing a new wind' as part of shoring up adherence to the *8 Point Regulations*.[38] The latest in a series of education campaigns amongst all Party members attacking formalism was launched in April 2023 to study and implement *Xi Jinping Thought on Socialism with Chinese Characteristics for a New Era*.[39]

[34] Central Committee of the CCP, Decision Concerning Some Major Questions in Comprehensively Moving Forward Governing the Country According to the Law (*Zhonggong Zhongyang guanyu quanmian tuijin yifa zhiguo ruogan zhongda wenti de jueding*) October 23, 2014, https://chinacopyrightandmedia.wordpress.com/2014/10/28/ccp-central-committee-decision-concerning-some-major-questions-in-comprehensively-moving-governing-the-country-according-to-the-law-forward/ (English translation).

[35] Incorporated into the Preamble of the Constitution at the 2018 NPC. It aims to achieve socialist modernization and national rejuvenation and to build China as a great modern socialist country that is prosperous strong democratic culturally advanced, harmonious and beautiful by the middle of the century. Xiang Bo ed., Backgrounder: Xi Jinping Thought on Socialism with Chinese Characteristics for a New Era Xinhua 17 March 2018 http://www.xinhuanet.com/english/2018-03/17/c_137046261.htm

[36] A specified for example in the General Office of the CPC Central Committee's 'Circular on Continuously Resolving the Formalism Problems Plaguing the Grassroots Units and Providing a Strong Work Style Guarantee for Decisive Victory in Building a Moderately Prosperous Society in an All-round Way.'

[37] Xi '"Don't Forget Your Original Intention and Keep Your Mission in Mind" Speech at the Conclusion of the Education Conference on the Theme of "Don't Forget Your Original Intention, Keep Your Mission in Mind"' supra note 9.

[38] Huang, Y and Bai, X) (2022) 'Xi Jinping Emphasised "Persevering in Rectifying the 'Four Winds' and Establishing a New Wind" (*guanyu qie'er bushi jiu sifeng shu xinfeng' Xi Jinping zheyang qiangdiao*)' *www.cpcnews.cn* Available at: <http://cpc.people.com.cn/n1/2022/0227/c164113-32360668.html>. also referred to as the Four Winds Problem (*si feng wenti*)

[39] Xinhua How the CPC empowers itself with Party-wide education campaigns Xinhua 3 April 2023 https://english.www.gov.cn/news/202304/03/content_WS642a277ac6d03ffcca6ec039.

WHY DO ANYTHING AT ALL? THE PROBLEMS OF WRONG CONSCIOUSNESS AND DISINCENTIVES TO BEING PROACTIVE

This section takes up the discussion on reasons for bureaucratic inertia, addressing both individual fault and institutional and structural causes, arguing that the institutional and structural issues are the most significant incentives to bureaucratic inertia.

Wrong consciousness, bad character

The description in the section above recounts the Party's long-standing and ongoing struggle against formalism and bureaucratism. It leans heavily on an account of the ideological weaknesses and failures of commitment by individuals. An illustration from the official Party news website of the problem of lying flat is the village Party official who was responsible for changing over toilets in the village with a RMB 90,000 'toilet revolution' (*cesuo geming*) fund but did not do any of the work as planned and left the toilet revolution fund in the village committee account. Or, the official in the land office who was so slack in the performance of duties that over a four year period, two farmers were unable to obtain a valid and accurate property rights certificate, with the seal not affixed to the document, and the land incorrectly described in the document.[40] Or the Director of the Housing Security Office whose negligent management of public rental housing led to misallocation of housing, chaotic management and severe rental arrears, who was punished by recording major demerits in performance of her government office (*zhengwu jì daguo chufen*)[41] and described as a stereotypical 'lying flat style official'.[42] They are too busy, the task is too insignificant, or too troublesome, they pass the responsibility on to someone else, their work is careless, they are too important to undertake the task. They are busy in a meeting, drinking tea, or reading the newspaper. They are not performing their responsibilities (*bu zuowei*) or doing so in a chaotic (inappropriate and unprincipled) manner (*luan zuowei*).[43] Their attitude is 'doing a task well or badly is the same, but it is better to do nothing at all' (*ganhao ganhuai*

html

40 'Practical Exploration of Managing "Lying Flat Style Officials"' supra note 16.

41 Law of the PRC on Government Penalties for Public Officials (Zhonghua renmin gonghe guo gongzhi renyuan zhengwu chufen fa) 20 June 2020, article 7(3)

42 Zhou, W (2023) 'Public Notification! An Anhui "Lying Flat Style Official" Has Been Sanctioned: Chuxiong Municipal Taxation Bureau Carries out a Specialist Rectification of a "Lying Flat Style Official' to Promote a Courageous, Can-Do Working Style (*gongkai tongbao! Anhui–'tangping shi ganbu' bei chufen: Chuxiong shi shuiwu ju kaizhan 'tangping she' ganbu zhuanxiang zhili ti zhen gangan shigan zuofeng*) Available at: <http://www.hyjsxy.com/jjjc/info/news-10816.html>.

43 Editorial Committee (2022) *Violating the Spirit of the Eight Regulations (weifan Zhongyang ba Xiang guiding jingsheng: anli pouxi)* Zhongguo Fangzheng Chubanshe (China Fangzheng Press) at 70-71.

yigeyang, buru bugan).[44] According to official rhetoric, they have lost any sense of responsibility to the wellbeing of the people.[45]

This approach characterises the problem as one of individual turpitude, laziness, a lack of responsibility and more seriously failure to properly embrace Party leadership and implement the mass line.[46] 'Lying flat style officials' and 'mediocre officials and lazy governance', are primarily referred to in terms of their individual failings in Party discipline and understanding and enacting ideological precepts of the mass line. [47] Lying flat officials lack motivation and enthusiasm for their daily work. They avoid work, are afraid of making mistakes, they muddle along with the old ways and do not study and implement innovations in the workplace and bluff their superiors with the illusion of being rushed and overworked.[48] They have become 'stumbling blocks' to achieving modernisation and rejuvenation of the nation.[49] In places they are also criticized as negative, wreckers and lacking a sense of responsibility.[50] They are also mistaken. In a 2019 article in the *China Discipline Inspection and Supervision News*, reporter Wang Zhuo attacks the prevalent view of officials that as long as they do not engage in corrupt conduct, failure to act is not a problem (*yiwei zhiyao bu chu fubai wenti, lan zheng dai zheng dou bushì wenti*). This, he argues, demonstrates a failure to 'comprehensively conform to the Party's demands'.[51]

Legal and institutional disincentives to being proactive

The individual culpability view of bureaucratic inertia, even in the Party's own terms, is partial and fails to engage properly with what I argue are

44 Waiting for retirement in your 40s? This lying flat cadre was dismissed twice *(40 duosui zuodeng tuixiu? zhe ge ' tangpingshi' ganbu bei shuang kai)*

China News 20 April 2023 https://m.huanqiu.com/article/4CZQERu6RGt

45 Xi "Don't Forget Your Original Intention and Keep Your Mission in Mind" Speech at the Conclusion of the Education Conference on the Theme of "Don't Forget Your Original Intention, Keep Your Mission in Mind"' supra note 9.

46 Ibid.

47 Ju Hua, (2022) 'Let the "Lying Flat" Cadres Who Are Messing about Have No Market (*rang hun rizi de 'tangping shi' ganbu mei shichang*)' *People's Forum (renmin luntan)* Available at: <http://paper.people.com.cn/rmlt/html/2022-04/01/content_25917755.htm>.

48 Li, S (2023) 'Heavy Handed Management "Mediocre Officials and Lazy Governance" (*zhong quan zhili 'yongguan lanzheng'*) *Lookout (liaowang)* Available at: <http://www.xinhuanet.com//politics/2017-02/20/c_1120494357.htm>.

49 Ju Hua 'Let the "Lying Flat" Cadres Who Are Messing about Have No Market' supra note 47.

50 Ibid.

51 Wang Zhuo, 'NPC delegate Yu Xuewen allows no place for bureaucratic inertia' (*quanguo renda daibiao Yu Xuewen rang lanzheng daizheng xingwei wu lizu de di*) *China Discipline Inspection and Supervision News* 15 March 2019, p 4

the more important institutional and structural underpinnings of inertia.[52] While blaming individuals for having the wrong consciousness and commitment appears prominently in officials diagnoses of the problem, at the same time the Party has recognised that at the local level, overwork resulting from bureaucratic workstyles is a contributing factor.[53]

In this section I explore how Party disciplinary, bureaucratic and legal systems combine to allocate costs and risks, create incentives and disincentives to administrative agents in the exercise of their powers and responsibilities. The analysis points to many and overlapping reasons why Party and government officials become reluctant to act.

Excessive and meaningless work at the local level

While bureaucratism has largely been associated with individual fault in Party accounts, the Party has also acknowledged that formalism, at the village and local government level at least, is exacerbated by the burdens faced by local officials of overwork and meaningless work.[54] Key problems are identified as being chronic work overload and lack of work autonomy and lack a sense of organizational fairness.[55] In response, the Party Central Committee designated 2019 as the 'Year of burden reduction at the grassroots level', focusing on solving the problems underlying formalism plaguing the grassroots level,[56] indicating that one cause of lying flat is that local officials are exhausted and disillusioned.[57]

[52] The Impact of Transparency and Accountability Mechanisms on Bureaucratic Inertia: A Case study of Work Safety Regulation in Biddulph, S and Biukovic, L eds., *Good Governance in Economic Development: International Norms and Chinese Perspectives* (2019) UBC Press

[53] Strengthening Party discipline comprises one of the 'Four Comprehensives' governance strategy' (*si ge quanmian' zhanlue bu ju*) formalised as an official slogan by Xi Jinping in December 2014. The four comprehensives comprise: comprehensively building a 'moderately prosperous society, comprehensively deepening reform, comprehensively promoting governance according to law, and comprehensively enforcing strict Party discipline. In 'Four Comprehensives' governance strategy' (*sige quanmian ' zhanlue bu ju*) 11 July 2022 http://keywords.china.org.cn/2022-07/11/content_78317098.html and see Gloria Davies 'The Four Comprehensives' *The China Story* 2016 at https://www.thechinastory.org/yearbooks/yearbook-2016/chapter-4-the-language-of-discipline/the-four-comprehensives/

[54] Ding and Thompson-Brusstar 'The Anti-Bureaucratic Ghost in China's Bureaucratic Machine' supra note 10 at 134.

[55] Ju Hua 'Let the "Lying Flat" Cadres Who Are Messing about Have No Market' supra note 47.

[56] General Office of the Central Committee of the CPC (2020) 'Notice on Continuously Resolving the Problems of Formalism Plaguing the Grassroots to Provide a Strong Work Style Guarantee for a Decisive Victory in Building a Moderately Prosperous Society in an All-Round Way. (*Zhonggong Zhongyang bangongting yinfa 'guanyu chixu jiejue kunrao jiceng de xingshi zhuyi wenti wei juesheng quanmian jiancheng xiaokang shehui tigong jianqiang zuofeng baozheng de tongzhi'*) Available at: <https://www.gov.cn/zhengce/2020-04/14/content_5502349.htm>.referring to 2019 as designated by the Central Committee as 'the year of local burden reduction'.

[57] General Office of the Central Committee of the CPC (2019) 'Notice on Solving Outstanding Issues of Formalism to Reduce Burdens on Grassroots Levels '*guanyu jiejue xingshi zhuyi*

The problem of too many meetings, too many reports, too many inspections and too little contact with the masses has been summarised in the slogan 'mountains of documents and oceans of meetings' (*wenshan huihai*).[58] An illustration is the Director of the Forestry department of a city directed all lower-level forestry officials travel to the city to meet to discuss the recent speech of the Director of the Provincial Forestry Office. Many had to stay overnight to attend the meeting because of long travel times. On the morning of the meeting, the attendees received a copy of the Director's speech (which they had previously been supplied) and the meeting comprised reading out the document ordering distribution of the speech. The meeting lasted for 5 minutes.[59] To address this type of formalism, in 2018 the *Chinese Communist Party Disciplinary Sanctions Regulations* were amended to punish this type of conduct. Article 122 (3) added a sanction for breaching Party work discipline 'where meetings are simply used to implement meetings, documents are used to implement documents and where no action is seen in actual work'.[60]

Party documents also point to another dimension of excessive workload at local level occurs where higher level departments and officials have delegated or allocated responsibility to lower levels of government for achieving certain targets by way of 'responsibility certificates' (*zeren zhuang*). For instance, highway safety management responsibilities may be transferred to the village committee by way of a responsibility certificate, performance against which the village committee is held responsible, or where work health and safety inspections are delegated downwards.[61] Failures to implement these responsibilities will render the local level officials liable to inspection and accountability.[62] Overuse of responsibility certificates and downward delegation has been identified as a way for higher level agencies to rid themselves of responsibilities.[63]

tuchu wenti wei jiceng jianfu de tongzhi' Available at: <https://www.gov.cn/zhengce/2019-03/11/content_5372964.htm>.

58 Ibid. at point 2

59 Editorial Committee (2018) *Formalism and Bureaucratism: Anatomy of Typical Cases (xingshi zhuyi guanliao zhuyi: dianxing anli pouxi)* Fanzheng Press.28-30

60 http://dangjian.people.com.cn/n1/2018/0827/c117092-30252331.html Article 122(3) *'danchun yi huiyi guanche huiyi, yi wenjian luoshi wenjian, zai shiji gongzuo zhong bu jian zhu xingdong de'*

61 State Council Safety Committee *2022 15 Measures for Production Safety to Further Strengthen the Implementation of Safety Production Responsibilities and Resolutely Prevent and Contain Major Accidents* at Measure 3.

62 Wang and Mou 'The Paradigm Shift in the Disciplining of Village Cadres in China: From Mao to Xi' supra note 3.

63 General Office of the Central Committee of the CPC 'Notice on Solving Outstanding Issues of Formalism to Reduce Burdens on Grassroots Levels' supra note 57. Xinhua News Agency (2020) 'The General Office of the Central Committee of the Communist Party of China Issued the "Notice on Continuously Solving Problems of Formalism Plaguing Grassroots Levels and Providing Strong Work Style Guarantees for a Decisive Victory in Building a Moderately Prosperous Society in an All-Round Way"' (Zhonggong Zhongyang bangong *ting yinfa 'guanyu jiejue xingshi zhuyi tuchu wenti wei jiceng jianfu de tongzhi'*). Available at:

Somewhat paradoxically, a survey of mid level Chinese bureaucrats at prefectural level conducted in 2015-2016 by Boittin, Distelhorst and Fukuyama found that Chinese bureaucrats scored higher than their US counterparts in terms of their rating of their individual autonomy and meritocracy in recruitment and promotion.[64] It is difficult to explain the divergence between Party concerns about dysfunction in the bureaucracy and evidence of the relatively positive evaluation by the bureaucrats surveyed. One possible explanation might be the different bureaucratic level of officials surveyed, with the main problems identified by Chinese literature and targeted by Party campaigns being village and local level officials as opposed to mid level bureaucrats at the higher, prefectural level. The evidence from this survey also directs our attention back to the unresolved question about the extent of the problem of bureaucratic inertia, as it suggests that one of the reasons given for unwillingness to act; disillusionment with unfairness in promotion and lack of agency, may not be as serious or widespread as the literature suggests. At least this survey result should invite us to interpret Party evaluations of the significance and prevalence of formalism and bureaucratism with a degree of caution.

Bureaucratic mandates and performance criteria

What Party accounts do not emphasise, and what is discussed in the sections that follow, are the organisational, institutional and legal structures that increase uncertainty, cost and risk in exercising administrative powers and responsibilities.

Bureaucratic mechanisms to evaluate work performance are a significant factor in directing work priorities.[65] Introduction of human resource and performance management systems in the reform era have been used to drive professionalization of the administration and to promote the quality of performance as well as accountability.[66] As these systems allocate costs, risks, rewards and punishments, they provide incentives and disincentives to act or not to act in particular ways. Administrative mandates and performance indicators provide strong incentives for officials to act in particular ways. Mayling Birney, John Burns, Susan Whiting and Melanie Manion's work have documented how performance indicators that privilege social order and stability (as defined and identified from time to time) have impacted on how officials (and judges) exercise their powers.[67]

<https://www.gov.cn/zhengce/2020-04/14 /content_5502349.htm>.

64 Boittin, M; Distelhorst, G and Fukuyama, F (2016) 'Reassessing the Quality of Government in China' *Osgoode Legal Studies Research Paper Series* 197.

65 Jie, G (2009) 'Governing by Goals and Numbers: A Case Study in the Use of Performance Measures to Build Governance Capacity in China' (29) *Public Administration and Development* 21.

66 Burns, J (1987) 'Civil Service Reform in Contemporary China' (18) *The Australian Journal of Chinese Affairs* 47; Burns, J (1999) 'The People's Republic of China at 50: National Political Reform' (159) *The China Quarterly* 580.

67 Birney, M (2014) 'Decentralization and Veiled Corruption under China's "Rule of Mandates"' (53) *World Development* 55; Manion, M (2004) *Corruption by Design, Building Clean Government in Mainland China and Hong Kong* Harvard University Press; Whiting, S (2004)

Targets are an institutional mechanism to evaluate performance and are a convenient way for political and enforcement priorities to be incorporated into performance appraisal.[68] Where performance is measured by quotas – for example, imposing a certain number of fines or inspecting a certain number of enterprises – failure to meet these targets may have a negative impact on the payment of performance bonuses or on promotion. Veto targets (*yipiao foujue*) are particularly significant as failure to meet the veto target negates all other good work and achievements. Veto targets have been commonly used in relation to social stability, under which a single protest or social order incident is sufficient to negate work and achievements in relation to other aspects of the official's responsibilities. Veto targets are often imposed during campaigns or concerted actions to rectify regulatory failures to ensure officials give priority to implementing the campaign.[69] However, in many cases the veto targets are retained after the cleanup has finished.[70]

The Central Committee has repeatedly identified the excessive and arbitrary use of veto targets, particularly retaining veto targets after the end of a campaign, as contributing to the problem of overwork by local level officials.[71] But performance indicators, even if counterproductive, are also the outcome of bureaucratic processes and, as many have commented, are difficult to change and need to balance a range of different, even competing, priorities.

Costs and Risks of Campaigns

Campaigns impact on performance in two distinct ways. The first is when officials are targeted by the campaign. Two of the most notable are the longstanding anti-corruption campaign, and the Saohei Chu' E (Sweeping Black and Eliminating Evil) specialist struggle (*saohei chu e zhuanxiang douzheng*) against local gangsters and their protective umbrellas (local officials). This campaign builds on the ongoing anticorruption campaign that has been used as a disciplinary tool against officials.[72] The *Saohei Chu'e*

'The Cadre Evaluation System at the Grassroots: The Paradox of Party Rule' in Naughton, B and Yang, D (eds) (2004) *Holding China Together: Diversity and National Integration in the Post-Deng Era* Cambridge University Press 101; Burns 'The People's Republic of China at 50: National Political Reform' supra note 66.

68 Civil Servants Law articles 35- 39

69 Biddulph et al 'Rule of Law with Chinese Characteristics: The Role of Campaigns in Law-Making' supra note 7.

70 General Office of the CPC Central Committee *Notice on Continuously Resolving the Problems of Formalism Plaguing the Grassroots to Provide a Strong Work Style Guarantee for a Decisive Victory in Building a Moderately Prosperous Society in an All-round Way*. supra note 56 https://www.gov.cn/zhengce/2020-04/14/content_5502349.htm

71 General Office of the Central Committee of the CPC 'Notice on Solving Outstanding Issues of Formalism to Reduce Burdens on Grassroots Levels' supra note 57, General Office of the CPC Central Committee *Notice on Continuously Resolving the Problems of Formalism Plaguing the Grassroots to Provide a Strong Work Style Guarantee for a Decisive Victory in Building a Moderately Prosperous Society in an All-round Way*. supra note 56

72 Andreas, J and Dong, Y (2017) '"Mass Supervision" and the Bureaucratisation of

campaign has been used to target official misconduct at the local level. Waged as a three-year nationwide campaign from 2018, its targets in the first year were local tyrants and criminal gangs. In the second year, local officials providing protective umbrellas for these activities were targeted.[73] This campaign is seen as a way to make the existing anti-corruption campaign more effective and to extend its scope to strengthen discipline at local levels. It is an additional mechanism to extend the anti-corruption campaign to those local officials resistant to attempts by the central authorities to strengthen discipline and rectitude at the local level through mechanisms like the *8 Point Regulations*.[74]

Both campaigns have contributed to an unwillingness by officials to take initiatives that might expose them to investigation by central discipline inspection teams. In these circumstances, officials perceive increasing risk of being investigated for corruption when they take initiatives or spend funds on projects. The anti-corruption campaign has resulted in officials becoming much more hesitant to take initiatives for economic development.[75] The logic is that it is far better to do nothing than risk investigation and punishment.

The second way campaigns impact on performance is the longer-term consequence of being responsible for implementing campaigns. In campaigns designed to address regulatory failures, officials at all levels are called upon to direct their full attention to the targeted problem, to punish the targeted transgressions severely and quickly and to deal with the underlying problems that led to the campaign being initiated. Examples are wide-ranging and include wages arrears[76] and police enforcement campaigns.[77] Campaigns effectively divert resources from day to day work and over time lead to passivity while officials wait for the next campaign to be initiated.[78] Campaigns to address the periodic crises resulting from

Governance in China' in Shue, V and Thornton, P (eds) (2017) *To Govern China: Evolving Practices of Power* Cambridge University Press 123. Li, L (2019) 'Politics of Anticorruption in China: Paradigm Change of the Party's Disciplinary Regime 2012-2017' (28) *Journal of Contemporary China* 47.

73 Central Committee of the CCP, State Council 'Notice on launching a specialist struggle to Sweep Black and Eliminate Evil' (Zhonggong Zhongyang, Guowuyuan '*guanyu kaizhan saohei chu'e zhuanxiang douzheng de tongzhi*'), *Xinhua*, 24 January 2018, http://www.xinhuanet.com/legal/2018-01/24/c_1122309773.htm

74 Biddulph, S (2022) 'Transformation in Policing Minor Offending in China' in Fu, H and Chen, W (eds) (2022) *Beyond Regime Type: The Transformation of Police in Asia* Cambridge University Press chapter 4 at 108.

75 Ang, YY (2016) 'With Its Corruption Crackdown, China Is Also Stamping out Innovation' *The Conversation* Available at: <https://theconversation.com/with-its-corruption-crackdown-china-is-also-stamping-out-innovation-68223>.

76 Biddulph et al 'Rule of Law with Chinese Characteristics: The Role of Campaigns in Law-Making' supra note 7.

77 Scoggins and O'Brien 'China's Unhappy Police' supra note 7. Scoggins, S (2021) *Policing China: Steet-Level Cops in the Face of Protest* Cornell University Press.

78 Biddulph, S (2015) *The Stability Imperative: Human Rights and Law in China* UBC Press; Biddulph 'Democratic Centralism and Administration in China' supra note 7; Biddulph et

failures in enforcement have become so common as to support a conclusion that they are now a regular part of administration rather than a measure used in more exceptional circumstances.[79]

Legal dimensions of the problem: fragmentation of jurisdiction and powers

Law also adds to costs and risks of exercising administrative power in a number of ways that contribute to bureaucratic inertia. Fragmentation of institutional powers and responsibilities is one. Fragmentation may be in terms of jurisdiction or of powers, where there are overlapping responsibilities amongst several different agencies for a certain sphere of regulation.

While fragmentation of both jurisdiction and powers is widespread, here I illustrate the problem through an analysis of fragmentation in the regulation of work health and safety. Overlapping jurisdictional powers and responsibilities have long contributed to ongoing weak enforcement of work health and safety laws.[80] In March 2018 a major reorganisation of the regulatory structure of work health and safety saw the Ministry of Emergency Management (MEM) taking over the work health and safety jurisdiction, with responsibility lying in its the Production Safety Law Enforcement Bureau (PSEB).[81] The occupational safety and health supervision and management duties of the former State Administration of Coal Mine Safety (SACMS) were transferred to the National Mine Safety Administration within the National Health Commission (NHC).[82] Inspection and enforcement power is shared by local health departments and inspectors from PSEB and there is a clear overlap between jurisdictions in workplaces such as coalmines, for example, where dust diseases such

al 'Rule of Law with Chinese Characteristics: The Role of Campaigns in Law-Making' supra note 7; Scoggins 'Policing Modern China' supra note 7.

79 Biddulph 'Democratic Centralism and Administration in China' supra note 7.

80 Including the Work Safety Law (amended on 10 June 2021) and the Law on the Prevention and Control of Occupational Diseases of the People's Republic of China NPC, October 27, 2001 (entered into force May 1, 2002, amended 31 December, 2011 2 July, 2016 and 29 December 2018) (Law on Occupational Diseases).

81 *State Council Institutional Reform Plan*, approved by the NPC in March 2018, reform details see https://www.gov.cn/zhengce/2018-11/13/content_5339918.htm

82 The State Mine Safety Administration was renamed National Mine Safety Administration in September 2020, https://www.gov.cn/zhengce/2020-10/09/content_5549984.htm Responsibilities of the Work Safety Law Enforcement Bureau, renamed the Work Safety Law Enforcement and Industrial and Trade Safety Supervision Administration Anquan Shengchan Zhifa he Gongmao Anquan Jiandu Guanli Ju were also expanded in October 2020 https://www.gov.cn/zhengce/2020-10/09/content_5549986.htm At that time the functions of industry associations were separated from government under the *Implementation Opinions on Comprehensively Rolling Out the Decoupling of Industry Associations and Administrative Organs* issued by the National Development and Reform Commission, https://www.gov.cn/xinwen/2019-06/17/content_5400947.htm. Under this reform the China Occupational Safety & Health Association (COSHA) and the China Association of Production Safety Production were no longer subordinated to or financially supported by the Ministry of Emergency Management.

as pneumoconiosis and mine explosions and collapses are prevalent.[83] In addition, a range of other state agencies exercise jurisdiction in relation to health and safety in different sectors including the Ministry of Construction, the Ministry of Agriculture, the Ministry of Public Security, the Ministry of Transport, the Ministry of Water Resources, and the General Administration of Quality Supervision, Inspection and Quarantine, among others.[84] Another layer of regulatory overlap is with the powers to inspect workplaces and enforce work law exercised by the labour inspectorate within the Ministry of Human Resources and Social Security (MOHRSS). These reorganisations have not resolved the problem of fragmentation and the problems of regulatory overlap that create lacunae in exercise of regulatory responsibilities in relation to production safety continue.[85]

Superimposed over the top of this complex of regulatory responsibilities, at the time of the reorganisation of the administration of work health and safety in 2018, an additional layer of regulatory responsibility was allocated to the local Party and government. In the Central Committee General Office and the State Council General Office jointly issued the *Regulations on the Safety Production Responsibility System for Local Party and Government Leading Cadres* issued in April 2018, local governments and Party Committees at or above county level were required jointly to coordinate and supervise implementation of work health and safety laws (articles 1 and 2).[86]

As the problems of weak management of work health and safety continued, and spurred by a series of major incidents, in March 2022 the State Council's Work Safety Committee issued *Fifteen Measures for Production Safety* exhorting firmer attention be paid to the exercise of supervisory powers and compliance.[87] This document referred again to the need to clarify regulatory responsibilities where there is an overlap. This document reiterated the joint responsibility shared by government agencies and Party Committees for implementation of work health and safety laws under

[83] Zhu, C; Yang, N and Wang, Y (2012) 'National Profile Report on Occupational Safety and Health in China' ILO March 2012 1 Available at: <http://www.ilo.org/wcmsp5/groups/public/@ed_protect/@protrav/@safework/documents/policy/wcms_186991.pdf>. Zou, M (2016) 'Falling through the Legal Cracks: The Fragmentation of China's Occupational Safety and Health Regime' (2016) *Chinese University of Hong Kong, Faculty of Law Research Paper* 1.

[84] Zhu et al 'National Profile Report on Occupational Safety and Health in China' supra note 83; Zou 'Falling through the Legal Cracks: The Fragmentation of China's Occupational Safety and Health Regime' supra note 83. p 18.

[85] Work Safety Committee of the State Council *Fifteen Measures for Work Safety* 10 April 2022 https://www.gov.cn/xinwen/2022-04/10/content_5684337.htm

[86] Central Committee General Office, State Council General Office '*Regulations on the Production Safety Responsibility System for Local Party and Government Leading Cadres*' 18 April 2018 https://www.gov.cn/gongbao/content/2018/content_5288814.htm

[87] The State Council Safety Committee formulated and deployed 15 Measures for Production Safety to further strengthen the implementation of safety production responsibilities and resolutely prevent and contain major accidents.(*Guowuyuan an wei hui zhiding bushu anquan shengchan shiwu tiao cuoshi jinyibu qianghua anquan shengchan zeren luoshi jianjue fangfan ezhi zhong teda shigu*) 4 April 2022 https://www.gov.cn/xinwen/2022-04/10/content_5684337.htm

the 2018 *Regulations on the Safety Production Responsibility System for Local Party and Government Leading Cadres* and added an ideological dimension by requiring study of 'Xi Jinping's expositions of production safety'.[88] The *Fifteen Measures for Production Safety* also acknowledged the problems caused by excessive downward delegation of regulatory responsibilities to local level governments in requiring the Emergency Management Department to take responsibility for planning, coordination and implementation of inspections including revoking delegation of responsibilities to grassroots organizations where they are unable to implement these responsibilities (Measure #3). Documents such as this give us a good indication that problems of lack of coordination between enforcement agencies and downward delegation are unresolved and that problems with work safety remain serious.

The second form of fragmentation relates to powers. Inspection, enforcement and punitive powers follow this jurisdictional fragmentation and, as a result, are also overlapping, fragmented and affected by problems of poor coordination between agencies. Recent amendments to both the *Work Safety Law* and the *Law on Occupational Diseases* have expanded both enforcement and punitive powers of implementing agencies.[89] Where there are overlapping responsibilities, the *Work Safety Law* merely requires that different agencies cooperate with each other.[90] Many of the most serious sanctions cannot be executed by the decision-making agency itself and depend upon cooperation of other agencies to enforce. Both require cooperation across administrative silos that cannot be assumed.

For example under the *Work Safety Law*, inspectors from the Emergency Management Department exercise the power to enter premises, access documents and interview employees, issue fines or correction orders,[91] and, where there is failure to comply, order the suspension of the business, order the evacuation of workers from dangerous areas, and impound facilities and equipment that are in breach of national safety standards.[92] Where there is a breach, the business may be ordered to suspend production and the responsible person may be fined, or subjected to criminal sanctions.[93] Many of these sanctions must be imposed or approved by a different government agency and so require their cooperation. A decision to impose administrative detention on an offender must be made by the public

[88] Central Committee General Office, State Council General Office 'Regulations on the Production Safety Responsibility System for Local Party and Government Leading Cadres' 18 April 2018 https://www.gov.cn/gongbao/content/2018/content_5288814.htm

[89] The Law of the PRC on Work Safety (Adopted 29 June 2002, amended 31 August 2014 and on 10 June 2021) Law on the Prevention and Control of Occupational Diseases.

[90] Work Safety Law art. 69 (62,65)

[91] Work Safety Law arts. 93-114

[92] Work Safety Law, arts. 102-105.

[93] Ibid., arts. 101-105.

security agency.[94] The public security agencies must also decide whether to investigate and file a criminal charge. The ultimate power to order an enterprise to cease operations is exercised by the local government through the State Administration of Industry and Commerce, and, thus, its cooperation must be obtained for this penalty to be imposed.[95] Where an offending enterprise fails to comply with a fine or order, the work safety agency must commence enforcement action in court, exposing the agency both to increased bureaucratic costs and the risk that the court may not support the agency's application. In situations such as these, the agency is successful in obtaining an order only some of the time.[96]

These mechanisms are ordinary enforcement and penalty mechanisms that are common to many jurisdictions and are necessary to ensure appropriate and legally justifiable exercise of enforcement powers. The point here is merely that these mechanisms also impose costs and risks on the enforcement agency when determining its appetite and capacity to enforce the law.

Risks and disincentives to positive performance: costs, liability and accountability mechanisms

Law also creates costs and disincentives to administrative enforcement action through imposition of sanctions and punishments on enforcement officials through mandatory procedures and accountability and supervision mechanisms. The intent of these provisions is to regularise administration and to improve transparency and accountability for decision-making, which is a desirable rule of law objective. But these supervision mechanisms can also act as a disincentive to enforcement, particularly in circumstances where the administrative agency is understaffed and under-resourced, not necessarily strongly supported by local government, and where the object of regulation is comparatively influential and highly motivated to resist regulation. In part because of the difficulties in enforcement through the lack of resources and power, when administrative agencies do exercise enforcement powers, they often selectively target certain known serious offenders (though detecting breaches is often difficult), and adopt collaborative, rather than deterrence-oriented, approaches to enforcement, resulting in weaker and fewer sanctions being imposed for breaches.[97]

The legal prescription of how powers must be exercised, coupled with liability provisions, provide an additional perspective in understanding bureaucratic inertia. Article 90 of the *Work Safety Law* sets out circumstances in which officials with work safety regulatory functions may be sanctioned,

94 Ibid., art. 115.

95 Ibid., art. 115.

96 Ho 'From Contracts to Compliance? An Early Look at Implementation under China's New Labor Legislation' supra note 6 at 52.

97 van Rooij 'Implementing Chinese Environmental Law through Enforcement' supra note 6 at 154.

either by an administrative sanction such as demotion or dismissal or subjected to criminal liability. These circumstances mostly relate to positive acts, but also include some failures to act. Positive acts include granting approvals where the approval should not have been granted (article 90(1)). Failures to act include failing to perform a regulatory duty such as revoking an approval after discovering the entity is in breach of standards (article 90 (3)) and failing to deal with hidden risks of a serious accident, but only after it has been discovered (article 90(4)). Failures to act thus become punishable only after the agency has knowledge or after a serious accident.

Citizen generated supervision: online complaints, administrative litigation and review

There are now many forms for individual complaint making, from telephone hotlines, government websites, online complaint mechanisms and complaints to the media.[98] From 2013, online portals have been established to receive and handle citizen complaints.[99] Originally this was a mechanism designed to divert petitioners away from complaining in person.[100] Online complaint mechanisms are now mandated for local governments and departments and require officials to respond to complaints in a timely manner, thus adding a disciplinary dimension to the complaint handling process. The stakes for officials to respond to complaints in a timely manner were raised with issue by the Central Committee of the CCP and the State Council on 21st January and 25th February 2022 respectively of the *Regulations on Letters and Visits Work*.

These regulations combine Party disciplinary and administrative sanctions by providing that failure to perform this work may be sanctioned as a Party disciplinary offence, as well as a breach of regulations. Party disciplinary sanctions are brought to bear through the Regulations' emphasise on the importance of handling citizen complaints as a matter of Party discipline and as a key component of mass line work.[101] The Regulations add to workload and add an internal oversight body in their requirement to establish local work groups to ensure that complaints are handled in a timely and effective manner.[102] The problem though is that

[98] Andreas and Dong '"Mass Supervision" and the Bureaucratisation of Governance in China' supra note 72 at 142.

[99] Gui, X and Luo, Z (2021) 'China's Online *Xinfang* Channel: Absorbing Grievances through Institutionalisation' (21, 3) *China Perspectives* 53.

[100] VOA News (2013) 'China Digitises Complaints: Please Sign In' *VOA News* Available at: <https://www.voanews.com/a/china-complaints-please-sign-in/1799655.html>.

[101] https://www.gov.cn/zhengce/2022-04/07/content_5683923.htm

[102] Yuan, W and Rong, H (2023) 'Cosmetic Responsiveness: Why and How Local Governments Respond to Mundane Online Complains in China' (28) *Journal of Chinese Political Science* 187. who point out that Response times to complaints are often included in performance evaluations, providing an incentive to respond within the prescribed time. But even where mundane complaints are not subject to performance evaluations, local officials will often still respond. Here, as well, informal dimensions of performance evaluation are

while response time may be mandated, there are not mechanisms in place for citizens to judge how effectively complaints are handled. This thus creates incentives for officials to respond even if in a formalistic manner, but not necessarily to resolve the underlying problem unless additional pressure is applied in response to some form of socially disruptive protest.

Similarly, supervision mechanisms, such as administrative litigation and review, impact on the decision-maker by adding costs and risks to decision-making. The academic interest in these mechanisms is generally directed to determining their capacity to protect the interests of those who are the subject of the administrative decision-making.[103] However, they also have important impacts on the administrative decision-maker. Virginia Ho suggests that the prospect of a well-resourced and connected local enterprise commencing either administrative litigation or review to challenge a sanction imposed by the labour inspectorate for breaches of work law has a considerable dampening effect on both the decision to impose a sanction and the severity of the sanction imposed.[104] Proposed revisions to the *Administrative Review Law* such as expanding the operation of the Administrative Review Committee may also, perversely, increase the administrative costs of administrative review to government agencies.[105] If the challenge against the administrative decision is successful, not only is the sanction overturned, but the individual decision-maker is at risk of being penalized, either directly through liability to pay compensation or indirectly through the negative evaluation of the department overall.[106]

Lifetime responsibility

Lifetime responsibility for decisions made in office also factor into decisions to undertake conduct or make decisions that might ultimately end up being 'wrong' and the official rendered liable.[107] While the 4th Plenary of the 18th Central Committee *Decision on Several Major Issues on Comprehensively*

present as responses in these circumstances are often driven by the need to please higher authorities and to project an image of a caring government to citizens.

103 See, for example, Pei, M (1997) 'Citizens v Mandarins: Administrative Litigation in China' (152) *The China Quarterly* 832 at 420-424.

104 Ho 'From Contracts to Compliance? An Early Look at Implementation under China's New Labor Legislation' supra note 6 at 35-37, 52.

105 For a discussion of the proposed revisions see Horsley, J (2023) 'Further Observations on the Second Revision Draft of the Administrative Reconsideration Law' *China Law Translate* Available at: <https://www.chinalawtranslate.com/en/arldraft2/>.

106 See, for example, Administrative Punishment Law of the People's Republic of China, National People's Congress (NPC) Standing Committee, March 17, 1996 (effective on October 1, 1996, as amended on August 27, 2009), art. 6(55) (Administration Punishment Law); Biddulph, Cooney, and Zhu, *supra* note 16, 123. In relation to individual liability of police officers for administrative decision-making, see Biddulph *Legal Reform and Administrative Detention Powers in China* supra note 20 at 310-312.

107 Mou, Y (2022) 'Accountable for a Lifetime: Reforms in Prosecutorial Accountability in China' (6) *China Law and Society Review* 36 at 36-78.

Governing According to Law mandated implementation of a system of lifetime accountability for judicial officials including judges and prosecutors,[108] the spirit of lifetime accountability for government officials has also taken hold.[109] The expansion of concepts of lifetime responsibility to government officials is partly in response to problems of unbalanced pursuit of economic development goals at the expense of other policy priorities such as pollution control and work health and safety. It is also partly in response to careless or negligent decision-making by officials, where the attitude prevailed that accountability for negative outcomes of decision-making or failing to pay attention to issues by the official could be avoided by simply leaving their post.[110]

The discussion in this section suggests that the costs of exercising enforcement powers and risks of punishment have been greater for wrongful conduct than they have been for wrongful failure to act. However, while the balance of cost, risk and accountability applies in respect of (mis) conduct, some provisions exist in both law and policy to enable punishment of omissions and failures to enforce responsibilities of office, particularly where failure, such as the case of work health and safety, results in damage and death. The point is that, until the costs and risks of inaction are raised through other complementary mechanisms, the focus of discipline and law has been on (mis)conduct. In seeking to address perceived problems of bureaucratic inertia in the section below I examine the ways in which legal and Party disciplinary sanctions for omission have increased and resolve to punish bureaucratic inertia has stiffened.

WHAT TO DO ABOUT IT – REDRESS AND PUNISHMENT

Fixing the problem

It is not that the Party has refused to recognise that lying flat has real causes. It has acknowledged that overwork and meaningless work are two objective problems. The designation of 2019 as the 'Year of burden reduction at the grassroots level', focused on solving some of the problems underlying formalism plaguing the grassroots level.[111] Several reports on

[108] 28 October 2014 Section IV, 'Guarantee judicial fairness, raise judicial credibility', point 3

[109] Regulations on Implementing the Responsibility System for Constructing Party Style and Clean Government 10 November 2010 https://news.12371.cn/2015/10/28/ARTI1446023500885270.shtml

[110] Dai, C (2016) 'How to implement the lifelong accountability system for officials (*guanyuan zongsheng zhui ze zhi zenma luoshi*)' *Study Times (xuexi shibao)* 17 March 2016 Available at: <http://theory.people.com.cn/n1/2016/0317/c40531-28207088.html>.

[111] General Office of the Central Committee of the CPC 'Notice on Solving Outstanding Issues of Formalism to Reduce Burdens on Grassroots Levels' supra note 57. Xinhua News Agency 'The General Office of the Central Committee of the Communist Party of China Issued the 'Notice on Continuously Solving Problems of Formalism Plaguing Grassroots Levels and Providing Strong Work Style Guarantees for a Decisive Victory in Building a Moderately Prosperous Society in an All-Round Way' supra note 63, referring to 2019 as designated by the Central Committee as 'the year of local burden reduction'.

implementation of the work of this 'Year' have since noted that successes have been achieved, but have also acknowledged that ongoing vigilance is required,[112] which is code for acknowledging that these successes are, at best, incomplete. The Party has also sought, since the 19th Party Congress in 2019,[113] to redress objective problems for local officials including long and meaningless meetings, the obligation to write unnecessary and excessively lengthy reports for higher level agencies, cleaning up performance targets, particularly veto targets, and excessive delegations of responsibility for implementing policies to village and local governments. [114] It has also strengthened ideological education and focused attention and punishment on bureaucratic inertia as part of the special rectification campaign against the lying flat official.

Education and punishment: the rectification campaign

The increased focus on strengthening enforcement of Party discipline[115] and sharpening political focus on eradicating formalism and bureaucratism has placed the problem of lying flat and other forms of bureaucratic inertia in the spotlight. Key meetings and documents include the 6th Plenary Session of the 19th Central Commission for Discipline Inspection in January 2022 when Xi Jinping exhorted strengthening the *8 Point Regulations* and 'persevering in correcting the 'four winds' and create new winds'.[116] Following this, the 20th National Congress of the Party in October 2022 resolved to continue to deepening rectification of the 'four winds' (formalism, bureaucratism, hedonism and extravagance) and to focus on

[112] In October 2022 Xinhua reported that the Central Committee received a report that summarised the achievements of this 'rectification of formalism', noting that significant results had been achieved which significantly reducing the burden of overwork on local officials: Wang, Q; Fan, SX and Dong, BT (2022) 'Reducing Burdens, Increasing Efficiency, Focusing on Hard Work, Taking on Responsibilities and Opening a New Chapter - A Review of the Party Central Committee's Rectification of Formalism with Comrade Xi Jinping as the Core since the 19th National Congress of the Communist Party of China to Reduce Burdens on the Grassroots (*Jianfu zeng xiao zhong shigan dangdang jinze kai xin pian- dang de shijiu da yilai yi Xi Jinping tongzhi wei hexin de dang zhongyang zhengzhi xingshi zhuyi wei jiceng jianfu zongshu*) *Xinhua News Agency* Available at: <https://www.gov.cn/xinwen/2022-10/10/content_5717091.htm>.

[113] General Office of the Central Committee of the CPC 'Notice on Solving Outstanding Issues of Formalism to Reduce Burdens on Grassroots Levels supra note 57.

[114] Shi, YF (2017) 'The Responsibility Certificate Must Not Become a "Fig Leaf" to Evade Responsibility, (*Zeren zhuan mo chengle taobi zeren de zhexiubu*') *People's Daily Online (Renmin Wang)* Available at: <http://theory.people.com.cn/n1/2017/1221/c409497-29721819.html>. General Office of the Central Committee of the CPC 'Notice on Solving Outstanding Issues of Formalism to Reduce Burdens on Grassroots Levels' supra note 57.

[115] Strengthening Party discipline comprises one of the 'Four Comprehensives' governance strategy formalised as an official slogan by Xi Jinping in December 2014. The four comprehensives comprise: comprehensively building a 'moderately prosperous society, comprehensively deepening reform, comprehensively promoting governance according to law, and comprehensively enforcing strict Party discipline. Davies supra note 53

[116] Huang and Bai 'Xi Jinping Emphasised "Persevering in Rectifying the 'Four Winds' and Establishing a New Wind" supra note 38.

formalism and bureaucratism.[117] This political focus has been accompanied by periodic campaigns against inertia[118] and the special rectification against lying flat officials. Together, they have all significantly increased the risks and costs of failure to act.

The special rectification campaign has been implemented as part of a nationwide education campaign. In contrast with regular regulatory failure campaigns, this campaign is addressed against government and Party officials themselves. Launched in April 2023, the special rectification has been folded into the education campaign for all Party members is to study and implement *Xi Jinping Thought on Socialism with Chinese Characteristics for a New Era*.[119] This is the latest of many iterations of ideological study and education, self examination and self correction, criticism and self criticism that has been conducted to strengthen discipline amongst Party members.[120] In 2020, before this latest campaign began, the Supervision Commission reported that 62,595 people were given Party sanctions in respect of formalism/bureaucratism related transgressions.[121]

There is a double irony in using a campaign to rectify the problem of bureaucratic inertia. The first is that the bureaucracy is directed to implement the campaign against itself. A campaign is a highly technocratic and bureaucratic endeavour that depends upon a competent and effective bureaucracy to implement.[122] But the ill targeted by this campaign is bureaucratic inefficiency and inertia. The second irony is that campaigns mandate that government and Party organs at all levels give priority to

[117] 'A Special Working Mechanism Meeting on Rectifying Formalism at the Central Level to Reduce the Burden on the Grassroots Was Held in Beijing. We Will Not Relax Our Efforts to Rectify Formalism and Reduce the Burden on the Grassroots, and Demonstrate the Effectiveness of Thematic Education by Deepening and Expanding Practical Results. (*Zhongyang cengmian zhengzhi xingshi zhuyi wei jiceng jianfu zhuanxiang gongzuo jizhu huiyi zai jing juxing hao bu fangsong zhengzhi xingshi zhuyi wei jiceng jianfu yi shenhua tazhan shiji chengguo zhangxian juti jiaoyu chengxiao*') (2023) *Xinhua* Available at: <http://www.news.cn/politics/2023-06/15/c_1129697105.htm>.

[118] Central Discipline Inspection Commission, 'If You Have the Spirit of Responsibility, You Should Be Ashamed of "Official Non-feasance"', (Original in Chinese) January 31, 2016, http://www.ccdi.gov.cn/yaowen/201601/t20160129_140160.html (in Chinese). The Central Discipline Inspection Commission is now merged within the Supervision Commission. Wang, Shengxia (reporter) and Yang Shengjun (correspondent), "Resolutely Taking the 'Sword' to Lazy Officials, Qinghai's Specialist Rectification Campaign against the Problem of Inappropriate Non-feasance" (Original in Chinese) March 24, 2018

[119] 'Practical Exploration of Managing "Lying Flat Style Officials" supra note 16.

[120] Zhou 'Public Notification! An Anhui "Lying Flat Style Official" Has Been Sanctioned: Chuxiong Municipal Taxation Bureau Carries out a Specialist Rectification of a "Lying Flat Style Official' to Promote a Courageous, Can-Do Working Style' supra note 42.

[121] http://www.xinhuanet.com/politics/2021-01/27/c_1127030012.htm

[122] Dutton 'A Mass Line without Politics, Community Policing and Economic Reform' supra note 20 at 218-219; Biddulph et al 'Rule of Law with Chinese Characteristics: The Role of Campaigns in Law-Making' supra note 7; Biddulph *The Stability Imperative: Human Rights and Law in China* supra note 78; Biddulph 'Democratic Centralism and Administration in China' supra note 7.

the campaign objectives, the organisation and management of which requires meetings to study the requirements of the campaign and to make plans for implementation, production of documents to plan and evaluate performance and to report to higher level authorities on achievements. It also demands increased inspections by higher level authorities to check on this work. In short, campaigns employ meetings, reports and inspections to address problems of governance caused in large part by excessive meetings, reports and inspections.

Campaign against lying flat officials

The Special Central Level Working Mechanism for rectifying formalism and reducing the burden on the grassroots level (Special Central Level Working Mechanism) was established in 1 April 2019 and now acts as the leading group of the campaign.[123] The Special Central Level Working Mechanism met in Beijing on 15 June 2023 and resolved to deepen efforts to address formalism and to amplify the education campaign to study and implement *Xi Jinping Thought on Socialism with Chinese Characteristics for a New Era.*[124]

Campaigns such as this special rectification are marked by the coordinated enforcement by designated agencies that are required to concentrate their attention and enforcement activities on the targeted problem for a specified period and to punish transgressors severely. The sentiment of urgency in employing severe punishment to achieve the campaign targets has been expressed for example in the Mengla County Relocation and Resettlement Office campaign deployment meeting as 'implementing the specific requirements (of the 20th Congress of the Communist Party) to strictly govern the Party', 'daring to use strong medicine', 'to beat this gang of lying flat officials', 'to use iron discipline to get them to stand up, to dare to stand up, work and run.' [125]

Meetings across government departments, local governments, Party committees and Discipline Inspection and Supervision Committees have taken place to implement the special rectification. Some examples of the reports of meetings that have taken place following these decisions from a range of government departments and Discipline Inspection Commission/ Supervision Committees give a flavour of their diagnosis, priorities and work plans. Reports of one mobilizational meeting held by the Zhou Zi Bureau of Natural Resources (Xishuang Banna) on 8th July 2023, for example, set out the work plan for implementing the special rectification of lying

[123] see http://www.xinhuanet.com/politics/2019-04/01/c_1124313149.htm

[124] 'A Special Working Mechanism Meeting on Rectifying Formalism at the Central Level to Reduce the Burden on the Grassroots Was Held in Beijing. We Will Not Relax Our Efforts to Rectify Formalism and Reduce the Burden on the Grassroots, and Demonstrate the Effectiveness of Thematic Education by Deepening and Expanding Practical Results' supra note 118. 'How the CPC Empowers Itself with Party-Wide Education Campaigns' (2023) *Xinhua* 3 April 2023 Available at: <https://english.www.gov.cn/news/202304/03/content_WS642a277ac6d03ffcca6ec039.html>.

[125] Mengla County Relocation and Resettlement Office supra note 12.

flat officials in accordance with the *Implementation Plan for Carrying out the "Lying Flat" Cadres in the Study and Implementation of Xi Jinping's Thought on Socialism with Chinese Characteristics in the New Era Theme Education*.[126] The first is to 'fully grasp' the requirements of the rectification campaign: understand the objectives and tasks of the campaign, emphasise the importance of the campaign, mobilise to undertake necessary tasks quickly to improve workstyles, implement the campaign so as to achieve practical results and to engage in self reflection about their own working style.[127]

Another illustration is the Chuxiong City Taxation Bureau which launched a special rectification to 'administer the medicine required to deal with sickness' of lying down officials with an 8 point implementation plan that requires: ideological education, self-examination and self-correction, warning and education, supervision and inspection, (so that officials dare not lie down), performance evaluation, (to strengthen positive incentives), strict discipline to ensure the correct wind (positive conduct), error toleration and correction of errors, and model reports.[128] The stated objective here is to employ a mixture of education, admonition, positive incentives to encourage good behaviour and severe punishments to create a lasting deterrent. The interesting point is that these targets appropriate the rhetoric of the anti-corruption campaign to ensure that officials are 'unable to lie flat, are unwilling to lie flat, do not lie flat again, don't think about lying flat and do not dare to lie flat' (borrowing the formulation used by Wang Qishan when addressing the strategy for eradicating corruption).[129] [130] This appropriation of this terminology for the campaign is not surprising as Andreas and Dong have argued that under Xi Jinping, anti-corruption campaigns have become the primary form for supervision and discipline of officials.[131] This campaign is an extension of and a different iteration of the overall objective of strengthening the reach of Party and state discipline over bureaucrats.

126 Guanyu Zai Xuexi Guanche Xi Jinping Xi Shidai Tese Shehui Zhuyi Sixiang Juti Jiaoyu Zhong Kaizhan Tangpingshe Ganbu de Zhuanxiang Zhengzhi de Shishi Fang'an Zhao, HS (2023) 'The State Natural Resources and Planning Bureau Held a "Lying Flat Style Official" Special Rectification Mobilization and Deployment Meeting. (*Xishuangbanna zhou ziran he guihua ju, Zhou ziran Zhiyuan he guihua ju zhaokai 'tangping shi' ganbu zhuanxiang zhengzhi dongyuan bushu hui) Xishuangbanna Prefecture Natural Resources and Planning Bureau* Available at: <https://www.xsbn.gov.cn/xsbnzgtzyj/19727.news.detail.dhtml?news_id=2892148>.

127 Ibid.

128 Zhou 'Public Notification! An Anhui "Lying Flat Style Official" Has Been Sanctioned: Chuxiong Municipal Taxation Bureau Carries out a Specialist Rectification of a "Lying Flat Style Official' to Promote a Courageous, Can-Do Working Style supra note 42.

129 Ibid.,

130 Ding and Thompson-Brusstar 'The Anti-Bureaucratic Ghost in China's Bureaucratic Machine' supra note 10.

131 Andreas and Dong '"Mass Supervision" and the Bureaucratisation of Governance in China' supra note 72 at 126.

Another illustration is the Zhenkang County Discipline Inspection Commission Supervision Committee which held a mobilizational and deployment meeting on 15 August 2023 to study and implement the spirit of *Implementation Plan for Carrying out the "Lying Flat" Cadres in the Study and Implementation of Xi Jinping's Thought on Socialism with Chinese Characteristics in the New Era Theme Education*. The meeting was framed as an opportunity to implement *Xi Jinping's Thoughts on Socialism with Chinese Characteristics in the New Era* and a special rectification to deepen the revolutionary style and efficiency of the discipline and inspection supervision team.[132] Unlike the report of the Chuxiong City Taxation Bureau, this meeting focused on ideology rather than the specific objectives and means of implementation. It is not surprising that local agencies have so far taken different approaches to this special rectification. It is, after all, a Party ideological education and rectification campaign addressed at officials, including, potentially, the ones attending these meetings. These approaches also reflect the confusion of the primary target of the rectification which contains dimensions of the ideological and ethical failings of individuals as well as systemic problems of overwork. As many of these meetings are held in local areas, it is arguably difficult for them to address the broader, systemic issues, even if minded to do so.

State and party sanctions for inertia

One feature of a campaign is that it concentrates attention and political will on the issue to be resolved. A consequence is that the different dimensions of the issue are better understood. Another consequence is that the campaign is implemented by allocating responsibilities and targets, which act as imperatives to enforcement, and requires that the problem be addressed quickly and punishments for offending be severe.[133] While programs to redress the underlying problems of bureaucratic inertia continue, at the same time, sanctions for lying flat have become more likely and more severe in light of this 'specialist rectification'. Launching a special rectification against lying flat officials indicates that there is now an increased willingness to adopt a punitive stance in addressing this issue. The special rectification against lying flat draws upon existing sanctions, both Party and state, and intensifies critical scrutiny and incentives to punish the targeted conduct severely. The campaign facilitates the expansion of existing sanctions.

[132] Zhenkang County Commission for Discipline Inspection and Supervision (2023) 'The Zhenkang County Commission for Discipline Inspection and Supervision Held a Mobilization and Deployment Meeting for the Special Rectification of "Lying Flat" Cadres (zhen kang xian jiwei jianwei zhaokai 'tangping shi' ganbu zhuanxiang zhengzhi dongyuan bushu huiyi fa') Available at: <http://www.lcjjjc.gov.cn/info-14-17823.html>.

[133] Biddulph et al 'Rule of Law with Chinese Characteristics: The Role of Campaigns in Law-Making' supra note 7; He, X (2003) 'Sporadic Campaigns as a Means of Social Control' (17) *Columbia Journal of Asian Law* 121; Trevaskes, S (2003) 'Yanda 2001: Form and Strategy in a Chinese Anti-Crime Campaign' (36) *Australian and New Zealand Journal of Criminology* 272; Trevaskes, S (2007) 'Severe and Swift Justice in China' (47) *British Journal of Criminology* 23; Trevaskes, S (2003) 'Yanda 2001: Form and Strategy in a Chinese Anti-Crime Campaign' (36) *Australian and New Zealand Journal of Criminology* 272.

Of significance in sanctioning formalism and bureaucratism are the 2018 *Chinese Communist Party Disciplinary Sanctions Regulations* which set out sanctions that may be imposed for breaches of Party Discipline as well as aggravating (article 19) and mitigating factors (article 17). Any person and those with leadership responsibilities may be liable to Party sanctions of a warning, serious warning, probation, or expulsion from the Party depending on the seriousness of the circumstances. Formalist behaviours such as talking about Party decisions but not implementing them or using meetings to implement meetings and documents to implement documents but not taking any action to do actual work (article 122) are subject to sanction. The Party official who failed to spend the funds to implement the toilet revolution received a Party warning. A veterinarian, Huang Jun, who lay flat was expelled from the Party and dismissed from public office for violating Party discipline. He was also convicted of the crime of favouritism in animal and plant quarantined and imprisoned for a year.[134]

The ways in which Party policy and discipline impact on the severity of sanctions particularly during campaigns can be seen in a set of standardised instructions for punishing omissions falling under the rubric of formalism. For example, timing of formalist conduct constitutes an aggravating factor where it has occurred after the 18th Party Congress (November 2012), with further aggravation after the publication of the Party's *8 Point Regulations* (December 2012) and then again after the Party initiated the education campaign on studying and implementing the mass line (commencing in June 2013). The prescription is that the later the conduct the more the punishment should be exacerbated.[135] Timing of the conduct in this case is important as it indicates the official has failed to embrace and implement Party policy and discipline relating to the conduct of their office.

Even though state laws in particular sectors have tended to target misuse of power for punishment, I have documented in the section above how omission may also be punished, particularly where the omission leads to death, property damage or injury or where an official fails to perform a positive duty. Campaigns give incentives to existing law reform proposals in ways that reflect campaign objectives. For example, the *Civil Servants Law* article 59(4) has been amended to enable punishment of officials for bureaucratic inertia: failure to take responsibility, failure to act, dereliction of duty and delaying in doing work (*bu dandang, bu zuowei, wanhu zhishou, yiwu gongzuo*).[136]

Other extant law reform proposals are also scrutinised through the campaign lens. For example, the law is now also being changed to increase the scope of citizen complaints about official inaction under both administrative litigation and review. The jurisdiction to complain about

[134] China News Net (2023) 'Sitting in Your 40s Waiting to Retire, This Lying Flat Official Was Expelled Twice supra note 44.

[135] Editorial Committee *Violating the Spirit of the Eight Regulations* supra note 43 at 73.

[136] PRC Civil Servants Law adopted 27 April 2005, amended 29 December 2018.

the failure to perform a duty under the *Administrative Litigation Law* has been expanded.[137] The list of reviewable inactions has been substantially increased in the 2017 revisions to the law but it still addresses only a specified list (as opposed to a general class) of circumstances where the law imposes a positive duty to make a decision within specified time limits, or where there is a legal obligation to perform an agreement. The second draft of the amendment to the *Administrative Review Law* also expands the list of decisions for which administrative review may be sought in relation to omissions. The existing law at Article 6(9) enables review of an omission on two grounds: where there has been a failure to respond to an application to perform a statutory duty or to protect the rights of the person or property or the right to receive an education and article 6(10) where there is a failure to issue a pension, pay social insurance money, or make minimum subsistence payments.[138] The draft revision authorises an application for review where an administrative organ fails to respond to an application for a licence within the legally prescribed period (article 11(3)), where the administrative organ refuses to perform or, fails to perform statutory duties to protect lawful rights and interests, such as the rights of the person, property rights, the right to receive education, and other lawful rights and interests, or does not respond (article 11(9)); fails to pay a pension, social insurance benefits, minimum living allowance or other social security (article 11(10)); or (article 11 (11)) fails to conclude or fulfill an administrative agreement, or perform as agreed such as a government franchise agreement or land and housing expropriation compensation agreement.

Increased interchangeability of Party and state sanctions

The Party has recently been working to rationalise and make its internal rules more akin to legal rules. One objective has been to expand the reach and scope of its disciplinary sanctions.[139] A consequence has been to create overlapping Party and state regulation over the same (mis)conduct or omission. An illustration, in the area of work health and safety, is the 2018 Central Committee General Office and the State Council General Office *Regulations on the Safety Production Responsibility System for Local Party and Government Leading Cadres*[140] which allocated responsibility jointly to local

[137] Administrative Litigation Law of the People's Republic of China April 4, 1989 (effective October 1, 1990, as amended November 1, 2014 and June 27, 2017, with amendments to take effect from July 1, 2017). Article 12(3) (where an agency fails to reply within the statutory period to an application for an administrative licence), article 12(6) (refusal to perform or failure to respond to a request to protect personal rights, property rights, and other lawful rights and interests), article 12(10) (failure to pay consolation money, minimum subsistence, or social insurance benefits), and article 12(11) (failure to perform an agreement)

[138] Administrative Review Law of the People's Republic of China, April 29, 1999 (amended August 27, 2009).

[139] Seppanen, S (2019) 'Interrogating Illiberalism Through Chinese Communist Party Regulations' (52) *Cornell International Law Journal* 267 at 272.

[140] Central Committee General Office, State Council General Office *Regulations on the Safety Production Responsibility System for Local Party and Government Leading Cadres* 18 April 2018

governments and Party Committees at or above county level to coordinate and supervise implementation of work health and safety laws (articles 1 and 2). Liability for failures to properly enforce work safety laws is also part of this joint responsibility. The State Council's Work Safety Committee *Fifteen Measures for Production Safety* requires that Party and government officials who fail to exercise leadership or implement their regulatory responsibilities will be liable for failures where there is a major accident (Measure #4) and exhorts safety inspections to be performed in a substantial and not superficial manner (Measure # 11).

The *Accountability Regulations of the Communist Party of China* also impose accountability in respect of work health and safety issues that include both failures to identify potential issues and to take action, as well as circumstances where ineffective supervision has resulted in serious work safety accidents (article 7(8)). Article 7(9) imposes liability where, as a result of the failure to perform management and supervision duties, major and extraordinarily large production safety accidents, mass incidents, public safety incidents, or other serious accidents or incidents occur within the scope of duties, which cause major losses or other adverse impacts.[141] Party sanctions that may be imposed under article 8 in relation to these breaches are investigation, notification to rectify, admonition, restructure or adjustment in the form of suspension, adjustment of duties, order to resign, removal, demotion and other measures and disciplinary sanctions under the provisions of the *Communist Party of China, Regulations on Disciplinary Sanctions* under article 10.[142]

The special rectification campaign also places obligations for its implementation on Party Committees and government organs. It allocates particular responsibilities to the Discipline Inspection and Supervision departments (a combination of Party and state supervision agencies under the National Supervision Commission). In addition to the blurring of Party and legal rules under a merged Party and state body such as those under the Supervision Commission, this campaign blurs the ideological with the regulatory dimensions of the problem of inertia. The *Regulations on Disciplinary Sanctions* mandate imposing Party sanctions along with administrative or criminal sanctions. During the special rectification campaign, a consequence of combining Discipline Inspection and

https://www.gov.cn/gongbao/content/2018/content_5288814.htm

141 Revised on 4 September 2019 https://www.gov.cn/zhengce/2019-09/04/content_5427269.htm

142 https://www.gov.cn/test/2005-06/27/content_9927.htm Effective from 1 October 2018 Article 10 punishments include warning, with no promotion within 1 year; serious warning with no promotion within 1 year; removal from internal party positions which includes removal from all positions or the highest position they hold within the Party and recommend removal from governmental positions and no appointment to positions of similar level within 2 years); Party probation which includes removal from all positions within the Party and deprived of the right to vote and be elected, and either expulsion from the Party or ability to recover Party membership after a 1-year probation period (may be extended to 2-year); and expulsion from the party: being forbidden from re-joining the Party within 5 years.

Supervision functions at all levels has been that Party and government sanctions may be imposed interchangeability or cumulatively. The veterinarian, Huang Jun, who was found to have laid flat and showing favouritism in animal and plant quarantine, received Party sanctions of being expelled from the Party, administrative sanctions of dismissal from office and was later convicted of a criminal offence and sentenced to one year in prison.[143]

CONCLUSION

What does the analysis of the lying flat officials and steps taken to get them back onto their feet reveal more broadly about the Chinese mode of governance?

As a case study, bureaucratic inertia and the rectification campaign illustrate the mismatch between diagnosis of causes and modes of redress. Bureaucratic inertia, and its latest manifestation framed as the lying flat official, has been largely characterised by the Party as a problem of individual failing, of failure to follow the Party line and lack of motivation and commitment to the core purpose of governing: to wholeheartedly serve the people. This framing replicates the decades-old characterisation of this problem which calls for redoubled efforts to improve ideological education and Party discipline through study, criticism and self criticism, to rectify wrong consciousness and cure self serving use of power. Unlike many other reform era campaigns, this is an ideological campaign, directed at rectifying the individual rather than rectifying a social problem, or a failing in bureaucratic performance. Ideological work is designed to strengthen fealty to the Party under Xi Jinping and the Party's direct control over the bureaucracy.

My analysis here demonstrates that the institutional and structural disincentives, the costs and risks of proactive enforcement are far broader than officially acknowledged. It is not only workstyle and the shape of bureaucratic governance in the form, for example, of veto targets that adds to this cost, but also dimensions of legalisation and professionalization that contribute. One illustration of this dynamic is the range of accountability mechanisms for wrong decision-making and how these feed into lifetime accountability. It might not be overstated to say that the techniques used to try to strengthen control over officials and their conduct has also squeezed the life out of them. The campaign exacerbates the very problem of overwork and meaningless work that even the Party has acknowledged led to formalist performance of responsibilities.

I return now briefly to the two propositions I set out in the introduction about what the Party's efforts to address the problem of bureaucratic inertia might reveal the characteristics of the Chinese mode of governance more broadly.

[143] China News Net 'Sitting in Your 40s Waiting to Retire, This Lying Flat Official Was Expelled Twice' supra note 44.

The first is to demonstrate how Party leadership, governance by law, governance by virtue and Xi Jinping leadership interact in day-to-day administration. Measures taken to rectify the problem of inertia combine ideological and bureaucratic measures. Ideological approaches to rectify the wrong consciousness and motivation include the education campaign requiring all Party members to study and implement *Xi Jinping Thought on Socialism with Chinese Characteristics for a New Era*. Bureaucratic measures to ameliorate some of the institutional causes include restricting downward delegations, reducing the burden of meaningless work and cleaning up the problems of too many competing veto targets. Both ideological and bureaucratic measures in turn draw on and are supported by Party disciplinary rules and state legal sanctions.

The account here of the problems of bureaucratic inertia and the campaign used to address it is one illustration of an oft repeated pattern of governance. Even though campaigns are rarely effective, except in the glowing reports written at the conclusion of the campaign, they are employed almost reflexively whenever there is a difficult problem of governance or when regulatory failure threatens key targets or social stability. Samson Yuen has aptly characterised the anti-corruption campaign as a 'Party-building' tool to promote centralisation of political power.[144] Similarly, this latest campaign against lying flat is clearly a Party building tool designed to strengthen Party discipline down to the level of the local official.

The ongoing use of the campaign format (with the specialist rectification of lying flat style officials being only the latest iteration) has facilitated expansion of the range and interchangeability of Party and legal punitive measures. The Discipline Inspection and Supervision departments responsible for leading this special rectification are able, through their merged form, to impose Party sanctions and legal sanctions either singly or together. So, in terms of both the structure of power and modes of enforcement, the campaign against bureaucratic inertia illustrates the seamless merging of governance according to (Party) morality, governance according to law, and the dimensions of personalised rule in practice.

In the introduction I characterised the relationship between bureaucratic and mobilizational (campaigns) approach to governance as being both interdependent and in tension and ultimately contributing to the problems of bureaucratic inertia and maladministration. That tension plays out in the mechanisms adopted to ameliorate the problem of bureaucratic inertia. The special rectification of lying flat officials, I think perfectly illustrates this tension. At one level the Party seeks to reduce the load of meaningless work in the forms of excessive meetings and reports. At the same time the campaign requires officials to demonstrate their firm resolve, as a matter of Party discipline, to implement the campaign through holding meetings and writing reports. The irony is that the primary mechanism adopted to address the problem of bureaucratic dysfunction depends for its success

144 Yuen, S (2014) 'Disciplining the Party: Xi Jinping's Anti-corruption Campaign and its Limits' (3) Yuen, S (2014) 'Disciplining the Party: Xi Jinping's Anti-corruption Campaign and its Limits' (14, 3) *China Perspectives* 41 at 41-47.

on a competent and functional bureaucracy and demands implementation using methods that exacerbate the conditions underlying both overwork and lying flat.

GLOSSARY OF CHINESE TERMS

Romanisation (Hanyu Pinyin)	Chinese Characters	English Translation
zhongyang baxiang guiding	中央八项规定	8 Point Regulations
bu dandang, bu zuowei,	不担当，不作为	failure to take responsibility,
wanhu zhishou, yiwu gongzuo in	玩忽职守，贻误工作	failure to act, dereliction of duty and delaying doing work
bu zuo wei	不作为	not performing their responsibilities.
cesuo geming	厕所革命	'toilet revolution'
gan hao gan huai yige yang, buru bu gan' but	干好干坏一个样，不如不干	doing a task well or badly is the same, it is better to do nothing at all
lan zheng dai zheng	懒政怠政	bureaucratic inertia
luan zuo wei (inappropriate	乱作为	performing responsibilities in a chaotic and unprincipled) manner
saohei chu'e zhuanxiang douzheng	扫黑除恶专项斗争	sweeping black and eliminating evil specialist struggle
sige quanmian zhanlüe Comprehensives *buju*	四个全面 战略布局	Four governance strategy

tangping shi ganbu	躺平式干部	the lying flat style officials
wenshan huihai	文山会海	mountains of documents and oceans of meetings
yipiao foujue	一票否决	Veto targets
yiwei zhiyao bu chu fubai wenti, lan zheng dai zheng dou bushi wenti	以为只要不出腐败问题，懒政怠政都不是问题	as long as they do not engage in corrupt conduct, failure to act is not a problem
yong guan lan zheng	庸官懒政	mediocre officials and lazy governance
yundong	运动	movements or campaigns
zeren zhuan	任状	responsibility certificates
zhengwu ji daguo chufen	政务记大过处分	punished by recording major demerits in performance of her government office

Tightening up the Regulatory Enforcement of Pollution Control Regulations: Local Environmental Officials under Stress in China

CARLOS WING-HUNG LO
The Chinese University of Hong Kong
JINGWEN CAI
The Chinese University of Hong Kong
NING LIU
The City University of Hong Kong
PANSY HON YING LI
The Polytechnic University of Hong Kong

INTRODUCTION

Following the global trend of gearing up the fight against industrial pollution to address climate change problems, the mainland People's Republic of China (hereafter, 'China' or 'PRC') has gradually stepped up its regulatory control of industrial pollution. Indeed, China has been on a greening trajectory in its development pathway since the adoption of sustainable development as its national strategy for the country's long-term development in 1992. Manifested in the continuous enhancement of this strategic positioning of sustainability by the last three decades of political leaders, which mainly resulted from growing concern of the heavy environmental cost of rapid economic growth, has been the increasing pressure for local jurisdictions to tighten up their enforcement of pollution control regulations issued by the Central government.[1] The momentum of strong regulatory enforcement was eventually gathered under President XI Jinping's ecological paradigm of national development when the environmental protection administrative system was expanded to cover ecology domain; pollution control regulations were revised with stricter penalties; and a system of Central Environmental Inspectorate was instituted to supervise closely local enforcement.[2]

[1] Liu, Nicole Ning, et al. (2015) 'Campaign-style Enforcement and Regulatory Compliance' (75) *Public Administration Review* 85; Xue, Lan; Simonis, Udo E. and Dudek, Daniel J. (2007) 'Environmental Governance for China: Major Recommendations of a Task Force' (16) *Environmental Politics* 669.

The work for this paper has been supported in part by the Research Grants Council of the Hong Kong Special Administrative Region: "Campaign-Style Enforcement and Environmental Compliance in China: A Comparative and Longitudinal Study"(RGC No.: 15699815) and also "Government-Sponsored Voluntary Environmental Programs and Firm Exits: A Longitudinal and Comparative Study" (Project No. CityU 21610019).

[2] Li, Ruoqi, et al. (2020) 'Does the Central Environmental Inspection Actually Work?' (253)

Recent research on China's pollution regulatory control has detected that the enforcement gap at the local level has been narrowing under the wider adoption of a more legalistic approach of enforcement. The regulatory ecology for stricter enforcement has been generally developed with stronger support from local governments to local EPBs (Environmental Protection Bureaus; restructured as Ecology and Environment Bureaus after 2018) under the environmental quality leadership system,[3] greater citizen worries over the environmental quality reflected in the rise of pollution complaints figures,[4] and wider public monitoring in the proliferation of eNGOs (environmental non-governmental organisations) and the increase in media's industrial pollution reporting coverage.[5] It follows that most localities have been able to seek continuous improvement in pollution control as reflected in recording better air and water quality nation-wide.

While most studies of the regulatory control of pollution in China have focused on local enforcement agencies from institutional perspectives, few have paid close attention to environmental officials in regard to their actual enforcement of pollution control regulations in behavioural terms. In this article, we address this gap in the literature by asking the question: what is the role and experience of these street-level bureaucrats? This is important because these local officials are the foot soldiers who directly interact with the regulatory entities in carrying out their duties of regulatory enforcement to seek corporate compliance and punish violated enterprises. Based on the interviews of leading officials from all enforcement teams of Guangzhou EPB, we aspire to provide their stories of street-level environmental officials in conducting regulatory enforcement under growing pressure for stringent enforcement for achieving more effective industrial pollution control. We will start by reviewing the legal regime for industrial pollution control in China, following this by considering local regulatory pressure created by the newly established Central Environmental Inspectorate system. We then move on to look at the way Guangzhou environmental officials undertake their enforcement tasks, before concluding our major observations.

Journal of Environmental Management 109602.

[3] Lo, Carlos Wing-Hung, et al. (2016) 'Controlling Industrial Pollution in Urban China: Towards a More Effective Institutional Milieu in the Guangzhou Environmental Protection Bureau?' (30) China Information 232; van der Kamp, Denise S (2021) 'Blunt Force Regulation and Bureaucratic Control: Understanding China's War on Pollution' (34) *Governance* 191.

[4] Buntaine, Mark T.; Zhang, Bing and Hunnicutt, Patrick (2021) 'Citizen monitoring of waterways decreases pollution in China by supporting government action and oversight' (118) *Proceedings of the National Academy of Sciences* e2015175118.

[5] Tang, Yaru, et al. (2023) 'Informal Regulation by Nongovernmental Organizations Enhances Corporate Compliance: Evidence from a Nationwide Randomized Controlled Trial in China' *Journal of Policy Analysis and Management* published: 11 September 2023 at https://doi.org/10.1002/pam.22530

DYNAMIC IN THE ENVIRONMENTAL OFFICIAL'S ENFORCEMENT OF POLLUTION CONTROL REGULATIONS

Increasing scholarly efforts have been devoted to unpacking the dynamic of regulatory enforcement of pollution control regulations with the focus on the street-level bureaucrats in adjusting their enforcement approaches, particularly in response to the growing pressure for reducing industrial pollution as nations all over the world have generally proclaimed their determination to combat climate change. A wide spectrum of research studies can be detected. Notably, legal research looks at the progress of building the legal regime for pollution control with concerns centring on the improvement of the enforceability of regulations, the broadening of the scope of regulatory control, the strengthening of the deterrent effect with heavier penalties, and most important of all, the increase of the legal authority granted to enforcement officials.[6] Policy research examines whether the changes in the institutional contexts are conducive to providing the political ecology that is increasingly favourable to stringent enforcement while reducing policy uncertainties.[7] Regulatory research explores the improvement of environmental agencies' organisational capacity to support their officials in performing their enforcement duties.[8] Enforcement research spots how enforcement officials' adoption of different approaches to secure corporate compliance in response to all these changing dynamics for achieving industrial pollution reduction.[9] Based on these four streams of environmental governance research, our conceptualisation to study the role

[6] McAllister, Lesley K (2010) 'Dimensions of Enforcement Style: Factoring in Regulatory Autonomy and Capacity' (32) *Law & Policy* 61; van Rooij, Benjamin and Lo, Carlos Wing-Hung (2010) 'Fragile Convergence: Understanding Variation in the Enforcement of China's Industrial Pollution Law' (32) *Law & Policy* 14; Wang, Alex L (2013) 'The Search for Sustainable Legitimacy: Environmental Law and Bureaucracy in China' (37) Harvard Environmental Law Review 365; Zhao, Yuhong (2022) 'Adjudication of Environmental Administrative Disputes in China' (17) *Journal of Comparative Law* 393.

[7] He, Guojun, et al. (2023) 'Reducing Single-use Cutlery with Green Nudges: Evidence from China's Food-delivery Industry' (381) *Science* eadd9884; May, Peter J and Winter, Søren (1999) 'Regulatory Enforcement and Compliance: Examining Danish Agro-environmental Policy' (18) *Journal of Policy Analysis and Management* 625; Tilt, Bryan (2007) 'The Political Ecology of Pollution Enforcement in China: a Case from Sichuan's Rural Industrial Sector' (192) *The China Quarterly* 915.

[8] Kang, Inkyu. (2023) 'How Does Technology-based Monitoring Affect Street-level Bureaucrats' Behavior? An Analysis of Body-worn Cameras and Police Actions' Journal of Policy Analysis and Management; Liu, Ning, et al. (2022) 'Enforcement Officials' Coping Strategies in a Changing Regulatory Environment' (100) *Public Administration* 408.

[9] Earnhart, Dietrich H. and Glicksman, Robert L. (2015) 'Coercive vs. Cooperative Enforcement: Effect of Enforcement Approach on Environmental Management' (42) *International Review of Law and Economics* 135; Liu, Ning; van Rooij, Benjamin and Lo, Carlos Wing-Hung (2018) 'Beyond Deterrent Enforcement Styles: Behavioural Intuitions of Chinese Environmental Law Enforcement Agents in a Context of Challenging Inspections' (96) *Public Administration* 497; Lo, Carlos Wing-Hung; Fryxell, Gerald E. and van Rooij, Benjamin (2009) 'Changes in Enforcement Styles among Environmental Enforcement Officials in China' (41) *Environment and Planning* A 2706.

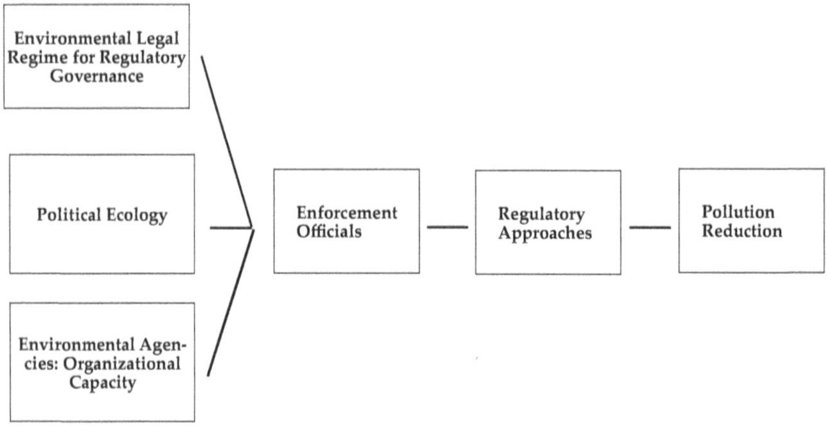

Figure One: Theoretical Conceptualisation of Regulatory Enforcement

and experience of street-level enforcement officials in a dynamic setting is shown in Figure One below:

CHINA'S EVOLVING ENVIRONMENTAL LEGAL REGIME FOR POLLUTION CONTROL

The inclusion of the cause of environmental protection in the 1982 Constitution and the promulgation of the Environmental Protection Law of the People's Republic of China in 1989 (replacing the provisional version adopted in 1979) marked the beginning of China's organised effort to build an environmental legal regime with industrial pollution control as a core focus. After more than four decades of environmental legislative action, a system of national laws, individual regulations and decrees down to local ordinances has now taken shape with increasing sophistication and comprehensiveness. Witnessed in the legal build-up process is the steady improvement and development of the body of pollution control laws and regulations in response to the growing determination of the Central government in the nation-wide reduction of pollution from the industrial sector, as reflected in the expanding scope of pollution control, clearer indication of regulatory specification, the imposition of heavier fines and other penalties, accordance of greater enforcement power, and the increase of local government accountability in regulatory enforcement.

With the Environmental Protection Law as its legal basis, China's industrial pollution control regime mainly consists of laws and regulations on air pollution, water pollution, solid waste, noise pollution, marine protection, and environmental impact assessment. As shown in the Table 1 below, starting with laws on marine environmental protection law in 1982, the Central government completed the legislation of the main body of pollution control with the enactment of solid waste law in 1995 and later added the proactive one of environmental impact assessment law in 2002. The momentum of tightening up these laws, set by the 1996 amendment of water pollution control law, have seen to be aligned with the pollution control strategy and priority adopted by different generations of political leadership's strategic choice of nation rebuilding. The pace of amendment and revision has been accelerated under XI Jinping's progressive eco-centric concept of sustainable development on stricter control of industrial pollution to serve for advancing his aggressive climate change roadmap.

Table 1: National Legal Regime for Industrial Pollution Control in China

Pollution Control Law	Date of Promulgation	Date(s) of Amendment(A)/Revision (R)
Environmental Protection Law	1989 (1979 – for Trial Implementation)	2014(R)
Air Pollution Control Act	1987	1995(A) 2000(R), 2015(R), 2018 (A)
Water Pollution Prevention and Control Law	1984	1996(A), 2008(R), 2017(A)
Law on the Prevention and Control of Environmental Pollution by Solid Wastes	1995	2004(R), 2013(A), 2015 (A), 2016(A), 2020(R)
Marine Environment Protection Law	1982	1999(R), 2013(A), 2016(A), 2017(A)
Law on Prevention and Control of (Environmental) Noise Pollution	1996	2018(A), 2021(R)
Environmental Impact Assessment Law	2002	2016(A), 2018(A)

This series of efforts commenced with the revision of the Environmental Protection Law which laid down the framework and foundations for later revision of all other industrial pollution control laws and related regulations. The revisions of individual laws were detailed in Table 2 (The Marine Environmental Protection Law is excluded below as its enforcement is general outside the jurisdiction of local EEPs, particularly that of Guangzhou EEP, while the revision of Law on Prevention and Control of (Environmental) Noise Pollution is not listed since it is out of the time frame of this paper).

Table 2: Major Revisions of Industrial Pollution Related Laws before 2018

Environmental Protection Law, Revised in 2014

1. Broadened scope of regulatory control

   Legitimation of NGOs' environmental lawsuits against violators

2. Added regulation specificity
   Increased transparency and whistle-blower protection for reporting environmental illegal actions
3. Stricter penalties
   Consecutive daily penalties introduced
4. Strengthened enforcement power
   Greater power granted to local EEPs in seizure and detention; administrative detention for non-criminal environmental offences
5. Increased (local) government accountability
   Enhanced accountability: environmental protection performance of government officials; heavy penalties for non-performance

Air Pollution Control Law: Revised in 2016

1. Broadened scope of regulation
   The control over greenhouse gases with measures on controlling coal use and transportation emission.
2. Added regulation specificity
   a. Stricter enforcement standards for coal operation and coal-free zone introduced
   b. Standards raised for public data disclosure and protection measures for public participants
   c. Differentiated the scope of fines for individuals (RMB500 – 2,000) and units (RMB10,000 - 100,000) that burn substances that produce toxic, harmful smoke, dust and odorous gases
3. Stricter penalties
   a. Use of high-pollution fuels in no-burn zones fined up to RMB200,000
   b. Violation related to boiler fined up to RMB200,000
4. Increased (local) government accountability
   Local governments required to regularly release and submit definitive plans to ensure they are on track to meet national air quality targets

Water Pollution Prevention and Control Law: Amended in 2017

1. Broadened scope of regulation
   Inclusion of the river chief system for water pollution monitoring
2. Added regulatory specificity
   Water pollution from agricultural sources and drinking water resources protection
3. Stricter penalties
   Maximum fine increased to RMB 1 million
4. Increased (local) government accountability
   Punishment for Party and government leaders for lax enforcement: fines and loss of promotion opportunities

Law on the Prevention and Control of Environmental Pollution by Solid Wastes, Amended in 2016 1. Added regulatory specificity a. Stricter approval procedures for closing, idling and demolishing domestic waste treatment facilities and sites b. Stricter approval procedures for the transfer of hazardous wastes across provinces, autonomous regions and municipalities under central administration
Environmental Impact Assessment Law, Revised in 2016 1. Stricter penalties Penalties intensified from a maximum of RMB200,000 to 1% to 5% of the total investment quota of the construction projects

As shown in Table 3, the Guangzhou municipal government has been steps ahead of the Guangdong provincial government in environmental legislation in formulating a system of local regulations for the control of local industrial pollution. The legislation in Guangzhou takes the form of a two-level process, that is, a regulation passed by the municipal people's congress has to be approved by the Provincial People's Congress before it can be put into effect. Indeed Guangzhou is one of the few municipalities that can propose its own regulations, instead of having all its laws imposed on it directly by the Central or provincial governments. This legislative arrangement has helped to ensure that all the regulations adopted in pollution control meet local circumstances. In a decentralisation setting, both the Guangdong and Guangzhou governments have the autonomy to enact their own specific measures and decrees to put national laws into local contexts. In this respect, the central effect has become increasingly visible as there has been a notable tendency for the local adoption of national laws by repealing their local regulations.

Table 3: Local Legal Regime for Industrial Pollution Control in Guangdong and Guangzhou

Pollution Control Regulation	Date of Promulgation: Guangdong Province	Date of Promulgation: Guangzhou	Date of Revision: Guangdong Province	Date of Revision: Guangzhou
Environmental Protection Regulation	2004	1997	2015, 2018, 2019, 2022	2015, 2019 (Repeal)
Water Pollution Prevention and Control Regulation	2020	1987	2021	2011, 2015, 2018, 2020

Regulation on the Prevention and Control of Environmental Pollution by Solid Wastes	2004	2001	2012(twice), 2018, 2022	2015, 2019 (Repeal)
Air Pollution Control Regulation	2018	1992	2022	1997, 2005, 2015, 2019 (Repeal)
Regulation on Noise Pollution	1998 (implementation decree for the national law)	1994	2004, 2010, 2018	1996, 2001, 2015, 2019 (Repeal)
EIA regulation for construction projects	1987 (decree) 1994 (regulation)	1984 (measures)	1997, 2004, 2010, 2012, 2018 (Repeal)	2007 (Repeal)

To enforce the substantive pollution control laws, the national environmental protection bureau formulates administrative rules based on the National Law on Administrative Penalties. Table 4 lists the related changes. In 2010, the updated Environmental Administrative Penalty Measures explicitly outlined that, barring specific designated circumstances, administrative penalty decisions must be made public. Notably, this revision introduced the concept of discretionary power for the first time, providing detailed provisions for investigation and evidence collection. For example, it clearly stated that online monitoring data can be used as evidence, and that a minimum of two investigators be involved in the investigation and evidence collection process. On this basis, provincial and municipal government in Guangdong have instituted their own regulations to govern the enforcement activities of local environmental protection bureaus. The Guangzhou EPB enacted three provisions concerning the Regulation of Discretionary Power in Environmental Administrative Penalties in 2014, 2016 (specifically addressing the Air Pollution Prevention and Control Law), and 2018, respectively. While the 2014 provision outlined 30 major environmental violations across 8 categories, the 2018 revision expanded the scope to cover 214 environmental violations spanning 18 categories. Despite the broader coverage offered by these new regulatory frameworks concerning administrative penalty scenarios, prior research suggest that frontline enforcement officials might face challenges when there is a disparity between increasing policy demands and limited implementation capacity.[10]

[10] Fernández-i-Marín, Xavier, et al. (2023) 'Bureaucratic Overburdening in Advanced Democracies' *Public Administration Review* at https://onlinelibrary.wiley.com/doi/

Table 4: Legal Regime on Administrative Penalties

Title	Authority	Date of Promul-gation	Date(s) of Revision
Law on Administrative Penalties	National People's Congress	1996	2009, 2017, 2021
Measures on Environmental Administrative Penalties	State Environmental Protection Agency (before 2005) Ministry of Environ-mental Protection (2005-2018)	1992	1999, 2003, 2010, 2023
Provisions on the regulation of Discretionary Power over Administrative Penalties (Environment)	Guangdong Envi-ronmental Protection Bureau	2011	2013, 2016, 2022
Provisions on the regulation of Discretionary Power over Administrative Penalties (Environment)	Guangzhou Envi-ronmental Protection Bureau	2010	2014, 2016, 2018, 2021, 2023

CONTEXTUAL AND INSTITUTIONAL DEVELOPMENT FOR REGULATORY ENFORCEMENT

The critical reversal of weak regulatory enforcement started with the establishment of the environmental quality administrative leadership system by the State Council under the Hu-Wen leadership. This was done with the strategic choice of active industrial pollution control, which make the entire government at both provincial and local levels, not the environmental protection bureau (EPB) alone, responsible for overall environmental quality.[11] However, the effect was restricted under the decentralised regulatory enforcement system dominated by local governments' policy priorities. More determined efforts came from President Xi's ecological vision of sustainable development, which led the central government to assert its leadership in the alignment of local enforcement with its hard-line regulatory stance against industrial pollution by strengthening the central command over the decentralised enforcement mechanism. In stepping up local governments' environmental regulatory responsibility, it was specified

full/10.1111/puar.13725; Liu, Ning, et al. (2022) 'Enforcement Officials' Coping Strategies in a Changing Regulatory Environment' supra note 8.

[11] Lo, Carlos Wing-Hung and Tang, Shui-Yan Tang (2006) 'Institutional Reform, Economic Changes, and Local Environmental Management in China: The Case of Guangdong Province' (15) *Environmental Politics* 190.

that local officials from both parties and governments at the county-level or above are to be dismissed for causing serious ecological damages due to lax enforcement.[12] Institutionally, the provincial-level EPB was now entrusted with the authority to exercise direct vertical control over local EPB's enforcement teams at the county-level or above in the enforcement hierarchy, rendering local regulatory enforcement more independent from the domination of local governments' policy priorities—typically manifested in tensions between GDP growth and industrial pollution control.

To strengthen central monitoring of local enforcement, inspection teams have been sent since 2016 at short notice under the newly instituted system of a Central Environmental Inspection Inspectorate to conduct on-site supervision of individual localities' regulatory control of industrial pollution–from provincial to local levels–with the power to make party committees and governments accountable for their EPBs' ineffective enforcement activities. The focus of central supervision was shifted from polluting enterprises to local governments to ensure their close adherence to the central policy line of strict regulatory enforcement of pollution control regulations, with greater involvement of non-state actors such as citizens, media, and NGOs in the inspection process. The first round of central supervision was completed in all 31 provinces in 2017, followed by two rounds in 2018. In this first wave of central supervision, a total of 875 leading cadres above departmental levels were unprecedently punished for the dereliction of duties in the regulatory control of industrial pollution. The deterrent effect was firmly established with the step-up effort to upgrade the leading group of central supervision from the State Council to the CPC Central Leadership Group for Ecological and Environmental Supervision in 2019.[13] The trend of tightening regulatory control with tougher enforcement and heavier fines was increasingly pronounced after 2001 as shown in Table 5.

Table 5: National Statistics on Enforcement of Environmental Regulations

Year	Administrative enforcement cases	Average fine per case (RMB)	Number of enforcement official	Complaint via letters	Complaint via visits	Complaint via phone/ Internet	Complaints via WeChat
2001	71,089	3,377	37,934	369,712	80,575	n/a	n/a
2002	100,103	3,017	41,878	435,420	90,746	n/a	n/a
2003	92,818	3,546	44,250	525,988	120,246	n/a	n/a

[12] Xinhua News Agency, 'Zhonggong zhongyang bangongting, guowuyuan bangongting yinfa "dangzheng lingdao ganbu shengtai huanjing sunhai zeren zhuijiu banfa (shixing)"' (The General Office of the CPC Central Committee and the General Office of the State Council Issuing the "Measures for the Accountability of Party and Government Leaders for Damage to the Ecological Environment (for Trial Implementation)", August 17, 2015, available at: https://www.gov.cn/zhengce/2015-08/17/content_2914585.htm.

[13] Lo, Carlos Wing-Hung, et al. (2022) '18. Sustainable Development Governance in Action: China' in Russel, Duncan and Kirsop-Taylor, Nick (eds) (2022) *Handbook on the Governance of Sustainable Development* 274.

2004	80,079	5,747	47,189	595,852	130,340	n/a	n/a
2005	93,265	6,868	50,040	608,245	142,360	n/a	n/a
2006	92,404	10,427	52,845	616,122	110,592	n/a	n/a
2007	101,325	n/a	57,427	123,357	77,399	n/a	n/a
2008	89,820	n/a	59,477	705,127	84,971	n/a	n/a
2009	73,719	n/a	60,896	696,134	73,708	n/a	n/a
2010	112,025	n/a	62,468	701,073	65,948	n/a	n/a
2011	119,333	n/a	64,426	201,631	107,597	852,700	n/a
2012	117,308	n/a	61,081	107,120	96,145	892,348	n/a
2013	139,059	n/a	62,696	103,776	107,165	1,112,172	n/a
2014	97,084	n/a	63,389	113,086	109,426	1,511,872	n/a
2015	102,084	n/a	66,379	121,462	104,323	1,646,705	n/a
2016	124,706	53,186	80,104	n/a	n/a	n/a	49,087
2017	233,167	49,666	94,929	n/a	n/a	n/a	129,423

Note: Data from the *China Environment Yearbook 2002-2018*. 'n/a' means not available.

Before long, the Guangdong Provincial Government also received central monitoring when the Central Environmental Inspection Team held a working meeting in Guangzhou in November 2016 to assert its presence and thereby assuring governments at all levels in the province on their need for close compliance with the central policy line on effective ecological protection and stringent pollution control.[14] Throughout the team's one-month station in the province, the Guangzhou government, and specifically its environmental protection bureau and enforcement teams, were the main inspection target. In the process, the inspection team reviewed enforcement records, undertook in-depth interviews with municipal government and party officials, conducted on-site investigation of six districts, handled local citizens' complaints, and received management executives of industrial enterprises to identify problems on local regulatory enforcement. Immediate rectification actions were taken, including the arrest of the deputy Chief of the EPB in Conghua District for abuse of power and neglect of duty in environmental supervision and the shut-down of seventy-six enterprises (mostly bleaching and dyeing factories) in a local industrial park in Zengcheng District following citizens' complaints and the onsite investigation, alongside a large number of pollution cases and citizens' petitions. Responsibility was placed the municipal government and EPB to handle these matters. This wave of central monitoring in Guangdong Province, which ended with a follow-up visit in late 2018, has effectively made the central environmental instructions heard and implemented at local

[14] Ministry of Ecology and Environment of the People's Republic of China 'No.4 Central Environmental Protection Inspection Team holds a Mobilisation Meeting on Inspection in Guangdong', December 6, 2016, available at: https://english.mee.gov.cn/News_service/news_release/201612/t20161206_368643.shtml.

levels. On the whole, the political ecology for strict regulatory enforcement and compliance of industrial pollution control has emphatically constituted through this central inspection effort, which has triggered the Guangdong government to organise provincial inspections on local governments under its jurisdiction to ensure that problems identified by the central inspection team were fully addressed.

REGULATORY ENFORCEMENT IN GUANGZHOU: LOCAL ENFORCEMENT OFFICIAL'S UNTOLD STORIES

To unpack the complexity of enforcement of pollution control regulation and its dynamics, there is no better way than getting the local enforcement officials' narratives on the delivery of their regulatory enforcement duties in the front line directly interacting with polluting enterprises. For this purpose, we performed two rounds of interviews with enforcement teams in the Guangzhou Environmental Protection Bureau (GEPB). The first round was conducted with eleven of out of the GEPB's twelve enforcement teams between August 2006 and July 2007, while the second round took place between January and March 2017 with interviews of all GEPB's enforcement teams. In most of these interviews, there was at least one leading official (chief or deputy team leader) with two to three enforcement officials from that enforcement teams. These semi-structured interviews were officially arranged with questions covering seven aspects of regulatory enforcement, namely, major tasks of enforcement, regulatory strategies, enforcement difficulties, sources of enforcement pressure, government and public expectations and possible improvements.

Based on individual district's locations, industrial structure, and development positioning, we divide the twelve districts into three groups. The first group is a city cluster consisting of five districts of Yuexiu, Haizhu, Liwan, Tianhe and Baiyun. The second group is positioned to be a cluster of economic and environmentally friendly development, including three districts of Nansha, Huadu and Kaifa (formerly Luogang). The third group is framed as cultural and ecology cluster making up of four districts of Panyu, Huangpu, Conghua and Zengcheng. Table 6 provides a snap shot of the regulatory background of each of the district enforcement team.

Table 6: Regulatory Background of Administrative Districts in Municipal Guangzhou

District	Enforcement team interviewed (Year in position): Background	Team capacity: Staff establishment/deployed	Geographical areas[15]	Development positioning	Government support
City Districts					
Haizhu	Leader (n/a): fire security and services	23/14	92 km^2	Modern city and business district with high quality environment	The district party secretary was with a strong environmental protection administration background.
Yuexiu	Leader (n/a): Labour and social welfare	25/12	34 km^2	Modern city and business district with high quality environment	The district was under strong pressure from the municipal government for air pollution control.
Liwan	Deputy leader (2): urban management	438/438 (an integrated capacity of all local enforcement)	63 km^2	Modern ecological city and tourist district	Under the pilot run of pooling up all administrative law enforcement officials in the district under an integrated bureau to strength the holistic enforcement capacity.
Baiyun	Leader (1): public security	30/15	665 km^2	Modern ecological city district	Government support had been significantly strengthened since 2016.
Tianhe	Leader (13); environmental protection	25/14	137 km^2	'Two suitable city' district in social and environment terms	The government attached great importance to pollution control: forerunner of the non-coal burning district.
Economic and Environmentally Friendly Districts					
Nansha	Deputy leader (2): environmental protection	20/20	697 km^2	Modern new coastal city with home to high-tech industries	The district government only required that there was no significant decline of environmental quality.

[15] Ministry of Civil Affairs of the People's Republic of China, "National Administrative Division Information Inquiry Platform", available at: http://xzqh.mca.gov.cn/map; Department of Commerce of Guangdong Province 'Guangzhou jingji jishu kaifaqu jianjie' (Introduction to Guangzhou Economic and Technological Development Zone), February 14, 2022, available at: https://com.gd.gov.cn/ztzl/jjjskfqhgtsjgq/jbqk/content/post_3814686.html.

Huadu	Deputy leader (1): military	24/17	968 km^2	Garden city district with strong economic development zones	District leaders took environmental protection seriously, setting pollution control as a most important task of the District government in 2017.
Kaifa (Development)	Leader (4): environmental protection	17/11	Old Luogang (before 2015): 393.22 km^2 New Huangpu since 2015 (includes Kaifa and Huangpu District): 481 km^2.	New city district for entrepreneurial business development and residential living.	The district government set high standards for industrial pollution control.
Cultural and Ecological Districts					
Conghua	Leader (7), public security organ	16/7	1984 km^2	Back garden-yard of Guangzhou	District government had increasingly paid greater attention to environmental protection, demanding the achievement of set pollution control targets and standards.
Zengcheng	Leader (n/a), military	24/18	1615 km^2	A rural ecological district for the modern manufacturing, agricultural and servicing, and tourist industries	District government took environmental protection highly seriously and understood the enforcement team's under capacity.
Panyu	Deputy leader (6): environmental protection	37/37	515 km^2	An affluent middle-class community and modern business city centre	District government had consistently lent great support to the enforcement team with street-level environmental units set up in 1989.
Huangpu	Leader (11), environmental protection: 28 years	18/11	Old Huangpu: 90.95 km^2 New Huangpu (includes Kaifa and Huangpu District): 481 km^2	New city district in Eastern Guangzhou with a culture and ecological focus	The district government was under strong pressure from the municipal government for meeting pollution control indicators.

Cluster Case One: The City Cluster

In this city cluster, the three districts of Yuexiu, Haizhu and Liwan are the older parts of the city centre with mainly residential and commercial areas. Tianhe is a new business centre, while Baiyun is a periphery city district with busy business activities where the airport is located. All interviewees were leaders of the enforcement team in these districts.

Major tasks:

In all these residential and commercial districts, pollution sources mainly came from the service sector including oil fumes and excessive noise from the catering industry and clinical waste from local community health and medical clinics. The regular enforcement tasks specified by the leader of the enforcement teams in the four city districts, namely Yuexiu, Haizhu, Tianhe and Baiyun, revolved around three key areas. The first one was inspecting and monitoring polluting enterprises and business entities to collect pollution evidence in case of violation for possible sanctions to be decided by the district environmental protection bureau. The second was the collection of pollution fee which mainly come from charges over oil fumes and excessive noise with the gradual disappearance of factories and manufacturing plants in city areas. The third was how best to handle citizens' pollution complaints and petitions with a notable increase in workload following the rise of popular environmental awareness.

For these city-based enforcement teams, pollution monitoring over the catering industry featured by a large number of restaurants with various operation sizes and formats was the most time consuming assignment among all. The measures mainly adopted were: tightening up the issuance of pollution discharge permits with strict adherence to current pollution control procedures and standards; target management of catering pollution including mandatory installation of oil fume purification devices and round the clock on-line monitoring to ensure the full operation of these devices; and standardising the supervision of catering pollution through the scrutiny and review of individual restaurants' compliance with all legal requirements of pollution control for operations. Control of clinical pollution was to be achieved by strengthening the monitoring of hospitals and medical clinics through the formulation of industry-specific standards.

Regulatory strategies

Enforcement approaches varied across these districts. The three districts of Yuexiu, Liwan and Tianhe tended to lean towards coercion with specific tactics, while the other two of Baiyun and Haizhu emphasised the use of education. Some shared practices were mentioned by the enforcement team of Yuexiu District, which included the grid-based format with streets as units of enforcement to overcome the problem of manpower constrains, used random periodic spot checks to increase the unpredictability and hence the deterrence of enforcement, and set up hotlines and other reporting channels to collect pollution information and receive complaint cases. For them, legalistic and stricter penalties were their watchwords of enforcement. While acknowledging the importance of employing educational methods to prevent direct confrontation and hostility from the regulatees, particularly in initial interactions, the enforcement teams of Baiyun and Haizhu Districts regarded the need of maintaining a certain degree of coercion in order to create the needed deterrent effect, particularly in facing non-compliance. As clearly pointed out by the team leader of Baiyun District, while education was their major regulatory strategy, the reality was that they could not do their job without resorting to coercion.

Enforcement difficulties

A common challenge across these city and sub-city districts was limited enforcement capacity, exacerbated by the overwhelming stress among the enforcement teams under the increasingly demanding governmental accountability system. Specifically, manpower shortage constituted the root of all sorts of enforcement difficulties. Most notably, Yuexiu District's enforcement team negotiated its heavy enforcement duties of monitoring over 2,000 regulatory entities and handling over 2,000 complaints cases every year with a small staff establishment of twenty-five dividing into two task forces for respective tasks, forcing pervasive overtime work but without compensation. Even Liwan District, which stood out as a unique case of reform with an integrated administrative law enforcement bureau over four hundred officials, was said to experience manpower deficit.

The career structure with the current staff establishment system had created considerable frustration among enforcement officials in these teams. Most serious of all was the limited advancement prospect which has adversely affected the team morale and individual job motivations as expressed by the team leaders from Tianhe, Baiyun, and Yuexiu Districts. This rendered the attraction of young talent a challenge, necessitating systematic training in enforcement skills for both new and experienced members. In Haizhu district, concerns arose about older officials lacking adequate training, passing on sub-standard skills and practices to newer recruits. In contrast, Yuexiu District praised the dedication of senior members to pollution control works but expressed concerns about younger members taking enforcement job as merely a steppingstone. Interestingly, Baiyun District emphasised the benefits of collaboration between experienced members and newer recruits, leveraging diverse insights and specialised knowledge. As summed up by the leader of the enforcement team in the Yuexiu District, 'whether in terms of career prospects or remuneration package, the enforcement team cannot be compared with that of other government departments. This constitutes a big problem'.

Other difficulties include limited resources, uncooperative enterprises, and citizens' misunderstanding of enforcement duties. The Baiyun and Yuexiu districts faced challenges in regulating small catering enterprises, urging refinement of related laws and regulations to stipulate the power and responsibilities of the environmental protection bureaus. Experiences with regulated enterprises varied, with some struggling to gain compliance, especially from SOEs and large enterprises that possessing close connections with higher-level government officials. Finally, personal danger during performing enforcement duties was still a concern in certain districts. While some team leaders reported violence as a resistance tactic, others, like Yuexiu, mentioned no such risks. After all, the enforcement team had much difficulty building its professional image to command the regulatees' respect, particularly they were enforcement officials without uniforms, unlike their counterparts in other disciplinary forces.

Sources of enforcement pressure

Environmental regulatory enforcement in these city districts faces mounting pressure due to heightened popular environmental awareness and an influx of citizen complaints, especially through the 'letters and visits' system, allowing citizens to conveniently lodge their pollution grievances. According to these enforcement teams, such grievance systems were prone to abuse, amplifying accountability pressures unfairly laid on enforcement officials. There was wide-spread frustration with other government departments' ignorance of environmental compliance when issuing business licenses or failing to timely ban unlicensed enterprises. Moreover, the easy access to petition channels leads to their exploitation, with instances of malicious reporting by enterprises against competitors.

Government and public expectations

The public's satisfaction with enforcement efforts varies across these five districts. While Yuexiu District garnered general satisfaction, other Districts struggled to meet societal expectations due to misunderstandings, rising expectations, procedural delays, negative media coverage, and personnel shortages. For example, residents may misunderstand the scope of local EPB and its enforcement teams' responsibilities, holding it accountable for matters beyond its jurisdiction. Many teams thus indicated the need for more publicity and communication with local citizens. Despite societal challenges, most districts believed they have effectively met government expectations, though Liwan District found it hard to determine. Yuexiu District contested judgments based solely on air quality rankings inconclusive, attributing its low ranking to city-centric air circulation rather than enforcement lax.

Possible improvements

According to our conversations with these city district enforcement teams, possible improvements were multi-fold, encompassing revising the regulations to be more enforceable and more in line with local conditions, increasing manpower and resources, addressing the rigid staff establishment system, preventing the abuse of petition channels, publicising the enforcement team's regulatory responsibilities, and improving the enforcement officials' inspection and monitoring power. Outside the jurisdiction of local enforcement teams, these team leaders suggested that pollution control requirements should be fully considered before the industry and commerce bureaus issuing business licenses to individual enterprises with pollution operations.

Cluster Case Two: The Economic and Environmentally Friendly Cluster

The three districts of Nansha, Huadu and Kaifa (Development) Districts form this economic and environmentally friendly cluster. All of them are suburban districts with considerable industrial areas positioning as home for technologically high-end and innovation enterprises, alongside the development of environmentally friendly and modern residential areas. The interviewees were the team leader of the enforcement team in Kaifa District and deputy leaders of that in Nansha and Huadu Districts.

Major tasks

The regular enforcement tasks common across these three suburban districts were pollution fee collection, enterprise inspection and monitoring, and complaints handling. Both Huadu and Kaifa Districts also listed handling pollution emergencies as their major tasks as well. For Nansha District, air pollution control from manufacturing plants was the core regulatory focus, which at the same time, constituted the major source of public complaints. The Huadu enforcement team grieved that their scope of environmental duties was too board to focus their regulatory sharply on industrial pollution control, even food safety was part of their task portfolio. Even worst in the case of Kaifa enforcement team with their Bureau covering the functional jurisdictions of both construction and environmental protection, extending the regulatory domains to construction projects, municipal gardening, local traffic and environmental sanitation.

Regulatory strategies

The enforcement teams in these three suburban districts exhibited contrasting regulatory strategies deliberately designed to fit respective local industrial development contexts. With a large portion of land in the district as home for many manufacturing plants recently moved in and operated with latest production technologies, the Nansha enforcement team set control priorities on the chemical and heavy industries and district areas close to residential zones that flushed with citizens' pollution complaints. The enforcement deterrence was built on randomly arranged inspection of polluting enterprises performed by locally stationed units in a highly coercive manner. Quite differently, the enforcement team in the Kaifa District greatly relied on monitoring technology with on-line devices to perform real-time monitoring on wastewater emissions, heavy metals, large boilers, and restaurant fumes. To achieve this end, the team leader told us that the district EPB had actively funded aging enterprises to finance their purchasing and installation costs, while making it mandatory for all new enterprises. As the largest suburban district with polluting enterprises in a wide range of industrial sectors, Huadu District's enforcement team emphasized the adoption of a 'double-randomness' inspection strategy in that both inspection groups and inspected enterprises were randomly assigned right before action. The deputy leader pointed out that the unpredictable effect created has made these inspection arrangements turn out to be quite effective.

Enforcement difficulties

Resource deficit in terms of manpower and equipment has severely constrained the regulatory capacity of all enforcement teams in these three suburban Districts. Most puzzled of all was the gap between the staff establishment and the actual number of enforcement officials assigned to the enforcement team. As pointed out by the leader of the enforcement team in the Kaifa District, only eleven out of the seventeen quota in the enforcement staff establishment were eventually deployed in the enforcement team, with six were either retained by the bureau or seconded to other environmental administrative units, which also suffered from severe shortage of manpower. Likewise, the actual number of enforcement officials in the Huadu District team was seventeen, despite a staff establishment of twenty-four being given. As compensation, these two teams were allowed to use contracted staff to make up the necessary regulatory strength, with more than ten employed by the Kaifa District team and eight in the Huadu District team respectively. However, these contracted staff could not undertake regulatory duties on their own as they were legally not rested with any enforcement power. The considerable number of young female officials in the enforcement team in Huadu District has disturbed the deputy team leader in that the enforcement capacity would be greatly weakened when any of them were on maternity leave.

Handling pollution complaints has created all kinds of difficulties for individual enforcement teams. For the Huadu enforcement team, the administrative requirement of written reply to every complaint received within a prescribed short period of time was a nightmare for their members as close to 6,000 complaints were received last year with difficult cases mainly from social media like Weibo and WeChat. In the Kaifa District, the complexity of pollution complaints came from the close distance between residential areas and industrial zones with the figure soared from around 400 to over 3,000 in four years' time. The difficulties rested mainly with the growing organised pressure from local residents to keep on pressing for relocating the nearby polluting enterprises despite no violation of emission standards being detected. In the words of the team leader, 'residential complexes are being built in industrial areas, resulting in continuous complaints'. In a similar pattern, the pressure of citizens' pollution complaint was mounting in Nansha District as a lot of former industrial lands had been converted to residential purposes, leading to problem-ridden residential-industrial mixed zones.

In the interactions with polluting enterprises in the regulatory process, enforcement teams in these districts got a wide range of different experiences. In the Nansha District, foreign enterprises from Japan and the Western countries were most cooperative with enforcement teams and compliance in strict legal terms, while those from Taiwan were most difficult to regulate and SOEs performed mostly passive compliance. A noticeable tactics for non-compliant enterprises was to seek for administrative review with the hope to find faults in pollution evidence for reversing the penalty decision or simply delay the sanction, when their unlawful polluting operations were got caught. The leader of enforcement team in the Kaifa District judged that the local industrial pollution situation was on the whole under control as enterprises exceeding pollution standards in emission were in a manageable number due to the high environmental thresholds set for enterprises to enter into the development zones. Most of these high-end enterprises were even steps ahead of the enforcement teams in their corporate environmental management concepts and practices, among them over a hundred were Fortune 500 companies in the world. As for the Huadu District, most regulatory difficulties for the enforcement team came from small private enterprises where the cost of relocation was low when got caught in their polluting operations. Top on their hit lists for targeted stringent enforcement were those polluting enterprises which operated without proper business license or pollutant discharge permits.

The threats for personal safety in undertaking the enforcement duties were commonly felt among enforcement officials in these three Districts. The leader of the enforcement team in the Kaifa District reported that it was quite often that owners of small factories and business entities who threatened to use force again them in order to stop them from entering into their premises for pollution inspection. Some enterprises in the Huadu District even hired hooligans to follow the enforcement officials' route to their workplace in the District EPB, suggesting a threat of revenge over their inspection actions. However, the team's suggestion for setting up a public security unit in the District EPB for better protection of enforcement officials was not approved. The situation in the Nansha District was less threatening, with potential danger mostly coming from small restaurants' owners for losing control when asked for rectifying their pollution operations involving costly investment. Joint enforcements with public security organs were more frequently organised than with other government agencies among these enforcement teams, partly because of personal safety reasons and partly because of limited inspection power to force entry into pollution sites.

Sources of enforcement pressure

Enforcement pressures were strongly felt across all the three suburban enforcement teams. In particular, the Huadu team leader complained that the newly established performance accountability system was too demanding in that their team alone could not ensure the improvement of environmental quality through their enforcement actions. The consequence of receiving any administrative warning or getting a demerit record because of poor performance was salary reduction for six months. Together with limited manpower capacity, the team members had to performed their inspection duties at night and very often until mid-night. In respect of the manpower issue, the Nansha District leader pointed out that the high turnover in their enforcement team due to less attractive remuneration package has created considerable pressure on local enforcement capacity. Fortune seesawed among different enforcement teams in interacting with the media. Despite the appointment of a press spoke-person, pressure from the media had been growing on the Nansha team coming mostly from negative reporting on the pollution problems in their Districts and the critical remarks on their enforcement works. Very differently in the case of the Kaifa District, apart from receiving supporting and positive coverage on the enforcement team's performance, the team leader even considered them helpful as media had once openly questioned the planning bureau's approval of residential projects inside industrial zones.

Government and public expectations

How far had these suburban district teams met government and public expectations under tremendous pressure for effective industrial pollution control? In general, the public expectations of 'clear water and blue sky' were too high to meet as reflected in the rising compliant figures. Specifically, the challenge for the Huadu and Nansha enforcement teams mainly came from new homeowners with an expectation of an environmentally friendly living surroundings free from industrial pollution in a suburban setting. A popular approach was adopted by the Kaifa enforcement team with positive effect through public engagement in their on-site monitoring on local pollution standards. In contrast, district governments set their own perspectives on industrial pollution control. Most notably, the local government in the Nansha District would accord the team a satisfactory rating in their performance as long as there was no noticeable deterioration of environmental quality despite a higher level of economic development. In comparison, the district government of the Kaifa District was quite willing to use its relative rich financial resources to support the team's industrial pollution control effort, enabling the district to achieve a third rank last year in the environmental assessment conducted by the Guangzhou Municipal government.

Possible improvements

When asked about possible improvements, the team leaders in these three suburban districts appeared to have their own ideas. The deputy team leader of the Huadu District realistically pointed out that a full team strength would help to relieve their heavy load pressure but admitted that it was wishful thinking to get a full staff establishment enforcement team. The wish list of the leader of the Kaifa District team was quite long, including additional manpower, setting up basic level environmental protection units, and greater support from related government agencies in joint enforcement actions. The deputy team leader of the Nansha District focused on addressing the balance between enforcement power and responsibilities, asking for granting direct enforcement authority in ordering plant closure and operation suspension without going through court proceedings, imposing heavy fines to increase the deterrence effect of sanction, and providing adequate resource support for performing the enforcement tasks into meet the required accountability.

Cluster Case Three: The Cultural and Ecological Cluster

The Conghua, Zengcheng, Panyu and Huangpu Districts together make up the Cluster Case Three, which is featured by cultural and ecological development positioning. The former two are former county-level cities with quite a sizeable rural setting, while the latter two are suburban districts with industrial areas. Among these four districts, the Conghua District is known as the ecological garden of Guangzhou with active prevention of industrial pollution, the Zengcheng District is struggling to recover a countryside feel, the Panyu District is under the transformation to a modern and affluent urban district, and the Huangpu District is in the process of being converted from an industrial zone to a new town. Participating in our interviews were the leaders of the enforcement teams in the Conghua and Huangpu Districts, the deputy leader in the Panyu District, and both the leader and the deputy leader in the Zengcheng District.

Major tasks

All the four districts in this culture and ecology cluster undertook typical pollution control related tasks of inspection and monitoring enterprises with industrial pollution, collection of pollutant discharge fees and handling public complaints and petitions. Specifically, with ecological well-being as the development core, the Conghua District enforcement team set the protection of the Liuxi River from any pollution as the overarching mission. The enforcement effort of the Panyu team was extended to cover radiation monitoring and vehicular emission control in an urbanising setting surrounded by power plants and plagued by heavy traffic. As a traditional heavy industrial centre, the Huangpu team's regulated entities were mainly large factories like Sinopec Guangzhou Petrochemical Company and logistic enterprises operating with a large fleet of heavy vehicles. Quite dissimilar, the Zengcheng team handled a wide range of manufacturing factories in smaller scales, normally operating without any valid environmental permits and proper pollution control facilities.

Regulatory strategies

Each team in this cluster tailored their regulatory strategy according to specific local industrial pollution structures in the light of their own limited enforcement strength. In a regulatory setting of few polluting enterprises in a large district area of 2,000 km^2, Conghua team leader targeted their enforcement at twenty plus heavy polluting factories in electroplating, bleaching & dyeing, tanneries, garment and rare earth with the inspection frequency ranging from monthly to annually, depending on the enterprises' level of pollution. Likewise, in admitting the inability of conducting regular inspection of every polluting enterprise, the Panyu team widely practiced a focus strategy with the method of 'double-randomness' in arranging the on-site monitoring. With air pollution coming from a handful of identifiable large heavy industrial enterprises like GAC Honda Automobile Co., Ltd., the Huangpu enforcement team leader indicated that these polluting plants appeared to be quite cooperative in meeting the needs of their regulation. In a jurisdiction of 1,615 km^2 filled with a large number of polluting enterprises in different scales of operation, the Zengcheng District team employed the strategy of organising high profile inspection led by District EPB leading officials over the polluting enterprises in industrial parks in order to create an overwhelming deterrent effect for all others. Their core enforcement principle was leniency to lesser polluting operations, and toughness against all heavy pollution.

Enforcement difficulties

All these four district teams faced the reality of workload exceeding the team capacity without exception even for the relatively well-off Panyu District team, which possibly had the best pay for its team members and was the most equipped in advanced technologies. Among the various challenges they faced, the deputy leader of the Panyu team found it difficult for the team to get the penalty decision letters delivered to the owners of small enterprises who deliberately evaded from their delivery in order to leave the judicial requirement of a signed return from the recipient unable to complete. The Conghua District leader was discontent with the simplified 'three licenses in one' regulations which allowed enterprises to operate once obtained a business license without the need to meet pollution requirement in the form of an environmental permit in the past. Backward in equipment has created all sorts of enforcement difficulties for the Huangpu District team, including the reliance on manual record taking and there was no schedule for setting up a digital on-line system for real-time pollution monitoring. Despite being equivalent to a prefecture-level city in both economic terms and industrial scale, the Zengcheng District team complained the lack of enforcement power accorded to the township and village enforcement units, rendering them unable to delegate enforcement duties to these local units.

No less difficulties were handling pollution complaints and petitions that had drained excessive time and effort from individual enforcement teams in these four districts. As reported by the leader of the Conghua District team, sheer volume which made up of 60-70% their daily workload had indeed distracted them from the core regulatory task of pollution inspection and monitoring. In facing the influx of pollution complaints as more convenient channels were open for the public, the Panyu District team had specifically set up a petition unit to handle over 1,900 cases received last year–in fact, the figure was as high as 8,000 if repeated and returned complaints were counted. The situation was not much better for the Huangpu District team to handle over 1,000 cases with a specific taskforce of eight officials. Though the load was slightly better for the Zengcheng District team which absorbed 50% of their work capacity, its two leaders had emphatically pointed out the core of the problem that 'until the relocation of industrial parks that are adjacent to the residential areas, there is no way to lower the complaint figures'.

Who were the main troublemakers within these regulatory jurisdictions? Most of the time they were small factories and restaurants, particularly those operated in a polluting way and without a valid business license. Surprisingly, the Panyu District team tended to be quite considerate in their pollution control actions to these restaurants and food caterers, giving them chances to rectify their polluting operations without imposing any sanctions. Difficult polluting enterprises had given rise to the need for the enforcement teams to organise joint action, particularly with public security organs in cases of high-risk operations involving resistance and unlawful discharge at nighttime with potential threats to personal safety. There were quite positive experiences for the Zengcheng District team which had often got active assistance from local residents in support of their enforcement actions.

Sources of enforcement pressures

In the situation of excessive workload and rising desire for an ecologically friendly living environment, no district enforcement teams could get away from all kinds of pressures. The leader of the Conghua District team frankly pointed out the pressure point was that 'many tasks cannot be completed'. Added to their grievance was the media's critical and negative reports on the ways they discharged their duties. Similarly, the Panyu District deputy team leader spelt out that their inability to timely and satisfactorily solve the industrial pollution problems raised by public complaints had exposed all the inadequacies of their works. Making him feel better was the media's increasingly considerate in reporting their works and performance. Quite the contrary, the Huangpu District team had made deliberate efforts to get away from media attention for fear of unfavourable coverage. The deputy leader of the Zengcheng District team admitted that they were unable to complete their inspection and monitoring tasks over all problematic enterprises, giving rise to the fear of the call for accountability from the District's disciplinary committee. In particular, he was quite annoying to see that the public had increasingly brought their complaints to the media whenever the pollution problems raised through official channels could not receive quick or satisfactory settlement.

Government and public expectations

When discussing whether the performance of their team had met government and public expectations, leaders look at it from different perspectives. With the best environmental quality among all districts, the Conghua District team leader expressed with confidence that its pollution control work had on the whole effectively met social expectation. Interestingly, the deputy team lead of the Panyu District looked at the rising figure of public complaints positively as an expression of growing citizens' trust in them to solve their pollution problems, while critical of government's harsh assessment of denying them an excellent rating because of the record of a lower water quality indicator despite achieving an overall score higher than the excellent line. For the Huangpu District, the leader was satisfied with the district government's positive assessment with full consideration of their diligent efforts but not happy with the municipal government to base the assessment exclusively on the district's quantifiable environmental indicators. Equally considerate was the Zengcheng district government in assessing the enforcement team's performance, particularly the district's air quality index was ranked high at the top in the last two years.

Possible improvements

While most suggestions focused on resource issues and regulatory power for capacity strengthening, a few District team leaders had sounded out the importance of localising industrial pollution control to township and street levels. In this respect, the Panyu District was institutionally a step ahead of all other districts in setting up local level regulatory units with enforcement power for inspection and monitoring. The Zengcheng District deputy leader found the local units' lack of enforcement power required the presence of District team's officials to take charge of all enforcement actions. Though local regulatory units were still non-existence in the Conghua District, the team leader considered the delegation of inspection and monitoring duties to township and street level setups would enable them to fit enforcement actions to local circumstances.

REFLECTIONS AND CONCLUSION

The three cluster cases above provide a unique set of narratives with ample insiders' stories from leading officials in all the twelve district enforcement teams of the GEPB around their regulatory tasks and activities for an in-depth exploration of the regulatory reality. Table 7 highlights the regulatory enforcement in individual districts.

Table 7: An Overview of District Enforcement

Districts	Sources of Industrial Pollution	Enforcement Tasks	Regulatory Approaches	Enforcement Difficulties	Enforcement Pressures	Performance/ Expectations Gaps	Possible Improvement
City Districts							
Haizhu	Catering industry and small factories	Driven by public complaints	Education and communication	Private enterprises operating without licence or permits	Public & media	Unable to meet public expectation	Greater environmental consideration from industry and commerce agencies when issuing business licence and approving site selection
Yuexiu	Catering industry & food services	Restaurants and catering services: oil fumes & noise nuisance	Legalistic with relatively heavier penalties	Low professional quality of enforcement officials	Public	Able to meet public expectation	Establishment of a proper environmental concept and attitude among all parties
Liwan	Catering industry & food services	Restaurants and catering services: oil fumes & noise nuisance	Legalistic and coercive	Small enterprises discharging pollutants without treatment	Public: repeated complaints	Unable to meet public expectation	Quality of enforcement officials
Baiyun	Industrial pollution	Driven by public complaints	Education and communication	High complexity in the types of polluting enterprises	Public & media	Unable to meet public expectation	Education of enterprises for the environmental obligation
Tianhe	Catering industry, hospitals, food factories, traffic	Restaurants and catering services: oil fumes & noise nuisance	Legalistic and stringent	Low environmental awareness among business owners	Municipal government & disciplinary committee	Unable to meet public expectation	Additional manpower & setting up street-level enforcement unit.
Economic and Environmentally Friendly Districts							

Nansha	Industrial pollution	Chemical and heavy industries	Legalistic and very strict	High turnover of enforcement officials	Public & media	Unable to meet public expectation	Strengthening enforcement and penalty power
Huadu	Industrial pollution	Driven by public complaints	Legalistic and strict	Small enterprises, particularly those operating without licence or permits	Public & media	Unable to meet public expectation	Full deployment of officials in the enforcement team
Kaifa	Industrial pollution	Power plants and manufacturing enterprises with effluent discharge in large quantity	Collaboration with opportunities for rectification	Small factories and small business operations with pollution	Public	Unable to meet public expectation	Establishment of street-level enforcement units
Cultural and Ecological Districts							
Conghua	Catering industry & food services	Protection of Liuxi River	Education and communication	Large area to cover for industrial pollution control	Public & media	Able to meet public expectation	Establishment of township and street level enforcement units
Zengcheng	Industrial pollution	Polluting manufacturing enterprises	Relatively considerate & lenient	Small enterprises, particularly those operating without licence or permits	Public & media	Unable to meet public expectation	Direct enforcement power granted to township and street level enforcement units
Panyu	Industrial pollution, Catering industry, and traffic	Power plants and vehicle emissions	Legalistic on the stricter side	Delivery of Judgments to sanctioned enterprises' & restaurants' owners	Public & media	Unable to meet public expectation	Refinement of pollution control regulations to make the provisions more specific to operate
Huangpu	Industrial pollution	Large petrochemical industry and logistic enterprises	Legalistic	Backward equipment	Public & media	Unable to meet public expectation	Improvement of the quality of enforcement officials

How did these foot soldiers see the latest legislative efforts to improve the legal regime for industrial pollution control? All enforcement teams were disappointed that this wave of revisions fell short of addressing their core regulatory concerns in legal terms. Most critical of all was the scapegoat effect of local government's increased accountability to pollution control in that the burden had been effectively shifted to the enforcement team with the immediate consequence of making their enforcement duties heavier and demanding but without receiving additional resources support. Similarly, no direct enforcement power was granted to enforcement teams as they were still required to seek court orders for closing or suspending polluting production or business operations, preventing them from taking forceful and timely actions. Finally, the legal basis for setting up the enforcement team as a professional disciplinary force with uniform was not provided, which rendered them difficult to command the respect from all regulated entities.

The emerging favourable political ecology for tougher regulatory control of industrial pollution control, attributed to the increased dedication of municipal and district governments to environmental well-being and growing public demand for improving the quality of their living environment, had turned out to be pressure but not support for the enforcement teams. On the one hand, local government had set higher and moving pollution control targets for the enforcement team to achieve but without empowering them to command interagency support. On the other hand, the rising number of complaints, with most of them on visible but not necessarily unlawful polluting operations, had all of sudden emerged as the major assignment for each district enforcement team, leaving them less capacity to regulate heavy polluting enterprises. Despite all these odds, all of these district enforcement teams had met or exceeded respective district governments' expectation on the levels of industrial pollution control.

The high-profile top-down monitoring over individual district enforcement teams through the Central Enforcement Inspection Team had immediately led to the tightening up of local regulatory control over industrial pollution to hit hard on polluting enterprises. However, the first impression among most enforcement team was quite miserable as their presence had made the enforcement team exhausted, working over time until late night without any weekend breaks throughout the inspection period. There was a strong feeling shared among local enforcement teams that this hit-hard effect of this campaign style of inspection was more less 'a gust of wind' which would not last long to ensure continuous and stronger local government support for their enforcement tasks.

No shortage of positive experiences can be identified from these district enforcement teams. Most notably, not all district enforcement teams were hostile to media and a few of them had made organised effort to actively communicate with media to assure accurate reporting of their regulatory works. Nor citizens' complaints were always seen negative as one district enforcement team took the rising number of complaint cases as a sign of increasing popular trust on them. A district enforcement team had even actively engaged local citizens to join and assist in their enforcement actions, while another one was happy to receive positive comments from local residence on their diligent regulatory efforts. Again, not all polluting enterprises refused to cooperate with enforcement officials in the control of their polluting operations and voluntary compliance could be achieved by the enforcement teams through close and friendly communication.

Finally, regulatory variations among all district enforcement teams were widely detected. Despite the salient legalistic trend in regulatory control across the board, each district enforcement team tailored their regulatory approaches according to the local contexts of industrial features, pollution structure, development positioning and district profile. Such variations were most pronounced between city district enforcement teams and their rural counterparts. The disparities in regulatory capacity across districts were also presence as some district enforcement teams enjoyed stronger local government resource support to build a larger team with better remuneration package for its officials and better pollution monitoring equipment. A few district teams were even able to extend their enforcement capability to the township or street level by setting up local inspection units, though not all of them were vested with enforcement power.

More illuminating reflections and further observations on local enforcement of industrial pollution control regulations can be drawn from their work experiences. Suffice it to conclude with a few remarks on the tough enforcement reality from individual team leaders: we work really hard and tiredly; our enforcement power is weak; and holding us accountable is unfair because of the imbalance of power and responsibility.

The Sword of Damocles: Enterprises' Strategies Under Campaign-Style Enforcement

JINGWEN CAI
The Chinese University of Hong Kong
CARLOS WING-HUNG LO
The Chinese University of Hong Kong
NING LIU
City University of Hong Kong

INTRODUCTION

Administrative justice concerns 'how justice is achieved through the delivery of public services and the actions, inactions, and decision-making of public bodies.'[1] Central to this notion is understanding how fairness and legitimacy are experienced by those subject to administrative power. This study contributes to this literature by examining environmental justice through the lens of regulatory enforcement in China. while previous research has emphasized the importance of formalism and procedural fairness in fostering intrinsic compliance—particularly in contexts where coercive capacity is limited[2]—less is known about how administrative bodies sustain compliance under conditions marked by legal ambiguity and episodic enforcement. we address this gap by focusing on how enterprises navigate the looming threat of campaign-style enforcement (CSE). Drawing on past research that examines campaign-style regulatory enforcement and the cyclical alternation between it and regular enforcement, this study proposes that the intermittent nature of CSE acts as a significant deterrent. Interviews with frontline managers in highly regulated coal power plants show that enterprises internalize the ever-present threat of CSE and incorporate it into their compliance strategies. We adopt a deterrence perspective to scrutinise how regulatory agencies leverage unpredictability in target selection, consistency in punitive severity, and the periodic recurrence of CSE to construct a form of cumulative pressure. The axiom of cumulative inertia and stress is used to explore the diverse strategies of regulated enterprises to cope with such deterrence. The findings suggest that CSE continues to

[1] Hertogh, M; Kirkham, R; Thomas, R and Tomlinson, J (eds) (2022) *The Oxford Handbook of Administrative Justice* Oxford University Press at xvi.

[2] Liu, N; Van Rooij, B and Lo, CWH (2018) 'Beyond Deterrent Enforcement Styles: Behavioural Intuitions of Chinese Environmental Law Enforcement Agents in a Context of Challenging Inspections' (96) *Public Administration* 497 at 510.

significantly influence enterprise behaviour, ensuring compliance even when not actively employed as the primary regulatory approach.

Since its inception, Lieberthal and Oksenberg's fragmented authoritarianism framework has been a cornerstone for analysing the Chinese government and its policy dynamics.[3] Zhan and Qin suggest that higher-level governments can use political ambiguity to 'enhance the adaptability and resilience of the Chinese political system.'[4] Campaign-style enforcement (CSE) is considered an unconventional governance method that addresses the shortcomings of regular enforcement. It is usually applied to political systems with a high degree of centralisation to cross bureaucratic gaps through top-down commands and resource mobilisation to achieve a specific goal within a limited time.[5] This approach usually underscores political mobilisation at the central level and necessitates local governments drastically tightening up regulatory enforcement to align with local conditions, thus effectively supporting the central government's directives. For example, in the CSE of environmental regulations, all levels of government and regulated entities perceive and act upon a strong political commitment to environmental issues from the central authority.[6]

Large-scale CSE initiatives, whether aimed at environmental protection or infrastructure development, are tools for the central government to strengthen control and foster better integration of local economies and societies with national policy lines.[7] Although campaign-style and regular enforcement often exist concurrently, they typically alternate in dominance.[8] Some studies critique CSE for its harsh and somewhat arbitrary methods, questioning its long-term effectiveness.[9] A common view is that under fragmented authoritarianism, there may be poor coordination between the central government and local governments on policies, resulting in

[3] Lieberthal, K and Oksenberg, M (1988) *Policy Making in China: Leaders, Structures, and Processes* Princeton University Press.

[4] Zhan, JV and Qin, S (2017) 'The Art of Political Ambiguity: Top–down Intergovernmental Information Asymmetry in China' (2) *Journal of Chinese Governance* 149 at 149.

[5] Liu, NN; Lo, CWH; Zhan, X and Wang, W (2015) 'Campaign-style Enforcement and Regulatory Compliance' (75) *Public Administration Review* 85; Zhou, X (2012) 'Mobilisational State: Further Exploration in the Institutional Logic of State Governance in China' (9) *Open Times* 105.

[6] Liu, NN; Lo, CWH; Zhan, X and Wang, W (2015) 'Campaign-style Enforcement and Regulatory Compliance' (75) *Public Administration Review* 85.

[7] Goodman, DS (2004) 'The Campaign to 'Open up the West': National, Provincial-level and Local Perspectives" (178) *The China Quarterly* 317; McNally, CA (2004) 'Sichuan: Driving Capitalist Development Westward' (178) *The China Quarterly* 426.

[8] Zhou, X (2012) 'Mobilisational State: Further Exploration in the Institutional Logic of State Governance in China' (9) *Open Times* 105.

[9] Huang Y (2023) '"Tentative Violations" and "Selective Tolerance": An Organisational Interpretation of the Failure of Campaign-style Regulations' (2) *China Public Administration Review* 25; Zhou, X (2012) 'Mobilisational State: Further Exploration in the Institutional Logic of State Governance in China' (9) *Open Times* 105.

local governments' ineffective implementation of the policies promoted by the central government. For example, Qian and Mok suggested that the dual decentralisation and fragmented authoritarianism in China's governance could lead to policy ineffectiveness.[10] Following the fragmented authoritarianism perspective, studies like those conducted by Tian and Zheng on straw burning and Huang on private tutoring indicate that fluctuations in the intensity of CSE are often mirrored by local governments' varying stringency in enforcement.[11] In this study, a critical inquiry is how CSE can maintain its distinct impact and avoid assimilation into regular enforcement mechanisms, thereby preserving its unique role in addressing systemic gaps when not at the forefront.

China's power industry is a classic example under CSE's looming threat. To reveal CSE's mechanism, it is crucial to observe the implementation and outcome of environmental protection supervision in the power industry, to study the power industry's perception and reaction to various regulatory policies, and to analyse factors that promote or restrict the development of the power industry's environmental protection. The Five-Year Plan (FYP), formulated by the Central Committee of the Communist Party of China (CPC) every five years, is a national blueprint for economic and social development. This cyclical planning process, which involves all government departments at every level, epitomises the top-down influence of the CPC Central Committee, providing a relatively stable research context to examine CSE's background operation mechanism. Specifically, the environmental sector's FYPs focus on ecological construction and pollution control. These plans review the environmental progress made over the previous five years and set forth policy directives and objectives for the forthcoming period. In Guangdong Province, the 11th, 12th and 13th Five-Year Environmental Protection Plans reflect the evolution of local environmental policies. These plans have systematically addressed air pollution by tightening pollutant treatment and discharge standards, using economic incentives to encourage power plants to undertake environmental upgrades, and improving both the online pollution monitoring system and environmental data sharing mechanism.[12] These strategic measures are promoted in a five-year cycle, cumulatively enhancing environmental governance. This progressive tightening of regulations provides the backdrop for analysing the impact of CSE, particularly in the context of the strict environmental standards and

[10] Qian, J and Mok, KH (2016) 'Dual Decentralisation and Fragmented Authoritarianism in Governance: Crowding out among Social Programmes in China' (36) *Public Administration and Development* 185.

[11] Tian, X and Zheng, J (2016) 'Enveloped State: The Action Logic of Grassroots Governance and Rural Autonomy — A Case Study Based on "Straw Burning" in Huangjiang' (2) *Journal of Public Management* 141; Huang Y (2023) "'Tentative Violations' and 'Selective Tolerance': An Organisational Interpretation of the Failure of Campaign-style Regulations" (2) *China Public Administration Review* 25.

[12] Available at: < http://www.gd.gov.cn/gkmlpt/content/0/136/post_136809.html#7>.
Available at: < http://gdee.gd.gov.cn/ghjh3128/content/post_2333841.html>.
Available at: < http://gdee.gd.gov.cn/ghjh3128/content/post_2333878.html>.

round-the-clock emission monitoring that power plants are currently facing as key monitoring objects.

BACKGROUND

China's bureaucratic system tends to transform administrative matters into the political arena, whereas Weberian bureaucracy traditionally converts political issues into administrative tasks.[13] Reflecting this, the language of China's environmental policy frequently resonates with CSE — from the Patriotic Health Campaign to the more recent Winning the Blue Sky Defense War. Launched by the State Council in 2018, this three-year action aimed to improve air quality through measures targeting the coal-fired power generation industry.[14] The plan employed both administrative guidance and economic incentives, signalling a clear political commitment to increasing the use of clean energy, limiting coal consumption, and strictly regulating pollutant treatment and discharge in power plants.

Despite not being one of the Blue Sky Defense War's primary focus areas, Guangdong Province, particularly its Pearl River Delta (PRD) region, was withdrawn from the three key national regions for air pollution prevention and control in 2018.[15] In 2019, the Ministry of Ecology and Environment highlighted Guangdong's proactive measures in winning the Blue Sky Defense War in a special article and praised the Pearl River Delta as a model for air pollution prevention and control.[16] Two notable aspects of the article were its framing and emphasis. It both opened and concluded with references to President Xi Jinping's progressive concept of ecological civilisation, illustrating a shift in environmental governance from a purely administrative issue to a political one. Furthermore, the article stressed that the most stringent regulatory system must be used to achieve the action plan's goals, reflecting the Chinese government's tendency to use strict regulatory enforcement to achieve regulatory goals within a set timeframe.

Guangdong Province's exemplary performance in the Blue Sky Defense War is largely attributed to its sustained commitment to environmental governance. Guangzhou is the capital city of Guangdong Province, the epitome of such commitment. A prime example of Guangzhou's leadership in environmental governance is the '50355' project, first launched by the Guangzhou Municipal Government in February 2014. This project targets transforming the city's coal power plants to 'ultra-clean emission'. Specifically, the project sets stringent standards: nitrogen oxides must be below $50mg/Nm^3$, sulphur dioxide below $35mg/Nm^3$, and soot below five

[13] Zhou, X (2012) 'Mobilisational State: Further Exploration in the Institutional Logic of State Governance in China' (9) *Open Times* 105.

[14] Available at: <https://www.cnemission.com/article/news/DomesticNews/201807/20180700001499.shtml>.

[15] Available at: <https://www.mee.gov.cn/ywgz/xcjy/shxc/201909/t20190909_733028.shtml>.

[16] Available at: <https://www.mee.gov.cn/ywgz/xcjy/shxc/201909/t20190909_733028.shtml>.

mg/Nm^3 in key regions,[17] way stricter than China's 2012 Emission Standard of Air Pollutants for Thermal Power Plants which requires nitrogen oxides below 100mg/Nm^3, sulphur dioxide below 50mg/Nm^3, and soot below 20mg/Nm^3 for key regions.[18]

This initiative is part of a broader trend of rectifying local thermal power plants that began over a decade ago. Since 2007, Guangzhou has progressively shut down coal-fired and fuel-fired small thermal power units annually, aligning with directives from various central government departments to reduce energy consumption and to achieve emission reduction.[19] The shutdowns, enforced through administrative orders, represent a definitive CSE method. This approach was notably evident during preparations for the 2010 Asian Games in Guangzhou, which were themed the 'Green Asian Games'. As part of the environmental quality assurance for the Game, the city government adopted drastic measures, including the immediate shutdown of pollution sources. In February 2010, the pre-Games air quality assurance plan mandated the shutdown of small thermal power units judged as 'high pollution and high energy consumption', among other significant sources of pollution in industries such as metallurgy, coking, building materials, chemicals, and ore mining.[20] These small thermal power units faced the most severe action, with a complete shutdown required in key control areas before the Games.[21] Subsequently, in October 2010, the 'Guangdong Provincial Asian Games Air Quality Guarantee Measures Program' was released, necessitating that 72 industrial enterprises reduce or stop production during the event.[22] Guangdong's power supply and demand relationship was still in a short-supply stage at that time. Despite the ongoing energy supply challenges in the region at the time, the targeted and temporary enforcement of these shutdowns was crucial to achieve specific environmental goals. The policy of shutting down small thermal power units continues in Guangdong, with public announcements made each time a unit is closed. Most recently, on January 26, 2024, the Nanlang Thermal Power Plant shut down two of its gas thermal power units.[23] This ongoing strategy underscores a clear, consistent approach to environmental governance, with the affected enterprises fully aware of the potential for closure.

Institutional dynamics have been widely studied by the research on administrative justice, particularly in efforts to understand how rule-making

[17] Available at: <http://www.gz.gov.cn/zwgk/zdxm/2014n/content/post_2851885.html>.

[18] Available at: <https://www.mee.gov.cn/ywgz/fgbz/bz/bzwb/dqhjbh/dqgdwrywrwpf-bz/201109/W020130125407916122018.pdf >.

[19] Available at: <http://www.gd.gov.cn/gkmlpt/content/0/136/post_136795.html#7>.

[20] Available at: <http://gdee.gd.gov.cn/shbtwj/content/post_2303946.html>.

[21] Available at: <http://gdee.gd.gov.cn/shbtwj/content/post_2303946.html>.

[22] Available at: <http://finance.sina.com.cn/roll/20101026/03078840984.shtml>.

[23] Available at: <http://drc.gd.gov.cn/snyj/tzgg/content/post_4361394.html>.

shapes, and is shaped by, frontline decision-making.[24] One promising line of inquiry examines the degree to which formal regulatory frameworks interact with the discretionary practices of street-level enforcement agents. As the capital city of Guangdong Province, a pioneer in regulatory reform, Guangzhou provides a revealing case. The city not only enforces national and provincial environmental regulations but also historically maintained its own set of local rules, including the *Environmental Protection Regulation of Guangzhou*, the *Water Pollution Prevention and Control Regulation of Guangzhou*, and several *Regulatory Files Related to Discretionary Power over Environmental Administrative Penalt*ies. However, a notable institutional trend in recent years has been the streamlining of regulatory authority, with local rules gradually repealed to avoid duplication with higher-level laws. For instance, in 2019, Guangzhou repealed both its local *Regulation on the Prevention and Control of Environmental Pollution by Solid Wastes* and its local *Air Pollution Control Regulation*. These institutional changes have tangible effects at the enforcement level. An analysis of the 2024 administrative penalty cases published by the Guangzhou Municipal Ecological Environment Bureau reveals that nearly all penalties—34 cases in total—were grounded in national or provincial legal instruments (see Table 1). Only one case cited a municipal-level regulation as a basis for administrative sanction.[25]

Table 1 Administrative Penalty Bases of Announced Cases of Guangzhou Municipal Ecological Environment Bureau in 2024

Level	Law/Regulation Name	Times of Being Used as the Basis
National	Regulations on the Administration of Construction Project Environmental Protection	12
	Air Pollution Control Act	8
	Regulations on the Administration of Pollutant Discharge Permits	4
	Water Pollution Prevention and Control Law	4
	Law on Noise Pollution Prevention and Control	2
	Law on the Prevention and Control of Environmental Pollution by Solid Wastes	2

[24] Hertogh, M; Kirkham, R; Thomas, R and Tomlinson, J (eds) (2022) *The Oxford Handbook of Administrative Justice* Oxford University Press at xvii.

[25] Available at: < https://data.gz.gov.cn/dataDetail.html?sid=1838779158815432704&openStatus=1&dsDataTableSid=1838779158815432704>.

Provincial	Environmental Protection Regulation	4
	Regulations on the Prevention and Control of the Exhaust Pollution of Motor Vehicles	1
	Water Pollution Prevention and Control Regulation	1
	Regulation on the Discretionary Power over Environmental Administrative Penalty	1
Municipal	Guangzhou's Municipal Standards on the Discretionary Power over Environmental Administrative Penalty Applicable to The Law on Noise Pollution Prevention and Control of the People's Republic of China and The Measures for the Administration of the Law-based Disclosure of Environmental Information by Enterprises	1

RESPONDING MECHANISM TO CSE'S LOOMING THREAT

In China, Guangdong Province has long been at the forefront of reform and opening-up, aiming to lead nationally environmental initiatives. This ambition drives Guangdong Province to pre-emptively set and enforce stricter environmental standards. To actively respond to the central government's call for environmental protection and governance, the province frequently employs CSE to maintain its status as a pioneer.

CSE's Looming Threat

Entities affected by these policies recognise the cyclical dominance of CSE and anticipate its periodic resurgence as the main regulatory approach. Given its tendency to impose stricter measures than regular enforcement, CSE looms like a sword of Damocles over these entities, who must stay prepared for its sudden and strict applications.

On the one hand, technological advances have enabled the government to monitor environmental compliance with minimal administrative resources. Modern technologies enable continuous, 24-hour monitoring of environmental data, thereby diminishing the distinction between the inspection frequencies of CSE and routine enforcement. On the other hand, the prevailing trend of prioritising political directives — especially within state-owned enterprises (SOEs) — means that top-down environmental priorities continue to exert significant pressure. Regulated entities are well aware that monitoring will intensify, and standards will tighten. Recognising this, many have adapted by incorporating potential CSE into their environmental strategies. Direct administrative actions, such as factory shutdowns, are anticipated and factored into operational planning. This ongoing readiness underscores how CSE, even when not active, maintains a pervasive influence, shaping corporate behaviour continuously rather than episodically.

Deterrence, Compliance, and Beyond Compliance

When used to analyse regulation and compliance, deterrence theory corresponds to calculating the gains and losses of the regulators and the regulated parties under different regulatory scenarios. "Deterring future undesirable acts" is one of the reasons governments engage in regulatory activities, aiming to prevent socially harmful behaviours through public law enforcement.[26] The optimal outcome of such enforcement is to deter undesirable actions at the lowest possible social cost.[27]

In the realm of environmental regulations, the government's toolkit for enforcing compliance includes two main types of deterrence: fines, which are relatively costless for the government to impose, and imprisonment, which entails significant costs.[28] In China, environmental laws provide for both these sanctions in response to violations, underscoring their role in the regulatory framework. Monetary penalties for environmental non-compliance can extend to shutting down enterprises, a measure representing potential tax revenue losses and, thus, a costly sanction for the government. However, the decision to close a business is not made lightly and is influenced by local political and economic conditions, which can affect the likelihood of harsh sanctions being applied.[29] Despite these complexities, when environmental protection is prioritised over economic interests, shutting down non-compliant enterprises may still be regarded and applied as a deterrent measure in which the overall social gains outweigh the losses.

It is interesting to look at to what extent the deterrence generated by shutting down as a potential sanction can drive regulatees towards compliance and even beyond compliance. Shimshack and Ward found that fines have significant marginal impacts, and "large improvements follow even from modest sanctions, as long as they have economic 'teeth'."[30] Being

[26] Raskolnikov, A (2021) 'Deterrence Theory: Key Findings and Challenges' in Van Rooij, B and Sokol DD (eds) (2021) *The Cambridge Handbook of Compliance* Cambridge University Press 179 at 179.

[27] Id.

[28] Id.

[29] Shimshack, JP and Ward, MB (2005) 'Regulator Reputation, Enforcement, and Environmental Compliance' (50) *Journal of Environmental Economics and Management* 519.

[30] Shimshack, JP and Ward, MB (2005) 'Regulator Reputation, Enforcement, and Environmental Compliance' (50) *Journal of Environmental Economics and Management* 519 at

shut down directly stops the lives of enterprises as economic entities and is undoubtedly one of the most severe monetary sanctions. Even the partial closure of operations, such as closing down one or a few factories within a larger enterprise, can serve as a powerful economic deterrent. Past research has pointed out that modest monetary sanctions can lead to significant improvements because enterprises would observe the experience of other enterprises being sanctioned and adjust their expectations for the possibility of penalties for violations.[31] Thus, it can be inferred that enterprises might adjust their expectations and compliance strategies based on the severe sanctions observed during previous instances of CSE.

Raskolnikov contrasts two frameworks: the optimal deterrence framework, where uncertainty about penalties can lead to behaviour that both exceeds and falls short of the social optimum, and the probabilistic compliance framework, which suggests that greater certainty about penalties enhances compliance.[32] The optimal deterrence framework challenges regulators to find a balance that maximises social welfare, which is often unrealistic in practice.[33] This study suggests CSE introduces a mix of certainty and uncertainty that places regulatees under the constant threat of severe regulatory actions. It corresponds to such a process: by leveraging the history of strict regulations in the past CSE and the alternation between it and regular enforcement, enterprises anticipate the potential return of stringent measures and adjust their compliance levels accordingly. Ideally, the looming threat of CSE serves as a continual reminder to enterprises of their responsibilities and the risks of non-compliance, prompting them to prepare for future risks in advance. In this way, CSE promotes compliance and fosters an environment where enterprises are incentivised to surpass minimum standards, preparing more robustly for future regulatory landscapes.

Responsive regulation is characterised by the regulator's ability to develop sophisticated strategies through a balance of persuasion and coercion. This model benefits from repeated interactions between regulators and regulated entities, which allow for increasingly deterrent-oriented measures against entities that consistently underperform.[34] However, the effectiveness of responsive regulation hinges on the frequency and quality of these interactions; insufficient interaction reduces its feasibility.[35] In the context of this study, the metaphor of the Sword of Damocles in CSE reflects a scenario where sufficient interactions are commonplace. This is particularly evident in the coal-fired power generation industry, which is historically

538.

[31] Id.

[32] Raskolnikov, A (2017) 'Probabilistic Compliance' (34) *Yale Journal on Regulation* 101.

[33] Id.

[34] Gunningham, N (2023) [2017] 'Compliance, Deterrence and Beyond' in Faure, M (eds) (2023) *Elgar Encyclopaedia of Environmental Law* Edward Elgar Publishing 63.

[35] Id.

subject to stringent regulation. Entities in this sector are monitored through a 24-hour electronic real-time system, routine and sporadic inspections by government departments, and investigations following public complaints. Such repeated interactions can provide sufficient knowledge for responsive regulation and, in turn, enable regulated enterprises to anticipate potential enforcement actions (both strength and scope), and adapt their responsive compliance strategies accordingly.

Thornton et al. suggested that while the punishment of the uncompliant may not necessarily heighten peer enterprises' perception of sanction threats, they do remind them to reassess their compliance routines, especially since most firms are already compliant.[36] A later study on Chinese companies found that a penalty deters peer enterprises and drives them to increase environmental investment.[37] The cases from the coal power plants interviewed in this study align with these findings. All interviewed plants are compliant and operate under ultra-clean emission standards and frequent inspections. Analysing their responding mechanism will give us a deeper understanding of how deterrence and compliance dynamics operate under CSE.

Cumulative Inertia and Cumulative Stress in Response to CSE

Enterprises facing the material threat of CSE and potential factory closures exhibit a range of responses. Active responses may include exceeding environmental management tasks ahead of schedule, pre-emptively relocating factories to less stringent regulatory environments, or transitioning to cleaner energy sources. Conversely, passive responses are characterised by inertia: no relocation, no power generation transformation, and no environmental technology improvement until compelled by new governmental standards.

The theoretical framework to analyse these responses involves the concepts of cumulative inertia and cumulative stress. The axiom of cumulative inertia suggests that accumulated residence generates inertia, such as deeper ties, which reduces the possibility of state changes.[38] Gilbert differentiates inertia into two categories, 'resource rigidity' (the reluctance to change investment patterns in resources) and 'routine rigidity' (the reluctance to modify organisational processes that use these resources).[39]

[36] Thornton, D; Gunningham, NA and Kagan, RA (2005) 'General Deterrence and Corporate Environmental Behaviour' (27) *Law & Policy* 262 at 262.

[37] Wang, Y; Li, Y; Ma, Z and Song, J (2019) 'The Deterrence Effect of a Penalty for Environmental Violation' (11) *Sustainability* 4226.

[38] McGinnis, R (1968) 'A Stochastic Model of Social Mobility' *American Sociological Review* 712; Myers, GC; McGinnis, R and Masnick, G (1967) 'The Duration of Residence Approach to a Dynamic Stochastic Model of Internal Migration: a Test of the Axiom of Cumulative Inertia' (14) *Eugenics Quarterly* 121; Li, SX and Rowley, TJ (2002) 'Inertia and Evaluation Mechanisms in Inter-organisational Partner Selection: Syndicate Formation among US Investment Banks' (45) *Academy of Management Journal* 1104.

[39] Gilbert, CG (2005) 'Unbundling the Structure of Inertia: Resource versus Routine Rigidity'

He notes that while threat perception weakens resource rigidity, it tends to reinforce routine rigidity.[40] A later study on environmental dynamism further indicates that in an environment characterised by frequent and directional, yet with low environmental variance, high levels of organisational inertia are likely to be selected.[41]

Integrating these theoretical insights with empirical data on deterrence, environmental enforcement dynamics, and corporate responses to the perceived looming threat in CSE will help better explore the dynamism of the forces shaping enterprise behaviour. This holistic approach allows for a more nuanced exploration of the dynamics at play in environmental enforcement and the underlying mechanisms driving enterprise responses to such enforcement.

RESEARCH METHODS

Case Descriptions

The power industry is crucial in China's environmental governance. It has long faced the threat of shutdowns and mandates for compliance enhancements. Given its central role and the high stakes involved, the power industry presents a proper case to study the dynamics of CSE in environmental governance. This study focuses on seven coal power plants in Guangzhou. Table 2 shows the basic information about these coal power plants.

Table 2 Interviewed Power Plants' Basic Information

Plant ID	Ownership	Power Generation Purpose
A	State-owned enterprise	Self-supply power plant
B	State-owned enterprise	Ordinary power plant
C	State-owned enterprise	Self-supply power plant
D	State-owned enterprise	Ordinary power plant
E	State-owned enterprise	Ordinary power plant
F	Joint venture	Ordinary power plant
G	State-owned enterprise	Ordinary power plant

While these plants were chosen via convenience sampling, the selection criteria included various dimensions to ensure a diversity of perspectives and operational contexts for a comprehensive analysis. In terms of ownership, the sample includes six SOEs and one joint venture (between an SOE and a Hong Kong enterprise). This is consistent with the dominant position of SOEs in China's power industry and reflects

(48) *Academy of Management Journal* 741.

40 Id.

41 Stieglitz, N; Knudsen, T and Becker, MC (2016) 'Adaptation and Inertia in Dynamic Environments' (37) *Strategic Management Journal* 1854 at 1863.

different governance structures and decision-making processes. Regarding the establishment period, the plants vary from those established decades ago to those initiated in the 2000s, indicating different levels of technology adoption and regulatory adaptation. For power generation purposes, the sample includes five ordinary power plants and two self-supply power plants. More than half of these plants cooperate with other factories in surrounding industrial parks, which may face different operational pressures and regulatory expectations. Overall, these plants differ in terms of profitability, environmental investment, environmental protection driving forces, subsidy policies, and the environmental regulations they face. These differences are pivotal as they influence the plants' responses to CSE, allowing us to uncover patterns and predictors of enterprises' strategic decisions under the looming threat of severe regulatory action.

Interviews and Data Analysis

China's application of the central environmental protection inspection is often used as an entry point for observing its campaign-style enforcement. The No.4 Central Environmental Protection Inspection Team conducted the environmental inspection in the Guangdong Province from November to December 2016 and provided feedback in April 2017, affirming the Pearl River Delta region's leading environmental supervision of the thermal power industry and praising the region as a benchmark for air pollution control.[42] In June and July 2018, the No.5 Central Environmental Protection Inspection Team reviewed Guangdong Province's rectification after the first round of central environmental protection inspection. The team reported the results in October 2018, also praising the Pearl River Delta region's exemplary role in regional air governance.[43]

This study's interviews were conducted with managers of these plants between 2017 and 2019 to form a comprehensive understanding of environmental management practices within thermal power plants. The interviewees were asked about the coal power plants' basic conditions, the environmental protection conditions, and their responses to government supervision. The research materials used in this study include interview scripts and government-published policy documents. This blend of primary and secondary data helps triangulate the findings and enhances the conclusions' validity.

The case study is employed to dissect and understand the nuances of each power plant's approach to environmental management. Through an inductive approach, the analysis seeks to identify commonalities among plants that actively respond to the looming threat of CSE as well as among those that display more passive behaviours. Integrating these empirical findings with existing theoretical frameworks facilitates a deeper interpretation of the strategic choices made by regulated enterprises

[42] Available at: <https://www.mee.gov.cn/gkml/sthjbgw/qt/201704/t20170413_411481.htm>.

[43] Available at: <https://www.mee.gov.cn/xxgk2018/xxgk/xxgk15/201810/t20181020_663312.html>.

regarding their future environmental management paths. This synthesis aims not only to describe but also to explain why certain responses are favoured over others in the face of stringent environmental regulations.

FINDINGS

Impact of Environmental Policies on Profitability

The government's environmental policies could influence coal power plants' profitability. First, stricter environmental requirements can force competitors who are unable to meet these enhanced standards to exit the market. Plant A exemplifies this scenario; although it operates at a loss, it benefits from stringent government policies that are expected to eliminate competitors reliant on high pollution for low-cost competitive advantage and to potentially increase Plant A's main product's market share in the long term, as it provides auxiliary services like steam and electricity to main product lines rather than relying solely on power generation for revenue.

Second, while the government's environmental electricity price subsidy may not fully cover the costs associated with environmental compliance, it still helps to mitigate financial burdens on coal power plants. However, as self-supply plants, Plants A and C face challenges in qualifying for these subsidies. Plant C, in particular, has engaged in unsuccessful negotiations with the government to obtain such financial support. Other economic factors mentioned that affect profitability include the price of raw materials, labour costs, the efficiency of power generation equipment, and financial pressures from loan repayments.

Power Generation and Economic Dynamics

The primary operational cost for coal power plants is coal consumption, which fluctuates based on coal prices and the efficiency of coal-fired generating units. However, other factors also significantly affect the profitability of these plants. For example, Plant E is an older facility with lower loan repayment pressures than new power plants, allowing it to remain profitable despite its high coal consumption. Conversely, new plants might struggle with both high operational costs and loan repayments.

Plants B, D, E, F, and G have undergone environmental transformation to meet government standards, qualifying them for electricity price subsidies that are helpful to them. Plant D diversifies its revenue by supplying heating, cooling, and steam to other enterprises, adding profitable services that also enhance its clients' environmental and energy efficiency. Plants E, F, and G also generate revenue through heating services. In contrast, Plant B, located near a residential area, faces a unique challenge as its potential to sell heat and steam is limited by the government's relocation of large-scale factories from the area, leading to wasted potential resources.

During the interview, it was noted that Guangdong's electricity market was experiencing an oversupply, which affects power plants differently depending on their operational model. Ordinary power plants, which sell electricity on the market, face intense competition. The electricity pricing structure at that time of the interviews was divided into planned electricity by the government based on enterprise conditions — allocated by the government based on enterprise conditions — and market electricity, which power plants had to sell independently. Plants selling planned electricity are subject to benchmark electricity prices, whereas those selling market electricity face reduced prices due to market oversupply. Reforms aimed at phasing out planned basic electricity have also significantly impacted coal power plants. First, the West-East Power Transmission Policy prioritises the distribution of lower-cost hydropower from other regions into Guangdong's market. Second, the mandated consumption hierarchy favouring renewable sources over coal places coal power plants at a competitive disadvantage. This hierarchy requires that new energy consumption prioritise wind and solar energy, followed by hydropower, with coal power being the last resort, further challenging coal plants' market positions.

Environmental Regulation, Urban Development, and Community Relations

At the time of this study, the Guangzhou municipal government focused on factory-emitted air pollutants. The seven interviewed coal power plants were all subject to Guangzhou's stringent ultra-clean emission standards, the aforementioned '50355' standard, which covers nitrogen oxides, sulphur dioxide, and particulate matter emissions. All interviewed plants met the current emission standards. Although the costs of achieving these standards represent a small portion of the total power generation cost, the interviewees expressed concerns about the future. They predict government standards will become even more stringent, nearing zero emissions. Achieving further reductions in emissions might require significant technological advancements and substantial financial investments, making compliance economically challenging for power plants.

It is also concerned that, as the city develops, the encroachment of residential areas on existing industrial zones, including areas around power plants, has increased friction between residents and power plants. Our interviewees voiced frustrations, noting that their facilities were established before nearby residential developments. Despite this, the daily operations of these plants, essential for the local community's energy needs, have led to conflicts. Guangzhou has established a comprehensive environmental complaint resolution mechanism, allowing residents to lodge anonymous complaints. Each complaint triggers mandatory inspections by the environmental protection bureau, ensuring that any grievances are promptly addressed. However, misunderstandings remain, particularly regarding the nature of emissions. For instance, the white smoke emitted from the stacks, which is non-polluting water vapour, has been a point of contention. Residents' concerns over these emissions have compelled plants to invest in additional modifications, such as heating the water vapour to render it colourless at the point of exit from the chimneys. Coal power plants have adopted several communication strategies to mitigate such issues and improve community relations. These include organising open house visits for residents and publicly displaying emission data, which helps demystify plant operations and reassure the community about the environmental impacts.

Driving Forces Behind Environmental Compliance

Our interviewees mentioned explicit government regulations, broader political directives, corporate social responsibility (CSR), and the exemplary role expected of SOEs as primary motivators for environmental transformation.

There is a difference between regulatory mandates and political requirements. Government requirements refer to clear government policies and administrative orders, such as the implementation of pollutant emission standards, the requirements for the environmental transformation of power stations, the collection of environmental protection taxes, and the design of carbon emission quotas. Political requirements often relate to a more general direction or a broader appeal. It can come from the abstract 'central' or a specific central leader, such as President Xi Jinping's speech on 'lucid waters and lush mountains are invaluable assets.'[44] As discussed earlier, CSE has the overtones of political mobilisation. The naming of environmental campaigns in China also shows a style of political mobilisation, such as the Patriotic Health Campaign and the Blue Sky Defense War. The distinction between government mandates and political expectations underscores a strategic alignment where political mobilisation enhances the implementation of structured governmental policies. This synergy is particularly effective in promoting environmental compliance and even proactive measures among SOEs, as these entities are often positioned to lead by example in alignment with both government policies and political aspirations.

Many interviewees emphasised their enterprises' SOE status, which traditionally carries heightened responsibilities for environmental stewardship compared to private enterprises. One manager from a central SOE highlighted their proactive compliance, stating that their plant often exceeds government environmental standards to showcase leadership in the sector.

Technological advancements have revolutionised how emissions are monitored, allowing for real-time, 24-hour surveillance of emissions data. This capability enables immediate alerts when emission levels exceed standards, facilitating rapid response and compliance. Regular government inspections, both scheduled and random, along with third-party audits, maintain a high level of oversight, ensuring that plants consistently meet stringent emission standards. An interviewee from Plant B expressed that the routine disclosure of monitoring data, though legally mandated, is seen as less impactful by the plants themselves. The perception is that compliance is obligatory, regardless of public data transparency: 'I don't think disclosing online monitoring data to citizens can play a role in

44 Available at: <http://www.xinhuanet.com/english/special/2017-11/03/c_136725942.htm>.

supervision... Even if the data is not public, we still have to meet the legal requirements. Disclosure of data does not matter to us'.

Despite current compliance, there is apprehension among plant managers about future regulatory tightening, which could impose even more stringent standards or potentially conflict with broader regional development plans. This anticipation of future challenges reflects a proactive mindset, preparing for potential scenarios where compliance might become even more demanding, possibly leading to significant economic implications or operational constraints.

Proactive and Adaptive Strategies

Under CSE's looming threat, the interviewed enterprises adopted different responses.

Many SOEs choose to over-fulfil environmental management tasks ahead of the government schedule. This proactive approach is driven by the lengthy approval processes typical within SOEs, the need to uphold a leadership role in environmental responsibility, and a risk-averse stance towards potential non-compliance penalties. Several plants are actively transitioning or planning to transition to cleaner energy forms. For instance, despite the significant costs, Plant B is prepared to invest heavily in converting to new energy or gas-fired power. Plant E is exploring alternative energy sources but remains a crucial part of the power grid for peak-shaving purposes with its coal-fired units. With government support, Plant G has already begun installing two gas-fired generator sets, though it anticipates operational losses.

Conversely, Plant D halted its transition to gas-fired power generation due to the high cost, and Plant F, the only joint venture, views its future as uncertain as a coal power plant. In the interview with Plant F, it is expected that there may be no coal power plants in the Greater Bay Area in 10-20 years. However, Plant F finds it difficult to transform because power plants are a relatively professional industry with high technical requirements and intensive capital investment, making its transformation of power generation unrealistic.

Relocation to areas with more lenient environmental requirements in advance is generally unpopular among the interviewed plants. Most have either rejected or resisted suggestions to relocate, citing various concerns on such moves. For instance, Plant G explained the reasons for not relocating after receiving requests and complaints from surrounding residents, pointing out that the power plant itself cannot decide whether to relocate and that relocation involves various intertwined interests, which are difficult to handle. Plant C has opted to remain in its current location despite government advice to relocate, betting on its significance as a major taxpayer and its central-SOE visibility to senior central leaders to shield it from forced closure. For Plant C, CSE in the form of political mobilisation seems to have little effect on it.

Plant A represents a unique case of employing a passive response. Its main business is not power generation. Having relocated just before the enforcement became more stringent, Plant A has no immediate plans to move again. Instead, it plans to respond reactively to new government environmental requirements. Despite compliance with current standards, the plant remains wary of future regional development plans that could necessitate its closure.

To sum up, in the face of deterrence brought by CSE, the interviewed coal power plants listed various reasons to defend the legitimacy of their continued normal operation at their current sites. The reasons given by the interviewed coal power plants include: the country has abundant coal resources, and for energy security, it is necessary to maintain a certain proportion of coal power; the characteristics of stable and controllable power supply of coal power generation make it helpful to maintain the stability of the power grid; after the implementation of ultra-low emission standards for coal power plants, their pollutant emission levels have been consistent with those of gas-fired power plants. Self-supply power plants point out that society needs their main business products. Most of the reasons the coal power plants give are equal to listing the social welfare they would bring if they continue running normally or suggesting that the social welfare will not increase even if they relocate or close down.

Coal power plants also list the obstacles that may be encountered if more active response strategies are adopted, such as the considerable investment required for infrastructure construction and the technical and personnel costs required for power plant energy transformation. Considering that the coal power plants interviewed are all wholly-owned or jointly owned by SOEs, and the assets of SOEs are owned by the whole people, even if the coal power plants analyse the costs of active response strategies from their standpoint, the essence is that costs are paid by the whole people. That is to say, when calculating the increase or decrease of corresponding social welfare, environmental benefits and the costs of environmental practices should be considered comprehensively.

DISCUSSION AND CONCLUSION

Cumulative Inertia in Response Strategies

When choosing response strategies to the pressure of CSE, regulated enterprises encounter several forms of cumulative inertia, stemming from both administrative and economic factors. These inertial forces significantly influence the decision-making process regarding operational changes and adaptations.

The administrative factor primarily lies in regulatory licensing. In China, operating a power plant requires a government-issued license specific to the type of power generation technology employed. SOEs, which have contemplated or initiated transitions to cleaner energy technologies, must navigate the complexities of obtaining new licences that accommodate these changes. For joint ventures like Plant F, the risk of not securing a new licence poses a significant barrier to investing in and transitioning to new power generation technologies.

Economic inertia stems from several factors. First, the substantial initial capital investment for establishing a power plant creates a significant barrier to changing technology. Any transition not only involves discarding previous capital investments in existing generators but also necessitates substantial new investments in setting up alternative technologies. Second, established management and operational processes are tailored to the current technology. Changes in power generation technology would require comprehensive adjustments to these systems, disrupting established practices and potentially affecting operational efficiency. The third factor is related to market adaptation challenges. Relocating to a different province involves not just physical and logistical challenges but also adapting to a new local electricity market. This can be daunting as it requires understanding and integrating into different regulatory and market dynamics. For example, an interviewee from Plant B highlighted the market's competitive nature even within Guangdong Province, indicating the difficulties involved in expanding or shifting operations geographically: 'Even in Guangdong Province, we have to fight to break our heads to sell electricity'.

Overall, the cumulative inertia faced by coal power plants under CSE influences their ability to respond flexibly to evolving environmental regulations. Administrative hurdles, significant financial commitments, and operational disruptions form a complex web that can impede rapid or drastic changes. Understanding these inertial forces is crucial for policymakers and regulators who aim to design effective environmental policies that encourage compliance while considering the operational realities of the power industry.

Cumulative Stress

Cumulative stress for coal power plants arises from both social dynamics and government actions, exerting significant pressure on these enterprises to adapt and transform in response to environmental concerns and regulatory changes. First, as urban expansion shortens the distance between residential areas and factories, environmental complaints from residents become more frequent. This leads to increased government scrutiny and stricter environmental regulations, pressuring power plants towards considering relocation or transitioning to cleaner energy sources to mitigate conflicts and comply with enhanced standards. Second, for SOEs, maintaining employment is a crucial aspect of their social responsibility. The potential shutdown of facilities due to non-compliance with environmental standards during CSE poses a significant threat, as it could lead to job losses, impacting the SOEs' duty to sustain employment.

Government factors also contribute to cumulative stress. Past CSE have shown that the government might resort to direct administrative actions, such as the abrupt shutdown of industrial enterprises, to meet environmental goals swiftly, often disregarding the economic implications or market-based solutions. This history of stringent enforcement practices serves as a warning to power plants about potential future actions. Meanwhile, the local governments have historically set high environmental standards, often exceeding national requirements to establish themselves as leaders in environmental governance. This proactive stance sends a clear political signal to all enterprises about the serious commitment to environmental standards at the local level.

The combination of these social and governmental pressures creates a landscape of cumulative stress for coal power plants. This stress not only dictates immediate responses but also shapes long-term strategic planning. Plants must navigate these pressures while balancing operational viability with environmental responsibility, leading to complex decision-making scenarios regarding compliance, technological innovation, and community relations.

CSE: Deterrence and Sustainable Impact

CSE operates as a continuous deterrent over enterprises, instilling a lasting sense of vigilance due to its potential reactivation at any time. This enforcement style alternates with regular enforcement, keeping enterprises in a state of readiness for its return to predominance.

Our findings showed that even when regular enforcement is the norm, enterprises are deterred by CSE when looking into the future and planning their development. Most are willing to invest extra in advance to deal with CSE that may come to them in the future. This investment is not merely a response to current regulations but a strategic move to mitigate future risks associated with potential CSE. From an economic perspective, responding actively to CSE may seem counterintuitive due to the substantial initial costs and disruptions involved. However, the analysis of cumulative inertia and stress shows that if coal power plants anticipate future regulations that could drastically impact their operations (eg, potential shutdowns), they are more likely to take proactive steps. This anticipatory behaviour is driven by the understanding that non-compliance could lead to severe consequences under CSE. This unpredictability ensures that enterprises continually maintain a high level of environmental performance. It parallels the effect of random inspections in conventional regulatory frameworks, where the unpredictability of inspections forces enterprises to adhere consistently to environmental standards. Moreover, the randomness of target selection in CSE compels all enterprises to consider themselves potential subjects of stringent regulatory actions. This unpredictability ensures that enterprises continually maintain a high level of environmental performance. It parallels the effect of random inspections in conventional regulatory frameworks, where the unpredictability of inspections forces enterprises to adhere consistently to environmental standards.

On the one hand, as mentioned previously, researchers regard China as being characterised by fragmented authoritarianism, which could influence CSE's effectiveness. Contrasting with those findings, our research reveals a different dynamic. The constant threat posed by CSE acts as a powerful deterrent, reducing potential opportunistic non-compliance during periods of lighter enforcement. One possible explanation is that coal-fired power plants operate under strict environmental surveillance, with real-time monitoring around the clock, enhancing transparency and accountability. Second, SOEs typically experience lengthy internal approval processes for new environmental measures, which slows down their ability to make rapid operational changes but ensures thorough vetting of compliance strategies. Third, given their public ownership and high visibility, SOEs are particularly cautious in the environmental domain, prioritising compliance to avoid potential repercussions that could arise from environmental infractions.

CSE maintains its influence over time by ensuring that its return—and the stringent enforcement accompanying it—is always a possibility. This unpredictability, along with the severe consequences of non-compliance, compels enterprises to not only meet but often exceed governmental environmental standards. Even during periods when CSE is not in effect, the lingering possibility of its resurgence motivates continuous compliance and proactive environmental stewardship.

Practical Implications

Merely relying only on the deterrence of CSE may not be sufficient to mobilise regulated enterprises towards more proactive environmental actions. The government should consider a comprehensive approach to calculate the gains and losses associated with environmental transformation in the regulated industry. Administrative and economic instruments can be used jointly to reduce the obstacles that coal power plants will encounter when responding actively. This includes simplifying the application and approval process for permits required for transitioning power generation technologies, which can reduce administrative barriers, and using monetary incentives to promote coal power plants' relocation or energy transformation.

This study concludes that the intermittent yet persistent threat of CSE acts as a significant motivator for regulated enterprises to go beyond minimum compliance. This sustained pressure created by the possibility of sudden, high-intensity enforcement compels firms not only to meet current regulatory standards but also to anticipate and prepare for stricter future requirements. This illustrates how CSE remains effective even during periods of routine enforcement, reinforcing its role as a tool of sustained regulatory control. Moreover, this study situates these enforcement dynamics within a broader administrative context increasingly shaped by digitisation and automation — trends that both complicate and enrich the normative aspirations of administrative justice. As regulatory processes become more technologically mediated, they invite new frameworks for understanding how fairness, accountability, and legitimacy are constructed under complex and evolving governance conditions. This study contributes to this rethinking by examining the complex mechanisms between environmental compliance and regulatory justice in China. These include the coexistence of dual enforcement systems, the inherently political nature of the administrative system, the top-down command structure, and the role of SOEs as role models in environmental compliance. By using deterrence — specifically, the looming threat of CSE—as the core analytical lens, this study unpacks the differentiated strategies of SOEs to demonstrate how administrative justice operates in contemporary China.

Future research directions are implicit in the study's limitations. First, the interviews are limited to one city. Future research may consider conducting comparisons to explore potential regional differences. Second, the study is limited to the context of electricity oversupply. After the interviews, China faced power shortages. With the changed enforcement context, the discussed mechanism might change as well. Third, the interviewees come from strictly regulated and restricted coal power plants, which may be more sensitive to deterrence than other industries and are more likely to tend to make more pessimistic forecasts for their own industry's development prospects. Therefore, the intensity of regulation in other industries needs to be assessed and considered before generalising the findings to other industries.

The Authority Deficit: How does China's Pharmaceutical Administration Work?

SONG YUECHAN

Research Fellow, Centre for Medical Ethics and Law, The University of Hong Kong

INTRODUCTION

China's administrative system comprises central administration, local administration at various levels, and the intermediate regime between central and local. Within this system, administrative legislation occurs mostly centrally, while implementation relies heavily on lower levels.[1] Given China's vast size and social heterogeneity, tiered implementation inevitably experiences high degrees of 'slippage'.[2] Such slippage remained unobtrusive under Mao's strongly imposed ideological control but became prominent as post-Mao reformers transformed administrative institutions.[3]

In the post-Mao era, as the economy underwent extensive liberalization and rapid growth, Chinese reformers embraced decentralization principles, allowing devolution of administrative power from central to local levels.[4] However, decentralized reforms proved imperfect and incomplete, causing fragmented bureaucracy and local protectionism that hindered grassroots implementation.[5]

Since Xi Jinping came to power in 2012, China has implemented policies to recentralize (*zai zhongxin hua*) power and reassert central control.[6] For example, the 2013 'super-ministry reform' (*dabuzhi gaige*) streamlined

[1] Chung, JH (2016) 'Implementation: Changing Norms, Issue-Variance, and Unending Tugs of War' in Donaldson, J (ed) (2016) *Assessing the Balance of Power in Central–Local Relations in China* Routledge 138.

[2] ibid 138-139.

[3] ibid 140-142.

[4] Li, Linda Che-lan (2010) 'Central-Local Relations in the People's Republic of China: Trends, Processes and Impacts for Policy Implementation' (30) *Public Administration and Development* 177; Donaldson, JA (2016) 'China's Administrative Hierarchy: The Balance of Power and Winners and Losers within China's Levels of Government' in Donaldson, J (ed) (2016) *Assessing the Balance of Power in Central–Local Relations in China* Routledge 105.

[5] Lieberthal, KG and Lampton, DM (2018) *Bureaucracy, Politics, and Decision Making in Post-Mao China* University of California Press; Wedeman, AH (2003) *From Mao to Market: Rent Seeking, Local Protectionism, and Marketization In China* Cambridge University Press; Van Rooij, B and Lo, CW-H (2010) 'Fragile Convergence: Understanding Variation in the Enforcement of China's Industrial Pollution Law' (32) *Law & Policy* 14.

[6] Donaldson 'China's Administrative Hierarchy' supra note 4 at 127.

elements of government and clarified divisions among parallel and vertical departments. This has raised a critical question—does recentralization curb implementation slippage? Few studies address this problem and those that do present contradictory findings. Kostka and Nahm argue increased central control improves environmental outcomes by changing local officials' conduct and making information falsification harder.[7] Conversely, van Rooij and colleagues contend that centralizing trends may spur stronger but uneven enforcement, with only minor benefits in terms of reducing pollution and local protectionism.[8] Given these contradictory findings, further analysis is required.

China's pharmaceutical administration provides an appropriate yet overlooked area for examining recentralization's impact on law enforcement. Drug policies have been weakly implemented; problems including high prices, low research productivity, and counterfeit drugs remain obstinate obstacles.[9] Previous literature attributes these persistent weaknesses to decentralization. Yu argues 1990s decentralized pharmaceutical administration caused power conflicts leading to inefficiency and corruption.[10] Similarly, Feng proposes that different departments overseeing various pharmaceutical circulation aspects was a process that generated inefficiency and coordination problems.[11] Under Xi's leadership, the 2013 and 2018 reforms established 'synthesized market regulation, specialized drug supervision', centralizing pharmaceutical administrative power to some extent. However, little attention has been given to the importance of local implementation of the Pharmaceutical Administrative Law (PAL, Yaopin Guanli Fa) under this system. If decentralization has created drug implementation issues, does recentralization improve enforcement?

This Chapter examines the recentralizing trend and assesses its impact on local pharmaceutical administrative law implementation.[12] The first

[7] Kostka, G and Nahm, J (2017) 'Central–Local Relations: Recentralization and Environmental Governance in China' (231) *The China Quarterly* 567.

[8] Van Rooij, B and others (2017) 'Centralizing Trends and Pollution Law Enforcement in China' (231) *The China Quarterly* 583.

[9] Chen, Yixi and others (2016) 'Drug Pricing Reform in China: Analysis of Piloted Approaches and Potential Impact of the Reform' (4) *Journal of Market Access & Health Policy* 1.

Meng, Qinyue and others (2015) *'The Impact of China's Retail Drug Price Control Policy on Hospital Expenditures: A Case Study in Two Shandong Hospitals'* (20) Health Policy and Planning 185.

Wong, Natasha (2004) 'Counterfeit Medicine: Is It Curing China?' (5) *Asian-Pacific Law & Policy Journal* 155.

[10] Yu, Hui (1997) 'Zhongguo yaoya zhengfu guanzhi zhidu xingcheng zhang'ai de fenxi (shang)' (['Analysis of the Obstacles in the Government Control System of the Chinese Pharmaceutical Industry (Part 1)'] (5) *Guanli Shijie* [Journal of Management World 10.

[11] Feng, Xin (2021) Big Market-Specialized Drugs: Research on My County's Drug Regulatory Model' (Da shichang-zhuan yaopin: woguo yaopin jianguan moshi yanjiu)(MA thesis, Shanxi University 2021).

[12] This Chapter draws on the author's PhD dissertation (*Why do Retail Pharmacies Violate*

section reviews China's pharmaceutical administration evolution since 1949. While numerous pharmaceutical administrative laws exist, this Chapter specifically examines retail pharmacy regulations. The second section briefly discusses these rules. Using Northeast China data, the third section argues recentralization has defeated pharmaceutical administrative practices and caused 'authority deficit'—a dilemma where local drug regulatory departments issue more licences than their regulatory capacity covers. The conclusion revisits the effects of administrative reforms on implementation issues.

PHARMACEUTICAL ADMINISTRATION IN CHINA

In China, administrative legislation primarily takes place at the central level, while implementation relies heavily on local governments.[13] Since 1949, China has undergone numerous administrative reforms that have shaped both the enactment and enforcement of pharmaceutical administrative laws through changes to state departments, legal systems, and administrative hierarchies.

Pharmaceutical Administration as a State Department

China's path to establishing pharmaceutical administration as a state (central government) department has been marked by four distinct phases, each reflecting different approaches to centralizing or decentralizing administrative power.

The Era of 'Decentralization and Subordination' (1950s–1978)

Initially, the Ministry of Health (MoH) was assigned to rebuild the pharmaceutical industry,[14] establishing key institutions including the Division of Pharmaceutical Affairs (Yaozhengchu), the Chinese Pharmaceutical Company (Zhongguo Yiyao Gongsi), the Chinese Pharmacopoeia Commission (Zhongguo Yaodian Weiyuanhui), and the Institute for the Control of Pharmaceutical and Biological Products

the Law? —An Empirical Study from Northeastern China, University of Hong Kong, 2023) preparation for which included four-month fieldwork in Changchun, Jilin Province, China. This location was chosen for several reasons: Jilin has a pharmaceutical industry that is quite typical for China, and Changchun and has experienced compliance problems that are widespread across China. Changchun is also the provincial capital and centre of Jilin's pharmaceutical industrial belt. It is the author's hometown, thereby providing effective access to local social networks, Research into issues of business compliance is especially challenging because firms treat compliance information as confidential and are reluctant to share regulatory responses with external researchers. To address this sensitive issue, a mixed methodology approach combining interviews with observations was used, supplemented by using *"guanxi"* (relationship networks) to establish trust with respondents and encourage them to be more forthcoming.

[13] Chung 'Implementation' supra note 1 at 138

[14] Pan, Xuetian (1994) 'Forty-Five Years of Chinese Pharmaceutical Administration' (Zhongguo yaozheng guanli de sishiwu nian) (10) *Zhongguo Yaoxue Zazhi* [Chinese Pharmaceutical Journal] 579.

(Weishengbu Yaopin he Shengwu Zhipin Jiandingsuo) in 1950, thus creating the country's primary pharmaceutical administrative system. However, the socialist transformation (1953-1956) fragmented this system. To adapt to the new economic order, the state constructed a 'government-enterprise integrated' (*zhengqi heyi*) system in which every major industry was owned and managed by a specialized department directly under the State Council. As the pharmaceutical industry was not recognized as a major industry warranting its own ministry, regulatory power was dispersed across multiple departments. In the early 1950s, the responsibility for regulating pharmaceutical institutions was transferred from the MoH to the Ministry of Commerce, while the responsibility for regulating chemical pharmaceuticals and medical devices was transferred to the Ministry of Light Industry. The MoH retained only drug examination duties and general pharmaceutical affairs.

During five rounds of institutional reforms between 1951 and 1975, pharmaceutical administrative functions changed hands frequently, with departments lasting an average of only three to five years.[15] For example, chemical pharmaceuticals were managed by six different departments between 1952 and 1978, pharmaceutical businesses by five departments, and traditional Chinese medicine by eight departments. Each sector changed hands several times, with some departments being extremely short-lived while others lasted longer. This created a fragmented authority structure by 1978 that would profoundly impact subsequent reform attempts, when China attempted to reintegrate pharmaceutical administration, and in so doing encountered significant resistance.

The Exploratory Stage of 'Centralization and Independence' (1978–2003)

Recognizing the pharmaceutical industry's enormous economic potential in the late 1970s, China established the State Medical and Pharmaceutical General Administration (SMPGA, Guojia yiyao guanli ju) on 22nd August 1978, as a department directly under the State Council but temporarily managed by the MoH.[16]The SMPGA, to some degree, integrated the fragmented power of pharmaceutical administration; functionally, it generally supervised the production, distribution, and usage of medical devices and western and Traditional Chinese medicines, while structurally, it assimilated the China National Pharmaceutical Industry Co. (Guojia Yiyao Gongye Gongsi) previously affiliated to the Ministry of Chemical Industry), the China Medical Device Industry Co. (Zhongguo Yiliao Qixie Gongye Gongsi), previously affiliated to the MoH),the China National Pharmaceutical Co. (Zhongguo Yiyao Gongsi, previously affiliated to the Ministry of Commerce [MofC]), and the China Medicinal Materials

[15] Yu 'Analysis of Obstacles' supra note 10; Liu Peng (2007) 'Mixed Regulation: Analysis of Drug Safety Regulation Mechanism in Contemporary China' (Hunhe xing jianguan: dangdai zhongguo yaopin anquan jianguan jizhi fenxi) 14 *Public Management Research* (Gonggong guanli yanjiu) 12.

[16] Yu 'Analysis of Obstacles' supra note 10

Co. (Zhongguo Yaocai Gongsi, previously affiliated to the MoC).[17] The establishment of the SMPGA was officially characterised in positive terms, as a pioneering undertaking, with the implication that China sought to make pharmaceutical administration a state department.

However, subsequent reforms repeatedly undermined any such centralization effort. In the 1982 institutional reform, the SMPGA was incorporated into the National Economic Council and renamed the State Medical and Pharmaceutical Administration (SMPA, Guojia yiyao guanli ju); in the 1988 reform, it was elevated to department status directly under the State Council. But then in the 1994 reform, it was downgraded to a component of the State Economic and Trade Commission. It was not until the reform of 1998 that it finally achieved an independent status, with the establishment of the National Medical Products Administration (NMPA, Guojia yapin jiandu guanli ju) as China prepared to enter the World Trade Organization.[18] Despite this achievement, the legacy of fragmentation persisted, reflecting the nearly three decades of institutional instability. By the 1990s, different pharmaceutical categories remained under various departments' control—the State Pharmaceutical Administration was responsible for medical devices, the Ministry of Health controlled biological products and medicinal preparations, the State Administration of Traditional Chinese Medicine oversaw Chinese medicines, while other ministries controlled veterinary medicine, narcotic drugs, radiopharmaceuticals, sports medicine, and biochemical drugs. This created a situation described as 'nine dragons taming a river' (*jiu long zhi shui*), a situation in which meaningful coordination was nearly impossible.[19]

The Era of 'Segmentation and Combination' (2003–mid-2010s)

At the beginning of the 21st century, various appalling food safety events occurred in China, prompting the Central Government to resurrect the NMPA as the State Food and Drug Administration (SFDA, Guojia shipin yapin jiandu guanli ju) in the 2003 institutional reform, initiating a decade of joint food-drug management.[20] The 2008 'super-ministry' reform—which aimed to reduce the number of ministries and commissions—temporarily merged the SFDA with the MoH. This reunion resulted in incongruities in terms of working mode, regulatory style, and governmental culture, as the administration of pharmaceuticals had been kept distinct from the MoH for decades. Moreover, as the SFDA transitioned from an independent department to a subordinate entity, it relinquished a portion of its communicative autonomy.[21] In 2013, China reorganized it into the

17 Ibid; Liu 'Mixed Regulation' supra note 15.

18 Notice of the State Council on Institution Setting (1998).

19 Yu 'Analysis of Obstacles' supra note 10

20 'To the Passing FDA: 40 Years of Ups And Downs' *Health Front Line* (21 April 2023) https://www.vodjk.com/news/180315/1464522.shtml.

21 Liu Peng (2009) 'Exploration towards Quality Regulation—Some Observations on

State Food and Drug General Administration (SFDGA, Guojia shipin yapin jiandu guanli zongju), permanently separating it from the MoH by abolishing the latter.

During this period, the fragmented 'nine dragons' system evolved into multi-department 'segmented' supervision (*duobumen fenduan jianguan moshi*) based on distribution links rather than drug categories. The health administrative department was responsible for examining qualifications and enacting drug policies; the industrial and commercial administration oversaw drug distribution; the quality assurance department supervised drug production; and the food and pharmaceutical administration handled overall drug safety across all links. However, this merely shifted fragmentation from one dimension to another. Under this segmented system, manpower and technological resources were dispersed across self-contained departments, hindering trans-departmental coordination and cooperation.[22]

The New Era of 'Synthetization and Specialization' (mid-2010s–present)

After Xi Jinping came to power in 2012, China introduced a new round of reforms. In 2015, the Central Government introduced a policy of '*fang guan fu*' intended to 'streamline administration, delegate power and strengthen regulation, and improve services' (*jianzheng fangquan, fang guan jiehe, youhua fuwu*).[23] Guided by this policy, China began exploring 'synthesized market regulation' *(dashichang*). Some regions experimented with 'two-in-one' patterns which merged quality assurance and industrial and commercial administration while retaining separate food and drug administration; others adopted 'three-in-one' modes merging all three departments. By the end of 2016, over half of municipalities and counties had completed these institutional innovations.

The 2018 institutional reform, adhering to the 'super-ministry' paradigm, completely dismantled the State Administration of Industry and Commerce. The State Administration of Quality Supervision, Inspection and Quarantine, and the State Administration of Food and Drug, together became the State Administration for Market Regulation (SAMR, Guojia shichang jiandu guanli zongju) directly under the State Council. To take into account the unique needs of pharmaceuticals, the SAMR established the NMPA as a secondary department. This system was characterised as

Drug Regulatory Reform in 2008' (zouxiang youzhi jianguan de youyi tansuo——2008 nian yaopin jianguan gaige de ruogan guancha, zhongguo chufang yao) 2 *Journal of China Prescription Drugs* 14

22 Feng 'Big Market' supra note 11 at 15.

23 The policy slogan *fang guan fu* translates to 'streamline administration, delegate power, and improve services.' It refers to China's administrative reform initiative that emphasizes: 放 (*fang*)–releasing/delegating', that is, reducing administrative approvals and delegating powers; 管 (*guan*)–regulating', that is, strengthening regulation and supervision; and 服 *(fu)* –'serving', that is, improving public services. This reform initiative aims to make government more efficient and business-friendly.

'synthesized market regulation, [with] specialized drug administration' (*dashichang, zhuanyaopin*), and represented a compromised mode of 'centralization and independence.'

Thus, learning from earlier experiences, China's political leaders did not simply centralize pharmaceutical administrative power but, rather, synthesized market regulation power while specializing pharmaceutical administration. This approach considered the unique characteristics of pharmaceuticals, as distinctive commodities. The Central Government established the specialized NMPA, thereby integrating all pharmaceutical administrative functions previously shared by the SAIC, SAQSIQ, and SGAFD. Considering the pharmaceutical supplies need to adhere to market regulations, the NMPA was placed under the auspices of SAMR management. Unlike previous subordinations that ignored compatibility (SMPGA under NEC in 1982, SMPA under SETC in 1994, SFDA under MoH in 2008), the SAMR-NMPA relationship is perceived as synergistic: the general and the specific, the leader and the subordinate, united by common objectives and a shared essence. Therefore, the pharmaceutical administrative authority has been recentralized at the state level.

Table: The Historical Evolution of Pharmaceutical Administration as State Department

Stage	Period	Department	Superior Department
Decentralization and Subordination	1950s-1978	None (dispersed across multiple ministries)	Ministry of Health, Ministry of Commerce, Ministry of Light Industry, etc.
Centralization and Independence	1978	SMPGA (State Medical and Pharmaceutical General Administration)	State Council; Ministry of Health
	1982	SMPA (State Medical and Pharmaceutical Administration)	National Economic Council
	1988	SMPA	State Council
	1994	SMPA	State Economic and Trade Commission
	1998	NMPA (National Medical Products Administration)	State Council

Segmentation and Combination	2003	SFDA (State Food and Drug Administration)	State Council
	2008	SFDA	Ministry of Health
	2013	SFDGA (State Food and Drug General Administration)	State Council
Synthetization and Specialization	2018-present	NMPA (National Medical Products Administration)	State Administration for Market Regulation

Pharmaceutical Administration: A Legal Framework

The 'Rule of Man' (1950s–1978)

In the 1950s and 1960s, under the decentralized system, various departments independently or cooperatively formulated a series of regulations and normative documents. Major legislation included the 1950 Notice on the Prohibition of Opium (Government Administration Council), the 1950 Interim Regulations on Narcotic Drugs (Ministry of Health), and the 1964 Interim Regulations on Poisons and Restricted Acute Drugs (co-enacted by the Ministry of Health, the Ministry of Chemical Industry, and the Ministry of Commerce). Most regulations focused on managing drugs, toxicants and narcotics, helping China to quickly eliminate problems of drug dependency left over from the pre-Liberation days (pre-1949)

The 1963 Provisions on Pharmaceutical Administration (PDA, Guanyu yaozheng guanli de ruogan guiding), co-enacted by the MoH, the Ministry for the Chemical Industry, and the Ministry of Commerce, represented China's first comprehensive act in this field. It defined new drugs, outlined approval procedures, clinical criteria, and production conditions, and specified supervision authority levels of health administrative departments.[24] However, these acts were essentially 'official documents' rather than state laws. Political movements in the 1960s-1970s halted China's progress in developing a sound legal system, leaving pharmaceutical administrative law very underdeveloped by the late 1970s.[25]

[24] Li, Tianquan and Zeng, Ya 'A Brief History of the Evolution of China's Drug Registration System (I): First there are Boundaries, then there are Rules' *Yaozhi News* (22 April 2023) https://news.yaozh.com/archive/22773.html.

[25] 'Legislation has evolved from nothing to something, from fragmented to complete, keeping pace with the times and the reform' *Legal System Daily* (22 April 2023) https://baijiahao.baidu.com/s?id=1703221751704723501&wfr=spider&for=pc.

The 'Rule of Law' (1978–present)

THE 1985 PAL

In the late 1970s, as the pressure from political movements declined and legislative work resumed, the MoH issued the Provisions on Drug Administration (Trial) on July 30, 1978. However, this was merely transitional legislation, with an extremely simple content, so that most rules were compulsory provisions which lacked corresponding penalty clauses. In 1980, the State Council endorsed the Report on Strengthening Pharmaceutical Administration and Prohibiting the Production and Distribution of Counterfeit and Inferior Drugs, explicitly asking the MoH to draft a more comprehensive PAL.

China's first Pharmaceutical Administration Law took effect July 1, 1985, establishing a licensing system requiring enterprises to obtain Drug Production Licenses (Yaopin shengchan xuke zheng), Drug Distribution Licenses (Yaoping jingying xuke zheng), and Dispensing Permits for Medical Organizations (Yiliao jigou zhiji xuke zheng).This law paved the way for numerous regulations including the 1985 Provisions for New Drug Approval, 1989 Implementation Regulations, and various measures controlling narcotic drugs, psychotropic drugs, toxic drugs, and radioactive drugs. By the 1990s, over one hundred types of licence[26]existed, covering narcotics, production, transportation, and distribution all required pre-licensure.

The licensing system reflected China's transition from planned to market economy in the 1980s. Adapting to the changing environment, the central government no longer exercised control through administrative orders but resorted to a process of administrative examination and approval—and all economic and social activities became subject to 'licensure.'[27] More generally, this was a transformation of government's role from regulatory control to service provision, and this change involved examination of both the theoretical foundations and practical reform measures. However, the government's reluctance to fully yield to market rules resulted in a large number of administrative examinations and approval–nearly three thousand by the early 1990s.

The 1985 PAL had fatal flaws. The MoH drafted it without granting substantial authority to the then SMPGA, reserving much authority for itself. Health administrative departments at all levels made the decisions on whether or not to issue licences while pharmaceutical administrative departments only reviewed applications. The 1985 PAL also failed to consider subsequent institutional changes—the SMPA and NMPA established in later

[26] Zhang, Kangzhi '(2003) Reform of Administrative Examination and Approval System: The Government Moves from Control to Service' [Xingzheng shenpi zhidu gaige: zhengfu cong guanzhi zouxiang fuwu, lilun yu gaige] 6 *Theory and Reform* 42

[27] Ibid

reforms still lacked clearly outlined statutory authority. This very imperfect legislation failed to bring order to China's pharmaceutical market.[28]

The 2001 PAL

The 2001 revision established Good Manufacturing Practice and Good Supply Practice systems, replaced local with national drug standards, created a prescription/non-prescription drug classification, and set up a Basic Medical Insurance System with the National Medical Insurance Directory. Major implementing regulations included the 2002 Implementation Regulations, 2002 Measures for Drug Registration, various certification measures for GMP (Yaopin shengchan guanli guifan, Good Manufacturing Practice) and GSP, and the 2005 comprehensive Regulation on Control of Narcotic Drugs and Psychotropic Drugs.

Amendments enacted in 2013 and 2015 were a direct consequence of the reform of the administrative examination and approval system. As the century drew to a close, this system had continued to pose significant barriers to development, engendering inefficiency and incurring substantial costs. On September 24, 2001, the State Council established the Leading Group for Reform, which issued implementation opinions on October 18, 2001. Over the next decade, the state cancelled, adjusted, or delegated thousands of approval items in six batches (2002, 2003, 2004, 2007, 2010, and 2012).[29]

This process streamlined the licensing system of pharmaceutical administration by removing superfluous elements. In 2002, the NMPA cancelled 20 of 70 approval items;[30]so that by 2012, half had been eliminated. The 2010 and 2012 batches shifted responsibilities like toxic drug retail/wholesale approval from state to provincial level, and medical device distribution approval and GSP certification from provincial to municipal level.

Table: Items Cancelled, Adjusted, or Delegated in Administrative Approval Reforms

Year	Cancelled	Adjusted	Delegated	Total
2002	789 (NMPA: 20)	-	-	789
2003	406 (NMPA: 4)	82 (NMPA: 1)	-	488
2004	409 (SFDA: 9)	39 (SFDA: 1)	47	495
2007	128 (SFDA: 5)	58 (SFDA: 7)	-	186
2010	113 (SFDA: 1)	-	71 (SFDA: 3)	184

[28] Yu 'Analysis of Obstacles' supra note 10.

[29] Wang, Kewen (2014) 'Reform and Legal Regulation of Administrative Approval System in China (*Woguo xingzheng shenpi zhidu de gaige ji qi falü guizhi, faxue yanjiu*)' 36(2) *Chinese Journal of Law* (*Faxue Yanjiu*) 3.

[30] The State Medical Products Administration announced the cancellation of 20 Administrative Approval Items' (2003) 01 *World Science and Technology* 9.

2012	171 (SFDA: 3)	143 (SFDA: 12)	-	314
Total	2016	322	118	2456

THE 2019 PAL

In the 2000s, 'feeding hospitals on drug revenue' (*yiyao yangyi*) became a severe worry in China.[31]The April 2009 New Healthcare Reform proposed 'separating medical treatment from drug sales' (*yiyao fengkai*). Subsequently, China implemented numerous drug policies: formulating a national essential medicine list and low-price drug list in order to maintain lower prices; launching consistency evaluation of indigenous generic drugs in 2016; and implementing volume-based procurement in 11 pilot cities in 2018. In 2015, the Central Government further proposed 'coupling medicine, medical security, and medical service' (*sanyi liandong*) as a new reform policy.

As these policies were enforced, the 2001 PAL became outdated. The 2019 PAL contained 155 articles with only 11 retained from the previous version.[32] It redefined fake and substandard drugs, promoted drug innovation, established a system of permit-holders for pharmaceutical sales (*yaoping shangshi xuke chiyouren zhidu*), and clarified responsibilities of different government levels.[33]

Dubbed the 'hardest-ever' PAL, it expanded property penalty ranges, introduced freedom penalties, increased qualification penalties, and adopted the 'double penalty system' punishing both legal entities and responsible individuals.[34] The 2019 PAL raised new supervision standards for pharmaceutical distribution and supply. However, the legal framework regulating it remains under construction—while some regulations like the 2021 Regulation on Supervision and Administration of Medical Devices and 2022 Measures for Administration of Radioactive Pharmaceuticals have been revised, many others await updating.[35]

[31] Chen and others 'Drug Pricing Reform' at supra note 9.

[32] Xu, Anbiao (2020) 'On the Essence, Innovation and Development of Revised Drug Administration Law' (Yaoping guanli fa xiugai de jingshen yaoyi, chuangxin yu fazhan) (2020, 1) *Administrative Law Review (Xingzheng Faxue Yanjiu)* 3.

[33] Xuan, Guan (2019) 'Implement "the Four Strictest Principles" and Strictly Observe Drug Safety—Publicity and Implementation of the Newly Revised Drug Administration Law of the People's Republic of China (Guanche 'sige zuiyan' yanshou yaopin anquan—xin xiuding zhonghua renmin gongheguo yaoping guanli fa)' 28(24) *China Pharmaceuticals* (Zhongguo yaoyie) 1.

[34] 'The Strictest Pharmaceutical Administration Law Implemented on 1st December! Fake and Substandard Drugs Have Been Redefined By "4+7"' *Sohu* (22 April 2023) https://www.sohu.com/a/356723911_120111344.

[35] Ibid. The concept of *tiao* may be briefly characterised as the vertical lines of functional

Pharmaceutical Administration as an Administrative Hierarchy

The 'Tiao–Tiao' Fragmented Departmental Administrative Hierarchy (1950s–2000)

After the creation of a People's Republic in 1949, the Central Government established four levels of local government and devised various sub-departments under them, parallel to State Council components. Since pharmaceutical administrative power was decentralized across various state-level departments in the 1950s, a 'tiao/tiao' fragmented departmental administrative hierarchy *(tiaotiao fenge de bumen guanli)* emerged.[36]

For example, the Division of Pharmaceutical Affairs of the MoH dispatched agencies and personnel to provincial, municipal, and county regions; the Institute for the Control of Pharmaceutical and Biological Products dispatched substations at health administrative departments at all levels. The MoC transformed the Chinese Pharmaceutical Company from a state-owned company into an administrative department (Medical Trade Bureau), with hundreds of drug distribution enterprises managed by local commercial bureaus except for two chemical reagent stations and four pharmaceutical procurement stations directly under MoC supervision. [37]

Under this tiao/tiao system, various local government sub-departments operated independently, preventing synergy in PAL enforcement. Between the 1960s-1970s, regular pharmaceutical administrative work was treated as 'managing, blocking, and pressing' (*guan, ka, ya*); departments of pharmaceutical affairs and institutes for drug control at all levels were suspended.[38]

Recovery began in the late 1970s when the MoH and other departments launched movements to inspect pharmaceutical factories and crack down on counterfeit drugs. By 1982, all levels of government had eradicated unqualified producers and removed over a hundred substandard drugs from the market. However, the fragmented hierarchy persisted. Despite the legal framework taking shape in the 1980s, implementation remained poor. Spontaneous drug markets emerged despite repeated prohibitions; by the 1990s, unlicensed business activities were ubiquitous throughout China.[39]

The Vertical Administrative Hierarchy Below the Provincial Level (2000–2008)

agencies (*tiao*) extend from central government ministries down through the state structure, while horizontal networks of territorially based government units (*kuai*) facilitate coordination within local jurisdictions. See, for example Mertha, Andrew 'China's "Soft" Centralization: Shifting Tiao/Kuai Authority Relations' (2005) 184 *The China Quarterly* 792.

[36] Yu 'Analysis of Obstacles' supra note 10.

[37] Ibid.

[38] Pan supra note 14

[39] 'The Disorder in the Drug Market Needs to be Resolved by the Rule of Law' China Youth Daily (7 February 1999) https://news.sina.com.cn/richtalk/news/society/9902/020701.html.

In 2000, the NMPA, backed by the State Council, issued the Reform Plan establishing vertical management below the provincial level (*sheng yixia chuizhi guanli xitong*).[40] Under this system, provincial medical products administrations supervised all pharmaceutical and medical device production stages. Pharmaceutical administration below provincial level was no longer beholden to local government superiors (*kuai*) but directly controlled by functional administrative superiors (*tiao*), maintaining only consultative relationships with former local government bosses.

This system emphasized professionalism. On June 24, 2002, the NMPA held its first training class for prefecture-level drug administration directors, providing necessary legal and pharmacological knowledge. All administrative levels began training officials, building a well-qualified enforcement team. However, trained implementers did not result in better regulation. The system was accompanied by 'two distinct avenues of fee collection' *(shou zhi liang tiao xian)*, leaving some provincial offices unable to make ends meet or afford municipal- and county-level bureau operations. Local regulators received little money but gained many responsibilities.[41]

Furthermore, local pharmaceutical administrations and governments frequently passed on responsibilities to each other. In complicated cases requiring cooperation from public security or industry of commerce, these local departments rejected pharmaceutical administration as an independent agency. The system also bred corruption and local protectionism, culminating in the 2006 scandal when SFDA head Zheng Xiaoyu was executed for corruption.[42]

Meanwhile, against the background of 'feeding hospitals on drug revenue,'', noted above, drugs became stable profit sources. Despite harsh crackdowns, profiteers built black markets of counterfeit drugs through low-price advantages. Estimates suggested 10-15% of circulating drugs were fake, accounting for about US$3 trillion in annual pharmaceutical sales. Another significant problem was drug procurement corruption—doctors colluded with dealers for kickbacks, overprescribing drugs and leading to prescription drug abuse, especially antibiotics.

The Tiered Administrative Hierarchy in Local Governments (2008–2018)

To address vertical hierarchy limitations, the 2008 reform built a tiered administrative hierarchy in local governments (*difang zhengfu fenji guanli zhidu*).[43] Local governments at all levels assumed overall pharmaceutical

[40] Notice of the State Council Approving the Plan of the State Drug Administration to Reform the Drug Supervision and Administration System (2000).

[41] See Mertha,AC 'China's 'Soft' Centralization:' supra note 37.

[42] Drakulich, A (2007) 'Former Chinese SFDA Chief Executed for Taking Bribes; Agency Cracks Down on Regulation' *Pharmtech*, July 12, 2007, at https://www.pharmtech.com/view/former-chinese-sfda-chief-executed-taking-bribes-agency-cracks-down-regulation.

[43] Notice of the General Office of the State Council on Issues related to Adjusting the Food and Drug Supervision and Administration System at or below the Provincial Level (2008)

administration responsibility, with every administrative level subject to both its superior department and same-level health administration.

This system emphasized local government responsibility but had significant shortcomings. First, it failed to fix the financial problems. Under this tiered system, pharmaceutical administration was funded locally. Without central funding, local governments could not even pay officials—salaries reportedly dropped from 2600 yuan to 1690 yuan per month, forcing resignations. Second, the system allowed local protectionism to resurface. Local governments often neglected regulatory enforcement and colluded with pharmaceutical enterprises for illegal profits.[44] Third, the central government suffered information asymmetry. Though inspectors were dispatched to local governments, they were few and prone to corruption. The tiered system's problems highlighted the persistent challenge of balancing central control with local implementation capacity.

The 'Single Row Above and Synthesis Below the Provincial Level' System (2018–present)

Following the 2018 institutional reform from central to local, the NMPA only dispatches provincial-level agencies while SAMR dispatches provincial, municipal, county, and three-level agencies. This administrative hierarchy, in which entities above the provincial level are listed and treated individually, while those below the provincial level are handled in a comprehensive or integrated manner (*sheng yi shang danlie, sheng yi xia zonghe*), represents China's first experiment with a top-down, non-parallel administrative structure—an 'inverted pyramid.[45]

This system reduces departments to 'one per level': at state and provincial levels, medical products administrations specialize in pharmaceutical administration; at grassroots levels, market regulation administrations execute PALs. With the thorough abolition of health administrative departments, industrial and commercial administrations, and quality assurance departments locally, power conflicts and communication gaps were structurally eradicated.

The new hierarchy brought clear functional division among all department levels. The NMPA drafts supervision systems and handles licensing, inspection, and R&D promotion for drugs, medical devices, and cosmetics. Provincial medical product administrations licence and inspect drug wholesalers, chain retailer headquarters, internet third-party platforms, and production facilities. Municipal- and county-level market

[44] Müller, A (2019) ‹Public Services and Informal Profits: Governing Township Health Centres in a Context of Misfit Regulatory Institutions' 237 *The China Quarterly* 108.

[45] Provisions on the Functions, Structure and Staffing of the State Administration for Market Regulation (2018). It might be added here that the phrase *'sheng yi shang danlie, sheng yi xia zonghe'* is used in this context to refer to an administrative management principle meaning 'separate listing for above provincial level, comprehensive management for below provincial level', referring to different management approaches for government entities above versus below the provincial administrative tier.

regulation departments licence and inspect the distribution and use of drugs, medical devices, and cosmetics.

This distribution considers pharmaceutical administration's characteristics. Supervising drug production and R&D, which relates to public health and requires high professionalism, was assigned to higher levels. Meanwhile, supervising drug distribution and use, which follow market rules and involve curbing irregular conduct, was devolved to lower levels. While reducing departments to 'one per level' structurally eliminates some coordination problems, its effectiveness remains to be evaluated.

Table: Single Row Above and Synthesis Below the Provincial Level System

Level	Department	Main Responsibilities
State	NMPA (under SAMR)	Policy making, system design, major licensing
Provincial	Medical Products Administration	Production licensing, wholesale licensing, chain headquarters
Municipal	Market Regulation Administration	Retail licensing, distribution supervision
County	Market Regulation Administration	Retail licensing, use supervision

In summary, China's pharmaceutical administration has evolved through repeated attempts at centralization consistently undermined by institutional instability and fragmentation. Only in the past decade has meaningful integration occurred through the current 'synthetization and specialization' model, though questions remain about its implementation effectiveness at local levels.

REGULATING DRUG RETAILING

China's drug retailing industry burgeoned in the 2000s after decades of stagnation. Following the 1999 Guidelines on Deepening the Reform of the Pharmaceutical Distribution System, which aimed to forge a new retail pattern, the number of retail pharmacies soared from 70,000 in 2000 to over 550,000 by 2020, with a market value reaching 200 billion yuan.[46]

In order to regulate this rapidly expanding industry, China established a licensing system requiring multiple permits for retail pharmacy operations. Currently, three-licences are mandatory: the Business License for Legal Person (BLLP), Drug Distribution License (DDL), and Good Supply Practice Certificate (GSP). Four additional optional licences further

[46] 'Perspective Top 100 Chain! The Number of Pharmacies in the Country Continues to Grow' *Financial World* (22 April 2023), available at: https://baijiahao.baidu.com/s?id=1706503817763600820&wfr=spider&for=pc; Huang, LQ (2023) 'A Decade Of Chain Retail Pharmacy' *Journal of Medical Economics* (22 April 2023) http://www.linkshop.com/web/article_news.aspx?articleid=136826.

expand operational scope: the Food Distribution License (FDL), Medical Device Distribution License (MDDL), Medical Insurance Designated Retail Pharmacy Agreement (MIDRPA), and Practicing License for a Medical Institution (PLMI).

These licences determine what products may be distributed by pharmacies–prescription/non-prescription drugs, Traditional Chinese herbal medicine, medical devices, supplements) and distribution methods (retail/wholesale, cash/insurance). Pharmaceutical administrations at all government levels issue licences and supervise licencees, with violations punishable by administrative penalties (warnings, fines, suspension, revocation) or criminal penalties including imprisonment and, in extreme cases, death.

The Business License for Legal Person (BLLP)

China's enterprise legal person registration system requires all corporations to obtain a BLLP before commencing operations.[47] The Administrative Regulations, enforced since 1998 and revised four times through 2019, were superseded by the 2021 Administrative Regulations on the Registration of Market Entities. Responsibility shifted from the State Administration for Industry and Commerce (1988-2018)[48] to the State Administration for Market Regulation thereafter.[49]

Registration covers corporate name, type, business scope, premises, capital, legal representative, and establishment date.[50] Business scope divides into general items (requiring no additional permits) and licensed items (requiring departmental approval).[51] Drug distribution falls under licensed items, necessitating a Drug Distribution Licence (DDL) before operation.

The Drug Distribution License (DDL)

Established by the 1985 PAL and refined through subsequent revisions, the DDL system formally created China's drug distribution licensing framework. According to law, retail pharmacies can only operate after obtaining the DDL. The 2004 Measures for the Administration of Pharmaceutical Trade License (revised 2017) further complemented this system.

The DDLs are divided into two types: wholesale and retail. Provincial-level pharmaceutical administration examines and approves wholesale DDLs, while municipal- or county-level administration handles retail

47 Administrative Regulations on the Registration of Market Entities (2021) Arts 2 and 3.

48 Administrative Regulations on the Registration of Legal Corporations (1988) Art 4.

49 Administrative Regulations Market Entities (2021) supra note 49, at Art 5.

50 Registration of Market Entities, supra note 49, Art 8.

51 Ibid Art 12.

DDLs.[52] Wholesale licensees cannot engage in retail, and vice versa. Therefore, retail pharmacies must apply for a retail DDL from their regional municipal or county-level pharmaceutical administration.

Retail pharmacy establishments also must adhere to the principle of 'making it convenient for people to buy drugs', taking into account the facts of local permanent population, geographical conditions, traffic conditions, and actual demand. Specific requirements include: (1) regulations ensuring pharmaceutical quality; (2) legally certified pharmaceutical technicians including licensed pharmacists; (3) no enterprise revocation record and no writ of prohibition for responsible persons; (4) appropriate business premises, equipment, warehouse facilities, and sanitary conditions suitable for drug distribution; and (5) ability to meet consumer demand and ensure 24-hour supply.[53]

Applications require extensive documentation: (1) quality control documents and inventory of storage facilities/equipment; (2) qualification certificates and appointment letters of pharmaceutical technical personnel; (3) personal resumes of legal representatives, responsible persons, and quality control personnel; (4) floor plans of business place and warehouse with property right or use proof; and (5) a BLLP. The competent department examines DDLs case-by-case, clearly indicating authorized business scope on the license.[54] Based on DDL content, retail pharmacies are classified into three types and three grades for better management. The state distinguishes traditional Chinese medicine from western drugs and classifies drugs into prescription and non-prescription categories. Prescription drugs are further categorized as prohibited (narcotic drugs, radioactive drugs, class I psychotropic drugs, pregnancy termination drugs), restricted (toxic drugs for medical use, class II psychotropic drugs, stimulants), and ordinary. Non-prescription drugs divide into Class A and Class B. Only ordinary prescription drugs and non-prescription drugs can be freely traded in pharmacies.

The three-type classification system creates a hierarchy:

- **Type III**: All drugs except prohibited prescriptions (narcotics, radioactive drugs, psychotropics). Must have at least 2 licensed pharmacists, 2 pharmacy technicians with senior pharmacist title or above, and 1 licensed Chinese medicine pharmacist if selling Chinese herbal pieces.
- **Type II**: Ordinary prescriptions and Class A non-prescriptions. Must have at least 1 licensed pharmacist, 1 pharmacy technician with senior pharmacist title or above, and 1 licensed Chinese medicine pharmacist if selling Chinese herbal pieces.
- **Type I**: Class B non-prescriptions only. No pharmacist requirement.

[52] Pharmaceutical Administration Law (2019) Art 51.

[53] Measures for the Administration of Drug Distribution Licenses (2017) Art 5.

[54] Ibid.

Higher types require stricter standards and larger business scope. Additionally, Types II and III pharmacies are further graded A, AA, or AAA based on service capacity:

- **A Grade**: Basic information equipment; no serious breach of trust within one year
- **AA Grade**: Drug traceability and information management systems; no serious breach within two years; 24-hour service capability
- **AAA Grade**: Mature traceability and information systems; no serious breach within three years; 24-hour drug supply and consultation service

Higher grades improve chances for medical insurance designation.[55]

In addition to business scope, the DDL specifies enterprise name, legal representative/person in charge, operation mode (wholesale/retail), registered address, warehouse address, certificate number, serial number, issuing authority, issuing date, and validity period.[56] DDLs remain valid for five years; licencees intending to continue must apply for renewal six months before expiration.[57] Issuing authorities regularly inspect licencees through written inspection, on-site inspection, or both. Violations result in appropriate punishment including fines, DDL revocation, and punishment of responsible persons.

The Good Supply Practice Certificate (GSP)

In 1984, the then State Pharmaceutical Administration enacted the Quality Management Standards of Pharmaceutical Commodities (Trial), the genesis of China's GSP. After joining the WTO, China issued the Good Supply Practice for Pharmaceutical Products in 2000 and revised PAL in 2001, requiring drug distributors to obtain both DDL and GSP certificates before operation. As the pharmaceutical market developed and administrative reforms advanced, the GSPPP underwent two revisions (2012, 2015) and one amendment (2016).

Like DDL, GSP has both wholesale and retail subcategories. For retail pharmacies, chained retail pharmacy headquarters must obtain wholesale GSP, while chained outlets and monomer retail pharmacies must obtain retail GSP.[58]

GSP standardizes pharmaceutical distribution through systematic quality control. Retail pharmacies obtain GSP by implementing quality control through system construction in procurement, storage, distribution,

[55] 'Pharmacy Classification Management is the Trend; A Group of Pharmacies Will Not Be Able to Sell Prescription Drugs' *Yaosu* (22 April 2023). Available at: http://news.yaosuce.com/xinwen/3663681797925509772.html.

[56] Measures for the Good Supply Practice of Drug Distribution (2016) Art 179.

[57] Measures for the Administration of Drug Distribution Licenses (2017) Art 32

[58] Measures for the Administration of Drug Distribution Licenses (2017) Art 19.

transportation, and trace.[59] According to law, after obtaining a DDL, retail pharmacies must apply to the same issuing authority for GSP before formally opening. GSP grants follow case-by-case examination, but unlike DDL's document review, GSP requires on-site examination.[60] Applicants failing to obtain a GSP may not run retail pharmacies; their DDLs are revoked if already obtained.

In recent years, China has streamlined administrative examination and approval procedures. Following state guidance,[61] some regions implement 'two-in-one' licensure systems with one-stop examination and approval for both DDL and GSP.[62] This reform reflects efforts to reduce administrative burden while maintaining regulatory standards.

The Medical Devices Distribution License (MDDL)

The 1999 Administrative Regulations (revised 2014, 2017, 2021) established a risk-based classification system. Class III devices (infusion sets, syringes, contact lenses) require municipal-level licences, whilst Class II (condoms, thermometers, blood pressure monitors) need only registration; Class I (band-aids, ice packs) trade freely. As retail pharmacies increasingly distribute medical devices, compliance with these regulations becomes essential.

The Medical Insurance Designated Retail Pharmacy Agreement (MIDRPA)

With China's Basic Medical Insurance System covering 95% of the population[63] and accumulating over one trillion RMB (one-third in individual accounts).[64] Designation as an insurance-accepting pharmacy provides a significant competitive advantage. The 1999 Interim Administrative Measures established qualification procedures, with competent departments shifting from the Ministry of Labor and Social Security (1998-2008) to Human Resources and Social Security (2008-2018) to the National Healthcare Security Administration (2018-present). Designated pharmacies face strict prohibitions against cashing out insurance funds, with violations resulting in termination and severe punishment.

[59] Measures Good Supply supra note 57, at Art 2.

[60] Ibid Art 4.

[61] Notice of the State Food and Drug Administration on Matters Related to the Current Drug Trade Supervision and Administration (2020) Art 2

[62] 'Two Certificates in One! Drugstore People Can Finally Stop Waiting for the Process!' *Sohu* (22 April 2023) https://www.sohu.com/a/398672708_100099933

[63] 'The National Health Commission Reported that the Coverage Rate of Basic Medical Insurance Reached 96.8 Percent' *People News* (22 April 2023) available at: http://news.china.com.cn/txt/2021-01/28/content_77163948.htm

[64] 'The National Health Care Bill of 2020 is out, Reflecting What Reform Achievements?' *China Healthcare* (22 April 2023) available at: https://www.cn-healthcare.com/articlewm/20210615/content-1231919.html.

The Food Distribution License (FDL)

Since nutritional supplements are classified as food rather than drugs under the 2009 Food Safety Law, retail pharmacies distributing them require an FDL from county-level authorities (formerly food and drug administrations, now market regulation administrations). The licence specifies 'specially prepared food (nutritional supplements)' among eleven distribution subcategories.[65]

The Practicing License for a Medical Institution (PLMI)

In 2007, the National Administration of Traditional Chinese Medicine (TCM) enforced the Administration Measures of In-house Clinics of TCM (applicable only in pilot areas), allowing retail pharmacies to employ TCM doctors and offer treatments. In 2008, the NATCM selected 48 districts as pilots,[66] and 'retail pharmacies with in-house doctors of TCM' (*zhongyi zuotang lingshou yaodian*) became a popular business model.

Setting up such pharmacies must follow medical institution rules.[67] According to the Regulation on the Administration of Medical Institutions, health administrative departments—the Health and Family Planning Commission before 2018 and National Health Commission after 2018—at all levels examine and approve applications for medical institutions and issue PLMIs.[68] TCM doctors are subject to the Practicing Doctors Law. In order to practise at retail pharmacies, they must have over 5 years' clinical experience and register at specific outlets; unregistered practice is forbidden.[69]

[65] Administrative Measures for Food Distribution Licensing (2017) Art 10.

[66] Notice of the Office of the State Administration of Traditional Chinese Medicine on Determining the List of Pilot Areas for Drug Retail Enterprises to Set up Traditional Chinese Medicine Clinics (2008).

[67] Management Measures for Sit-in Clinics of Traditional Chinese Medicine (for Pilot Exercise only) (2007) Art 5

[68] Regulation on the Administration of Medical Institutions (2022) Art 6.]

[69] Management Measures for Sit-in Clinics of Traditional Chinese Medicine (for Pilot Exercise only) (2007) Art 8.

Table: The Licensing Laws for Drug Retailing

License	Legal Basis	Competent Department	Key Requirements
BLLP	Administrative Regulations on Registration of Market Entities (2021)	SAMR (2018-present); formerly SAIC	Corporate registration, business scope
DDL	Pharmaceutical Administration Law (2019); Measures for Administration of Pharmaceutical Trade License (2017)	Provincial MPA or Municipal/ County AMR	Pharmacists, premises, quality systems
GSP	Good Supply Practice for Pharmaceutical Products (2016); PAL (2019)	Same as DDL	Quality control systems, on-site inspection
MDDL	Administrative Regulations on Medical Devices (2021)	Municipal/ County AMR	Risk-based requirements
FDL	Food Safety Law (2015)	County AMR	Food safety standards
MIDRPA	Interim Administrative Measures (1999)	NHSA (2018-present)	Service standards, no fund misuse
PLMI	Regulation on Administration of Medical Institutions (2022)	NHC	Medical standards, registered doctors

This complex licensing system reflects China's attempt to balance market development with public safety, creating multiple regulatory touchpoints throughout the pharmaceutical retail chain. However, as the following section demonstrates, the gap between regulatory design and implementation capacity has created significant challenges for local enforcement.

HOW DOES RECENTRALIZATION AFFECT LOCAL IMPLEMENTERS?

This Chapter began by reviewing China's pharmaceutical administration as a state department, a legal framework, and an administrative hierarchy. The first section highlighted the recentralizing trend in pharmaceutical administrative power over the past decade. Although China has enacted a series of regulations regarding pharmaceutical administration, for reasons of space this Chapter concentrates exclusively on those pertaining to retail pharmacies. The subsequent section delineates the licensing statutes. In this section, drawing upon data gathered in Northeast China, we scrutinize the execution of these regulations within the framework of recentralization. I contend that recentralization has precipitated a weakening of the implementation team, hindered legislative cohesion, and obstructed collaborative enforcement. These elements have engendered a predicament that I characterize as an 'authority deficit,' wherein local implementers are granting a greater number of licences than their operational capacity can accommodate.

The Diluted Implementary Team

In comparison to the regulation of other types of commodity, pharmaceutical administration has distinctive characteristics. First, pharmaceutical administration is time-consuming and laborious; it involves every aspect of pharmaceutical distribution and supply chain processes and requires regulators to devote significantly more time and effort compared to the regulation of other commodities:

> The regulation of pharmaceuticals is different from that of other industrial goods. For example, we never care about the productive process of televisions and phones; we only care about whether they work or not–that is, the product quality. But when it comes to pharmaceuticals, from raw materials to manufacturing technique, curative effects to side effects, product transportation to product sales...in other words, from cradle to grave, we care about everything. This means our workload is exponentially more than that of other departments.[70]

Second, pharmaceutical administration is professional and specialized. This implies that, in addition to possessing legal skills, implementers must also attain a comprehensive understanding of pharmacological expertise.

> Pharmacological knowledge is critical to our work. Drugs have been categorized into chemicals, Chinese patent medicines, and biological products. For chemicals, regulation is comparatively easy. We only have to know their components and concentration. For example, normal saline is 0.9% sodium chloride. We can check whether a brand of normal saline is up to standard by experiments. Similar to this is the regulation of biological products. However, for Chinese patent medicines, regulation is comparatively difficult. The chemical components of these medicines are hard to determine; we must gain some knowledge on herbal medicine to be able to properly do our work.[71]

[70] Interview data, the regulator of the Provincial Drug Administration.

[71] Ibid.

Both 'manpower' and 'expertise' are indispensable for the successful implementation of the PALs. China once boasted a cadre of highly qualified implementers, meticulously distributed across the provincial, municipal, and county-level pharmaceutical administrations. As previously noted, this team was established by the NMPA alongside the various tiers of pharmaceutical administration in the 2000s. However, owing to the prevailing trend of recentralization, this team has been irreversibly diminished.

The dilution of the pharmaceutical administration team aligns with the '*fang guan fu*' policy, noted above. '*Fang guan fu*' requires all levels of government to streamline their component elements. However, as these component elements become fewer in number, their civil servants remain the same or even increase in number. To alleviate the workload on employees in certain departments, dilution is unavoidable. In practice, since 2015, local governments have integrated the law-enforcement teams for trademarks, patents, quality assurance, food supervision, commodity prices, and industry and commerce with the team for pharmaceutical administration.[72] Because the pharmaceutical regulatory team is disproportionately smaller than other law enforcement agencies, it has inadvertently absorbed a cadre of officials who lack experience in pharmaceutical regulation.

After China's 2018 administrative reforms, the provincial government first recruited all officials who previously worked for the abolished departments and then reassigned them to the newly established provincial, municipal, and county-level administrative branches. Since the NMPA exclusively delegates responsibilities to provincial-level agencies—whereas the SAMR extends its oversight to provincial, municipal, and county-level agencies—this three-tiered structure means that in reality the provincial government is the cornerstone of pharmaceutical administration at the provincial level. Meanwhile, the majority of officials from various departments, particularly those from the erstwhile expansive State Administration of Industry and Commerce, have been reassigned to municipal and county-level administrations for the purpose of market regulation. As a consequence, the integrity of drug supervision was preserved only to a limited extent at the provincial level, while its efficacy at the municipal and county levels was markedly diminished. The overall professionalism of the administrative hierarchy of pharmaceutical administration has clearly declined.

Furthermore, the dilution of the pharmaceutical administration team is exacerbated by the framework of 'synthesized market regulation and specialized pharmaceutical administration,' which has the effect of downsizing the team. Within this framework, the administrative hierarchy of pharmaceutical administration is top-heavy and resembles an inverted pyramid. At the provincial level, the medical products administration is a

[72] "Market Regulation Bids Farewell to 'Nine Dragons Governing the Waters'; Administration of Industry and Commerce, Quality Inspection, Food and Drug, and Price Control Enforcement Will Be 'Consolidated into One'" (*Beijing News* [*Xinjing Bao*], March 21, 2018; accessed April 22, 2023 at https://baijiahao.baidu.com/s?id=1595547618771281337&wfr=spider&for=pc.

component of the market regulation administration, but they function as two independent departments; they separately formulate and assign work plans to lower levels. However, at the municipal and county levels, only one department–the administration of market regulation–executes these plans. While these municipal- and county-level administrations of market regulation appear to be comprehensive and to have sufficient officials and resources, they have internal divisions of labour and staff, and in reality the funds allocated to pharmaceutical administration are limited. In practise, it is always an office where a small number of people handle a mountain of tasks:

> I have to say that our implementary capacity is weakened. Previously, it was possible to inspect a retail pharmacy twice a year; now, we are barely able to make it once a year.[73]
>
> '[I]n our country, under the administrative hierarchy, officials are dispatched from the municipal 'administrative offices' (*keshi*) to counties. This means the county-level administration is always short of hands. Furthermore, our professionalism is undermined. Now, my colleagues are mostly from the previous industrial and commercial administration, not the previous food and drug administration [....] .obviously, our regulatory capacity is weakened.[74]

The provincial medical products administration has recognized the problem of labour shortage at the lower levels. To address this issue, it has implemented some remedial measures, such as periodically conducting flight checks and steering inspections. However, these measures are insufficient and cannot compensate for the enforcement gap left by lower-level departments:

> [O]ur provincial competent department is not letting things slide, but we are incompetent. Our time and energy are limited. We resort to spot checks, flight checks, cross checks... Furthermore, we also annually announce new key works and enact concrete work programmes to lower-level sub-departments. But these top-down inspections are infrequent and always one-sided...the outcome, well, undoubtedly, is undesirable.[75]

The Delayed Legislative Unification

After every institutional reform, local governments must formulate new work regulations to coordinate old and new departments. Additionally, whenever the state revises the PAL and other related laws and regulations, local governments must enact corresponding implementation statutes.

[73] Interview data, the regulator of the Provincial Drug Administration.

[74] Ibid.

[75] Ibid.

However, an implementing statute often takes several months or even years to produce. Moreover, frequent top-down administrative reforms and state-law revisions further impede local legislative work. Consequently, the local implementation of legal principles and norms established at the national level persistently manifests crisis. Several distinctive attributes underscore this problem.

First, since the legal framework of pharmaceutical administration has grown considerably, adapting state laws to local conditions has become increasingly complex. For example, the PAL is the foundation of the entire legal framework of pharmaceutical administration. This means even a minor modification of the PAL can have a ripple effect: numerous state laws and departmental regulations must be amended, and local governments must create or revise their implementary statutes based on them. Although the latest revision of the PAL was passed in 2019, it has exerted limited influence on local practices. The legal framework based on the 2019 PAL is still under construction, and local implementers have yet to revise their implementing statutes accordingly:

> In my experience, each new version of PAL takes at least a decade to have an impact. I remember, in 2001, the PAL was revised; in 2002, its enforcement regulation was enacted; in 2004, the new GSP [Yaopin jingong guanli guifan, Good Supply Practice] was passed; in 2006, the Pharmaceutical Circulation Act was passed [...] Just as the enactment of these state laws or departmental regulations takes years, so too does that of the local statutes. The latest PAL (2019) was enacted two years ago, and departmental regulations have still not been revised accordingly. Even the slightest stir has not occurred at our department.[76]

Second, local legislation is impeded by inconsistencies in executive standards across various departments and levels of government. For example, for a long period, the power of pharmaceutical administration was decentralized. Various departments at different levels issued countless statutes within their authority that adopt different implementary standards (for example, different fines for the same misconduct). Therefore, when formulating new implementary statutes based on the 2019 PAL, local implementers are confused about which standard they should retain and which they should waive:

> Too many conflicting clauses exist among provincial, municipal and county-level implementary rules. These statutes were enacted by former departments, and although these departments have been dissolved, their officials are still there. Every standard has its supporters. It is extremely difficult to harmonize them in a short period of time.[77]

[76] Ibid

[77] Ibid

Furthermore, frequent administrative reforms disrupt and delay local legislation. Every time a restructuring administrative reform takes place, local governments must first spend a long period reconfiguring their components and then enacting new implementary regulations. A comprehensive examination of China's pharmaceutical administration history reveals that the enactments of laws alternate with reforms in administrative institutions and hierarchy. For example, the revision of the PAL typically occurs once every 15 years, and it takes at least five years to form the legal framework of each new version of PAL. Institutional reforms, on average, happen once every five years, while the reforms of administrative hierarchy basically occur once every nine years. Considering these transformations at the local level, it becomes evident that as the implementing statutes pertinent to old laws and administrative frameworks are being promulgated, new legislation and reforms are concurrently in progress. In essence, the incessant waves of administrative reform further impede the enactment of local statutes.

The Blocked Joint Implementation

In practice, even when implementary statutes are in place, joint law enforcement between superior and subordinate departments or even among departments at the same level is extremely difficult.

One significant drawback of the prevailing framework of 'a singular row above and synthesis beneath the provincial level' noted above is that while it delineates the responsibilities of various competent departments, it falls short in fostering collaboration amongst them. For instance, the provincial medical products administration is tasked with the oversight of the headquarters of retail pharmacy chains, whereas the municipal and county-level market regulation departments are entrusted with the supervision of both chains and independent retail pharmacy outlets. This arrangement engenders a dilemma in enforcement: should a municipal or county-level market regulation agency uncover a legal infraction at a branch of a chain pharmacy and harbour suspicions that the corporate headquarters might be implicated in analogous or even graver violations, it is compelled to navigate a protracted bureaucratic process of liaising with the provincial medical products administration prior to taking any action. This delay in action gives violators enough time to prepare for a possible investigation.

In addition, cooperation among departments at the same level is often hindered by various factors. For instance, a drug regulatory department may need an expert report from a same-level medicine appraisal agency to charge a violator, but insufficient resources can impede this process. Typically, within a municipal jurisdiction, only one medicine appraisal agency is established, with limited professionals and other resources. As a result, it may not be able to provide timely survey reports for numerous cases, resulting in investigations that exceed statutory time limits. Moreover, the report outcome may be unconvincing due to inadequate detection techniques, which undermine prosecution efforts.[78] In short, without timely and reliable test reports as evidence, the competent pharmaceutical department cannot smoothly proceed with the administrative procedure.

The Enlarging Authority Deficit

The three factors (the diluted implementation team, delayed legislative harmonization, and obstructed collaborative execution) identified above contribute to a conundrum wherein local pharmaceutical authorities issue a significantly greater number of licences than their regulatory capacity can adequately accommodate.

First, the dilution of the professional implementary team has caused an overflow of licences. Before 'recentralization', administrative reforms dispatched the authority of licensing to lower-level competent pharmaceutical departments. For example, the licensing right of retail pharmacies was devolved from the provincial level to the municipal level and finally to the county level, after which the subsequent recentralizing trend only reintegrated the pharmaceutical administrative framework, failing to reintegrate the licensing authority. Because county-level competent departments are more numerous than higher-level ones, they also issue far more licences than departments at other levels. However, county-level departments are more vulnerable to local protectionism than their higher-level counterparts. This means that when reviewing licence applications, a county-level market regulation administration does not only consider the statutory standards but also personal connections (*guanxi)* and 'personal interests'(*sili*)–in other words, applicants can easily leverage 'bribes' and use their social networks to intervene in the administrative examination and approval of licences. The decline in professionalism has further worsened this situation because less-professional officials who sense the weak constraining force of the law are more susceptible to external pressure. As a result, an increasing number of licences are issued to applicants that do not meet the statutory standard:

> The power of examination and approval has been delegated from municipal-level competent departments to county-level ones. This power is executed loosely at these lower-level departments, causing the number of licensed retail pharmacies to grow. From my point of view, I think the reasons are complex. First, as is known to all, our country is a 'human relationship society (*renqing shehui) guanxi*' does help in obtaining licences. Second, the officials in county-level departments are short of professional knowledge. They barely understand the essence of the pharmaceutical administration laws. Third, I think that local governments intend to promote the economy. Retail pharmacies, for one thing, create new jobs, and for another, create social and economic value. Finally, the human factor (discretionary power) is to blame; in the process of administrative examination and approval, some rules are unclear; you may either

[78] Ibid

understand them in a strict or a lax manner. Previously, municipal-level competent departments tended to be strict; however, the county-level departments are now lax.[79]

Second, because pharmaceutical administration involves both the issuing and supervising authority for drug retailing, the decline in professionalism also undermines the implementation of the PALs. The professionalism required for pharmaceutical administration involves mastering pharmacology as well as related laws, which is difficult to achieve in a short period. Officials from other departments may not be able to acquire this knowledge quickly, and there may also be mindset conflicts.[80]As stated above, pharmaceutical administration oversees the whole process of production, distribution and sale, whereas the regulation of other commodities primarily focuses on quality. Nowadays, in the practice of PALs at the lower levels, regulators who used to work for the industrial and commercial administration do not understand the necessity of licensure in drug retailing. When they encounter under-licensed distributors, they merely caution them to procure the necessary licences, as they have done in the past with other legitimate entities; however, from the standpoint of professional enforcers of PALs, this behaviour constitutes a transgression that warrants stringent penalties.[81]

Additionally, the implementation of PALs is hindered by the lack of trans-departmental joint implementation. Red-tape procedures and insufficient human and material resources have dampened the enthusiasm of local enforcers for collegial teamwork.[82]As a result, they choose to work independently, focusing on smaller violations and letting the larger ones go unnoticed (*guaxiao fangda*)–that is, for example, they focus on detecting violations at the retail outlets while leaving the headquarters unexamined.

Furthermore, the protracted legislative unification has exacerbated the issue at hand. Frequently, there exists a temporal disconnect between the promulgation of state laws and the enactment of local statutes, which often creates confusion among local enforcement officials. Some adhere to the antiquated laws, while others comply with the newly established regulations, occasionally referencing the old statutes when the new ones remain ambiguous.[83]This disarray can precipitate the exercise of discretion

79 Ibid

80 Ibid

81 Jingyi [净壹], 'Mindset Differences between the Old Industrial and Commercial People and the Old Food And Drug Regulatory People in the Market Supervision Enforcement Team [Shichang jianguan zonghe zhifa duiwu li lao gongshang ren yu lao shi yao jian ren siwei fangmian de chayi]'. *Weibo* (4 May 2021) https://weibo.com/ttarticle/p/show?id=2309404633071898198225 accessed 22 April 2023.

82 Interview data, the regulator of Municipal Drug Administration.

83 Interview data, the regulator of Municipal Drug Administration, and the regulator of Provincial Drug Administration.

and the enforcement of unambiguous rules. Despite the existence of a plethora of laws, only a select few are rigorously enforced.

Thus, alongside the recentralizing trend, unqualified local implementers are increasingly issuing licences to inadequately qualified applicants, while local implementation capacity is deteriorating due to an unprofessional implementation team, less collaborative bureaux, and less applicable regulations. These two facets have engendered a dilemma wherein the proliferation of licensed retail pharmacies stands in stark contrast to the diminishing capacity of pharmaceutical administration; this phenomenon has been designated as 'authority deficit' in this chapter. The consequence of 'authority deficit' is the perpetuation of the enforcement gap, which has not only remained stagnant but has also further compromised the integrity of pharmaceutical administration practices.

Characterising this situation as 'authority deficit' alludes to the fact that regulators often inappropriately allocate power in terms of duties. In the example of the regulation of drug retailing that was given, local implementers attach too much importance to the examination and approval of licences while ignoring their task of supervising the licencees. 'Authority deficit' is not a new phenomenon and indeed has existed for a long time. Therefore, we may assume that before the recentralization trend, China's pharmaceutical administration was already plagued by the overflow of licences. The specific origins of authority deficit are hard to trace, but through China's regulation of drug retailing, we see it enlarging at least at the local level.

Authority deficit helps our understanding in several ways in relation to regulation. On the one hand, it lets us know that regulators need to configure their power in practice using as the starting point of enforcement outcomes instead of depending on their personal imaginings. As Yan and others have pointed out, a paradox exists in the relationship between regulation and compliance; enforcers simply may not be aware of which rules are more likely to be complied with and which regulated actors are more likely to comply.[84] Thus, enforcement policies may be directed towards those regulations and entities for which infractions yield the most significant harm, rather than focusing on those regulations that are more susceptible to breaches and those entities that are more prone to contravening them.[85]

On the other hand, the implementary capacity of local government is impacted by various factors, and this cannot be simply improved with resource allocation. For example, Lo et al. argued that increased local government support for the enforcement of environmental regulations in China may not necessarily lead to more rigorous enforcement.[86] In other

[84] Yan, Huiqi, van Rooij, B and van der Heijden, J (2016) 'The Enforcement-Compliance Paradox: Implementation of Pesticide Regulation in China' 30(2) *China Information* 209.

[85] Ibid 209-231.

[86] Lo, Carlos Wing Hung; Fryxell, Gerald E; Van Rooij, Benjamin; Wang, Wei and Li, Pansy Honying (2012) 'Explaining the Enforcement Gap in China: Local Government Support and

words, increasing local government support in China will not necessarily close the enforcement gap.[87]

Furthermore, a point worth discussing is whether authority deficit benefits or impedes market development. This echoes the classic question–as the market economy develops in China, should China strengthen or weaken its state power and emphasize the leading role of the central or local governments?[88] Wang and Hu argue that, in the transitional period, the central government plays a prominent role; when it comes to the central-local relationship, the central government should gradually assimilate authority from the local level.[89]This point implies that while recentralization may better steer the country in the right direction, the authority deficit would in fact likely impede social development.

However, this Chapter also argues that the absence of administrative power in China's drug retailing–government control is present, but only loosely–benefits market development and public welfare in the pharmaceutical sector. Due to the authority deficit, China's pharmaceutical market is given free rein to allocate limited resources in ways that mostly run contrary to the law. In other words, if it adopts strict state control, China will not be able to meet the public's pharmaceutical demand as well as it does now. To some extent, this means the state only needs to ensure that there will be no serious drug safety events, rather than engage in intensive administrative control.

CONCLUSION

This Chapter has examined how China's recentralizing trend impacts local implementers in pharmaceutical administration. The first part reviewed the evolution of China's pharmaceutical administration system, noting that despite recognizing the need to centralize pharmaceutical administrative power in the 1970s, meaningful progress occurred only recently. The second and third parts, analyzing retail pharmacy regulation using Northeast China data, argued recentralization produces negative effects—diluting professional teams, blocking trans-departmental cooperation, delaying local legislation—creating 'authority deficit' where local departments approve far more licences than their capacity is able to handle. The Chapter introduces a conceptual innovation by coining the term 'authority deficit' to delineate a phenomenon more nuanced than existing notions such as 'implementation gap' or 'bureaucratic drift'. This concept encapsulates the particular dynamic wherein administrative reforms paradoxically create a context in which the exercise of licensing authority exceeds the capacity for effective implementation.

Internal Agency Obstacles as Predictors of Enforcement Actions in Guangzhou' (111) *Journal of Environmental Management* 227.

[87] Ibid.

[88] Ibid

[89] Ibid at 1 and at 160

This Chapter's findings have three immediate implications. First, they deepen understanding of how central-local relations affect implementation currently. Under Xi's leadership, China has recentralized administrative power to solve decentralization-era problems like local protectionism and fragmented bureaucracy. However, pharmaceutical administration reform has fallen short of expectations. Unprofessional local implementers remain hindered by '*guanxi*,' personal interests, corruption, and regional benefits, indicating persistent local protectionism. Poor trans-departmental cooperation reveals unresolved fragmented bureaucracy manifesting differently.

Second, the Chapter explored the side effects of incomplete administrative reform. While the literature notes China's incomplete reforms, this chapter has gone further by examining departmental impacts. In drug retailing licensing, recentralization integrates pharmaceutical administrative power into compound departments but does not recentralize examination and approval authority upward, causing license overflow. This highlights conflicts among administrative reforms and adverse regulatory implementation impacts.

Third, the findings of this study may benefit China's pharmaceutical administration. Early literature attributed enforcement gaps to decentralization, but this chapter shows gaps persist under recentralization. Given the identified reasons—unprofessional implementers, poor cooperation, legislative disunification—certain measures should be adopted to benefit drug retailing regulation and accelerate medical-drug separation.

Overall, the Chapter provides important insights into recentralization's impact on local pharmaceutical administration implementers and highlights needs for comprehensive administrative reforms improving the quality of regulatory implementation in China. The Chapter's findings illuminate the persistent tensions between competing institutional logics within China's administrative system. The recentralization reforms, ostensibly designed to harmonize fragmented authority, have instead generated new forms of institutional conflict. The 'authority deficit' phenomenon demonstrates how bureaucratic actors at different levels pursue divergent interests—provincial administrators seeking professional control, municipal regulators managing resource constraints, and county-level officials responding to local political pressures.

The dilution of professional expertise reflects broader struggles over symbolic and cultural capital within the administrative hierarchy. Former pharmaceutical specialists find themselves marginalized within integrated market regulation departments, while officials from industrial and commercial backgrounds lack the specialized knowledge required for effective drug regulation. The rules of the game change but existing power relations and forms of cooperation and thinking persist, creating institutional friction and implementation failures.

Moreover, the persistence of guanxi networks and local protectionism despite formal recentralization reveals the resilience of informal power structures. The chapter demonstrates how formal institutional change may actually strengthen informal mechanisms of influence, as reduced professional oversight creates more opportunities for discretionary decision-making and regulatory capture.

The findings also present something of a challenge to administrative justice and the rule of law in China. The 'authority deficit' creates a situation where formal legal frameworks exist but lack effective implementation mechanisms—a phenomenon that undermines the predictability and consistency essential to legal legitimacy. Citizens and businesses face regulatory uncertainty, as the same legal violations may be treated differently depending on the professional background of local officials, the availability of inter-departmental cooperation, or the currency of local implementing regulations. The delayed legislative unification documented in this study reveals a deeper problem: the temporal mismatch between rapid institutional reform and the slower process of legal adaptation. This creates periods of legal ambiguity where multiple, potentially conflicting regulatory frameworks coexist. Such conditions undermine legal certainty and may lead to arbitrary enforcement—fundamental violations of administrative justice ideals. Furthermore, the blocked joint implementation mechanisms demonstrate how structural reforms can inadvertently create accountability gaps. When no single agency has clear authority over complex regulatory challenges, the result is often regulatory avoidance rather than collaborative governance. This fragmentation of responsibility can shield both regulators and regulated entities from accountability, undermining the deterrent effect of regulatory frameworks.

GLOSSARY OF CHINESE TERMS

Romanisation (Hanyu Pinyin)	Chinese Characters	English Translation
Bumen	部门	Department
dabuzhi gaige reform'	大部制改革	'super ministry
duobumen fenduan jianguan moshi supervision	多部门分段监管模式	multi-department 'segmented'
difang zhengfu	地方政府	Local government
dashichang	大市场	synthesized market regulation
fang guan fu	放管服	Streamline administration, delegate power, and improve services

zhuaxiao fangda	抓小放大	focusing on smaller violations and letting the larger ones go unnoticed
guan, ka, ya	管, 卡, 压	managing blocking and pressing
guanxi	关系	Personal connections / relationships
Guojia shichang jiandu guanli zongju	国家市场监督管理总局	State Administration for Market Regulation (SAMR)
Guojia yaopin jiandu guanliju	国家药品监督管理局	National Medical Products Administration (NMPA)
Guojia yiyao guanli azongju	国家医药管理总局	State Medical and Pharmceutical General Administra tion (SMPGA)
Guojia yiyao guanliju	国家医药管理局	State Medical and Pharmaceutical Administration (SMPA)
jianzheng fangquan, fang guan jiehe, youhua fuwu	简政放权, 放管结合，优化服务	streamline administration and delegate power and strengthen regulation, and improve services
jiu long zhi shui	九龙治水	'nine dragons taming a river'
keshi	科室	municipal 'administrative offices'
renqing shehui	人情社会	human relationship society
sanyi liandong	三医联动	Three-medical-linkage (medicine, insurance, service)
shou zhi liang tiao xian	收支两条线	two distinct avenues of fee collection

sheng yishang danlie, shengyi xia zonghe	省以上单列，省以下综合	entities above the provincial level are listed and treated in dividually, while those below the provincial level are handled in a com prehensive or inte grated manner
sheng yixia chuizhi guanli xitong	省以下垂直管理系统	vertical management below the provincial level (in which higher administrative levels directly manage lower levels in a hierarchical structure)
sili	私利	personal interests
tiaotiao	条条	vertical departmental control line
tiaotiao fenge de bumen guanli	条条分割的部门管理	tiao/tiao' fragmented 'departmental admin istrative hierarchy
Weishengbu Yaopin he Shengwu Zhipin Jiandingsuo	卫生部药品和生物制品检定所	Institute for the Control of Pharmaceutical and Biological Products
Yaopin Guanli Fa	药品管理法	Pharmaceutical Ad ministration Law (PAL)
Yaopin jingying xukezheng	药品经营许可证	Drug Distribution License (DDL)
Yaopin jingong guanli guifan	药品进供管理规范	Good Supply Practice (GSP)
yaopin shangshi xuke chiyouren zhidu	药品上市许可持有人制度	system of permit-holders for pharmaceutical sales
Yaopin shengchan guanli guifan	药品生产管理规范	Good Manufacturing Practice (GMP)
Yaopin shengchan	药品生产许可证	Drug Production Licensexukezheng

Yaozhengchu	药政处	Division of Pharmaceutical Affairs
Yiliao jigou zhiji xukezheng	医疗机构制剂许可证	Dispensing Permit for Medical Organizations (DPMO)
yiyao yangyi	以药养医	feeding hospitals on drug revenue
yiyao fenkai	医药分开	separating medical treatment from drug sales
zhengqi heyi	政企合一	government-enterprise integrated
zai zhongxin hua	再中心化	recentralization
Zhongguo Yaodian Weiyuanhui	中国药典委员会	Chinese Pharmacopoeia Commission
Zhongguo Yiyao Gongsi	中国医药公司	Chinese Pharmaceutical Company
Zhongyang zhengfu	中央政府	Central government
Zhongyao	中药	Traditional Chinese Medicine

PART V

ADMINISTRATIVE POWER AND CITIZEN RIGHTS

Pandemic Control in China's Gated Communities

HUALING FU*
University of Hong Kong

INTRODUCTION

A key global strategy to contain the coronavirus disease 2019 known as COVID-19 has been the implementation of social distancing measures (SDMs), in particular Stay-at-Home (SaH) orders. Given the epidemiological consensus at the time that social distancing significantly reduces transmission and that the ability of a country to contain the spread of infections depends on the degree to which SaH orders and other SDMs are enforced and complied with, few countries, if any, have not imposed lockdowns of sorts to some degree, in particular a range of SaH orders, placing a significant part of their population, if not all, under quarantine for various durations.[1] To a large degree, the success or failure of these measures has depended on citizens' willingness to change their behaviours to comply with SaH orders.

The existing literature indicates a range of factors, both subjective and objective, to explain compliance. Subjective factors include substantive support for the measures, trust in the government, political values, and obligations to obey regulations, broadly defined to include the impact of deterrence and the sense of fairness.[2] Some studies show that civic and moral education, and the appeal to altruism or a sense of solidarity, have some short-term positive impact on compliance with SDMs; an invocation of a degree of fear is also found to have more explanatory power in motivating behaviour change.[3] Others have pointed out that one's political views

* The essay was originally published in Christine Loh (ed) *How COVID-19 Took over the World: Lessons for the Future* (Hong Kong University Press, 2023). The author would like to thank Calvin Ho, Eric Ip, Christine Loh, Shitong Qiao, and the reviewers for their insightful comments on the earlier version of this paper and Chloe Tang and Kinson Cheung for their research assistance. The *Journal of Comparative Law* thanks to Hong Kong University Press for permission to reproduce the essay, and Dr Amy Kellam and Dr. Ling Zhou for their assistance in converting the footnotes to the *Journal*'s style.

[1] Park, M; Cook, AR; Lim Jue Tao; Sun, Yinxiaohe and Dickens, BL (2020) 'A Systematic Review of COVID-19 Epidemiology Based on Current Evidence'(9) *Journal of Clinical Medicine* 967; Talic, S; Wild, H; Maharaj, A; Ademi, Z; Xu, Wei and Theodoratou, E et al (2021) 'Effectiveness of Public Health Measures in Reducing the Incidence of Covid-19, SARS-Cov-2 Transmission, And Covid-19 Mortality: Systematic Review Ad Meta-analysis' *British Medical Journal* 375.

[2] Reiders Folmer, CP; Brownlee, MA; Fine, AD; Kooistra, EB; Kuiper, ME and Olthuis, EH et al (2021) 'Social Distancing in America: Understanding Long-Term Adherence to Covid-19 Mitigation Recommendations' (16) *PloS one*, available at: <https://doi.org/10.1371/journal.pone.0257945>.

[3] Harper, CA; Satchell, LP; Fido, D and Latzman, RD (2021) 'Functional Fear Predicts Public

(Democrat or Republican in the American context) have some predictive power on whether or not one will adhere to SDMs.[4]

Compliance with SaH orders can hardly be achieved without coordinated action, effective enforcement, and adequate material and psychological support on the part of the government. In the United States, while people generally felt compelled to obey the law, supported the principle of social distancing, and were concerned with the consequences of non-compliance, 'only a minority of Americans indicate that they always follow social distancing measures'.[5] In Italy, public authorities struggled to deal with significant non-compliance with SaH rules.[6] Sheth and Wright reported significant violations of the SaH order in California, concluding that relying on risk aversion or altruism would not achieve compliance.[7] Even in Canada, where compliance was high across all provinces, there was still a substantial proportion of norm-breakers.[8]

In order to secure adequate compliance, objective factors also need to be factored in, including people's capacity to follow SaH orders, opportunities to violate the measures, costs and benefits of adherence, and social norms in terms of adherence, i.e. whether others around are also in compliance. A key factor is the practical capacity to adhere to SDMs—people do not follow rules that are hard, if not impossible, to follow. Effective implementation of SaH orders demands support for residents in isolation and monitoring to enforce the orders.

This chapter examines the unique role that grassroots residential social organisations in China have played in supporting and enforcing pandemic control measures. In explaining China's performance to date in containing the pandemic,[9] commentators have attributed this to the

Health Compliance in the COVID-19 Pandemic' (19) *International Journal of Mental Health and Addiction* 1875; Lau, JYC and Lee, Shui-Shan (2021) 'Legal Provisions for Enforcing Social Distancing to Guard against COVID-19: The Case of Hong Kong' (8) *Journal of Law and the Biosciences* 1.

[4] Painter, MO and Qiu, Tian (2021) 'Political Beliefs affect Compliance with Government Mandates' (185) *Journal of Economic Behavior and Organisation* 688.

[5] Reiders Folmer et al 'Social Distancing in America' supra note 2.

[6] Guglielmo, B; Lacetera, N; Macis, M and Tonin, M (2020) 'Compliance with COVID-19 Social-Distancing Measures in Italy: The Role of Expectations and Duration', National Bureau of Economic Research, IZA Discussion Papers No. 13092.

[7] Sheth, K and Wright, GC (2020) 'The Usual Suspects: Does Risk Tolerance, Altruism, and Health Predict the Response to COVID-19?' (18) *Review of Economics of the Household* 1041.

[8] For the Canadian case, see Daoust, JF; Bélanger, E; Dassonneville, R; Lachapelle, E and Nadeau, R (2022) 'Is the Unequal COVID-19 Burden in Canada Due to Unequal Levels of Citizen Discipline Across Provinces?'(48) *Canadian Public Policy* 124.

[9] China has been successful in reaching its zero-COVID-19 goal. For example, prior to the outbreak of the Omicron variant, 'China has reported only 0.05% of the total number of global cases despite making up 19% of the world's population'; Tang, Jin-Ling and Abbasi, K (2021) 'What Can the World Learn from China's Response to Covid-19?' *British Medical Journal* 375, available at: <https://www.bmj.com/content/375/bmj.n2806>.

Chinese Communist Party's decisive move to lock down cities at a high social and economic cost and to the capacity both to mobilise human and material resources to build hospitals to isolate those infected with the virus, and to send medics and support to the most infected cities to treat patients. Another feature that has characterised the Chinese strategy and is receiving increasing attention is the broad societal participation and the ability of residential communities to enforce SDMs and, in particular, SaH orders, enabling residents to respond to the pandemic and to comply with pandemic control measures with resources and confidence.[10] In what was dubbed by the Party as the people's war against the COVID-19 pandemic, Chinese urban communities have showcased the effectiveness of the unique governance style in activating participation and inducing compliance. What makes Chinese urbanites more willing to participate in pandemic control enforcement and more compliant with SaH orders?

EMERGENCIES AND AUTHORITARIAN ADVANTAGE

Chinese urban communities are part of the overall political system and need to be situated in that larger political context.[11] China's political system, with its democratic centralism, coupled with its ability to shape public opinion and exert discipline and control, is well-equipped to manage novel crises.[12] Chinese commentators have confidently and, nearly universally, pointed to that systemic advantage over liberal democracies. As Gao and Zhang put it:

[10] For a growing body of literature, see, for example, Chen, Quilan; Rodewald, L; Lai, Shengjie and Gao, GF (2021) 'Rapid and Sustained Containment of covid-19 Is Achievable and Worthwhile: Implications for Pandemic Response' *British Medical Journal* 375, available at: <https://www.bmj.com/content/bmj/375/BMJ-2021-066169.full.pdf>; Gao, Jinghua and Zhang, Penfei 'China's Public Health Policies in Response to COVID-19: From an "Authoritarian" Perspective' *Frontiers in Public Health*, 15 December 2021, available at: <https://doi.org/10.3389/fpubh.2021.756677>; Jiang, Jue (2022) 'A Question of Human Rights or Human Left?—The "People's War against COVID-19" under the "Gridded Management" System in China' (31) *Journal of Contemporary China* 491; Xu, Feng and Liu, Qian (2021) 'China: Community Policing, High-Tech Surveillance, and Authoritarian Durability' in Ramraj, VV (ed) (2021) *COVID-19 in Asia: Law and Policy Context* Oxford University Press 27; He, Xiaolin; Jiang, Ping; Wu, Qiong; Lai, Xiaobin and Liang, Yan (2022) 'Governmental Inter-Sectoral Strategies to Prevent and Control COVID-19 in a Megacity: A Policy Brief From Shanghai, China', *Frontiers in Public Health*, available at: <https://doi.org/10.3389/fpubh.2022.764847>; Yang, Guobin (2022) *The Wuhan Lockdown* Columbia University Press.

[11] Article 21 of the PRC Constitution explicitly mentions these organisations ('neighbourhood organisations') in the context of public health. It states: 'To protect the people's health, the state shall develop medical and health care, develop modern medicine and traditional Chinese medicine, encourage and support the running of various medical and health facilities by rural collective economic organizations, state enterprises, public institutions and neighbourhood organizations, and promote public health activities.'

[12] deLise, J and Kui, Shen (2020) 'Lessons from China's Response to COVID-19: Shortcomings, Successes, and Prospects for Reform in China's Regulatory State' (16) *University of Pennsylvania Asian Law Review* 66; Schwartz, J (2012) 'Compensating for the "Authoritarian Advantage" in Crisis Response: A Comparative Case Study of SARS Pandemic Responses in China and Taiwan' (17) *Journal of Chinese Political Science* 313; Shih, VC (2021) 'China's Leninist Response to COVID-19: From Information Repression to Total Mobilization' in Greer, SC; King, EJ; Massard da Fonseca, E and Peralta-Santos, A (eds) (2021) *Coronavirus Politics: The Comparative Politics and Policy of COVID-19* University of Michigan Press.

> Because collectivist societies are supposed to cooperate more for the benefit of the majority, individual interests need to be sacrificed when necessary. Democracies, on the other hand, advocate for individual freedom, and governments must implement policies within the limits of what is legally permissible. Such institutional constraints inevitably cause numerous inconveniences in responding swiftly to disasters and crises.[13]

Regime type seems to have mattered less in shaping states' initial responses during the crisis as the pandemic has created a global authoritarian movement that witnessed a sudden surge of executive power and steady weakening of democratic accountability.[14] The traditional liberal states have scrambled to impose some emergency measures suitable to their respective constitutional traditions and made a turn in their governance towards authoritarianism.[15] In managing the pandemic, the differences between democracies and statist/authoritarian states have diminished. As Fukuyama points out:

> In the end, I don't believe that we will be able to reach broad conclusions about whether dictatorships or democracies are better able to survive a pandemic. What matters in the end is not regime type, but whether citizens trust their leaders, and whether those leaders preside over a competent and effective state.[16]

Yet, as liberal democracies learn to act uncomfortably and often awkwardly in authoritarian ways, they encounter formidable political, legal, and social resistance.[17] The legislature may refuse to endorse pandemic control legislative initiatives or act to dilute the expansion of executive power that may be needed to implement effective control. Similarly, the judiciary, holding the executive legally accountable, may review and invalidate some of the executive excesses. More importantly, citizens, frustrated by continuous lockdowns and SaH orders, may rebel through non-compliance and open protest, as has been widely observed in democracies. [18]

[13] Gao and Zhang 'China's Public Health Policies in Response to COVID-19' supra note 10.

[14] Horton, R (2021) 'Offline: Is Democracy Good for Your Health?' (398) *The Lancet* 2060; Gilbert, D (2020) 'These 30 Regimes Are Using Coronavirus to Repress Their Citizens' (9 April 2020) *Vice*, available at: <https://www.vice.com/en_us/article/dygbxk/these-30-regimes-are-using-coronavirus-to-repress-their-citizens>.

[15] Thomas, S and Ip, EC (2020) 'COVID-19 Emergency Measure and the Impending Authoritarian Pandemic' (7) *Journal of Law and the Biosciences* 1.

[16] Fukuyama, F 'The Thing That Determines a Country's Resistance to the Coronavirus' *The Atlantic*, 30 March 2020, available at: <https://www.theatlantic.com/ideas/archive/2020/03/thing-determines-how-well-countries-respond-coronavirus/609025>; Alon, I; Farrell, M and Li, Shaomin (2020) 'Regime Type and COVID-19 Response' (9) *FIIB Business Review* 152. For a general survey of state capacities, see Ramraj *COVID-19 in Asia: Law and Policy Context* supra note 10.

[17] Engler, S; Brunner, P; Loviat, R; Abou-Chadi, T; Leemann, L and Glaser, A (2021) 'Democracy in Times of the Pandemic: Explaining the Variation of COVID-19 Policies across European Democracies' (44) *West European Politics* 1077.

[18] See for example, Kowalewski, M (2021) 'Street protests in times of COVID-19: adjusting

How to explain the different responses among different regimes to the pandemic control emergency measures? For liberal democracies in general, the gap between the normal and the exceptional was sharp, and the restrictions on rights and freedoms during the pandemic made real differences, both epistemologically and empirically. Under pandemic control measures, public gatherings were banned, rallies and processions were barred, and freedom of mobility was curtailed. These restrictive measures, which may be commonly accepted and even taken for granted under authoritarianism, may produce shocks, be met with resistance and are, in any event, hard to implement in democracies.

The Chinese political system is well-equipped to manage novel crises. The authoritarian advantage is referred to as democratic centralism, in which a constitutionally entrenched Communist Party monopolises political power to exercise 'absolute leadership'. There are no effective checks and balances, and the decision-making process is, in McCubbins' terms, 'decisive' or even 'tyrannical'.[19] Under democratic centralism, China's pandemic control efforts are defined as 'centralization, coercive intervention, and state paternalism'.[20] The decision to impose a total lockdown on first Wuhan, a city of over 11 million people, then Hubei, a province of 65 million people, and finally on most of the other provinces was a decisive moment in China's war against the virus,[21] a move that received initial disbelief, shock and suspicion in the international community, but later became a standard preventive measure that was widely adopted.[22] The lockdown illustrated the decisiveness and swiftness of the system in sharp contrast with some of the democratic gridlocks that have been commonly observed. By the time Shanghai was totally locked down in 2022, what the Party-state is capable of achieving its policy objectives regardless of the costs was laid bare. After all, this is the same Party that implemented the One Child Policy and other massive projects unprecedented in human history. Political systems with concentrated political power may be able to act decisively while others with more fragmented political powers—subjecting decisions to multiple veto points and excessive checks and balances—may succumb to gridlock and political paralysis in the process.[23]

tactics and marching 'as usual'' (20) *Social Movement Studies* 758; and Plümper, T; Neumayer, E and Pfaff, KG (2021) 'The strategy of protest against Covid-19 containment policies in Germany' (102) *Social Science Quarterly* 2236.

19 McCubbins, MD (2000) 'Gridlock' in Clarke, B and Foweraker, J (eds) (2000) *The Encyclopedia of Democratic Thought* Routledge 325. See also Cox, GW and McCubbins, MD (2001) 'Political Structure and Economic Policy: The Institutional Determination of Policy Outcomes' in Haggard, S and McCubbins, MD (eds) (2001) *Presidents, Parliaments, and Policy* Cambridge University Press.

20 Gao and Zhang 'China's Public Health Policies in Response to COVID-19' supra note 10.

21 Yu, E (2021) 'An Analysis of China's Strategy in Combating the Coronavirus Pandemic with the 3H Framework' (24) *Public Administration and Policy: An Asia-Pacific Journal* 76.

22 Bradsher, K 'As China Fights the Coronavirus, Some Say It Has Gone Too Far' New York Times, 20 February 2020, available at: <https://www.nytimes.com/2020/02/20/business/economy/china-economy-quarantine.html>.

23 McCubbins 'Gridlock' supra note 19 and Alon, Farrell, and Li 'Regime Type and

In addition, the Party-led system can mobilise national resources to launch a sustained political campaign, setting aside legal rules and marginalising legal institutions in accomplishing its goals,[24] leading to human rights abuses. [25] This whole national system, which has often been referred to when China demonstrates its ability to coordinate national resources to train athletes,[26] has a long history and goes far beyond sports. Facing a crisis or a challenging task of national significance with limited resources, the Party is razor-sharp in its focus. It can mobilise all available resources to achieve its goal. In the process, it does not tolerate doubts, distractions, or disobedience and is ready to silence and crush, if needed, any sign of resistance.[27] This type of multi-functional government with the power of total mobilisation is commonly regarded as a Chinese political advantage.[28] The capacity to mobilise resources, evidenced in the record-breaking speed in building specialised hospitals; manufacturing and supplying medical supplies, especially protective equipment, in large quantities; drafting 42,600 medical doctors and experts to affected areas at short notice;[29] and the seamless coordination, vertical and horizontal, of operations, is regarded as a strength that can barely be matched in any liberal democracy.[30]

The Chinese political and constitutional design demonstrates fewer differences between normal operations and crisis management. One may even argue that part of the Chinese system has already normalised and routinised exceptional or emergency measures, so it is ready to encounter crises with a high degree of preparedness. Examples abound. Political rules of the Party have *de facto* legal effect in normal times or during a crisis, as Article 1 of the Chinese Constitution declares that 'Leadership by the

COVID-19 Response' supra note 16.

[24] Thornton, PM (2021) 'Of Constitutions, Campaigns and Commissions: A Century of Democratic Centralism under the CCP' (248) *The China Quarterly* 52.

[25] Jiang, Jue (2022) 'A Question of Human Rights or Human Left? – The 'People's War against COVID-19' under the 'Gridded Management' System in China' (31) *Journal of Contemporary China* 491.

[26] Wei, Fan; Hong, Fan and Lu, Zhouxiang (2010) 'Chinese State Sports Policy: Pre- and Post-Beijing 2008' (27) *The International Journal of the History of Sport* 2380.

[27] Cox and McCubbins 'Political Structure and Economic Policy: The Institutional Determination of Policy Outcomes' at supra note 19.

[28] Initium Media (2020) 'Sha mao, feng lu, qiangzhi geli, Zhongguo shi kang yi shi ruhe xingcheng de?' (Killing cats, closing roads, and enforced isolation, how did the Chinese style of fighting against the epidemic take shape?) *Initium Media*, March 4, 2020, available at https://thein- itium.com/article/20200309-mainland-coronavirus-mergency-management/

[29] Jin, Hao; Lu, Ligong; Liu, Junwei and Cui, Min (2021) 'COVID-19 Emergencies around the Globe: China's Experience in Controlling COVID-19 and Lessons Learned' (33) *International Journal for Quality in Health Care* 1; Yu 'An Analysis of China's Strategy' supra note 19.

[30] He et al 'Governmental Inter-Sectoral Strategies' supra note 10; Yan, Jingjing and Zhao, Dahei (2020) 'Administrative Mechanism of Joint Participation and Cooperation in the Early Stages of the COVID-19 Outbreak in Wuhan' (13) *Risk Management and Healthcare Policy* 723.

Communist Party of China is the defining feature of socialism with Chinese characteristics'. There are few if any veto points in the decision-making process; the Party controls the press and imposes censorship of news; it routinely punishes rumours through criminal law and police power; prohibits demonstration and protest at all times; the routine police monitoring and control of population movement and residence is a feature of China's urban management, and the mass surveillance does not spark significant privacy concerns from the society; and Chinese courts encourage and subtly enforce the settlement of disputes expediently through mediation. What is regarded as normalcy in China could be possible only under emergency measures elsewhere. Due to the lack of a clear distinction in the conceptual framework and institutional choices between normalcy and emergency, China can move into crisis management mode with far less resistance.

Authoritarian advantages notwithstanding, the political design and the power to mobilise *per se* cannot fully explain the Chinese ability to enforce the SaH order and SDMs. The world is not short of authoritarian leaders who can act decisively and expediently or political systems that do not admit any checks and balances or external accountability. States that are able to pull in national resources to achieve certain political goals or manage a crisis also abound. This is the 'despotic power', in Mann's terms, to assert control *over* society, which explains Chinese decisiveness and resourcefulness.[31] China's success depended, however, on more than despotism and autocratic decision-making. When China launched a people's war against the pandemic, the battleground was shifted to residential communities at the grassroots level, and the despotic power had to penetrate the social fabric and become what Mann referred to as the 'infrastructural power' *through* society that is manifested through the routine.[32] The pre-crisis neighbourhood organisations, as they were mobilised by the Party-state to combat the pandemic, coupled with a high level of political trust in the government and the resulting voluntary compliance, proved to be the most crucial aspect of the Chinese ability to trace, monitor, and control, which in turn further legitimised, solidified, and reinforced the operating system.

SHEQU, XIAOQU, AND GATED COMMUNITIES

The Chinese residential community (*shequ*) is the place where SaH orders and other measures are enforced. It is the site where the Party-state displays its infrastructural power. A Chinese community is composed of three

[31] Mann, M (1985) 'The Autonomous Power of the State: Its Origins, Mechanisms and Results' (25) *European Journal of Sociology/Archives européennes de sociologie* 185; Mann, M (2008) 'Infrastructural Power Revisited' (43) *Studies in Comparative International Development* 355, available at: <https://doi.org/10.1007/s12116-008-9027-7>; Mann, M (2005) 'The Sources of Social Power Revisited: A Response to Criticism' in Hall, JA and Schroeder, R (eds) (2005) *An Anatomy of Power: The Social Theory of Michael Mann* Cambridge University Press 343.

[32] Ibid Mann, 'Sources of Social Power Revisited'. For an application of Mann's conceptualisation of power on China, see Dowdle, MW (2019) 'Infrastructural Power and Its Possibilities for the Constitutional Evolution of Authoritarian Political Systems: Lessons from China' in Garcia, HA and Frankenberg, G (eds) (2019) *Authoritarian Constitutionalism* Edward Elgar 76.

elements on a long spectrum that includes government offices, parastate and civil society organisations, and commercial firms, which together formed the backbone of the people's war against the pandemic.[33] The government includes the Street Office (SO), the lowest level of Party-state power in urban China. Within the SO jurisdiction, there is a neighbourhood police station called a *paichusuo* (PCS) in charge of population management and public order. Under the SO, there is a parastate organisation called the Residential Committee (RC), a semi-autonomous organisation elected by and composed of local residents to manage neighbourhood affairs. Each RC is composed of a number of small communities (*xiaoqu*), often in the form of a gated community with walls to mark its boundaries and protect it from outsiders. The RC may set up a service station at a *xiaoqu* to maintain contact with residents in the jurisdiction. Under Chinese law, residents in a *xiaoqu* are entitled to form a homeowners' association (HoA) through an election among the homeowners. An HoA is a self-regulatory body formed to protect the rights and interests of homeowners. Each *xiaoqu* may engage a Property Management Company (PMC) to manage the residential buildings and provide services for the residents. A *shequ* is often a high-density ecosystem with complicated hierarchical and horizontal relations in which the Party-state, society, and market interact with each other to maximise their respective interests.

The *shequ* is a unique political design. At its core, as Read noted, is 'a dense network of standardized cells, with state-defined boundaries, covering all or virtually all of the urban geography'. The structure and designs are inherited from long historical practice and in significant ways, 'grow out of a more regimented vision of how society is to be ordered'.[34] Underlining this unique infrastructure is the Chinese *hukou* system, which registers persons by household and assigns each individual, at birth, to a community. The Party has upgraded the system into a panopticon to allow the state, through the neighbourhood police, to monitor and control the entire population.[35] The neighbourhood community exists first and foremost for government control over urban societies.

Significantly, control is extended through a parastate organisation, the RC, and a network of social groups, whose leaders, often endorsed, and from time to time chosen, by the residents, work for and with government officials on a wide range of matters concerning the community. Beyond extending government control to the fabric of the communities, the RC and the social groups also represent local interests in their interaction and bargaining with

[33] Tang, Beibei (2020) 'Grid Governance in China's Urban Middle-class Neighborhoods' (241) *The China Quarterly* 43. For studies of Chinese urban communities, see Whyte, MK and Parish, WL (1984) *Urban Life in Contemporary China* University of Chicago Press; Read, BL (2012) *Roots of the State: Neighborhood Organisation and Social Networks in Beijing and Taipei* Stanford University Press; Tomba, L (2014) *The Government Next Door: Neighborhood Politics in Urban China* Cornell University Press.

[34] Ibid Read *Roots of the State* at 3.

[35] Dutton, MR (1992) *Policing and Punishment in China: From Patriarchy to 'the People'* Cambridge University Press.

the local state. Policing, public health, and poverty alleviation are concerns of both the government and the community. The dialogical, 'socialised',[36] or 'associative'[37] process in which both contention and accommodation take place,[38] and through which the state integrates residents into state projects and residents make their claims, not only allows the state to calibrate its control but also solidifies and strengthens the social fabric. Through formal and informal links, the community structure engenders dynamic state–society synchronisation and mutual support. Under this structure, citizens' 'belonging, participation and entitlement, and state obligation' all gravitate towards the residential communities, and the neighbourhood becomes the site of political action in China's urban governance.[39]

Shequ is a hodgepodge of organisations with different identities, interests, and priorities, which interact hierarchically and horizontally. The RC is legally an autonomous organisation, the PMC is a commercial entity serving the interests of residents who pay them, and the HoA jealously guards the interests of the Chinese middle classes. The SO is the lowest organ in the Party-state system and is staffed by low-ranking bureaucrats whose duties are to coordinate the bread-and-butter affairs of the urban communities. When the COVID-19 pandemic hit, the Party started to intervene directly in community management, connecting the SO, RC, PMC, and HoA into a network to form a defensible space against the virus.

Since the outbreak of COVID-19, local people's congresses and city governments in most provinces have enacted local legislation and rules to require *shequ* organisations, especially the PMC and HoA, to follow the leadership of the SO and RC and to take active steps to implement pandemic control measures, in particular in posting information flyers, disinfecting public areas, taking the temperature of visitors, monitoring residents who returned from other regions, enforcing social distancing rules, and so on, all contingent on evolving circumstances.[40] The *xiaoqu*—the little gated community—formed the basic unit in China's people's war on the pandemic; and China's massive SaH order was enforced under the leadership of the SO

[36] Woodman, S (2016) 'Local Politics, Local Citizenship? Socialized Governance in Contemporary China' (226) *The China Quarterly* 342.

[37] Read *Roots of the State* supra note 33 at 4.

[38] Tomba *The Government Next Door* supra note 33 at 165.

[39] Woodman 'Local Politics' supra note 36 at 343.

[40] Guangzhou shi renmin zhengfu (The People's Government of Guangzhou Municipality) 'Guangzhou shi renda changweihui biaojue tongguo "Guanyu yifa quanli zuohao xinguan feiyan yiqing fangkong gongzuo de jueding",' (The Standing Committee of the Guangzhou Municipal People's Congress votes to pass the 'Decision on the Prevention and Control of the Covid-19 Epidemic'), February 12, 2020 available at: https://www.gz.gov.cn/zt/qlyfdyyqfkyz/gzzxd/content/post_5660732.html; Tieling shi zhufang he chengxiang jianshe ju (Tieling Housing and Urban-Rural Development Bureau) 'Guanyu yiqing fangkong qijian jinyibu jiaqiang zhuzhai xiaoqu wuye guanli de tongzhi' (Notice on Further Strengthening the Property Management of Residential Areas During the Epidemic Prevention and Control Perio) *PMCEO.com* 2 July 2020 available at: http://www.pmceo.com/show/202005/226290.html.

and RC, with the active participation of the PMC and *xiaoqu* residents, all supported and reinforced by the police in the PCS. Through this particular organisational structure, national pandemic control policies are announced and sent to residents, individuals are isolated, monitored and supported, and those who test positive are sent to designated places for quarantine. A well-led, resourceful, and well-organised community structure with disciplined participation is a necessity to make the SaH order practical and enforceable. However China's pandemic control strategy is perceived and assessed, the gated communities are an essential part of it.

The Street Office and the Residential Committee

Let us examine these community structures in more detail. The SO and the RC are the two key institutions in Chinese urban communities. The SO and the RC were institutionalised in Chinese cities in 1954 according to the particular social and political environment at the time. They played an important role in mobilising politically isolated social groups into a unified leadership, extending administrative control, and offering a more systematic way of political recruitment.[41] An SO is established as a sub-agency of a district or city government to take charge of an area referred to as an administrative street. To avoid any possible 'fragmentation of power', an SO was restricted to a minimum level in terms of resources and responsibilities.[42]

Despite the drastic social and economic changes that have taken place in Chinese cities, the role of the SO remains largely unchanged in that, as the most basic level of government, its principal function is to enhance the governance capacity at the basic level, framed as to work with stakeholders to build streets that are 'civilised', 'vibrant', 'convenient', and 'peaceful', with its work clearly identified as 'local', 'social', and 'mass-oriented'. In concrete terms, the SO should respond to complaints to the city government from local residents and address their concerns; in addition, SO officials should appear on the frontline in coordinating works and services from different government departments and solve whatever problems may arise in the locality.[43] The SO is front and centre in the Party's effort to build a responsive state.

The RC is a 'basic level' parastate organisation that was established directly by the Constitution and is governed by national law. The RC is designed as a 'self-management, self-education and self-service entity'

[41] Salaff, J (1967)'The Urban Commune in Communist China' (29) *The China Quarterly* 82; Salaff, J (1971) 'Urban Residential Committees in the Wake of the Cultural Revolution', in Lewis JW (ed) (1971) *The City in Communist China* Stanford University Press 289.

[42] Schurmann, FH (1968) *Ideology and Organisation in Communist China* University of California Press 379.

[43] Beijingshi Tongzhouqu Renmin Zhengfu (People's Government of Tongzhou District of Beijing Municipality) (2020) 'Beijing shi jiedao bangong chu tiaoli' (Regulations on the Neighborhood Offices of Beijing Municipality) available at: http://www.bjtzh.gov.cn/tzzfxxgk/c109720/202101/1332302.shtml; & at: https://www.sohu.com/a/361259169_99960504

and is tasked with community public affairs, such as policing, poverty alleviation, and dispute resolution. It also has a legal duty to promote the implementation of laws and policies, and to reflect the views and complaints of residents to the government. As a self-regulatory body, its members are elected either by all eligible residents and households, or by representatives from small groups within an RC. An RC receives supervision, guidance and, above all, financial support from the SO. It is commonly observed that members of an RC maintain 'affective connections' with officials and at the same time build 'personal relations' with residents in the community,[44] in which 'an active, proximate, and responsive state' is interacting and coping with 'disagreement, contentions, and resistance' from the communities.[45]

Property Management Companies and Homeowners Associations

The traditional neighbourhood system has gone through a period of renewal with the privatisation and commodification of residential housing, forming the typical Chinese gated residential communities. With the rise of the Chinese middle class and the availability and popularity of privately owned condominiums, Chinese cities have witnessed a fundamental shift towards clear demarcation, assertion, and protection of property rights. With this broad background, PMCs emerged to manage residential communities in high-density, high-rise residential buildings.[46]

The PMC, as a commercial entity, operates on a contract basis with the residents in a community to offer management services on a fee-for-service basis. The PMC is well-resourced, commercially organised, and embedded in the community to offer routine services. It is a formidable player in China's urban community with a staggering influence on people's livelihoods. Take Hangzhou, for example, where over 700 PMCs manage over 4,000 *xiaoqu* and buildings in the city and where over 50,000 employees of those PMCs were on the frontline in enforcing SDMs. Another notable example is Vanke Property Development, a single company that has 2,663 residential projects and 639 business projects. Its more than 50,000 employees participated in the services of over 5 million households during the pandemic.[47]

Side-by-side with the PMC is another prominent organisation—the HoA, a companion entity that has grown together with the PMC. Both are products of China's burgeoning residential housing market. As it happens,

[44] Schurmann *Ideology and Organisation* supra note 42 at 346; Read *Roots of the State* supra note 33 at 4

[45] Read *Roots of the State* supra note 33 at 4.

[46] Qiao ST (2023) 'The Authoritarian Commons: Divergent Paths of Neighborhood Democratization in Three Chinese Megacities' (2023) (71, 3) *American Journal of Comparative Law* 388

[47] 'Xinhua News Agency (2020)'Xinhua she jingji fenxi baogao: Qianghua wuye guanli goujian shequ yiqing fang kong "anquán xiàn", ' ('Xinhua News Agency Economic Analysis Report: Strengthen property management and build a "safety line" for community epidemic prevention and control'), February 19, 2020, available at: https://www.sohu.com/a/374168882_214444

disputes over property rights and management issues abound, and the PMC, as a matter of routine, often gets into disputes with residents. The PMC is often controlled or owned by the developers that built the housing projects and occupies an advantageous position vis-à-vis the often-disorganised residents. In response, aggrieved residents use the HoA platform to protect their rights in legal and political ways.[48]

Ownership of private property in urban condominiums creates a common identity and shared interest for the owners, who, united under a common cause, demand the protection of their legal rights, efficient management of their property, and good governance of the neighbourhood. The government clearly recognises property rights and has created procedures to form HoAs under the guidance of the SO and the RC, and with the limited participation of the developers. While the government grants the right to organise the HoA through a democratic process, a rare situation in the Chinese political system, and to seek legal and political protection of rights in a collective and organised manner, these rights are strictly limited to their implementation in the immediate neighbourhood.[49]

Riding on the tide of social management innovation, the government has become more interventionist in pre-empting disputes between the two entities. Clearer rules have been made, and the SO and RC are more proactive in establishing co-governance involving all stakeholders and are more ready to take political action to root out networking, public protests or other 'radical actions' on the part of some of the HoAs.[50] In the urban management setting, the HoA is regarded as a potential spoiler of the established arrangement, whereas the PMC and the developers behind them are able to build and maintain a close alliance with the government, which is interested in little more than maintaining stability.[51]

Beyond giving the SO and RC more resources and mandates to manage urban communities and, in particular, to improve relations between the PMC and HoA to maintain local stability, the other step that has been taken is the building of the Party at the community level and the invocation of Party mechanisms. While the RC does not have any legal or administrative authority over the PMC, just as the SO does not have any direct authority over the RC, the political mechanism of the Party serves as the golden thread to tie all the loose pieces together. While the local government, the PMC, and the HoA may have their unique interests and concerns, the political interest of the Party transcends all. Each autonomous unit has a Party cell,

[48] Yip, Ngai-Ming; Huang, Ronggui and Sun, Xiaoyi (2014)'Homeowners' Activism and the Rule of Law in Urban China' (7) *China Journal of Social Work* 175.

[49] Qiao 'The Authoritarian Commons' supra note 46.

[50] Yip, Ngai-ming and Jiang, Yihong (2011) 'Homeowners United: The Attempt to Create Lateral Networks of Homeowners' Association in Urban China' (20) *The Journal of Contemporary China* 735; Xia, Ying and Guan, Bing (2014) 'The Politics of Citizenship Formation: Homeowners' Collective Action in Urban Beijing' (19) *Chinese Journal of political Science* 405.

[51] Qiao 'The Authoritarian Commons' supra note 46.

which can be used to exercise political leadership over Party members in the PMC and Party members in the whole community.[52]

When the pandemic broke out, the government immediately tapped into the resources and organisational capacity of PMCs in China and folded them into the pandemic control mechanisms. PMCs, being a permanent presence in the gated community, had no choice but to participate. While accusations that PMCs may have shed their responsibilities from time to time, they worked hand-in-glove with the government and the residents and by and large performed extra, out-of-contract tasks at their own expense for pandemic control purposes. Indeed, they have been treated as if they were a government entity in performing a wide range of pandemic control responsibilities such as checking the identities and conditions of vehicles and individuals entering or leaving a community, disinfecting public places, enforcing SDMs, arranging food deliveries to households, and any other tasks that needed to be done. In order to recognise PMCs' contributions, some well-off cities provided them with subsidies for the additional costs that PMCs may have incurred.[53]

The institution that is conspicuous by its absence from the entire pandemic control campaign is the HoA, which has gained much popularity in its fight for property rights since its inception. As many studies have shown, the government is hostile to the formation of any independent organisations, including HoAs, and has taken steps to limit their growth.[54] According to some statistics, about 20–30 per cent of eligible residential communities have created HoAs, and a very small percentage of the established HoAs (5–10%) operate actively. The difficulty of collective action has prevented them from expanding as the legislation allows.

Despite their high profile, HoAs have not been able to grow into a formidable force to reckon with and have played a marginal role, if any, as institutions in enforcing pandemic control rules in their own *xiaoqu*. In the best-case scenarios where an HoA has played an active role, it was its members who volunteered their services in their personal capacities, using their social and political capitals to serve their communities.[55] Two main reasons may explain the marginalisation of HoAs. First, pandemic control measures are regarded as a highly politicised activity, and SO and RC leaders are hands-on in directing and organising enforcement and coordinating support. The heavy presence of officials, including those civil servants or Party members who are seconded to the communities—to be

52 Zhong, Fuliang & Liu, Le (2018) 'Chengzhen hua jincheng zhong chuangxin shequ dangjian gongzuo', (Innovating Community Party Building Work in the Process of Urbanization), (17, 10) *Guangzhou daxue xuebao (shehui kexue ban)* (Journal of Guangzhou University, Social Science Edition) 66-73

53 ' Xinhua She, supra note 47

54 Qiao 'The Authoritarian Commons' supra note 46.

55 One report from Shanghai, where the HoAs were better developed than those elsewhere and developed a cooperative relationship with the government, said the level of volunteerism of the HoA members reached 80 per cent (Qiao 'The Authoritarian Commons' supra note 46.

discussed below—crowded the HoA out, except for its members' voluntary participation under government leadership. The democratic procedure in the decision-making of the HoA is such that participation in pandemic control work would require the authorisation of the Owners' Committee with the support of half of the owners of the units, which may have rendered it impossible for an HoA to use its resources to support the pandemic control work, given the isolation and social distancing requirements. The historical image of the HoA as a representative organ of homeowners standing against the PMC on economic matters and against the local government on political matters has not helped either.

The neighbourhood police

The neighbourhood police station, the PCS, is at the heart of the system in maintaining public order in general but has only played a supplementary role in pandemic control enforcement. Their presence is mainly to ensure compliance, take action when voluntary compliance and persuasion of community leaders have failed, and punish delinquents when required.[56]

The principal duty of the PCS is to maintain order within its jurisdiction, including maintaining and updating a population/household database, organising community crime control, monitoring suspicious populations, and carrying out other matters related to law and order within a defined territory. Policing in the neighbourhood is preventive, aiming to pre-empt potential disorder. In that sense, the police, through their deep-rooted, proactive policing, make the community and the people visible and legible to the state, thus enhancing the state's capacity to know, monitor, and control.

Chinese police forces, compared to their Western counterparts, are small in size and have less visibility. One of the key features of the Chinese policing system is the embedding of policing and maintenance of order in the communities where the police serve. This mass-line policing, as it is known, promotes the concept of co-governance and shared responsibility, where the police receive public input and support while at the same time enhancing the self-policing capacity of the communities. The strength of the Chinese police lies in the development of a mode of policing by people who know the community and have routine interactions with residents on non-policing matters, rather than by strangers who remain at arm's length from the communities. It is both 'bottom up' and 'inside out',[57] making police work subtler, less confrontational, and often more effective.[58]

In China, some efforts have been made, especially in the 1980s, to create what was called dynamic policing—highly visible and quick to respond

[56] Lin, Kai; Shen, Shan; Sun, IY and Wu, Yuning (2022) 'Policing pandemic in China: investigating the roles of organizational adjustment, procedural justice, and police trustworthiness on public compliance' *Police Practice and Research*, available at: <https://doi.org/10.1080/15614263.2022.2127717>.

[57] Wong, Kam C (2017) *Police Reform in China* Routledge.

[58] Zhong, LY (2009) *Communities, Crime and Social Capital in Contemporary China* Routledge.

and adapt to the changing social and economic environment. With the arrival of migrant workers en masse in the mid-1990s and the increase in social mobility, traditional community control and policing styles were placed under great stress and, from time to time, were criticised for being too static and ill-equipped to control a dynamic society in great social and economic transition. Instead of embedding policing in community work to enhance self-policing capacity, police were asked to withdraw from the community and to launch swift and effective responses to crimes; instead of visiting households and chatting in the neighbourhood, police were forced to put their limited resources on the streets so as to become visible through routine patrols. There was a clear shift from maintaining order to enforcing the law and from preventive community work to rapid response to crime scenes and emergency calls. Doubts were even cast on the viability of the PCS as an institution, and suggestions were made to uproot the police from the community so as to professionalise the service. This was a paradigmatic shift in strategic thinking about policing, crime, and punishment in China.[59]

By the late 1990s and early 2000s, China was facing new challenges. While the periodic crackdowns on crime had achieved an impact in terms of incapacitating and deterrence, suppressing the crime rate to a comparatively low level, social conflict and protest had increased at speed and to a degree that exceeded the capacity of the existing institutions. Petitions to Party authorities and public protests were perceived to be spiralling out of control and posed a threat to the political order. Not surprisingly, the vast majority of conflicts came from local communities and could have been prevented, resolved, or otherwise stopped at the level where they arose in the first place. Institutions were required to go back to the basics to halt the further escalation of social conflict—courts were forced to settle cases through mediation so that matters would truly end when the case files closed, and police were ordered to go back to the communities where the root causes of China's social problems were located.

At that particular juncture, community policing (*shequ jingwu*) became fashionable and was systematically promoted within the police in partnership with other relevant authorities. Some coastal cities piloted it in the late 1990s, and by the early 2000s, community policing was rolled out nationwide.[60] A contentious issue was why China resorted to US policing for inspiration in developing community policing rather than reflecting on its own experiences from the not-so-distant past and whether there were any meaningful differences between the neighbourhood policing that the PCS had developed and the newly imported community police.[61] Nevertheless, the police did return to the communities, and when they did so, they

59 Fu, Hualing (1990) 'Patrol Police: A Recent Development in the People's Republic of China' (13) *Police Studies* 111.

60 Wu, Yuning; Jiang, Shanhe and Lambert, E (2011) 'Citizen Support for Community Policing in China' (34) *Policing: An International Journal of Police Strategy & Management* 285.

61 Zhong, LY (2009) 'Community Policing in China: Old Wine in New Bottles' (10) *Police Practice and Research: An International Journal* 157.

encountered residential communities that had been transformed beyond recognition, with high-rise residential towers dotting the city landscape and where strangers of different social and economic backgrounds came together to rebuild their communities, now referred to as 'little communities'.

The new community police in China addressed the security concerns of the *xiaoqu*, and the resulting policing measures, in turn, reinforced the *xiaoqu* identity and a shared sense of community. The Ministry of Public Security, together with the Ministry of Civil Affairs, which has jurisdiction over community development, jointly issued instructions to establish community policing in China.[62]

Part of the reform was, in fact, to return to the old-style neighbourhood policing with which the Chinese police were familiar. Under community policing orders, local police are required to participate in the RC activities and coordinate the management of local affairs;[63] in particular, they are required to give guidance and offer supervision on community mediation, monitor the rehabilitation of offenders on probation, and carry out neighbourhood patrols.[64] The main thrust of the police reform, especially since 2003, has been to enhance local and community capacity and, within the police, to 'sink' the workforce and resources all the way down to support the PCS and reengage the community. A heavy presence of the police on the streets was no longer a priority; instead, the urgent work was to equip *shequ* organisations to develop their self-policing capacity, with the understanding and expectation that disputes mostly arose at a low level and should be solved, if not pre-empted, at this low level. Not directly related to the pandemic, the police in 2020 launched a nationwide campaign of one million police officers entering households,[65] in which the police were required proactively to engage communities to improve police–society relations.

There is a new element to modern community policing, which China learnt from US criminology. In maintaining order in the new neighbourhoods with a high population density in high-rise towers, the police encouraged the creation of a 'defensible space' to control crime and disorder through physical design.[66] The new design resulted in a gated community with restricted membership, limited access, and extensive monitoring. It is a community with a strong sense of insiders versus outsiders and one that treats outsiders as strangers with great suspicion, if not outright hostility.

[62] Wu et al 'Citizen Support' supra note 60 at 288.

[63] Ibid.

[64] Messner, SF; Zhang, Lening; Zhang, SX and Gruner, CP (2017) 'Neighborhood Crime Control in a Changing China: Tiao-Jie, Bang-Jiao, and Neighborhood Watches' (54) *Journal of Research in Crime and Delinquency* 544.

[65] Liu,Yang (2021) 'Quanguo gong'an jiguan shenru kaizhan "bai wan jing jin qian wan jia" huodong reqing fuwu qunzhong shouhu yifang ping'an'(National public security organs carry out in-depth activities of "millions of policemen entering thousands of households" to serve the masses enthusiastically and protect the safety of one place) *Renmin Ribao* (People's Daily) July 1, 2021 available at: http://www.gov.cn/xinwen/2021-01/07/content_5577609.htm

[66] Newman, O (1966) *Creating Defensible Space* Diane Publishing.

In its ideal form, retired residents are organised to serve as floor monitors, building monitors and block monitors. All the security measures are also maintained and reinforced by paid private security working closely with the PMCs, supported by the PCS and enhanced by surveillance technologies such as high-definition cameras and face-recognition tools. Thus, the small communities are all fortified against criminals or 'bad elements' in society. When COVID-19 broke out and the government demanded isolation, Chinese communities were immediately mobilised and prepared for it.

Grids and grid monitors

Perceiving a declining governance capacity at the grassroots level and the potential of technology-enhanced social management, the Party created a grid system in 2013 to upgrade and renew shequ management so as to entrench the stability (*weiwen*) of the mechanism that had been initiated a decade earlier.[67] The new grid system was mapped onto the existing shequ structure, injecting more resources into the communities and enhancing the monitoring capacity of the state.[68]

Under the grid system, each RC is further divided into several zones, or 'grids', clearly demarcated and identified, with specific allocations of responsibility. In a pilot district for grid reform in Beijing, for example, the 17 SOs and 205 RCs were further divided into 589 grids in 2010, and each was allocated a person living within the grid as a grid monitor. The grid system was finalised in Beijing in 2014, and by 2017, Beijing had been able to integrate urban administration, policing, and social services within the grid system. The grid was introduced as an urban governance reform and designed as a system of total control: where there is a community, there are grids; where there is a grid, there is someone in charge; and when there is someone in charge, that person is held accountable—a visible return of a technology-enhanced *baojia* system.

The grid system serves two functions: one is to solidify control, and the other is to address specific concerns of residents and enhance services. Distinct from the traditional RC mechanisms that rely on face-to-face contact between community leaders and residents, the grid offers a digital platform that contains comprehensive personal and community data. Indeed, a key duty of a grid monitor is the responsibility to collect and update the data to facilitate control and service. The dataset would create a transparent *shequ*, exposing individuals and communities to the state. The creation of the digital grid would be transformative, shifting the control of the old style that is 'traditional, reactive, qualitative and diverse' to a new style

[67] Yang, DL (2017) 'China's Troubled Quest for Order: Leadership, Organisation and Contradictions of the Stability Maintenance Regime' (26) *Journal of Contemporary China* 35; Benney, J (2016) 'Weiwen at the Grassroots: China's Stability Maintenance Apparatus as a Means of Conflict Resolution' (25) *Journal of Contemporary China* 389.

[68] Tang 'Grid Governance in China's Urban Middle-Class Neighborhoods' supra note 3; Jiang 'A Question of Human Rights' supra note 10.

that will be 'modern, proactive, quantitative and systematic'.[69] The grid is a sophisticated tool to maximise control by identifying events promptly, allocating responsibilities swiftly and offering solutions effectively. In essence, the grid governance system refocuses on pre-emptive control at the grassroots level. It aims to streamline and rationalise management responsibilities at different levels of government and to enhance multi-institutional coordination of police, social services, and other government departments—which had previously operated in isolation—into a single control network. The grid makes rapid and targeted actions possible.[70]

The second function is to improve public services and, in so doing, enhance government accountability. Once a request for service is made on the online platform, it triggers an upward information flow that demands swift and effective action from those with responsibility. The grid system, while not making the government's responsibilities transparent and comprehensible to residents, does create a mechanism to hold officials accountable to the rhetoric of the Party.

At the heart of the system is the grid monitor, who feeds information to the government for action. Each grid generally has one monitor, who may be assisted by a few other grid workers. They are supported by SO officials, RC members, and also by PCS police. The backgrounds of grid monitors vary. When the grid was created, local governments recruited a large number of full-time grid monitors to work in the communities. For example, in one district in Changde city, Hunan province, in 2014, the district government contracted a technology company to build a grid information platform for the district. It created 577 grids out of 92 *shequ,* with an average of 350 to 500 households per grid.[71] It then recruited over 500 grid monitors, who were said to be young and well-educated. There is a clear trend to professionalise grid monitors, as evidenced by the use of uniforms, recruitment of recent university graduates, and training before deployment. Grid monitors see themselves as the chiefs of staff of their respective grids, giving answers to residents and at the same time monitoring behaviour, entering data, solving disputes, and reporting suspicious individuals to the police, all similar functions to those that RC members used to and continue to play.[72] Many grid workers are indeed recruited from residents in the grids working part-time or full-time.[73]

[69] Tang 'Grid Governance in China's Urban Middle-Class Neighborhoods' supra note 33.

[70] Ibid at 44.-

[71] Kang, Peipei and Han, Bingxi (2014) 'Wang ge hua dangjian tongling shequ zhili chuangxin' (Grid-based party building leads community governance innovation), November 27, 2014, *Remin Wang*（People's Daily Online）available at: http://theory.people.com.cn/n/2014/1127/c40531-26105462.html

[72] Sa, Ze (2021) 'Nage zhongguan xiaoqu zonghezhili "shenjing moshao" derén' (The persons in charge of the "nerve endings" of the comprehensive management of the community)) *Zhongguo shuzi shidai* (China Digital Times) July 24, 2021 available at: https://chinadigitaltimes.net/chinese/668681.html

[73] ' Liu Ziyang (2020) 'Youyi zhongliliang， jiao "Zhongguo wanggeyuan",' (There is a force

It is difficult to estimate how many grid workers there are in China. *Legal Daily* reported that four and a half million grid workers went into a 'state of war' in China after the COVID-19 outbreak.[74] Reports from the grassroots level are more informative. In one street in Luohu, Shenzhen, there are 81 grids, covering a total of 100,000 people. Another community with 15,000 people is divided into nine grids with six grid monitors.[75]

Grid monitors, like other community leaders and volunteers, play an indispensable role in the pandemic control operation. They serve multiple functions. First, they are the police within the gated community, checking and verifying the movement of residents, and especially isolating those who have returned from high-risk areas, persuading and forcing residents to comply with social distancing rules, stopping outsiders from entering their communities, deciding who can leave the community and for how long, and from time to time physically restraining or even assaulting residents who are trying to sneak out. Grid monitors and other grid workers may not be government officials, but they enjoy government powers.

Second, they serve as social workers and medics. They provide public health information and remind residents to take preventive measures; they answer questions from residents, offer comfort and therapies as best as they can, and in any event, maintain near-constant communications; they facilitate COVID-19 testing as the government requires; liaise with hospitals and quarantine facilities on behalf of residents who need quarantine at designated places; and they persuade senior citizens to get vaccinated.[76] Finally, they are service providers for residents under the SaH order, doing the tedious work of receiving food and other daily necessities ordered by residents and organising and coordinating deliveries and pick-ups.

'Sinking' and volunteering

The Party did not leave the *shequ* alone, of course, to enforce the SaH order. Effective enforcement of the regulations on the Chinese scale requires direct state support and also state supervision. China's President Xi Jinping called on 10 February 2020 for the construction of a people's frontline and demanded government officials and Party members 'sink' (*xiachen*) to the

called the "Chinese grid member") *Zhongguo shuzi shidai* (*China Digital Times*) October 3, 2021 available at: https://chinadigitaltimes.net/chinese/663429.html.

[74] Liu, Ziyang (2020) 450 wan wanggeyuan zhu lao yiqing shequ "di yi dao fangxian",' (4.5 million grid members build the first line of defense' for community prevention and control of the epidemic) Xinhua March 10, 2020 available at: http://www.xinhua- net.com/legal/2020-03/10/c_1210507945.htm.

[75] Sa, Ze 'Nerve endings' supra note 72.

[76] Wu, Lumu (2020) 'Chongqing Yubei: Wanggehua guanli "shi daowei" zhu lao fangyi zuihou yi gongli' (Chongqing Yubei: grid management 'ten in position' to strengthen the last mile of epidemic prevention') *Zhongguo Jingjiwang* (China Economic Net) February 7, 2020 available at: http://www.ce.cn/xwzx/gnsz/gdxw/202002/07/t20200207_34231032.shtml.

shequ during the lockdown.[77] In Wuhan, by 27 February 2020, close to half a million civil servants, employees in public institutes, and Party members were sent to communities to enforce the lockdown.[78] When Xi'an imposed its lockdown in late 2021, it sent 64,000 cadres to monitor and serve the 13 million people in the city.[79] There was a certain specificity as to who went where and a degree of stability in the temporary assignments. In a Wuhan example, eight Party members from a District Bureau of Justice, divided into two groups, were sent to assist the 9th and 10th grids of a community with a total of 760 households.[80] But there was no clear division of labour among these cadres, which led to complaints from those who had to perform whatever tasks were presented to them, including getting to know the communities by memorising the names and addresses of the residents, helping to check and verify the travel histories of residents, taking temperatures, or simply purchasing and delivering goods for residents.

The 'sinking' process is decisive, and even war-like and military in style. Mobilising cadres and marching them to specific grids requires rigid organisation and careful coordination. Life as a 'sinking' official was tough and risky, but working on the frontlines was a political mission of the highest order and a test of one's political loyalty. In addition to civil servants assigned by administrative decisions, the Party has also mobilised its members in other public sectors to serve in the *xiaoqu*. For example, school teachers are not civil servants and are not normally required to work at *xiaoqu* even if they are available. But teachers who are Party members were still called upon, as Party members, to 'volunteer' at a *xiaoqu*. Like civil servants, these Party members were assigned to a specific *xiaoqu* to join the pandemic control teams. The sheer size of the population under SaH orders necessitates societal support beyond those in the public sectors, and there were isolated calls by city governments for non-government organisations (NGOs) to also participate in serving the communities. When a new wave of the pandemic hit Xi'an at the end of 2021, the provincial government

77 Zhang, Xiaosong (2020)' Xi Jinping: Ganbu zhongxin xia yi, zhiyuan shequ yiqing fang kong', (Xi Jinping: The focus of cadres has shifted downward to support community epidemic prevention and control) Xinhua, February 10, 2020 available at http://www. xinhuanet.com/ politics/leaders/2020-02/10/c_1125556265.htm.

78 Cheng, Rongxing; Wang, Chenglong; Li, Yuan; Huang, Lei; and Wu, Chunxinxin (2020) 'Wuhan 4.45 wan dangyuan ganbu xia chen fang kong yixian'(44,500 party members and cadres in Wuhan go down to the front line of prevention and control), Hubeisheng Renmin Zhengfu (The People's Government of Hubei Province) February 28 2020 available at: http:// www.hubei.gov.cn/hbfb/ szsm/202002/t20200228_2161484.shtml.

79 He, Bin (2020) 'Xi'an yiqing zhi xia, shehui zuzhi dou qu nalile?' (Where did social organizations go during the Xi'an epidemic?), *Zhongguo cishan jia zazhi* (China Philanthropist Magazine), January 5, 2022 available at: https://mp.weixin.qq.com/s/ PnDMdX6flK6h99ynTDZ_Tw.

80 He, Xin (2020) 'Wuhan 1.7 wan yu dangyuan ganbu xia chen shequ da paicha quebao ying shou jin shou' (More than 17,000 party members and cadres in Wuhan have a large-scale investigation deep in the community to ensure that all receivables [that should be received] are collected) *Zhongguo Jingji Wang* (China Economic Net) February 11, 2020, available at http://www.ce.cn/xwzx/gnsz/gdxw/202002/11/t20200211_34245935.shtml.

made an uncharacteristic appeal to social organisations, largely those under government control, requesting them to reach out to their members to support the pandemic control work.[81] In general, the NGO sector did not play any visible role during the pandemic, due both to the crackdown on NGOs in China since 2013 and the demand for social distancing, although the spirit of volunteerism and charitable donations have continued and are highly visible in Chinese cities.[82] Through WeChat groups, volunteers in Guangzhou were assigned to RCs and, after some brief training, helped out at the many COVID-19 test centres.[83] Services that volunteers provided included looking after pets while their owners were placed under non-residential quarantine;[84] assisting with COVID-19 testing; providing online psychological therapy; or receiving calls from residents, registering their requests, and passing them on to *xiaoqu* leaders for further action.[85]

MAKING SAH ORDERS WORK

The pandemic control work, particularly the enforcement of SaH orders at the micro-level in *shequ* and *xiaoqu*, requires a supporting macro environment to succeed. This includes a high degree of political trust, positive and consistent messaging, and effective legal enforcement. The disciplined participation of residents in and their support of SaH orders are often conditioned on the existence of a positive environment.

Political trust

The relationship between social/political trust and levels of compliance with SaH orders and other SDMs is a contentious one. Some studies find positive correlations between trust and compliance. Thus, trust in decision-makers predicts higher levels of compliance with lockdown rules, with people in high-trust regions reducing their mobility significantly more than those

81 Yang, Xiaoling (2021) 'Shaanxī shèhuì zǔzhī "hélì kàng yì",' (Social Organizations in Shaanxi 'work together to fight the epidemic') *Shaanxi Sheng Renmin Zhengfu* (The People's Government of Shaanxi Province) December 31, 2021 available at: http://www.shaanxi.gov.cn/xw/ldx/bm/202112/t20211231_2206111_wap.html

82 Hu, Ming and Sidel, M (2020) 'Civil Society and COVID in China: Responses in an Authoritarian Society' (49) *Nonprofit and Voluntary Sector Quarterly* 1173.

83 Zou, Ling and Ye, Ziwen (2021) 'Shendi guancha: Guangzhou shequ fangyi yixian beihou de zhiyuan zhe liliang' (In-depth observation: Volunteers behind the frontline of community epidemic prevention in Guangzhou) *Nanfang Dushi Bao* (Southern Metropolis Daily), 4 June 2021 available at https:// xw.qq.com/partner/vivoscreen/20210604A0B0XO00.

84 Yang *Wuhan Lockdown* supra note 10.

85 Some of the requests were urgent. One household reported that it has nothing left to eat except some sugar and another requested medicines for an elderly person who had recently gone through an operation. Zhang, Yiyi (2021)'Feng cheng qi ri: Yi wei tonghua zhiyuan zhe de mi yu mang' (Seven days of closure of the city: the obsession and workload of a Tonghua volunteer) *Zhongguo Shuzi Shidai* (China Digital Times) January 25, 2021 available at https:// chinadigitaltimes.net/chinese/661993.html

in low-trust regions.[86] Others find a weak link. Mehari's study finds that people in traditionally high-trust countries behave more individualistically in defiance of SaH orders and, on the contrary, countries with low trust levels outperform their high-trust counterparts in following SaH orders—the fear of the virus and the mistrust of authorities may have forced people in low-trust countries to reach the conclusion that staying at home is the safest option.[87]

Trust is an anomalous issue in China. While China is a low-trust society in terms of interpersonal relations due to the prevailing familism,[88] political trust is high, and the Chinese population, in general, has shown a high level of trust in institutions. However, the trust is hierarchical, and, in China's vertically fragmented state, people place their trust predominantly in the central government rather than local government.[89] As the pandemic control narrative and rules, like other rules, come down from the central to the grassroots level for enforcement, the level of trust in government diminishes. The Chinese pandemic control experiences both reflect and reinforce Chinese political trust, though the lockdown in Shanghai may have caused a fresh challenge to the long-held political trust thesis in China.[90]

How is trust in government built and sustained? Facing a significant pandemic, the central government has put its heart, head, and hands to work in designing the people's war and has reiterated the priority of people's safety, health, and welfare.[91] This purposive mission, crystalised in a clear, positive, and confident tone, promotes solidarity and builds confidence.[92] At the city level, the people's war is multi-dimensional,

[86] Bargain, O and Aminjonov, U (2020) 'Trust and Compliance to Public Health Policies in Times of COVID-19' (192) *Journal of Public Economics*, available at: <https://doi.org/10.1016/j.jpubeco.2020.104316>.

[87] Mehari, Y (2020) 'The Role of Social Trust in Citizen Mobility During COVID-19' SSRN 3607668, 20 May 2020, https://dx.doi.org/10.2139/ssrn.3607668.

[88] Fukuyama, F (1996) *Trust: The Social Virtues and the Creation of Prosperity* Free Press at 87. For the development of the concept of amoral familism, see Huysseune, M (2020) 'Theory Travelling through Time and Space: The Reception of the Concept of Amoral Familism' (33) *International Journal of Politics, Culture, and Society* 365; Putnam, RD (1993) *Making Democracy Work. Civic Traditions in Modern Italy* Princeton University Press.

[89] Wu, G and Wilkes, R (2018) 'Local-National Political Trust Patterns: Why China Is an Exception' (39) *International Political Science Review* 436; Li, Lianjiang (2004) 'Political Trust in Rural China'(230) *Modern China* 228. For a revised and more nuanced view, see Li, Lianjiang (2016) 'Reassessing Trust in the Central Government: Evidence from Five National Surveys' (225) *The China Quarterly* 100. For a study on the relationship between political trust and effective enforcement of pandemic control measures, see Min, Chen; Shen, Fei; Yu, Wenting and Chu, Yajie (2020) 'The Relationship Between Government Trust and Preventive Behaviors during the COVID-19 Pandemic in China: Exploring the Roles of Knowledge and Negative Emotion' (141) *Preventive Medicine*, available at: <https://doi.org/10.1016/j.ypmed.2020.106288>.

[90] Minter, A 'Lockdown Anger in Shanghai Won't Fade Anytime Soon' *Bloomberg*, 12 April 2022, available at: <https://www.bloomberg.com/opinion/articles/2022-04-12/shanghai-s-lockdown-anger-won-t-fade-anytime-soon>.

[91] Yu 'An Analysis of China's Strategy' supra note 21.

[92] *The Lancet* (editorial) (2020) 'COVID-19 and China: Lessons and the Way Forward' (396) *The Lancet* 213.

combining paternalistic admonition with patient education, effective services, and punishment. There is close surveillance, but community surveillance is mostly embedded in and carried out through an interactive and dialogical process within the communities between sent-down officials, community leaders, volunteers, and residents. Residents under SaH orders are not mere recipients of a repressive system imprisoned in their homes just out of fear. They are active parties to a containment strategy that they share and have confidence in. Despite the initial failures, dismal in some aspects, the Wuhan lockdown showcased the faith that people had in the Party and their resilience to carry SaH orders through regardless of their pains, sufferings, and grievances.[93]

There are constant communications between the residents and community leaders through which concerns and anxieties are expressed, grievances aired, and suggestions made, all part of the semi-regulatory process of a close-knit community. Residents and the *shequ* leaders live together throughout the lockdown, sharing the same anxiety, fear, confidence and hope.[94] As the lockdown diaries have powerfully shown, residents followed and enforced all the pandemic control measures to protect their homes and their loved ones, and they cooperated 'out of a sense of civic responsibilities'.[95] Through the technologies-enhanced communicative process in crisis management, the communities become more transparent to the government, and their grievances, claims, and contentions become clear and better known. As a result, government controls and services become more tailor-made, subtle, and responsive. In an organic way, the grid system, which effectively embeds government control in service provisions and merges state surveillance of communities with residents' participation in neighbourhood affairs, offers a platform that has performed multiple and often conflicting functions in the grass-roots urban management. The grid is perhaps the most unique, effective, and significant instrument in the Party's toolkit of order maintenance.[96]

Standard and positive messaging

It requires more than adequate food and other daily necessities to maximise compliance and to make the lengthy and harsh SaH orders sustainable. Consistent with best practices in public health, the ability of a government to communicate with residents using clear and consistent messaging is indispensable to the effective enforcement of SDMs.[97] Indeed, a standardised and reassuring message is a Chinese strength unmatched by other countries, as the government is able to shape the tone of official and social media, with government officials, epidemiologists, reporters, and other stakeholders all

93 Yang *Wuhan Lockdown* supra note 10 at 79.

94 Ibid.

95 Ibid at 220.

96 Tang 'Grid Governance in China's Urban Middle-class Neighborhoods' supra note 33.

97 Boin, A; McConnell, A and 't Hart, P (2008) *Governing after Crisis: The Politics of Investigation, Accountability and Learning* Cambridge University Press.

speaking with one voice to the public.[98] Xi himself reiterated the importance of strengthening Party propaganda to reinforce the guidance of public opinion in crisis management.[99] Clear messages about the infectious nature of the virus could create fear, which might then reduce risky behaviours, while guidance for citizens would reduce anxieties and build confidence at moments of panic, ensuring the smooth implementation of SDMs.[100] Local media, new and traditional, offered a psychological safe house for residents by providing guidance and health education of various kinds by experts and regular briefings on recent developments.[101]

Standardised messaging requires censorship, and the Chinese government has achieved this with rigour. It has effectively silenced any alternative reporting, curbed public discussion and, in particular, punished rumour-mongering. Chinese law is well-equipped to subject anyone who spreads 'rumours' relating to the pandemic to police sanctions and criminal punishment, and police have been aggressive in placing those who spread rumours in police detention. In Beijing, for example, the police imposed the penalty of administrative detention, which could last for up to 15 days under Chinese law, on 610 individuals for violating pandemic control measures, and among them, 97 were for making or spreading pandemic-related rumours.[102]

In the meantime, government propaganda has been in full force to admonish residents not to generate, spread or believe in rumours, a message accompanied by regular clarification of facts and policies relating to the pandemic. This combination of proactive propaganda and education on the one hand, and rigorous censorship and police punishment on the other allows the government to generate a single narrative, convincing people that whatever measures have been taken are absolutely necessary for public safety and beneficial to individual interests. Whether the official narrative can be effective and persuasive is largely contingent on the evolving threat that COVID-19 poses and China's relative international standing

98 Schwartz 'Compensating for the "Authoritarian Advantage"' supra note 12.

99 Hart, M and Link, J 'Chinese President Xi Jinping's Philosophy on Risk Management' Center for American Progress, 20 February 2020, available at: <https://www.americanprogress.org/article/chinese-president-xi-jinpings-philosophy-risk-management>.

100 On how rumours caused panic in the society and reduced the effectiveness of the pandemic response in Taiwan in 2003, see Schwartz 'Compensating for the "Authoritarian Advantage"' supra note 12.

101 Zhang, Ni; Shi, Tianqin; Zhong, Heng and Guo, Yijia (2020) 'COVID-19 Prevention and Control Public Health Strategies in Shanghai, China' (26) *Journal of Public Health Management and Practice* 334, available at: <https://doi.org/10.1097/PHH.0000000000001202>.

102 Beijing Shi Renmin Zhengfu (2021) '2020 nian yiqing fangkong yilai chachu raoluan zhengchang fangyi zhixuIlei anjian 785 qi xingzheng juliu 513 ren' (Since the prevention and control of the epidemic in 2020, 785 cases of disrupting the normal epidemic prevention order have been investigated and dealt with, and 513 people have been administratively detained) Beijing Shi Renmin Zhengfu (The People's Government of Beijing Municipality) January 15, 2021 available at: http://www.beijing.gov.cn/ywdt/zwzt/yqfk/zxxx/202101/t20210115_2220826.html. 1

in pandemic control. The Shanghai lockdown seems to have created a remarkable decline in the narrative power of the government.

Rigid enforcement

The rigidity in the enforcement of SaH orders is staggering, often leading to human tragedies commonly regarded as preventable by exercising discretion. The political goal to contain COVID-19 and the assignment of designated officials to specific *xiaoqu* generates tremendous pressure on local government and community leaders, in particular sent-down cadres, to enforce SaH orders with little concern for costs, consequences, or responsibilities. As it happens, officials who were held responsible for even a tiny COVID-19 breakout by international standards were punished harshly and swiftly, often with immediate removal from leadership positions if not criminal prosecution, sending a sharp message that the responsibility to contain the pandemic is absolute and that negligence will not be tolerated. The flip side is equally true that no major officials have been held liable for taking harsh and excessive measures to prevent the spread of the virus.

Given the zero-COVID-oriented incentives, it would not be surprising that there is a great deal of local variation with leaders racing to the bottom in competing to design and enforce the toughest measures to prevent a pandemic breakout or even a single positive case.[103] Thus, while rules made at the central or provincial levels may balance effectiveness, fairness, and humanity, when the same rules are enforced at lower levels, fairness and humanitarian concerns are watered down, and more restrictions and additional controls would be added. This may be repeated at every stage in the process, and when the rules are enforced at the grassroots level, excessiveness and distortion become abundant. Those manning the gates literally decide who is allowed to leave the compound, who is prohibited from entering, how one should behave in the community, and what infractions of rules warrant police intervention. Under the enabling Contagious Disease Control Law, often broadly interpreted and rigorously enforced, any lack of compliance with a SaH order or SDMs has the potential to be regarded as a violation of the law and thus subject to police and criminal law sanctions.

New technologies, in particular the use of health codes, have enhanced China's capacity to monitor the travel and medical history of residents, track suspect cases for quarantine, and regulate social mobility in vulnerable times.[104] There is also the need to collect near-total information about citizens to make a sound assessment of public health risks and countries with different political systems have also used contact-tracing

[103] For an analysis of the distortion caused by target-oriented policy implementation, see Yang, DL (2017) 'China's Illegal Regulatory State in Comparative Perspective' (2) *Chinese Political Science Review* 114.

[104] Chaturvedi, A 'The China Way: Use of Technology to Combat Covid-19' *Geospatial World*, 5 November 2020, available at: <https://www.geospatialworld.net/article/the-sino-approach-use-of-technology-to-combat-covid-19>.

technologies to enforce pre-emptive and restrictive measures against the pandemic.[105] The Chinese government, working with tech giants, developed a monitoring design that can be easily and effectively used to determine whether a resident is entitled to leave their apartment and the degree of personal freedom that they can enjoy in public spaces. The deployment of the smartphone-based health code, coupled with the use of a massive surveillance system and AI-enhanced analytics, makes the Chinese *xiaoqu* the most closely monitored place in the world, 'rendering citizens to a state of permanent visibility'.[106]

There are few legal or political constraints on mass surveillance, and government surveillance and monitoring of individuals are taken for granted and commonly accepted if not welcomed. Personal data, in China's collective society, does not enjoy the same level of appreciation and protection as has been the case in liberal counterparts, allowing the government to monitor citizens, gather their information, and develop a data-driven pandemic control strategy without giving much consideration to privacy.[107]

At the same time, the state has aggressively prosecuted and otherwise punished residents who may have violated social distancing rules. In 2020, there were 5,474 pandemic-related criminal trials in China,[108] and the number rose to 9,653 in 2021, a 76 per cent increase.[109] However, the number of prosecutions that were instituted by the procuratorate in pandemic-related cases witnessed a 63.7 per cent decline from 11,234 in 2020[110] to 4,078 in 2021,[111] indicating a likely decline in convictions in 2022.

The number of police punishments far exceeded that of criminal prosecutions. For example, the numbers of criminal detentions (which may lead to prosecution) and those of administrative detention were: 88 and 3,458 respectively in Heilongjiang between January and March 2020;[112] 74 and 1,910 in Inner Mongolia between January and February 2020;[113] 261

105 Liang, Fan (2020) 'COVID-19 and Health Code: How Digital Platforms Tackle the Pandemic in China' (6) *Social Media + Society* 2.

106 Ibid at 3.

107 Ibid.

108 ' Xinhua (2021) 'Lianghui shouquan fabu) zuigao renmin fayuan gongzuo baogao (As authorized by the two sessions, the Work Report of the Supreme People's Court) *Xinhua* (New China News Agency) March 15, 2021 available at: http://www.xinhuanet.com/politics/2021lh/2021-03/15/c_1127212486.htm.

109 'Supreme People's Court 'Zuigao Renmin Fayuan Baogao' (Report of the Supreme People's Court) March 8, 2022 available at: https://www.court.gov.cn/zixun-xiangqing-349601.html.

110 Xinhua Supra note 108

111 Supra note 109.

112 ''Heilongjiang sheng gong'an jiguan banli 4825 qi she yi weifa fanzui anjian' (Heilongjiang Provincial Public Security Organs Handled 4,825 Epidemic-related Illegal and Criminal Cases) *Baidu*, 15 March 2020 available at: https://baijiahao.baidu.com/s?id=1661228712202321617&wfr=spider&for=pc.

113 'Neimenggu kuai zhen kuai po she yi anjian 2078 qi'(Inner Mongolia quickly detects and

and 278 in Hunan between January and April 2020; 521 and 2,942 in Henan between January and March 2020.[114]

CONCLUSION

The Chinese success to date in containing COVID-19 relies on its ability to mobilise the entire society to participate in the people's war against the pandemic,[115] particularly in organising residents, through persuasion and discipline, into compliance. The social structure in place prior to the outbreak involves multiple government departments, commercial firms, and civil society organisations, combining state guidance and community volunteerism in developing co-governance at the grassroots urban level. That structure, energised by the strong will of the Party, has proved indispensable to China's containment strategies.[116] The same *shequ* system was used in the past to enforce the One Child Policy, root out 'evil cults' like Falun Gong, and keep suspicious outsiders at a distance. City lockdowns and efficient hospitalisation are strategies that can be replicated in different societies, but the Chinese way of community organising and participation, based on the unique Chinese urban governance design and social ecosystem, as demonstrated in this essay, is hard to transplant.[117]

Politics is also local in China, and it is at the basic level of SOs and RCs that millions of Chinese residents participate in national politics. Through socialised governance within their own gated communities, they interact with government departments, air their grievances, and settle their daily disputes. Life in the gated communities is rich, thick, and largely

solves 2,078 epidemic-related cases) *Baidu*, February 21, 2020, available at: https://baijiahao.baidu.com/s?id=1659127177068731591&wfr=spider&for=pc.

[114] Li Guigang, '河南加强境外输入性疫情防控 查处6757宗涉疫犯罪案', *Eastday*, 12 March 2020, available at: <http://news.eastday.com/eastday/13news/auto/news/society/20200312/u7ai9153153.html>. Wan Qingli (2020) 'Henan chachu sheyi weifa fanzui anjian 6,757qi huhang fugong renyuan 380 wan renci' (Henan investigated and dealt with 6,767 cases of ilegal and criminal cases related to the epidemic, escorting 3.8 million returnees.), March 13, 2020, *China Radio International*, available at: https://hn.cri.cn/2020-03-13/2fe05bf4-4d5a-9d19-2660-4ea553db2276.html

[115] 'Shequ, shehui gongzuo, shehui zuzhi canyu yiqing fang kong zhuanjia tan (Qinghua Daxue Li Qiáng jiàoshòu, Nankai Daxué Guan Xinping jiaoshou, Shanghai Jiaotong Dàxué Xu Jialiang jiaoshou)' (Community, social work, and social organizations' participation in epidemic prevention and control expert talks [Professor Li Qiang from Tsinghua University, Professor Guan Xinping from Nankai University, and Professor Xu Jialiang from Shanghai Jiaotong University') December 20, 2021 available at: https://www.163.com/dy/article/G39VSBKR0523 N11P.html.

[116] Yang, Tuan (2020) 'Shehui liliang zai shequ fangyi zhong de zuoyong he nanti' (Yang Tuan: Zhongguo shehui kexueyuan shehuixue yanjiusuo yanjiuyuan, shehui zhengce yanjiu zhongxin guwen Yang Tuan)'(The role and problems of social forces in community epidemic prevention) (Yang Tuan, researcher at the Institute of Sociology, Chinese Academy of Social Sciences, consultant of the Social Policy Research Center)', *Fenghuang Xinwen* (Pheonix News) April 1, 2020 available at: https://ishare.ifeng.com/c/s/v002PNvo9-_YcmquDjEqn9UmMDV49S0ulodYR-_ceabFN1dxw; also available at: https://ishare.ifeng.com/c/s/7vJmslTYe1N

[117] Ibid.

autonomous, forming what Yang refers to as the 'moral communities', the constant gaze of the state notwithstanding.[118]

Be they elderly residents, retired cadres, or the newly recruited grid monitors, all are simultaneously agents of the government and representatives of the communities, continuing to serve as a transmission belt to connect the Party with society. For the Party, these local agents make the numerous gated communities that dot Chinese cities observable, comprehensible and manageable. For citizens, their representatives provide easier access to power to have their personal and community concerns heard and maybe even addressed. The government, with all its power and resources, is too important to hide from and definitely not to be pushed away. Through the platform of the parastate, now actively organised by grid monitors, local welfare is promoted, and local problems are addressed, but more importantly, promoted and addressed with the participation and input of the local communities themselves.

China's pandemic control measures and the SaH orders take place within neighbourhood structures. Community mobilisation forms the core of the Chinese pandemic containment strategy and has proven to be the most crucial aspect of China's strategy to date. Even the experiences in Shanghai's lockdown in 2022, when the *shequ* system was stretched to a breaking point, prove, in a negative way, that there is no alternative to the existing urban design, calling for further solidification, reinforcement, and legitimisation of the existing social and political system of the Chinese neighbourhood in the post-crisis era. In coming out of the crisis, *shequ* governance, with all its innovation and upgrading, will remain a public-private partnership under the renewed leadership of the Party at the grassroots level.

GLOSSARY OF CHINESE TERMS

Romanisation (Hanyu Pinyin)	Chinese Characters	English Translation
baojia	保甲	neighbourhood watch system
paichusuo	派出所	police station
shequ	社区	residential community
shequ jingwu	社区警务	community policing
weiwen	维稳	to maintain social stability
xiachen	下沉	to sink
xiaoqu	小区	small community

[118] Yang *Wuhan Lockdown* supra note 10 at 221.

Police Powers to Punish Law and Order Violations: Controversies and Recurring Issues

YAN MEI NING

Institute of Advanced Legal Studies (University of London)

INTRODUCTION

The Law on Penalties for Administration of Public Security (LPAPS) is the key legislation upon which the Chinese police rely to administer law and order at the community level.[1] LPAPS authorizes and regulates all-encompassing police powers against individuals who have allegedly committed relatively minor unlawful acts that are not subject to prosecution under the Criminal Law (CL) but which are considered to cause harm to society by disrupting public order, endangering public safety, infringing upon the rights of others, or impeding the management of society.[2]

The police are entrusted with the sole responsibility for investigating LPAPS offences, determining whether to impose penalties on alleged offenders, and executing any penalties imposed. Such LPAPS police powers, classified as administrative, do not fall under the purview of the criminal justice system. Individuals summoned, interrogated, and ultimately punished by the police under LPAPS are denied access to lawyers throughout the process. Furthermore, the police may impose administrative detention, without a court trial, on LPAPS offenders for up to 20 days. As such, LPAPS has granted police officers enormous powers, posing a significant threat to the rights and freedoms of ordinary people in China. Over the years, controversial incidents related to LPAPS enforcement

[1] The Standing Committee of the National People's Congress (hereafter, NPCSC) (2005) 'Zhonghua renmin gongheguo zhi'an guanli chufafa' (The Law of the People's Republic of China on Penalties for Administration of Public Security) (hereafter, LPAPS) (Enacted on 28 August 2005; amended on 26 October 2012). Available at *Beida Fabao*. An English version is available at http://www.npc.gov.cn/zgrdw/englishnpc/Law/2007-12/13/content_1384114.htm. The author has made modifications to the English translations where appropriate. The main parts of this book chapter were written in early 2025. In late June 2025, the NPCSC completed a major revision of LPAPS. The revised legislation will take effect on 1 January 2026. Available at *Beida Fabao*.

[2] When referring to cases of LPAPS offences, the Chinese authorities use the term "law-and-order cases" (*zhi'an anjian*) to differentiate them from "criminal cases" (*xingshi anjian*). See, for example, 'Anquan zhishu lianxu baochi gaoshuiping: renmin qunzhong anquanqan buduan tisheng' (Safety Index Continues to Remain at a High Level – People's Safety Feeling Continues to Rise) *Renmin Ribao* (*People's Daily*) 28 August 2024. Available at <https://www.gov.cn/lianbo/bumen/202408/content_6970925.htm>. In plain terms, "law-and-order cases" address neighbourhood petty law-and-order violations, while "criminal cases" deal with more serious unlawful acts. This chapter uses "law-and-order cases", "law-and-order violations", and "cases involving LPAPS offences" interchangeably.

have sparked public outcry and alarm. Complaints included the misuse of the legislation, exercise of broad police discretion, and the abuse of police power. Chinese law expert Jerome Cohen characterised the main thrust of LPAPS as generating low-level, low-visibility police oppression.[3]

This chapter begins with an overview of LPAPS police powers, highlighting safeguards introduced in 2005 and the related criticism.[4] It is followed by a recount of six notable incidents related to controversial LPAPS police powers. The primary task of this chapter is to examine the first-instance court judgments in 225 administrative lawsuits appealing police penalty decisions made shortly before or during the COVID-19 pandemic. The survey aims to identify recurring issues in LPAPS enforcement and assess whether these six notable cases were isolated incidents or part of a more prevalent phenomenon.

The research questions concerning police powers and LPAPS enforcement considered in this Chapter are: 1) How frequently and pervasively were complaints regarding the misuse of LPAPS, the exercise of broad police discretion, and abuses of police power? 2) Were LPAPS's built-in safeguards and appeal mechanisms effective? 3) Has LPAPS enabled police oppression or even facilitated political oppression? 4) Has LPAPS offered an efficient and lenient approach to resolving local disputes and tackling petty unlawful acts? And lastly, 5) Have LPAPS rationales been met, justifying the legislation's continuation in its existing form?

LPAPS AND POLICE POWERS TO PUNISH: AN OVERVIEW

LPAPS and Its Historical Evolution

The origin of LPAPS dates to 1908 when the Qing Dynasty promulgated the Great Qing Code on Police Offences (*Daqing Weijinglü*) to enhance the authority of a new modern police force.[5] During the Republican era, the legislation was renamed the Law for the Punishment of Police Offences (LPPO) (*Weijing Fafa*) and was thoroughly revised in 1943.[6] By then, it was

[3] Cohen, J (2020) 'Implications of the Coronavirus Crisis for China's Legal System' 10 February 2020. Available at <https://www.jeromecohen.net/jerrys-blog/2020/2/10/implications-of-the-coronavirus-crisis-for-chinas-legal-system>.

[4] This chapter focuses on LPAPS enforcement by the police. For recent research on policing in China, see, generally, Scoggins, SE (2021) *Policing China: Street-Level Cops in the Shadow of Protest* Cornell University Press; Biddulph, S (2023) 'Transformation in Policing Minor Offending in China' in Chen, WT and Fu, HL (eds) (2023) *Regime Type and Beyond: The Transformation of Police in Asia* Cambridge University Press.

[5] Shen, L (2011) 'Zhongguo jindai zhi'an chufa fagui de yanbian: yi weijingfafa de quxingfahua wei shijia' (Evolution of the Legislation on Penalties Against Law-and-Order Violations: The Decriminalization of 'The Law for the Punishment of Police Offences') 29(4) *Zhengfa Luntan* (*Tribune of Political Science and Law*) 179.

[6] For an English account of the evolution of the legislation from 1915 to 1987, see Bracey,

firmly established that the police were granted administrative powers to punish unlawful acts at the community level without judicial oversight, curbing various problems arising from rapid urbanization.[7] This impacted almost every aspect of daily life, and the legislation also made people submissive to the ruling regime.[8]

The Chinese Communist Party (CCP) came into power in 1949, repealing all laws of the Republican era.[9] In the early 1950s, local police officers were instructed, first informally and later by an internal document, to refer to the 1943 LPPO when addressing law-and-order violations at the community level.[10] In late 1957, the Standing Committee of the National People's Congress, the national legislature, promulgated the Regulations on Penalties for Administration of Public Security (RPAPS).[11] As a watered-down version of the 1943 LPPO, RPAPS existed long before CL was promulgated in 1979. The legislation aimed to maintain social order by punishing "bad elements" who were not considered "counter-revolutionaries" and other less well-behaved individuals with undesirable habits, lifestyles or corrupt morals.[12] RPAPS remained unchanged for three decades and fell into disuse during the Cultural Revolution. A new RPAPS came into effect in 1987, with further amendments made in 1994, but the legislation was still rudimentary.

D (1989) 'The Regulation of the People's Republic of China Concerning Punishments for Disturbing Order: The Police and Administrative Punishment' 14 (2) *Criminal Justice Review* 154.

[7] Shen 'Evolution' supra note 5.

[8] Article 58, for example, punishes those who did not salute, when directed, the National Flag and Anthem, or a portrait of the Republic's founding father. See also Shen, L (2012) 'Xinshenghuo yundong yu zhongguo jindai de zhi'an chufafa – yi fanghai fengsulei zhi'an chufa de lifa yanbian wei shijiao' ('New Life Movement and Modern China's Legislation on Penalties Against Law-and-Order Violations: Legislative Evolution of Penalties on Offending Public Morals) 2012(1) *Bijiaofa Yanjiu* (*Journal of Comparative Law*) 16.

[9] Zhongguo gongchandang diqijie zhongyang weiyuanhui (Chinese Communist Party 7th Central Committee) (1949) 'Zhonggong zhongyang guanyu feichu guomindang de liufaquanshu yu queding jiefangqu de sifa yuanze de zhishi (The CCP Central Committee Instructions on Abolition of Kuomintang Six Codes and Confirmation of Liberated Zone's Judicial Doctrines). See also Chen, A (2018) *An Introduction to the Legal System of the People's Republic of China* (5th ed) LexisNexis at 28-34.

[10] 'Xinzhongguo zhi'an lifa wushinian: cong tiaoli dao fa jiannan qicao qingyi tongguo' (New China's Fifty Years of Law-and-Order Legislation: From Regulations to Law, Painstaking Drafting and Readily Enactment) *Jiancha Ribao* (*Procuratorate Daily*) 27 August 2009. Available at <https://news.ifeng.com/c/7fYTQrKES42>.

[11] NPCSC (1957) 'Zhonghua renmin gongheguo zhi'an guanli chufa Tiaoli' (People's Republic of China Regulations on Penalties for Administration of Public Security) (hereafter, RPAPS) (Enacted on 22 October 1957 and repealed on 1 January 1987).

[12] Luo, RQ (1957) 'Guanyu zhonghua renmin gongheguo zhi'an guanli chufa tiaoli cao'an de shuoming' (Explanatory Notes to the Bill of 'Regulations on the Penalties for Administration of Public Security'), reprinted in 120 *Guowuyuan Gongbao* (*State Council Gazette*) 979. Luo was the then Minister for Public Security.

LPAPS: Offences and Penalties

Following a major revamp and significant expansion in 2005, RPAPS was renamed LPAPS, with further minor amendments made in 2012.[13] As it stands, LPAPS has six chapters. comprising 119 provisions.

Chapter 3 stipulates various law-and-order violations, along with the associated police penalties. There are four categories: a) acts that disrupt public order, including "picking quarrels and provoking trouble" (*xunxin zishi*) (Article 26); b) acts that endanger public safety; c) acts that infringe upon the rights of others, such as "assault" (Article 43), "theft" and "damage to property" (Article 49), etc.; and d) acts that impede the management of society. The last category is the broadest, a total of 26 provisions, ranging from the prohibition of prostitution, drugs, gambling, and noise pollution, to the keeping of animals that threaten others. For a violation committed by a unit (*danwei*), individuals directly in charge or directly responsible would be penalized.[14]

Chapter 2 stipulates four types of penalty: a) warnings; b) fines; c) detention; and d) revocation of licences issued by the police. The maximum detention period for one offence is 15 days, and 20 days for two or more offences. Detention is mandatory for many offences, including Articles 26 and 49. In addition, those offenders who repeatedly commit unlawful acts relating to organizing or facilitating prostitution, producing or disseminating pornographic materials, or gambling, etc., can be subject to compulsory educational measures.[15] Police penalty decisions can be appealed by filing an administrative review or bringing administrative litigation.[16]

LPAPS: New Safeguards and Protection of Human Rights

Article 5 of Chapter 1 (General Provisions), introduced in 2005, stipulates that the imposition of LPAPS penalties must be based on facts and proportionate to the nature and circumstances of the violation, as well as the extent of harm caused to society. Penalty enforcements are required to be open and fair, respecting and safeguarding human rights and protecting the dignity of citizens. The long-standing socialist penal principle of "integrating education into punishment" is to be upheld in handling law-and-order cases. A new and separate chapter on "law enforcement

[13] Pei, ZB and Wang, LL (2015) 'The Evolution and Survey of Chinese Legal System of Penalties for Administration of Public Security' 12 *US-China Law Review* 695.

[14] Article 18.

[15] Article 76.

[16] Article 102. For detailed rules and regulations on administrative review, see NPCSC (2023) 'Zhonghua renmin gongheguo xingzheng fuyifa' (Administrative Reconsideration Law of the People's Republic of China) (Enacted on 29 April 1999; latest revision on 1 September 2023). For detailed rules and regulations on administrative litigation, see NPCSC (2017) 'Zhonghua renmin gongheguo xingzheng susongfa' (Administrative Litigation Law of the People's Republic of China) (Enacted by NPC on 4 April 1989; amended by NPCSC in 2014 and 2017).

supervision" (Chapter 5) was included. Article 116 stipulates more than ten types of police malpractices that attract administrative sanctions or criminal liability. Topping the list are coerced confessions, the use of physical punishment, torture, or insult. Moreover, anyone can report or complain to public security organs (*gong'an jiguan*), the procuratorates or administrative supervisory bodies concerning police misconduct.[17]

Chapter 4 details the procedures that police officers must follow when investigating LPAPS offences and deciding and executing penalties. Recusal arrangements have been introduced to prevent conflicts of interest. Several new provisions strengthen safeguards for alleged offenders. These include informing the suspect of the reason and basis of the summons and notifying a family member. At least two officers must be present when conducting searches, and female officers shall conduct searches of female offenders. The interrogation period shall not exceed eight hours, but can be extended to 24 hours if the case is complicated, and a detention penalty may be imposed. Parents, guardians, or adults in specified categories must be present when youngsters under 16 are interrogated. Suspects are to cross-check and countersign interrogation records. Moreover, a penalty decision cannot be based solely on a confession. The offender shall receive the penalty decision in written form containing specific details. Family members shall be notified if detention is imposed.

In sum, LPAPS not only authorizes police powers and their exercise, but also attempts to regulate these powers strictly. Notably, the new safeguards are strikingly similar to those stipulated in criminal procedure laws. Around 2005, several favourable factors contributed to the birth of this revamped legislation, which placed greater emphasis on balancing police powers with individuals' rights. These included China's signing of the International Covenant on Civil and Political Rights (ICCPR) in 1998 and the insertion of a clause on respecting human rights in the revised PRC Constitution of 2004.

Reactions towards LPAPS were mixed. Some hailed it as modernized legislation with sufficient safeguards.[18] Some others, including overseas human rights bodies, maintained that LPAPS had not gone far enough to protect ordinary people from possible police abuses. Amnesty International proposed that punitive administrative detention, incompatible with Articles 9 and 14 of the ICCPR, should be eliminated altogether and that all sanctions resulting in deprivation of liberty should be brought within the scope of CL and Criminal Procedure Law.[19]

[17] Article 114. See also 'Dui zhi'an anjian zhifa xingwei ji chufa jueding bufu, nengfou xiang jianchayuan shenqing jiandu' (If Dissatisfied with Law-and-order Enforcement and Penalty Decisions, Can Apply to Procuratorate for Supervision?) 23 August 2021. Available at <https://www.spp.gov.cn/spp/zdgz/202108/t20210823_527315.shtml>.

[18] Wang JG (2006) 'Public Security Penalties Law Respects, Protects Human Rights' 5(1) *Human Rights* 31.

[19] Amnesty International (2006) 'China: Abolishing "Re-education Through Labour" and Other Forms of Punitive Administrative Detention: An Opportunity to Bring the Law into

The United Nations (UN) General Comment No. 35 (on Liberty and Security of Person, Article 9 of the ICCPR) regards administrative detention as presenting serious risks of arbitrary deprivation of liberty.[20] Shortly before the enactment of LPAPS, a UN working group on arbitrary detention visited China, and stated in its report: "Even if the Chinese authorities might be led by the good intention to provide a milder system of sanctions for petty criminals, the result of removing them from the criminal system is ultimately that they are stripped of the guarantees surrounding criminal procedures."[21] Widespread criticisms of China's punitive administrative detention have led to the abolition of "Re-education Through Labour" (laodong jiaoyang) in late 2013, but police-administered penalties under LPAPS remained (and still remain) intact.

LPAPS: Rationales for Its Continuing Existence

Criminal Law and LPAPS have formed a two-tier sanctions system.[22] MZ Wang summarized reasons for the continued existence of LPAPS police powers to punish law-and-order violations.[23] First, for the CCP, LPAPS offenders were not class enemies, and their unlawful acts were considered "internal contradictions among the people." Second, influenced by the Soviet legal traditions during the 1950s, minor unlawful acts causing less harm to society were differentiated from crimes and handled differently. Lastly, there was a practical consideration for the Chinese authorities: the police could swiftly deal with these minor offences, sparing the courts' time and resources. In brief, LPAPS has been offering an efficient and lenient approach to tackling minor unlawful acts.

NOTABLE INCIDENTS ARISING FROM USE OF LPAPS POLICE POWERS

This section recounts six notable incidents that occurred in the past decade. They illustrate how vulnerable ordinary people, including well-educated

Line with the International Covenant on Civil and Political Rights. Memorandum to the State Council and the Legislative Committee of the National People's Congress of the People's Republic of China.' Available at <https://www.amnesty.org/en/documents/asa17/016/2006/en/>.

[20] United Nations Human Rights Committee (2014) 'General Comment No. 35 (Article 9, Liberty and Security of Person)' UN Doc CCPR/C/GC/35.

[21] United Nations Commission on Human Rights (2004) 'Report of the Working Group on Arbitrary Detention, Addendum: Mission to China' 29 Dec 2004 UN Doc E/CN.4/2005/6/Add.4 at para 55. Available at <https://docs.un.org/en/E/CN.4/2005/6/Add.4>.

[22] NPCSC (2023) 'Zhonghua renmin gongheguo xing fa (2023 xiuzheng)' (Criminal Law of the People's Republic of China, 2023 Revision) (Enacted by NPC on 1 July 1979; latest revision by NPCSC on 29 December 2023).

[23] Wang, MZ (2024) 'Zhi'an guanli xingzheng chufa de zhengdangxing zhengcheng ji zhidu wanshan' (A Study of Law-and-Order Administrative Penalties: Legitimacy and Improvements) 99 *Zhongguo Zhengfa Daxue Xuebao (Journal of Chinese University of Political Science and Law)* 121 at 128.

professionals, could be when encountering use of the controversial LPAPS police powers.

The Case of Dr Li Wenliang

In Wuhan, Dr Li Wenliang warned his fellow medics in late December 2019 through a chat group after learning several patients had contracted a new deadly coronavirus (later known as COVID-19) in a market.[24] He was cautious enough to remind them not to disseminate his messages further. Within days, Dr Li was summoned to a local police station (*paichusuo*) for violating LPAPS. There, he was interrogated and made to sign an admonition letter, confessing to the unlawful act of spreading untrue statements regarding coronavirus cases and seriously disrupting social order.

Dr Li contracted COVID-19 a week later, and he posted the admonition letter online from his hospital bed. He told the *New York Times*: "I felt I was being wronged, but I had to accept it."[25] He died in early February 2020. Dr Li was widely hailed as the COVID-19 Whistleblower. His ordeal at the local police station and subsequent death aroused immense public anger throughout China. In a rare move, the central authorities in Beijing retracted the police decision, noting it was improper and contained procedural irregularities.[26]

In this incident, the police also reprimanded seven other doctors for violating LPAPS.[27] In mid-February 2020, state media reported that the Chinese police had taken swift action nationwide against approximately 5,000 cases of fabricating or disseminating false and harmful information about the spread of a new coronavirus.[28]

[24] Hegarty, S (2020) 'The Chinese Doctor Who Tried to Warn Others About Coronavirus' *BBC* 6 February 2020. Available at <https://www.bbc.co.uk/news/world-asia-china-51364382#:~:text=Dr%20Li%2C%2034%2C%20tried%20to,for%20at%20least%20three%20weeks>.

[25] 'He Warned of Coronavirus. Here's What He Told Us Before He Died' *New York Times* 7 February 2020. Available at <https://www.nytimes.com/2020/02/07/world/asia/Li-Wenliang-china-coronavirus.html>.

[26] Guojia jiancha weiyuanhui diaochazu (National Supervisory Commission Investigation Team) (2020) 'Guanyu qunzhong fanying de sheji liwenliang yisheng youguan qingkuang diaocha de tongbao' (A Public Circular on The Investigation Regarding Concerns of the Mass for Dr Li Wenliang) 19 March 2020. Available at <http://politics.people.com.cn/n1/2020/0320/c1001-31640288.html>.

[27] Hegarty 'The Chinese Doctor' supra note 24.

[28] Xiong, J (2020) 'Quanguo yiliao jiuzhi zhixu zongti pingwen youxu' (Medical Treatment and Care Nationwide Is Smooth and Orderly) *Renmin Ribao Haiwaiban* (*People's Daily Overseas Edition*) 22 February 2020. Available at <http://paper.people.com.cn/rmrbhwb/html/2020-02/22/content_1972481.htm>.

The Case of Lei Yang, A Young Scholar

The case of Lei Yang, a young scholar, also attracted widespread attention.[29] One evening in May 2016, Lei left his home to travel to Beijing Airport to pick up his grandmother.[30] However, Lei did not appear at the airport but died soon afterwards. The police claimed Lei was caught visiting a foot massage parlour during an LPAPS enforcement operation.[31] Lei resisted forcibly and suddenly became very ill and was pronounced dead upon arrival at a hospital. Lei's family did not believe in the police account.[32] The authorities refuted an accusation of police entrapment.[33]

Lei's autopsy report and later investigations by the Beijing procuratorate confirmed that the police's forceful actions and delays in offering medical treatment contributed to Lei's death. The procuratorate also found that five police officers had committed "dereliction of duty" under the CL but decided against prosecuting them, considering the circumstances as minor. Instead, they would be subject to the CCP's internal disciplinary measures.[34]

The Case of Simon Cheng, who Worked for the UK Government

Simon Cheng was a local employee at the United Kingdom (UK) Consulate in Hong Kong. On 8th August 2019, he went missing during a one-day business trip in mainland China. By 20th August, China's Foreign Ministry spokesman confirmed that Cheng was in detention in Shenzhen for 15 days for soliciting a prostitute.[35] On 24th August, Cheng was released and returned to Hong Kong.[36]

[29] United States Congressional Executive Commission on China (2017) 'Chinese Authorities Decided Not to Prosecute Police Officers Found to Have Caused a Beijing Resident's Death' 16 May 2017. Available at <https://www.cecc.gov/publications/commission-analysis/chinese-authorities-decided-not-to-prosecute-police-officers-found>.

[30] Kaiman, J 'A Mysterious Death in China Raises Suspicions of Police Brutality' *Los Angeles Times* 10 May 2016. Available at<https://www.latimes.com/world/asia/la-fg-china-police-brutality-20160510-snap-story.html>; 'Qingnian xuezhe lei yang shepiao beizhua siwangqian de zuihou liangxiaoshi' (The Last Two Hours Before Death of Young Scholar Lei Yang who was Arrested for Allegedly Soliciting a Prostitute) *Pengpai Xinwen* (*The Paper*) 11 May 2017. Available at <https://m.thepaper.cn/kuaibao_detail.jsp?contid=1467561&from=kuaibao>.

[31] Id.

[32] Wu, WC (2016) 'Guanyu yaoqiu beijingshi jianchayuan li'an zhencha lei yang beihaian de xingshi baoanshu' (A Copy of the Filing of a Criminal Case Requesting the Beijing Procuratorate to Investigate the Killing of Lei Yang) 16 May 2016. Available at <https://wqw2010.blogspot.com/2016/05/blog-post_25.html> Wu was Lei's wife.

[33] 'Leiyang'an wuming she'an jingwurenyuan buyu qisu' (Five Police Officers in Lei Yang's Case Won't be Prosecuted) *Ciaxin* 23 December 2016. Available at <https://china.caixin.com/2016-12-23/101030078.html>.

[34] Id; US CECC 'Chinese Authorities' supra note 29.

[35] 'Hong Kong: China Confirms Detention of UK Consulate Worker' *BBC* 21 August 2019. Available at <https://www.bbc.co.uk/news/world-asia-china-49419711>.

[36] 'China Releases British Consulate Worker Detained at Border' *BBC* 24 August 2019.

Cheng later claimed in a *BBC* interview that he had been tortured and forced to confess to the LPAPS offence.[37] According to Cheng, the Chinese police sought to extract information from him regarding the UK government's involvement in the 2019 Hong Kong political unrest. The then-British Foreign Secretary, Dominic Raab, summoned the Chinese Ambassador to express outrage at Cheng's brutal and disgraceful treatment.[38] In response, the Chinese state media, *The People's Daily*, published a confession video by Cheng, showing that he had visited a massage parlour three times in the summer of 2019. [39] *The Global Times*, affiliated with *The People's Daily*, also quoted a woman who maintained Cheng was willing to pay more for extra services.[40]

Rare Convictions of Three Police Officers in Early 2025

In early 2025, several Chinese media outlets reported the rare convictions of three police officers in Xining, Qinghai.[41] In late August 2023, Mr Sun and his mother were taken to a local police station because the elderly woman had skipped the daily COVID-19 tests.[42] Once there, she was severely scolded by the police. Several officers dragged Sun into a female toilet and assaulted him. He suffered multiple injuries, with broken ribs and a swollen face. Sun initially agreed to settle the case through mediation. But he later lodged a formal complaint after learning a police officer who had assaulted him was still on duty and denied any wrongdoing. The local procuratorate intervened, resulting in the criminal prosecution of the three police officers for wilful assault. Nonetheless, they were only each given a nine-month

Available at <https://www.bbc.co.uk/news/world-asia-china-49445555>.

[37] Sudworth, J (2019) 'Simon Cheng: Former UK Consulate Worker Says He was Tortured in China' *BBC* 20 November 2019. Available at <https://www.bbc.co.uk/news/world-asia-china-50457262>.

[38] UK Foreign and Commonwealth Office (2019) 'Foreign Secretary statement on Simon Cheng' 20 November 2019. Available at<https://www.gov.uk/government/news/foreign-secretary-statement-on-simon-cheng-20-november-2019>.

[39] Chan, H (2019) 'Chinese State Media Publish "Confession" Video of Former UK Consulate Staffer Simon Cheng' *Hong Kong Free Press* 21 November 2019. Available at <https://hongkongfp.com/2019/11/21/chinese-state-media-publish-confession-video-former-uk-consulate-staffer-simon-cheng/>.

[40] Tang, D (2019) 'China Releases Video of Former UK Official Simon Cheng "in Massage Parlour"' *The Times* 21 November 2019. Available at <https://www.thetimes.com/world/article/china-releases-video-of-former-uk-official-simon-cheng-in-massage-parlour-ph83c67jm>.

[41] 'Nanzi paichusuo zao jingyuan qunou, jianfang jianyi shiyong huanxing helima?' (Five Police Officers Assaulted a Man at Local Police Station, Reasonable for Procuratorate to Suggest Suspended Sentences?) *QQ.com* 26 January 2025. Available at <https://news.qq.com/rain/a/20250126A07Y8Y00>.

[42] 'Muqin paichusuo li zao minjing zema, nanzi chahuahou bei tuojin nüce qunou, jingfang duoci tensiliao' (Mum Scolded in Local Police Station, Man Intervened but then Dragged into Female Toilet and Assaulted by Police Officers, Police Tried Many Times Asking the Man to Settle the Case Privately) *Dafeng Xinwen* 4 July 2024. Available at <https://news.qq.com/rain/a/20240704A06L4200>.

suspended sentence upon conviction because they had confessed to the crime and paid damages to Sun.

The Case of Chris Zhang, an IT Worker

On 13 October 2022, a lone protester, Peng Zaizhou, boldly criticized China's Zero-COVID policy and lack of democracy by displaying two banners on the Sitong Bridge in Beijing.[43] To show his support for Peng, Chris Zhang, an IT worker, disseminated Peng's protest slogans four days later in Chengdu via the Apple Airdrop function to more than 300 subway train passengers. One recipient reported Zhang to the police.[44]

Within days, the police arrived at Zhang's office, slapped him, and took him to a police station. He was strip-searched and then handcuffed throughout the interrogation, which lasted into the next day. Zhang was scolded repeatedly and warned to expect a jail term of three to four years. However, he was given a 15-day administrative detention instead. Upon release, Zhang obtained a note from the police certifying that he had completed his detention for "picking quarrels and provoking trouble."[45]

Arriving at a detention centre, Zhang was asked to read a letter of repentance aloud in front of a camera. The room he was staying in was cold, filthy, small, and crowded. Zhang was forbidden from calling his family and was placed under constant CCTV surveillance throughout. Soon after his detention, Zhang was fired by his employer. Landlords repeatedly evicted him after knowing the authorities closely monitored him.

The Case of Sun Shihua, a Defence Lawyer

On 20 September 2018, Sun Shihua, a lawyer with 20 years' experience in civil law practice, visited a local police station to handle her first criminal case involving a petitioner in a land acquisition dispute.[46] When Sun inquired about the bail procedures of her client, a police officer became agitated and accused Sun of assaulting him.

According to Sun, several officers charged at her, and one grabbed her by the neck. After being strip-searched, photographed, fingerprinted, and forced to undergo a urinary drug test, Sun was then interrogated for hours.

[43] Zhang, C (2025) 'Ai weiwei, AirDrop he sanfeng youjian: yige tongxinglian zhengzhifan de chengzhangshi' (Ai Weiwei, AirDrop, and Three Emails: The Maturing of a Homosexual Political Prisoner) 1 January 2025. Available at <https://women4china.substack.com/p/airdrop>.

[44] Jiang, S and Liu, J (2022) 'Apple Curbs AirDrop File Sharing on Devices in China' *CNN* 11 November 2022. Available at <https://edition.cnn.com/2022/11/11/business/china-apple-airdrop-function-restricted-hnk-intl/index.html>.

[45] The author emailed the website that published Zhang's article, requesting further details. Zhang provided the note issued by the police through the website's editor.

[46] Sun, S (2018) 'The Day when Police Showed Their True Colours: My Frightening and Humiliating Experience of Being Framed and Detained by the Guangzhou Police' 3 December 2018. Available at <https://archive.frontlinedefenders.org/fr/node/4778>.

She was eventually released around midnight without any explanation. Sun lodged complaints the next day, but to no avail.

LPAPS: A Major Vehicle of Police Oppression and Political Oppression?

Chinese law expert Jerome Cohen described Dr Li's experience at the local police station as humiliating and intimidating.[47] Cohen estimated that LPAPS accounted for more imposed punishments each year than the criminal process and viewed the legislation as a major vehicle for low-level, low-visibility police oppression. YJ Chen and Cohen also observed that administrative detention could be arbitrary and frequently served as a warning for people whom the police consider potential criminals.[48] However, as demonstrated in Dr Li's case, said Cohen, detention is often unnecessary.[49] An informal chat or a stern warning would be enough. Cohen did not define "police oppression". Here, in my view, "police oppression" refers to the use of physical violence, verbal abuse, threats, deception, and other coercive tactics by police officers to instil fear, exert pressure, or force compliance with their orders.

As we have noted, Dr Li, Cheng, and Zhang were penalized for the offences of "spreading rumours", "soliciting a prostitute", and "picking quarrels and provoking trouble". They fell victim to police powers. However, their ordeals as LPAPS offenders did not arise from police oppression at the community level but could be traced to wider political oppression. Here, political oppression refers to local or central authorities seeking to make the population submissive and behave accordingly, through various means, including instructing local police officers to exert pressure or compel individuals to comply with orders. In short, in these three cases, LPAPS was a convenient tool for the CCP regime to "maintain stability" (*weiwen*).

Lei and the two Suns suffered police violence. Cheng and Zhang also complained about police torture. Such physical violence took place either on the street or in police stations where CCTV cameras were installed. Police officers in Lei and Mr Sun's cases managed to avoid criminal punishments despite proven police violence. Ms Sun's complaints were ignored. As such, all six incidents involved the misuse of LPAPS, the exercise of broad police discretion, and abuses of police power. LPAPS's built-in safeguards were not functioning as well. It also begs the question: Has police violence or police oppression often been tolerated and not incurred any liability because LPAPS police powers are instrumental in realizing political oppression? The validity of these tentative observations of LPAPS police powers will be further examined below when analyzing the selected court judgments.

[47] Cohen 'Implications' supra note 3.

[48] Chen, YJ and Cohen, J (2023) 'Freedom from Arbitrary Detention' in Law, D et al (eds) *The Oxford Handbook of Constitutional Law in Asia.* Available at <https://doi.org/10.1093/oxfordhb/9780198825463.013.47>.

[49] Cohen 'Implications' supra note 3.

STATISTICS ON LPAPS CASES AND APPEALS

This section examines nationwide statistics, which provide an overview of law-and-order cases and estimate the percentage of administrative lawsuits appealing police penalty decisions.[50]

LPAPS Cases Nearly Doubled That of Criminal Cases

In recent years, the number of law-and-order cases handled by the police ranged from 8.63 million in 2020 to 8.69 million in 2023, with a peak of around 9 million in 2021 (see Figure 1). Criminal cases filed for police investigation ranged from 4.78 million in 2020 to 4.5 million in 2023, with a peak of around 5 million in 2021. As such, annual law-and-order cases nearly doubled that of criminal cases and matched Cohen's estimation.

Figure 1: Cases handled by the Police

Year	Criminal Cases# (Accepted and Filed by the Police)	Law-and-Order Cases##	
		Cases Received	Cases Completed (Investigated and Decided)
2020	4,780,624	8,628,053	7,723,930
2021	5,027,829	9,060,786	8,205,100
2022	4,423,259	8,648,819	7,828,809
2023	4,496,359	8,685,252	7,880,992

Gong'an jiguan li'an de xingshi an'jian; ## *Gong'n jiguan shouli he chachu zhi'an anjian*

Source: National Bureau of Statistics of China. 'China Statistical Yearbook' (2021-2024). Available at <https://www.stats.gov.cn/english/Statisticaldata/yearbook/>.

The China Statistical Yearbook divides law-and-order cases into 20 categories. The author grouped several categories into two tables. Figure 2a lists those categories that the police handled frequently. "Theft" cases consistently ranked top, averaging 25.7%. This is followed by cases of "assault" (25.1%), "fraud" (7.1%), "gambling" (3.5%), and "drug" (2.6%). Meanwhile, "prostitution" cases (1.7%) were on a rising trend in 2022 and 2023. In sum, theft, assault, fraud, gambling, drugs, and prostitution formed the bulk of LPAPS enforcement. Chinese police have been more proactive in gambling and prostitution cases, conducting annual combat campaigns and sporadic raids.[51]

50 These official statistics are taken at their face value.

51 See, for example, Ministry of Public Security (hereafter MPS) (2022) 'Gong'an jiguan zai "bairi Xingdong" zhong zhongquan daji huan du weifa fanzui' (Public Security Organs Launched "Hundred Days" Operation Striking a Hard Blow to Illegal Activities Involving Prostitution and Gambling) 21 July 2022. Available at <https://www.shdf.gov.cn/shdf/contents/767/447431.html>.

Figure 2a: Law-and-Order Cases – Top Categories

Year	Case Total	Theft	Assault	Fraud	Gambling	Drugs	Prostitution	Others
2020	8,628,053	2,119,503 (24.6%)	2,063,483 (23.9%)	716,115 (8.3%)	249,655 (2.9%)	324,301 (3.7%)	103,148 (1.2%)	2,197,509 (25.5%)
2021	9,060,786	2,337,264 (25.8%)	2,316,131 (25.6%)	657,489 (7.3%)	275,765 (3%)	241,500 (2.7%)	135,171 (1.5%)	2,276,942 (25.1%)
2022	8,648,819	2,285,899 (26.4%)	2,195,005 (25.4%)	542,576 (6.3%)	307,175 (3.6%)	161,979 (1.9%)	152,130 (1.8%)	2,246,011 (26%)
2023	8,685,252	2,245,846 (25.9%)	2,215,010 (25.5%)	568,830 (6.5%)	388,901 (4.5%)	169,530 (2%)	184,827 (2.1%)	2,068,460 (23.8%)
Average Percentage		25.7%	25.1%	7.1%	3.5%	2.6%	1.7%	25.1%

Source: National Bureau of Statistics of China. 'China Statistical Yearbook' (2021-2024). Available at <https://www.stats.gov.cn/english/Statisticaldata/yearbook/>.

Worldwide, police maintain peace within their respective communities. However, public order and obstruction offences, along with their enforcement by the police, often give rise to controversies. This is especially true in China. Figure 2b lists four such LPAPS categories: disturbing order in public venues, disturbances in work units and enterprises, etc, and obstructing government officials in the performance of their duties. The last category is the infamous and unique Chinese offence of "picking quarrels and provoking trouble", and annual cases ranged from approximately 100,000 in 2020 to around 125,000 in 2023.

Figure 2b: Law-and-Order Cases – Notable Categories

Year	Case Total	Disturb Order in Public Venues	Pick Quarrels and Provoke Trouble	Disturb Order in Work Units and Enterprises, etc.	Obstruct Government Officials in Their Performance of Duties
2020	8,628,053	196,380 (2.3%)	103,192 (1.2%)	45,151 (0.5%)	39,179 ((0.5%)
2021	9,060,786	165,149 (1.8%)	111,555 (1.2%)	47,483 (0.5%)	34,780 (0.4%)
2022	8,648,819	135,485 (1.6%)	113,011 (1.3%)	47,352 (0.5%)	34,347 (0.4%)
2023	8,685,252	151,070 (1.7%)	125,511 (1.4%)	57,513 (0.6%)	29,418 (0.3%)
Average Percentage		1.9%	1.3%	0.5%	0.4%

Source: National Bureau of Statistics of China. 'China Statistical Yearbook' (2021-2024). Available at <https://www.stats.gov.cn/english/Statisticaldata/yearbook/>.

Few LPAPS Offenders Filed Lawsuits Against Police Penalty Decisions

The 1987 RPAPS introduced a provision allowing offenders to appeal to the court. This evolved into administrative litigation, facilitating judicial review of police penalty decisions. Figures 3a and 3b are based on statistics published by the Supreme People's Court (SPC) on first-instance court cases. Figure 3a shows that administrative lawsuits have consistently formed a small fraction of the total number of court cases, ranging from a high of 1% in 2022 to a low of 0.6% in 2023.

The SPC statistics further divide administrative lawsuits into 44 subcategories. The "public security" (*gong'an*) subcategory ranged from 8.9% in 2020 to 11.9% in 2023. No details are given about this subcategory. A 2021 study by N Zhang and R Qiao concluded that LPAPS penalty cases accounted for approximately one-half of the "public security" subcategory.[52] Given the enormous LPAPS cases handled by the police each year, which exceeded 8.6 million in 2023 (see Figure 2a), the number of administrative lawsuits brought against such cases in the same year was comparatively very small, i.e., a halving of 35,541 cases (see Figure 3a), representing only 0.2%.

Figure 3a: Court Cases Received

Year	All Types of Cases	First-Instance Administrative Cases	
		Total	Public Security
2020	28,283,204	260,220	23,406
2021	31,539,810	319,977	32,292
2022	30,314,250	278,304	28,216
2023	45,573,652	298,711	35,541

Source: Judicial Statistical Report of Chinese Courts (2021-2024). Available at <http://gongbao.court.gov.cn/ArticleList.html?serial_no=sftj>.

The reasons why so few administrative lawsuits are brought to appeal against police penalty decisions are unknown, and multiple reasons may exist. One possible reason is that most offenders found police penalty decisions acceptable and did not appeal. Two other possible reasons are far more likely. First, offenders might fear retaliation. Second, offenders were

52 Zhang, N and Qiao, R (2021) 'Jingcha xingzhengquan de shifan yu guizhi: ji yu gong'an xingzheng susong caipan wenshu de shizheng fenxi' (Unruliness and Regulation of Police Administrative Powers: An Analysis of Court Judgments on Administrative Litigation Involving Public Security) 210 *Zhongguo Renmin Gong'an Daxue Xuebao (shehui kexue ban)* (*Journal of People's Public Security University of China* (*Social Sciences Edition*)) 116 at 119.

deterred by the unfavourable outcomes of "public security" lawsuits (see Figure 3b). Fewer than half reached the final stage, i.e. handing down of court judgments (49%). Also notable is the percentage of withdrawals by plaintiffs, which peaked at 31% in 2023. Moreover, only 0.15% were settled through mediation.

Figure 3b: Completed First-Instance Cases (Administrative Total and Public Security Sub-category) – A Breakdown

Year	Types of Cases	Judgments Delivered After Full Trial	No Judgments Delivered				Others	Total
			Refused Filing (Inadmissible)	Struck Out During Trial	Withdrawn	Mediated		
2020	AL Total	130,271 (48.9%)	13,837 (5.2%)	56,239 (21.1%)	53,423 (20%)	1,448 (0.5%)	11,094 (4.2%)	266,312
	P.S.	11,476 (48.8%)	1,347 (5.7%)	3,304 (14%)	6,851 (29.1%)	39 (0.1%)	514 (2.2%)	23,531
2021	AL Total	144,010 (48.3%)	15,194 (5.1%)	66,589 (22.3%)	59,095 (19.8%)	2,142 (0.7%)	11,271 (3.8%)	298,301
	P.S.	#14,581 (48.2%)	1,893 (6.3%)	4,880 (16.1%)	8,189 (27%)	31 (0.1%)	704 (2.3%)	30,278
2022	AL Total	139,373 (49.2%)	13,998 (4.9%)	56,614 (20%)	62,537 (22%)	1,965 (0.7)	9,045 (3.2%)	283,532
	AL P.S.	14,064 (49.4%)	1,575 (5.5%)	4,092 (14.4%)	8,175 (28.7%)	52 (0.2%)	517 (1.8%)	28,475
2023	AL Total	145,081 (49%)	13,647 (4.6%)	52,728 (17.8%)	71,963 (24.3%)	3,556 (1.2%)	8,990 (3%)	295,965
	P.S.	16,745 (48.5%)	1,741 (5%)	4,580 (13.3%)	10,706 (31%)	69 (0.2%)	653 (1.9%)	34,494

AL Total (Administrative cases: Total); P.S. (Public Security Sub-Category)

Source Judicial Statistical Report of Chinese Courts (2021-2024). Available at <http://gongbao.court.gov.cn/ArticleList.html?serial_no=sftj>.

Official statistics regarding the "plaintiffs' win rate" against LPAPS offences are not publicly available. However, recent research indicates that the rate can be very low. YJ Tang examined 674 court judgments on LPAPS appeals in Inner Mongolia and found that the "police loss rate" ranged from 16.9% in 2017 to 22.4% in 2020.[53] N Zhang and R Qiao surveyed 71,513 first-instance court judgments of "public security" lawsuits nationwide. The results indicated that the "police loss rate" ranged from 14.3% in 2017

[53] Tang, YJ (2024) 'Fazhi beijing xia neimenggu jiceng zhi'an xingzheng chufa changjian wenti yanjiu: jiyu neimenggu gong'an xingzheng susong caipan wenshu de shizheng fenxi' (A Study of Common Problems of Law-and-Order Administrative Penalties at Grassroot Level in Inner Mongolia in the Rule of Law Setting: From An Analysis of Court Judgments of Inner Mongolia Administrative Litigation Involving Public Security) 10 *Hebei Falü Zhiye Jiaoyu (Hebei Vocational Education of Law)* 50 at 52.

to 16.9% in 2020, with a peak of 17.1% in 2019.[54] This is despite a study conducted by YZ Zhang and Z Liu on 237,751 first-instance administrative adjudications of all kinds, not limited to "public security" lawsuits, which found that the "plaintiffs' success rate" rose steadily from 33.2% in 2014 to 42.2% in 2020.[55]

A SURVEY OF SELECTED LAWSUITS APPEALING LPAPS PENALTY DECISIONS

The following section examines court judgments on administrative lawsuits appealing LPAPS penalty decisions made by the police shortly before or during the COVID-19 pandemic. On 28 January 2025, the author conducted a keyword search in *Beida Fabao* using two phrases: "治安管理处罚法" (*zhi'an guanli chufafa,* i.e., LPAPS) and "新冠" (*xinguan*, i.e., the Chinese abbreviated term for COVID-19).[56] This resulted in a selection of 225 first-instance court judgments. These judgments originated in various parts of China, except Xinjiang, Tibet, Qinghai, and Hainan. The judgments often mentioned why offenders were punished, investigation procedures, sentencing guidelines, etc. Also disclosed are the arguments against police penalty decisions and, sometimes, complaints about police malpractices and abuses of power.

The author grouped these judgments into two categories: a) 176 lawsuits brought by LPAPS offenders appealing their penalties (hereafter referred to as "offenders"); and b) 49 lawsuits brought by complainants or victims objecting to police's inaction or leniency (hereafter referred to as "complainants"). The following study focuses on the "offenders" category, which typically contains more details. Figure 4 shows 176 lawsuits in the "offenders" category, comprising 185 penalty decisions. In some lawsuits, an offender was penalized for two offences, and the sign ^ is used for indication.

Figure 4: Lawsuits Brought by LPAPS Offenders – A Breakdown of Offences

Assault	71 ^3	Gambling	3
Picking Quarrels and Provoking Trouble	28	Trespass	3 ^1
Damage to Property	9 ^2	Theft	2
Disturbing Order in Work Units and Enterprises, etc.	8	Spreading False Information about Epidemics	2
Disturbing Order in Public Venues	7	Disturbing Order on Public Transport	1
Non-compliance with Orders Issued During an Emergency	7 ^1	Disrupting Traffic	1
Obstructing Officers in Their Performance of Duties	3 ^5	Disturbing Others by Sending Messages that are Threatening, Insulting, Obscene, etc.	2
Obstructing Police	^5	Invasion of Privacy	1
Insult	6	Threatening Others	^1
Soliciting a Prostitute	6	Producing, Disseminating, etc. Obscene Materials	1
Drugs	5	Improper Storage of Explosives	1
Sub-Total	150 ^16		17 ^2
Total			167 ^18 (176) [185]

^ In some cases, the offenders were penalized for two offences. There are a total of 176 lawsuits, comprising 185 penalty decisions.

[54] Zhang and Qiao 'Unruliness' supra note 52.

[55] Zhang, YX and Liu, Z (2023) 'The Rise of the Chinese Judiciary and Its Limits: Administrative Litigation in the Reform Period' 7 May 2023. Available at <https://papers.ssrn.com/sol3/papers.cfm?abstract_id=4696197>.

[56] *Beida Fabao* is the largest Chinese law database available in China and beyond.

Violating COVID-19 Restrictive Measures: Penalties and Lawsuits

Figure 5 indicates that only 30 penalty decisions (27 plus ^3) were due to violations of COVID-19 restrictive measures (16.2% of the total 185). Most court judgments referred to the phrase "新冠 *xinguan*" simply as an explanation for postponed police investigations, decisions, penalty enforcement, or court hearings. Thirteen lawsuits arose directly from COVID-19 restrictive measures and 17 (14 plus ^3) indirectly. In the "indirect" category, several lawsuits arose from refusals to follow pandemic safety instructions given in communities or queue-jumping during COVID-19 tests, and these trivial disputes led to fighting, with some individuals penalized for assault.

Figure 5: Lawsuits Brought by LPAPS Offenders – Arising from COVID-19 Restrictive Measures

Directly		Indirectly	
Failure to Comply with Orders Issued in an Emergency	7#	Assault	7
Spreading False Information about the Epidemic	2	Picking Quarrels and Provoking Trouble	2
Disturbing Order on Public Transport	1	Damage to Property	3
Disturbing Traffic	1	Insult	2
Gambling	1	Threatening Others	^1
Picking Quarrels and Provoking Trouble	1	Obstructing Officers in Their Performance of Duties	^1
		Obstructing Police	^1
Sub-Total	13		14 ^3
Total			27 ^3

Four cases arose from the same set of facts.

As for the "direct" category, seven lawsuits were brought by offenders penalized for "failing to comply with orders issued in an emergency."[57] Four lawsuits arose from the same incident.[58] Each of the four was given a 10-day detention and fined 500 yuan. Court judgments revealed that as many as nine individuals were penalized on that occasion, but only four appealed. All were veterans working in a prison in Heilongjiang Province. Dissatisfied with their salaries, they attempted to gather at a public square to sign a petition. However, once they arrived, the police took them away for violating COVID-19 restrictive measures. The offenders maintained that restrictions had already been lifted, that some people were exercising in the square, and that their planned gathering did not take place. The same judge dismissed all four lawsuits.

Two lawsuits were brought by offenders penalized for the offence of "spreading false information about an epidemic."[59] One offender, as was

[57] Article 50 (1)(1).

[58] *Wang Liang v Jixi Shi Gong'anju Jiguan Gong'an Fenju (Jiquan branch of Jixi City Public Security Bureau, Heilongjiang Province)* (2020) Hei 0302 Xingchu No. 50; *Chai Shouguang v Jixi Shi Gong'anju Jiguan Gong'an Fenju (Jiquan branch of Jixi City Public Security Bureau, Heilongjiang Province)* (2020) Hei 0302 Xingchu No. 60; *Wang Qixin v Jixi Shi Gong'anju Jiguan Gong'an Fenju (Jiquan branch of Jixi City Public Security Bureau, Heilongjiang Province)* (2020) Hei 0302 Xingchu No. 62; *Zhang Jian v Jixi Shi Gong'anju Jiguan Gong'an Fenju (Jiquan branch of Jixi City Public Security Bureau, Heilongjiang Province)* (2020) Hei 0302 Xingchu No. 63.

[59] Article 25(1).

the case with Dr Li Wenliang, was a doctor.[60] In late January 2020, Dr Li Juan told a shop owner in Anhui Province that her hospital had recently admitted two patients from Wuhan who had a fever. The shop owner later spread Li's words via a chat group. As a result, Li was fined 300 yuan. Handing down the judgment in November 2020, the court ruled that the police evidence did not prove Li committed the offence. However, the judgment also revealed that the police had already retracted their original penalty decision after the court heard the case in August. The court concluded that no revocation order was necessary, and that a confirmation of the unlawfulness of the original penalty decision would suffice. Meanwhile, in another lawsuit, an offender was given a 2-day detention for spreading messages in a chat group in late January 2020, accusing another man of contracting COVID-19.[61] The court dismissed the case, even after finding procedural irregularities in the penalty decision.

Another noteworthy lawsuit was brought by Ms Li, who flew from Shenzhen to Beijing in early February 2021.[62] Ignoring repeated instructions from crew members, Li refused to return to her assigned seat and preferred to sit elsewhere, maintaining social distancing from other passengers. Arriving at Beijing Airport, she was taken to a local police station and fined 200 yuan for "disrupting order on public transport."[63] In bringing the lawsuit, Li maintained that she had no intention of disrupting order on the plane. She also complained about police malpractices during interrogation and that her confession was made under duress. In addition, Li argued that her case was very trivial and that a police warning would suffice. The judge dismissed Li's appeal, emphasizing the importance of flight safety rules, public order maintenance, and citizens' obligations to observe such regulations.

Assaults (Article 43 Offences): Penalty Decisions and Lawsuits

Interestingly, out of the 185 penalty decisions heard by the court, 74 concerned Article 43 offences (see Figure 4). This percentage is significantly higher than that of "assault" cases handled by the police (25.1%, see Figure 2a). Most of these 74 assaults arose from disputes of a private nature, and community, neighbour, and family disputes formed the bulk (see Figure 6a).[64] Some disputes occurred sporadically, while others involved old foes, and several were related to land issues.

[60] *Li Juan v Xiaoxian Gong'anju Longcheng Chengdong Paichusuo* (*Longcheng East Local Police Station of Xiao County Public Security Bureau, Anhui Province*) (2020) Wan 1322 Xingchu No. 98.

[61] *Zhu Zhipeng v Jiangxi Sheng Poyangxian Gong'anju* (*Poyang County Public Security Bureau, Jiangxi Province*) (2020) Gong 1129 Xingchu No. 55.

[62] *Li Yazhu v Shoudu Jichang Gong'anju Beijing Shoudu Guoji Jichang Donghangzhanqu Paichusuo* (*Eastern Terminal Local Police Station of Beijing Capital Airport Public Security Bureau*) (2021) Jing 0105 Xingchu No. 109.

[63] Art 23(1)(3).

[64] Here, "community disputes" refer to conflicts between individuals from the same community or township, but these individuals do not necessarily know each other.

Figure 6a: The Offence of Assault – Nature of Incidents

Incidents of Public Nature	Breaking COVID-19 Restrictions/ Disputes Arising from COVID Restrictions	7	15
	Land (Acquisition) Disputes	3	
	Disputes about Village/Community Management	5	
Incident of Public/Private Nature	Medical Disputes (Arising from Treatment)	1	1
Incident of Private Nature	Family Disputes (Land, Money, Affairs, Custody, etc.)	11 ^3	55 ^3
	Neighbour Disputes (Some Involving Land)	13	
	Community Disputes (Some Involving Land)	17	
	Traffic Disputes	4	
	Economic Disputes (Debt etc.)	8	
	Labour Disputes (Salary)	2	
Total			71 ^3

Figure 6b: The Offence of Assault: Penalties Imposed

No Penalty		1
A Fine Only (100-500 yuan)		11
Detention Only	The Shortest: one day	1
	2-7 days	20 ^1
	The Longest: 10 days	1
Detention with a Fine	The Lowest: 5 days and a Fine (Ranging from 200 yuan to 500 yuan)	8
	6-9 days with a Fine (Ranging from 200 yuan to 500 yuan)	9 ^2
	10 days with a Fine (Ranging from 200 yuan to 500 yuan)	18
	12 days with a Fine (Ranging from 500-600 yuan)	2
	Total	71 ^3

Most "assault" offenders were subjected to detention only or both detention and a fine (see Figure 6b). As many as 18 offenders were given a 10-day detention with fines ranging from 200 to 500 yuan. Figure 6c indicates that only about one-third of the "assault" offenders applied for administrative review before resorting to administrative litigation. Courts upheld most "assault" penalty decisions, even though five contained police procedural irregularities (see Figure 6d). Only six penalty decisions were revoked, and three penalties were reduced. This is despite approximately half of the "assault" offenders having hired lawyers in their litigation.

Figure 6c: The Offence of Assault – Any Administrative Review Before Bringing Litigation

	"Assault" Offenders
Applied for Administrative Review	26 ^2
Did not Apply for Administrative Review	45 ^1
Total	71 ^3

Figure 6d: The Offence of Assault – Litigation Outcomes

	Lawyer Hired	No lawyer	Total
Case Dismissed	27 ^3	30	57 ^3
Case Dismissed (but procedural irregularities found)	2	3	5
Penalty Decision Revoked	3	3	6
Penalty Reduced	3	0	3
Total	35 ^3	36	71 ^3

Family, Neighbour or Community Disputes

Assaults arising from family disputes were disheartening and often quite dramatic. Two lawsuits from Sichuan Province arose from the same incident.[65] Ten members from extended families gathered to celebrate Lunar New Year Eve, but fighting soon erupted over financial disputes. The police were called after several members suffered injuries. Mediation was held twice but failed. Eventually, two individuals were penalized for assault. Both brought administrative lawsuits, one insisting he had only acted in self-defence. Dismissing the appeals, the court noted that it was impossible to reconstruct the fight through testimonies because witnesses were related to one another.

Another "Article 43" lawsuit from the "complainants" category concerned a fight between opposite factions of a family that occurred outside a courtroom right after matrimonial proceedings.[66] The police imposed LPAPS penalties on six individuals. Meanwhile, another dramatic incident led to four lawsuits. Joined by her daughter and two other individuals, a woman entered an apartment and assaulted her husband's mistress. The wife was handed an 8-day detention and fined 200 yuan for assault and trespassing.[67] The other three were penalized for trespassing and detained for 6 to 7 days, each with a fine of 200 yuan. [68] These three offenders

[65] *Song Shifeng v Yibin Shi Gong'anju Cuiping Qu Fen Ju (Cuiping Branch of Yibin City Public Security Bureau, Sichuan Province)* (2020) Chuan 1502 Xingchu No. 42; *Xiao Bing v Yibin Shi Gong'anju Cuiping Qu Fen Ju (Cuiping Branch of Yibin City Public Security Bureau, Sichuan* Province) (2020) Chuan 1502 Xingchu No. 43.

[66] *Yang Xuying v Fengyang Xian Gong'anju (Fengyang County Public Security Bureau, Anhui Province)* (2020) Wan 1126 Xingchu No. 36.

[67] *Mao Xuemei v Changzhou Shi Gong'anju Wujin Fenju, Changzhou Shi Wujin Qu Renmin Zhengfu (Wujin Branch of Changzhou City Public Security Bureau, Wujin District People's Government, Changzhou City, Jiangsu Province)* (2020) Su 0411 Xingchu No. 130.

[68] *Jing Cheng v Changzhou Shi Gong'anju Wujin Fenju and Changzhou Shi Wujin Qu Renmin Zhengfu (Wujin Branch of Changzhou City Public Security Bureau and Wujin District People's Government, Changzhou City, Jiangsu Province)* (2020) Su 0411 Xingchu No. 131; *Zhu Qi v Changzhou Shi Gong'anju Wujin Fenju and Changzhou Shi Wujin Qu Renmin Zhengfu (Wujin Branch of Changzhou City Public Security Bureau and Wujin District People's Government, Changzhou City, Jiangsu Province)* Su 0411 Xingchu No. 132; *Cui Jianshun v Changzhou*

complained to the court that police had lured them into confession. The court dismissed all four appeals.

Thirteen "Article 43" lawsuits concerned neighbour disputes, and another 17 arose from community disputes, often originating from trivial matters. Two neighbouring families in Sichuan Province broke into a fight, and a woman suffered injury.[69] Mediation was held twice but failed. A daughter and her father were then penalized for assault, with each given a 10-day detention and a fine of 500 yuan. The 86-year-old father was spared detention because of his age. His application for an administrative review was dismissed, and he died soon afterwards. In early 2020, his wife filed an administrative lawsuit on his behalf, complaining that the elderly man was too frail to have committed an assault, that the penalty was actually revenge for his report on embezzlement by village cadres, and that the neighbours had colluded in their testimonies of what exactly happened at the "assault" scene. Dismissing the lawsuit, the court asked both families to learn to be good neighbours, not to get embroiled in further disputes, and to resolve any issues lawfully.

Disputes of a Public Nature

Only 15 of the "Article 43" lawsuits arose from disputes of a public nature, and eight of them could be traced to land acquisition or village/community management disputes (see Figure 6a). In Sichuan Province, after tensions ran high in a land dispute, a villager was taken to a local police station for allegedly assaulting a local party secretary at the scene.[70] The police extended the interrogation to 24 hours, and the villager was eventually given a 7-day detention and fined 200 yuan. Both her administrative review and administrative lawsuit were dismissed. Another villager got a 2-day detention for insulting a police officer.[71] This offender maintained she was assaulted by the police at the scene and produced her own video to prove she did not insult anyone. However, the court ruled that her video did not capture all that happened during the conflict. Despite finding police procedural irregularities, the court dismissed her lawsuit.

"Assault" cases arising from medical disputes are unfortunate and alarming. In Anhui Province, a hospital doctor and the son of an elderly

Shi Gong'anju Wujin Fenju and Changzhou Shi Wujin Qu Renmin Zhengfu (*Wujin Branch of Changzhou City Public Security Bureau and Wujin District People's Government, Changzhou City, Jiangsu Province*) (2020) Su 0411 Xingchu No. 133.

[69] *Wang Guiying v Jiajiang Xian Gong'anju and Jiajiang Xian Renmin Zhengfu* (*Jiajiang County Public Security Bureau and Jianjiang County People's Government, Sichuan Province*) (2020) Chuan 1102 Xingchu No. 33.

[70] *Xie Juan v Qianwei Xian Gong'anju and Leshan Shi Gong'anju* (*Qianwei County Public Security Bureau and Leshan City Public Security Bureau, Sichuan Province*) (2020) Chuan 1102 Xingchu No. 177.

[71] *Xie Li v Qianwei Xian Gong'anju and Leshan Shi Gong'anju* (*Qianwei County Public Security Bureau and Leshan City Public Security Bureau, Sichuan Province*) (2020) Chuan 1102 Xingchu No. 179.

patient quarrelled over medical treatment, which escalated into a fight.[72] The doctor was handed a 3-day detention for causing bodily harm to the son. The doctor maintained he had acted in self-defence, but the court dismissed his lawsuit.

Another "Article 43" lawsuit arising from a medical dispute falls into the "complainants" category.[73] In Henan Province, an elderly woman repeatedly scolded the doctor treating her baby grandson. The doctor phoned her husband, who then hurried to the hospital. Fighting soon erupted. The woman suffered injury, having five teeth fall out. The doctor's husband was given an 8-day detention and fined 500 yuan. The woman filed an administrative lawsuit complaining about the LPAPS penalty decision, maintaining that the assailant should be criminally prosecuted instead. The court dismissed her lawsuit, ruling her injury had been certified as minor (the five teeth were rotten and weak) and did not meet the threshold for criminal prosecution.

Picking Quarrels and Provoking Trouble (Article 26 Offences): Penalty Decisions and Lawsuits

In the 176 lawsuits brought by offenders, 28 appealed penalty decisions concerning "picking quarrels and provoking trouble" (Article 26), accounting for 15.9% of the total (see Figure 4). This is significantly higher than the 1.3% of law-and-order cases handled by the police (see Figure 2a). Moreover, 21 arose from incidents of a public nature, and 15 were brought by petitioners (see Figure 7a). Article 26 mandates detention penalties. A maximum 15-day detention was imposed on seven offenders, and two other offenders were given 15-day detention and also fined 1,000 yuan each (see Figure 7b). Half of the 28 offenders applied for an administrative review before bringing their lawsuits (Figure 7c). The court dismissed 24 lawsuits, 16 of which had hired lawyers (Figure 7d).

Figure 7a: The Offence of Picking Quarrels and Provoking Trouble – Nature of Incidents

			Sub-total
Incidents of Public Nature	Petition	15	21
	Disputes about Village/Community Management	3	
	Breaking Covid Restrictions/ Disputes Arising from COVID Restrictions	2	
	Making and Disseminating a Video (Dancing Wearing a Japanese military outfit)	1	
Incidents of a Private Nature	Land dispute	2	7
	Traffic dispute	2	
	Assault (One Relating to COVID Restrictions)	2	
	Damage to Property	1	
Total			28

[72] *Wang Xiang v Hanshan Xian Gong'anju and Ma'anshan Shi Gong'anju* (*Hanshan County Public Security Bureau and Ma'anshan City Public Security Bureau, Anhui Province*) (2020) Wan 0504 Xingchu No. 27.

[73] *Shi Zhenglan v Nanyang Shi Gong'anju Wancheng Qu Gong'an Fenju* (*Wencheng Branch of Nanyang City Public Security Bureau, Henan Province*) (2020) Yu 1302 Xingchu No. 138.

Figure 7b: The Offence of Picking Quarrels and Provoking Trouble – Penalties Imposed

The Lowest Penalty (3 days)	1
4-7 days	8
8-14 days	12
15 days	5
The Highest Penalty (15 days and 1000 yuan)	2
Total	28

Figure 7c: The Offence of Picking Quarrels and Provoking Trouble – Any Administrative Review Before Bringing Litigation

	Lawyer Hired	No lawyer	Total
Applied for Administrative Review	10	3	13
Applied for Administrative Review but Later Retracted	0	1	1
Did not Apply for Administrative Review	8	6	14
Total	18	10	28

Figure 7d: The Offence of Picking Quarrels and Provoking Trouble – Litigation Outcomes

	Lawyer Hired	No lawyer	Total
Case Dismissed	15	8	23
Case Dismissed (but procedural irregularities found)	1	0	1
Penalty Decision Revoked	1	2	3
Decision Revoked and New Decision Demanded	1	0	1
Total	18	10	28

Eight "Article 26" lawsuits originated from Shandong Province. Shortly before the PRC's 70th anniversary, six individuals went to Beijing to petition about the demolition of their houses.[74] Two offenders appealed their penalties – a 15-day detention and a fine of 1,000 yuan each–and the court dismissed both appeals. Three other lawsuits concerned another incident that occurred in March 2019. After losing their land dispute litigation, 11 individuals went to Beijing to petition during the annual national legislative and consultative meetings. All three offenders got a 15-day detention, and the court dismissed their appeals. Another "Article 26" lawsuit was brought by a petitioner who also threatened to stage a protest outside the Embassy of the United States.[75] The police imposed a 10-day detention on him. The court also dismissed his appeal.

Only on rare occasions would the court revoke "Article 26" penalty decisions. This happened to two petitioners from Jiangsu Province. Having previous LPAPS penalty records for petitioning in Beijing, they went to the capital again shortly before the PRC's 70th anniversary. Once there, they were intercepted and repatriated by Jiangsu police. Each was then given a 7-day detention. They brought administrative lawsuits, arguing they

[74] *Zhao Dan v Shan Xian Gong'anju* (*Shan County Public Security Bureau, Shangdong Province*) (2020) Lu 1721 Xingchu No. 1; *Zu Naizhi v Shan Xian Gong'anju* (*Shan County Public Security Bureau, Shangdong Province*) (2020) Lu 1721 Xingchu No. 2.

[75] *Liu Xianghua v Qihe Xian Gong'anju and Qihe Xian Renmin Zhengfu* (*Qihe County Public Security Bureau and Qihe County People's Government, Shandong Province*) (2020) Lu 1425 Xingchu No. 21.

were in Beijing seeking medical treatment and did not bring any petition material. The court revoked their LPAPS penalty, ruling that they were in Beijing to make enquiries about their previous petitions, and that they did not engage in any petition activity as they were intercepted immediately.

The outcome of another "Article 26" lawsuit from Shandong Province was also exceptional.[76] A drunken man, Mr Ji, broke a car's mirror, worth 210 yuan, on a street. The car owner agreed to settle the case after Ji paid 1,000 yuan for the damage. But the police insisted Ji had violated Article 26 and imposed a 3-day detention on him. The CCP disciplinary committee at Ji's work unit was also notified about this LPAPS penalty record. Ji then filed an administrative lawsuit. He also made a complaint to the court about police procedural irregularities and malpractices, including spending half an hour reading his mobile phone. The court ruled the police did not follow the sentencing manual on administrative penalties issued by the Shandong authorities. It revoked the penalty decision on the grounds of procedural irregularity, wrongful application of the law, and inappropriate penalty decision.

In another "Article 26" lawsuit, also of a private nature and from Shandong, the offender was less fortunate. A roadside strawberry seller was embroiled in a fight with a neighbouring seller.[77] He was given a 12-day detention and fined 500 yuan. Bringing an administrative lawsuit, he argued he should be penalized for "assault" instead of contravening Article 26. The court dismissed his case, ruling that the police were right to rely on Article 26, which carries a heavier penalty, because the offender had provoked a fight in a public place, causing personal injuries.

Two other "Article 26" lawsuits are also noteworthy. In Liaoning Province, Mr Jing was so bored by the COVID-19 pandemic lockdown that he uploaded a dancing video of himself wearing a Japanese military outfit, which he had retained from a previous freelance acting role.[78] The video attracted 40,000 views. The police considered Jing's act and video a promotion of extreme militarism and imposed a 10-day detention on him for violating Article 26. Jing appealed, maintaining that his sole aim was entertainment and that he had done nothing provocative. Dismissing the lawsuit, the court sided with the police, ruling that Jing's act had violated public order and decency and hurt the Chinese people's patriotic feelings. Also, during the lockdown, Mr Wang in Shanxi Province quarrelled with guards at a COVID-19 control point.[79] Even after publicly apologizing on

[76] *Ji Tengfei v Jinan Shi Gong'anju Huaiyin Qu Fenju* (*Huaiyin Branch of Jinan City Public Security Bureau, Shandong Province*) (2020) Lu 0104 Xingchu No. 124.

[77] *Liang Mounan v Xixia Shi Mouju and Xixia Shi Renmin Zhengfu* (*Mr Liang v A public security bureau in Xixia City and Xixia City People's Government, Shandong Province*) (2023) Lu 0682 Xingchu No. 37.

[78] *Jing Jianhua v Benxi Shi Gong'anju Pingshan Fenju* (*Pingshan Branch of Benxi City Public Security Bureau, Liaoning Province*) (2020) Liao 0502 Xingchu No. 53.

[79] *Wang Yamin v Lingchuan Xian Gong'anju* (*Lingchuan County Public Security Bureau,* Shanxi Province) (2020) Jin 0581 Xingchu No. 12.

television the next day for quarrelling, Wang was given a 5-day detention for violating Article 26. The court dismissed his appeal.

Soliciting A Prostitute (Article 66(1) Offence): Penalty Decisions and Lawsuits

Six lawsuits arose from "soliciting a prostitute" (Article 66(1)). However, not a single offender was caught in bed with a prostitute. Three were in the hotel rooms or on some other private premises, fully dressed.[80] One was stopped in the street after leaving a bathing centre.[81] The other two were penalized after the police searched the WeChat records of prostitutes.[82] One of these two offenders was summoned by the police in late November 2019 based on his chats with a prostitute made in early October.[83] All offenders complained about police coercion, torture, or other malpractices during interrogation.[84]

The penalties imposed ranged from 500 yuan to 15 days of detention. One offender was especially desperate to appeal after a circular publicising his penalty was sent to his work unit.[85] Only one offender managed to persuade the court to revoke his penalty.[86] In another lawsuit, the court asked the police to reinvestigate the case and reach a new decision.[87]

Theft and Damage to Property (Article 49 Offences): Penalty Decisions and Lawsuits

Only two of 176 lawsuits concerned "theft" (see Figure 4). This is far lower than the 25.7% recorded in law-and-order cases handled by the police (see Figure 2a). In early July 2020, a noodle bar operator in Shandong Province

[80] *Li Xianglong v Loudi Shi Gong'anju louxing Fenju (Louxing Branch of Loudi City Public Security Bureau, Hunan Province)* (2020) Xiang 1321 Xingchu No. 102; *Dong Weiwei v Huangshi Shi Gong'anju Xialu Fenju (Xialu Branch of Huangshi City Public Security Bureau, Hubei Province)* (2020) E 0204 Xingchu No. 13; *Zheng Jianji v Lanzhou Shi Gong'anju Chengguan Fenju Yanyuanlu Paichusuo and Lanzhou Shi Chengguan Qu Renmin Zhengfu (Yanyuanlu Local Police Station, Chengguan Branch of Lanzhou City Public Security Bureau and Lanzhou City Chengguan District People's Government, Gansu Province)* (2020) Gan 0103 Xingchu No. 91.

[81] *Li Zhengnan v Dalian Shi Gong'anju Shahekou Fenju (Shahekou Branch of Dalian City Public Security Bureau, Liaoning Province)* (2020) Liao 0203 Xingchu No. 98.

[82] *Wang Yu v Taiyuan Shi Gong'anju Yingze Fenju (Yingze Branch of Taiyuan City Public Security Bureau, Shanxi Province)* (2020) Jin 0110 Xingchu No. 86; *Zhang Yang v Tianjin Shi Gong'anju Heping Fenju, Tianjin Shi Heping Qu Renmin Zhengfu (Heping Branch of Tianjin City Public Security Bureau and Tianjin City Heping District People's Government)* (2020) (Tian)Jin 0101 Xingchu No. 260.

[83] *Zhang Yang* id.

[84] *Wang Yu* supra note 82; *Zhang Yang* id; *Li Zhengnan* supra note 81; *Dong Weiwei* supra note 80; *Zheng Jianji* supra note 80; *Li Xianglong* supra note 80.

[85] *Dong Weiwei* supra note 80.

[86] *Li Xianglong* supra note 80.

[87] *Zheng Jianji* supra note 80.

reported to the police that her mobile phone had gone missing. After inspecting the CCTV in the shop, the police summoned a customer. She was also ordered to take a drug test a few days later, and the result was negative. In late July, the woman was given a 6-day detention for stealing the seller's mobile phone valued at 500 yuan. The woman brought an administrative lawsuit, maintaining that she had taken the phone by mistake.[88] The court dismissed her case despite her arguing that the CCTV footage did not show her intentionally grabbing the phone and that she had a witness to support her claim.

The other lawsuit originated from Zhejiang Province.[89]A man reported to the police that two pots of flowers placed outside his house across the street had gone missing. After inspecting the CCTV footage nearby, the police summoned a married couple. The husband was then handed a 3-day detention for theft of the two pots, valued at 72 yuan. He later brought an administrative lawsuit, seeking to revoke the penalty decision and requesting compensation of 50,000 yuan for his wife for suffering bodily harm during police interrogation, and another 50,000 yuan for the police's inflicting on her emotional stress.

The husband complained to the court that he and his wife were detained for more than 24 hours. His wife had been handcuffed, deprived of food and medicine, barred from going to the toilet, and subjected to verbal abuse and pressure to confess. Through the court, he also requested the police to produce the CCTV footage showing their 28-hour interrogation. The police rejected the request, saying that the footage had been overlaid with new images, rendering it irretrievable—this was to be expected as four months had already elapsed between the incident and the filing of the lawsuit. The court dismissed the suit, ruling that the penalty decision was sound and appropriate. The court further noted that it would not rule on the compensation claims, as the wife was not a plaintiff in the lawsuit.

Article 49 also punishes intentional damage to property. In a village in Hebei Province, a deputy party secretary broke a drawer of the village party secretary's desk when searching for a duty logbook.[90] He immediately hired a workman to repair it and paid a fee of 10 yuan. But he was still handed a 5-day detention. The court dismissed his appeal, ruling that the damage was intentional because the man did not phone the party secretary for permission to open the drawer before his search.

Also in Hebei Province, a 7-day detention was imposed on a man who kicked the door of the village party committee office, which was shut during

[88] *Shen Xiujuan v Weifang Shi Gong'anju Fangzi Fenju* (*Fangzi Branch of Weifang City Public Security Bureau, Shandong Province*) (2020) Lu 0705 Xingchu No. 97.

[89] *Yu Xingkang v Shaoxing Shi Gong'anju keqiao Qu Fenju* (*Keqiao Branch of Shaoxing City Public Security Bureau, Zhejiang Province*) (2020) Zhe 0603 Xingchu No. 100.

[90] *Sun Fushan v Chengde Xian Gong'anju and Chengde Shi Gong'anju* (*Chengde County Public Security Bureau and Chengde City Public Security Bureau, Hebei Province*) (2020) Ji 0802 Xingchu No. 84.

the COVID-19 lockdown.[91] The man brought an administrative lawsuit, maintaining that his kick did not damage the sturdy door. Despite being summoned by the court as a third party, the village party committee did not send any representative to attend the trial. The court dismissed the lawsuit, upholding the penalty decision.

Discussion on LPAPS Safeguards, Appeal Mechanisms, and Efficiency

Compared to CL, LPAPS provides milder penalties. Moreover, unlike convicts, LPAPS offenders are not marred by criminal records. However, the adverse impact of LPAPS penalties cannot be underestimated. As seen, some LPAPS offenders experienced trauma during interrogation and detention, and faced devastating publicity and consequences for their penalties. Convicts often had their suspended prison sentences revoked and were jailed immediately if they committed LPAPS offences during probation.[92] LPAPS offenders who received detention sentences have been barred from applying for postgraduate studies or civil service vacancies.[93]

Are In-Built Safeguards Functioning?

LPAPS stipulates various safeguards, in effect encouraging greater attention to due process. The surveyed court judgments also reveal that police officers must follow detailed normative documents and manuals on mediation, investigation procedures, sentencing, etc., when handling LPAPS cases.[94] For example, the Ministry of Public Security (MPS) issued guidelines spanning 43 pages for sentencing.[95] Local sentencing manuals are even

[91] *Cui Er'long v Bo'ye Xian Gong'anju and Baoding Shi Gong'anju* (*Bo'ye County Public Security Bureau and Baoding City Public Security Bureau, Hebei Province*) (2020) Ji 0683 Xingchu No. 9.

[92] *Chen Xing Zhiwu Qinzhan Zui Xingfa Biangeng zhixing Caidingshu* (Decision on alteration of punishment enforcement of Chen Xing's appropriation of entity property offence) (2020) Zhe 0523 Xinggeng No. 2; *Song Mou Guyi Shanghai Zui Xingfa Biangeng Xingshi Caidingshu* (Decision on the alteration of criminal punishment of Mr Song's wilful assault offence) (2020) Nei 0521 Xinggeng No. 1.

[93] 'Reyi xia de zhi'an guanli chufafa xiuding, you neixie zhide guanzhu de wenti?'(Hotly Debated LPAPS Amendments: What are the Noteworthy Issues?) *Sanlian Shenghuo Zhoukan* (*Sanlian Life Weekly*) 10 September 2023. Available at <https://www.lifeweek.com.cn/h5/article/detail.do?artId=210872>.

[94] See, for example, *Cui Jianshun* supra note 68, quoting MPS (2020) 'Gong'an jiguan banli xingzheng anjian chengxu guiding' (Regulations Governing Public Security Organs' Handling Procedures of Administrative Cases) (MPS Order No. 125; Latest revision on 6 August 2020). Available in *Beida Fabao*; *Zhang Weibing v Huaian Shi Gong'anju Jingji Jishu Kaifaqu Fenju and Huaian Shi Gong'anju* (*Economic and Technology Development Zone Branch of Huaian City Public Security Bureau and Huaian City Public Security Bureau, Jiangsu Province*) (2019) Su 0812 Xingchu No. 578, quoting MPS (2007) 'Gong'an jiguan zhi'an tiaojie gongzuo guifan' (Specifications Governing Public Security Organs' Law-and-Order Mediation) (Gongtongzi [2007] No. 81, issued on 8 December 2007). Available in *Beida Fabao*.

[95] MPS (2018) 'Gong'an jiguan dui bufen weifan zhi'an guanli xingwei shishi chufa de cailiang zhidao yijian' (Sentencing Guidelines Regarding Penalties Administered by Public Security Organs on Some Law-and-Order Violations) (Gongtongzi [2018] No. 17, issued on 5 June 2018). Available in *Beida Fabao*.

more detailed; the one prepared by the Beijing Public Security Bureau is about 290 pages long.[96] Additionally, police officers are often burdened with extensive paperwork in LPAPS cases. Numerous forms must be filled out, signed, delivered, and filed throughout the penalty decision process.

When scrutinizing LPAPS penalty decisions, the court examines whether the police have satisfied the following requirements: that the facts of the unlawful acts were clear; that the evidence was sufficient and sound; that the police procedures were lawful; that the application of the law was correct; and that the penalty was proportionate.[97] In sentencing, police officers must comprehensively consider the following factors: the offender's malicious intent, the unlawful purpose and act, the harm caused, and any previous offence record.[98]

However, in practice, several issues have affected the effectiveness of these intended in-built safeguards and procedures. First, although LPAPS offences target only petty unlawful acts, police interrogation can last eight hours and be extended to 24 hours. Since no lawyer is present throughout the interrogation, individuals summoned by the police are deprived of legal assistance and can be very vulnerable. An "Article 43" lawsuit from Shaanxi Province revealed that no guardian was present when a minor was interrogated.[99] Second, the surveyed court judgments have indicated that complaints about police abuses of power are not isolated incidents. All six Article 66(1) offenders mentioned above complained that they had been lured or coerced into confession. Some other offenders also alleged that they were subjected to police duress and misconduct during their interrogation. Nonetheless, it is difficult to tell if the presence of a lawyer can help LPAPS suspects because some criminal lawyers themselves have experienced police violence.[100]

[96] Beijingshi Gong'anju (Beijing Public Security Bureau) (2024) 'Fujian: beijingshi gong'anju zhi'an guanli xingzheng chufa cailiang jizhunbiao (2024 nian ban)' (Appendix: Beijing Public Security Bureau Sentencing Manual Regarding Administrative Penalties on Law-and-Order Violations (2024 ed)) (issued on 12 August 2024, Jinggongzhi zi [2024] No. 703). Available at <https://www.bjfsh.gov.cn/ztzx/wqzt/xzzfgs/qzfbm_22985/fsgafj/jbxx/202204/P020240117373671907475.docx>.

[97] See, for example, *Li Yazhu* supra note 62; *Shen Xiujuan* supra note 88; *Yu Xingkang* supra note 89.

[98] For considering LPAPS offence records, see *Wu Lunfei v Rugao Shi Gong'anju* (*Rugao City Public Security Bureau, Jiangsu Province*) (2019) Su 0691 Xingchu No. 283; *Ling Xiaochun v Taizhou Shi Gong'anju Hailing Fenju* (*Hailing Branch of Taizhou City Public Security Bureau, Jiangsu Province*) (2020) Su 1291 Xingchu No. 105.

[99] *Zhang Xiru v Lantian Xian Gong'anju* (*Lantian County Public Security Bureau, Shaanxi Province*) (2020) Shaan 7102 Xingchu No. 1312.

[100] Sun 'The Day' supra note 46. See, generally, International Service for Human Rights (2024) 'UN Expert Condemns Targeting of Human Rights Lawyers in China,' including the link to a letter sent by M Satterthwaite, UN Special Rapporteur on the independence of judges and lawyers, to the PRC government on 14 February 2024. Available at <https://ishr.ch/latest-updates/in-letter-to-china-un-expert-condemns-targeting-of-human-rights-lawyers/>.

Third, police officers enjoy obvious discretion in enforcing some LPAPS offences, collecting blood and body samples,[101] and imposing sentences. For example, there is significant controversy over whether the police should have pursued and punished the suspects in the four "Article 49" cases mentioned above. All were trivial incidents involving a tiny sum of money: a stolen phone, two stolen flowerpots, damage to a drawer, and the kicking of a door. The same observation applies to several "Article 26" cases: breaking a car mirror, uploading a video of oneself dancing while wearing a Japanese military outfit, and a fight between roadside strawberry sellers.

Article 26 consists of four subsections: the first three punish gang fighting, interception of other persons, forceful possession or damage to property, etc. Article 26(4) is a catch-all clause applicable to any other acts considered picking quarrels and provoking trouble. In addition, Article 26 has a parallel provision in the Criminal Law. Indeed, numerous overlaps exist between LPAPS offences and the crimes stipulated in the Criminal Law. As such, various vague LPAPS provisions and their overlaps with CL contribute to the broad discretion of the police.

How Effective Are the Appeal Mechanisms?

Appeals against LPAPS penalty decisions can be lodged via administrative review or administrative lawsuits. Articles 107-110 provide detailed arrangements for postponing administrative detention pending the outcome of an appeal. However, most LPAPS offenders only managed to bring their appeals after serving detention.[102] Administrative reviews, mentioned in the surveyed court judgments, were primarily conducted on paper.[103] One offender complained that such an administrative review process was a mere formality, not allowing offenders to argue their cases.[104] The success rate of administrative review applications remains unknown. Many offenders skipped administrative review and filed administrative lawsuits directly (see Figures 6c and 7c).

Many offenders hired lawyers to represent them in administrative lawsuits, indicating that they attached much importance to their lawsuits

[101] *Shen Xiujuan* supra note 88; see also *Lin Wenxue v Qingle Shi Gong'anju* (*Qingle City Public Security Bureau, Zhejiang Province*) (2020) Zhe 0303 Xingchu No. 40, in which the court justified the taking of blood and DNA samples by quoting MPS (2014) 'Gong'an jiguan zhifa ban'an changsuo ban'anqu shiyong guanli guiding' (Regulations on Public Security Organs' Case Handling Offices and Areas) (Issued on 1 January 2014). Available in *Beida Fabao.*

[102] Gao, ZJ (2023) 'Duli xingzheng juliu chengxu zhi tichang: lun xingzheng juliu chengxu gaige de "zhongjian fangan"'(A proposal on Administrative Detention Independent Procedures: On a 'Middle Ground Solution' for Reforming Administrative Detention Procedures) 2023 (3) *Xingzheng Faxue Yanjiu* (*Administrative Law Review*) 30 at 32.

[103] These administrative reviews were conducted before the recent revision of 'Administrative Reconsideration Law', which took effect in early 2024.

[104] *Tian Fengtong v Beijing Shi Gong'anju Daxing Fenju and Beijing Shi Daxing Qu Renmin Zhengfu* (*Daxing Branch of Beijing City Public Security Bureau and Beijing City Daxing District People's Government*) (2020) Jing 0115 Xingchu No. 313.

(see Figures 6d and 7d). However, some third parties did not attend court trials when summoned.[105] On some occasions, even public security bureaus summoned were absent from court trials.[106] As mentioned, the police in one "theft" lawsuit could not produce the interrogation CCTV footage when requested. In another lawsuit, a local police station and a detention centre refused to produce CCTV footage showing police dealing with pre-detention procedures.[107] Judges only noted these refusals without proceeding further. As such, complaints about police abuses could not be verified. Judges also readily endorsed the police's extension of interrogation to 24 hours.[108] Some penalty decisions were upheld despite procedural irregularities (see Figures 6d and 7d). This approach by the court is in stark contrast to the revocation made by the central authorities of the police penalty decision in the case of Dr Li Wenliang.

Indeed, it is doubtful whether most courts conduct any meaningful and effective judicial review. A reasoned, well-written judgment running more than ten pages is rare.[109] Typically, a first-instance court judgment is brief, averaging five pages in length. It appears that judges have often copied and pasted the police submissions, endorsed them, and dismissed the lawsuits. For example, many "assault" offenders maintained that they had acted in self-defence. Most judges rejected such a defence without giving any explanation. Only a handful tackled the issue. One judge relied on an MPS normative document.[110] Another judge referred to a 2020 SPC Judicial Interpretation, which only applied to criminal cases.[111]

105 See, for example, *Lu Dongqian v Baoying Xian Gong'anju and Baoying Xian Renmin Zhengfu (Boaying County Public Security Bureau and Boaying County People's Government, Jiangsu Province)* (2020) Su 1084 Xingchu No. 41; *Cui Er'long* supra note 91.

106 *Pan Xingying v Hanyin Xian Gong'anju and Ankang Shi Gong'anju (Hanyin County Public Security Bureau and Ankang City Public Security Bureau, Shaanxi Province)* (2020) Shaan 7101 Xingchu No. 212; *Dang Linlin, Dang Zhongjun, and Yuli v Ankang Shi Gong'anju Hanbin Fenju Chengjiao Paichusuo and Ankang Shi Gong'anju Hanbin Fenju (Countryside Local Police Station, Hanbin Branch of Ankang City Public Security Bureau and Hanbin Branch of Ankang City Public Security Bureau, Shaanxi Province)* (2020) Shaan 7101 Xingchu No. 240.

107 *Guo Lixin v Beijing Shi Gong'anju Shijingshan Fenju (Shijingshan Branch of Beijing City Public Security Bureau)* (2020) Jing 0107 Xingchu No. 97.

108 *Yu Xingkang* supra note 89.

109 *Li Yazhu* supra note 62.

110 *Mou Lanmei v Rugao Shi Gongaju Jiang'an Zhongxin Paichusuo and Rugao Shi Gong'anju (Jiang'an Central Local Police Station and Rugao City Public Security Bureau, Jiangsu Province)* (2019) Su 0691 Xingchu No. 1145, quoting MPS (2007) 'Gong'an zhixing zhonghua renmin gongheguo zhi'an guanli chufafa youguan wenti de jieshi (No. 2)' (Explanatory Note No. 2 on Issues Regarding LPAPS Enforcement by Public Security Organs) (Gongtongzi [2007] No.1, issued on 26 January 2007). Available in *Beida Fabao*.

111 *Wu Enyu v Laifeng Xian Gong'anju (Laifeng County Public Security Bureau, Hubei Province)* (2020) E 2826 Xingchu No.52, quoting SPC, Supreme People's Procuratorate, MPS (2020) 'Guanyu yifa shiyong zhengdang fangwei zhidu de zhidao yijian' (Guidelines on Lawful Use of Self-Defence) (Fafa [2020] No.31, promulgated on 28 August 2020). Available in *Beida Fabao*.

How Efficient is LPAPS?

The two "theft" lawsuits mentioned vividly illustrate how public resources have been wasted. First, before police penalties were imposed, the stolen mobile phone and two flowerpots were sent to assessing agencies to determine their actual value – 500 yuan and 72 yuan, respectively. Second, in each lawsuit, the police produced approximately 30 items of evidence to the court. Meanwhile, the police and the court in the "Beijing Airport" lawsuit also spent plenty of time and resources. But questions arise. a) Can a fine of 200 yuan deter other passengers from repeating what Li had done? b) Should passengers be allowed to opt for social distancing during the COVID-19 pandemic on a plane with plenty of empty seats? And c) Are there better means of handling such an incident?

In "assault" cases, many offenders were reluctant to admit any wrongdoing. Some "assault" offenders even complained that police officers had sided with local authorities or interested parties in their handling of local disputes, especially those involving land issues. Questions arise: a) Is LPAPS a proper mechanism for tackling assaults that occur at the community level? b) How well-equipped and trained are local police officers in handling "assault" cases? c) Would having early intervention by professional social workers in family disputes be better? And d) Nearly all assault cases resulted in certified "minor" injuries that could include bruises, bleeding, swollen faces, broken teeth, twisted limbs, and fractured bones – are such injuries too broadly characterised as "minor", and should some assailants be criminally prosecuted instead?

In recent decades, the prostitution industry has been flourishing in China. Apparently, LPAPS penalties have done little to curb the business or to stop clients from soliciting prostitutes. Moreover, police operations to combat prostitution are often seen by some members of the public as a form of entrapment or even a means of extorting money and other benefits from prostitutes and their clients. Are there any other better measures to control or regulate the industry? Similar queries also apply to LPAPS gambling offences.

Is LPAPS a Tool of Political Oppression?

Article 66(1) punishes both prostitutes and their clients. This LPAPS provision has been used, at times, as a detention tool or a smearing tactic, as in Simon Cheng's case. Meanwhile, local police frequently used Article 26 to prevent, stop, or punish villagers who travelled to Beijing to petition. Indeed, Article 26 of LPAPS and its sister provision, Article 293 of the CL, are well-known for their role as the CCP's convenient tools for maintaining stability (*weiwen*). Moreover, some other vague LPAPS provisions allow police officers broad discretion when dealing with petitioners, as seen in the case of the Heilongjiang prison employees. In the case of Dr Li Juan from Anhui Province, she was fined 300 yuan for "spreading false information about an epidemic." Did this penalty form a part of the nationwide campaign to stop the news of COVID-19 from spreading? If yes, did both the police retraction and the court judgment serve the political purpose of righting the wrongs of the campaign?

Recent Revision of LPAPS

As of May 2025, LPAPS is still undergoing another major revision. There have been long delays due to several highly controversial proposed changes contained in the first draft of the amendment bill.[112] A second draft was tabled before an NPCSC meeting in June 2024.[113] Discussion on the pending revision is beyond the scope of this chapter. For years, Chinese scholars have made numerous LPAPS reform proposals. These include a stipulated right to access lawyers;[114] formation of a specialized court to hear LPAPS cases;[115] a reduction in the duration of detention;[116] and the introduction of community service orders.[117]

Some proposals were made in light of reforms that took place in Taiwan. There, the 1943 LPPO was ruled unconstitutional and eventually replaced by the Social Order Maintenance Act (SOMA) in 1991.[118] Under the latter, detention for social order violations is limited to five days and imposed by

[112] Bhole, O (2023) 'Increasing Moral Policing in China' *News Bharati* 5 October 2023. Available at <https://www.newsbharati.com/Encyc/2023/10/5/Increasing-Moral-Policing-in-China.html>.

[113] Wang, F (2024) 'Zhi'an guanli chufafa xiuding caoan er'shen: wanshan youguan chufa chengxu guiding' (Second Reading of LPAPS Amendment Bill: Improvements on Penalty Procedures) *www.21jingji.com* 26 June 2024. Available at <https://www.21jingji.com/article/20240626/herald/2fe543cc8fc36fdb8260afb957766090.html>.

[114] Liu, SP et al (2019) 'Zhi'an anjian banli jieduan de lüshi jie'ru jizhi: xuqiu, kunjing yu goujian lujing' (Access to Lawyer During the Processing of Law-and-Order Cases: Demands, Dilemmas, and Construction Pathway) 35 (11) Wujing Xueyuan Xuebao (Journal of Armed Police Academy) 41. https://chinadigitaltimes.net/chinese/719540.html. Not having access to a lawyer has become a common practice. However, there have been exceptions on rare occasions. In July 2025, with the assistance of two lawyers, two alleged LPAPS offenders had their penalty decisions stayed pending the outcome of their appeal. See Jiusihaihun (Spikemoss Blog) (2025) 'Jianguo Xiongdi he Zheng Hongbin bei xingju yi'an, bei zanhuan zhixing' (The Case Concerning Administrative Detention of Jianguo Brother and Zheng Hongbin, Stay of Execution) Reprinted in *China Digital Times* 12 July 2025. Available at https://chinadigitaltimes.net/chinese/719540.html.

[115] Wang, PP and Wang, XD (2022) 'Lun sheli zhi'an fating de biyaoxing he kexingxing' (Introducing Law-and-Order Court: Necessity and Feasibility) 37(2) *Guangxi Zhengfa Guanli Ganbu Xueyuan Xuebao (Journal of Guangxi Administrative Cadre Institute of Politics and Law)* 12.

[116] Zhang, YQ (2015) 'Lun ICCPR yujing xia xingzheng juliu zhidu de "sifahua" gaige' (The ICCPR and the Judicialized Reform of Administrative Detention) 17(5) *Xinan Zhengfa Daxue Xuebao (Journal of Southwest University of Political Science* and Law) 72 at 80-81.

[117] Li, Q (2021) 'Zhi'an guanli chufa de xianshi kunjing yu zhidu fansi' (Penalties on Law-and-Order Violations: Dilemmas and Reflections) 2021 (3) *Zhongguo Renmin Gong'an Daxue Xuebao (shehui kexue ban) (Journal of People's Public Security University of China (Social Sciences Edition))* 133 at 140.

[118] Lifayuan (Legislative Yuan of the Republic of China) (1991) 'Shehui zhixu weihufa' (Social Order Maintenance Act) (Enacted on 29 June 1991; latest revision on 7 May 2021).

a court, not the police. There have been criticisms of SOMA and arguments for its abolition, but the legislation has never been perceived as a convenient tool for police oppression, let alone political oppression.

CONCLUSION

The court judgments surveyed in this chapter certainly do not represent all LPAPS cases. Nonetheless, they indicate that the six notable and controversial incidents mentioned are not isolated but illustrative of the recurrent issues in LPAPS enforcement: frequent complaints about the misuse of LPAPS, the exercise of broad police discretion, and abuses of police powers. In combination, these issues have at times led to police oppression at the community level. The major contributing factors include vaguely worded LPAPS provisions, non-functioning safeguards, and ineffective appeal mechanisms. The lax attitudes of courts and the tolerance of procuratorates towards police misconduct can probably be traced to LPAPS being used as a convenient tool to facilitate political oppression with the ultimate aim of maintaining the CCP regime's control of power.

Meanwhile, LPAPS has not proven efficient or lenient in dealing with local disputes and petty unlawful acts. The police and the court have often spent unjustifiable time and resources on trivial cases and issues. It is also questionable whether LPAPS has been integrating education into punishment. As seen, administrative detention without judicial oversight risks arbitrary deprivation of personal liberty. In addition, the court's regular dismissals of appeals by aggrieved LPAPS offenders and ignoring complaints about police misconduct may harden public attitudes towards the police and the authorities, creating more petitioners, disputes, and even unrest. These are certainly not conducive to good governance of the local community and the country. In short, LPAPS has not performed well in its existing form. That said, this system of two-tier sanctions in tackling unlawful acts will continue to exist for the foreseeable future, as the proposed LPAPS amendments expand police powers.

GLOSSARY OF CHINESE TERMS

Romanisation (Hanyu Pinyin)	Chinese Characters	English Translation
danwei	单位	Unit (work unit, organization)
Daqing weijinglü	大清违警律	Great Qing Code on Police Offences
gong'an	公安	Public security (police)

gong'an jiguan	公安机关	Public security organs
Gong'anbu	公安部	Ministry of Public Security
laodong jiaoyang	劳动教养	Re-education Through Labour
paichusuo	派出所	Local police station
Shehui zhixu weihufa	社会秩序维护法	Social Order Maintenance Act (SOMA) (Taiwan)
weijingfa	违警罚	Police offences
Weijing fafa	违警罚法	Law for the Punishment of Police Offences (LPPO)
weiwen	维稳	Maintaining stability
xinguan	新冠	COVID-19 abbreviation in Chinese)
xingshi anjian	刑事案件	Criminal cases
xunxin zishi	寻衅滋事	Picking quarrels and provoking trouble
zhi'an anjian	治安案件	Law-and-order cases
Zhi'an guanli chufafa	治安管理处罚法	Law on Penalties for Administration of Public Security (LPAPS)
Zhi'an guanli chufa	治安管理处罚条例	Regulations on Penalties *tiaoli* for Administration of Public Security (RPAPS)

Administered Divorce in China: Reflecting on the 2020 Civil Code's Restrictive Turn

LING ZHOU

Shenzhen Technology University

IALS, School of Advanced Study, University of London

INTRODUCTION

The purpose of this chapter is to examine a particular aspect of state-citizen relations following the introduction in the People's Republic of China (hereafter 'PRC') of a new Civil Code (2020, in force, January 1, 2021). This aspect is the growing use, over the past two decades or so, of the right to seek divorce by mutual consent (*fuqi shuangfang ziyuan lihun; xieyi lihun*), the ways in which this important trend has impacted on official thinking about divorce, and the resulting restrictive rules in the Civil Code 2020 on the procedure of consensual divorce through the administrative process. In contextualising the issues involved, we consider the nature of state-family relations in China, in particular the idea that state and family are inextricably linked and mutually dependent.

In Chinese society today, there is a continuing public perception that it is the government's responsibility for the welfare of citizens across a wide range of issues. In my earlier work on consumer protection in a southern Chinese city,[1] I concluded that many consumers looked in the first instance to government (and quasi-governmental organisations) to resolve their complaints, rather than (say) the courts, or other agencies. For more than two decades, there has been a growing reliance on administrative processes to meet the need for divorce. Public perceptions of the government's responsibility for provision of matrimonial uncoupling is one factor helping us to understand what determines processual preferences in divorce. The state has much power, and in popular consciousness therefore bears wide-ranging responsibilities. The difficulties encountered, especially by women, in contested judicial divorce are another factor, of course.

The current system of divorce by mutual consent has been a part of family law in the PRC since shortly after 'liberation' in 1949 when the new Marriage Law 1950 provided at Article 17

> Divorce shall be granted when husband and wife both desire it [....] In eases where divorce is desired by both husband and wife, both parties shall register with the subdistrict people's government

[1] See, in particular, Ling Zhou (2020) *Access to Justice for the Chinese Consumer: Handling Consumer Disputes in Contemporary China* Hart Publishing.

> in order to obtain divorce certificates. The subdistrict government, after establishing that divorce is desired by both parties and that appropriate measures have been taken for the care of children and property, shall issue the divorce certificates without delay.[2]

This provision was continued in the revised Marriage Law 1980 at Article 24, and the further revisions in 2001, at Article 31. China's Marriage Registration Regulations make similar provision at Articles 10 to 13 in the version currently in force (2003). Moreover, the previous version (1994) provided for a month-long period of examination for processing the divorce, at Article 16

> The marriage registration authority shall examine the divorce application submitted by the parties and shall, within one month from the date of accepting the application, register the divorce, issue them a divorce certificate and revoke their marriage certificates where the parties conform to the divorce conditions.

The husband-and-wife relationship is rescinded as soon as they acquire the divorce certificate. As a result of the relaxation of the Article 16 provision on the examination period, the popular observation was that at least in theory, one could get married and divorced in China on the very same day.

The 2003 Regulations at Article 14, we should add here, also provide for a reverse process:

> Where, after divorce, both the man and the woman desire to resume their husband-and-wife relationship (*huifu fuqi guanxi*) on a voluntary basis, they shall undergo the formalities for registration of resumption of marriage with the marriage registration office. The provisions of these Regulations on marriage contract registration shall apply to registration of resumption of marriage.[3]

This suggests that despite the relatively liberal system of divorce by registration, conservative values supportive of marriage and indirectly critical of divorce could be found sitting alongside it.

Moreover, in reaction to the increases in divorce rate over the past two decades or more, the state has come to the view that the rise is facilitated primarily through the availability of divorce by the administrative process of mutually agreed divorce by registration. As a result, the system which has been in place for some 70 years has now been revised. The chapter on Marriage and Family in the PRC Civil Code, which officially came into effect on the first day of 2021, is transformative legislation. In Article 1077,

2 Divorce by mutual consent was found in traditional Chinese law, in the Republic of China Civil Code 1930, and was embraced by socialist China in its attempt to reform the Chinese family post-1949. See Meijer, Marinus (1971) *Marriage Law and Policy in the Chinese People's Republic*, Hong Kong University Press.

3 The 2003 Regulations at Article 14.

provision is made to create a 'divorce cooling-off period' (*lihun lengjing qi*)[4] system applicable to divorce by registration at the legislative level for the first time:

> Where either husband or wife is unwilling to divorce within 30 days after the relevant marriage registration authority has received the divorce registration application, husband or wife may withdraw the divorce registration application from the marriage registration authority.
>
> Husband and wife shall apply in person to the marriage registration authority for the issuance of a divorce certificate within 30 days following the expiry of the time limit prescribed in the preceding Paragraph, failing which, they shall be deemed to have withdrawn their divorce registration application.

The Civil Code, in this Article, thus stipulates that after the marriage registration authority receives the application for divorce registration the parties are entitled to change their mind. If one or both parties conclude that they do not really want to divorce within 30 days, then there is a withdrawal of the divorce registration application that has been lodged with the marriage registration authority organ. If, however, within another 30 days after the expiration of that initial time limit both parties apply in person to the marriage registration organ for a divorce certificate, then that certificate is granted. Nevertheless, and very importantly, if no such application is made, the application for divorce registration is deemed to have been withdrawn. So, there is a requirement that the parties seeking divorce have to remain pro-active. If the necessary steps are not taken, then the presumption is that they have withdrawn their application. Implicit in the restrictions placed on parties divorcing by registration is the idea that many divorces in recent years are 'reckless divorce' (*qingshuai lihun*), namely, divorce having been carried out in an impulsive, rash and unthinking manner.

Coming into effect on the same day as the Civil Code itself, (January 1, 2021) a Judicial Interpretation offered by the Supreme People's Court elaborated on many parts of the Chapter on Marriage and Family in the Code (hereinafter, the SPC Interpretation).[5] This is, as might be expected, primarily focused on contested divorces—matrimonial cases that necessitate the intervention of the court. However, in Article 89 the SPC Interpretation does provide an interesting gloss on one aspect of consensual divorce by registration:

[4] A popular expression not used in the Code itself.

[5] Interpretation of the Supreme People's Court on Application of the Part on Marriage and Family under the 'Civil Code of the People's Republic of China' (1) (Zuigao renmin fayuan guanyu shiyong 'zhonghua renmin gongheguo minfadian' hunyin jiating jiufen bian de jieshi, 1), published in December 2020, effective from January 1st, 2021.

> Where a party concerned, after going through the procedures for divorce registration with a marriage registration authority, makes a request claiming compensation to the competent people's court in accordance with Article 1091 of the Civil Code the people's court shall accept the request. However, the people's court will not uphold the request if the party concerned has explicitly waived this request when going through divorce by agreement.

The reference to Article 1091 of the Civil Code is to a provision allowing for compensation to an injured party in the marriage unless that specific waiver has been given:

A 'no-fault spouse' has the right to claim compensation where divorce is caused by one of the following acts done by the other spouse:

(1) has committed bigamy;

(2) has cohabited with another person;

(3) has committed domestic violence;

(4) has maltreated or deserted a family member; or

(5) has acted with other serious faults.

This suggests, again, continuing concerns reflective of moral conservatism, with the possible identification even in mutually agreed divorce by registration of parties with 'fault' and parties with 'no fault', and with the latter empowered to sue the former for compensation for suffering caused during their marriage.

CHANGING PATTERNS OF DIVORCE

The process of divorce by registration does in practice require the local Civil Affairs officials (in effect, the marriage and divorce registration authority) to attempt mediation so that the couple might consider continuation rather than dissolution of the marriage, and to be assured that appropriate child custody and property and financial arrangements have been agreed. Nevertheless, procedurally the process of divorce by registration until the 2020 Civil Code came into force at the very beginning 2021 has been much easier. As noted above, an examination period of one month was not continued in the 2003 Marriage Registration Regulations, and this has been one factor facilitating greater use of the track of registered divorce by mutual consent. Another factor, I surmise, is a growing sophistication on the part of many people about the nature of marriage, including a recognition that many couples are not suited to each—they have 'incompatible personalities' (*xingge buhe*), which means that both parties may be quite agreed that they want to get a divorce.[6] Nowadays in the major cities of China many women are financially independent, and no longer see their role as one of providing

[6] Data provided by the Supreme People's Court suggests that over 77.51% of the parties getting a divorce in the court say that they have a break-up of relationship because of, inter alia, 'incompatible personalities'. See Judicial Big Data on Divorce Cases, available at: https://www.court.gov.cn/fabu-xiangqing-87622.html.

husbands with sons. The effects of these changing attitudes include a decline in the birth rate, and an increase in the divorce rate. Especially because of the single-child policy in force in the 1980s, 1990s, and 2000s daughters in more developed cities were (and still are) regarded as equally precious as sons to the family. When they mature into women they are much more reluctant in the past to endure misconduct by their husband. And these women usually have a supportive original family who can help with childcare and give financial assistance when buying residential property in the large urban areas.

The relative ease of consensual divorce by registration is reflected in the official statistics on divorce over the past twenty years or so.

Figure 1. Graph of statistics on divorce registered with the civil affairs department from 2006 to 2021. [7]

Year	Number
2006	1,291,000
2007	1,457,000
2008	1,609,000
2009	1,802,000
2010	2,010,000
2011	2,207,000
2012	2,423,000
2013	2,815,000
2014	2,957,000
2015	3,149,000
2016	3,486,000
2017	3,704,000

[7] Statistics adapted from the website of the Ministry of Civil Affairs, available at: https://www.mca.gov.cn/

2018	3,812,000
2019	4,047,000
2020	3,736,000
2021	2,141,000

Figure 2. Table of number of divorces registered with the civil affairs department from 2006 to 2021.[8]

THE MORAL PANIC

A combination of pressures has impacted on official policy thinking about the divorce situation, creating what sociologists might well characterise as a moral panic.[9] In addition to the factors noted above of changing social attitudes in the area of gender and reproduction, the close association in Chinese society and culture of the paternalistic state with the family, and of the felt need for stability in both the state and the family have also been important factors encouraging conservative attitudes to divorce, and official fear of climbing divorce rates. Moreover, China has been taken through a demographic transformation in the post-Mao era of reform, most obviously in the form of the birth limitation programme and policies promoting the ideal of one-child families. Although generally benefitting the status of urban women, it has also left China with a population that is aging, and which continues to age. The increasing costs of bringing up children and of schooling have also encouraged a decline in fertility rates, and contributed also to decreasing rates of marriage. Since childbirth is still officially seen as something that should take place within marriage, high divorce rates are easily characterised as bearing negative demographic consequences .

It should be added, nevertheless, that despite the recent increases, even at its highest levels, China falls some way down the list of countries with high divorce rates. Of the 13 countries with the highest divorce rates, China ranks only seventh (at 3.2 annually, per 1000 people) significantly below for example Russia (3.9) and tied with Belgium (3.2).[10] While recognising that divorce can indeed be problematic and may lead to social and individual difficulties, that divorce is still seen intrinsically as a 'social problem' in need of curative treatment reflects conservative official thinking. This perspective continues to see matrimony between persons of the opposite sex as the preferred and normal mode of conjugal union, and as performing

[8] Ibid.

[9] By moral panic is meant a situation in which public reports create a much-exaggerated sense of uncertainty and unease about a particular social problem or social group so that there is a popular demand of the authorities that something is done about it – even though the information which has created the panic is often limited and inaccurate. See, for example, Stanley Cohen (1980) *Folk Devils and Moral Panics: The Creation of the Mods and Rockers*: St. Martin's Press.

[10] This data is provided at: https://worldpopulationreview.com/country-rankings/divorce-rates-by-country.

a socialization role, and a social regulating function. Conventional marriage needs to be defended, and divorce reflects individual failings, and sometimes creating social problems. For this reason, couples should persist with their relationship, despite disagreements.

From the point of view of couples divorcing by the process of registration, the growing disparity between the figures for divorce by registration and those for judicial divorce should be seen as a realisation of their right to divorce. Article 49 of the PRC Constitution provides that it is prohibited to undermine freedom of marriage, and this is generally taken to include freedom of divorce. It should be a matter of choice by the parties as to how and when they get divorced. In addition, it should be added here, much English language discourse on divorce issues in China have hitherto focused on the difficulties encountered in the process of contested, judicial dissolving of marriage. While this focus is rewarding in terms of the rich data and complex issues that it reveals, there is sense—given the figures above—that this approach is court-centric, and that the picture of divorce in China can only be painted fully by extending the existing analysis to mutually agreed divorce by registration.

The practice of contested divorce, as many observers have noted, has remained problematic in various ways for quite some time. A number of the most important difficulties have been analyzed in a recent collection of studies on issues in family law and practice in China.[11] Thus, despite the introduction of an anti-domestic violence law in 2015, judges, police and other authorities are inclined still to treat domestic abuse as a relatively minor issue and to give emphasis instead on the need for family unity. To a significant extent there remains an under-criminalization of the law in this sensitive area. Judges handling divorce cases, especially in rural areas, continue to tend to downplay allegations of husband on wife violence and to allow an abusive husband to retain principal custody over a child, especially a male child. Abused women who depart the family home for self-protection often leave their child or children behind. In some areas of China, the courts have experimented for nearly a decade with their own cooling off system (*lihun lengjiqi zhidu*). A wife usually will have to ensure a rejected divorce application and a delay of a year before her divorce petition will be accepted by a court. Such delays are intended to give the parties time to restore harmony in their broken relationship, but in effect work against the interests of women. Moreover, in general terms rural women tend to suffer poor legal services and are at a general disadvantage when attempting to secure their interests in the matrimonial home. Given that many of the problems are matters of practice and attitude rather than law, it seems unlikely that the new Civil Code will in itself significantly improve matters.

The 2020 Civil Code brings together the pre-existing Marriage Law and Adoption Law within a single Part 5, entitled 'Marriage and Family', with

[11] See, in particular, Xin, He, Moscati, Maria Federica and Palmer, Michael (2020) 'China's Family Law in Action: An Introduction' 15 (2) *Journal of Comparative Law* 1-21, and the various essays in the special issue introduced by He, Moscati and Palmer.

the inclusion also of some additional provisions.[12] The two preexisting laws ceased to have effect on January 1, 2021. Part V is in effect supplemented, as we have noted above, by the SPC Interpretation of that Part which came into effect on the same day. It is divided into five chapters, namely General Provisions (1040-1045); Marriage (1046-1054), Family Relationships (*'Jiating Guanxi'*, 1055-1075) Divorce (1076-1092) and Adoption (1093-1163).[13] The General Provisions now include an exhortatory term at Article 1043 'A family shall establish a good family style (*youliang jiafeng*), promote family virtues (*hongyang jiating meide*) and stress the development of a civilized family (*zhongshi jiating wenming jianshe*)'. This section continues to declare basic principles found in the earlier legislation including freedom of marriage, gender equality, protection of vulnerable categories of person (women, children, the elderly and persons with disability). Additionally, fundamental prohibitions are also restated, including prohibition of bigamy, domestic violence, and transactions in children disguised as 'adoptions'.

In the Chapter on Marriage, the Code persists with the legal position that only woman and men may marry. Same-sex relationships receive no legal recognition. Marriage is created by the process of registration and the issue of marriage certificates, not by celebration. The minimum legal ages of marriage, which in comparative terms are rather high, remain at 22 for men, and 20 for women. Spouses have equal status within marriage and family. They may also retain their respective surnames names after marriage and, depending on the agreed wishes of the two parties, the wife may become a member of her husband's family or vice versa—the latter arrangement being important during the era of the single-child family policy, when the wife's parents may have been in need of domestic support. Any property acquired during the marriage becomes the joint property of the spouses. Nevertheless, ownership is not joint where the property was owned by one of the spouses prior to marriage, derives from compensation for personal injury, or where specified in—for example—a will, or consists of goods used on a daily basis. In some respects, these provisions work to the disadvantage of women—for example, where a husband is gifted an apartment prior to marriage which in reality will serve as the matrimonial home.

The Chapter on Family Relations in the Code continues the strong emphasis on the family (including where relevant, grandparents) as a unit of care and mutual respect and support.[14] This has long been an important part of the welfare policies of the state. The wife and husband are expected to

[12] A succinct English-language account of the major features of the provisions on marriage and family in the 2020 Civil Code is provided in Chinese Justice Observer 'PRC Civil Code Series […] About Part V Marriage and Family', 18 July 2020 available at: https://www.chinajusticeobserver.com/a/prc-civil-code-series-05-the-thing-about-part-v-marriage-and-family%C2%A0.

[13] The Civil Code provides a corpus of rules governing the processes of adoption of children, and adoptive relations, but adoption is not directly relevant for the analysis of administered divorce by mutual consent and so is not dealt with here.

[14] A policy further strengthened in the 2021 Law of the People's Republic of China on the Promotion of Family Education (*Zhonghua renmin gongheguo jiating jiaoyu cujin fa*).

support each other, and enjoy equal entitlement to, and are equally obliged to take care of, their children. Among the consequences of this policy as that mature children are under a duty to support their elderly parents, reciprocating the support given to them by their parents when they were growing up. On the other hand, if parents fail in their obligation to provide care and properly bring up their offspring, then the child or children may seek maintenance costs from the parents.

The Civil Code Part V in its Chapter regarding divorce, as noted above, provides for two processes of divorce. The first, which is the subject of this paper, is the system of divorce by mutual consent, in which the parties seek official registration of the termination of their matrimonial relations. The second, in contested cases, is by the process of judicial proceedings. In the latter case, however, the court will likely attempt mediatory intervention in order to try to secure a reconciliation between the parties. It is only if the judge concludes that the relationship between the couple is irrevocably broken (*ganqing polie*) that divorce will be permitted. For young children (especially under the age of two years) the general position is that the mother is awarded custody. In the case of children above the age of age, her or his wishes are to be considered. Up to that age, custody is a matter of negotiation between spouses—which, as we have noted, may well work against the interests of the wife. This Chapter also details the legal norms governing payment of child support and other financial aspects of the dissolved marriage, as well as contact rights of a non-custodial parent. As noted above, in cases where there has been domestic abuse, or one partner has cohabited with a third party, the partner who has thereby suffered harm may claim damages. As also noted earlier, the divorce chapter also provides for consensual restoration of marriage—such provision also, arguably, reflecting policy reluctance to accept the idea of divorce.

Many of these provisions in Part V are a matter of particular debate within China, and some are clearly reflective of a moral conservatism in Chinese family law. But it is also clear that one the most controversial issues is to be found in the relatively small number of provisions—Articles 1076, 1077, and 1078—which deal with mutually consented divorce by registration, in particular the 30-day cooling-off period introduced into system for registered divorce for the first time, and justified as an attempt to prevent 'reckless' divorce.

DEBATES AND DISAGREEMENTS

As might be imagined, the introduction of the cooling off period has attracted considerable controversy. Perhaps the two most important areas of debate, and which are focussed on here, are the impact on gender equality and the actual process of divorce registration. Of course, there have been other areas of disagreement including, for example, in the years before the provision was introduced, what might be the most appropriate length of time for the cooling period. Despite the controversies, as we have seen in this essay, it does not stand alone as a provision reflective of the moral conservatism in Chinese family law, and I surmise that the new system will remain in place for some considerable length of time. In general, we may say that in the period before the Civil Code came into force at the start of 2021, the disagreements were mainly focussed on the substantive issue of whether or not there should be a cooling-off period. After the Code came into force, the focus has been on procedural issues, especially how best to shape the process of confirming the intention to divorce within the additional one-month period.

Impact on Gender Equality and Freedom of Marriage

Those who support the cooling-off period believe that the additional time required before the divorce may proceed will likely reduce the number of 'reckless divorces' (*caoshuai lihun*) —the divorce decision is seen as having been made by parties without due consideration and is regarded as an abuse of the freedom of divorce. For example, one of China's leading family law specialists, Ma Yinan, argues that although imperfect, the cooling-off period is the still best available policy choice for preventing parties from proceeding with a divorce that they might later regret, so that overall in China the divorce rate is reduced and a good family environment and social order is maintained.[15] Other possible methods, such as requiring a recommendation from the work unit, creating a one-month period in which the administrative body could investigate a proposed divorce, and a better system of separation before divorce, are no better than a simple cooling-off period. In the past ten years, Ma reminds us, most divorces in China have been handled by the marriage registration authority through administrative procedures. In 2003, following the promulgation of the revised Marriage Registration Regulations, the divorce rate rose dramatically—in the Regulations, the process of administrative divorce may proceed if it is mutually agreed by the parties, and this represented respect for the parties' free will. The 2003 Regulations cancelled two important restrictions on divorce previously in force—the requirement to obtain a recommendation letter from the work unit before a divorce is granted, and the one-month period for marriage registration authority to investigate a proposed divorce. As a result, the marriage registration authority simply checked the completeness of documentation, and did not seek to explore the reasons for the application for divorce.

Since then, the divorce rate has maintained a relatively high level, so that the overall divorce rate increased from 0.9‰ in 2002 to 3.2 ‰ in 2017. Also, the rate for divorce by mutual consent exceeded the rate judicial divorce for the first time in 2003, and continued to rise so that by 2020 more than four-fifths of divorces granted were for administrative divorce by mutual consent. Empirical research by Song Jian and Li Lingchun has shown that the introduction of cooling-off period did reduce the divorce rate significantly in 2021,[16] though the negative impact of Covid 19 on social life as a contributing

[15] Ma, Yinan (2020) 'Lengjingqi shi dui qingshuai lihun de xianzhi he yueshu' (Divorce cooling-off period is a restriction and restraint on reckless divorce) (2020, 4) *Funü Yanjiu Luncong* (Journal of Chinese Women's Studies) 103-107.

[16] Song Jian and Li Lingchun (2022) 'Lihun lengjingqi" zhengce nengfou jiangdi lihun shuiping', (Can the 'Divorce Cooling-Off Period' Policy Reduce the Divorce Rate?) *Tansuo yu*

factor should also not be ignored. Their work also points to other strategic motives for divorce, so that some divorces are also driven by strategies intended to enhance the possibilities of buying more properties—a kind of a 'pseudo divorce' that is also to be discouraged from a policy perspective. Those who submit a mutual consent divorce application but who then decide not to break up after the cooling-off period constitute 29.6% of such divorce applications[17]—that is, around one third of applicants for administrative divorce by mutual consent choose not to proceed with the divorce.[18]

At least in the short term, as Song and Li suggests, the cooling-off period has helped and will continue to help achieve the policy goal of the state to reduce the actual divorce rate. However, the cooling-off period can also be a double-edged sword—the increase of cost for getting a divorce may frighten those who have not yet entered into a marriage, so that their approach to getting married is more cautious, thus, leading to a reduce in the marriage rate. In fact, Korea used to face a situation in which the cooling-off period policy was effective in reducing the number of divorces by mutual consent, but indeed also increased the number of contested divorces through the court. Because it is only one year since the publication of the Civil Code, Song and Li cannot provide more statistics to show the trend of divorce rate affected by the cooling-off period, and they argue that it will take time to see the true effectiveness of the policy.

Another commentator, Ma Zhiyong observes that China's decision makers have been oscillating between different ideologies of divorce policy at different development stages post Liberation in 1949.[19] On the one hand, China is deeply affected by ideologies of Confucianism which stress that marriage is bound to family, and hold that people should prioritise their moral responsibilities to family and society. On the other hand, there have been periods times when freedom of marriage and women's rights to divorce have been emphasised. For example, when the first marriage law in the PRC was published in 1950, decision-makers supported the ideology of freedom of marriage and of personal emotional fulfilment, in large part so as to gain political supportive for the new government by demolishing what was characterised as the old feudalistic marriage system. But this support for freedom of marriage did not last too long and soon in judicial practice the court was back on the trail of prioritising family responsibilities and being cautious in rendering divorces, and using mediation to promote reconciliation rather than amicable dissolution. Again, in 1980, the ideology of freedom of marriage (including of divorce) was re-emphasized by the revised Marriage Law of that year. However, what was associated with the more

Zhengming (Exploration and Free Views) 119-128.

17 As illustrated in the popular film directed by Feng Xiaogang, 'I am not Madam Bovary' (Wo bushi Pan Jinlian) 2016.

18 Song and Li 'Divorce Cooling-off Policy' supra note 16 at 127.

19 Ma Zhiyong (2022) 'Lihun Lengjingqi' zhidu de shengcheng luoji jiqi fansi (The General Logic of the Cooling Off Period System and its Reflection), 3 *Faxue Jia* (The Jurist) 14-28.

relaxed policy on divorce in the 1980s was the emerging social problems of economically successful men taking second wives, third wives and mistresses publicly, especially in developed areas such as Guangdong. In the eyes of the party-state, this misconduct was an important cause of social instability. Thus, in practice, the court became more cautious in rendering divorces and agreed that parties should not be granted a divorce, especially at their first attempt. But, while the court was holding back on granting divorces, there was the relaxation on getting a divorce by mutual consent. In particular, in 2003, the revised Marriage Registration Regulations had removed the restrictions for investigating the conduct of couples in a marriage applying for divorce, and as time progressed, as we have seen, this became the preferred avenue for many couple's intent on divorce. Now in 2022, the pendulum leans to the ideology of prioritising family responsibilities again, so as to counter the low birth rate and high divorce rate in China.

Obviously, China has adopted a utilitarian approach in shaping its divorce policy. Whenever problems of social instability in family life are thought to be on the rise, there is increased reliance on the escape route of reviving traditional Confucius values prioritising family responsibilities over individual needs. The application of a cooling-off period, in this context, should be seen as another such attempt of restricting freedom of divorce in the face of perceived social difficulties—especially demographic difficulty of the now entrenched low birth rate. It seems clear that women's rights have not been sufficiently dealt with when the authorities introduced the cooling-off period in the processes of consensual divorce. In his analysis, Ma Zhiyong adds that unless there are changes in policy and practice, that women will become alienated from the new system restricting divorces. They will not accept the policy over-emphasis on family responsibility, especially the wife being subordinated to husband and sacrificing herself for the family.[20] Indeed, as Supreme People's court data shows, over 70% of the divorces at first instance are the result of suits brought by women rather than by men, indicating that women are more likely to feel dissatisfied in their marriage.[21] The legitimacy of the policy can only be justified when it reflects the core value of equality of men and women—a basic socialist value that China also strives to promote.

Impact on Actual Process of Divorce Registration

Some scholar argues that the one-month period is actually not primarily driven by the idea that it is needed for parties to 'cool off' their emotions and to avoid making reckless decisions. It is more of a practical failure—the

[20] Ma Zhiyong 'The General Logic', supra note 19, at 24.

[21] Data published by the Supreme People's Court available at: https://www.court.gov.cn/upload/file/2018/03/23/09/33/20180323093343_53196.pdf. The data also shows that over 91% of the divorce cases at the first instance in the courts are those in which only one party wants to get a divorce.

divorcing parties often struggle to reach a satisfactory divorce agreement on issues of matrimonial property, childcare, eldercare and so on. Many marriage registration officers see the meaning of a 'cooling-off period' in these terms—as a period for the formation of an agreement on matters surrounding the divorce. Those who fail to reach a divorce agreement within the limited time, will have to put aside the application for the divorce temporarily. They may come back again, either to the court or to the marriage registration authority for such a divorce. In this sense, what the parties truly regret is perhaps not the break-up of the relationship itself, but the benefits and losses sharing plan for their dissolving marriage.

Some reports also suggest that marriage registration authorities may be employ certain strategies to deliberately hold up a divorce. For example, parties may not be able to make an appointment for confirming the divorce after the 30-day cooling-off period.[22] In this sense, parties may have reached an agreement on divorce but they fail to proceed with it because of restrictive practices set up by the officials. As the default position is that the agreed divorce then lapses, and the parties remain married, this is a serious divorce impediment. Without thorough empirical research I cannot comment on this processual barrier, but on the surface at least it does suggest that there may now be issues of administrative injustice in mutual consent divorce. The fact that there is a restriction for a divorce through administrative processes for mutual consent divorce, may also affect judges' view on granting a divorce through a court trial—which is already a tough process under the current Chinese judicial divorce system.[23] Indeed, it should be pointed out here that the cooling-off period was first used in the court for contested divorce applications. On July 2018, the Supreme People's Court issued 'Opinions of the Supreme People's Court on Further Deepening the Reform of Modes and Working Mechanisms of Family Trials (for Trial Implementation)',[24] which stipulates that 'With the agreement of the two parties, the people's court adjudicating a divorce case may set up a cooling-off period of no more than 3 months. It is likely that this judicial provision has encouraged the establishment of such a period with divorce by mutual consent through the administrative process. However, as with

[22] See for example, Davidson, Helen 'China divorces drop 70% after controversial "cooling off' law", *The Guardian*, 18 May 2021, at: https://www.theguardian.com/world/2021/may/18/china-divorces-drop-70-after-controversial-cooling-off-law.

[23] Zhang Li (2022) '"Minfadian" lihun lengjingqi tiaokuan de shiyong yuanli: neihan yu waiyan' (The Applicable Principle of the Cooling-off Period Clause of Divorce in the Civil Code: Connotation and Extension), (2022, 1) *Fazhi yanjiu* (Research on Rule of Law) 36-44. For example, article 147 of the Civil Procedure Law (revised 2021), states that 'Divorce cases that are not allowed to divorce by judgment and by mediation, and cases in which the adoptive relationship is maintained by judgment or mediation, if there are no new circumstances and new reasons, the plaintiff files another lawsuit within six months, shall not be accepted.' Also, article 179 of the Civil Code also states that only 'Where one party is declared as missing and the other party files divorce proceedings, divorce shall be approved.'

[24] Opinions of the Supreme People's Court on Further Deepening the Reform of Modes and Working Mechanisms of Family Trials (for Trial Implementation) (Guanyu jinyibu shenhua jiashi shenpan fangshi he gongzuo jizhi gaige de yijian [shixing]), published on August 2018 by the Supreme People's Court.

divorce by mutual consent, some scholar argues that the temporary trial of a cooling-off period in the process of judicial divorce should be abandoned because there are already too many obstacles for getting a divorce in the court, including the deliberate 6-month waiting time for parties to rethink about their marriage before making another attempt for divorce following a rejected divorce application. Clearly, both the court and the civil affairs administrative organs have gone back to supporting the more traditional family values, prioritising family interests over individual rights.

It is questionable that whether the policy of a cooling-off period will achieve the goal of reducing 'reckless divorces', because it is not at all clear that a substantial number of divorces are in reality decided recklessly. One research paper suggests that most of the cases in which parties fail to get divorce are those where the parties have agreed on the divorce itself, but fail to agree on certain terms in the divorce contract during the 30-day period—parties have a genuine intention to secure a divorce, but lack the time to reach a unanimous decision on the divorce agreement.[25] However, there are already existing mechanisms that protects parties' interests over their divorce agreement, when the parties get a divorce through administrative procedure—article 70 of the SPC Interpretation provides that 'parties [may change their minds on] the terms in a divorce agreement if they are divorced through the administrative process, and bring suit in a court.'[26] This means that the court will not re-determine on the divorce itself, but will re-handle the issues in the divorce agreement on properties, child care, elder care, and so on upon parties' request. Therefore, it would be unnecessary to set another barrier—the cooling-off period—for getting a divorce, if the period mainly serves as extra time for parties to reconsider their divorce contract and to make post-divorce arrangements more responsibly. The parties can always revise the divorce contract reached through the administrative procedures and seek remedies from the court.

Other scholars suggest that, in order to achieve the goal of reducing the number of 'reckless divorces', it would be more conducive to set up a 30-day 'period of regret' after the divorce is registered, so that parties may cancel their divorce registration and unite again easily, instead of a 30-day period before the divorce is registered.[27] If the parties have differences of view on the terms of a divorce agreement, there is always a remedial process for the parties to correct the terms in the divorce agreement through the court, without changing their marriage status and limiting their freedom of divorce. By nature, the only criteria for deciding whether a divorce is granted, as mentioned above, should be that 'the relationship between the couple is irrevocably broken'. So long as the parties are willing to get a

[25] Zhang Li 'The Applicable Principle', supra note 23, at 37-38.

[26] See supra note 5.

[27] Wang, Xinyu (2021) 'Eryuanlun shiye xia de linhun lengjingqi' (The Divorce Cooling-Off Period under Dualism), 6 *Zhonghua nü zi xueyuan xuebao* (Journal of China Women's University) 79-86, at 86.

divorce through mutual consent, their decision on a divorce should not be affected by the execution of their divorce agreement.

As the cooling-off period comes into effect, it is expected that there will be more and more disputes surrounding a divorce which will need to be handled by the community and local administrative body rather than by the court. As a result, scholars call for a better role to be played by the Women's Federation, so that matrimonial disputes are better resolved by the community.[28] The local administrative body and the local community can work together on the prevention of 'reckless divorce'—instead of a cooling-off period, it is more important for a third party, such as therapists sent by the Women's Association, to intervene in the relationship of the couple and provide psychological support and counselling to diagnose, repair or even heal the marital relationship.[29] For years, with an emphasis on employing mediation in handling family disputes, the state has been working on a collaborative 'judicially, administratively and socially' combined family dispute resolution mechanism and the next step should be to enhance the cooperation between the administrative bodies and social organisations to ensure that couples get a fair treatment for the closing of their relationship.

CONCLUSIONS

The purpose of this essay has been to examine the effectiveness of the new marriage law in 2021 on the protection of rights and interests of vulnerable party upon divorce. Considering the relatively low social status of women for a long period of time in Chinese history, reform to marriage law to better protect women's rights in marriage is necessary and generally expected by the public. The provisions in the chapter on Marriage and Family of 2021 Civil Code mutually agreed divorce by administrative procedure, however, do not seem to have been introduced in a spirit of the promotion and realization of the principle of equality between men and women. The worries are that this new regulation for administrative divorce by registration is very unfavourable for women who want to exit their marriage for the husband can withdraw the application unilaterally during the cooling-off period even after his wife has convinced him to agree to divorce, and perhaps encourage more people to attempt judicial divorce, despite its many difficulties.

[28] See news article at: http://www.women.org.cn/art/2020/7/8/art_25_164605.html.

[29] Ibid.

GLOSSARY OF CHINESE TERMS

Romanisation (Hanyu Pinyin) Translation	Chinese Characters	English
fuqi shuangfang ziyuan lihun	夫妻双方自愿离婚	voluntary divorce
caoshuai lihun	草率离	reckless divorce
ganqing polie	感情破裂	irrevocably broken relationship
Hunyin Dengji Tiaoli	婚姻登记条例	Marriage Registration Regulations
hongyang jiating meide	弘扬家庭美德	promote family virtues
huifu fuqi guanxi	恢复夫妻关系	resume the husband-and-wife relationship
lihun lengjiqi	离婚冷静期	divorce cooling off period
lihun lengjiqi zhidu	离婚冷静期制度	divorce cooling off period system
qingshuai lihun	轻率离婚	reckless divorce
youliang jiafeng	优良家风	good family style
xingge buhe	性格不合	incompatible personalities
xieyi lihun	协议离婚	divorce by mutual consent

A Comparative Study of Administrative Enforcement of Copyright Protection in China and Europe

FAYE FANGFEI WANG*
Brunel University of London

INTRODUCTION

Social media platforms are now key spaces for user-generated content and video monetization. AI technology increasingly supports dispute resolution, including internal content claims, notice-and-takedown procedures and ODR services. AI can be applied in civil or criminal enforcement to implement blocking injunctions and facilitate alternative administrative blocking mechanisms. However, questions persist regarding the reliability and legal clarity of AI-powered content moderation tools in these procedures.

In Europe, content owners can address copyright infringement by first using social media platforms' internal content claim services. If unresolved, they may initiate a notice-and-takedown procedure, pursue alternative or online dispute resolution (ADR/ODR), or, as a last resort, file a civil or criminal lawsuit, or both.

In most countries, service providers are responsible for managing notice-and-takedown procedures. In China, rightsholders also have access to administrative enforcement through the National Copyright Administration of China and its branches.[1] This administrative system is often more time effective in resolving complaints compared to civil litigation, as it requires fewer documents and less evidence from complainants.[2] A key drawback of China's administrative enforcement system is the lack of consistent processes across provinces, leading to varying outcomes.[3] For

* This paper mainly draws upon the author's previous publication in JCL: Wang, F (2022) 'Resolving Online Content Disputes in the age of Artificial Intelligence: Legal and Technological Solutions in comparative perspective' 17 (2) *Journal of Comparative Law* 491-517.

[1] Administrative Enforcement of Intellectual Property in China: Guidance for British companies seeking administrative enforcement against IP infringements in China, 13 November 2023 available at <https://www.gov.uk/government/case-studies/uk-china-cooperation-on-intellectual-propert> last accessed 31 March 2025. (This factsheet was written for the British Embassy Beijing and the UK Intellectual Property Office by Joshua Mandell on 23 October 2023).

[2] *Ibid*, p.2.

[3] Factsheet on Administrative Enforcement of Copyright in China, 6 December 2019 available at <https://assets.publishing.service.gov.uk/media/5f5b4f488fa8f5106910058d/Admin-

highly complex cases or when complainants are seeking damages, court litigation remains the only route, as administrative enforcement can only provide infringement findings, cease-and-desist orders, or fines.[4]

In contrast to China, neither the UK nor the EU has an administrative enforcement system within their respective copyright offices. In the United Kingdom (UK), there is general academic interest in establishing an 'administrative justice' framework for disputes between individuals and the state[5] within the context of the modern administrative system.[6] Similar debates occur in the US over granting administrative adjudicative authority to copyright offices for resolving online video-sharing disputes,[7] as administrative agencies' expertise could enhance copyright enforcement. In the EU, while the Copyright Directive 2019 in its Recital (66) acknowledges the role of administrative authorities in issuing injunctions under national law, it primarily focuses on liability mechanisms for content-sharing service providers rather than users uploading content.[8]

This paper explores a potential administrative justice framework for copyright protection in the UK and EU by examining how digital technologies are transforming administrative justice in China through digital case management and AI-powered decision automation and execution, while also evaluating the possibility of granting adjudicative authority to copyright offices based on insights from China's system. It recommends legal and technological improvements to notice-and-takedown procedures for generative-AI copyright disputes, advocating for stronger platform regulations, more efficient digital case management, and the use of explainable AI-powered content moderation tools. This paper advocates for streamlining the notice-and-takedown process across administrative and civil justice systems to create a more efficient and accessible dispute resolution mechanism, promoting a fairer balance between rightsholders and platform providers. It seeks to promote collaboration among policymakers and stakeholders for harmonized best practices on copyright protection and enforcement.

istrative_Enforcement_of_Copyright_-_IP_in_China_Factsheet.pdf> last accessed 31 March 2025.

4 *Ibid*, p.3.

5 Partington, TM (1999) 'Restructuring administrative justice? The redress of citizens' grievances' 52 *Current Legal Problems* 173-179.

6 Anthony, G (2015) 'Administrative Justice in the United Kingdom' 7(1) *Italian Journal of Public Law* 9-33.

7 Gocha, AJ (2018) 'Modern system for resolving online copyright infringement disputes: administrative rulemaking and adjudication, one-stop fix to the digital millennium copyright act. IDEA' 58(2) *The Journal of the Franklin Pierce Center for Intellectual Property* 131-172 at 168.

8 EC Copyright Directive 2019, Recital (66) and Article (29).

AI-POWERED CONTENT MODERATION: THE NEED FOR HARMONISED ADMINISTRATIVE ENFORCEMENT

Constraints of AI-powered Content Moderation

AI-powered content moderation tools embed AI technology including machine learning and natural language processing to analyse audio and video to detect and manage online content automatically, assisting the enforcement of guidelines and removal of harmful and copyright infringing materials. While AI may improve efficiency, it may also struggle with contextual understanding.[9] AI's current limited contextual understanding can lead to the wrongful removal or alteration of legal content, making human review essential for detected violations. When AI algorithms independently detect and remove infringing content, it raises concerns about determining liability and accountability for wrongful takedowns. the deployment of AI-powered moderation tools for self-executing copyright enforcement may be subject to technological, legal, and self-regulatory constraints.

Technological Constraints[10]

AI-powered content recognition/moderation tools may not accurately monitor or determine infringing content, in particular live streaming. Identifying specific music tracks, videos, or images is challenging due to various factors. Audio misrecognition can occur if the track is played at a different speed, has altered equalization, or includes background noise or echoes. Similarly, video misrecognition may result from changes in playback speed, frame cropping, colour adjustments or heavy compression.[11]

Currently, AI technology remains limited in its ability to comprehend nuanced contexts, such as those involving fair use. Fair use generally entails the reproduction of a limited portion of an original work for a legitimate purpose, which often requires careful consideration of legal and contextual factors. Using the US legislation as an example, there are four consideration factors to determine fair use to unauthorised work of copyrighted work, which include the purpose and character of the use (i.e., educational use); the nature of the copyrighted work; the amount and substantiality of the portion used against the entire work; and the effect of such use (i.e., market value). [12] It was noted that in industries there were attempts to 'incorporate fair use metrics into copyright policing algorithms, both to protect against automated overdeterrence and to inform users of their compliance with

[9] Wang, F (2017) *Online Arbitration* (1st ed.) Informa Law from Routledge at 94.

[10] Wang, F (2022) Resolving Online Content Disputes in the age of Artificial Intelligence: Legal and Technological Solutions in comparative perspective 17(2) *Journal of Comparative Law* 491-517 at 495.

[11] *Ibid.*

[12] 17 USC § 107.

copyright law' but with very limited success.[13] In the case of *Lawrence Lessig v Liberation Music Pty Ltd*,[14] it was argued that using automated takedown requests/notices often increases the number of requests/notices being wrongly flagged and investigated.[15] This, in turn, may impose a significant burden on manpower, escalate costs, and negatively affect the well-being of the parties involved.

The determination of fair use in a borderless digital environment is a complex process, as it will be subject to different national laws and culture interpretations. In addition, its assessment also needs to be contextual on a case-by-case basis. An AI algorithm would be able to determine which portion of the original work has been reproduced and therefore calculate the total proportion that had been reproduced. This may be only one factor in determining fair use. Identifying the reason for the reproduction may be far harder for an AI algorithm to determine. For example, identifying that a detailed commentary followed a reproduced movie clip would require an understanding of not just the words, but the context of the commentary relating to the clip. Likewise, if an audio clip was unreasonably reproduced for the purpose of providing a professional sounding video intro, it would also be difficult for an AI algorithm to determine whether this was the case.

Given the limitations of AI technology in accurately assessing infringing content online, it is worth considering whether current legislation adequately supports the use of AI-powered content moderation tools to address copyright infringement. Additionally, it raises the question of whether existing rules and provisions provide sufficient clarity and legal certainty.

Legal Constraints

Constraints on Substantive Law

From a substantive law perspective, to hold AI legally accountable would require the recognition of AI as a legal entity—a concept that remains highly debated.[16] While advanced AI can mimic human tasks through deep learning, it still lacks full emotions and consciousness, making legal personality unsuitable for AI in the foreseeable future. It has been argued

[13] Burk, DL(2019) 'Algorithmic Fair Use' 86(2) *The University of Chicago Law Review* 283.

[14] Case 1:13-cv-12028, *Lawrence Lessig v Liberation Music Pty Ltd*, 22 August 2013, United States District Court for the District of Massachusetts.

[15] Williams, J (2015) 'Absurd Automated Notices Illustrate Abuse of DMCA Takedown Process' *Electronic Frontier Foundation* 24 February 2015, available at < https://www.eff.org/deeplinks/2015/02/absurd-automated-notices-illustrate-abuse-dmca-takedown-process> last accessed 31 March 2025.

[16] Kurki, VAJ 'The Legal Personhood of Artificial Intelligences' in Kurki, VAJ *A Theory of Legal Personhood* (Oxford Scholarship Online, 2019), Chapter 6. DOI:10.1093/oso/9780198844037.003.0007. It argues that AI is capable of performing similar tasks as human beings and thus should function as legal persons.

that if AI algorithms could possess human consciousness, they should be given legal personality.[17]

There is ongoing debate over whether AI-generated work should be eligible for intellectual property rights (IPR) protection. There is a growing trend of consensus among jurisdictions that an AI algorithm should not be granted legal personality.[18] For example, in China in the case of *Shenzhen Tencent Computer System v Shanghai Yingxun Technology* (2019), the court did not recognize legal personality for Tencent's Dreamwriter software.[19] The US courts have consistently ruled that AI-generated work is not eligible for copyright protection due to the absence of human authorship. For example, in the recent US Federal Appeal Case of *Stephen Thaler v Shira Perlmutter* (representing register of Copyrights and Director of the United States) in 2025, Dr Stephen Thaler, a computer scientist, had created a generative AI named the 'Creativity Machine,' which generated an artwork titled 'A Recent Entrance to Paradise.'[20] He applied for copyright registration with the United States Copyright Office, listing the Creativity Machine as the sole author and himself as the owner. The Copyright Office rejected the application, stating that only works created by human beings qualify for copyright protection, excluding AI-generated works without human authorship under the human-authorship requirement. The appeals court upheld the district court and copyright office's rejection of Dr Thaler's argument that he should be recognized as the author because he created and used the Creativity Machine. The appeal court also rejected the claim that there was an employment relationship between Dr Thaler (as employer) and Creative Machine (as employee). The appeals court therefore affirmed that Dr Thaler's claim did not meet the requirements of the Copyright Act 1976, which allows individuals and organizations to own copyrights for works created by others only through a contractual agreement known as a 'work made for hire.' The court reaffirmed that the Creativity Machine may not be considered the author of a copyrighted work, as the Copyright Act 1976 requires authorship by a human being. Consequently, Dr Thaler could not be recognised as the author of the work.[21]

[17] Papakonstantinou, Vagelis & Paul De Hert, 'Refusing to award legal personality to AI: Why the European Parliament got it wrong', 20 November 2020 available at <https://europeanlawblog.eu/2020/11/25/refusing-to-award-legal-personality-to-ai-why-the-european-parliament-got-it-wrong/> last accessed 31 March 2025.

[18] Wang, F (2023) Copyright Protection for AI-Generated Works Solutions to Further Challenges from Generative AI, Series 2 Vol. 5 No. 1 *Amicus Curiae* 88-103 at 91.

[19] *Shenzhen Tencent Computer System Co Ltd v Shanghai Yingxun Technology Co Ltd* (2019) Yue 0305 Min Chu 14010, Judgment decision on 24 December 2019 by Shenzhen Nanshan District People's Court.

[20] *Stephen Thaler v Shira Perlmutter* (representing register of Copyrights and Director of the United States), Decision 18 March 2025, Appeal from the United States District Court for the District of Columbia (No. 1:22-cv-01564).

[21] *Ibid*, page 23 IV.

This ruling is unsurprising, as unlike many other jurisdictions, the US does not grant copyright protection to 'computer-generated works' and only protects original works created by human authors.[22] According to the US Supreme Court (1879), copyright applies to 'the fruits of intellectual labor' derived from 'the creative powers of the mind.'[23] This principle was reinforced in *Naruto v. Slater* (2018), where the court ruled that a selfie taken by a monkey that accidentally pressed a camera button could not be protected under US copyright law, as it lacked human authorship.[24]

There have been a series of class actions against OpenAI for usage of copyrighted materials for AI data training.[25] For example, in the pending US trial case of *Andersen v. Stability AI*[26] (scheduled in autumn 2026), artists alleged Stability AI and others of copyright infringement by using their works to train AI models and generate similar styled images. Further investigation may be required to understand how AI companies use copyrighted materials to train their systems and whether such usage for data training may infringe copyright law. The decisions of all these pending cases may potentially influence the direction of AI-generated art protection and how courts interpret the balance between AI innovation and IP rights in the US.

Recently the US Copyright Office's Report on Copyright and AI Generative Copyright and Artificial Intelligence in its Part 2 on Copyrightability (2025) affirms that AI outputs are only eligible for copyright protection if a human author contributes sufficient expressive elements, such as incorporating perceptible human-authored content or making creative modifications, but merely providing prompts is insufficient.[27] It concludes that changes to existing law for AI-generated outputs protection is unnecessary.

In the UK, the final Judgment in *Getty Images (US) Inc v Stability AI Ltd*[28] is expected to address substantive legal issues and ethical questions

22 Wang, F (2023) 'Copyright Protection for AI-Generated Works Solutions to Further Challenges from Generative AI' Series 2 Vol. 5 No. 1 *Amicus Curiae* 88-103, p.94. See also United States Copyright Office. 'Copyrightable Authorship: What Can Be Registered.' In *Compendium of US Copyright Office Practices*. 3rd edn, ch 300, 21 August 2021.

23 United States Supreme Court. Trademark Cases, Syllabus from US Supreme Court, 100 US 82, 94 (1879).

24 Naruto v Slater, 2018 WL 1902414 (9th Cir April 23, 2018).

25 Case No 1:23-cv-8292 Class Action Complaint – Authors Guild, et al v Open AI, Inc, et al, United States District Court Southern District of New York, lawsuit field 19 September 2023 (consolidated with *Alter v OpenAI* and *Basbanes & Ngagoyeanes v Microsoft and OpenAI*); Case No 3:23-cv-03416-AMO *Sarah Silverman, et al v OpenAI, Inc, et al*, United States District Court Northern District of California, San Francisco Division, lawsuit filed 27 September 2023 ((consolidated with *Tremblay v OpenAI and Chabon v OpenAI*).

26 Case No 23-cv-00201-WHO *Andersen v. Stability AI Ltd.* (N.D. Cal. Aug. 12, 2024).

27 Copyright and Artificial Intelligence Part 2: Copyrightability, United States Copyright Office, January 2025 available at <https://www.copyright.gov/ai/Copyright-and-Artificial-Intelligence-Part-2-Copyrightability-Report.pdf> last accessed 31 March 2025.

28 *Getty Images (US) Inc and Ors v Stability AI Ltd* [2025] EWHC 38 (Ch).

concerning the use of copyright protected materials in training and developing GenAI models, particularly where rights-holder consent is absent. The case may potentially clarify UK's position on the interpretation of AI training practices and copyright protection.

Although a consensus may be reached among jurisdictions that an AI algorithm should not be granted authorship or ownership for copyright due to various reasons, it will be difficult to reach an agreement on whether or not AI-generated work should be eligible for IPR protection. In the author's opinion, AI-generated work should receive appropriate IPR protection to promote technological development while striving a balanced protection among different rightsholders.[29] The most appropriate persons/authors/beneficiaries for such protection are individuals who make primary necessary arrangements for the development and operation of AI, including creators, programmers, developers, algorithm designers as well as those selecting, inputting, and training data, and the operators or users of the AI. [30] Establishing clear legal and technical mechanisms is essential to identify and protect these contributors.[31] In addition, specialized administrative offices, such as copyright management organizations for AI-generated works, could be established for publishers, and all who make arrangements necessary for the work to be generated, to join and receive awards efficiently in case of their works being in commercial use.

Constraints on Procedural Law

From a procedural law perspective, when global social media platforms (such as YouTube, Tiktok and Facebook) offer AI-powered content moderation tools, they must comply with national laws on notice and takedown requests for copyright infringement, depending on the location of the user or where the content is accessed. For example, YouTube offers a Copyright Match Tool to support the notice and takedown process. Available to users who have submitted a valid copyright takedown request, the tool automatically detects videos that match or resemble others on the platform. Content owners can then review these matches to assess whether they fall under fair use, fair dealing, or similar copyright exceptions.[32] YouTube will encounter legal challenges and uncertainties due to varying national and regional legislation regarding content moderation and copyright enforcement.

[29] Copyright, Designs and Patents Act 1988, s.9(3). See also Wang, F (2022) 'AI and Intellectual Property Rights: IPR Protection for AI-Created Work' (Speech at the Evidence Meeting of AI and Intellectual Property Rights: IPR Protection for AI-Created Work for All-Party Parliamentary Group (APPG), 24 January 2022) available at <https://www.youtube.com/watch?v=E3wMWldnIPM> last accessed on 31 March 2025.

[30] Wang, F (2022) 'AI and Intellectual Property Rights: IPR Protection for AI-Created Work' *Speech at the Evidence Meeting of AI and Intellectual Property Rights: IPR Protection for AI-Created Work for All-Party Parliamentary Group (APPG)*, 24 January 2022 available at <https://www.youtube.com/watch?v=E3wMWldnIPM> last accessed 31 March 2025.

[31] *Ibid.*

[32] Use the Copyright Match Tool, available at <https://support.google.com/youtube/answer/7648743> last accessed 31 March 2025.

In the EU, it is arguable that although the Copyright Directive 2019 'does not impose upload filters nor does it require user-uploaded platforms to apply any specific technology to recognise illegal content',[33] the Copyright Directive in 2019 may still appear to encourage hosting service providers to use technological measures (such as 'content recognition technologies'[34] which is also known as 'automated content recognition tool'[35]) to detect illegal content to avoid liability, which may appear to contradict with the principle of prohibiting imposing 'general monitoring obligations' as set out in the EC E-Commerce Directive and the Digital Service Act 2022. This is due to the wording set out in Article 17(4)(c) of the Copyright Directive 2019 that online content-sharing service providers shall be liable for unauthorized public communication of acts of communication to the public, unless they act quickly to remove or disable access to infringing content upon receiving a valid notice from rights holders and 'make best efforts to **prevent their future uploads**'[36] [emphasis added] Although the European Commission has clarified that the 'best efforts' obligation does not specify any specific means or technology,[37] it is not clear how it is possible to prevent any future uploads without monitoring in line with the principle of prohibiting imposing 'general monitoring obligations'. It was argued that Article 17 of the EC Copyright Directive 2019 may place additional burden on hosting service providers to demonstrate their best efforts by using more stringent content recognition algorithms to scan users' content 'more rigorously and pre-emptively'.[38] In a CJEU (Court of Justice of the European Union) case on April 26, 2022, the Republic of Poland sought to annul Article 17 of the EC Copyright Directive 2019. Poland argued that Article 17(4)(b) and (c) effectively require service providers to conduct 'preventive monitoring' of user-uploaded content using automated filtering tools.[39] Poland claimed

[33] Questions and Answers – New EU copyright rules, 4 June 2021 available at <https://ec.europa.eu/commission/presscorner/detail/en/QANDA_21_2821> last accessed 31 March 2025.

[34] 'Effective Content Recognition Technologies' were proposed in Article 13(1) within Chapter 2 'Certain uses of protected content by online services' in the *Proposal for a Directive of the European Parliament and of the Council on copyright in the Digital Single Market*, COM/2016/0593 final, 14.9.2016. However, such wording was removed in the final adopted Copyright Directive 2019 in its Chapter 2 'Certain uses of protected content by online services'.

[35] Communication from the Commission to the European Parliament and the Council: Guidance on Article 17 of Directive 2019/790 on Copyright in the Digital Single Market, COM(2021) 288 final, 4 June 2021, Section VI.

[36] Directive (EU) 2019/790 of the European Parliament and of the Council of 17 April 2019 on copyright and related rights in the Digital Single Market and amending Directives 96/9/EC and 2001/29/EC, OJ L 130, 17.5.2019, p. 92-125. Article 17(4)(c).

[37] Questions and Answers – New EU copyright rules, 4 June 2021 available at <https://ec.europa.eu/commission/presscorner/detail/en/QANDA_21_2821> last accessed 31 March 2025.

[38] Tie, A. (2020) 'Copyright law issues in the context of video game Let's Plays and livestreams' 3(2) *Interactive Entertainment Law Review* 121 at 128.

[39] CJEU Case C-401/19, ACTION for annulment under Article 263 TFEU, brought on 24 May

that these provisions lack sufficient safeguards to protect the right to freedom of expression and information, resulting in a disproportionate and unjustified limitation on this fundamental right.[40]

In the UK, general monitoring obligations remain prohibited, and there is no legal requirement to use automated filtering software for detecting illegal content. The UK Government's 2020 Online Harms White Paper confirms that service providers will not be required to conduct general monitoring of online content but must swiftly remove illegal material once aware of it, ensuring being comparable with EU e-Commerce Directive liability rules.[41] Platforms are only required to remove or disable illegal content once they become aware of it in order to avoid liability. General monitoring is not mandated due to concerns about excessive burdens on service providers and potential harm to freedom of expression and user privacy.[42] Notably, the UK chose not to implement the EU Copyright Directive 2019, despite its connection to the EC Directive on Electronic Commerce.

In the US, the Digital Millennium Copyright Act (DMCA) provides a notice and takedown procedure, known as the 'safe harbor' provisions, to shield online intermediaries from legal liability for hosting infringing content.[43] While this procedure applies broadly to remove online infringing materials, including counterfeit goods,[44] it is not explicitly covered under the Lanham Act.[45] Section 512(m) of the DMCA imposes no duty on a service provider to 'monitor its service or affirmatively seek facts indicating infringing activity, except to the extent consistent with a standard technical measure'.[46] However, the US Copyright Office has clarified that if automated filtering technology flags repeated infringers, such infringers should be referred for human review, because the rule of no general monitoring

2019, *Republic of Poland v European Parliament and Council of the European Union*, Judgment of the Court (Grand Chamber) 26 April 2022, para. 24.

[40] CJEU Case C-401/19, ACTION for annulment under Article 263 TFEU, brought on 24 May 2019, *Republic of Poland v European Parliament and Council of the European Union*, Judgment of the Court (Grand Chamber) 26 April 2022, para. 24.

[41] 'Consultation Outcome - Online Harms White Paper: Full government response to the consultation' UK Government, 15 December 2020.

[42] *Ibid.*

[43] US Digital Millennium Copyright Act (DMCA), Section 512.

[44] *Tiffany (NJ) Inc. v. eBay Inc.* 600 F.3d 93 (2nd Cir. 2010).

[45] Ballon, I. C. (2019) *E-Commerce & Internet Law: Treatise with Forms* (2nd ed) Thomson/West Publishing 135.

[46] US Digital Millennium Copyright Act (DMCA), Section 512(I)(2). 'The term 'standard technical measures' means technical measures that are used by copyright owners to identify or protect copyrighted works and - (A) have been developed pursuant to a broad consensus of copyright owners and service providers in an open, fair, voluntary, multi-industry standards process; (B) are available to any person on reasonable and non-discriminatory terms; and (C) do not impose substantial costs on service providers or substantial burdens on their systems or networks.')

obligation does not mean that online service providers 'may simply ignore information of potential repeated infringement on their system once obtained'.[47] This approach aligns with recent legislation and court rulings in the EU, supporting the use of automated filtering technology.[48]

In the People's Republic of China (hereafter 'PRC' or 'China') China, the notice and takedown procedure has been regulated by E-Commerce Law of PRC, adopted in 2018 and enforced in 2019 (hereafter 'China E-Commerce Law 2019')[49] in accordance with China Civil Code. This Code provides that rightsholders shall notify the network service provider to take such necessary measures such as deletion, block, or disconnection to tackle a tortious act on the network service.[50] The China E-Commerce Law at Article 42 provides that an IPR holder could notify any content infringement to the e-commerce operator, however any such notice must include prima facie evidence, whilst upon the receipt of such notice, the e-commerce platform operator should 'take such necessary measures as deletion, blocking, disabling the link, termination of transaction and service' in a timely manner.[51] Compared with the relevant legislation in the UK, EU and US, this Article 42 of China E-Commerce Law 2019 provides the threshold of liability, instead of providing general liability exemption like other countries. It stipulates that an IPR holder's wrong notice may result in civil liability or double liability depending on the severity, whilst an 'e-commerce platform operator' may bear the joint and several liability for magnified damage, due to undue delay in taking necessary measures, along with 'operators on platform' who are allegedly engaging in content infringing activities.[52] An e-commerce platform operator should be understood as an e-commerce service provider or 'hosting service provider' (as used in EC Directive on Electronic Commerce, Article 14), whilst operators on platform should be understood as the content generators/providers on platform, 'subscribers' on platform (as used in US DMCA, Section 512), or 'the recipient of the service' (as used in EC Directive on Electronic Commerce, Article 14).

If operators on platform submit a counter notice ('a statement of no infringement') with prima facie evidence to the e-commerce platform operator, an IPR holder should be informed about his/her right to file a complaint to relevant competent authorities or bring a lawsuit in courts.[53]

47 'Section 512 of title 17: A Report of the Register of Copyrights', United States Copyright Office, May 2020, p.3.

48 Joined Cases C-682/18 and C-683/18, *Frank Peterson v Google LLC and Others* and *Elsevier Inc.v Cyando AG*, Judgment of the Court (Grand Chamber) of 22 June 2021.

49 People's Republic of China E-Commerce Law 2019, Articles 41-46.

50 People's Republic of China Civil Code 2020, Article 1195.

51 China E-Commerce Law 2019, Article 42. See the English version available at <https://ipkey.eu/sites/default/files/documents/resources/PRC_E-Commerce_Law.pdf> last accessed 31 March 2025.

52 *Ibid.*

53 China E-Commerce Law 2019, Article 43. See the English version available at <https://

Comparing with relevant legislation in the UK and EU which is currently unclear on the counter notice procedures,[54] the provision in Article 43 of the China E-Commerce Law 2019 provides an additional timeframe to enable the e-commerce operator to lift any measures taken, in that ' if the e-commerce platform operator has not received any notice within fifteen days as of the arrival of the forwarded statement at the IPR holder that the right holder has filed a complaint or lawsuit, it shall immediately stop the measures it has taken'.[55] Such timeframe is helpful to reduce the legal uncertainty as to how the e-commerce platform operator should react upon receipt of a counter notice. This is also in line with the current legislation in the US Digital Millennium Copyright Act (DMCA) that 'unless the copyright owner files an action seeking a court order against the subscriber, the service provider must put the material back up within 10-14 business days after receiving the counter notification.'[56] Unlike China (15 days) and the US (10-14 days), EU legislation lacks clarity on counter-notices and the timeframe for reinstating removed content after receiving counter-notices from uploaders.[57] While counter-notice measures aim to protect uploaders' rights, they have been seen as inadequate in the US.[58]

Additionally, neither the EU, US, nor China require service providers to offer out-of-court settlement options for unresolved content disputes after a counter-notice. However, China's amended Copyright Law (2020) in its Article 60 encourages mediation or arbitration to resolve disputes.[59] WIPO's recent report highlights the benefits of using technology for ODR in B2B digital copyright disputes, such as reducing legal costs and avoiding adversarial processes. Since 2021, WIPO has promoted ODR with initiatives like the WIPO Rules for Expert Determination for User-Uploaded Content,

ipkey.eu/sites/default/files/documents/resources/PRC_E-Commerce_Law.pdf> last accessed 31 March 2025.

[54] Reform of the EU liability regime for online intermediaries - Background on the forthcoming digital services act, European Parliamentary Research Service, May 2020 available at <https://www.europarl.europa.eu/RegData/etudes/IDAN/2020/649404/EPRS_IDA(2020)649404_EN.pdf> last accessed 31 March 2025.

[55] China E-Commerce Law 2019, Article 43. See the English version available at <https://ipkey.eu/sites/default/files/documents/resources/PRC_E-Commerce_Law.pdf> last accessed 31 March 2025.

[56] The Digital Millennium Copyright Act of 1998, U.S. Copyright Office Summary, December 1998 available at <https://www.copyright.gov/legislation/dmca.pdf> last accessed 31 March 2025.

[57] China E-Commerce Law 2019, Article 43. See the English version <https://ipkey.eu/sites/default/files/documents/resources/PRC_E-Commerce_Law.pdf> last accessed 31 March 2025. See also The Digital Millennium Copyright Act of 1998, U.S. Copyright Office Summary, December 1998 available at <https://www.copyright.gov/legislation/dmca.pdf> last accessed 31 March 2025.

[58] Urban, JM, Karaganis, J and Schofield, BL (2017) 'Notice and Takedown in Everyday Practice Urban' *UC Berkeley Public Law Research Paper No. 2755628* available at <http://dx.doi.org/10.2139/ssrn.2755628> last accessed 31 March 2025.

[59] China Copyright Law (amended in 2020 and enforced in 2021), Article 60.

model mediation agreements, and expedited arbitration agreements for digital copyright disputes.[60]

Another comparable feature of the China E-Commerce Directive 2019 with corresponding UK, EU and US legislation is that it applies the knowledge standard to determination of the liability of an e-commerce platform operation. Under the knowledge standard, the e-commerce platform operator should be liable only if it knows or should know any infringing or illegal activities and does not take necessary or appropriate measures expeditiously.[61] The underlying differences among the rule of the knowledge standard among China, the UK, EU and US are that the UK, EU and US, different from China, emphasize that such knowledge must be actual, though there is no harmonised interpretation as to what constitutes 'actual knowledge' in judicial cases or regulations. The US Copyright Office provides limited interpretation to 'actual knowledge' being 'the requisite level of knowledge' of infringing materials by the service provider.[62] In the EU, the notice-and-takedown procedure has faced criticism for its lack of clarity, particularly due to the absence of a clear definition of 'actual knowledge' and a standardized benchmark for determining 'illegal activities.' [63] The EC Directive on Electronic Commerce 2000 outlines three core interconnecting factors influencing a hosting service provider's liability under Article 14(1): 'actual knowledge', actions (to 'remove/disable') and manners ('expeditiously').[64] The Digital Services Act (DSA) 2024 builds on and updates the E-Commerce Directive by providing clearer guidelines. Under the DSA, actual knowledge is presumed when service providers receive a clear and detailed notice containing sufficient information to identify and assess illegal content, including the URL, legal justification, and notifier's details. Reports from trusted flaggers, recognized for their expertise in detecting illegal content, also establish actual knowledge. Additionally, providers are considered to have actual knowledge upon receiving a legally binding order from a court or regulatory authority to remove specific content.

[60] Alternative Dispute Resolution Mechanisms for Business-to-Business Digital Copyright- and Content-Related Disputes: A report on the results of the WIPO–MCST survey, WIPO 2021 at 53-58 available at <https://www.wipo.int/edocs/pubdocs/en/wipo_pub_969.pdf> last accessed 31 March 2025.

[61] China E-Commerce Law 2019, Articles 42 and 45; EC Directive on Electronic Commerce 2000, Article 14; and the US Digital Millennium Copyright Act (DMCA), Section 512(c).

[62] The Digital Millennium Copyright Act of 1998, U.S. Copyright Office Summary, December 1998 available at <https://www.copyright.gov/legislation/dmca.pdf> last accessed 31 March 2025.

[63] Reform of the EU liability regime for online intermediaries - Background on the forthcoming digital services act, European Parliamentary Research Service, May 2020 available at <http://dx.doi.org/10.2139/ssrn.2755628> last accessed 31 March 2025.

[64] Wang, F (2012) 'Response to Public Consultation on Procedures for Notifying and Acting on Illegal Content hosted by Online Intermediaries' (December 2012) Issue 91 *Journal of Intellectual Property Forum*, 93 at 95.

One of the fundamental differences of the safe harbour regime in China, as compared with the UK, EU and US, is that there is no explicit provision confirming that the e-commerce platform operator has 'no general monitoring obligation' on their platform. China E-Commerce Law 2019 is also silent on the legality of using automated filtering software (such as AI algorithms) to detect illegal content and take actions automatically. Based on the wording of China E-Commerce 2019, it could be interpreted that the e-commerce operator has no general monitoring obligation, because necessary measures to delete or disable infringing materials, would only be initiated by the operator upon the receipt of a manual notification from IPR holders with prima facie evidence.

Even if there is no monitoring obligation under relevant legislation, there is still legal uncertainty as to what extent the deployment of AI-powered content moderation tools may be considered as undertaking general monitoring obligation on their services, which may conflict with the prohibition on general monitoring for hosting services in current legislation in Europe,[65] US[66] and China.[67] On the other hand, the deployment of notice and takedown procedures with no general monitoring obligation from hosting services in the UK, EU and US has raised concerns over the effectiveness of tackling illegal content uploads, in particular with the use of AI-powered content moderation tools, because: (1) hosting service providers may receive a large volume of notice requests which places them with an unreasonable and difficult to handle burden;[68] (2) once an approved illegal content is taken down, the same content may be uploaded repeatedly; or (3) hosting service providers may not have the incentives to arrange licensing agreements as they may profit from the dissemination of illegal uploads. In order to improve the efficiency and effectiveness of the notice and takedown procedures, the interpretation of knowledge standard/ requirements and the threshold of allowance and limitation on 'monitoring' need to be further clarified in law and courts. Thus, it is crucial to determine an appropriate relationship between 'knowledge requirements' and 'no general monitoring obligation'.[69]

[65] EC Directive on Electronic Commerce 2000, Article15. UK Regulation on E-Commerce 2000, Article 19 (Provisions in the e-Commerce Regulations 2002 and the e-Commerce Regulations 2018 implementing Articles 12-14 of the Directive are unaffected by the Electronic Commerce (Amendment etc.) (EU Exit) Regulations 2019.) See also 'Consultation Outcome - Online Harms White Paper: Full government response to the consultation', UK Government, 15 December 2020. It sets out that 'the regulator would not compel companies to undertake general monitoring on their online services, as this would place a disproportionate burden on companies and raise concerns about freedom of expression and user privacy.'

[66] US Digital Millennium Copyright Act (DMCA), Section 512(m).

[67] China E-Commerce Law 2019, Articles 41-46.

[68] For example, between 2012 to 2022, there were 5,589,764,758 URL requests for content delistings due to copyright. See Google Transparency Report available at <https:// transparencyreport.google.com/copyright/overview?hl=en_GB> last accessed 31 March 2025.

[69] See also 'Section 512 of title 17: A Report of the Register of Copyrights', United States Copyright Office, May 2020, p.3.

In both Europe and the US, hosting service providers are generally not liable for illegal content unless rightsholders notify them with sufficient evidence. However, if AI algorithms detect illegal content and generate notifications that meet legal standards for evidence, this may constitute actual knowledge of the content. This could raise concerns about whether using AI-powered content moderation tools implies that platforms are monitoring content, potentially increasing their liability if they fail to act quickly on flagged content. Additionally, while YouTube offers AI-powered content moderation tools to assist copyright owners, applying these tools without consent across all videos could be seen as imposing a prohibited general monitoring obligation.

A possible solution is to limit the use of AI-powered content moderation tools to specific issues, like detecting 'manifestly infringing uploads,' instead of employing them as broad, indiscriminate policing tools.[70] AI-powered moderation tools should also be subject to risk assessments under relevant legislation, such as the EU AI Act 2024, to ensure they do not manipulate behaviour or cause harm before their implementation on online platforms.

Self-regulatory Constraints

In the absence of specific legislation and international guidelines, many social media platforms rely on self-regulation to implement AI-powered content moderation tools. Notable examples include YouTube's voluntary Content ID Claims, Meta's moderation tools on Facebook, and Weibo's community-driven content moderation system.

In contrast to Chinese platform Douyin (internationally known as 'Tiktok') which only offers notice and takedown process,[71] YouTube offer voluntary Content ID Claims tools. A content ID claim on the YouTube platform is not a copyright strike within the formal notice and takedown legal procedure. When content creators/generators receive a Content ID claim, it means that their video and audio uploads have been found to contain potentially copyright infringing materials after being automatically checked. The content creators will be given three choices: trim out segment, replace or mute/erase audio.[72] Otherwise, they can share revenue within YouTube Partner Program or dispute the claim. If disputed, the notice will be sent to the content owner. While waiting for the dispute to be resolved, content creators could choose to wait to make their content go live or just publish it. If it is published, any revenue will be held until the dispute is

[70] Wang, F (2022) Resolving Online Content Disputes in the age of Artificial Intelligence: Legal and Technological Solutions in comparative perspective 17(2) *Journal of Comparative Law* 491-517 at 511.

[71] 'Douyin E-commerce Intellectual Property Protection Platform User Guide' 17 January 2024 available at < > last accessed 31 March 2025.

[72] What is a Content ID claim? available at < https://support.google.com/youtube/answer/6013276> last accessed 31 March 2025.

resolved.[73] The content owner can either accept or reject the claim. If rejected, the video creator can choose to accept or appeal. If the video creator's appeal is rejected, the content owner may initiate a takedown notice. This self-regulatory process demonstrates that YouTube's Content ID system is primarily automated, with human oversight mainly provided by content creators and copyright owners who can manually claim or dispute claims through YouTube's voluntary review process.

Facebook (now Meta) first experimented with crowdsourced content moderation in 2010. In 2020 it took a different approach from YouTube and officially established the Oversight Board, a 'quasi-judicial body of third-party experts', to review and provide oversight on its disputed content decisions.[74] The Oversight Board is an independent entity, operating separately from Meta's internal structure and control. Similarly, in 2021 Twitter introduced Birdwatch (now known as 'Community Notes'), which is a community-driven note-taking feature on Twitter (now on 'X') that enables contributors to identify potentially misleading information in Tweets and add notes that provide informative context.[75]

In 2012, Sina launched the Weibo Community Management Centre along with the 'Weibo Community Convention,' which operates like a jury of users resolving disputes.[76] Last updated in 2021, 'Weibo Community Convention' is a set of self-regulatory rules in compliance with relevant Chinese laws. It is believed to operate independently, offering a unique opportunity to observe genuine user behaviour as conflicts are resolved through reasoning, persuasion, and voting instead of authoritative orders. However, it was observed that frequent reporters on Weibo often act as community enforcers or participate in coordinated trolling. Reporting behaviour can be contagious and is sometimes motivated by retaliation. Moreover, potential selection bias may exist, as analysis can only draw upon user-reported cases, leaving uncertainties about unreported moderation activities in this community-driven content moderation system.[77]

As discussed above in the absence of specific international legislation, many social media platforms opt for self-regulation for AI-powered content moderation tools, incorporating human oversight to ensure fair and

[73] *Ibid.*

[74] Zhao, A & Hu, L (2025). Rule social media with users: Unveiling Strategical Governance and User Dynamics in Weibo's Community-driven Content Moderation System, available at <https://osf.io/preprints/socarxiv/da8fz_v1> last accessed 31 March 2025.

[75] Coleman, K (2021) Introducing Birdwatch, a community-based approach to misinformation, available at <https://osf.io/preprints/socarxiv/da8fz_v1> last accessed 31 March 2025.

[76] BBC News: Sina launches Weibo community convention and management regulations, 28 May 2012 available at <https://www.bbc.com/zhongwen/trad/chinese_news/2012/05/120528_sina_byraymondli> last accessed 31 March 2025.

[77] Zhao, A & Hu, L (2025). Rule social media with users: Unveiling Strategical Governance and User Dynamics in Weibo's Community-driven Content Moderation System, available at <https://osf.io/preprints/socarxiv/da8fz_v1> last accessed 31 March 2025.

compliant decisions. This approach may help reduce legal liability if AI systems fail to remove illegal content or mistakenly censor lawful materials.

Administrative Enforcement Measures

The deployment of AI-powered content moderation tools on social media platforms is likely to lead to deeper and more extensive interventions by copyright law in the structure of complex and dynamic markets. Administrative authorities may effectively resolve online content-sharing conflicts by ensuring the consistent implementation of notice and takedown procedures, especially if they are well-regulated and trained in specialized dispute resolution. Administrative authorities could be delegated to resolve AI-related content disputes by applying notice and takedown procedures consistently and effectively, and by contributing to harmonised best practices for copyright enforcement within administrative justice. This approach can also support the judicial system in addressing legal uncertainties surrounding the use of AI-powered content moderation tools on social media platforms.

Laws such as the EU Digital Services Act, the US Digital Millennium Copyright Act (DMCA), and China's Civil Code and E-Commerce Law require platforms to balance content moderation with safeguarding users' rights, primarily using the 'notice and takedown' process.

Technological, legal and self-regulatory constraints have led to a considerable degree of uncertainty of protection for rightsholders on social media platforms. Although there have been fifty-eight countries including China, France, Australia and India signing an international AI declaration to promote AI accessibility, transparency, security, trust and inclusivity,[78] UK and US refused to sign it due to various concerns including national security and global governance.[79] The Council of Europe Framework Convention on Artificial Intelligence, Human Rights, Democracy and the Rule of Law is the first treaty open to non-European countries.[80] Eight Council of Europe member states including the UK, along with the European Union, the United States, and Israel have taken the first step to sign this treaty,[81]

[78] Statement on inclusive and sustainable artificial intelligence for people and the planet, 14 February 2025 available at <https://my.ambafrance.org/Statement-on-inclusive-and-sustainable-artificial-intelligence-for-people-and> last accessed 31 March 2025.

[79] 'UK and US refuse to sign international AI declaration', BBC News, 11 February 2025 available at <https://www.bbc.co.uk/news/articles/c8edn0n58gwo> last accessed 31 March 2025.

[80] Council of Europe Framework Convention on Artificial Intelligence and Human Rights, Democracy and the Rule of Law, Vilnius, 5.IX.2024 available at <https://rm.coe.int/1680afae3c> accessed 31 March 2025.

[81] Press release: UK signs first international treaty addressing risks of artificial intelligence, Ministry of Justice 5 September 2024; Bureau of Democracy, Human Rights, and Labor, US Department of State, 5 September 2024 available at <https://www.state.gov/bureau-of-democracy-human-rights-and-labor/the-council-of-europes-framework-convention-on-artificial-intelligence-and-human-rights-democracy-and-the-rule-of-law> last accessed

however, the treaty still requires ratification to take effect. Reaching an international AI agreement or legislation will be highly challenging, if not infeasible, due to the diverse political and legal cultures, as well as varying economic and technological capacities across countries. Global platforms still need to comply with varying national and regional laws concerning copyright protection, depending on the location of the user or where the content is accessed.[82]

Besides relevant laws, China primarily relies on administrative measures to enforce platform responsibility. For example, in China, the National Copyright Administration of China (NCAC) has been established to provide administrative regulations and administrative dispute resolution service on illegal activities concerning copyright infringement.[83] When rightsowners report a concern to NCAC by post or via their online reporting/complaint platform, rightsowners are advised to provide samples of pirated materials and their sources when reporting.[84] When a complaint is accepted, the copyright administrative authority will investigate the suspected infringement and make decisions to dismiss the case; impose an administrative penalty on the infringer if the infringement is not minor; or to transfer to judicial courts if there is any criminal suspicion.[85] The administrative authority for copyright may give the infringer administrative penalties by 'ordering the infringing act to cease; confiscating the illegal gains; confiscating or destroying the infringing copy; imposing a fine; confiscating the materials, tools, equipment, etc. mainly used to make the infringing copy if the circumstances are serious; or giving other administrative penalties provided for by laws and regulations'.[86] Although NCAC provides a general system for copyright administrative enforcement, it was reported that there are considerable differences in copyright case filing systems set up by individual administrative authorities in different cities and provisions which may result in inconsistent investigation outcomes.[87] Comparing with

31 March 2025; and Canada and Japan sign Council of Europe's first ever global treaty on AI, Council of Europe,11 February 2025 available at <https://www.coe.int/en/web/portal/-/canada-and-japan-sign-council-of-europe-s-first-ever-global-treaty-on-ai> last accessed 31 March 2025.

82 Wang, JF (2025) 'Platform Responsibility with Chinese Characteristics' in Chakravorti B & Trachtman, JP (eds.) *Defeating Disinformation: Digital Platform Responsibility, Regulation and Content Moderation on the Global Technological Commons* Cambridge University Press at 59.

83 National Copyright Administration of China (NCAC) available at <https://www.ncac.gov.cn/> last accessed 31 March 2025.

84 National Copyright Administration of China (NCAC) Online Reporting Platform available at <https://www.ncac.gov.cn/chinacopyright/channels/12578.shtml> last accessed 31 March 2025.

85 National Copyright Administration of China (NCAC) Complaint Guideline, Section 7 available at <https://www.ncac.gov.cn/chinacopyright/channels/12577.shtml> last accessed 31 March 2025.

86 *Ibid.*

87 Factsheet on Administrative Enforcement of Copyright in China available at <https://

China's administrative copyright enforcement system, in the UK, Ofcom, a public funded national regulator/authority for communication services has provided the UK Video-sharing platform guidance - Guidance for Providers on Measures to Protect Users from Harmful material,[88] though Parliament has not given Ofcom powers to resolve complaints concerning illegal content.[89] Unlike China, neither the UK nor the US has an administrative enforcement system within their copyright offices.

In the EU, while IP offices are not currently tasked with handling administrative copyright enforcement, there is a growing trend toward adopting administrative measures to address the emerging enforcement challenges posed by AI and generative AI. For example, on 24 January 2024, the European Commission established European Artificial Intelligence Office (AI Office), which may be granted enforcement authority to implement relevant AI regulations within the EU.[90] The AI Office has formed task forces to develop guidelines, establish codes of conduct, and foster cross-sectoral and international cooperation.[91] Collaboration between the European Union Intellectual Property Office (EUIPO) and the EU AI Office could facilitate the creation of harmonized guidelines and enforcement mechanisms for notice and takedown procedures, particularly in addressing AI-related content-sharing disputes.

Appeals Centre Europe (ACE) was established on 26 September 2024 under the EU's Digital Services Act (DSA) as an independent out-of-court dispute settlement (ODS) body.[92] It reviews content moderation decisions made by platforms like Facebook, TikTok, and YouTube, offering users a fast, low-cost, fair and impartial avenue to challenge such decisions.[93] By ensuring an independent review process, ACE promotes fairness and accountability in online content moderation, serving as a check on administrative actions by platforms. However, ACE has faced criticism over its ties to Meta, having received $15 million in start-up funding from Meta's

www.gov.uk/government/publications/factsheet-on-administrative-enforcement-of-copyright-in-china> last accessed 31 March 2025.

88 Ofcom Video-sharing platform guidance - Guidance for providers on measures to protect users from harmful material, 6 October 2021 available at <https://www.ofcom.org.uk/__data/assets/pdf_file/0015/226302/vsp-harms-guidance.pdf> last accessed 31 March 2025.

89 What is Ofcom? available at <https://www.ofcom.org.uk/about-ofcom/what-is-ofcom> last accessed 31 March 2025.

90 Commission Decision Establishing the European AI Office, 24 January 2024, available at <https://digital-strategy.ec.europa.eu/en/library/commission-decision-establishing-european-ai-office> last accessed 31 March 2025.

91 European AI Office, available at <https://digital-strategy.ec.europa.eu/en/policies/ai-office#ecl-inpage-tasks-of-the-ai-office> last accessed 31 March 2025.

92 Out-of-court dispute settlement bodies under the Digital Services Act (DSA), European Commission, 26 September 2024 available at <https://digital-strategy.ec.europa.eu/en/policies/dsa-out-court-dispute-settlement> last accessed 31 March 2025.

93 Appeals Centre Europe, available at <https://www.appealscentre.eu/about-us/> last accessed 31 March 2025.

Oversight Board. While ACE asserts its independence with strict conflict-of-interest policies, its non-binding decisions are intended to reduce legal disputes. The Irish media regulator stressed that ACE would maintain financial independence through fees from social media companies and assured continuous oversight to ensure compliance with the Digital Services Act.[94] Although ACE's decisions are non-binding, platforms are required to engage in good faith and may reverse their previous stance on the content in question based on ACE's recommendations. ACE has promised to explain the reasons for its decisions and ensure transparency, but it remains unclear whether AI-powered decision-making tools will assist in the ACE dispute process, including the expert review, and whether the reasoning behind algorithmic decisions will be provided alongside human expert reviews.

HARMONISING ALGORITHMIC ADMINISTRATIVE JUSTICE

Effective redress mechanisms should be available to users/uploaders to address concerns over any disabled or removed content by AI-powered content recognition tools in particular a) where an exception, limitation and fair use has not been sufficiently considered; b) where it materially distorts an uploader's behaviour in his/her future content creation and uploads; or c) where it causes psychological and economic harm. Currently, there is no international harmonisation regarding effective redress mechanisms that national legislation should regulate within their notice and takedown or safe harbour regimes. Additionally, courts and tribunals have been notably slower in adopting new technologies and online processes compared to private initiatives[95] and administrative justice systems.

An administrative justice system governs how government decisions affect citizens' rights and entitlements and provides avenues for challenging those decisions. As the largest part of the state, the administration translates high-level policies into direct actions impacting citizens.[96] Administrative justice is intended to ensure fairness and offer redress, providing benefits such as quicker resolutions, greater accessibility, and a more informal process compared to complex civil justice system. It has also been argued that administrative dispute resolution systems, due to their flexibility and specialisation, may be better positioned than courts to lead technological innovation.[97] With the rapid pace of technological advancements,

[94] Burns, J (2024) 'Regulator insists body with links to Meta is 'independent': Appeals Centre Europe was given start-up costs by Meta's Oversight Board', *Irish Independent,* Dublin. 12 October 2024.

[95] Alternative Dispute Resolution Mechanisms for Business-to-Business Digital Copyright- and Content-Related Disputes: A report on the results of the WIPO–MCST survey, WIPO 2021 at 53 available at <https://www.wipo.int/edocs/pubdocs/en/wipo_pub_969.pdf> last accessed 31 March 2025.

[96] Tomlinson, J (2019) *Justice in the Digital State: Assessing the Next Revolution in Administrative Justice* (1st ed) Bristol University Press at 1.

[97] Sossin, L and Thompson, D (2021) 'Digitalisation and Administrative Justice: An Access to

there is significant potential to reshape and improve the effectiveness of administrative justice, particularly in how redress mechanisms are implemented and accessed.

If a national copyright office could be granted administrative adjudicative authority, such administrative system could offer impartial adjudication and reduce the need of a costly court proceeding. It may also discourage invalid takedown requests and relieve hosting service provider's burden of dealing with notice and takedown legal process.[98]

In China, the Cyberspace Administration of China (CAC) has enhanced its supervision of online law enforcement by encouraging local administrations to improve enforcement quality through regular inspections, self-assessments, and annual reviews. It promotes the development of certified online law enforcement teams, ensuring personnel meet qualification standards. Additionally, the CAC supports comprehensive training programs to strengthen the political and professional competence of internet law enforcement officials, ensuring the effective implementation of national laws and regulations. For example, in 2024 the national network information system severely cracked down online violations of laws and regulations to clean cyberspace which led to interviewing 11,159 platforms, issuing warnings or fines to 4,046 platforms, ordering 585 websites to suspend relevant functions or information updates, removing 200 mobile applications, disposing of 40 mini programs, shutting down 10,946 illegal websites and closing 107,802 user accounts.[99] In 2023 China's cyberspace regulator also fined Tencent 1 million yuan for hosting illegal content on its Tencent QQ platform's 'Little World' section, with additional penalties including a 30-day suspension and profit confiscation.[100] Tencent QQ's security centre accepted the penalties and pledged to enhance the platform through technological upgrades and improved content moderation.

This example shows that Chinese administrative agencies or authorities have managed to effectively resolve online copyright infringement issues. China Copyright Offices have copyright enforcement administrative functions,[101] compared with other nations and regions which IP offices were

Justice Perspective' in Marc Hertogh (ed.) et al., *The Oxford Handbook of Administrative Justice* Oxford University Press at 503-520.

98 Gocha, AJ (2018) 'Modern system for resolving online copyright infringement disputes: administrative rulemaking and adjudication, one-stop fix to the digital millennium copyright act. IDEA' 58(2) *The Journal of the Franklin Pierce Center for Intellectual Property* 131 at 176.

99 'Maintaining Cyberspace Cleanliness: the national network information system severely cracking down online violations of laws and regulations,' China Network Information Network 25 February 2025 available at <https://www.cac.gov.cn/2025-02/25/c_1742186054989836.htm> last accessed 31 March 2025.

100 'China watchdog fines Tencent over illegal content on its messaging platform' by Reuters, 13 September 2013 available at <https://www.reuters.com/technology/china-watchdog-fines-tencent-over-illegal-content-its-messaging-platform-2023-09-13/> last accessed 31 March 2025.

101 Administrative Enforcement of Intellectual Property in China: Guidance for British

not tasked for administrative enforcement functions. China's Copyright Offices at the city, provincial, and regional levels should consider adopting measures to enhance and harmonize their practices by applying notice and takedown procedures consistently, developing suitable AI tools, and establishing a code of practice to effectively address generative-AI content infringement.

Regarding administrative policies development, since 2020 China National Copyright Administration Office (also known as 'Copyright Bureau') has improved consistency in its administrative copyright enforcement, issuing a Circular (known as 'Notification') on Further Improving the Examination and Identification of Evidence for Administrative Enforcement of Copyright Law.[102] This Circular gives guidance to three areas of administrative enforcement, namely concerning 'proof of rights', 'evidence of infringement', and 'determination of infringement'[103] with the intent to improve the efficiency and clarity of the copyright administrative enforcement process. However, there is still scope for further clarification and interpretation as to admissible evidence of AI-related copyrighted materials. For example, it lacks explanation as to the format of admissible evidence, concerning AI-generated work. It is also silent on the mechanism and process that administrative authorities may use to collect, analyse and determine copyright infringement.

With regard to 'proof of rights', the Circular specifies that complainants are required to provide evidence concerning alleged copyright infringement, whilst respondents will be given an opportunity to provide evidence to the contrary. If there is no contrary evidence, the administrative authority shall presume the authors of work, publishers of publications, performers of performance, or producers of sound recordings, signed in the usual manner, as rightsholders if appropriate.[104] It is not clear as to who should be considered as authors, publishers, performers or producers if such work is AI-generated. Therefore, it would be helpful for the administrative authority to provided guidelines as to how authorship is determined concerning AI-generated work.

With regard to 'evidence of infringement', The Circular outlines the types of admissible evidence for infringement cases, including infringing works, performances, sound recordings, purchase records, contracts, production documents, photos, videos, webpage screenshots, and proof of forged or

companies seeking administrative enforcement against IP infringements in China, 13 November 2023 available at <https://www.gov.uk/government/case-studies/uk-china-cooperation-on-intellectual-property> last accessed 31 March 2025.

102 Circular on Further Improving the Examination and Identification of Evidence for Administrative Enforcement of Copyright Law, 15 November 2020, available at <https://www.gov.cn/gongbao/content/2021/content_5582649.htm> last accessed 31 March 2025.

103 *Ibid.*

104 *Ibid,* Section 1.

unauthorized documents.[105] However, it does not specify the required format of this evidence. Establishing clearer guidelines on evidence formats would enhance certainty, particularly in disputes involving AI-generated works.

Concerning 'determination of infringement', the copyright administrative enforcement authority shall conduct investigation and verification; and punish infringements of illegal dissemination.[106] A 'punishment decision' is usually issued along with a fine, and an order to stop infringement. It was noted that although the administrative enforcement authority may also deal with cases of online infringement, it is more appropriate for more complex cases of online infringement to be resolved via civil litigation due to their technical nature, which may require the evidence of expert witnesses.[107] However, referring all complex cases to civil litigation may not be a sustainable solution, given the rapidly increasing volume and complexity of online infringement cases in our digital society. As the majority of copyright infringement cases are likely to involve digital elements with increasing complexity, expert determination could offer an effective alternative to civil litigation. This procedure, regulated under the World Intellectual Property Organization (WIPO) Expert Determination Rules, [108] allows parties to submit disputes to one or more experts for resolution.[109] If both parties agree, expert determination could provide a streamlined and specialised approach to handling complex online copyright infringement cases. Expert determination is best suited to determine 'technical, scientific or related business nature' of cases, which may be binding if agreed, or at least may serve as a recommendation.[110] China's copyright administrative enforcement authorities could potentially help to reduce court caseloads by adopting expert determination for online copyright infringement cases. This method would offer a specialized and efficient resolution process, leveraging expert knowledge to address complex digital copyright disputes

Currently China lacks a national guideline on expert determination mechanisms for copyright-related disputes. However, on March 5, 2024, Shenzhen, as one of the pilot areas for the rapid settlement of intellectual property disputes, introduced the Guidelines for Neutral Assessment of Intellectual Property Disputes.[111] This 'neutral assessment' functions

[105] *Ibid*, Section 2.

[106] *Ibid*, Section 3.

[107] *Ibid.*

[108] WIPO Expert Determination Rules, effective from 1 July 2021, available at < https://www.wipo.int/amc/en/expert-determination/rules/index.html > last accessed 31 March 2025.

[109] What is Expert Determination? by WIPO, available at <https://www.wipo.int/amc/en/expert-determination/index.html> last accessed 31 March 2025.

[110] Why Expert Determination in Intellectual Property? By WIPO, available at <https://www.wipo.int/amc/en/expert-determination/why-is-exp.html> last accessed 31 March 2025.

[111] Interpretation of Guidelines for Neutral Assessment of Intellectual Property Disputes, Shenzhen Government, 5 March 2024, available at <https://www.sz.gov.cn/

similarly to expert determination, where neutrals — typically experts or trusted third parties — provide expert opinions.

An important omission in the Circular on Further Improving the Examination and Identification of Evidence for Administrative Enforcement of Copyright Law is the lack of clarity on the tools and processes administrative authorities may use to collect, analyse and determine the three areas. It remains uncertain whether AI-assisted content moderation tools are permitted, and if so, whether these tools adhere to ethical, safe, and trustworthy standards, comparable to the European AI Act 2024.

At the industry level, the Cybersecurity Administration of China has implemented regulations such as the Administrative Provisions on Algorithm Recommendation for Internet Information Services (2022) [112] and the Interim Administrative Measures for Generative AI Services (July 2023) to provide guidance on AI technologies and services. [113] At the national level, ethical oversight in China is guided by the Ethical Norms for New Generation Artificial Intelligence (September 2021) issued by the National New Generation Artificial Intelligence Governance Specialist Committee,[114] and the Scientific and Technological Ethics Review Regulation (September 2023) issued by the Ministry of Science and Technology alongside nine other government agencies.[115]

Digitalisation, using digital technologies and digitised data to transform process, does not automatically result in lower costs and greater ease of use, as poorly designed digital interfaces can complicate otherwise simple processes; additional risks may relate to accessibility barriers and algorithmic biases; and ambiguous or insufficient administrative policies can undermine fair and consistent enforcement. It has been observed that digital administrative initiatives often prioritize procedural justice over substantive justice, remaining focused on processes rather than outcomes.[116] It has been argued that there are no significant barriers to adopting algorithmic administrative enforcement, provided the algorithmic decision-

attachment/1/1424/1424526/11184207.pdf> last accessed 31 March 2025.

112 Administrative Provisions on Algorithm Recommendation for Internet Information Services 2022, available at <https://www.gov.cn/zhengce/zhengceku/2022-01/04/content_5666429.htm> last accessed 31 March 2025.

113 Interim Administrative Measures for Generative Artificial Intelligence Services 2023, available at <https://www.cac.gov.cn/2023-07/13/c_1690898327029107.htm> last accessed 31 March 2025.

114 Ethical Norms for New Generation Artificial Intelligence (25 September 2021), Ministry of Science and Technology of People's Republic of China, September 2021 available at <https://www.most.gov.cn/kjbgz/202109/t20210926_177063.html> last accessed 31 March 2025.

115 Scientific and Technological Ethics Review Regulation (September 2023), National Science and Technology Development and Supervision [2023] No. 167 available at <https://www.gov.cn/zhengce/zhengceku/202310/content_6908045.htm> last accessed 31 March 2025.

116 Raso, J (2021) 'Implementing Digitalisation in an Administrative Justice Context' in Marc Hertogh (ed.) et al., *The Oxford Handbook of Administrative Justice* Oxford University Press at 521-544.

making system can demonstrate that it outperforms humans in making accurate, efficient, and fair decisions, as human decision-making is often unclear and susceptible to errors, biases, and delays.[117]

A more contextualised and holistic approach has been advocated, emphasising user needs, thoughtful design and the structure of administrative justice systems.[118] A more balanced approach has also been promoted on procedural fairness with substantive outcomes in algorithm-driven administrative enforcement environments.[119] The responsible design and use of algorithms to promote administrative justice requires governments to rigorously engage in developing and overseeing these systems, with appropriate investments in budgetary (e.g., infrastructure improvements), informational (e.g., data training), and human (e.g., expertise) resources. [120]

Algorithmic administrative enforcement for copyright protection may enable access to administrative justice instead of expensive processes of civil justice by levelling the playing field between rightsholders and platform providers. If decision-making algorithms are trained appropriately and used responsibly, they may help accelerate dispute resolution process and increase consistency of administrative enforcement in local, provincial and national administrative offices. Algorithmic administrative enforcement systems should adopt an 'ethics by design' approach, integrating internationally established AI ethics best practices from alternative dispute resolution (ADR) and online dispute resolution (ODR) systems into their own administrative dispute resolution processes, ensuring accessibility, transparency, accountability, fairness, impartiality, neutrality, competency, security, and confidentiality.[121] Ensuring AI-powered administrative decision-making enhances rather than undermines administrative justice requires the addressing of two key challenges: data quality and algorithmic accountability through explainability. High-quality data is essential for accurate and fair decisions, while explainability ensures transparency and accountability in automated processes.

[117] Appel, SM and Coglianese, C (2021) 'Algorithmic Administrative Justice' in Marc Hertogh (ed.) et al., *The Oxford Handbook of Administrative Justice* Oxford University Press 481-502 at 494.

[118] Sossin, L and Thompson, D (2021) 'Digitalisation and Administrative Justice: An Access to Justice Perspective' in Marc Hertogh (ed.) et al., *The Oxford Handbook of Administrative Justice* Oxford University Press at 503-520.

[119] Raso, J (2021) 'Implementing Digitalisation in an Administrative Justice Context' in Marc Hertogh (ed.) et al., *The Oxford Handbook of Administrative Justice* Oxford University Press at 544.

[120] Appel, SM and Coglianese, C (2021) 'Algorithmic Administrative Justice' in Marc Hertogh (ed.) et al., *The Oxford Handbook of Administrative Justice* Oxford University Press 481-502 at 495.

[121] Wang, F (2023) AI Ethics of Online Commercial Arbitration in Comparative Perspective, (18) 2 *Journal of Comparative Law* 529-556 available at <https://www.lawbookexchange.com/pdf/JCL_18-2_07_Wang_AIEthicsOfOnlineCommercialArbitrationInComparativePerspective.pdf> last accessed 31 March 2025.

CONCLUSION AND A WAY FORWARD

Technological, legal, and self-regulatory constraints create uncertainty for rightsholders on social media platforms. While digitalisation in administrative enforcement has the potential to simplify these issues, it can also introduce new complexities. Although algorithms can improve accuracy, efficiency, and fairness compared to human decisions, poor design may lead to complications, accessibility problems and biases. A user-centred approach, supported by investments in infrastructure, data training/management and expertise, is crucial. To strengthen administrative justice in copyright enforcement, a combination of technological, legal, and policy measures including self-regulation should be implemented to ensure transparency, accountability and fairness in AI-powered decision-making.

China's administrative justice system effectively leverages administrative agencies for rapid and streamlined enforcement, as evidenced by the Cyberspace Administration of China's (CAC) initiatives. The Cyberspace Administration of China (CAC) has implemented policies and promoted legal frameworks for internet information dissemination, along with guiding, coordinating, supervising relevant departments to strengthen the management of online content, investigating and penalising illegal and non-compliant websites.[122]

If the UK and EU could establish specialised administrative bodies like China's CAC to oversee copyright enforcement, the case burden on courts could be reduced. The Appeals Centre Europe (ACE), established under the EU's Digital Services Act, provides independent dispute resolution for content moderation cases. While it offers transparency and fairness, ACE has faced criticism over financial ties to Meta's Oversight Board. ACE's non-binding decisions limit its enforcement power, reducing its effectiveness in holding platforms accountable. Providing ACE with binding authority for certain decisions could enhance its credibility and effectiveness. ACE should ensure robust financial and operational independence through stronger oversight mechanisms and diversified funding sources. ACE should also provide clear policies or guidelines on expert review/determination for resolving technically complex content disputes.

In contrast, China's Copyright Offices possess administrative enforcement authority, which offer quicker resolutions and reduce the reliance on complex court proceedings. Administrative enforcement also offers the potential to enhance accessibility and reduce financial barriers for rightsholders. The UK and EU could consider granting their national copyright offices administrative enforcement authority to resolve ordinary copyright disputes, while reserving highly complex matters for civil courts. National administrative offices and agents could also help developing detailed guidelines on admissible evidence in AI-related copyright cases, establishing standards for assessing authorship and ownership

[122] Cyberspace Administration of China Questions and Answers to its Establishment and Responsibilities, 5 May 2011. Available at <https://www.gov.cn/jrzg/2011-05/05/content_1858131.htm> last accessed 31 March 2025.

of AI-generated works, and encouraging transparency and fairness in administrative investigations.

China's regulatory framework encompasses various guidelines on AI governance in administrative justice, focusing on ethical norms and safety standards to promote accountability and transparency in AI-powered decision-making. If the UK and EU were to grant their copyright offices administrative enforcement authority, they could establish comprehensive ethical frameworks for AI-driven copyright enforcement. The UK could draw on its Guidance on Ethics, Transparency, and Accountability Framework for Automated Decision-Making (2023), while the EU could develop AI-specific ethical guidelines aligned with the EU AI Act 2024.

By granting copyright offices adjudicative authority, establishing clear evidence standards, leveraging AI technology and incorporating expert determination mechanisms, the UK and EU can enhance the efficiency and accessibility of copyright dispute resolution. Additionally, robust ethical oversight and technological literacy among administrators will ensure just and transparent decisions, and foster a balanced, fair, and technologically advanced administrative justice system.

Moreover, streamlining the notice and takedown process globally is crucial for both civil and administrative justice. The notice and takedown procedures for copyright infringement vary across the UK, EU, US, and China, leading to challenges for social media platforms with global reach. In the EU, the Copyright Directive 2019 requires platforms to demonstrate 'best efforts' to prevent unauthorised content uploads, which may indirectly encourage automated content recognition tools. However, general monitoring obligations are prohibited under the E-Commerce Directive and the Digital Services Act, resulting in legal ambiguity. In the UK, platforms are similarly protected under the E-Commerce Regulation 2002, with no requirement for general monitoring. The UK maintains a traditional notice and takedown procedure, requiring platforms to act upon receiving valid copyright infringement notices. The UK did not implement the EU's Copyright Directive 2019, reducing regulatory complexity. The US follows the Digital Millennium Copyright Act (DMCA), which offers safe harbour protection to service providers. Platforms are not required to monitor content proactively, but repeated infringements identified through automated tools may lead to liability. The US has also established counter-notice mechanisms to ensure fair treatment of uploaders. China's E-Commerce Law 2019 adopts a stricter approach. Platforms must act quickly upon receiving valid infringement notices and can face joint liability if they fail to do so. Unlike other jurisdictions, China's law emphasizes timely removal of content and allows for counter-notices, with a clear 15-day window for rights holders to pursue legal action.

Establishing harmonised procedures and best practices for managing infringement notices and counter-notices is essential to promote transparency and fairness on social media platforms worldwide. AI-powered content moderation tools can be used to detect manifestly infringing content, but human oversight should be maintained to reduce removal errors.

Harmonising the interpretation of 'actual knowledge' and clarifying the scope of AI monitoring obligations will help reduce legal uncertainties across different jurisdictions. From a substantive law perspective, while there is broad agreement worldwide that AI algorithms should not be granted authorship or copyright ownership, opinions differ on whether AI-generated works should receive intellectual property protection. Some advocate for recognizing the contributions of developers, programmers, creators and algorithm designers, while others argue that only substantial human-authored elements in AI outputs should be copyrightable. Harmonizing this debated issue would enhance legal certainty.

Harmonised AI ethics standards will also play a crucial role in ensuring that AI algorithms are developed and applied in line with ethical principles to support administrative justice and remain aligned with the public interest. With responsible implementation, AI-powered tools can enhance the efficiency and fairness of both administrative and civil justice systems, fostering more equitable enforcement practices.

REFLECTIONS

Reflections: Administrative Justice Between Innovation and Control

MICHAEL PALMER

University of London

ZHOU LING

Shenzhen Technology University

YANG LIN

University of Hong Kong

The analysis presented by the contributions to this volume reveals that administrative justice in China operates according to logics that challenge fundamental assumptions about the relationship between institutional development and accountability. Rather than representing either simple authoritarian oppression or gradual democratization, China's administrative justice system demonstrates a complex pattern of institutional adaptation that manages governance challenges while preserving political control. This finding has implications that may well extend to other authoritarian systems, offering insights into how administrative power operates in diverse political contexts and under different constitutional arrangements. Various domains of law provide safeguards for individual rights in relation to the state. These encompass legislation that enshrine citizens' rights, enacted by an elected parliament and upheld by a judiciary whose independence is constitutionally guaranteed. Furthermore, since the early 1990s, China has cultivated a substantial body of administrative laws and regulations to govern the conduct of officials in the execution of their responsibilities. Nevertheless, the protection of rights has yet to emerge as a central focus within the operational framework of the system.

Marc Hertogh's conceptualization of administrative justice, as outlined in *The Oxford Handbook of Administrative Justice*, and noted in our introduction, adopts three key parts: the steps for making decisions, the rules or laws that guide those decisions, and the systems in place to resolve disputes and handle complaints. At the same time, he advises flexibility in identifying the particular forms that these three analytical dimensions manifest, and in identifying the types of form that are found across different legal cultures:

> The precise meaning of 'administrative justice' is contestable and fluctuates over time, context, and place. Nonetheless, the core animating feature of this field of research is a desire to understand how justice is achieved through the delivery of public services and the actions, inactions, and decision-making of public bodies.

> Administrative justice also encompasses the redress systems by which people can challenge public bodies in order to seek the correction of injustices. Perhaps the most compelling imperative for researchers to focus on these activities of the state is that they constitute the primary way that citizens across the world actually experience justice (or injustice) vis-à-vis public power. In other words, 'administrative justice' is just as much a core function of the modern state as 'criminal justice' and 'civil justice' and needs to be fully recognized as such.[1]

While Hertogh's three components are an especially useful mapping of the components of administrative justice, his additional insight that understandings are flexible and fluctuating–that is, what the actual meaning of the components is in different settings is not necessarily clear, and varies with time and place. We suggest that each of the components can be usefully analysed comparatively in terms of several differing perspectives: empirical, prescriptive, and phenomenological. The 'empirical perspective' focuses on 'what is'—how the system operates in practice. It looks at how decision-makers actually make decisions, what legal rules currently govern those decisions, and what systems exist to resolve disputes and how they function. This perspective is about observing and understanding the system as it works in reality. The 'prescriptive perspective' considers 'what ought to be'—how the system should function to meet standards such as those of fairness and justice. It asks what decision-making should look like, what laws would best ensure values such as justice in the relationship between citizens and the government, and how dispute resolution systems should be designed to deliver outcomes such as justice effectively. This perspective evaluates the system against ideals such as fairness and justice. The 'phenomenological perspective' focuses on 'what is experienced'—the lived reality of individuals interacting with the system. It examines how people experience decision-making processes, whether they understand them, and if they feel heard. It also considers the manner in which laws affect people's lives, whether they know their rights, and whether they can access and trust the systems designed to resolve disputes. This perspective involves considering how governance is experienced by the people to whom it applied. Hertogh's initial framework takes us so far, but as he also suggests, we need to extend the analysis beyond seeing how systems formally exist on paper, and these three analytical dimensions provide a framework for understanding how administrative justice operates in different contexts.

DESCRIPTIVE DIMENSION:

This dimension focuses on the structures, processes, and mechanisms through which administrative justice is delivered. In the Chinese context, administrative justice is heavily mediated through institutional mechanisms

[1] Hertogh, M (2022) 'Administrative Justice as a Field of Study' in Hertogh, M; Kirkham, R; Thomas, R and Tomlinson, J (eds) (2022) *The Oxford Handbook of Administrative Justice* Oxford University Press.2 at xvi.

such as procuracy-initiated litigation, which redistributes power among state institutions. The 'mandarins v. mandarins' framework exemplifies this descriptive aspect, as it highlights the horizontal competition between bureaucratic entities (for example, the procuracy and administrative agencies) as a means of ensuring oversight and compliance. While this may not align with the liberal democratic ideals of administrative justice, it reflects a distinct institutional arrangement that serves the governance priorities of the Chinese party-state.

In the Chinese context, administrative justice is heavily mediated through institutional mechanisms that reflect the governance priorities of the party-state. One prominent example is the system of procuratorate-initiated Administrative Public Interest Litigation (APIL), as explored in Ding Chunyan's Chapter Seven. This mechanism represents a shift from traditional 'citizens v. mandarins' litigation to a 'mandarins v. mandarins' framework, where the procuracy gains new authority to sue administrative agencies for failing to protect public or national interests. Through mandatory pre-litigation procedures, enhanced investigative powers, and unique burden-of-proof arrangements, the procuratorate addresses issues such as local non-compliance with central environmental policies. This system exemplifies how administrative justice operates through horizontal institutional competition, redistributing power among state entities rather than focusing on direct citizen-state accountability.

Another example is the 'judicial review of administrative rules', as discussed by Xiao Shiling and Yang Lin (Chapter 5). China's 'weak-form' judicial review allows courts to refuse to apply illegal administrative rules but not to invalidate them outright. Procedural barriers, such as strict time limits and the exclusion of higher-level administrative rules from review, limit citizens' access to justice. Courts often consult administrative authorities about the legality of their own rules, reflecting a deferential relationship between judicial and administrative institutions. This highlights how administrative justice is mediated through mechanisms that prioritize state control over individual rights. In the realm of environmental governance, Yuhong Zhao's chapter (Six) demonstrates how specialized environmental courts and cross-provincial jurisdictional arrangements address local protectionism and ensure compliance with national environmental regulations. These courts employ innovative institutional designs, such as centralized jurisdiction and ecosystem-based boundaries, to reduce local government interference. For example, cross-provincial environmental courts review cases where local governments prioritize economic development over environmental protection, ensuring that national environmental goals are upheld. This approach shows us how administrative justice is delivered through structural innovations that address governance challenges.

The campaign-style enforcement of pollution control regulations, as examined by Cai, Liu, and Lo (Chapter 11) further illustrates the institutional dynamics of administrative justice. Local environmental officials operate under intense pressure from central inspections, navigating a dual enforcement system that combines routine bureaucratic processes with politically charged campaigns. Mechanisms like 'dual random selection' inspections and 'positive lists' aim to systematize enforcement, but officials often face a power-responsibility imbalance, being held accountable for outcomes they cannot directly control. This example reveals the structural constraints and institutional tensions that shape the delivery of administrative justice.

The phenomenon of blaming local officials for failing to meet unattainable targets, as highlighted by Biddulph (Chapter 10), further underscores the systemic challenges within campaign-style governance. When central authorities impose ambitious mandates, such as pollution control or safety enforcement, local officials often lack the resources, jurisdictional clarity, or institutional support to achieve these goals. Yet, failure to meet these targets frequently results in severe disciplinary actions, including public reprimands, demotions, or even criminal charges. This dynamic not only exacerbates the power-responsibility imbalance but also fosters a culture of risk aversion, where officials prioritize avoiding blame over initiative-taking governance. The resulting cycle of overburdened local administrations and punitive oversight mechanisms illustrates how campaign-style enforcement can undermine both administrative justice and the broader objectives of governance.

Yang Lin's contribution (Chapter Eight) on cross-border data governance in the Greater Bay Area highlights the challenges of administrative justice in a fragmented legal landscape. While Hong Kong and Macao maintain robust internal appeal mechanisms, these safeguards do not extend across jurisdictional boundaries, creating procedural voids. Mainland China's authoritarian framework prioritizes substantive security control over procedural fairness, leaving affected parties with limited recourse against administrative decisions. This fragmented accountability landscape demonstrates the complexities of delivering administrative justice in a multi-jurisdictional context.

Finally, Song Yuechan's chapter (Thirteen) on pharmaceutical administration introduces the concept of 'authority deficit,' where local authorities issue more licences than they can regulate effectively. Frequent institutional restructuring creates regulatory uncertainty, while licensing authority is devolved to local levels that lack the capacity for effective oversight. Local governments often prioritize economic development over regulatory compliance, leading to gaps in pharmaceutical regulation. This example highlights how administrative justice is shaped by structural misalignments between authority distribution and implementation capacity.

Together, these examples illustrate how in the essays contributed to this volume, administrative justice in China is delivered through institutional mechanisms that emphasize horizontal competition, innovative structural designs, and governance priorities. While these mechanisms address specific challenges, they often reflect a system that prioritizes state control and bureaucratic efficiency over individual rights and direct citizen engagement.

NORMATIVE DIMENSION

The normative dimension of administrative justice focuses on the values and principles that guide how justice is delivered, such as fairness, accountability, and adherence to the rule of law. In China, however, the goals of administrative justice differ significantly from those in liberal democracies. Instead of prioritizing the protection of individual rights, the Chinese system places greater importance on maintaining party-state authority, ensuring the smooth functioning of government institutions, and achieving policy goals. Accountability in this context is more about holding government agencies and officials responsible for their performance within the state system, rather than fostering accountability between the government and individual citizens. This approach reflects a normative framework that values the stability and efficiency of the state apparatus over personal rights. This understanding differs considerably from the ideals of liberal democracies, reflecting instead China's distinctive political-legal structure and cultural traditions.

The normative dimension addresses the values and principles that underpin administrative justice. In many legal systems these include fairness, accountability, and the rule of law. In China, however, the normative goals of administrative justice are less about protecting individual rights substantively and procedurally, and more about maintaining state control, ensuring bureaucratic efficiency, and achieving policy objectives. The emphasis on institutional accountability (rather than citizen-state accountability) reflects a normative framework that prioritizes the stability and functionality of the state apparatus. This of course is a departure from liberal democratic ideals, but aligns with the Chinese political and cultural context, emphasizing collective harmony, state-led governance, and socio-political stability."

EXPERIENTIAL DIMENSION:

This dimension considers how individuals experience administrative justice in their interactions with public institutions. In China, citizens' direct experiences of administrative justice are often mediated through state institutions rather than through direct legal recourse. For example, the procuratorate's role in addressing administrative misconduct may indirectly benefit citizens by improving governance and reducing maladministration, but it does not necessarily empower individuals to seek redress or assert their rights. The experiential dimension in China, therefore, reflects a system where justice is often experienced as an outcome of institutional processes rather than as a direct interaction between citizens and the state.

THREE DIMENSIONS REVISITED

The China case reflects Hertogh's three dimensions of administrative justice, but in a way that is uniquely shaped by the PRC'S political and institutional context. The descriptive dimension is evident in the institutional mechanisms of oversight and power redistribution. The normative dimension is shaped by the state's priorities of control and efficiency rather than individual rights. The experiential dimension is indirect, with citizens benefiting from improved governance rather than direct engagement with justice mechanisms. This reflects the adaptability of Hertogh's framework to different governance systems, while also underscoring the need to contextualize administrative justice within specific political and cultural settings.

EMERGENT PATTERNS

Three interconnected patterns emerge consistently across the diverse policy domains and institutional contexts examined in this volume. Each pattern illuminates different aspects of how administrative justice functions when fundamental political constraints remain unchanged, yet each also demonstrates the possibilities and limitations of procedural reform within authoritarian governance structures.

The first pattern concerns the coexistence of procedural sophistication with persistent structural authoritarianism. Across multiple chapters, the analysis reveals how China has achieved remarkable procedural innovations—from due process expansion and environmental jurisdiction reform to comprehensive legal codification and technological integration—without altering the fundamental relationship between state authority and individual rights. Palmer's analysis of population policy transformation exemplifies this pattern, showing how the elimination of invasive surveillance, birth permits, and punitive social maintenance fees significantly improved procedural fairness while preserving state control over reproductive autonomy. Similarly, Zhao's environmental cases demonstrate how specialized courts and cross-jurisdictional arrangements represent creative institutional responses to local protectionism, yet judicial deference patterns persist and citizen success rates remain low. Fu's study of pandemic control in China's gated communities also offers a striking illustration of this pattern. The sophisticated community governance system, with its intricate network of grid monitors, property management companies, and technological surveillance, represents a remarkable procedural innovation. Yet, these mechanisms ultimately served to enhance state control rather than constrain it, enabling unprecedented levels of pandemic management while preserving fundamental power structural imbalance.

This pattern challenges conventional assumptions about the relationship between procedural reform and systemic change. The evidence suggests that procedural improvements can serve legitimating functions rather than constraining state power, creating what we see as 'authoritarian administrative justice' that reduces certain administrative injustices while maintaining fundamental power imbalances. This finding has broader relevance for understanding how authoritarian systems adapt to governance challenges without accepting liberal democratic constraints on state power.

The second pattern reveals how administrative justice in China may operate through horizontal inter-institutional competition rather than vertical citizen-state accountability. As we have noted, Ding Chunyan's analysis (Chapter Seven) of procuracy-initiated litigation exemplifies this dynamic, showing how the procuratorate system gained new oversight powers to compensate for lost anti-corruption functions, fundamentally altering the relationship between different state institutions rather than enhancing citizen rights. Also, Yang Lin's cross-border data governance study demonstrates how jurisdictional fragmentation creates accountability gaps that undermine administrative justice even when individual jurisdictions maintain robust internal procedures.

This horizontal dimension of administrative justice has received insufficient attention in comparative scholarship, which typically focuses on citizen-state relationships rather than inter-institutional dynamics. The Chinese experience demonstrates how bureaucratic institutions adapt to maintain relevance and authority within the party-state apparatus, using legal innovations as resources in ongoing jurisdictional conflicts. Administrative justice becomes more complex when operating across multiple legal fields with competing logics, as state institutions negotiate power relationships that may have little connection to citizen welfare.

The third pattern concerns the systematic implementation failures that undermine administrative justice despite comprehensive legal frameworks and policy reforms. The chapters in Part IV document how street-level bureaucrats face impossible institutional constraints that create what Song terms 'authority deficit'—systematic misalignments between licensing authority and regulatory capacity that generate regulatory outcomes neither reformers nor local officials intended. Biddulph's analysis of bureaucratic inertia reveals how campaigns against 'lazy officials' misdiagnose structural problems as individual failings, while Lo, Liu, Cai, and Li's Chapter (Eleven) shows how officials lack legal tools to achieve their assigned responsibilities. Bureaucrats operate under severe resource constraints while facing mounting accountability pressures from multiple directions. They identify how enforcement officials find themselves ensnared in an institutional paradox—they lack sufficient legal authority to directly mandate plant closures or suspensions without judicial proceedings, yet bear full responsibility for environmental outcomes within their jurisdiction.

These implementation challenges illustrate significant tensions between authoritarian governance structures and the autonomy of professional bureaucracies—tensions that procedural reforms alone are ill-equipped to resolve. When authority is misaligned with operational capacity, when resources are insufficient for the responsibilities at hand, and when performance incentives are at odds with procedural mandates, even the most sophisticated systems of administrative justice will yield arbitrary outcomes. In the absence of genuine judicial independence and robust legal constraints against political interference, enhancements in administrative justice remain precarious and susceptible to reversal amid shifts in policy.

It might also be pointed out that in these implementation challenges, actors will likely often prioritize appearances of compliance and performance over substantive outcomes. Goffman's concept of impression management could be borrowed for this analysis by framing the campaigns as performative acts designed to project an image of control, efficiency, and ideological alignment to central authorities and the public. The frontstage of governance—meetings, reports, and inspections—becomes a space where officials perform their roles to meet the expectations of superiors, while the 'backstage' reveals the disillusionment, overwork, and risk aversion that undermine genuine administrative effectiveness. This approach could help explain why campaigns often seem to exacerbate the very problems they aim to solve, as the focus shifts from substantive governance to maintaining the appearance of compliance.[2] At the same time , however, campaigns may be self-defeating for another reason, as Randall Collins suggests with his concepts of 'emotional energy' and 'emotional fatigue'.[3] While initial campaigns may generate bursts of emotional energy and compliance, repeated cycles of high-pressure enforcement without addressing structural issues can deplete emotional energy, leading to disengagement, risk aversion, and the very bureaucratic inertia the campaigns aim to combat. This dynamic highlights a fundamental tension in authoritarian governance: in which reliance on emotionally charged rituals to sustain control risks alienating the very officials they target.

IMPLICATIONS FOR ADMINISTRATIVE JUSTICE STUDIES

These findings encourage significant revision of existing theoretical frameworks in administrative justice scholarship. Hertogh's three-dimensional analysis—procedures, legal frameworks, and dispute resolution mechanisms—provides a useful starting point for analyzing non-democratic contexts, but may require adaptation to account for how these dimensions function differently when embedded within authoritarian political structures.

The procedural dimension is best understood not merely as technical arrangements for decision-making but as political instruments that serve different functions within different constitutional systems. In liberal democratic contexts, procedural fairness serves to protect individual rights against arbitrary state action. In authoritarian contexts, procedural fairness may serve instrumental functions related to governance efficiency, social stability, or regime legitimacy without providing meaningful constraints on state power. This distinction has important implications for evaluating procedural reforms and predicting their effects.

[2] Goffman, E (1959) *The Presentation of Self in Everyday Life*: Doubleday. We might also draw on Randall Collins' work on rituals of interaction to provide a framework for understanding the repetitive nature of meetings, inspections, and reports in campaign-style governance. These rituals, while ostensibly aimed at improving governance, often serve as symbolic acts that reaffirm the authority of the Party and the ideological commitment of officials. At the same time, however, they may be self-defeating, as Randall Collins suggests with his concepts of emotional energy and emotional fatigue.

[3] Concepts developed primarily in his 2004 work *Interaction Ritual Chains* Princeton University Press.

The legal framework dimension requires recognition that law serves different functions within different political systems. In democratic contexts, law constrains state power through constitutional limitations and judicial oversight. In authoritarian contexts, law may serve primarily as an instrument of state policy rather than a constraint on state action. Legal reforms do not necessarily produce the accountability benefits typically associated with rule of law development, particularly when courts remain politically subordinate and individual rights are treated as instrumental rather than inherent values.

The dispute resolution dimension must account for how different political systems structure accountability relationships. In democratic contexts, dispute resolution mechanisms provide channels for citizens to challenge state power and seek redress for administrative harm. In authoritarian contexts, dispute resolution may serve primarily to manage social tensions and provide safety valves for grievances without fundamentally altering power relationships. Understanding these functional differences is essential for analyzing how administrative justice operates across different political contexts.

Hampshire's justice as conflict framework also offers a valuable lens for understanding the systemic tensions within China's administrative justice system. Rather than viewing conflict as a failure of governance, Hampshire's approach suggests that in social life conflict is inevitable, and that if long-term stability and justice and to be secured, they need to be based on the fair resolution of inevitable competing interests and perspectives. In the Chinese context, the persistent tension between central mandates and local implementation exemplifies such conflicts, as local officials are often tasked with achieving ambitious targets without the necessary resources or institutional support. Campaign-style governance, while designed to enforce compliance, suppresses these underlying conflicts by framing them as individual failings rather than structural issues. This approach not only exacerbates the power-responsibility imbalance but also undermines the potential for administrative justice by denying officials and citizens meaningful opportunities to contest or negotiate these demands. China, in this sense, would require institutional mechanisms that openly acknowledge and mediate these conflicts, ensuring that both local officials and citizens have a voice in shaping governance priorities and outcomes. Without such processes, the system risks perpetuating cycles of blame, disengagement, and inefficiency, ultimately weakening the legitimacy of governance itself.[4]

[4] Hampshire's views are primarily articulated in his books *Innocence and Experience* (1989, Penguin) and *Justice is Conflict* (2000, Princeton UP).

COMPARATIVE LEGAL STUDIES

The Chinese experience offers important insights for comparative legal scholarship concerned with understanding how legal institutions function across different political systems. The analysis demonstrates that formal legal empowerment can coexist with continued political control in ways that challenge conventional assumptions about the relationship between judicialization and democratization.

Mou's historical research on the Dali Yuan system during China's Northern Warlords era (1912-1928) provides a nuanced case study of legal institutional development. By examining why an American-style judicial review system was not adopted, Mou reveals the complex interplay between legal transplantation, political constraints, and institutional adaptation. His analysis demonstrates that the resistance to judicial review was not a simple rejection of constitutional accountability, but reflected deeper structural challenges—including the weak independence of judicial organs, the political instability of the era, and the framers' perception of courts as insufficiently autonomous from government control.

Mou's work illuminates how emerging legal systems negotiate between imported institutional models and local governance structures. Rather than viewing legal development as a linear process of Western-style modernization, his research shows how legal institutions are shaped by specific historical, political, and cultural contexts. The Dali Yuan's 'unified law interpretation system', for instance, represented not a failure of legal reform, but a distinctive approach to managing legal interpretation within the constraints of early 20th-century China. This perspective aligns with the volume's broader argument about the need to understand institutional change as a complex, contextual process that cannot be reduced to simple narratives of convergence or divergence. The concept of 'weak-form judicial review' analyzed by Xiao and Lin provides a useful framework for understanding how courts in the PRC today can gain formal powers without achieving meaningful independence from political control. Courts may review administrative decisions without being able to invalidate illegal administrative rules, creating symbolic review processes that fail to provide effective constraints on administrative power. This finding has broader relevance for understanding judicial roles in hybrid political systems worldwide.

The 'mandarins v. mandarins' framework introduced by Ding Chunyan, and noted above, offers an alternative to assumptions that administrative law primarily involves citizen-state conflicts. The Chinese experience demonstrates how state institutions can assume adversarial roles against each other in ways that redistribute power within the state apparatus without necessarily enhancing citizen rights. This insight challenges conventional frameworks for analyzing administrative accountability and suggests new directions for comparative administrative law scholarship.

The analysis of campaign-style enforcement by Cai, Lo, and Liu reveals how different political systems structure relationships between rule application and political authority. Unlike liberal democratic systems that emphasize predictable rule application, China transforms administrative matters into political mobilization exercises that create strategic uncertainty for regulated entities. This finding illustrates how identical legal texts can generate fundamentally different governance experiences depending on their political context.

In the study of authoritarian systems, a number of scholars have found the 'dual state' framework helpful in characterising key aspects of the system. In this study too, we see some value in its application. Dual state theory, developed by Ernst Fraenkel in his book *The Dual State: A Contribution to the Theory of Dictatorship* (1941)[5] describes a political system where two distinct forms of governance coexist: a normative state that follows legal rules and a prerogative state that operates outside of legal constraints. The systematic exclusion in today's China of party-issued documents from judicial review, as Xiao and Lin demonstrate, reflects a clear boundary between formal legal processes and political authority that operates outside legal constraints. Similarly, the 'one institution with two names' phenomenon creates precisely the kind of parallel authority structures that dual state theory anticipates—administrative agencies operating simultaneously through bureaucratic hierarchies and party control mechanisms.

The book's implementation chapters reveal this duality particularly clearly. Song's 'authority deficit' concept and Lo and colleagues' environmental enforcement studies show street-level bureaucrats caught between formal legal requirements and political imperatives that can override procedural constraints. The campaign-style enforcement patterns documented by Lo and colleagues represent classic prerogative state interventions—periodic suspension of routine legal processes in favour of intensive political mobilization that achieves compliance through unpredictability rather than consistent rule application. The framework would also illuminate the puzzle of why formal legal empowerment consistently fails to deliver meaningful constraints on administrative power. Courts can expand procedural protections within the normative state sphere while remaining structurally subordinate to prerogative state authority that intervenes when politically necessary.

However, applying dual state theory to China faces significant analytical challenges. The original Fraenkel formulation assumed tension between normative and prerogative elements, with the latter representing deviation from legal norms. China's system appears more integrated, with party authority constitutionally recognized rather than operating as an exception to legal order. The chapters in this book suggest that the boundaries between formal and informal authority are more fluid and context-dependent than dual state theory typically assumes. Environmental courts can operate with relative autonomy in technical cases while remaining politically constrained on sensitive issues. Procuratorate-initiated litigation creates hybrid

[5] Fraenkel, Ernst (2017) *The Dual State: A Contribution to the Theory of Dictatorship* (Edward A. Shils trans., Jens Meierhenrich ed.) Oxford University Press.

mechanisms that combine formal legal procedures with political oversight functions. The framework might also obscure distinctive features of Chinese governance that do not fit either normative or prerogative categories. The systematic deployment of algorithmic governance tools documented in Wang's chapter represents neither traditional legal administration nor arbitrary political intervention, but rather technological rationalization that operates according to computational rather than legal or political logics. Rather than relying on dual state theory per se, the challenge to be faced is one of developing an analytical framework more attuned to China's specific institutional arrangements. The evidence in the chapters of this book suggests something closer to 'layered governance' where multiple authority systems—legal, political, technological, and administrative—operate simultaneously with complex interaction effects rather than clear jurisdictional boundaries.[6] Hualing Fu's analysis of pandemic control mechanisms provides a vivid illustration of this layered governance approach. The mobilization of community organizations, technological platforms, and state bureaucracies during COVID-19 management showed how multiple administrative logics can operate simultaneously—legal, political, technological, and social—creating a complex governance ecosystem that defies simple categorization. Administrative justice in China involves ongoing negotiation between different institutional logics rather than simple dominance of political over legal authority.

Björn Ahl's Chapter (Four) on due process development in Chinese administrative law offers a sophisticated lens for understanding judicial innovation within authoritarian institutional constraints. His research illuminates how courts strategically expand procedural principles not through direct confrontation, but through careful, incremental interpretative strategies. By focusing on procedural errors rather than challenging substantive administrative decisions, Chinese courts create a nuanced space for administrative accountability. This approach reveals a complex mechanism of institutional adaptation, where judicial actors navigate political limitations by introducing accountability mechanisms that appear technically neutral. Ahl demonstrates that administrative justice in such contexts is less about wholesale systemic transformation and more about creating interstitial spaces of procedural review. The due process principle becomes a subtle instrument of institutional agency, allowing courts to introduce modest yet meaningful reforms while maintaining the appearance of deference to state authority. Such insights are crucial for understanding how legal institutions can incrementally develop accountability mechanisms in political systems where direct challenges to power are prohibitively risky.

The comparative insights extend beyond judicial mechanisms. Goo's research on stakeholder representation in Chinese state-owned enterprises (Chapter Nine), for instance, demonstrates how institutional innovations

[6] This analysis aligns closely with Geertz's approach of providing rich, layered descriptions that capture the complex meanings that infuse social practices, encapsulated in his concept of 'thick description': Geertz, (1973) *The Interpretation of Cultures: Selected Essays* Basic Books.

can address governance challenges while maintaining fundamental power structures. By proposing stakeholder committees or boards that operate within existing party-state frameworks, Goo illustrates how administrative justice can be reimagined through procedural mechanisms that enhance accountability without fundamentally challenging political control. This approach exemplifies the book's broader argument about procedural sophistication coexisting with persistent authoritarian governance.

IMPLEMENTATION CHALLENGES AND GOVERNANCE IMPLICATIONS

The implementation analysis provides crucial insights into why formal institutional reforms often fail to achieve their stated objectives. The concept of 'authority deficit' introduced by Song captures a phenomenon that extends beyond China's specific context—systematic misalignments between formal authority distribution and practical implementation capacity that undermines effective governance regardless of political system.

These misalignments emerge from multiple sources. Administrative restructuring can dilute professional expertise, as Song's pharmaceutical study demonstrates. Recentralization efforts can paradoxically create new forms of fragmentation, with specialized knowledge concentrated at higher levels while implementation occurs through generalized departments lacking necessary expertise. Performance pressures can create incentive systems that reward short-term compliance over sustainable governance, as Lo and colleagues environmental studies reveal.

The persistence of these challenges despite repeated reform efforts suggests that implementation problems reflect deeper structural features of complex administrative systems rather than technical deficiencies amenable to procedural solutions. Effective administrative justice requires not merely formal procedures but institutional structures capable of implementing those procedures consistently and fairly. When these structural requirements are not met, procedural reforms may actually exacerbate rather than resolve administrative justice problems.

Lo and colleagues' empirical studies of enforcement issues in Guangzhou (Chapters Eleven and Twelve) provide a nuanced illustration of how administrative justice operates at the street-level bureaucracy. Their research reveals the complex challenges faced by local environmental protection officials, highlighting the gap between formal institutional reforms and the practical realities of implementation. The study demonstrates how enforcement teams navigate limited resources, increasing accountability pressures, and diverse local contexts, while still attempting to achieve regulatory compliance. By documenting the granular experiences of street-level bureaucrats, Lo and colleagues illuminate the adaptive strategies officials employ to implement environmental regulations, showing how administrative justice is not just about formal procedures, but about the daily negotiations and improvisations of officials working within constrained institutional environments. Their work offers further insights into administrative justice in China by revealing the nuanced strategies enterprises employ when navigating regulatory pressures. Their research on coal power plants illustrates how administrative justice is not simply a matter of formal compliance, but a dynamic process of negotiation between regulatory bodies and regulated entities. By examining how enterprises internalize and respond to the threat of campaign-style enforcement, the study demonstrates the complex ways administrative power operates—not through straightforward coercion, but through creating a persistent sense of potential intervention. This perspective highlights how administrative justice functions as a continuous process of adaptation, where regulatory expectations and enterprise strategies are constantly recalibrated. The study's insights underscore that administrative justice in China is often about creating an environment of 'anticipatory compliance', where the mere possibility of stringent action can drive proactive behavioural changes.

Mei Ning Yan's comprehensive analysis (Chapter Fifteen) of the Law on Penalties for Administration of Public Security (LPAPS) provides a critical examination of how administrative justice operates at the intersection of law enforcement and political control. Her study reveals the complex ways administrative powers can be used to suppress individual rights under the guise of maintaining social order. Yan demonstrates how seemingly procedural mechanisms can become tools of political oppression, with police powers allowing for arbitrary detention and punishment without meaningful judicial oversight. The research exposes the gap between formal legal safeguards and their actual implementation, showing how administrative justice can be manipulated to serve state interests rather than protect individual rights. Her findings illuminate the subtle ways administrative systems can be used to exert social control, highlighting how procedural mechanisms can be designed to prioritize state power over individual protections. This nuanced analysis reveals that administrative justice in authoritarian contexts is often more about managing potential dissent than providing genuine legal recourse.

Ling Zhou's detailed examination (Chapter Sixteen) of the 2020 Civil Code's divorce provisions offers a nuanced perspective on how administrative mechanisms can be used to reinforce traditional social values and state control. Her analysis reveals how seemingly procedural changes, such as introducing a mandatory 'cooling-off period' for divorce registration, can effectively constrain individual rights under the guise of protecting social stability. Dr. Zhou demonstrates that such administrative interventions are not neutral mechanisms, but rather deliberate policy tools designed to shape social conduct. By making divorce more bureaucratically complex, the state attempts to discourage what it perceives as 'reckless' relationship dissolution, prioritizing family preservation over individual autonomy. This approach reflects a broader pattern of administrative justice in China, where procedural mechanisms are strategically employed to manage social dynamics and reinforce state-preferred normative frameworks. Particularly striking is Zhou's observation that these regulations disproportionately impact women, who are often more likely to initiate divorce proceedings and bear the greater social and economic consequences of marital constraints.

Yuhong Zhao's comprehensive analysis (Chapter Six) noted above of environmental administrative disputes provides critical insights into the evolving mechanisms of judicial review in China's administrative system. Her research reveals how courts are gradually expanding their role from mere procedural arbiters to active participants in environmental governance. Zhao demonstrates that judicial review is not simply about determining the legality of administrative actions, but increasingly serves as a mechanism for protecting public environmental rights, ensuring transparency, and compelling administrative agencies to act responsibly. By examining cases across different environmental domains, she illustrates how courts are developing nuanced approaches to judicial review that balance procedural rigidity with substantive justice. Particularly noteworthy is Zhao's observation that courts are moving beyond strict legalistic interpretations to consider the broader implications of administrative decisions on environmental protection and public interests. This shift suggests an emerging understanding of judicial review as a dynamic process of governance, where courts act not just as passive arbiters but as active participants in shaping environmental policy and protecting citizens' environmental rights.

TECHNOLOGY AND ADMINISTRATIVE JUSTICE

Wang's analysis of AI-powered copyright enforcement (Chapter Seventeen) reveals how technological innovation creates new challenges for administrative justice that existing theoretical frameworks struggle to address. Automated content moderation tools make decisions about legal violations without the transparency, reasoned explanation, or human oversight that characterize legitimate administrative action. These systems create new forms of unaccountable administrative power that operate according to algorithmic rather than legal logics.

The technological dimension of administrative justice deserves greater attention in comparative scholarship. Digital transformation is accelerating across administrative systems worldwide, creating both opportunities and risks for procedural fairness, accountability, and citizen participation. Understanding how different political systems approach these challenges provides insights into broader questions about the compatibility of technological efficiency with administrative justice values.

The Chinese experience suggests that technological solutions cannot substitute for institutional accountability mechanisms. While digital systems may enhance procedural efficiency and reduce certain forms of arbitrary action, they may also create new opportunities for discrimination and abuse without corresponding accountability mechanisms. The relationship between technological innovation and administrative justice requires careful analysis that considers both technical capabilities and political context.

METHODOLOGICAL CONTRIBUTIONS AND FUTURE RESEARCH

This volume, we have suggested, suggests the value of multi-method approaches to administrative justice research that combine institutional analysis with implementation studies and citizen experience research. Historical analysis reveals continuities that contemporary analysis might miss. Comparative case studies illuminate how similar formal institutions produce different outcomes across contexts. Empirical surveys expose gaps between formal procedures and actual implementation. Statistical analysis enables systematic assessment of administrative justice outcomes across large numbers of cases.

The methodological diversity enables comprehensive analysis that captures both institutional dynamics and individual experiences across multiple levels of governance. This approach addresses limitations in existing administrative justice scholarship, which often focuses on either formal institutional analysis or individual case studies without connecting these different levels of analysis.

Future research should build on this methodological foundation while addressing several important gaps revealed by the analysis. More systematic comparison across different authoritarian contexts would help assess whether China's patterns represent broader authoritarian governance features or reflect distinctive characteristics of Chinese political development. Longitudinal analysis tracking administrative justice changes over extended time periods would illuminate how institutional reforms interact with broader political transformations. Cross-national survey research examining citizen experiences with administrative justice across different political systems would provide crucial evidence about how institutional differences affect individual outcomes.

LIMITATIONS AND CAVEATS

Several significant limitations constrain the analyses presented in this volume. The emphasis on China's experience, while offering intricate insights into a pivotal case, restricts generalizability to alternative contexts. Authoritarian regimes exhibit considerable variation in their institutional frameworks, political dynamics, and interactions with civil society. Whether the patterns discerned in China are applicable to other non-democratic environments remains an empirical inquiry necessitating further comparative research.

The temporal scope of the analysis also creates limitations. Most chapters focus on developments within the past two decades, and this relatively limited historical perspective makes assessment of long-term trends in administrative justice development rather difficult. Whether current patterns represent stable features of Chinese governance or transitional phenomena remains unclear. The swift pace of economic and social transformation in contemporary China signifies that research findings need constant monitoring.

Data availability constraints affect several dimensions of the analysis. Many chapters rely on official statistics and published legal decisions that may not reflect the full range of administrative justice experiences. Access to internal government documents, comprehensive citizen survey data, field research and detailed implementation studies remain limited. These constraints mean that important aspects of administrative justice operations may well remain invisible to external researchers, as well as those on the mainland.

POLICY IMPLICATIONS AND PRACTICAL APPLICATIONS

The analysis presented in this volume offers several insights relevant to policymakers and practitioners working on administrative reform in diverse contexts. The Chinese experience demonstrates that procedural improvements can achieve meaningful governance benefits even within constrained political environments. Environmental jurisdiction reforms, pharmaceutical regulation restructuring, and judicial review expansion have produced real improvements in administrative decision-making quality despite persistent political constraints.

However, the analysis also reveals important limitations of reform strategies that focus primarily on procedural innovation while leaving fundamental power relationships intact. Without constitutional constraints on administrative power, independent judicial review, and meaningful citizen participation in governance processes, procedural reforms remain vulnerable to reversal based on changing political priorities. Sustainable administrative justice requires institutional foundations that extend beyond technical procedures to encompass broader questions about power, authority, and accountability.

For international development organizations and technical assistance providers, the Chinese experience offers both insights and cautionary lessons. Legal technical assistance that focuses solely on formal institutional development may achieve limited results if it fails to address broader political constraints on institutional effectiveness. Understanding how different political contexts affect administrative justice operations is essential for designing effective reform strategies.

CONCLUDING THOUGHTS

The Chinese experience with administrative justice reveals both the possibilities and limitations of institutional reform within constrained political environments. The analysis demonstrates that authoritarian systems can achieve remarkable procedural sophistication while preserving fundamental power imbalances that limit transformative change. This finding challenges both optimistic assumptions about the democratizing effects of legal modernization and pessimistic assumptions about the impossibility of governance improvements within authoritarian contexts.

The broader significance lies in demonstrating how administrative justice scholarship must grapple with diverse forms of state power and citizen-state relationships that extend far beyond liberal democratic assumptions. Understanding administrative justice as a field requires acknowledging how institutional conflicts, power dynamics, and political constraints shape governance outcomes across different contexts, while recognizing that procedural fairness and accountability mechanisms may serve different functions within different political systems.

China's administrative justice system represents neither a failed attempt at democratization nor a successful model for authoritarian governance, but rather a distinctive approach to managing complex governance challenges within specific political constraints. Understanding this approach provides insights into broader patterns of institutional development, political adaptation, and governance transformation that have relevance far beyond China's borders. As administrative systems worldwide face new challenges from technological change, social complexity, globalization and political polarization, the Chinese experience offers both innovative solutions and sobering reminders about the persistent influence of political context on institutional effectiveness.

The analysis suggests that meaningful administrative justice requires more than technical reform or institutional innovation. Without fundamental restructuring of power relationships, constitutional constraints on administrative authority, and genuine mechanisms for citizen participation in governance processes, procedural improvements will remain limited in their transformative potential. Yet the Chinese experience also demonstrates that within existing constraints, institutional reforms can achieve meaningful improvements in governance quality, procedural fairness, and administrative effectiveness. Understanding both the possibilities and limitations of such reforms provides essential insights for scholars, policymakers, and practitioners working to enhance administrative justice across diverse political contexts.

It remains to draw together the two framings that have organised this volume. Our introduction proposed that administrative justice be understood through three cumulative layers — a domain (the procedures, the law, and the dispute-resolution mechanisms that Hertogh's framework marks out), the distinctive functions those elements perform within the party-state, and, finally, the critical question of how administrative power renders itself legitimate — and we suggested that the argument of the book was the passage from the first of these to the third. In these reflections we have proceeded instead through three perspectives — the descriptive, the normative, and the experiential — asking of each Hertoghian component what it is, what it is taken to require, and how it is lived. The two schemes are not rivals, and the appearance of divergence is an artefact of their running on different axes. The layers describe the deepening of the question we are ultimately asking; the perspectives describe the standpoints from which the evidence can be read. Far from competing, each completes the other.

Read together, they intersect at every point. The descriptive perspective populates the domain: it tells us what China's procedures, rules, and redress mechanisms actually are and do. The functional layer — the inversions by which procedure comes to legitimise rather than to constrain, law to assert authority rather than to limit it, and dispute resolution to manage stability rather than to check power — becomes visible only when the descriptive is set against the normative, for it is the gap between what these institutions do and what the prescriptive account assumes they ought to do that discloses the inversion. And the experiential perspective, which asks how the governed encounter, accept, or contest administrative power, is what carries the analysis to the critical layer, since legitimacy is in the end a matter of how power is made to appear lawful to those subject to it. The normative perspective thus enters our account not as an external template against which China is found wanting, but as one of the standpoints whose friction with the descriptive record exposes the work of self-justification that 'authoritarian administrative justice' performs. The three perspectives, in short, are the means; the movement from domain to function to legitimation is the end they serve. To study administrative justice in the Chinese party-state is, on both framings and in the end on a single account, to study how administrative power is exercised, justified, and contested — and how, under law, it is made to appear just.

References

Abbott, KW. and Snidal, D (2000) 'Hard and Soft Law in International Governance' (54, 3) *International Organization* 421.

Adams, HC (1886) *Relation of the State to Industrial Action and Economics and Jurisprudence* AMS Press.

Adams, HC (1886) *Relation of the State to Industrial Action and Economics and Jurisprudence* AMS Press .

Ahl, B (2014) 'Retaining Judicial Professionalism: The New Guiding Cases Mechanism of the Supreme People's Court' (217) *The China Quarterly* 121.

Ahl, B (2019) 'Judicialisation in Authoritarian Regimes: The Expansion of Powers of the Chinese Supreme People's Court' (17) *International Journal of Constitutional Law* 255.

Ahl, B (2021) 'Post-2013 Reforms of the Chinese Courts and Criminal Procedure: An Introduction' in Ahl, B (ed) *Chinese Courts and Criminal Procedure: Post-2013 Reforms*, Cambridge University Press.

Ahl, B and Sprick, D (2018) 'Towards Judicial Transparency in China: The New Public Access Database for Court Decisions' (32) *China Information* 3.

Ahl, B; Cai, L; and Xi, C (2019) 'Data-Driven Approaches to Studying Chinese Judicial Practice: Opportunities, Challenges, and Issues' (19, 2) *The China Review* 1.

Alon, I; Farrell, M and Li, Shaomin (2020) 'Regime Type and COVID-19 Response' (9) *FIIB Business Review* 152.

Amnesty International (2006) 'China: Abolishing "Re-education Through Labour" and Other Forms of Punitive Administrative Detention: An Opportunity to Bring the Law into Line with the International Covenant on Civil and Political Rights. 'Memorandum to the State Council and the Legislative Committee of the National People's Congress of the People's Republic of China', available at <https://www.amnesty.org/en/documents/asa17/016/2006/en/>.

Andreas, J and Dong, Y (2017) '"Mass Supervision" and the Bureaucratisation of Governance in China' in Shue, V and Thornton, P (eds) (2017) *To Govern China: Evolving Practices of Power* Cambridge University Press 123.

Ang, YY (2016) 'With Its Corruption Crackdown, China Is Also Stamping out Innovation' *The Conversation,* available at: <https://theconversation.com/with-its-corruption-crackdown-china-is-also-stamping-out-innovation-68223>.

Anthony, G (2015) 'Administrative Justice in the United Kingdom' 7(1) *Italian Journal of Public Law* 9.

Apacible-Bernardo, A and Bushey, K (2025) 'Data Protection and Privacy Laws Now in Effect in 144 Countries' *International Association of Privacy Professionals*, at https://iapp.org/news/a/data-protection-and-privacy-laws-now-in-effect-in-144-countries/

Au, AK. and Witzleb, N(2024) 'Data Flows and Data Protection in the Greater Bay Area: The Need for a Coordinated Legal Framework' (12) *Chinese Journal of Comparative Law*, at cxae013, https://doi.org/10.1093/cjcl/cxae013

Ayuso, S and Argandone, A (2007) 'Responsible Corporate Governance: Towards a Stakeholder Board of Directors' *IESE Business School Working Paper* No 701.

Bargain, O, and Aminjonov, U (2020) Trust and compliance to public health policies in times of COVID-19' (192) *Journal of Public Economics*, 10431, available at: https://doi.org/10.1016/j.jpubeco.2020.104316.

BBC (2019) 'China Releases British Consulate Worker Detained at Border' BBC 24 August 2019. Available at <https://www.bbc.co.uk/news/world-asia-china-49445555>.

BBC (2019) 'Hong Kong: China Confirms Detention of UK Consulate Worker' BBC 21 August 2019. Available at <https://www.bbc.co.uk/news/world-asia-china-49419711>.

Beijing Shi Renmin Zhengfu (2021) '2020 nian yiqing fangkong yilai chachu raoluan zhengchang fangyi zhixu lei anjian 785 qi xingzheng juliu 513 ren' (Since the prevention and control of the epidemic in 2020, 785 cases of disrupting the normal epidemic prevention order have been investigated and dealt with, and 513 people have been administratively detained) *Beijing Shi Renmin Zhengfu* (The People's Government of Beijing Municipality) 15 January 2021, available at: http://www.beijing.gov.cn/ywdt/zwzt/yqfk/zxxx/202101/t20210115_2220826.html.

Beijingshi Gong'anju (Beijing Public Security Bureau) (2024) 'Fujian: beijingshi gong'anju zhi'an guanli xingzheng chufa cailiang jizhunbiao (2024 nian ban)' (Appendix: Beijing Public Security Bureau Sentencing Manual Regarding Administrative Penalties on Law-and-Order Violations (2024 ed)) (issued on 12 August 2024, Jinggongzhi zi [2024] No. 703), available at <https://www.bjfsh.gov.cn/ztzx/wqzt/xzzfgs/qzfbm_22985/fsgafj/jbxx/202204/P020240117373671907475.docx>.

Beijingshi Tongzhouqu Renmin Zhengfu (People's Government of Tongzhou District of Beijing Municipality) (2020) 'Beijing shi jiedao bangong chu tiaoli' (Regulations on the Neighborhood Offices of Beijing Municipality) available at: http://www.bjtzh.gov.cn/tzzfxxgk/c109720/202101/1332302.shtml.

Benney, J (2016) 'Weiwen at the Grassroots: China's Stability Maintenance Apparatus as a Means of Conflict Resolution' (25) *Journal of Contemporary China* 389.

Bhole, O (2023) 'Increasing Moral Policing in China' *News Bharati* 5 October 2023. Available at <https://www.newsbharati.com/Encyc/2023/10/5/Increasing-Moral-Policing-in-China.html>.

Biddulph, S (2001) 'Through a Glass Darkly: China, Transparency and the WTO' (3) *Australian Journal of Asian Affairs* 59.

Biddulph, S (2007) *Legal Reform and Administrative Detention Powers in China* Cambridge University Press;

Biddulph, S (2015) *The Stability Imperative: Human Rights and Law in China* UBC Press at 183–186;

Biddulph, S (2018) 'Democratic Centralism and Administration in China' in Fu, H; Gillespie, J; Nicholson, P and Partlett, W (eds) (2018) *Socialist Law in Socialist East Asia* Cambridge University Press.

Biddulph, S (2019) 'The Impact of Transparency and Accountability Mechanisms on Bureaucratic Inertia: A Case Study of Work Safety Regulations' in Biddulph, S and Biukovic, L (eds) (2019) *Good Governance in Economic Development: International Norms and Chinese Perspectives* UBC Press.

Biddulph, S (2022) 'Transformation in Policing Minor Offending in China' in Fu, H and Chen, W (eds) (2022) *Beyond Regime Type: The Transformation of Police in Asia* Cambridge University Press 87

Biddulph, S (2023) 'Transformation in Policing Minor Offending in China' in Chen, WT and Fu, HL (eds) (2023) *Regime Type and Beyond: The Transformation of Police in Asia* Cambridge University Press.

Biddulph, S; Cooney, S; and Zhu, Y (2012) 'Rule of Law with Chinese Characteristics: The Role of Campaigns in Law-Making' (34) *Law and Policy* 373;

Bird, M (2014) 'China Just Overtook The US As The World's Largest Economy' *Business Insider* (8 October 2014).

Birney, M (2014) 'Decentralization and Veiled Corruption under China's "Rule of Mandates"' (53) *World Development* 55.

Boin, A; McConnell, A; and Hart, P (2008) *Governing after Crisis: The Politics of Investigation, Accountability and Learning* Cambridge University Press.

Boittin, M; Distelhorst, G and Fukuyama, F (2016) 'Reassessing the Quality of Government in China' (197) *Osgoode Legal Studies Research Paper Series* 1.

Bracey, D (1989) 'The Regulation of the People's Republic of China Concerning Punishments for Disturbing Order: The Police and Administrative Punishment' (14, 2) *Criminal Justice Review* 154.

Bradford, A(2020) *The Brussels Effect: How the European Union Rules the World* Oxford University Press (New York, 2020; online edn, Oxford Academic, 19 Dececember 2019), https://doi.org/10.1093/oso/9780190088583.001.0001

Bradsher, K (2020) 'As China Fights the Coronavirus, Some Say It Has Gone Too Far' *New York Times* 20 February 2020, available at: https://www.nytimes.com/2020/02/20/business/economy/china-economy-quarantine.html.

Buntaine, MT.; Zhang, B and Hunnicutt, P (2021) 'Citizen monitoring of waterways decreases pollution in China by supporting government action and oversight' (118*) Proceedings of the National Academy of Sciences* e2015175118.

Burns, J (1987) 'Civil Service Reform in Contemporary China' (18) *Australian Journal of Chinese Affairs* 47.

Burns, J (1999) 'The People's Republic of China at 50: National Political Reform' (159) *The China Quarterly* 580.

Cai, Y (2015) *State and Agents in China: Disciplining Government Officials* Stanford University Press

Caixin (2016) 'Leiyang'an wuming she'an jingwurenyuan buyu qisu' (Five Police Officers in Lei Yang's Case Won't be Prosecuted) Ciaxin 23 December 2016. Available at <https://china.caixin.com/2016-12-23/101030078.html>.

Campbell DE (2007) *A Matter of Faith: Religion in the 2004 Presidential Election* Brookings Institute Press.

Cang, W (2023) 'Provinces find couples are marrying later in life' *China Daily* (15 February 2023) available at: <https://global.chinadaily.com.cn/a/202302/15/WS63ebb6dea31057c47ebaec5f.html>.

Central Committee of the CCP(2018) 'Plan for Deepening the Reform of Party and State Institutions' (Shenhua dang he guojia jigou gaige fang'an) 21 March 2018 Section 1.10 reproduced at https://www.gov.cn/zhengce/2018-03/21/content_5276191.htm#1

Central Committee of the CCP, State Council '(2018)Notice on launching a specialist struggle to Sweep Black and Eliminate Evil (Zhonggong zhongyang, guowuyuan 'Guanyu kaizhan saohei chu'e zhuanxiang douzheng de tongzhi'), Xinhua, 24 January 2018, http://www.xinhuanet.com/legal/2018-01/24/c_1122309773.htm

Central Discipline Inspection Commission, 'If You Have the Spirit of Responsibility, You Should Be Ashamed of 'Official Non-feasance' (Yao you dandang jingshen, yinggai dui wei guan bu wei gandao xiuchi) January 31, 2016, http://www.ccdi.gov.cn/yaowen/201601/t20160129_140160.html.

Chan, H (2019) 'Chinese State Media Publish "Confession" Video of Former UK Consulate Staffer Simon Cheng' Hong Kong Free Press 21 November 2019. Available at <https://hongkongfp.com/2019/11/21/chinese-state-media-publish-confession-video-former-uk-consulate-staffer-simon-cheng/>.

Chander, A and Lê, UP (2015) 'Data Nationalism' (64) *Emory Law Journal* 686.

Chaturvedi, A (2020) 'The China Way: Use of Technology to Combat Covid-19' *Geospatial World* 5 November, available at: https://www.geospatialworld.net/article/the-sino-approach-use-of-technology-to-combat-covid-19.

Chen, A (2018) *An Introduction to the Legal System of the People's Republic of China* (5th ed) LexisNexis.

Chen, AHY (2011) *An Introduction to the Legal System of the People's Republic of China* (4th edn) LexisNexis.

Chen, H and Zhao, Y (2024) 'Enhancing Legal Convergence in the GBA through Harmonization of the Digital Dispute Resolution Legal Framework' (12) *Chinese Journal of Comparative Law* cxae007, https://doi.org/10.1093/cjcl/cxae007

Chen, JF (2016) *Chinese Law: Context and Transformation* (revised and expanded edition) Brill.

Chen, Q (2008) 'Xingzhengfa jiben yuanze sifa shiyong de fazhan – yi zhengdang chengxu yuanze zai woguo de fazhan wei li' (The Development of the Administrative Principles in Judicial Application - Taking the Development of the Due Process Principle in China as an Example) (2008) (3) *Fujian jingcha xueyuan xuebao* (Fujian Police College Journal) 93 at 95.

Chen, QL; Rodewald, L; Lài, SJ; and Gao, GF (2021) 'Rapid and Sustained Containment of COVID-19 is Achievable and Worthwhile: Implications for Pandemic Response' (375) *British Medical Journal*, available at: https://www.bmj.com/content/bmj/375/BMJ-2021-066169.full.pdf.

Chen, R (2016) 'Legal Informality and Human Capital Development in China' in Liebman, BL and Milhaupt, CJ (eds) (2016) *Regulating the Visible Hand? The Institutional Implications of Chinese State Capitalism* Oxford University Press.

Chen, R (2016) 'Legal Informality and Human Capital Development in Ciepley, D (2013) 'Beyond Public and Private: Towards a Political Theory' (107) *American Political Science Review* 139.

Chen, YJ and Cohen, J (2023) 'Freedom from Arbitrary Detention' in Law, D & Ors (eds) *The Oxford Handbook of Constitutional Law in Asia*. Available at <https://doi.org/10.1093/oxfordhb/9780198825463.013.47>.

Chen, YX & Ors (2016) 'Drug Pricing Reform in China: Analysis of Piloted Approaches and Potential Impact of the Reform' (4) *Journal of Market Access and Health Policy* 1.

Cheng, RX; Wang, CL; Li, Y; Huang, L; and Wu, CX (2020) 'Wuhan 4.45 wan dangyuan ganbu xia chen fang kong yixian' (44,500 party members and cadres in Wuhan go down to the front line of prevention and control) *Hubeisheng Renmin Zhengfu* (The People's Government of Hubei Province) 28 February 2020, available at: http://www.hubei.gov.cn/hbfb/szsm/202002/t20200228_2161484.shtml.

Cheng, S (2025) 'Unions Call for Better Protection of Female Jobseekers, Employees: Employers Warned Against Biased Hiring and Unfair Treatment of Women' *China Daily* 14 March 2025.

China Healthcare (2023)'The National Health Care Bill of 2020 is out, Reflecting What Reform Achievements?' *China Healthcare* (22 April 2023) available at: https://www.cn-healthcare.com/articlewm/20210615/content-1231919.html.

China News (2023) Waiting for retirement in your 40s? This lying flat cadre was dismissed twice (40 duosui zuodeng tuixiu? zhe ge ' tangpingshi' ganbu bei shuang kai) *China News* 20 April 2023 https://m.huanqiu.com/article/4CZQERu6RGt

China Youth Daily (1999) 'The Disorder in the Drug Market Needs to be Resolved by the Rule of Law' *China Youth Daily* (7 February 1999) available at: https://news.sina.com.cn/richtalk/news/society/9902/020701.html.

Chinese Justice Observer (2020) 'PRC Civil Code Series […] About Part V Marriage and Family', 18 July 2020 available at: https://www.chinajusticeobserver. com/a/prc-civil-code-series-05-the-thing-about-part-v-marriage-and-family%C2%A0.

Chung, JH (2016) 'Implementation: Changing Norms, Issue-Variance, and Unending Tugs of War' in Donaldson, J (ed) (2016) *Assessing the Balance of Power in Central–Local Relations in China* Routledge.

Chung, S and Wong, CK (2013) 'Regulatory and Policy Control on Food Safety in China' (67) *Journal of Epidemiology and Community Health* 476.

Ciepley, D (2013) 'Beyond Public and Private: Towards a Political Theory' (107) *American Political Science Review* 139 at 158.

Clarke, D (2016) 'Blowback: How China's Efforts to Bring Private-Sector Standards into the Public Sector Backfired' in Liebman, BL and Milhaupt, CJ (eds) (2016) *Regulating the Visible Hand? The Institutional Implications of Chinese State Capitalism* Oxford University Press.

Coase, RH (1960) 'The Problem of Social Cost' (3) *Journal of Law and Economics* 1.

Cohen, J (2019) 'Law's Relation to Political Power in China: A Backward Transition' (86) *Social Research: An International Quarterly* 231.

Cohen, J (2020) 'Implications of the Coronavirus Crisis for China's Legal System' 10 February 2020. Available at <https://www.jeromecohen.net/jerrys-blog/2020/2/10/implications-of-the-coronavirus-crisis-for-chinas-legal-system>.

Cohen, Stanley (1980) *Folk Devils and Moral Panics: The Creation of the Mods and Rockers* St. Martin's Press.

Cooney, S; Biddulph, S and Zhu, Y (2013) *Law and Fair Work in China* Routledge.

Cory, N and Dascoli, L, 'How Barriers to Cross-Border Data Flows Are Spreading Globally' (202, *Information Technology and Innovation Foundation Report* at https://www.researchgate.net/publication/353368028_How_Barriers_to_Cross-Border_Data_Flows_Are_Spreading_Globally_What_They_Cost_and_How_to_Address_Them

Cox, GW and McCubbins, MD (2001) 'Political Structure and Economic Policy: The Institutional Determination of Policy Outcomes' in Haggard, S and McCubbins, MD (eds) *Presidents, Parliaments, and Policy* Cambridge University Press.

Cyberspace Administration of China Questions and Answers to its Establishment and Responsibilities' 5 May 2011. Available at <https://www.gov.cn/jrzg/2011-05/05/content_1858131.htm> last accessed 31 March 2025.

Dai, C (2016) 'How to implement the lifelong accountability system for officials (Guanyuan zongsheng zhui ze zhi zenma luoshi)' Study Times (Xuexi shibao) 17 March 2016 Available at: <http://theory.people.com.cn/n1/2016/0317/c40531-28207088.html>.

Daoust, JF; Bélanger, E; Dassonneville, R; Lachapelle, E and Nadeau, R (2022) 'Is the Unequal COVID-19 Burden in Canada Due to Unequal Levels of Citizen Discipline Across Provinces?' (48) *Canadian Public Policy* 124.

Davies, G 2016 'The Four Comprehensives' *The China Story* at https://www.thechinastory.org/yearbooks/yearbook-2016/chapter-4-the-language-of-discipline/the-four-comprehensives/

DeLisle, J (2015) 'The Rule of Law with Xi-Era Characteristics: Law for Economic Reform, Anticorruption, and Illiberal Politics' (20) *Asia Policy* 23.

deLisle, J and Kui, S (2020) 'Lessons from China's Response to COVID-19: Shortcomings, Successes, and Prospects for Reform in China's Regulatory State' (16) *University of Pennsylvania Asian Law Review* 66.

Deloitte China (2024) 'Regulations on Promoting and Regulating Cross-border Data Flow—Key Takeaways' (25 March 2024).

Deng, F (2016) 'Indigenous Evolution of SOE Regulation' in Liebman, BL and Milhaupt, CJ (eds) *Regulating the Visible Hand? The Institutional Implications of Chinese State Capitalism* Oxford University Press.

Ding CY (2022) Mandarins v. Mandarins: Procuratorate-initiated Administrative Public Interest Litigation in China. (17) *Journal of Comparative Law* 286.

Ding, CY (2015) 'Surrogacy litigation in China and beyond' (2015) *Journal of Law and the Biosciences* 33.

Ding, I and Thompson-Brusstar, M (2021) 'The Anti-Bureaucratic Ghost in China's Bureaucratic Machine' (248, S1) *The China Quarterly* 116.

Donaldson, JA (2016) 'China's Administrative Hierarchy: The Balance of Power and Winners and Losers within China's Levels of Government' in Donaldson, JA (ed) (2016) *Assessing the Balance of Power in Central–Local Relations in China* Routledge.

Dowdle, MW (2019) 'Infrastructural Power and Its Possibilities for the Constitutional Evolution of Authoritarian Political Systems: Lessons from China' in Garcia, HA and Frankenberg, G (eds) *Authoritarian Constitutionalism* Edward Elgar 76.

Dragos, D (2021) 'Administrative Justice in Transitional States' in Tomlinson, J; Thomas, R; Hertogh, M and Kirkham, R (eds) (2021) *The Oxford Handbook of Administrative Justice* Oxford University Press.

Drakulich, A (2007) 'Former Chinese SFDA Chief Executed for Taking Bribes; Agency Cracks Down on Regulation' *Pharmtech* (12 July 2007), available at: https://www.pharmtech.com/view/former-chinese-sfda-chief-executed-taking-bribes-agency-cracks-down-regulation.

Duan, RQ (2019) 'How to Coordinate Cases? The Development and Reformed Functions of the Party Political and Legal Affairs Committee's Power of Law Implementation and Supervision' (6) *Shenzhen Social Science* 144.

Dutton, M (1992) 'A Mass Line without Politics, Community Policing and Economic Reform' in Watson, A (ed) (1992) *Economic Reform and Social Change in China* Routledge.

Dutton, M (1995) 'Dreaming of Better Times: "Repetition with a Difference" and Community Policing in China' (3, 2) *positions east asia cultures critique* (Positions: East Asia Cultures Critique) 418.

Dutton, MR (1992) *Policing and Punishment in China: From Patriarchy to 'the People'* Cambridge University Press.

Earnhart, DH and Glicksman, RL (2015) 'Coercive vs. Cooperative Enforcement: Effect of Enforcement Approach on Environmental Management' (42) *International Review of Law and Economics* 135.

Editor (2023) 'Nine Keywords to Look at Ten Years after the Centre Introduced the Eight Point Regulations (Jiu ge guanjian ci fan zhongyang ba xiang guiding ding chutai zhe shi nian) cpcnews.cn Available at: <http://cpc.people.com.cn/n1/2023/0103/c164113-32598816.html>.

Editorial Committee (2018) *Formalism and Bureaucratism: Anatomy of Typical Cases* (Xingshi zhuyi guanliao zhuyi: dianxing anli pouxi) Fanzheng Press.

Editorial Committee (2022) *Violating the Spirit of the Eight Regulations* (Weifan zhongyang ba xiang guiding jingsheng: anli pouxi) Zhongguo Fangzheng Chubanshe, China Fangzheng Press.

Engler, S; Brunner, P; Loviat, R; Abou-Chadi, T; Leemann, L and Glaser, A (2021) 'Democracy in Times of the Pandemic: Explaining the Variation of COVID-19 Policies across European Democracies' (44) *West European Politics* 1077.

European Data Protection Board (2021) 'Recommendations 01/2020 on Measures that Supplement Transfer Tools to Ensure Compliance with the EU Level of Protection of Personal Data' (final, 18 June 2021).

Factsheet on Administrative Enforcement of Copyright in China' 6 December 2019 available at <https://assets.publishing.service.gov.uk/media/5f5b4f488fa8f5106910058d/Administrative_Enforcement_of_Copyright_-_IP_in_China_Factsheet.pdf> last accessed 31 March 2025.

Fahey, BA (2022) 'Data Federalism' (135) *Harvard Law Review* 1007.

Fazhi Ribao (Legal System Daily) (2023) 'Legislation has evolved from nothing to something, from fragmented to complete, keeping pace with the times and the reform' *Legal System Daily* (22 April 2023) available at: https://baijiahao.baidu.com/s?id=1703221751704723501 and wfr=spider and for=pc.

Feng XG (2016) 'I am not Madam Bovary' (Wo bushi Pan Jinlian) (a film directed by Feng Xiaogang and written by Liu Zhenyun, based on Liu's 2012 novel I Did Not Kill My Husband).

Feng, L (2021) 'Lying flat': The millennials quitting China's '996' work culture to live 'free of anxiety' 23 September 2021 ABC News https://www.abc.net.au/news/2021-09-23/tang-ping-lying-flat-generation-rejecting-chinas-work-culture/100477716.

Feng, X (2021) *Big Market-Specialized Drugs: Research on My County's Drug Regulatory Model* (Da shichang-zhuan yaopin: woguo yaopin jianguan moshi yanjiu) (MA thesis, Shanxi University 2021).

Financial World 'Perspective Top 100 Chain! The Number of Pharmacies in the Country Continues to Grow' *Financial World* (22 April 2023) available at: https://baijiahao.baidu.com/s?id=1706503817763600820 and wfr=spider and for=pc.

Four Comprehensives' governance strategy' ('Sige quanmian'zhanlue bu ju) 11 July 2022 http://keywords.china.org.cn/2022-07/11/content_78317098.html and see

Fraenkel, E (2017) *The Dual State: A Contribution to the Theory of Dictatorship* (EA Shils trans; J Meierhenrich ed.) Oxford University Press.

Friedman, M (1962) *Capitalism and Freedom* University of Chicago Press.

Friedman, M (1970) 'A Friedman Doctrine: The Social Responsibility of Business Is to Increase Its Profits' *New York Times Magazine* (13 September 1970).

Fu, HL (1990) 'Patrol Police: A Recent Development in the People's Republic of China' (13) *Police Studies* 111.

Fu, HL (2016) 'Building Judicial Integrity in China' (39) *Hastings International and Comparative Law Review* 167.

Fu, HL (2019) 'The Secrets About State Secret: The Burden of Overclassification' in Fu, H; Palmer, M and Zhang, X (eds) (2019) *Transparency Challenges Facing China* Wildy, Simmonds and Hill Publishing.

Fu, HL (2019) 'Duality and China's Struggle for Legal Autonomy' (1) *China Perspectives* 5.

Fukuyama, F (1996) *Trust: The Social Virtues and the Creation of Prosperity* Free Press.

Fukuyama, F (2020) 'The Thing That Determines a Country's Resistance to the Coronavirus' *The Atlantic* 30 March 2020, available at: https://www.theatlantic.com/ideas/archive/2020/03/thing-determines-how-well-countries-respond-coronavirus/609025.

Gallagher, ME 'The Social Relations of Chinese State Capitalism' in Liebman, BL and Milhaupt, CJ (eds) (2016) *Regulating the Visible Hand? The Institutional Implications of Chinese State Capitalism* Oxford University Press.

Gallagher, ME 'The Social Relations of Chinese State Capitalism' in Goetzmann WN and Köl E (2005) 'The History of Corporate Ownership in China: State Patronage, Company Legislation, and the Issue of Control' in Morck RK (ed), *A History of Corporate Governance around the World: Family Business Groups to Professional Managers* University of Chicago Press, available at http://www.nber.org/chapters/c10269.pdf

Gao, JH and Zhang, PF (2021) 'China's Public Health Policies in Response to COVID-19: From an "Authoritarian" Perspective' *Frontiers in Public Health* 15 December 2021, available at: https://doi.org/10.3389/fpubh.2021.756677.

Gao, ZJ (2023) 'Duli xingzheng juliu chengxu zhi tichang: lun xingzheng juliu chengxu gaige de "zhongjian fangan"'(A proposal on Administrative Detention Independent Procedures: On a 'Middle Ground Solution' for Reforming Administrative Detention Procedures) 2023 (3) *Xingzheng Faxue Yanjiu* (Administrative Law Review) 30 at 32.

Geertz, C (2017) *The Interpretation of Cultures: Selected Essays* Basic Books.

General Office of the Central Committee of the CPC (2019) 'Notice on Solving Outstanding Issues of Formalism to Reduce Burdens on Grassroots Levels' (Guanyu jiejue xingshi zhuyi tuchu wenti wei jiceng jianfu de tongzhi), available at: <https://www.gov.cn/zhengce/2019-03/11/content_5372964.htm>.

General Office of the Central Committee of the CPC 'Notice on Solving Outstanding Issues of Formalism to Reduce Burdens on Grassroots Levels' supra note 84.

Gersen, JE (2007)'Temporary Legislation' (74,1) *University of Chicago Law Review,* at https://chicagounbound.uchicago.edu/public_law_and_legal_theory?utm_source=chicagounbound.uchicago.edu%2Fpublic_law_and_legal_theory%2F292 and utm_medium=PDF and utm_campaign=PDFCoverPages

Gilbert, CG (2005) 'Unbundling the Structure of Inertia: Resource versus Routine Rigidity' (48) *Academy of Management Journal* 741.

Ginsburg, T (2008) 'Administrative Law and the Judicial Control of Agents in Authoritarian Regimes' in Ginsburg, T and Moustafa, T (eds) *Rule by Law: The Politics of Courts in Authoritarian Regions* Cambridge University Press.

Ginsburg, T (2009) 'The Judicialization of Administrative Governance: Causes, Consequences and Limits' in Ginsburg, T and Chen, AHY. (eds) *Administrative Law and Governance in Asia: Comparative Perspectives* Routledge.

Ginsburg, T, and Simpser, A (2013) 'Introduction: Constitutions in Authoritarian Regimes', in Ginsburg, T and Simpser, A (eds) Comparative Constitutional Law and Policy Cambridge: Cambridge University Press, 2013, 1-18.

Gocha, AJ (2018) 'Modern system for resolving online copyright infringement disputes: administrative rulemaking and adjudication, one-stop fix to the digital millennium copyright act. IDEA' (58, 2) *The Journal of the Franklin Pierce Center for Intellectual Property* 131.

Goetzmann, WN and Köl, E (2005) 'The History of Corporate Ownership in China: State Patronage, Company Legislation, and the Issue of Control' in Morck, RK (ed) *A History of Corporate Governance around the World: Family Business Groups to Professional Managers* University of Chicago Press, available at: http://www.nber.org/chapters/c10269.pdf.

Goffman, E (1959) *The Presentation of Self in Everyday Life* Doubleday

Goffman, E (1963) *Stigma: Notes on the Management of Spoiled Identity* Prentice-Hall.

Goldstein, Leslie Friedman (2011) 'Judicial Review' in Bertrand Badie and others (eds), *International Encyclopaedia of Political Science* SAGE Press 1372.

Gong'an Bu (Ministry of Public Security) (2022) 'Gong'an jiguan zai "bairi Xingdong" zhong zhongquan daji huan du weifa fanzui' (Public Security Organs Launched "Hundred Days" Operation Striking a Hard Blow to Illegal Activities Involving Prostitution and

Gambling) 21 July 2022. Available at <https://www.shdf.gov.cn/shdf/contents/767/447431.html>.

Goo, SH (2017) 'An Economic Efficiency Approach to Reforming Corporate Governance: the Case of Multiple Stakeholder Board' (4) *Asian Journal of Law and Society* 387.

Goo, SH (2019) 'Corporate Governance Reform' in Institute of Comparative Law in Japan's 70th Anniversary Commemorative Book Series Editorial Committee (ed), *Beyond Globalization: Future of Comparative Law in Asia-Pacific* Chuo University Press.

Goo, SH and Hong, FXX (2011) 'The curious model of internal monitoring mechanisms of listed corporations in China: the Sinonization process' (12) *European Business Organization Law Review* 469.

Goodman, DS (2004) 'The Campaign to "Open up the West": National, Provincial-level and Local Perspectives' 178 *The China Quarterly* 317.

Greenleaf, G (2014) *Asian Data Privacy Laws: Trade and Human Rights Perspectives* Oxford University Press

Greenleaf, G (2021) 'China's Completed Personal Information Protection Law: Rights Plus Cyber-security' (2021) 172 *Privacy Laws and Business International Report* 20, at extension://mjdgandcagmikhlbjnilkmfnjeamfikk/https://classic.austlii.edu.au/au/journals/UNSWLRS/2021/91.pdf

Grote, Rainer (2018) 'Judicial Review', *Max Planck Encyclopaedia of Comparative Constitutional Law,* https://oxcon.ouplaw.com/display/10.1093/law-mpeccol/law-mpeccol-e334?prd=MPECCOL

Guangzhou Shi Renmin Zhengfu (The People's Government of Guangzhou Municipality) (2020) 'Guangzhou shi renda changweihui biaojue tongguo "Guanyu yifa quanli zuohao xinguan feiyan yiqing fangkong gongzuo de jueding"' (The Standing Committee of the Guangzhou Municipal People's Congress votes to pass the 'Decision on the Prevention and Control of the Covid-19 Epidemic') 12 February 2020, available at: https://www.gz.gov.cn/zt/qlyfdyyqfkyz/gzzxd/content/post_5660732.html.

Guglielmo, B; Lacetera, N; Macis, M; and Tonin, M (2020) 'Compliance with COVID-19 Social-Distancing Measures in Italy: The Role of Expectations and Duration' National Bureau of Economic Research, *IZA Discussion Papers* No 13092.

Gui, X and Luo, Z (2021) 'China's Online Xinfang Channel: Absorbing Grievances through Institutionalisation' (2021, 3) *China Perspectives* 53.

Gunningham, N, 'Compliance, Deterrence and beyond' in Faure, M (eds) (2023) *Elgar Encyclopaedia of Environmental Law* Edward Elgar Publishing.

Guojia jiancha weiyuanhui diaochazu (National Supervisory Commission Investigation Team) (2020) 'Guanyu qunzhong fanying de sheji liwenliang yisheng youguan qingkuang diaocha de tongbao' (A Public Circular on The Investigation Regarding Concerns of the Mass for Dr Li Wenliang) 19 March 2020. Available at <http://politics.people.com.cn/n1/2020/0320/c1001-31640288.html>.

Heilongjiang sheng gong'an jiguan banli 4825 qi she yi weifa fanzui anjian' (Heilongjiang Provincial Public Security Organs Handled 4,825 Epidemic-related Illegal and Criminal Cases) (2020) *Baidu* 15 March, 2020, available at: https://baijiahao.baidu.com/s?id=1661228712202321617 and wfr=spider and for=pc.

Halliday, S and Scott, C (2010) 'Administrative Justice' in Cane, P and Kritzer, H (eds) (2010) *The Oxford Handbook of Empirical Legal Research* Oxford University Press 469.

Hampshire, S (1989) *Innocence and Experience* Penguin

Hampshire, S (2000) *Justice is Conflict* Princeton University Press.

Hand, Keith (2011) 'Resolving Constitutional Dispute in Contemporary China' (7) *University of Pennsylvania East Asia Law Review* 109.

Harding, H (1981) *Organizing China: The Problem of Bureaucracy 1949-1976* Stanford University Press.

Harper, CA; Satchell, LP; Fido, D and Latzman, RD (2021) 'Functional Fear Predicts Public Health Compliance in the COVID-19 Pandemic' (19) *International Journal of Mental Health and Addiction* 1875.

Hart, M and Link, J (2020) 'Chinese President Xi Jinping's Philosophy on Risk Management' Center for American Progress 20 February, available at: https://www.americanprogress.org/article/chinese-president-xi-jinpings-philosophy-risk-management.

Hart, O and Zingales, L (2017) 'Companies Should Maximize Shareholder Welfare Not Market Value' (2) *Journal of Law, Finance, and Accounting* 247.

He, B (2022) 'Xi'an yiqing zhi xia, shehui zuzhi dou qu nalile?' (Where did social organizations go during the Xi'an epidemic?) *Zhongguo Cishan Jia Zazhi* (China Philanthropist Magazine) 5 January, available at: https://mp.weixin.qq.com/s/PnDMdX6flK6h99ynTDZ_Tw.

He, GJ, & Ors (2023) 'Reducing Single-use Cutlery with Green Nudges: Evidence from China's Food-delivery Industry' (381, 6662) *Science* eadd9884.

He, Haibo (2011) 'Litigations without a Ruling: The Predicament of Administrative Law in China' (3) *Tsinghua China Law Review* 257.

He, Haibo (2018) 'How Much Progress Can Legislation Bring: The 2014 Amendment of the Administrative Litigation Law of the PRC' (13) *University of Pennsylvania Asian Law Review* 137.

He, Haibo (2018) 'How Much Progress Can Legislation Bring: The 2014 Amendment of the Administrative Litigation Law of the PRC' (13) *University of Pennsylvania Asian Law Review* 137.

He, HB (2008) 'The Dawn of the Due Process Principle in China' (22) *Columbia Journal of Asian Law* 57.

He, X (2003) 'Sporadic Campaigns as a Means of Social Control' (17) Columbia Journal of Asian Law 121;

He, X (2009) 'Administrative Law as a Mechanism for Political Control in Contemporary China' in Balme, S and Dowdle, M (eds) (2009) *Building Constitutionalism in China* Palgrave Macmillan.

He, X (2020) 'Wuhan 1.7 wan yu dangyuan ganbu xia chen shequ da paicha quebao ying shou jin shou' [More than 17,000 party members and cadres in Wuhan have a large-scale investigation deep in the community to ensure that all receivables (that should be received are collected)] *Zhongguo Jingji Wang* (China Economic Net) 11 February, 2020, available at: http://www.ce.cn/xwzx/gnsz/gdxw/202002/11/t20200211_34245935.shtml.

He, X (2024) *The Judicial System of China* Oxford University Press.

He, X; Moscati, MF; and Palmer, M (2020) 'China's Family Law in Action: An Introduction' (15, 2) *Journal of Comparative Law* 1.

He, XL; Jiang, P; Wu, Q; Lai, XB and Liang, Y (2022) 'Governmental Inter-Sectoral Strategies to Prevent and Control COVID-19 in a Megacity: A Policy Brief From Shanghai, China' *Frontiers in Public Health*, available at: https://doi.org/10.3389/fpubh.2022.764847.

Hegarty, S (2020) 'The Chinese Doctor Who Tried to Warn Others About Coronavirus' BBC 6 February 2020. Available at <https://www.bbc.co.uk/news/world-asia-china-51364382#:~:text=Dr%20Li%2C%2034%2C%20tried%20to,for%20at%20least%20three%20weeks>.

Hertogh, M (2022) 'Administrative Justice as a Field of Study' in Hertogh, M; Kirkham, R; Thomas, R; and Tomlinson, J (eds) (2022) *The Oxford Handbook of Administrative Justice* Oxford University Press.

Hertogh, M; Kirkham, R; Thomas, R and Tomlinson, J (eds) (2022) *The Oxford Handbook of Administrative Justic*e Oxford University Press.

Ho, V (2009) 'From Contracts to Compliance? An Early Look at Implementation under China's New Labor Legislation' (23) *Columbia Journal of Asian Law* 35.

Hooghe, L and Marks, G (2001) *Multi-Level Governance and European Integration* Rowman and Littlefield.

Horsley, J (2023) 'Further Observations on the Second Revision Draft of the Administrative Reconsideration Law' *China Law Translate*, 23

January 2022, available at: <https://www.chinalawtranslate.com/en/arldraft2/>.

Horton, R (2021) 'Offline: Is Democracy Good for Your Health?' (398) *The Lancet* 2060.

Howson, NC (2016) 'Protecting the State from Itself? Regulatory Interventions in Corporate Governance and the Financing of China's "State Capitalism" ', in Liebman BL and Milhaupt CJ (ed) (2016) *Chinese State Capitalism and Institutional Change: Domestic and Global Implications* Oxford University Press.

Howson, NC (2017) 'China's 'corporatization without privatization' and the late 19th century roots of a stubborn path dependency' (50, 4) *Vanderbilt Journal of Transnational Law* 961.

Hu, DZ; Li, HB; Li, T; Meng, LS and Nguyen, BT (2023) 'The Burden of Education Costs in China: A Struggle for All, but Heavier for Lower-Income Families' available at: <http://dx.doi.org/10.2139/ssrn.4558282>.

Hu, M and Sidel, M (2020) 'Civil Society and COVID in China: Responses in an Authoritarian Society' (49) *Nonprofit and Voluntary Sector Quarterly* 1173.

Huang, LQ (2023) 'A Decade of Chain Retail Pharmacy' *Journal of Medical Economics* (22 April 2023) available at: http://www.linkshop.com/web/article_news.aspx?articleid=136826.

Huang, Y (2023) '"Tentative Violations" and "Selective Tolerance": An Organisational Interpretation of the Failure of Campaign-style Regulations' (2023, 2) *China Public Administration Review* 25

Huang, Y and Bai, X (2022) 'Xi Jinping Emphasised "Persevering in Rectifying the 'Four Winds' and Establishing a New Wind" (Guanyu qie'er bushi jiu sifeng shu xinfeng' Xi Jinping zheyang qiangdiao)' www.cpcnews.cn Available at: <http://cpc.people.com.cn/n1/2022/0227/c164113-32360668.html>, also referred to as the Four Winds Problem (Si feng wenti)

Huysseune, M (2020) 'Theory Travelling through Time and Space: The Reception of the Concept of Amoral Familism' (33) *International Journal of Politics, Culture, and Society* 365.

Initium Media (2020) 'Sha mao, feng lu, qiangzhi geli, Zhongguo shi kang yi shi ruhe xingcheng de?' [Killing cats, closing roads, and enforced isolation, how did the Chinese style of fighting against the epidemic take shape?] Initium Media 4 March 2020, available at: https://theinitium.com/article/20200309-mainland-coronavirus-mergency-management/.

Ip, Eric 'Administrative Justice in Authoritarian States' in Hertogh, M; Kirkham, R; Thomas, R; and Tomlinson, J (eds) (2022) *The Oxford Handbook of Administrative Justice* Oxford University Press.

Ip, Eric C. (2011) 'The Supreme People's Court and the Political Economy of Judicial Empowerment in Contemporary China' (24) *Columbia Journal of Asian Law* 374.

Ip, Eric C. (2012) 'Judicial Review in China: A Positive Political Economy Analysis' (8) *Review of Law and Economics* 334.

Ji, WD (1993) 'Falü chengxu de yiyi——dui zhongguo fazhidu jianshe de yi zhong sikao' (The Significance of Legal Procedures - Another Thinking on the Construction of the Chinese Legal System) (1993, 1) *Zhongguo Shehui Kexue* (China Social Science) 83.

Jian, B (2012) 'Xingzheng chengxu zhengdangxing de sifa shencha' (Judicial Review of the Administrative Due Process) (2012, 7) *Zhongguo shehui kexue* (Social Sciences in China) 123.

Jiancha Ribao (Procuracy Daily) 'Xinzhongguo zhi'an lifa wushinian: cong tiaoli dao fa jiannan qicao qingyi tongguo' (New China's Fifty Years of Law-and-Order Legislation: From Regulations to Law, Painstaking Drafting and Readily Enactment) *Jiancha Ribao* (Procuracy Daily) 27 August 2009. Available at <https://news.ifeng.com/c/7fYTQrKES42>.

Jiang, B and He, Y (2021) 'Guanche Xingzheng Chufa Fa xu Zhongdian Bawo de Jige Wenti' (Key Issues to Focus on in Implementing the Administrative Penalty Law) (2021, 5) *Falü kexue* (Xibeizhengfa daxue xuebao, Journal of Northwest University of Political Science and Law) 43.

Jiang, Bixin (2013) 'Reform of China's Administrative Adjudication' (4) *Administrative Law Studies* 3.

Jiang, BX (2009) 'Administrative Procedure Law and Abstract Administrative Act' (3) *Xingzheng Faxue Yanjiu* (Administrative Law Review 23.

Jiang, BX (2014) 'Improvement of the Administrative Litigation System from a Macroscopic Perspective' (9) *Frontiers of Law in China* 1.

Jiang, BX(2013) 'Reform of China's Administrative Adjudication' (4) Administrative Law Studies 3.

Jiang, DX (2018) 'Zhengzhi Zhengdang Yu Qiye : Zhengzhi Quanli Canyu Ziyuan Fenpei De Wenming Jiegou (Party Politics and Enterprises: The Civilized Structure for the Political Power to Participate in Resource Allocation' 2018 *Dangdai Faxue* (Contemporary Legal Studies) 11.

Jiang, H (2019) 'Zhengdang chengxu yuanze sifa shiyong de zhengdangxing: huigui guifan lichang' (Legitimacy of the Judicial Application of the Due Process Principle: Returning to the Normative Position) (2019, 3) *Zhongguo Faxue* (China Legal Science) 46 at 56.

Jiang, J (2022) 'A Question of Human Rights or Human Left? The "People's War against COVID-19" under the "Gridded Management" System in China' (31) *Journal of Contemporary China* 491.

Jiang, MA (1995) 'Woguo xingzheng chengxu lifa moshi de xuanzi' (Choice of China's Administrative Procedure Legislation Mode) (1995) (6) *Zhongguo Faxue* (Chinese Legal Science) 42.

Jiang, S and Liu, J (2022) 'Apple Curbs AirDrop File Sharing on Devices in China' CNN 11 November 2022. Available at <https://edition.cnn.com/2022/11/11/business/china-apple-airdrop-function-restricted-hnk-intl/index.html>.

Jiao, H; Dong, Y; Hou, W and Lee, E (2013) 'Independent Directors and Corporate Performance in China' in Cumming, D & Ors (2013) *Developing China's Capital Market* Palgrave Macmillan UK.

Jie, G (2009) 'Governing by Goals and Numbers: A Case Study in the Use of Performance Measures to Build Governance Capacity in China' (29) *Public Administration and Development* 21.

Jin, H,& Ors (2020) 'Empirical Study of the Cases Lost by Environmental Agencies' 46 *Environmental Protection Science* 7.

Jin, H; Lu, LG; Liu, JW; and Cui, M (2021) 'COVID-19 Emergencies around the Globe: China's Experience in Controlling COVID-19 and Lessons Learned' (33) *International Journal for Quality in Health Care* 1.

Jin, Hai,& Ors (2020) 'Empirical Study of the Cases Lost by Environmental Agencies' (46) *Environmental Protection Science* 7.

Jin, ZN (2015) 'Environmental Impact Assessment Law in China's Courts: A Study of 107 Judicial Decisions' (55) *Environmental Impact Assessment Review* 35.

Jin, ZN(2015) 'Environmental Impact Assessment Law in China's Courts: A Study of 107 Judicial Decisions' (55) *Environmental Impact Assessment Review* 35.

Jingyi [净壹] (2021) 'Mindset Differences between the Old Industrial and Commercial People and the Old Food And Drug Regulatory People in the Market Supervision Enforcement Team' [Shichang jianguan zonghe zhifa duiwu li lao gongshang ren yu lao shi yao jian ren siwei fangmian de chayi] *Weibo* (4 May 2021) available at: https://weibo.com/ttarticle/p/show?id=2309404633071898198225.

Ju Hua, (2022) 'Let the "Lying Flat" Cadres Who Are Messing about Have No Market (Rang hun rizi de 'tangping shi' ganbu mei shichang)' *People's Forum* (Renmin Luntan), available at: <http://paper.people.com.cn/rmlt/html/2022-04/01/content_25917755.htm>.

Judicial Big Data on Divorce Cases' available at: https://www. court.gov.cn/fabu-xiangqing-87622.html.

Kaiman, J 'A (2016) Mysterious Death in China Raises Suspicions of Police Brutality' Los Angeles Times 10 May 2016. Available at<https://www.latimes.com/world/asia/la-fg-china-police-brutality-20160510-snap-story.html>; '

Kang, I. (2023) 'How Does Technology-based Monitoring Affect Street-level Bureaucrats' Behavior? An Analysis of Body-worn Cameras and Police Actions' (42, 4) *Journal of Policy Analysis and Management* 971.

Kang, PP and Han, BX (2014) 'Wang ge hua dangjian tongling shequ zhili chuangxin' (Grid-based party building leads community governance innovation) *Renmin Wang* (People's Daily Online) 27 November, available at: http://theory.people.com.cn/n/2014/1127/c40531-26105462.html.

Kazuo, T (1967) *Introduction to Anglo-American Law* Yuhikaku Publishing.

Keith, RC, Lin, ZQ: and Hou, SM(2014) *China's Supreme Court* Routledge.

Kennedy, G and Lai, J (2024) 'Guangzhou Internet Court Decision on Cross-Border Data Transfer' *Mayer Brown Insights* at https://www.mayerbrown.com/en/insights/publications/2024/12/guangzhou-internet-court-issues-the-first-decision-on-cross-border-transfer-of-personal-data-under-pipl

Kenny, C (2024) 'The Inequitable Impacts of Data Localization' Center for Global Development, at https://www.cgdev.org/publication/data-localization-tax-poor

Kirby, WC (1995) 'China Unincorporated: Company Law and Business Enterprises in Twentieth-Century China' (54) *The Journal of Asian Studies* 43.

Kostka, G and Nahm, J (2017) 'Central–Local Relations: Recentralization and Environmental Governance in China' (231) *The China Quarterly* 567.

Kowalewski, M (2021) 'Street protests in times of COVID-19: adjusting tactics and marching "as usual" ' (20) *Social Movement Studies* 758.

Krygier, M (2021) 'Illiberalism and the Rule of Law' in Sajo, A; Uitz, R and Holmes, S (eds) (2021) *Routledge Handbook of Illiberalism* Routledge.

Kuner, C (2015)'Extraterritoriality and Regulation of International Data Transfers in EU Data Protection Law' (5, 4) *International Data Privacy Law* 235.

Lachaud, E (2020) What GDPR tells about certification' (38) *Computer Law and Security Review* 105457.

Lau, JYC and Lee, SS (2021) 'Legal Provisions for Enforcing Social Distancing to Guard against COVID-19: The Case of Hong Kong' (8) *Journal of Law and the Biosciences* 1.

Law Reform Commission of Hong Kong (1994) *Report on Reform of the Law Relating to the Protection of Personal Data.*

Li, C, and Zhao, WG (2018) 'Difficulties and Solutions: Study on the APIL Case Clue Discovery System' (45, 4) *Journal of Sichuan Normal University (Social Science Edition)* 55.

Li, H (2014) *Xingzhengfa shiyixue: Xingzhengfa xueli de gengxin* (Administrative Law Hermeneutics: A Renewal of Administrative Law Doctrine) Zhongguo Renmin Daxue Chubanshe.

Li, J; Ni, X and Wang, R (2021) 'Blame Avoidance in China's Cadre Responsibility System' (247) *The China Quarterly* 681.

Li, JR (2022) *Zhongguo Qiji Yu Zhongguo Zhidu* (The China Miracle and Chinese System) Kai Ming Bookstore.

Li, L (2015) ' "Rule of Law" in a Party-State: A Conceptual Interpretive Framework of the Constitutional Reality of China' (2) *Asian Journal of Law and Society* 93.

Li, L (2019) 'Politics of Anticorruption in China: Paradigm Change of the Party's Disciplinary Regime 2012-2017' (28) *Journal of Contemporary* China 47.

Li, LCL (2010) 'Central-Local Relations in the People's Republic of China: Trends, Processes and Impacts for Policy Implementation' (30) *Public Administration and Development* 177.

Li, LJ (2004) 'Political Trust in Rural China' (230) *Modern China* 228.

Li, LJ (2016) 'Reassessing Trust in the Central Government: Evidence from Five National Surveys' (225) *The China Quarterly* 100.

Li, Q (2021) 'Zhi'an guanli chufa de xianshi kunjing yu zhidu fansi' (Penalties on Law-and-Order Violations: Dilemmas and Reflections) 2021 (3) *Zhongguo Renmin Gong'an Daxue Xuebao (shehui kexue ban)* (Journal of People's Public Security University of China (Social Sciences Edition)) 133 at 140.

Li, QX and Di, X (2025) 'Fertility discrimination in the Chinese labour market: Evidence from a correspondence study and an employer survey' (92) *Labour Economics* 102668.

Li, RQ, & Ors (2020) 'Does the Central Environmental Inspection Actually Work?' (253) *Journal of Environmental Management* 109602.

Li, S (2023) 'Heavy Handed Management "Mediocre Officials and Lazy Governance" (Zhong quan zhili 'yongguan lanzheng') *Lookout* (Liaowang) Available at: <http://www.xinhuanet.com//politics/2017-02/20/c_1120494357.htm>.

Li, SX and Rowley, TJ (2002) 'Inertia and Evaluation Mechanisms in Inter-organisational Partner Selection: Syndicate Formation among US Investment Banks' 45 *Academy of Management Journal* 1104.

Li, TQ and Zeng, Y (2023) 'A Brief History of the Evolution of China's Drug Registration System (I): First there are Boundaries, then there are Rules' *Yaozhi News* (22 April 2023) available at: https://news.yaozh.com/archive/22773.html.

Liang, F (2020) 'COVID-19 and Health Code: How Digital Platforms Tackle the Pandemic in China' (6) *Social Media + Society* 2.

Lieberthal, K and Oksenberg, M (1988) *Policy Making in China: Leaders, Structures, and Processes* Princeton University Press.

Lieberthal, KG and Lampton, DM (2018) *Bureaucracy, Politics, and Decision Making in Post-Mao China* University of California Press.

Liebman, BL and Milhaupt CJ (eds.), (2016) *Regulating the Visible Hand? The Institutional Implications of Chinese State Capitalism* Oxford University Press.

Lin, K; Shen, S; Sun, IY and Wu, YN (2022) 'Policing pandemic in China: investigating the roles of organizational adjustment, procedural justice, and police trustworthiness on public compliance' *Police Practice and Research,* available at: https://doi.org/10.1080/15614263.2022.2127717.

Lin, LW (2010) 'Corporate Social Responsibility in China: Window Dressing or Structural Change' (28) *Berkeley Journal of International Law* 64.

Lin, LW (2015) 'Balancing Closure and Openness: The Challenge of Leadership Reform in China's State-Owned Enterprises' in Liebman, BL and Milhaupt, CJ (eds) (2016) *Regulating the Visible Hand? The Institutional Implications of Chinese State Capitalism* Oxford University Press.

Lin, LW and Milhaupt, CJ (2013) 'We Are the (National) Champions: Understanding the Mechanism of State Capitalism in China' (65) *Stanford Law Review* 697.

Lin, LYH (2021) 'Institutionalizing Political Influence in Business: Party-Building and Insider Control in Chinese State-Owned Enterprises' (45) *Vermont Law Review* 441.

Lin, LYH and Milhaupt, CJ (2021) 'Party Building or Noisy Signaling? The Contours of Political Conformity in Chinese Corporate Governance' (50) *Journal of Legal Studies* 187.

Lin, SL (2022) 'Fiscal Relationship between the Central and Local Governments' in *China's Public Finance: Reforms, Challenges, and Options* Cambridge University Press.

Lin, SL (2022) *China's Public Finance: Reforms, Challenges, and Options* Cambridge University Press.

Lin, YD; Zhang, BY; Hu, M; Yao, Q; Jiang, M and Zhu, CR (2024) 'The effect of gradually lifting the two-child policy on demographic changes in China' (39) *Health Policy and Planning* 363.

Liu, CX (2020) 'Judicial Review of Environmental Administrative Cases – A Study of Model Cases' (19) *Journal of Nanjing Tech University (Social Science Edition)* 1.

Liu, J; Liu, M; Zhang, S; Ma, Q and Wang, Q (2019) 'Intent to have a second child among Chinese women of childbearing age following China's new universal two-child policy: a cross-sectional study' (46, 1) *BMJ Sex Reproductive Health* 59.

Liu, JZ and Zhang, AH (2019) 'Ownership and Political Control: Evidence from Charter Amendments' (60) *International Review of Law and Economics* 1.

Liu, NN & Ors (2022) 'Enforcement Officials' Coping Strategies in a Changing Regulatory Environment' (100) *Public Administration* 408.

Liu, NN, & Ors (2015) 'Campaign-style Enforcement and Regulatory Compliance' (75) *Public Administration Review* 85.

Liu, NN; Lo, CWH; Zhan, X and Wang, W (2015)'Campaign-style Enforcement and Regulatory Compliance' (75) *Public Administration Review* 85

Liu, NN; van Rooij, B and Lo, Carlos Wing-Hung (2018) 'Beyond Deterrent Enforcement Styles: Behavioural Intuitions of Chinese Environmental Law Enforcement Agents in a Context of Challenging Inspections' (96) *Public Administration* 497.

Liu, P (2007) 'Mixed Regulation: Analysis of Drug Safety Regulation Mechanism in Contemporary China' (Hunhe xing jianguan: dangdai zhongguo yaopin anquan jianguan jizhi fenxi) (14) *Gonggong Guanli Yanjiu* (Public Management Research) 12.

Liu, P (2009) 'Exploration towards Quality Regulation—Some Observations on Drug Regulatory Reform in 2008' (Zouxiang youzhi jianguan de youyi tansuo—2008 nian yaopin jianguan gaige de ruogan guancha, zhongguo chufang yao) (2) *Journal of China Prescription Drugs* 14.

Liu, SP & Ors (2019) 'Zhi'an anjian banli jieduan de lüshi jie'ru jizhi: xuqiu, kunjing yu goujian lujing' (Access to Lawyer During the Processing of Law-and-Order Cases: Demands, Dilemmas, and Construction Pathway) (35, 11) *Wujing Xueyuan Xuebao* (Journal of Armed Police Academy) 41.

Liu, X (2018) 'Xingzheng chengxu zhongjian xingwei kesuxing biaozhun tantao – jiehe zuigao fayuan di 69 hao zhidao anli de fenxi' (Discussing the Standards of Justiciability of Intermediate Acts in Administrative Procedure: In Combination with an Analysis of Supreme Court Guiding Case No. 69) (2018, 2) *Xingzheng faxue yanjiu* (Administrative Law Review) 81.

Liu, Y (2020) 'People's will or the central government's plan? The shape of contemporary Chinese local governance' (9, 2) *Journal of Contemporary East Asia Studies* 226, available at: <https://doi.org/10.1080/24761028.2020.1744290>.

Liu, Y (2020) 'The Development Tendency and Improvements of the APIL system' (26, 4) *Journal of Chongqing University (Social Science Edition)* 176.

Liu, Y (2021) 'Quanguo gong'an jiguan shenru kaizhan "bai wan jing jin qian wan jia" huodong reqing fuwu qunzhong shouhu yifang ping'an' [National public security organs carry out in-depth activities of 'millions of policemen entering thousands of households' to serve the masses enthusiastically and protect the safety of one place] *Renmin Ribao* (People's Daily) 1 July, available at: http://www.gov.cn/xinwen/2021-01/07/content_5577609.htm.

Liu, ZY (2020) '450 wan wanggeyuan zhu lao yiqing shequ "di yi dao fangxian"' [4.5 million grid members build the first line of defense for community prevention and control of the epidemic] *Xinhua* 10 March, available at: http://www.xinhuanet.com/legal/2020-03/10/c_1210507945.htm.

Liu, ZY (2021) 'Youyi zhongliliang, jiao "Zhongguo wanggeyuan" ' [There is a force called the 'Chinese grid member'] *Zhongguo shuzi shidai* (China Digital Times) 3 October, available at: https://chinadigitaltimes.net/chinese/663429.html.

Lo, CWH, & Ors (2016) 'Controlling Industrial Pollution in Urban China: Towards a More Effective Institutional Milieu in the Guangzhou Environmental Protection Bureau?' (30) *China Information* 232.

Lo, CWH, & Ors (2022) '18. Sustainable Development Governance in Action: China' in Russel, Duncan and Kirsop-Taylor, Nick (eds) (2022) *Handbook on the Governance of Sustainable Development* 274.

Lo, CWH; Fryxell, GE; and van Rooij, B (2009) 'Changes in Enforcement Styles among Environmental Enforcement Officials in China' (41, 11) *Environment and Planning A* 2706.

Lo, CWH; Fryxell, GE; Van Rooij, B; Wang, W and Li, PHY (2012) 'Explaining the Enforcement Gap in China: Local Government Support and Internal Agency Obstacles as Predictors of Enforcement Actions in Guangzhou' (111) *Journal of Environmental Management* 227.

Loh, C (ed) (2023) *How COVID-19 Took over the World: Lessons for the Future* Hong Kong University Press.

Lü, ZM (2014) 'Environmental Administrative Adjudication: Problems and Responses' (4) *Journal of Law Application* 2.

Luo, H and Zhan, Z (2015) *Xingzheng Faxue* (Administrative Law) Beijing Daxue Chubanshe

Luo, RQ (1957) 'Guanyu zhonghua renmin gongheguo zhi'an guanli chufa tiaoli caoan de shuoming' (Explanatory Notes to the Bill of 'Regulations on the Penalties for Administration of Public Security'), reprinted in 120 *Guowuyuan Gongbao* (State Council Gazette) 979.

Muqin paichusuo li zao minjing zema, nanzi chahuahou bei tuojin nüce qunou, jingfang duoci tensiliao' (Mum Scolded in Local Police Station, Man Intervened but then Dragged into Female Toilet and Assaulted by Police Officers, Police Tried Many Times Asking the Man to Settle the Case Privately) *Dafeng*

Xinwen 4 July 2024. Available at <https://news.qq.com/rain/a/20240704A06L4200>.

Ma LF, Wang YF and Shen XX (2012) 'Zhongguo Guoyou Qiye Dang Zuzhi de Zhili Xiaoying Yanjiu' (Research on the Governance Effects of Party Organizations in Chinese State-Owned Enterprises] 83 *Zhongguo Gongye Jingji* (China Industrial Economics) 83.

Ma LF, Wang YF and Shen XX (2013)'Guoyou Qiye Dang Zuzhi Zhili, Rongyü Guyuan yu Gaoguan Xinchóu Qiyue' (Party Organization Governance, Redundant Employees and Executive Compensation Contracts in State-Owned Enterprises) *Guanli Shijie* (Management World) 100.

Ma ZY (2022) 'Lihun Lengjingqi' zhidu de shengcheng luoji jiqi fansi (The General Logic of the Cooling Off Period System and its Reflection) (3) *Faxue Jia* (The Jurist) 14-28.

Ma, G and Wu, H (2025) 'Cross-Border Data Flow Supervision in China's Free Trade Zones: Security and Compliance Rules' (2025) *Asia Pacific Law Review* 1.

Ma, YN (2020) 'Lengjingqi shi dui qingshuai lihun de xianzhi he yueshu' (Divorce cooling- off period is a restriction and restraint on reckless divorce) (2020, 4) *Funü Yanjiu Luncong* (Journal of Chinese Women's Studies) 103.

Mandell, J (2023) Administrative Enforcement of Intellectual Property in China: Guidance for British companies seeking administrative enforcement against IP infringements in China, 13 November 2023 available at <https://www.gov.uk/government/case-studies/uk-china-cooperation-on-intellectual-propert> last accessed 31 March 2025.

Manion, M (2004) *Corruption by Design, Building Clean Government in Mainland China and Hong Kong* Harvard University Press;

Mann, M (1985) 'The Autonomous Power of the State: Its Origins, Mechanisms and Results' (25) *European Journal of Sociology/Archives européennes de sociologie* 185.

Mann, M (2005) 'The Sources of Social Power Revisited: A Response to Criticism' in Hall, JA and Schroeder, R (eds) *An Anatomy of Power: The Social Theory of Michael Mann* Cambridge University Press 343.

Mann, M (2008) 'Infrastructural Power Revisited' (43) *Studies in Comparative International Development* 355, available at: https://doi.org/10.1007/s12116-008-9027-7.

Mashaw, JL. (1985) *Due Process in the Administrative State* Yale University Press.

May, PJ and Winter, S (1999) 'Regulatory Enforcement and Compliance: Examining Danish Agro-environmental Policy' (18) *Journal of Policy Analysis and Management* 625;

McAllister, LK (2010) 'Dimensions of Enforcement Style: Factoring in Regulatory Autonomy and Capacity' (32) Law *and Policy* 61;

McCubbins, MD (2000) 'Gridlock' in Clarke, B and Foweraker, J (eds) *The Encyclopedia of Democratic Thought* Routledge 325.

McGinnis, R (1968) 'A Stochastic Model of Social Mobility' (1968) *American Sociological Review* 712

McGregor, R (2012) *The Party: The Secret World of China's Communist Rulers* Harper Perennial.

McNally, CA (2004) 'Sichuan: Driving Capitalist Development Westward' 178 *The China Quarterly* 426

Mehari, Y (2020) 'The Role of Social Trust in Citizen Mobility During COVID-19' SSRN 3607668 20 May 2020, available at: https://dx.doi.org/10.2139/ssrn.3607668.

Meijer, M (1971) *Marriage Law and Policy in the Chinese People's Republic* Hong Kong University Press.

Meltzer, JP (2015) 'The Internet, Cross□Border Data Flows and International Trade; (2, 1) *Asia & the Pacific Policy Studie* 90-102.

Meltzer, JP (2015)'The Internet, Cross-Border Data Flows and International Trade' (2, 1) *Asia and The Pacific Policy Studies* 90.

Meng, QY, & Ors (2015) 'The Impact of China's Retail Drug Price Control Policy on Hospital Expenditures: A Case Study in Two Shandong Hospitals' (20) *Health Policy and Planning* 185.

Mengla County Relocation and Resettlement Office (Mengla xian banqian anzhi bangongshi) (2023) 'Deployment Meeting to Comprehensively Launch the Special Mobilisation Against the "Lying Flat Style" Official (Quanmian jidong 'tangping shi' ganbu zhuanxiang dongyuan bushu hui)' 14 August 2023 Available at: <https://www.ynml.gov.cn/93.news.detail.dhtml?news_id=1472493>.

Mertha, A (2005) 'China's "Soft" Centralization: Shifting Tiao/Kuai Authority Relations' (184) *The China Quarterly* 792.

Merton, RK (1936) 'The Unanticipated Consequences of Purposive Social Action' (1, 6) *American Sociological Review* 894.

Merton, RK (1968) *Social Theory and Social Structure* enlarged ed, Free Press.

Messner, SF; Zhang, LN; Zhang, SX and Gruner, CP (2017) 'Neighborhood Crime Control in a Changing China: Tiao-Jie, Bang-Jiao, and Neighborhood Watches' (54) *Journal of Research in Crime and Delinquency* 544.

Milhaupt, CJ and Zheng, WT (2015) 'Beyond Ownership: State Capitalism and the Chinese Firms' (103, 3) *Georgetown Law Journal* 49.

Milhaupt, CJ and Zheng, WT (2016) 'Reforming China's State-Owned Enterprises: Institutions, Not Ownership' in Liebman, BL and Milhaupt, CJ (eds) (2016) *Regulating the Visible Hand? The Institutional Implications of Chinese State Capitalism* Oxford University Press.

Milhaupt, CJ, and Zheng, WT (2015"Beyond ownership: state capitalism and the Chinese firms' (103, 3) *Georgetown Law Journal* 49.

Min, C; Shen, F; Yu, WT; and Chu, YJ (2020) 'The Relationship Between Government Trust and Preventive Behaviors during the COVID-19 Pandemic in China: Exploring the Roles of Knowledge and Negative Emotion' (141) *Preventive Medicine*, available at: https://doi.org/10.1016/j.ypmed.2020.106288.

Ministry of Ecology and Environment of the People's Republic of China (2016)'No.4 Central Environmental Protection Inspection Team holds a Mobilisation Meeting on Inspection in Guangdong', December 6, 2016 available at: https://english.mee.gov.cn/News_service/news_release/201612/t20161206_368643.shtml.

Minter, A (2022) 'Lockdown Anger in Shanghai Won't Fade Anytime Soon' Bloomberg 12 April, available at: https://www.bloomberg.com/opinion/articles/2022-04-12/shanghai-s-lockdown-anger-won-t-fade-anytime-soon.

Minzner, C (2006) 'Xinfang: An Alternative to Formal Chinese Legal Institutions' (42) *Stanford Journal of International Law* 103.

Mishra, N (2024) 'Regulatory Interoperability in the Digital Economy' (April 10, 2024), available at SSRN: https://ssrn.com/abstract=4990518 or http://dx.doi.org/10.2139/ssrn.4990518

Moerel, L (2011) 'Back to basics: when does EU data protection law apply?' (1) *International Data Privacy Law* 2.

Morris, RJ (2010) 'China's Marbury: Qi Yuling v Chen Xiaoqi – The Once and Future Trial of Both Education' (2) *Tsinghua China Law Review* 275.

Mou, MX (2022) 'Why Not American-Style Judicial Review? Judicial Power and the Constitutional Interpretation System in China's Northern Warlords Government Era (1912-1928) (17, 2) *Journal of Comparative Law* 331.

Mou, Y (2022) 'Accountability for a Lifetime: Reforms in Prosecutorial Accountability in China' (6, 1) *China Law and Society Review* 1.

Müller, A (2019) 'Public Services and Informal Profits: Governing Township Health Centres in a Context of Misfit Regulatory Institutions' (237) *The China Quarterly* 108.

Myers, GC; McGinnis, R and Masnick (1967) 'The Duration of Residence Approach to a Dynamic Stochastic Model of Internal Migration: a Test of the Axiom of Cumulative Inertia' (14) *Eugenics Quarterly* 121.

'Nanzi paichusuo zao jingyuan qunou, jianfang jianyi shiyong huanxing helima?' (Five Police Officers Assaulted a Man at Local Police Station, Reasonable for Procuratorate to Suggest Suspended Sentences?) QQ.com 26 January 2025. Available at <https://news.qq.com/rain/a/20250126A07Y8Y00>.

'Neimenggu kuai zhen kuai po she yi anjian 2078 qi' (Inner Mongolia quickly detects and solves 2,078 epidemic-related cases) (2020) *Baidu* 21 February 2020, available at: https://baijiahao.baidu.com/s?id=1659127177068731591 and wfr=spider and for=pc.

New York Times (2020) He Warned of Coronavirus. Here's What He Told Us Before He Died' New York Times 7 February 2020. Available at <https://www.nytimes.com/2020/02/07/world/asia/Li-Wenliang-china-coronavirus.html>.

Newman, O (1966) *Creating Defensible Space* Diane Publishing.

Ni, SB (2023) 'Young People's Fertility Intentions and Concerns Under the Two-Child Policy Context' in Ni, SB *From One Child to Two Children Opportunities and Challenges for the One-child Generation Cohort in China* Springer.

Ni, SB (2023)*From One Child to Two Children Opportunities and Challenges for the One-child Generation Cohort in China* Springer.

O'Brien, KJ and Li, LJ(2004) 'Suing the Local State: Administrative Litigation in Rural China' (51) *The China Journal* 75.

OECD (2023) *The Nature, Evolution and Potential Implications of Data-Localisation Measures* (OECD Trade Policy Paper No. 278, November 2023).

Painter, MO and Qiu, T (2021) 'Political Beliefs affect Compliance with Government Mandates' (185) *Journal of Economic Behavior and Organisation* 688.

Palmer, M (1995) 'The Re-Emergence of Family Law in Post-Mao China: Marriage, Divorce and Reproduction' (141) *The China Quarterly* 110.

Palmer, M (1997) 'Protecting the Health of Mothers and their Children? Developments in the Family Law of the People's Republic of China' in Bainham, A (ed) *Annual Survey of Family Law: 1995* Dordrecht: Kluwer (for The International Society on Family Law) 107 at 116.

Palmer, M (2006) 'Controlling the State?: Mediation in Administrative Litigation in the People's Republic of China' (16) *Transnational Law and Contemporary Problems* 165.

Palmer, M (2006) 'Controlling the State?: Mediation in Administrative Litigation in the People's Republic of China' (16) *Transnational Law and Contemporary Problems* 125

Palmer, M (2007) 'Transforming Family Law in Post-Deng China: Marriage, Divorce and Reproduction' (191) *The China Quarterly* 675.

Palmer, M; Xi, C and Zhou, L (2023) 'Special Section: Issues in Administrative Justice Part Two' (18) *Journal of Comparative Law* 417.

Pan, XT (1994) 'Forty-Five Years of Chinese Pharmaceutical Administration' (Zhongguo yaozheng guanli de sishiwu nian) (10) *Zhongguo Yaoxue Zazhi (Chinese Pharmaceutical Journal)* 579.

Panek, W (2024) 'People's Republic of China and the adequacy–Why Chinese data protection law is not adequate within the meaning of the GDPR' (18, 2) *Masaryk University Journal of Law and Technology* 143

Park, M; Cook, AR; Lim JT; Sun, YX and Dickens, BL (2020) 'A Systematic Review of COVID-19 Epidemiology Based on Current Evidence' (9) *Journal of Clinical Medicine* 967.

Partington, TM (1999) 'Restructuring administrative justice? The redress of citizens' grievances' 52 *Current Legal Problems* 173.

Peerenboom, R (2009) 'More Law, Less Courts: Legalized Governance, Judicialization, and Dejudicialization in China' in Ginsburg, Tom and Chen, AHY. (eds) *Administrative Law and Governance in Asia: Comparative Perspectives* Routledge.

Pei, MX (1997) 'Citizens v. Mandarins: Administrative Litigation in China' (152) *The China Quarterly* 832.

Pei, ZB and Wang, LL (2015) 'The Evolution and Survey of Chinese Legal System of Penalties for Administration of Public Security' 12 *US-China Law Review* 695.

Plümper, T; Neumayer, E and Pfaff, KG (2021) 'The strategy of protest against Covid-19 containment policies in Germany' (102) *Social Science Quarterly* 2236.

Potter, P (2003) 'Globalization and Economic Regulation in China: Selective Adaptation of Globalized Norms and Practices' (2) *Washington University Global Studies Law Review* 119.

Potter, P (2006) 'Selective Adaptation and Institutional Capacity: Perspectives on Human Rights in China' (61) *International Journal* 389.

Privacy Commissioner for Personal Data (Hong Kong) (2022) *Guidance on Recommended Model Contractual Clauses for Cross-border Transfer of Personal Data* (May 2022).

Pünder, H (2013) 'German Administrative Procedure in a Comparative Perspective: Observations on the Path to a Transnational Ius Commune Proceduralis in Administrative Law' (11) *International Journal of Constitutional Law* 940.

Putnam, RD (1993) *Making Democracy Work: Civic Traditions in Modern Italy* Princeton University Press.

Qian, J and Mok, KH (2016) 'Dual Decentralisation and Fragmented Authoritarianism in Governance: Crowding out among Social

Programmes in China' (36) *Public Administration and Development* 185

Qianan, RY and Teets, J (2020) 'Responsive Authoritarianism in China – a Review of Responsiveness in Xi and Hu Administrations' (25) *Journal of Chinese Political Science* 141.

Qiao, ST (2023) 'The authoritarian commons: Divergent paths of neighbourhood democratisation in three Chinese megacities' (71) *The American Journal of Comparative Law* 388.

Qing, J (2017) 'The Qinghai Provincial Commission for Discipline Inspection has deployed a special campaign to address issues of irresponsibility and inaction' www.cpcnews.cn 21 August 2017, available at: <http://fanfu.people.com.cn/n1/2017/0821/c64371-29483276.html>. (Qinghai sheng jiwei bushu kaizhan bu dandang bu zuowei wenti zhuanxiang zhili)

Qingmu CY (1994) Dui neibu ren kongzhi de kongzhi: zhuan gui jingji zhong gongsi zhili de ruogan wenti '(Control on internal control: several corporate governance problems in the transitional economy', (6) *Gaige* (Reform) 11.

Qingnian xuezhe lei yang shepiao beizhua siwangqian de zuihou liangxiaoshi' (The Last Two Hours Before Death of Young Scholar Lei Yang who was Arrested for Allegedly Soliciting a Prostitute) *Pengpai Xinwen* (The Paper) 11 May 2017. Available at <https://m.thepaper.cn/kuaibao_detail.jsp?contid=1467561 and from=kuaibao>.

Ramraj, VV (ed) (2021) *COVID-19 in Asia: Law and Policy Context* Oxford University Press.

Ran, R (2017) 'Understanding Blame Politics in China's Decentralized System of Environmental Governance: Actors, Strategy and Context' (231) *The China Quarterly* 634.

Ranchordás, S (2015) 'Sunset Clauses and Experimental Regulations: Blessing or Curse for Legal Certainty?' (36, 1) *Statute Law Review* 28.

Raskolnikov, A (2017) 'Probabilistic Compliance' 34 *Yale Journal on Regulation* 101

Raskolnikov, A, 'Deterrence Theory: Key Findings and Challenges' in Van Rooij, B and Sokol DD (eds), *The Cambridge Handbook of Compliance* (Cambridge University Press, 2021) 179

Read, BL (2012) *Roots of the State: Neighborhood Organisation and Social Networks in Beijing and Taipei* Stanford University Press.

Reiders Folmer, CP; Brownlee, MA; Fine, AD; Kooistra, EB; Kuiper, ME and Olthuis, EH & Ors (2021) 'Social Distancing in America: Understanding Long-Term Adherence to Covid-19 Mitigation Recommendations' (16) *PloS one*, available at: https://doi.org/10.1371/journal.pone.0257945.

Ren, Y; Cheng, X; Niu, C & Ors (2024) 'Fertility intention of young people of childbearing age in China after the implementation of the two-child policy—A systematic review and meta-analysis' (24) *BMC Public Health* 3518.

Renmin Ribao (People's Daily) (2023) 'Let the Willingness to Take Action, the Courage to Take Responsibilities Become Common Practice (Thoughts Going Up and Across), (Rang yuan dandang gan dangdang shang dangdang weiran chengfeng (sixiang zongheng)) (2023) People's Daily (Renmin ribao), available at: <http://paper.people.com.cn/rmrb/html/2023-07/20/nw.D110000renmrb_20230720_2-09.htm>.

Renmin Ribao (People's Daily) (2024) 'Anquan zhishu lianxu baochi gaoshuiping: renmin qunzhong anquanqan buduan tisheng' (Safety Index Continues to Remain at a High Level – People's Safety Feeling Continues to Rise) *Renmin Ribao* (People's Daily) 28 August 2024, available at <https://www.gov.cn/lianbo/bumen/202408/content_6970925.htm>.

Reuters (2024) 'China relaxes security review rules for some data exports' (22 March 2024).

Rodriguez, S (2023) *Reproductive Realities in Modern China: Birth Control and Abortion, 1911–2021* Cambridge University Press.

Rutkowski, R (2014)'Reform: the Long Wait for a Chinese Temasek Continues … ,' *Peterson Institute for International Economics* (PIIE), 23 January 2014, available at file:///Users/peterg/Documents/Documents%20from%20old%20mac%20pro/TOSHIBA/phd%20degree/sg%20columbia/JSD%20reading%20list/State-Owned%20Enterprise%20Reform:%20the%20Long%20Wait%20for%20a%20Chinese%20Temasek%20Continues…%20%7C%20PIIE.webarchive

'Shequ, shehui gongzuo, shehui zuzhi canyu yiqing fang kong zhuanjia tan (Qinghua Daxue Li Qiáng jiaoshou, Nankai Daxué Guan Xinping jiaoshou, Shanghai Jiaotong Daxue Xu Jialiang jiaoshou)' [Community, social work, and social organizations' participation in epidemic prevention and control expert talks (Professor Li Qiang from Tsinghua University, Professor Guan Xinping from Nankai University, and Professor Xu Jialiang from Shanghai Jiaotong University)] (2021) 20 December, available at: https://www.163.com/dy/article/G39VSBKR0523N11P.html.

Sa, Z (2021) 'Nage zhongguan xiaoqu zonghezhili "shenjing moshao" derén' (The persons in charge of the 'nerve endings' of the comprehensive management of the community) *Zhongguo shuzi shidai* (China Digital Times) 24 July 2021, available at: https://chinadigitaltimes.net/chinese/668681.html.

Salaff, J (1967) 'The Urban Commune in Communist China' (29) *The China Quarterly* 82.

Salaff, J (1971) 'Urban Residential Committees in the Wake of the Cultural Revolution' in Lewis, JW (ed) *The City in Communist China* Stanford University Press 289.

Sanlian Shenghuo Zhoukan (Sanlian Life Weekly) (2023) Reyi xia de zhi'an guanli chufafa xiuding, you neixie zhide guanzhu de wenti?'(Hotly Debated LPAPS Amendments: What are the Noteworthy Issues?) *Sanlian Shenghuo Zhoukan* (Sanlian Life Weekly) 10 September 2023, available at <https://www.lifeweek.com.cn/h5/article/detail.do?artId=210872>.

Schoenhals, M (1999) 'Political Movements, Change and Stability: The Chinese Communist Party in Power' (159) *The China Quarterly* 595.

Schurmann, FH (1968) *Ideology and Organisation in Communist China* University of California Press.

Schwartz, J (2012) 'Compensating for the "Authoritarian Advantage" in Crisis Response: A Comparative Case Study of SARS Pandemic Responses in China and Taiwan' (17) *Journal of Chinese Political Science* 313.

Schwartz, PM (2019) 'Global Data Privacy: The EU Way' (94, 4) *New York University Law Review* 771.

Scoggins, S (2018) 'Policing Modern China' (3) China Law and Society Review 79.

Scoggins, S (2021) *Policing China: Steet-Level Cops in the Face of Protest* Cornell University Press.

Scoggins, S and O'Brien, K (2016) 'China's Unhappy Police' (56) Asian Survey 225;

Scoggins, SE (2021) *Policing China: Street-Level Cops in the Shadow of Protest* Cornell University Press;

Seppanen, S (2019) 'Interrogating Illiberalism Through Chinese Communist Party Regulations' (52) *Cornell International Law Journal* 267 at 272.

Shen, K (2011) 'Xingzheng ziwo guizhi yu xingzheng fazhi: yige chushi kaocha' (Administrative Self-regulation and Rule of Administrative Law: A Preliminary Investigation) (2011, 3) *Xingzheng Faxue Yanjiu* (Administrative Law Review) 12.

Shen, L (2011) 'Zhongguo jindai zhi'an chufa fagui de yanbian: yi weijingfafa de quxingfahua wei shijia' (Evolution of the Legislation on Penalties Against Law-and-Order Violations: The Decriminalization of 'The Law for the Punishment of Police Offences') (29, 4) *Zhengfa Luntan* (Tribune of Political Science and Law) 179.

Shen, L (2012) 'Xinshenghuo yundong yu zhongguo jindai de zhi'an chufafa – yi fanghai fengsulei zhi'an chufa de lifa yanbian wei shijiao' ('New Life Movement and Modern China's Legislation on Penalties Against Law-and-Order Violations: Legislative Evolution of Penalties on Offending Public Morals) (2012, 1) *Bijiaofa Yanjiu* (Journal of Comparative Law) 16.

Sheth, K and Wright, GC (2020) 'The Usual Suspects: Does Risk Tolerance, Altruism, and Health Predict the Response to COVID-19?' (18) *Review of Economics of the Household* 1041.

Shi, YF (2017) 'The Responsibility Certificate Must Not Become a "Fig Leaf" to Evade Responsibility. (Zeren zhuan mo chengle taobi zeren de zhexiubu') *Renmin Wang* (People's Daily Online), available at: <http://theory.people.com.cn/n1/2017/1221/c409497-29721819.html>. General Office of the Central Committee of the CPC 'Notice on Solving Outstanding Issues of Formalism to Reduce Burdens on Grassroots Levels' supra note 84.

Shih, VC (2021) 'China's Leninist Response to COVID-19: From Information Repression to Total Mobilization' in Greer, SC; King, EJ; Massard da Fonseca, E and Peralta-Santos, A (eds) *Coronavirus Politics: The Comparative Politics and Policy of COVID-19* University of Michigan Press.

Shimshack, JP and Ward, MB (2005) 'Regulator Reputation, Enforcement, and Environmental Compliance' (50) *Journal of Environmental Economics and Management* 519

Shirk S (2018) China in Xi's "New Era" The Return to Personalistic Rule (29, 2) *Journal of Democracy* 22.

Sobotka, T (2021) 'World's Highest Childlessness Levels in East Asia' (595) *Population et Sociétés* 1.

Sohu (2023) 'The Strictest Pharmaceutical Administration Law Implemented on 1st December! Fake and Substandard Drugs Have Been Redefined By "4+7"' *Sohu* (22 April 2023) available at: https://www.sohu.com/a/356723911_120111344.

Sohu (2023) 'Two Certificates in One! Drugstore People Can Finally Stop Waiting for the Process!' *Sohu* (22 April 2023) available at: https://www.sohu.com/a/398672708_100099933.

Solove, DJ and Hartzog, W (2014)'The FTC and the New Common Law of Privacy' (114) *Columbia Law Review* 583.

Song J, and Li LC (2022) 'Lihun lengjingqi" zhengce nengfou jiangdi lihun shuiping', (Can the 'Divorce Cooling-Off Period' Policy Reduce the Divorce Rate?) Tansuo yu Zhengming (Exploration and Free Views) 119.

Song, YS (2023) *Why do Retail Pharmacies Violate the Law?—An Empirical Study from Northeastern China* PhD Dissertation, University of Hong Kong.

Stieglitz, N; Knudsen, T and Becker, MC (2016) 'Adaptation and Inertia in Dynamic Environments' 37 *Strategic Management Journal* 1854

Stoner, JR (2005) *Common Law and Liberal Theory: Coke, Hobbes, and the Origins of American Constitutionalism* Peking University Press.

Strauss, J (2020) *State Formation in China and Taiwan: Bureaucracy, Campaign and Performance* Cambridge University Press.

Sudworth, J (2019) 'Simon Cheng: Former UK Consulate Worker Says He was Tortured in China' BBC 20 November 2019. Available at <https://www.bbc.co.uk/news/world-asia-china-50457262>.

Sun, S (2018) 'The Day when Police Showed Their True Colours: My Frightening and Humiliating Experience of Being Framed and Detained by the Guangzhou Police' 3 December 2018, vailable at <https://archive.frontlinedefenders.org/fr/node/4778>.

Supreme People's Court (2022) 'Zuigao Renmin Fayuan Baogao' [Report of the Supreme People's Court] 8 March 2022, available at: https://www.court.gov.cn/zixun-xiangqing-349601.html.

Talic, S; Wild, H; Maharaj, A; Ademi, Z; Xu, Wei and Theodoratou, E & Ors (2021) 'Effectiveness of Public Health Measures in Reducing the Incidence of Covid-19, SARS-Cov-2 Transmission, and Covid-19 Mortality: Systematic Review and Meta-analysis' 18 November 2021 *British Medical Journal* 375

Tang, BB (2020) 'Grid Governance in China's Urban Middle-class Neighborhoods' (241) *The China Quarterly* 43.

Tang, D (2019) 'China Releases Video of Former UK Official Simon Cheng "in Massage Parlour"' *The Times* 21 November 2019. Available at <https://www.thetimes.com/world/article/china-releases-video-of-former-uk-official-simon-cheng-in-massage-parlour-ph83c67jm>.

Tang, JL and Abbasi, K (2021) 'What Can the World Learn from China's Response to Covid-19?' 2 November 2021 *British Medical Journal* 375, available at: https://www.bmj.com/content/375/bmj.n2806.

Tang, W (2013) 'Zhengdang chengxu yuanze zai xingzheng susong shiyong de kunhuo yu chulu – yi zuigao fayuan suo fabu de jiu ge quanwei anjian wei hexin de diaocha' (Problems and Solutions of the Application of the Due Process Principle in Administrative Litigation —Research Centered on Nine Authoritative Cases Issued by the Supreme People's Court). Quanguo fayuan di 25 jie xueshu taolunhui huojianglun wenji: gongzheng sifa yu xingzhengfa shishi wenti yanjiu (Award-winning Essays of the 25th National Court Academic Symposium: Research on the Issues of a Fair Judiciary and Administrative Law Implementation) 989 at 994.

Tang, Y; Liu, M; Xia, F; and Zhang, B (2024). Informal regulation by nongovernmental organizations enhances corporate compliance:

Evidence from a nationwide randomized controlled trial in China. 43(1) *Journal of Policy Analysis and Management* 234.

Tang, YJ (2024) 'Fazhi beijing xia neimenggu jiceng zhi'an xingzheng chufa changjian wenti yanjiu: jiyu neimenggu gong'an xingzheng susong caipan wenshu de shizheng fenxi' (A Study of Common Problems of Law-and-Order Administrative Penalties at Grassroot Level in Inner Mongolia in the Rule of Law Setting: From An Analysis of Court Judgments of Inner Mongolia Administrative Litigation Involving Public Security) 10 *Hebei Falü Zhiye Jiaoyu* (Hebei Vocational Education of Law) 50.

The Economist (2025) 'The Chinese Government Is Cracking Down on Predatory Law Enforcement' *The Economist* (27 March 2025) 26.

The Lancet (editorial) (2020) 'COVID-19 and China: Lessons and the Way Forward' (396) *The Lancet* 213.

Thomas, S and Ip, EC (2020) 'COVID-19 Emergency Measure and the Impending Authoritarian Pandemic' (7) *Journal of Law and the Biosciences* 1.

Thornton, D; Gunningham, NA and Kagan, RA (2005) 'General Deterrence and Corporate Environmental Behaviour' 27 *Law and Policy* 262

Thornton, PM (2021) 'Of Constitutions, Campaigns and Commissions: A Century of Democratic Centralism under the CCP' (248) T*he China Quarterly* 52.

Tian, X and Zheng, J (2016) 'Enveloped State: The Action Logic of Grassroots Governance and Rural Autonomy—A Case Study Based on "Straw Burning" in Huangjiang' (2016, 2) *Journal of Public Management* 141.

Tieling shi zhufang he chengxiang jianshe ju (Tieling Housing and Urban-Rural Development Bureau) (2020) 'Guanyu yiqing fangkong qijian jinyibu jiaqiang zhuzhai xiaoqu wuye guanli de tongzhi' [Notice on Further Strengthening the Property Management of Residential Areas During the Epidemic Prevention and Control Period] *PMCEO.com* 2 July 2020, available at: http://www.pmceo.com/show/202005/226290.html.

Tilt, B (2007) 'The Political Ecology of Pollution Enforcement in China: a Case from Sichuan's Rural Industrial Sector' (192) *The China Quarterly* 915.

Tomba, L (2014) *The Government Next Door: Neighborhood Politics in Urban China* Cornell University Press.

Trevaskes, S (2003) 'Yanda 2001: Form and Strategy in a Chinese Anti-Crime Campaign' (36) *Australian and New Zealand Journal of Criminology* 272.

Trevaskes, S (2007) 'Severe and Swift Justice in China' (47) *British Journal of Criminology* 23;

Tsang, S and Cheung, O (2024) *The Political Thought of Xi Jinping* Oxford University Press at 27.

Tu, WY and Gong, T (2022) 'Bureaucratic Shirking in China: Is Sanction-based Accountability a Cure?' (249) *China Quarterly* 259.

Underhill, K and Ayres, I (2022) 'Sunsets Are for Suckers: An Experimental Test of Sunset Clauses' (59) *Harvard Journal on Legislation* 101.

United Kingdom Government (2023) *Administrative Enforcement of Intellectual Property in China: Guidance for British companies seeking administrative enforcement against IP infringements in China,* 13 November 2023 available at <https://www.gov.uk/government/case-studies/uk-china-cooperation-on-intellectual-propert>

United Kingdon Foreign and Commonwealth Office (2019) 'Foreign Secretary statement on Simon Cheng' 20 November 2019. Available at<https://www.gov.uk/government/news/foreign-secretary-statement-on-simon-cheng-20-november-2019>.

United Nations Commission on Human Rights (2004) 'Report of the Working Group on Arbitrary Detention, Addendum: Mission to China' 29 Dec 2004 UN Doc E/CN.4/2005/6/Add.4 at para 55. Available at <https://docs.un.org/en/E/CN.4/2005/6/Add.4>.

United Nations Human Rights Committee (2014) 'General Comment No. 35 (Article 9, Liberty and Security of Person)' UN Doc CCPR/C/GC/35.

United States Congressional Executive Commission on China (2017) 'Chinese Authorities Decided Not to Prosecute Police Officers Found to Have Caused a Beijing Resident's Death' 16 May 2017. Available at <https://www.cecc.gov/publications/commission-analysis/chinese-authorities-decided-not-to-prosecute-police-officers-found>.

van der Kamp, DS (2021) 'Blunt Force Regulation and Bureaucratic Control: Understanding China's War on Pollution' (34) *Governance* 191.

van Rooij, B (2002) 'Implementing Chinese Environmental Law through Enforcement' in Chen, J; Li, Y and Otto, JM (eds) (2002) *Implementation of Law in the People's Republic of China* Kluwer Law International

van Rooij, B (2006) *Regulating Land and Pollution in China: Lawmaking, Compliance, and Enforcement: Theory and Cases* Leiden University Press.

van Rooij, B (2012) 'The People's Regulation: Citizens and Implementation of Law in China' (25) *Columbia Journal of Asian Law* 116.

van Rooij, B (2014) 'Regulation by Escalation: Unrest, Lawmaking and Law Enforcement in China' in Trevaskes, S; Nesossi, E; Sapio, F; and Biddulph, S (eds) (2014) *The Politics of Law and Stability in China* Edward Elgar Publishing.

van Rooij, B and Lo, CWH (2010) 'Fragile Convergence: Understanding Variation in the Enforcement of China's Industrial Pollution Law' (32) *Law and Policy* 14.

van Rooij, B and others (2017) 'Centralizing Trends and Pollution Law Enforcement in China' (231) *The China Quarterly* 583.

Vinx, L (2015) *The Guardian of the Constitution: Hans Kelsen and Carl Schmitt on the Limits of Constitutional Law* Cambridge University Press.

VOA News (2013) 'China Digitises Complaints: Please Sign In' VOA News, available at: <https://www.voanews.com/a/china-complaints-please-sign-in/1799655.html>.

Wan QL (2020) 'Henan chachu sheyi weifa fanzui anjian 6,757qi huhang fugong renyuan 380 wan renci' (Henan investigated and dealt with 6,757 cases of illegal and criminal cases related to the epidemic, escorting 3.8 million returnees) *China Radio International* 13 March 2020, available at: https://hn.cri.cn/2020-03-13/2fe05bf4-4d5a-9d19-2660-4ea553db2276.html.

Wang JG (2006) 'Public Security Penalties Law Respects, Protects Human Rights' (95, 1) *Human Rights* 31.

Wang Z (2019) 'NPC delegate Yu Xuewen allows no place for bureaucratic inertia' (Quanguo renda daibiao Yu Xuewen rang lanzheng daizheng xingwei wu lizu de di) *China Discipline Inspection and Supervision News* 15 March 2019, p 4

Wang, AL (2013) 'The Search for Sustainable Legitimacy: Environmental Law and Bureaucracy in China' (37) *Harvard Environmental Law Review* 365.

Wang, A and Gao, J (2010) 'Environmental Courts and the Development of Environmental Public Interest Litigation in China' (3) *Journal of Court Innovation* 42.

Wang, AL (2016) 'China State Capitalism and the Environment' in Liebman, BL and Milhaupt, CJ (eds) (2016) *Regulating the Visible Hand? The Institutional Implications of Chinese State Capitalism* Oxford University Press.

Wang, Chloe 'Party-led Corporate Governance: Embedded Party Organization in Chinese State-owned Enterprises' (unpublished SJD draft chapter at HKU being written under the supervision of Professor SH Goo).

Wang, F (2024) 'Zhi'an guanli chufafa xiuding caoan er'shen: wanshan youguan chufa chengxu guiding' (Second Reading of LPAPS Amendment Bill: Improvements on Penalty Procedures) www.21jingji.com 26 June 2024, available at <https://www.21jingji.com/article/20240626/herald/2fe543cc8fc36fdb8260afb957766090.html>.

Wang, FF (2017) *Online Arbitration* (1st ed.) Informa Law (Routledge).

Wang, FF (2022) 'Resolving Online Content Disputes in the age of Artificial Intelligence: Legal and Technological Solutions in comparative perspective' (17, 2) *Journal of Comparative Law* 491.

Wang, FF (2023) AI Ethics of Online Commercial Arbitration in Comparative Perspective, (18,2) *Journal of Comparative Law* 529-556, available at <https://www.lawbookexchange.com/pdf/JCL_18-2_07_Wang_AIEthicsOfOnlineCommercialArbitrationInComparativePerspective.pdf> last accessed 31 March 2025.

Wang, G (1973) 'Bureaucracy in Imperial China' (32) *Australian Journal of Public Administration* 62.

Wang, H (2019) 'China's approach to Belt and Road Initiative: Scope, Character and Sustainability' (22) *Journal of International Economic Law* 29.

Wang, J (2014) *Company Law in China* Edward Elgar.

Wang, J and Mou, Y (2021) 'The Paradigm Shift in the Disciplining of Village Cadres in China: From Mao to Xi' (248) *The China Quarterly* 181.

Wang, J(2021) 'Judicial Review of Regulatory Documents in Administrative Litigation in China' (16) *University of Pennsylvania Asian Law Review* 328.

Wang, JY (2014) 'The Political Logic of Corporate Governance in China's State-Owned Enterprises' (43, 3) *Cornell International Law Journal* 632.

Wang, KW (2014) 'Reform and Legal Regulation of Administrative Approval System in China' (Woguo xingzheng shenpi zhidu de gaige ji qi falü guizhi, faxue yanjiu) (36) (2) *Faxue Yanjiu* (Chinese Journal of Law) 3.

Wang, MZ (2024) 'Zhi'an guanli xingzheng chufa de zhengdangxing zhengcheng ji zhidu wanshan' (A Study of Law-and-Order Administrative Pe*nalties: Legitimacy and Improvements) 99 Zhongguo Zhengfa Daxue Xuebao* (Journal of Chinese University of Political Science and Law) 121

Wang, PP and Wang, XD (2022) 'Lun sheli zhi'an fating de biyaoxing he kexingxing' (Introducing Law-and-Order Court: Necessity and Feasibility) 37(2*) Guangxi Zhengfa Guanli Ganbu Xueyuan Xuebao* (Journal of Guangxi Administrative Cadre Institute of Politics and Law) 12.

Wang, Q; Fan, SX and Dong, BT (2022) 'Reducing Burdens, Increasing Efficiency, Focusing on Hard Work, Taking on Responsibilities and Opening a New Chapter - A Review of the Party Central Committee's Rectification of Formalism with Comrade Xi Jinping as the Core since the 19th National Congress of the Communist Party of China to Reduce Burdens on the Grassroots (Jianfu zeng xiao zhong shigan dangdang jinze kai xin pian- dang de shijiu da yilai yi Xi Jinping tongzhi wei hexin de dang zhongyang zhengzhi xingshi zhuyi wei jiceng jianfu zongshu) *Xinhua News Agency,* available at: <https://www.gov.cn/xinwen/2022-10/10/content_5717091.htm>.

Wang, XX (1998) 'Administrative Procedure Reforms in China's Rule of Law Context' (12) *Columbia Journal of Asian Law* 251.

Wang, XX (2007) 'Between Dreams and the Reality: Making of the Administrative Procedure Act in China' (7) *Journal of Korean Law* 157.

Wang, XY (2021) 'Eryuanlun shiye xia de linhun lengjingqi' (The Divorce Cooling-Off Period under Dualism) (6) *Zhonghua Nüzi Xueyuan Xuebao* (Journal of China Women's University) 79.

Wang, Y; Li, Y; Ma, Z and Song, J (2019) 'The Deterrence Effect of a Penalty for Environmental Violation' (11) *Sustainability* 4226

Wedeman, AH (2003) *From Mao to Market: Rent Seeking, Local Protectionism, and Marketization in China* Cambridge University Press.

Wei, F; Hong, F and Lu, ZX (2010) 'Chinese State Sports Policy: Pre- and Post-Beijing 2008' (27) *The International Journal of the History of Sport* 2380.

Wei, Y (2023) 'Household Expenditure on Education in China: Key Findings From the China Institute for Educational Finance Research-Household Surveys (CIEFR-HS)' (7, 3) *ECNU Review of Education* available at: <https://doi.org/10.1177/20965311241243389>.

Whiting, S (2004) 'The Cadre Evaluation System at the Grassroots: The Paradox of Party Rule' in Naughton, B and Yang, D (eds) (2004) *Holding China Together: Diversity and National Integration in the Post-Deng Era* Cambridge University Press 101.

Whyte, MK 'Who Hates Bureaucracy' available at https://deepblue.lib.umich.edu/bitstream/handle/2027.42/51105/337.pdf?sequence=1

Whyte, MK and Parish, WL (1984) *Urban Life in Contemporary China* University of Chicago Press.

Wong, Kam C (2017) *Police Reform in China* Routledge.

Wong, N (2004) 'Counterfeit Medicine: Is It Curing China?' (5) *Asian-Pacific Law and Policy Journal* 155.

Woodman, S (2016) 'Local Politics, Local Citizenship? Socialized Governance in Contemporary China' (226) *The China Quarterly* 342.

Woolf, H & Ors (2013) *De Smith's Judicial Review* (7th ed) Sweet and Maxwell.

World Economic Forum and OECD (2020) *Agile Governance for Emerging Technologies,* at: <https://www3.weforum.org/docs/WEF_Agile_Regulation_for_the_Fourth_Industrial_Revolution_2020.pdf>

World Science and Technology (2003) 'The State Medical Products Administration announced the cancellation of 20 Administrative Approval Items' (01) *World Science and Technology* 9.

World Trade Organization (2020) *World Trade Report 2020: Government policies to promote innovation in the digital age.*

Wu JT (2023) 'The National Health Commission Reported that the Coverage Rate of Basic Medical Insurance Reached 96.8 Percent' *Zhongguo Wang* (22 April 2023) available at: http://news.china.com.cn/txt/2021-01/28/content_77163948.htm.

Wu, G and Wilkes, R (2018) 'Local-National Political Trust Patterns: Why China Is an Exception' (39) *International Political Science Review* 436.

Wu, LM (2020) 'Chongqing Yubei: Wanggehua guanli "shi daowei" zhu lao fangyi zuihou yi gongli' (Chongqing Yubei: grid management 'ten in position' to strengthen the last mile of epidemic prevention] *Zhongguo Jingjiwang* (China Economic Net) 7 February 2020, available at: http://www.ce.cn/xwzx/gnsz/gdxw/202002/07/t20200207_34231032.shtml.

Wu, W (2017),'How the Communist Party Controls China's State-Owned Industrial Titans,' *South China Morning Post,* 17 June 2017.

Wu, WC (2016) 'Guanyu yaoqiu beijingshi jianchayuan li'an zhencha lei yang beihai an de xingshi baoanshu' (A Copy of the Filing of a Criminal Case Requesting the Beijing Procuratorate to Investigate the Killing of Lei Yang) 16 May 2016, available at <https://wqw2010.blogspot.com/2016/05/blog-post_25.html> Wu was Lei's wife.

Wu, YC (1995) 'Guoyou qiye neibu ren kongzhi wenti de chengyin ji duice (The causes and solutions to the problem of insider control in SOEs)' (4) *Gaige* (Reform) 73.

Wu, YN; Jiang, SH and Lambert, E (2011) 'Citizen Support for Community Policing in China' (34) *Policing: An International Journal of Police Strategy and Management* 285.

Xi JP (2021) There is no greater danger than forgetting the original intention and mission and becoming disconnected from the masses. (Xi Jinping: Meiyou bu wangji chuxin shiming, tuoli chunzhong geng da de weixian) 6 October 2021 QStheory.cn http://www.qstheory.cn/zhuanqu/2021-10/06/c_1127932976.htm

Xi JP 'Don't Forget Your Original Intention and Keep Your Mission in Mind' Speech at the Conclusion of the Education Conference on the Theme of 'Don't Forget Your Original Intention, Keep Your Mission in Mind' (Buwang chuxin, laoji shiming' Xi Jjinping "zai buwang chuxin, laoji shiming' juti jiaoyu zongjie dahui shang de jianghua) cpcnews.cn 8 January 2020, available at: <http://cpc.people.com.cn/n1/2020/0630/c64094-31765104.html>.

Xia, Y and Guan, B(2014) 'The Politics of Citizenship Formation: Homeowners' Collective Action in Urban Beijing' (19) *Chinese Journal of Political Science* 405.

Xiang B (ed) (2018) 'Backgrounder: Xi Jinping Thought on Socialism with Chinese Characteristics for a New Era' *Xinhua* 17 March 2018 http://www.xinhuanet.com/english/2018-03/17/c_137046261.htm

Xiao, SL (2024) *Judicial Review in Greater China: Activism and Deference of Four Apex Courts* Cambridge University Press.

Xinhua News (2016) 'Xi Stresses CCP Leadership of State-Owned Enterprises' *Xinhua News Agency* (11 October 2016).

Xinhua News Agency (2016) 'Xi Jinping: Adhere to the Combination of Governing the Country by Law and Governing the Country by Virtue (Xi Jinping: Jianchi yifa zhiguo he yide zhiguo xiangjiehe)' *Xinhua* 10 December 2016 Available at: <http://www.xinhuanet.com//politics/2016-12/10/c_1120093133.htm>.

Xinhua News Agency (2019) 'The Central Leading Group for Education on the Theme of "Don't Forget the Original Aspiration and Remember the Mission" Issued the "Work Plan on Finding Gaps in the Theme Education of "Don't Forget the Original Aspiration and Remember the Mission" in Comparison with the Party Constitution and Party Regulations (Zhongyang 'buwang chuxin, laoji shiming' zhuti jiaoyu lingdao xiaozu yinfa "Guanyu zai 'buwang chuxin, laoji shiming' zhuti jiaoyu zhong dui dangzhang danggui zhao chuju de gongzuo fang'an") www.gov.cn 21 July 2019.

Xinhua News Agency (2020) 'Xinhua she jingji fenxi baogao: Qianghua wuye guanli goujian shequ yiqing fang kong "anquán xiàn"' [Xinhua News Agency Economic Analysis Report: Strengthen property management and build a 'safety line' for community epidemic prevention and control] 19 February, available at: https://www.sohu.com/a/374168882_214444.

Xinhua News Agency (2021) 'Lianghui shouquan fabu zuigao renmin fayuan gongzuo baogao' [As authorized by the two sessions, the Work Report of the Supreme People's Court] *Xinhua* (New China News Agency) 15 March 2021, available at: http://www.xinhuanet.com/politics/2021lh/2021-03/15/c_1127212486.htm.

Xinhua News Agency (2023) 'A Special Working Mechanism Meeting on Rectifying Formalism at the Central Level to Reduce the Burden on the Grassroots Was Held in Beijing. We Will Not Relax Our Efforts to Rectify Formalism and Reduce the Burden on the Grassroots, and Demonstrate the Effectiveness of Thematic Education by Deepening and Expanding Practical Results. (Zhongyang cengmian zhengzhi xingshi zhuyi wei jiceng jianfu zhuanxiang gongzuo jizhu huiyi zai jing juxing hao bu fangsong zhengzhi xingshi zhuyi wei jiceng jianfu yi shenhua tazhan shiji chengguo zhangxian juti jiaoyu chengxiao') (2023) *Xinhua*, available at: <http://www.news.cn/politics/2023-06/15/c_1129697105.htm>.

Xinhua News Agency (2023) 'How the CPC empowers itself with Party-wide education campaigns' *Xinhua* 3 April 2023 https://english.www.

gov.cn/news/202304/03/content_WS642a277ac6d03ffcca6ec039.html

Xinhua News Agency (2023) 'How the CPC Empowers Itself with Party-Wide Education Campaigns' (2023) *Xinhua* 3 April 2023 Available at: <https://english.www.gov.cn/news/202304/03/content_WS642a277ac6d03ffcca6ec039.html>.

Xinjing Bao (Beijing News) (2018) 'Market Regulation Bids Farewell to "Nine Dragons Governing the Waters"; Administration of Industry and Commerce, Quality Inspection, Food and Drug, and Price Control Enforcement Will Be "Consolidated into One"' *Beijing News* (21 March 2018) available at: https://baijiahao.baidu.com/s?id=1595547618771281337 and wfr=spider and for=pc.

Xiong, J (2020) 'Quanguo yiliao jiuzhi zhixu zongti pingwen youxu' (Medical Treatment and Care Nationwide Is Smooth and Orderly) *Renmin Ribao Haiwaiban* (People's Daily Overseas Edition) 22 February 2020, available at <http://paper.people.com.cn/rmrbhwb/html/2020-02/22/content_1972481.htm>.

Xu, AB (2020) 'On the Essence, Innovation and Development of Revised Drug Administration Law' (Yaoping guanli fa xiugai de jingshen yaoyi, chuangxin yu fazhan) (1) *Xingzheng Faxue Yanjiu (*Administrative Law Review) 3.

Xu, C (2019) 'Zhengdang chengxu: linyong chengxuquan de panduan biaozhun' (Due Process Principle: Criteria for the Abuse of Administrative Discretionary Power) (2019, 2) *Faxue Pinglun* (Law Review) 53 at 56.

Xu, F and Liu, Q (2021) 'China: Community Policing, High-Tech Surveillance, and Authoritarian Durability' in Ramraj, VV (ed) *COVID-19 in Asia: Law and Policy Context* Oxford University Press.

Xuan, G (2019) 'Implement "the Four Strictest Principles" and Strictly Observe Drug Safety—Publicity and Implementation of the Newly Revised Drug Administration Law of the People's Republic of China' (Guanche 'sige zuiyan' yanshou yaopin anquan—xin xiuding zhonghua renmin gongheguo yaoping guanli fa) (28, 24) *Zhongguo Yaoyie* (China Pharmaceuticals) 1.

Xue GLand Xiao SY (2023) 'Holistic Administration Model with Chinese Characteristics: Practical Generation and Theoretical Construction (Zhongguo tese de zhengti xing xingzheng moshi: shijian shengcheng yu lilun chenggou)' (457) *Zhongguo Xingzheng Guanli* (Chinese Public Administration) 68.

Xue, L; Simonis, UE. and Dudek, DJ (2007) 'Environmental Governance for China: Major Recommendations of a Task Force' (16) *Environmental Politics* 669.

Yang, D (2017) 'Zhidao anli 6 hao de weijing zhiye' (Unresolved Issues of the Guiding Case No. 6) (2017, 3) *Fazhi Xiandaihua Yanjiu* (Research into Legal Modernisation) 124.

Yang, D (2020) 'Xingzheng chengxu defang xianxing lifa de zhuti, moshi yu guifan' (Subject, Mode and Norms of Advancing Local Legislation on Administrative Procedures) (2020, 3) *Zhengzhi yu Falü* (Politics and Law) 64.

Yang, DF (2018) 'Fa wu guiding shi zhengdang chengxu yuanze zhi shiyong' (The Application of the Due Process Principle in the Absence of Law) (2018, 1) *Falü Kexue* (Xibei Zhengfa Daxue Xuebao, Journal of Northwest University of Politics and Law) 191.

Yang, DF (2021) 'Reasonableness, Good Faith or Principle of Proportionality: Whither Legitimate Aim Test to Go' (4) *Peking University Law Journa*l 945.

Yang, DL (2017) 'China's Illegal Regulatory State in Comparative Perspective' (2) *Chinese Political Science Review* 114.

Yang, DL (2017) 'China's Troubled Quest for Order: Leadership, Organisation and Contradictions of the Stability Maintenance Regime' (26) *Journal of Contemporary China* 35.

Yang, GB (2022) *The Wuhan Lockdown* Columbia University Press.

Yang, P (2011) 'Competitions Must Be Real, and Monitoring Must Be Substantial' (10, 19) *Contemporary Workers Magazine* 10-11.

Yang, T (2020) 'Shehui liliang zai shequ fangyi zhong de zuoyong he nanti' [The role and problems of social forces in community epidemic prevention] Fenghuang Xinwen (Pheonix News) 1 April 2020, available at: https://ishare.ifeng.com/c/s/v002PNvo9-_YcmquDjEqn9UmMDV49S0ulodYR-_ceabFN1dxw.

Yang, XL (2021) 'Shaanxī shèhuì zǔzhī "hélì kàng yì"' [Social Organizations in Shaanxi 'work together to fight the epidemic'] Shaanxi Sheng Renmin Zhengfu (The People's Government of Shaanxi Province) 31 December 2021, available at: http://www.shaanxi.gov.cn/xw/ldx/bm/202112/t20211231_2206111_wap.html.

Yaosu (2023) 'Pharmacy Classification Management is the Trend; A Group of Pharmacies Will Not Be Able to Sell Prescription Drugs' *Yaosu* (22 April 2023) available at: http://news.yaosuce.com/xinwen/3663681797925509772.html.

Ye, B (2014) *Xingzheng xingwei yuanli* (The Theory of the Administrative Act) Shangwu Yinshuguan at 293.

Yip, NM and Jiang, YH (2011) 'Homeowners United: The Attempt to Create Lateral Networks of Homeowners' Association in Urban China' (20) *The Journal of Contemporary China* 735.

Yip, NM; Huang, RG; and Sun, XY (2014) 'Homeowners' Activism and the Rule of Law in Urban China' (7) *China Journal of Social Work* 175.

Yu, H(1997) 'Zhongguo yaoya zhengfu guanzhi zhidu xingcheng zhang'ai de fenxi (shang)' ('Analysis of the Obstacles in the Government Control System of the Chinese Pharmaceutical Industry [Part]') (5) *Guanli Shijie [Journal of Management World]* 10.

Yuan, W and Rong, H (2023) 'Cosmetic Responsiveness: Why and How Local Governments Respond to Mundane Online Complains in China' (28) *Journal of Chinese Political Science* 187.

Yuen, S (2014) 'Disciplining the Party: Xi Jinping's anti-corruption campaign and its limits' (2014, 3) *China Perspectives* 41.

Zelin, M (2005) *The Merchants of Zigong: Industrial Enterprise in Early Modern China* Columbia University Press.

Zeng, SJ (2022) 'Environmental Policy and Compensation in China: An Empirical Analysis of Article Eight of the Chinese Administrative License Law' (34) *Journal of Environmental Law* 287.

Zhan, JV and Qin, S, (2017) 'The Art of Political Ambiguity: Top–down Intergovernmental Information Asymmetry in China' (2017, 2) *Journal of Chinese Governance* 149

Zhang L (2022) '"Minfadian" lihun lengjingqi tiaokuan de shiyong yuanli: neihan yu waiyan' (The Applicable Principle of the Cooling-off Period Clause of Divorce in the Civil Code: Connotation and Extension) (1) *Fazhi Yanjiu* (Research on Rule of Law) 36-44.

Zhang, AHY (2017) 'The Antitrust Paradox of China Inc' (50) *New York University Journal of International Law and Politics* 9.

Zhang, C (2025) 'Ai weiwei, AirDrop he sanfeng youjian: yige tongxinglian zhengzhifan de chengzhangshi' (Ai Weiwei, AirDrop, and Three Emails: The Maturing of a Homosexual Political Prisoner) 1 January 2025, available at <https://women4china.substack.com/p/airdrop>.

Zhang, C; Tong, X and Liu, A (2025) 'Sociological studies on women/gender in China during the past 40 years' (11, 2) *Chinese Journal of Sociology* 161.

Zhang, CL (1995) 'Cong rongzi jiaodu fenxi guoyou qiye de zhili jigou gaige (An analysis of the reform of governance structure of SOEs from the perspective of fund raising)' (3) *Gaige* (Reform) 34.

Zhang, HT(2021) 'Study on the Issue of Time Limitation in APIL' (15, 3) *Tsinghua University Law Journal* 115.

Zhang, J (2001) 'Xiandai xingzheng chengxu de chengyin he gongneng fenxi' (Analysis of Origins and Functions of Modern Administrative Procedure) (2001, 1) *Zhongguo Faxue* (Chinese Legal Science) 79.

Zhang, J (2005) 'Lun xingzheng chengxu zhengdangxing de xianfa guifan jichu: yi guifan shizheng fenxi wei shejiao' (The Normative

Foundation of the Legitimacy of Administrative Procedure in the Constitution: From the Perspective of a Normative Empirical Analysis) (2005) (4) *Faxue Luntan* (Legal Forum) 95.

Zhang, J (2017) 'Cong difang dao zhongyang: woguo xingzheng chengxu lifa de xianshi yu weilai' (From Local to Central: The Reality and the Future of China's Administrative Procedure Legislation) (2017, 2*) Xingzheng Faxue Yanjiu* (Administrative Law Review) 54.

Zhang, KZ (2003) 'Reform of Administrative Examination and Approval System: The Government Moves from Control to Service' (Xingzheng shenpi zhidu gaige: zhengfu cong guanzhi zouxiang fuwu, (6) *Lilun yu Gaige* (Theory and Reform) 42.

Zhang, L and Lin, HM (2024) 'On the Improvement Approach of the Legal System for Cross-border Data Flows in the Guangdong-Hong Kong-Macao Greater Bay Area' (5) *Practice and Theory of Special Economic Zones* 91.

Zhang, LH (2023)'Research on the Legal Nature and Remedy Approach of Security Assessment of Outbound Data Transfers' (1) *Administrative Law Review* 45.

Zhang, N and Qiao, R (2021) 'Jingcha xingzhengquan de shifan yu guizhi: ji yu gong'an xingzheng susong caipan wenshu de shizheng fenxi' (Unruliness and Regulation of Police Administrative Powers: An Analysis of Court Judgments on Administrative Litigation Involving Public Security) 210 *Zhongguo Renmin Gong'an Daxue Xuebao (shehui kexue ban)* (Journal of People's Public Security University of China [Social Sciences Edition]) 116.

Zhang, X; Lou, H; Tang, X & Ors (2021) 'Socio-demographic characteristics and outcomes of pregnant women who delivered prior to and after the termination of the one-child policy in China: a comparative study' (21) *BMC Pregnancy Childbirth* 318.

Zhang, XJ (2010) *Shengyu quan ji qi jiuji zhidu yanjiu — yi "Deng Jun taoyao shengyu quan" deng sange anli wei li* (Research on Reproductive Rights and Their Relief System — Taking "Deng Jun Claiming Reproductive Rights" and Three Other Cases as Examples) Master of Law dissertation, Lanzhou University.

Zhang, Y (2024) 'Discrimination against Women in the Workplace' (27) *Humanities and Social Sciences* 135.

Zhang, YH and Cen, DZ (eds) (1981)*Zhonghua Minguo Xianfa Shiliao Shangbian* (Historical Documents on the Constitution of the Republic of China [I]) Wenhai chubanshe.

Zhang, YQ (2015) 'Lun ICCPR yujing xia xingzheng juliu zhidu de "sifahua" gaige' (The ICCPR and the Judicialized Reform of Administrative Detention) (17, 5) *Xinan Zhengfa Daxue Xuebao* (Journal of Southwest University of Political Science and Law) 72 at 80-81.

Zhang, YX and Liu, Z (2023) 'The Rise of the Chinese Judiciary and Its Limits: Administrative Litigation in the Reform Period' 7 May 2023, available at <https://papers.ssrn.com/sol3/papers.cfm?abstract_id=4696197>.

Zhang, Z (2014) *Xingzheng faxue zonglun* (General Introduction of Administrative Law) Beijing Daxue Chubanshe.

Zhao YH (2022) Adjudication of Environmental Administrative Disputes in China (17) *Journal of Comparative Law* 393.

Zhao, F and Dong, M 'How to Overcome Formalism (Zhenyang kefu xingshi zhuyi)' (2021, 1) *Qianxian Luntan* 54-55.

Zhao, HS (2023) 'Guanyu Zai Xuexi Guanche Xi Jinping Xi Shidai Tese Shehui Zhuyi Sixiang Juti Jiaoyu Zhong Kaizhan Tangpingshe Ganbu de Zhuanxiang Zhengzhi de Shishi Fang'an' 'The State Natural Resources and Planning Bureau Held a "Lying Flat Style Official" Special Rectification Mobilization and Deployment Meeting (Xishuangbanna zhou ziran he guihua ju, Zhou ziran Zhiyuan he guihua ju zhaokai 'tangping shi' ganbu zhuanxiang zhengzhi dongyuan bushu hui) *Xishuangbanna Prefecture Natural Resources and Planning Bureau*, available at: <https://www.xsbn.gov.cn/xsbnzgtzyj/19727.news.detail.dhtml?news_id=2892148>.

Zhao, YH (2022) 'Adjudication of Environmental Administrative Disputes in China' (17) *Journal of Comparative Law* 393.

Zheng, L; Liebman, BL and Milhaupt, CJ (2016) 'SOEs and State Governance: How State-Owned Enterprises Influence China's Legal System' in Liebman, BL and Milhaupt, CJ (eds) (2016) *Regulating the Visible Hand? The Institutional Implications of Chinese State Capitalism* Oxford University Press.

Zhenkang County Commission for Discipline Inspection and Supervision (2023) 'The Zhenkang County Commission for Discipline Inspection and Supervision Held a Mobilization and Deployment Meeting for the Special Rectification of "Lying Flat" Cadres (Zhenkang xian jiwei jianwei zhaokai 'tangping shi' ganbu zhuanxiang zhengzhi dongyuan bushu huiyi fa'), available at: <http://www.lcjjjc.gov.cn/info-14-17823.html>.

Zhong, FL and Liu, L (2018) 'Chengzhen hua jincheng zhong chuangxin shequ dangjian gongzuo' (Innovating Community Party Building Work in the Process of Urbanization) (17) *Guangzhou Daxue Xuebao (Shehui Kexue Ban)* (Journal of Guangzhou University, Social Science Edition) 66.

Zhongguo gongchandang diqijie zhongyang weiyuanhui (Chinese Communist Party 7th Central Committee) (1949) 'Zhonggong zhongyang guanyu feichu guomindang de liufaquanshu yu queding jiefangqu de sifa yuanze de zhishi (The CCP Central Committee Instructions on Abolition of Kuomintang Six Codes and Confirmation of Liberated Zone's Judicial Doctrines).

Zhongguo jijian jiancha bao) (China Discipline Inspection and Supervision News) (2023) Practical Exploration of Managing "Lying Flat Style Officials" (Zhili 'tangping shi ganbu' de shijian tansuo)' (2023) *China Discipline Inspection and Supervision News* (Zhongguo jijian jiancha bao), available at: <http://fanfu.people.com.cn/n1/2023/0303/c64371-32635521.html>.

Zhongyang Jiwei Guojia Jianwei'(Central Commission for Discipline Inspection and National Supervision Commission (2023) (There Is Something to Be Said in the Picture: Hitting Hard Against the "Lying Flat Style Officials" '(Huali you hua dui 'tangping shi' ganbu dong zhen pengying)' (2023) Website of the Central Commission for Discipline Inspection and National Supervision Commission (Zhongyang Jiwei Guojia Jianwei Zhan) 9 August 2023 Available at: <http://www.hebcdi.gov.cn/2023-08/09/content_9052328.htm>.

Zhou, L (2020) *Access to Justice for the Chinese Consumer: Handling Consumer Disputes in Contemporary China* Hart Publishing.

Zhou, W (2023) 'Public Notification! An Anhui "Lying Flat Style Official" Has Been Sanctioned: Chuxiong Municipal Taxation Bureau Carries out a Specialist Rectification of a "Lying Flat Style Official' to Promote a Courageous, Can-Do Working Style (Gongkai tongbao! Anhui–'tangping shi ganbu' bei chufen: Chuxiong shi shuiwu ju kaizhan 'tangping she' ganbu zhuanxiang zhili ti zhen gangan shigan zuofeng), available at: <http://www.hyjsxy.com/jjjc/info/news-10816.html>.

Zhou, X (2012) 'Mobilisational State: Further Exploration in the Institutional Logic of State Governance in China' (9) *Open Times* 105

Zhou, Y (2019) 'Sifa panjue dui zhengdang chengxu yuanze de fazhan' (The Development of the Due Process Principle in Court Decisions) (2019, 3) *Zhongguo Faxue* (China Legal Science) 26 at 28.

Zhou, Y (2023) 'Gender Inequality: A Key to Understanding China's Population Decline' *Australian Outlook* (8 March 2023) available at: <https://www.internationalaffairs.org.au/australianoutlook/gender-inequality-a-key-to-understand-chinas-population-decline/>.

Zhou, Y (2023) 'Toward a Feminist Re-problematization of China's Low Birth Rate' *Georgetown Journal of International Affairs* (6 January 2023) available at: <https://gjia.georgetown.edu/2023/01/06/toward-a-feminist-re-problematization-of-chinas-low-birth-rate/>.

Zhou, Y (2025) 'How gendered lived experiences shape sex preference attitudes in contemporary urban China' (87) (1) *Journal of Marriage and Family* 365.

Zhu, C; Yang, N and Wang, Y (2012) 'National Profile Report on Occupational Safety and Health in China' *ILO* March 2012 1, available at: <http://www.ilo.org/wcmsp5/groups/public/@ed_protect/@protrav/@safework/documents/policy/wcms_186991.pdf>.

Zhu, GB (2010) 'Constitutional Review in China: An Unaccomplished Project or a Mirage' (43) *Suffolk University Law Review* 625.

Zhu, X (2012) 'Xingzheng lanyong zhiquan de xin dingyi' (New Definition of the Abuse of Administrative Discretionary Power) (2012) (3) *Faxue Yanjiu* (Studies on Law) 30.

Zou, MM (2016) 'Falling through the Legal Cracks: The Fragmentation of China's Occupational Safety and Health Regime' (2016) *Chinese University of Hong Kong, Faculty of Law Research Paper* (2016-07).

Zuigao Renmin Fayuan Anli Zhidao Gongzuo Bangongshi (Case Guidance Office of the Supreme People's Court) (2012) 'Zhidao anli 6 hao Huang Zefu, He Boqing he He Yi su Chengdu shi Jintang gongshang xingzheng guanli ju xingzheng chufa an de lijie yu canzhao' (The Understanding and Reference of the Guiding Case No. 6 [Huang Zefu, He Boqiong, and He Yi v. The Jintang Administration for Industry and Commerce of Chengdu Municipality]) (2012) (15) *Renmin Sifa* (People's Judicature) 51.

Zuigao Renmin Jianchayuan (Supreme People's Procuracy) 'Dui zhi'an anjian zhifa xingwei ji chufa jueding bufu, nengfou xiang jianchayuan shenqing jiandu' (If Dissatisfied with Law-and-order Enforcement and Penalty Decisions, Can Apply to Procuratorate for Supervision?) 23 August 2021. Available at <https://www.spp.gov.cn/spp/zdgz/202108/t20210823_527315.shtml>.

Index

A

abstract administrative acts/ activities 78–79, 87, 153, 179
abstract executive acts 93, 95, 99
abuses 243, 307, 388, 412, 415, 421, 426, 440, 443
  of authority 75
  police 408, 411, 417, 434, 436, 439
  of power 143, 179, 262
academic cooperation 189–190
accidents 272, 277, 290
accountability 12, 221, 263, 268–9, 277–8, 491
  administrative 4, 7, 151–2, 160, 163, 496, 498
  benefits 6, 495
  citizen-state 489, 491
  gaps 7, 493
  government 100, 296, 396
  mechanisms 7, 10, 12, 259, 275, 498, 501, 504
ACE, see Appeals Centre Europe
ACL, see Administrative Compulsion Law
actions
  agency 125, 130, 132–134, 143–145
  collective 168
  disciplinary 20, 42, 280–2, 287, 289–90, 418, 494
  executive 91, 93, 104–105, 112
activism 167, 219, 230, 394
adaptability 220, 325, 496
administrative agency 67, 68, 72, 73, 74, 80, 81, 154, 155, 158, 160, 161, 162, 163, 164, 169, 171, 176, 179, 279
  county-level 304, 357, 358, 361, 364, 367
  enforcement 278–9, 297, 367
  government x, 38, 205, 277, 281, 314, 315, 483, 495
  implementing 57, 59, 278
  provincial-level 358, 367
  regulatory 12, 224, 254, 324
Administrative Appeals Board (AAB) 209
administrative authorities 23, 351, 477, 481
administrative authority 7, 13, 57, 60, 508
administrative bodies 19, 39, 147, 268, 324, 459
administrative cases 28, 30, 77, 118–119, 126, 127, 137–139, 142, 153
  power to decide 30–31
administrative compensation 78, 141
Administrative Compulsion Law (ACL) 128–129
administrative compulsory action 128–129
administrative compulsory enforcement 128–129
administrative control 38, 42, 54–55, 60, 370, 388
administrative courts 22, 30–31, 37, 209–210
administrative decision-making 65, 164, 180, 210, 280, 484, 507

AI-powered 6, 10, 13, 461, 462–4, 468, 473–476, 479, 484, 485–7, 505

administrative decisions 4, 54, 56, 65, 69, 70, 84, 86–87, 97, 107, 119, 500, 505

administrative detention 124, 126, 265, 278, 406, 408, 411, 415–416, 420, 421, 439, 443

punitive 415–416

administrative discretion 10, 75–6, 141, 143, 178, 209

administrative disputes 57, 117–147, 505

administrative divorce 454–455, 459

administrative enforcement 279, 461–487

algorithmic 479–80

of copyright protection 457–83

system 457–8

administrative examination 353–4, 363–4, 371

administrative fairness 209, 211

administrative governance 12, 152, 164–6, 172

judicialization 152, 164–78

administrative harm 4, 59–60, 499

administrative hierarchy 12, 356–60, 365–8, 370, 375

administrative injustices 39, 82, 87, 89, 496

administrative justice ix–xi, 3–9, 11–14, 38–9, 42, 53–4, 56–60, 88, 184, 187, 209, 214–5, 224, 253–4, 259, 324, 328, 344, 376, 462, 476, 479–87, 491–9

dynamics 4, 8, 11, 254, 493, 497, 504

failures xi, 10, 11

framework 10, 11, 58, 462, 492, 496

functions xi, 3–5, 496, 504

improvements 6, 56–7, 59, 60, 210, 496, 507, 508

outcomes 5, 137, 425, 484, 492, 494, 497, 498, 499, 502, 506, 508

reform ix, 3, 4, 5, 6, 7, 8, 9, 12, 13, 44, 46, 48, 52, 57, 58, 59, 60, 88, 209, 215, 224, 254, 265, 274, 276, 284, 288, 496, 497, 499, 502, 503, 506, 507, 508, 509

scholarship 3, 11, 498, 506, 508

system 5, 457, 479, 485–7, 491, 499, 508

administrative law ix, xv, xviii, 4, 7, 10, 38–39, 41, 65–66, 68, 70, 74–80, 87, 92, 94, 98, 106, 121, 137, 151, 157, 164, 178, 185, 209–210, 262–263, 307, 310, 346–347, 355, 412, 422, 424, 426, 430–434, 436–437, 439, 491, 500, 502

administrative lawsuits 412, 424, 426, 430, 433, 439

administrative licenses 68–9, 74, 85, 118, 120, 124–5, 129–32

Administrative Licensing Law 67–8, 74, 79, 84

administrative litigation 12, 20, 34, 51, 55–6, 62, 77, 91, 93–4, 97–100, 105, 107, 110–2, 117–27, 130, 136–44, 147, 151–82, 280–8, 414, 424, 429

citizens v. mandarins form 151–82

private party-initiated 152, 157, 165, 168–9

procuratorate-initiated xi, 7, 170–6, 179–80, 493, 501

system 93, 100, 118, 144, 147

Administrative Litigation Law 65, 70, 75, 84–6, 89, 96, 97, 105, 106,

117, 120, 153–4, 162–4, 178–9, 181, 289
administrative measures 42, 77, 88, 96, 104, 124, 360, 361, 476–8
administrative nonfeasance 160–1, 163, 169, 179, 181
administrative normative documents, see ANDs
administrative omissions 118, 120, 132–4
administrative orders 328, 338, 353
administrative oversight 54–5, 197
administrative penalties 10, 42, 50, 67–9, 73, 77–8, 117–8, 124–8, 140–3, 302, 303, 320, 360, 434, 477
  environmental 303–4
Administrative Penalty Law (APL) 67–8, 70–3, 92, 126
administrative policies 42, 170–1, 481
administrative power xi, 4–5, 7–11, 13, 21, 23, 28, 35, 60, 105, 164, 219, 224, 268, 276, 324, 345–7, 351, 356, 374–5, 491, 500, 504, 505, 507
  exercise of 164, 260
  unaccountable 10, 505
administrative procedures 5, 10, 11, 65–7, 69–71, 81, 87–9, 454, 458
administrative processes 3, 13, 65, 445–6, 457–81
administrative public interest litigation, see APIL
administrative reconsideration 51, 62, 65, 73, 80, 82, 83, 86, 123, 129, 147, 164, 209, 210
Administrative Reconsideration Law 73, 83, 123
administrative reforms 9, 12, 58, 60, 224, 254, 347, 350, 362, 367, 370, 375, 507
administrative regulations 69–70, 89, 95, 96, 125, 171, 244, 356, 361, 477
administrative review 13, 42, 55, 57, 59, 123, 281, 289, 314, 414, 429, 431, 432, 439
  bodies 123
  processes 57, 59
Administrative Review Law, see Administrative Reconsideration Law
administrative rulemaking 93–4, 96, 101, 103, 111
administrative rules 69, 93–4, 95, 96, 97, 99, 100–1, 103–7, 111, 112, 132, 144, 179, 180, 248–9, 302, 493, 500
  illegal 493, 500
  judicial review of 91–116, 493
  scope 99–111
administrative sanctions 166, 167, 280, 290, 415
administrative supervision 87, 117, 172, 199, 279, 286
administrative systems xi, 9, 12, 48, 59, 120, 224, 254, 295, 344, 345, 348, 375, 461, 462, 479, 503, 504, 505, 508
admissible evidence 481, 485
ADR (alternative dispute resolution) 461, 484
affordability, housing 44–5
age-appropriate marriage 51
ageing population 10, 39, 43, 44, 48, 53, 56
agencies (agency) x, 3, 9, 11, 12, 13, 19, 38, 40, 47, 49, 57, 59, 65, 67, 68, 72, 73, 74, 75, 77, 80, 81, 82,

83, 84, 88, 89, 98, 104, 111, 117, 119, 120, 121, 122, 123, 124, 125, 126, 127, 128, 129, 130, 132, 133, 134, 135, 137, 140, 142, 143, 144, 145, 146, 147, 151, 154, 155, 158, 160, 161, 162, 163, 164, 165, 166, 168, 169, 171, 176, 179, 183, 200, 205, 209, 210, 213, 224, 230, 236, 245, 250, 254, 261, 264, 272, 273, 276, 277, 278, 279, 280, 281, 282, 283, 285, 287, 288, 290, 296, 297, 303, 304, 314, 315, 324, 356, 357, 358, 367, 370, 374, 376, 392, 393, 408, 441, 445, 462, 480, 483, 485, 493, 495, 501, 502, 505

agency action 117, 119, 122, 125, 130, 132, 133, 134, 143, 144, 145

agency decisions 119–21, 123–5, 130, 134, 137, 142–4, 146, 209

agency enforcement 128, 132

aggrieved parties 57, 87, 120, 123, 134, 137, 138, 140, 141, 142, 144, 146

agreements 52, 125, 134–6, 138, 224, 453, 463

administrative 117–8, 124–5, 134–6, 138, 219, 285

divorce 457, 458, 459

executive 205

government franchise 125, 134, 284

public-private partnership 134–5

Retail Pharmacy Agreement 359, 361

AI 6, 461–4, 468, 469–72, 474, 477, 480, 481–4, 486

algorithms 461, 463, 469, 477, 481–3

algorithm designers 467, 486

algorithmic administrative enforcement 483, 484

algorithms, copyright policing 463

AI-generated works 461, 463, 477, 481–2

AI-powered content moderation tools 463, 469–72, 482

AI technology 461, 463, 464, 486

air pollution 123, 127, 298, 299, 300, 302, 316, 326, 327, 329, 335

air pollution control 299, 300, 329, 335

air pollution prevention 127, 302, 327

Air Pollution Control Act 295, 325

Air Pollution Control Regulations 298, 326

alternative dispute resolution (ADR) 484

altruism 383–384

ambiguity 100

legal 324, 376, 486

political 325

American-style judicial review 17, 18, 20, 22, 24, 26, 28, 30, 32, 34–36

ANDs (administrative normative documents) 96–98, 101, 104, 111

cases reviewed 97, 98, 111

illegal 111

impugned 99, 101

legality 97, 98, 101, 104

reasonableness and proportionality 101

reviewed 97, 98, 111

reviewing 96, 97, 101, 104
Anhui Higher People's Court 81, 82
Anhui Province 109, 428, 431, 432
anti-corruption campaign 161, 180, 274, 275, 286, 292
anti-corruption functions 7, 167, 171, 180, 497
APEC 204, 207, 208, 214, 218
APIL (administrative public interest litigation) 151–180, 493
cases 153–180, 493
procuratorate-initiated cases 151–180, 493
system 151–158, 161, 165, 167, 170–180, 493
APL (see Administrative Penalty Law)
appeal mechanisms 412, 437, 439, 494
appeals 6, 10, 13, 139, 209, 212, 213, 215, 219, 220, 422, 425, 430, 431, 433, 439, 443, 465, 478, 485
courts 465
Appeals Centre Europe (ACE) 478, 485
appropriateness 85, 142, 143
arbitration 199, 242, 463, 471, 484
Article 43 (Law on Penalties for Administration of Public Security) 412–441
Article 66 (Law on Penalties for Administration of Public Security) lawsuits 412–441
assault 401, 414, 419, 420, 422, 427–431, 434, 437, 440, 441
audit committees 241–242, 253
audits
third-party 338
authoritarian administrative justice 4, 59
authoritarian advantage 385, 387, 389, 406
authoritarian contexts 3, 12, 13, 89, 498, 499, 504, 506, 507
authoritarian governance 3, 60, 496–498, 503, 506, 508
structures 3, 60, 496–498, 503
authoritarian movement 386
authoritarian systems 4, 5, 92, 112, 491, 496, 501
authoritarianism 5, 169, 325, 326, 342, 386, 387, 496
legal 5
persistent structural 496
authority deficit 9, 12, 345–378, 494, 497, 501, 503
authorship 466, 467, 481
human 465, 466
autocracy 33
autonomy 23, 65, 157, 175, 184, 246, 251, 301, 349, 501
individual 10, 56, 60, 273, 504
institutional 6, 175, 497
local 33, 216
reproductive 43, 57–59
restriction 172, 175, 180

B

Baiyun 306, 309, 310
baojia (保甲 [neighbourhood watch system]) 410
Basic-level courts 138, 139
Beijing Airport 418, 428, 441
Beijing Public Security Bureau 438
Beiyang Zhengfu 26, 36

Belt and Road Initiative (BRI) 232, 252
biases 42, 46, 138, 232, 246, 475, 483, 484
bigamy 43, 448, 452
biological products 347, 366, 378
birth defects 51–52
birth planning (family planning) 38–57, 61
  birth limitation 38, 39, 42, 52, 55, 56, 450
  historical development of system 39–43
  limits to progress 44–47
  policy and regulatory changes 48–57
birth rates 10, 39, 44, 45, 46, 53, 449, 456
birth restrictions 40, 44, 46, 56
births 39–41, 43, 49, 56, 57
  encouragement 38, 39
  unregistered children 41, 61
Blue Sky Defense War 327, 338
board of directors 229–231, 235–238, 240–242, 245–247, 250, 253, 254
board of supervisors 226, 242, 245–247, 253, 254
boundaries 9, 112, 119, 143, 178, 185, 186, 191, 193, 197, 199, 202, 209, 213, 219, 352, 390, 493, 494, 501, 502
  jurisdictional 193, 209, 493, 494, 502
breastfeeding 51, 52
BRI (see Belt and Road Initiative)
Bribes 21, 357, 371
buchang (补偿) indemnity or compensation for administrative acts characterised as lawful]) 147
buildings 73, 74, 77, 79, 80, 82, 85–87, 89
  demolition 77, 79, 80, 82, 85–87
  expropriation 77, 80, 82, 86, 87, 89
bureaucracy 259, 264–266, 273, 284, 291, 292, 297, 327, 345, 375, 503
bureaucratic dysfunction 292
bureaucratic inertia 8, 259–270, 273, 276, 279, 282–284, 287, 288, 291–293, 498
bureaucratic institutions 3, 7, 8, 497
bureaucratisation 264–266, 274, 280, 286
bureaucratism 264–269, 271–273, 283, 284, 287
bureaucrats 8, 11, 89, 251, 259, 264, 266, 272, 273, 286, 296, 297, 391, 497, 501, 503
  street-level 8, 11, 296, 297, 501
business licences 359, 360
business operations 190, 238, 244, 322
businesses 20, 192, 193, 195, 196, 200, 202, 209–211, 215, 220, 221, 229, 348, 376
  scope 360, 362, 365

C

CAC (see Cyberspace Administration of China)
cadres 103, 106, 237, 247, 259, 261, 267, 270, 271, 272, 273, 277, 278, 286, 287, 289, 304, 367, 402, 407, 410, 431, 442
lying flat 259–71, 282–93
campaign-style enforcement (CSE) (see also campaign-style

governance) 8, 325, 326, 327, 335, 342, 493–4, 500–1
analysis 12, 500
findings 336
research methods 334–5
responding mechanism 330, 333
threat of 324, 332, 340, 504
campaign-style governance (see also campaign-style enforcement) 8, 494, 498–9
campaigns 8, 259, 260–1, 271, 280–4, 288, 493–4
costs and risks 271, 274
nationwide 275, 398, 441
childbirth 44, 46, 48, 51, 52, 56, 450
childcare 47, 50, 52, 53, 449, 457
children
unregistered (*heihaizi* [黑孩子 'black children'--that is, children born outside family planning policies and not registered])
China Copyright Offices 471, 480
China E-Commerce Law 470, 471, 472, 473, 476, 486
China Quarterly, The 41
China Railway Corporation (CRC) 252
China Securities Regulatory Commission (CSRC) 226, 227, 242
Chinese characteristics 71, 92, 156, 226, 248, 264, 268, 274, 275, 284, 285, 286, 287, 291, 389, 477
Chinese Communist Party (CCP) 156, 223, 287, 289, 413
chuli jianyi (处理建议 [disposition proposal]) 102, 112
cities 44, 69, 190, 227, 316, 355, 384, 385, 392, 393, 395, 397, 403, 409, 448, 449, 477 (See also individual cities)
citizen participation 4, 60, 505, 507, 508
citizen-state accountability 493, 497
citizen welfare 254, 497
citizens 3, 4, 5, 7, 8, 9, 11, 12, 39, 42, 43, 51, 54, 55, 56, 57, 58, 59, 60, 61, 65, 70, 84, 89, 99, 100, 111, 119, 120, 121, 123, 126, 134, 137, 138, 140, 141, 151, 152, 162, 163, 164, 165, 166, 168, 169, 170, 179, 180, 214, 254, 259, 262, 280, 281, 288, 296, 304, 305, 309, 310, 311, 312, 313, 318, 322, 323, 338, 376, 383, 384, 386, 391, 397, 398, 401, 404, 406, 407, 408, 409, 414, 428, 445, 462, 479, 491, 492, 493, 494, 495, 496, 497, 499, 500, 505, 506, 507, 508
complaints 305, 309, 312, 322
rights 5, 12, 51, 56, 59, 88, 479, 491, 505
citizens v. mandarins 7, 12, 151–182
city districts 309, 310, 311, 323
city governments 227, 328, 392 (see also individual cities)
civic and moral education 383
Civil Code 10, 22, 23, 52, 53, 55, 445, 446, 447, 448, 451, 452, 453, 454, 455, 457, 459, 470, 476
civil law
frameworks 41, 52, 212
systems 23, 58
civil litigation 20, 34, 38, 55, 173, 461, 482
Civil Procedure Law 154, 181, 457
civil public interest litigation 154, 174

civil servants 20, 24, 274, 288, 367, 395, 402
Civil Servants Law 274, 288
co-governance 394, 396, 409
Coal
consumption 327, 336
power plants 324, 327, 334, 335, 336, 337, 338, 339, 340, 341, 342, 343, 344, 504
coercion 10, 40, 42, 92, 140, 309, 310, 332, 435, 504
collective actions 168, 169, 394, 395
commerce 68, 73, 77, 185, 189, 191, 193, 279, 312, 348, 350, 351, 352, 357, 360, 367, 468, 469, 470, 471, 472, 473, 474, 476, 486
commercial administration 350, 358, 372
Commission for Discipline Inspection 262, 283, 286, 287
common law 29, 31, 32, 34, 35, 58, 66, 183, 204
communities 9, 58, 59, 227, 252, 253, 383, 384, 385, 386, 388, 389, 390, 391, 392, 393, 394, 395, 396, 397, 398, 399, 400, 401, 402, 404, 405, 406, 408, 409, 410, 423, 427, 496
community level 394, 411, 413, 421, 443
community policing (*shequ jingwu* [社区警务]) 397, 398, 410
community relations 337
companies
foreign 190
joint-stock 242
company law 226, 229, 230, 231, 236, 237, 239, 242, 243, 244
compensation
administrative 85, 141
agreements 125, 134, 289
claims 77, 88, 136, 436
fair 131
housing expropriation 289
competition
horizontal 493, 494
competitiveness 191, 212, 233, 246
complainants 426, 430, 432, 461, 462, 481
complaints 10, 43, 56, 93, 120, 127, 129, 135, 137, 140–2, 168, 214, 215, 280, 281, 288, 296, 304, 305, 309–13, 316–22, 333, 337, 339, 341, 392, 393, 402, 413, 421, 426, 438, 440, 443, 445, 461, 478, 491
compliance 8, 12, 40, 42, 47, 51, 103, 106, 296–97, 309, 324, 331
concrete administrative actions 93, 95, 108, 111, 120, 124
conditional openness 187, 192
condominiums 393, 394
conflicts
jurisdictional 8, 30, 214, 497
overt 60, 89
consensual divorce 10, 445, 447, 449, 456
consensus 75, 176, 383, 465, 467, 469
consent 171, 188, 192, 193, 194, 195, 196, 200, 222, 243, 445, 446, 448, 452, 453, 454, 455, 456, 457, 459, 460, 467, 474
conservatism, moral 448, 453
consistency
legal 12
mechanism 205, 216
Constitution
draft 20, 30, 31, 33

constitution making 20
constitutional constraints 201, 507, 508
constitutional interpretation 17, 25, 29, 32, 33, 34
constitutional protections 10, 58, 60
constitutional review 91, 103
Constitutionalism 5, 18, 28, 33, 35, 37, 91, 92, 389
constitutionality
  of laws 17, 29, 35, 36, 91, 103
constraints
  constitutional 201, 507, 508
  effective 7, 500
  institutional 8, 254, 386, 497, 502
  self-regulatory 463, 474, 476, 485
construction
  infrastructure 340
  projects 120, 146, 301, 312
consumer protection 156, 445
content
  illegal 468, 469, 472, 473, 475, 480
  infringing 463, 468, 486
  moderation 10, 461, 462, 463, 464, 467, 473, 474, 475, 476, 477, 478, 480, 483, 485, 505
  online 461, 463, 468, 469, 474, 476, 478, 485
  owners 461, 467
  user-uploaded 468, 471
content recognition tools
  automated 468, 486
contested divorces 447, 451, 455, 457
continuities 5, 6, 11, 56, 58, 506
contracts 97, 134, 168, 233
  GBA 195, 197, 198, 199, 200, 201, 205, 208, 214, 215, 217, 219, 221
  standard 186, 188, 189, 195, 197, 198, 199, 204, 208, 216, 217, 219, 221
control
  administrative 38, 39, 42, 43, 49, 54, 55, 60, 374, 392
  central 345, 346, 358
  insider 224, 229, 230, 238, 245
  pandemics 9, 11, 383, 384, 385, 386, 387, 388, 390, 391, 392, 394, 395, 396, 398, 400, 401, 402, 403, 404, 405, 406, 408, 410, 502
  political 3, 5, 6, 7, 105, 224, 235, 500, 503, 504
  regulatory 187, 215, 295, 296, 297, 299, 304, 322, 323, 343
  state 5, 9, 13, 60, 232, 233, 243, 254, 374, 494, 496
cooling-off periods 10, 11, 53, 447, 453, 454, 455, 456, 457, 458, 459, 504
cooperation
  academic 189, 190
  coordination
  failures 7
  mechanisms 186, 201
copyright (see also moderation AI-generated works infringing content)
  China Copyright Offices 471, 480
  enforcement 10, 462, 463, 467, 476, 477, 478, 480, 481, 482, 485, 505
  infringement 10, 461, 462, 464, 466, 467, 477, 480, 481, 482, 486

infringing materials 472, 473, 474
law 464, 466, 468, 471, 476, 481, 482
offices 462, 465, 466, 469, 471, 472, 473, 478, 479, 480, 481, 485, 486
Copyright Directive 462, 468, 469, 486
copyrighted work 463, 465, 469
corporate compliance 296, 297
corporate governance
standards 245, 246
Covid-19 9, 217, 265, 383, 384, 385, 386, 387, 388, 391, 399, 400, 401, 403, 404, 406, 407, 409, 412, 417, 419, 420, 426, 427, 428, 434, 437, 441, 444, 454, 502
CRC (China Railway Corporation) 252
criminal cases 21, 31, 34, 137, 161, 174, 408, 411, 418, 420, 422, 440, 444
criminal prosecution 407, 419, 432
criminal sanctions 278, 290
crises 7, 234, 275, 385, 386, 387, 388
crisis management 388, 389, 405
Cross-Border Privacy Rules (CBPR) 204, 207, 214
cross-border data
flows 184, 185, 186, 187, 188, 189, 190, 191, 196, 204, 211
governance 7, 13, 183, 184, 186, 187, 188, 190, 192, 194, 196, 198, 200, 202, 204, 206, 208, 210, 212, 214, 215, 216, 218, 220, 221, 222, 494, 497
rights 219
transfers 187, 189, 190, 192, 193, 200, 207, 210, 211
CSE see campaign-style enforcement
CSR see corporate social responsibility
CSRC (China Securities Regulatory Commission) 226, 227, 242
Cunmin Weiyuanhui (村民委员会 [Villagers' Committees]) 40, 61
cuoshang zuotanhui (磋商座谈会 [negotiation symposium]) 161, 181
cultural heritage 160
culture/s 4, 212, 248, 265, 316, 349, 450, 464, 477, 491, 494
cumulative inertia 324, 333, 341, 342
cumulative stress 333, 341, 342
cyber-sovereignty 186, 191
Cybersecurity Law (CSL) 184, 187, 188
Cyberspace Administration China (CAC) 171, 184, 186, 188, 193, 197, 210, 211, 480, 485

D

dabuzhi gaige (大部制改革 [super-ministry system reform]) 345, 376
Dali Si (大理寺 [Chamber of Revision]) 18, 36
Dali Yuan (大理院 [Provisional Supreme Court]) 17–26, 30, 32–36
Regulations 23–24, 26
role
system 17–18, 22, 36, 500
damages 77, 85, 97, 154, 168, 304, 420, 453, 462
punitive 168

dangwei fushuji (党委副书记 [deputy Party committee secretary]) 255
dangwei shuji (党委书记 [Party committee secretary]) 255
danwei (单位 [work unit]) 255, 414, 443
Daqing Wei Jing Lü (大清违警律 [Qing Dynasty Police Offences Law]) 412
dashichang (大市场 [large market]) 350, 376
data
- controllers 212–213
- emission 338
- exports 190, 194–195, 200, 206, 210
- federalism 184, 187, 208, 216, 222
- flows 7, 184–187, 191–192, 196, 199, 201, 203–206, 211, 214, 220, 222
- cross-border 184–185, 191, 203–204, 206, 211
- governance 6–7, 13, 183–184, 186–188, 190, 192, 194, 196, 198, 200, 202–216, 218, 220–222, 494, 497
- cross-border/-jurisdiction 7, 12, 183–184, 186–188, 190, 192, 194, 196, 198, 200, 202, 204, 206, 208, 210, 212, 214–216, 218, 220–222, 494, 497
- misuse 194, 200, 212
- protection 183–188, 191–196, 198, 201, 204–208, 211, 213–214, 216–217, 220
- regulation 190, 209, 212
- sovereignty 7, 184–185, 191, 222
- transfers 185–190, 192–193, 197–198, 205, 207, 210, 220
- Data Security Law (DSL) 186–188
- data subjects 219
- rights 214, 219
- data training 466, 484

democratic centralism 260, 262, 265, 275–276, 284, 385, 387–388, 511
democratic contexts 3–4, 60, 498–499
- liberal 4, 60, 498

democratization 393, 491, 500, 508
demographic goals/objectives 48, 59
demographic pressures 55
demolition of buildings 77, 79–80, 82, 85–87
departments, government 102, 109, 285, 310–311, 326, 328, 333, 392, 400, 409
deployment meeting 262, 285, 287
deputy team leaders 306, 313, 315, 318
dereliction of duty 288, 293, 418
despotism 32, 389
detention 71, 124, 126, 128, 153, 265, 278, 281, 300, 406, 408, 411, 414–416, 418, 420–421, 427–437 439–443, 504
- administrative, see administrative detention
- centres 153
- penalties 432

deterrence 279, 309, 312, 315, 324, 331–334, 340, 342–344, 383, 397
deterrent effect 297, 304, 310, 317, 376

developers 393–394, 467, 486

development

economic 7, 39, 78, 106, 169, 188, 234, 252, 259, 265, 271, 275, 282, 308, 315, 493–494, 511

institutional 250, 303, 491, 500, 507–508

legal 5–6, 39–40, 500

sustainable 119, 147, 227–228, 235, 246, 248, 295, 299, 303–304

digital economy 183, 185, 191, 196, 198, 200

digital enforcement 462, 463, 472, 481, 483, 484, 486

Digital Millennium Copyright Act (DMCA) 462, 469, 471–473, 476, 480, 486

Digital Services Act (DSA) 471–472, 476, 478, 485–486

digital sovereignty 183, 186–187, 221

digital trade 183, 185, 191

directives 12, 47–48, 50, 236, 240, 246, 249, 254, 325–326, 328, 330, 338, 468

central 47–48, 253

directors 223, 228–231, 234, 235–238, 240–242, 245–247, 250, 253–254

boards of 223, 246, 253

independent 230, 246

disciplinary actions 42, 494

discretion 10, 65, 75–76, 83, 88, 99–100, 108, 141–143, 178, 209, 249, 372, 407, 412, 421, 439, 441, 443

administrative 11, 141, 143, 178, 209

of courts 88, 99

police 412, 421, 443

procedural 75

discretionary power 54, 75–76, 302, 329–330, 371

regulation of 302

discrimination 40–42, 46, 52, 59, 505

dispute resolution 3–4, 13, 55, 59, 141, 169, 199, 202, 213, 216, 393, 459, 461–462, 472, 476–477, 479, 484–486, 492, 498–499, 513

mechanisms and processes 3–4, 13, 59, 199, 472, 479, 498–499

disputes

administrative, see administrative disputes

local 412, 441, 443

district enforcement teams 306–307, 311, 316, 318–320, 322–323

district governments 79–84, 86, 124, 307–308, 315, 318–319, 322, 400

Districts (see also individual districts)

city 307, 309–311, 320

divisions of labour 368, 402

divorce 10–11, 44, 53, 441–460

administrative 454–455, 459

agreements 457–459

applications 455, 457

certificates 446

changing patterns 448

consensual 10, 445, 447, 449, 456

contested 447, 451, 455, 457

debates and disagreements

freedom of 451, 454, 456, 458

judicial 445, 451, 454, 457–459

moral panics 450

by mutual consent 443, 447

mutual consent 443, 447
policy 455–456
rate 446, 449–450, 454–456
reckless 447, 454, 458–460
registration 447–448, 453, 456, 458
DMCA (see Digital Millennium Copyright Act)
domestic abuse 451, 453
domestic violence 448, 451–452
dominant shareholders
downward delegation 272, 278
draft constitution 20–22, 30
drinking water safety 123, 129, 131
duties 24, 26, 28, 77, 84, 104, 122, 127, 132, 134–135, 147, 160–162, 164, 183, 223, 228, 240–241, 254, 268–269, 276, 289–290, 296–297, 304, 306, 310–314, 317–319, 322, 348, 373, 391, 423
enforcement 297, 306, 310–311, 314, 317, 322
fiduciary 228, 240–241
legal 77, 241
performance 161–162, 269, 423
statutory 122, 132, 147, 289
DWSR (drinking water source reserves) 123
dynamics 4–7, 9, 11, 13, 66, 89, 221, 254, 297, 306, 325, 328, 333–334, 336, 341, 343, 475, 493, 497, 504, 506, 508
of administrative justice 11, 254, 493
institutional 4, 6, 11, 328, 493, 497, 506
social 341, 504
dysfunction 9, 225, 273, 292
bureaucratic 292
regulatory 9

E

e-commerce 185, 189, 468–474, 476, 486
economic costs 191, 384
economic development 7, 39, 78, 106, 169, 188, 234, 252, 259, 265, 271, 275, 315, 493–494
economic growth 44, 48, 224, 234, 295
economic incentives 50, 61, 326–327
economic integration 186, 191
economic losses 132, 134, 135
economic pressures 44, 48, 58, 228
economy 53, 66, 105–106, 135, 183, 185, 191–192, 196, 198–200, 224–227, 229–230, 232–234, 243–245, 248–251, 345, 353, 371, 374, 387
digital 183, 185, 191, 196, 198, 200
local 135
political 105–106, 232, 234, 248, 250
education 41–42, 45–46, 50–52, 61, 72, 74, 89, 97, 118, 244, 261, 264, 267–268, 270, 283–289, 291, 309–310, 383, 392, 405, 406, 414–416, 425, 443–444, 452
campaigns 264, 267–8, 283–4, 285, 291
ideological 283, 286–287, 291
sex 50
effectiveness 24, 68, 97, 101, 102, 174, 216, 223, 229, 247, 284, 285, 325–326, 332, 342, 359, 383, 385, 406–407, 438, 455, 459, 473, 480, 485, 498, 507–508
administrative 498, 508
institutional 507–508

efficiency 6, 175, 191, 223, 224, 240, 245, 260, 262, 263, 437, 463, 473, 481, 483, 485, 487, 494, 495, 496, 498, 505
  SOE/societal 223, 224, 239, 240, 244, 248, 249, 251, 252, 253
EIA (see environmental impact assessment)
electricity 146, 336–337, 341, 344
emission data 338
emission standards 127, 327, 333, 337, 339–340
empirical evidence 220, 223, 245
employees 46, 227, 239, 243–244, 248, 251, 252, 278, 367, 393, 402, 441
employers 46
empowerment 6, 89, 93–94, 97, 99–100, 105–106, 500–501
  formal legal 6, 500–501
  judicial 93, 100
enforcement 3, 7–8, 10, 12, 39–40, 42, 45, 49, 51, 53, 57–59, 67–68, 70–71, 79, 86, 96, 99, 102–103, 117, 119–120, 125, 127–129, 132–135, 139, 147, 153, 189, 195, 199–201, 203, 207–209, 212, 214–215, 218–220, 225–227, 229, 233, 238, 242, 260, 274–276, 278–279, 282–283, 285, 287, 291–292, 295–344, 346–347, 356–358, 365–370, 372–376, 384–385, 395–396, 401, 403–406, 411–412, 414–415, 418, 422–423, 427, 437, 440, 443, 461–464, 466–468, 470, 472, 474–478, 480–487, 493–494, 497–498, 500–501, 503–505
  actions 314–315, 318–319, 323, 333, 374
  administrative, see administrative enforcement
enterprises 8, 65, 113, 123, 130, 135, 170, 197–198, 223–224, 226–229, 231–233, 235, 238, 243–245, 247–248, 274, 296, 304–306 309–314, 316–318, 320–324, 328, 330–333, 335–339, 341–344, 353, 356, 358, 364, 385, 423, 502, 504
  industrial 305, 316, 328, 341
  polluting 304, 306, 309, 312–314, 316–318, 322–323
  private 249, 314, 338
  regulated 310, 324, 333, 336, 341, 343–344
  state-owned 8, 170, 226, 231–232, 235, 238, 244–245, 247, 331, 502
environment 6–8, 11, 42, 48, 58, 117–147, 153–154, 156, 159–160 165–166, 169, 174, 176, 192–193, 196, 202, 213, 221, 224–228, 234, 237, 241, 243–245, 248, 250, 252, 260–261, 279, 295–344, 346, 353, 373–374, 392, 397, 403, 454, 464, 484, 493, 496–497, 501, 503–507
  living 318, 322
environmental administrative disputes 117–147, 297, 505
  defendants 119–124
  plaintiffs 119–122
  prospects for more effective adjudication 118–119, 136–147
environmental administrative penalties 302, 329
environmental agencies 122, 127, 132, 137, 297
environmental compliance 133, 295, 311, 331–332, 336, 338, 344
environmental enforcement 8, 117, 120, 127, 133–135, 147, 297, 334, 501

environmental governance 117–119, 132, 145, 147, 261, 295, 297, 326–328, 334, 342, 346, 493, 505
role of courts 118–119, 145
environmental impact assessment (EIA) 120, 126, 137, 298–299, 301
environmental information 117, 132–134, 146, 226, 330
environmental law 11, 119–123, 125, 127, 131, 139, 147, 154, 165, 226–227, 260, 279, 297, 299, 324, 331–332
environmental management 296–297, 303, 314, 333, 335–336, 339, 374
environmental monitoring 127, 142
environmental policies 326, 336, 341, 493
environmental pollution, see pollution
environmental protection 117–118, 121–124, 126, 130–131, 133, 135–137, 142, 145, 146, 156, 160, 169, 176, 226–227, 234, 243–244, 260, 295–296, 298–300, 302–303, 305–310, 312, 315, 325–326, 329–331, 335, 338, 493, 503, 505
bureaux (EPBs) 121–123, 126–128, 135, 169, 176, 296, 302–306, 311–312, 315, 317
law (EPL) 117, 128, 131–134, 160, 298–299
environmental quality 131, 147, 296, 303, 307, 314–315, 318, 328
environmental regulation 119, 122, 131–132, 136, 145, 304, 325, 329, 331, 335–337, 341–342, 373, 493, 503
environmental rights 145, 505
environmental standards 253, 326, 330, 339, 342–343
environmental supervision 133, 304–305, 335
EPBs (see environmental protection, bureaux)
EPL (see environmental protection law)
equality 30, 41–42, 46, 48, 52, 452–454, 456, 459
gender 41–42, 46, 52, 452–454
errors 85, 86–88, 183, 286, 484, 486, 502
procedural 85, 86–88, 502
ethical oversight 42, 483
EU, see European Union
European Data Protection Board (EDPB) 205, 208, 211, 216–217, 220
European Parliament 465, 468–469, 471–472
European Union 203–204, 206, 210–211, 468–469, 476, 478
evidence 46, 50, 68, 79–80, 110, 126–127, 131, 134, 140, 142–143, 155, 162–163, 165, 176, 212, 217–218, 220–221, 223, 236, 245, 254, 273, 296–297, 302, 309, 314, 371, 383, 388, 400, 404, 428, 438, 441, 461, 467, 470, 473, 481–482, 485–486, 496, 502, 506
admissible 481, 485
empirical 220, 223, 245
prima facie 218, 470, 473
examination 79–80, 98, 104, 145, 152, 284, 286, 348, 353–354, 363
expropriation 77, 80, 82, 86, 87, 89, 102, 109–110, 116, 289
of buildings 77, 82, 86, 87, 89

F

Facebook 191, 205, 207, 219, 467, 474–475, 478

factories 305, 309, 314, 316–317, 332–333, 335, 337, 341, 356
  dyeing 305, 316
  small 314, 317
fagui（法规 [regulations]） 19–20, 89, 95, 104, 112, 412
fair decisions 483–484
fair treatment 46, 459, 486
fair trial 138
fair 463–464, 479
fairness 4, 12, 57–58, 60, 73, 155, 184, 187, 209, 211, 215, 221–222 271, 273, 282, 324, 343, 383, 407, 478–479, 484–487, 492, 494–496, 498, 505, 508
  administrative 57–58, 73, 184, 209, 211, 215, 221–222, 271, 281, 324
  organizational 271
  procedural 4, 12, 57–58, 60, 187, 211, 215, 221, 324, 484, 494, 496, 498, 505, 508
falü (法律 [law/statute])
falü shang lihai guanxi (法律上利害关系 ['legally relevant interests']) 120–121, 130, 147
families 39, 41–43, 45–46, 48–52, 58, 227, 430–431, 450
family disputes 428, 430, 441, 459
family law 10, 11, 38, 41, 43–44, 445, 451, 453–454
family members 227, 415, 448
family planning 38–43, 45, 49, 51–52, 54–56, 61, 364
family size 38, 40, 43–44, 52, 55, 58
fang guan fu (放管服, short form for: jianzheng fangquan, *fang guan jiehe, youhua fuwu,* 简政放权，放管结合，优化服务, streamline administration, delegate power and improve services) 376
favouritism 288, 290
FDLs (Food Distribution Licenses) 360, 364–365
federalism, data 184, 187, 216, 222
feedback 55, 186, 335
fertility rates 43–44, 48, 450
fiduciary duties 228, 241
fines 38–40, 42, 50, 56, 68, 124, 126, 128, 142–143, 170, 212, 274, 278, 279, 298, 300, 304, 315, 331–332, 360, 362, 369, 414, 429–431, 433, 441, 462, 477, 480–481
first-instance courts 86, 119, 129, 137–138, 424–426, 440
flows, data 7, 184–193, 196, 199, 201, 203–206, 211, 214, 220, 222
Food Distribution Licenses (FDLs) 360, 364–365
food safety 169, 260, 312, 349, 364–365
formal legal empowerment 6, 500–501
formal procedures 9, 11, 503, 506
formalism 194–195, 264–269, 271–274, 282–285, 287–288, 324
formality 198, 210, 267, 439
fragmentation 7, 9, 13, 184, 187, 195–196, 199, 202, 213, 215, 221, 254, 276–278, 349–350, 359, 376, 392, 497, 503
  jurisdictional 7, 278, 497
frameworks 3, 5, 7–8, 10, 12–13, 38, 41, 44, 47, 58, 92, 183, 185, 187, 194, 199–200, 204–205, 207, 213–214, 217, 224, 226, 302, 329, 332, 335, 343–344, 370, 376, 485, 497–498, 500, 503–506
  comprehensive 52, 186, 206

GBA 203, 206, 208, 215, 217, 220
institutional 234, 254, 506
legal 3, 5, 8, 43, 50, 52–53, 55–56, 58–59, 92, 196, 205, 216, 224, 226–227, 352, 355–356, 365, 369–370, 376, 485, 497–499
mandarins v. mandarins 7, 12, 151–152, 154, 156, 158, 160, 162–166, 168–170, 172, 174, 176, 178–180, 182, 492–493, 500
normative 12, 495, 504
theoretical 12, 178, 333, 335, 505

free trade zones (FTZs) 190

freedom 33–34, 124, 128, 163, 225–226, 239, 355, 386–387, 408, 411, 421, 451–452, 454–456, 458, 469, 473
of divorce 451, 454, 456
of marriage 451–452, 454–455
personal 128, 163, 408

FTZs (free trade zones) 190

Fukushima Shigeo 27

functions 3–7, 12–13, 22–23, 25, 51–52, 65–66, 103, 118, 122, 153–156, 167–168, 171, 175, 179, 202, 231, 241–242, 247, 263, 266–268, 279, 290, 348, 351, 358, 399–401, 405, 480, 482, 496–499
anti-corruption 7, 155, 157, 161, 167, 171, 176, 180, 274, 274, 286, 287, 292, 497

fundamental rights 66, 72, 83–84, 88, 92, 210, 469

Fuyang City 109, 114

G

gender 11, 34, 41–42, 44, 46, 48, 52, 56, 450, 452–454
`discrimination 42, 52
equality 41–42, 46, 52, 452–454
imbalance 44, 48

General Data Protection Regulation (GDPR) 204–206

generative AI 465–466, 478, 483

global trade 249–250

globalization 7, 185, 250, 508

gong'an (公安 [public security]) 398, 408, 415, 422, 424–425, 427, 432, 437, 439–440, 442–444

Good Supply Practice Certificate

governance 3–13, 27, 40, 47, 50, 55–56, 60, 70, 84, 92, 106, 117–119, 132, 145, 147, 151–153, 157–158, 160, 163–166, 171–172, 175–180, 183–188, 190–192, 194, 196, 198, 200–206, 208–212, 214–218, 220–225, 228–230, 232–233, 235–236, 238–240, 243–248, 250, 252–254, 259–268, 270–274, 276, 278, 280, 282–286, 288, 290–298, 304, 325–328, 330, 334–335, 342, 343, 346, 376, 385–386, 390–392, 394, 396, 399–400, 405, 409–410, 443, 475–476, 483, 486, 491–503, 505–508
administrative (see administrative governance)
authoritarian (see authoritarian governance)
campaign-style 8, 494, 498–499
capacity 262–263, 268, 273, 392, 399
challenges 5–6, 491, 493, 502, 508
corporate 223–224, 228–230, 232, 235–236, 238, 243, 245–248, 250, 253
data, see data, governance
environmental 117–118, 132, 145, 261, 295, 297, 326–327, 334, 342, 346, 493, 505

and ideology 259
by law 263–264, 291
lazy 259, 261, 265, 270, 294
multi-level 184, 218
objectives 12
of officials 263–264
philosophies 183
priorities 493–494, 499
private 10, 12
quality 508
redress and punishment 282
SOEs 223–224, 232–233, 245–247, 253–254, 334
structures 3, 5, 10, 223, 266, 335, 496–497, 500
authoritarian 3, 60, 496–497
corporate 223, 229, 235–236, 248, 253
systems 4, 399, 496
targeting omission 261
transformation 5, 13, 224, 254, 508
government accountability 101, 298, 300, 400
government agencies 38, 205, 277, 281, 314–315, 483, 495
government control 346, 374, 390, 402, 405, 500
government departments 109, 285, 310–311, 328, 333, 392, 400, 409
government officials 20, 106, 249, 259, 261, 271, 281, 290, 300, 311, 390, 401, 405
governments 47, 50–51, 70, 78, 96, 99, 102–105, 110, 120, 123–125, 129, 131, 134–135, 137–138, 140, 143–145, 170, 200, 202, 221, 248–249, 261, 277–278, 280, 283, 285, 289, 296, 300–301, 303–306, 315, 322, 325–326, 331, 342, 347, 357–358, 367–371, 374, 386, 391, 400, 402, 484, 493–494
municipal 76, 78–83, 85–86, 167, 301, 305, 315, 319, 327, 337
provincial 102, 138, 174, 176, 301, 305, 367, 402
grassroots 9, 20, 267–268, 271–274, 278, 282–283, 285, 326, 345, 358, 384, 389, 399–400, 404, 407, 409–410
courts 20
level 271–272, 274, 282–283, 285, 358, 389, 399–400, 404, 407, 410
organizations 278
Greater Bay Area (see GBA)
grid monitors 399–401, 409–410, 496
grid system 399–400, 405
grievance mechanisms/systems 57, 59
grievances 4, 13, 54, 57, 59, 120, 131, 280, 311, 318, 337, 405, 409, 462, 499
growth 35, 44, 48–49, 224, 226–227, 234, 246, 250, 295, 304, 345, 395
economic 44, 48, 224, 234, 295
GDP 304
population 44, 48
GSP (Good Supply Practice Certificate) 354, 359, 362–363, 365
Guangdong 72, 78–80, 84, 109, 116, 123, 131, 183–184, 186–187, 190–191, 193, 195–200, 208, 211, 213, 301–303, 305–306, 326–330
Guoziwei (国资委 [State-owned Assets Supervision and Administration Commission (SASAC)]) 224, 230–231, 255

H

He Haibo 66, 119, 141

Hainan 80, 127, 166, 426

Haizhu 306

harm, administrative 4, 59–60, 499

harmonization 196, 204, 215, 370, 478

health 40, 120, 133, 346, 348–9, 354, 359, 401

Health and Family Planning Commission (卫生和计划生育委员会 [Weisheng he Jihua ShengyuWeiyuanhui]) 40

healthcare 51–3, 185, 198

hearing procedures 69–70

hearing rights 81, 83, 86–7

Hebei Province 436

hedonism 266, 283

heihaizi [黑孩子 ('black child'; unregistered child)] 41, 61

heirs, male 41–3

Henan 78, 97–8, 129, 409, 432

 Higher People's Court 83, 124, 129

heritage, cultural 160

Hertogh, Marc 4, 56, 484, 491–2, 494

hierarchy 94–5, 333, 352, 354, 357, 366

 administrative 12, 343, 356, 361, 365, 368, 370

 political 7, 13, 88

 social 58

high courts 76–8, 80, 82–3, 124, 129, 131–2, 141, 212

 individual high courts)

Hiraga Letter Event 27

HoAs (homeowners' associations) [业主委员会, Yezhu Weiyuanhui]

 Hong Kong 183–4, 186–99, 201–6, 208–11, 215–6, 239, 418

 companies 198, 210–1, 216–7

 courts 193–4

 PDPO (Personal Data (Privacy) Ordinance) 183, 184, 192, 193, 197, 198, 199, 201, 204, 214, 210–1

hongtou wenjian [红头文件 ('red-headed documents'; official documents with red-printed headers)] 144, 147

*hongyang jiating meide [*弘扬家庭美德 ('promote family virtues')]

horizontal competition 493

hospitals 309, 355, 379, 385, 401, 417, 428

hosting service providers 468–9

household inspections 40, 54

household registration 52, 61

households 40, 44, 386, 390, 394, 396, 398–9

housing 44, 51, 114, 125, 390

 affordability 44–5

Huadu 306, 312, 315

Huangpu 306, 316–7

Hubei Higher People's Court 34, 87

hukou [户口 (household registration system)] 50, 52, 390

human authorship 465

human oversight 10, 475, 486

human resources 77

human review 464

human rights [人权 [*renquan*]] 40, 75, 385, 414, 476

Hunan Province 69, 109–10, 113–4, 135, 400
husbands [丈夫 [*zhangfu*]] 34, 430, 432, 445, 447–8, 452, 456

I

information 206, 401
ideological education 283, 287
ideology 227, 259, 455
Ienaga Saburo 27–8
illegal administrative activities 160, 166, 174, 176–7, 179
illegal content 468–9, 472, 476
illegality 28, 160, 162–3, 166, 170
impartiality 12, 147, 478, 480
implementation 23, 39–40, 53–4, 155–6, 280–2, 326, 338, 499–500
  capacity 9, 12, 13, 302, 358, 365, 373, 494, 503
  challenges 11, 53, 57, 493, 499
  effective 147, 220, 476
  gaps 5, 47, 60
  local 41, 342, 354, 365, 369, 495
  realities 4, 8–9
  regulatory 12, 371
implementers
  local 9, 361–71
  trained 357
implementing agencies 57, 59, 278
incentives 51, 229, 269
  economic 50, 61, 326–27
  positive 282
  independence 19, 21, 31–2, 348, 487, 497
  judicial 4–5, 18, 19, 25–8, 33, 147, 496–7
  individual autonomy 10, 56, 60
  individual rights 9–12, 58–60, 65, 89, 492–495, 499
  industrial and commercial administration [工商行政管理, *gongshang xingzheng guanli*]
  industrial pollution 295, 299, 311–2, 317–8
  control 291–2, 295, 299–300, 302, 308, 311, 315, 317–8
insider control 224, 229, 238
inspection teams 304, 335
inspections, on-site 127, 362
instability, social 168, 456
institutional adaptation 496, 497
institutional conflicts 6, 11, 224, 254, 508
institutional constraints 8, 494, 498
institutional design 3, 9, 122
institutional development 504
institutional dynamics 4, 6–8, 11, 325
institutional innovations 497, 505
institutional reform 157, 169, 233, 348, 368, 370, 502–4
institutional restructuring 9
institutional structures 9, 156, 499
integration 41, 184, 187, 192, 219, 247, 321
  economic 186
  regional 7, 196
intellectual property rights, see IPR
intentions 29, 454
interests
  public, see public interest
  state 134, 207, 500
interference 21, 27–8, 137–8, 234, 244
  local 147, 157, 169

political 245, 497
intermediate people's courts 127, 130, 132–3, 140, 142, 166
International Covenant on Civil and Political Rights (ICCPR) 415
International Covenant Economic, Social and Cultural Rights (ICESCR) 40
international trade 189, 218
interoperability 185, 186, 191, 196, 202, 205, 216–9
interpretation
applicants seeking 24
constitutional 17, 29, 31–4
contents 25
effect 24–5
judicial 25, 31–2, 34–6, 66, 99, 158–9, 162, 443
object 24
unified 24–5, 33
interviews 66, 72, 320, 331, 333, 340
investments 135–6, 228, 336–8
IPR (intellectual property rights) 465
holders 466–7
irregularities 430
procedural 427–8, 430, 434

J

Japan 17, 18, 19, 20, 26, 27, 28, 31, 204, 250, 251, 313, 434, 439, 477
Constitution 17, 18, 19, 20, 26, 27, 28, 31
jiancha jianyi (检察建议 [procuratorial suggestion]) 155, 179, 181
Jiancha Weiyuanhui (监察委员会 [Supervision Commission]) 152, 156, 181, 417
Jiangsu 69, 73, 76, 79, 83, 86, 113, 116, 130, 133, 139, 146, 170, 430, 431, 433, 437, 438, 440
Jiangsu EPB (Envornmental Protection Bureau) 130, 133, 146
Jiangsu High Court 86, 146
Jiangyin 133, 139
Jiangyin Court 133, 139
Jiangyin EPB (Envornmental Protection Bureau) 133
jianzheng fangquan fang guan jiehe youhua fuwu (简政放权 放管结合优化服务 [streamline administration and delegate power and strengthen regulation and improve services]) 350, 377
jiaocha renzhi (交叉任职 [concurrent/overlapping officeholding])
jihua shengyu (计划生育 [birth planning)] 38, 39, 40, 43, 49, 50, 52, 55, 56, 61
Jihua Shengyu Fuwu Zheng (计划生育服务证 [Birth Planning Service Certificate] 61
Jilin Province 347
jingji jili (经济激励 [economic incentives]) 50, 61
Jinshan District Court 127, 128
joint-stock companies 242
joint ventures 334, 339, 340
judges 17, 19, 21, 23, 25, 26, 27, 28, 30, 31, 32, 35, 36, 66, 76, 83, 92, 111, 118, 121, 137, 140, 147, 164, 174, 273, 281, 438, 440, 451, 457
judicial regulations 26, 165

judicial review 5, 6, 7, 12, 17, 18, 20, 22, 24, 26, 28, 29, 30, 32, 34, 35, 36, 55, 59, 60, 91, 92, 93, 94, 95, 96, 97, 98, 99, 100, 101, 102, 103, 104, 105, 106, 108, 109, 110, 111, 112, 114, 116, 117, 118, 119, 121, 122, 124, 125, 126, 129, 130, 132, 133, 134, 137, 139, 140, 143, 144, 145, 146, 147, 151, 209, 210, 212, 219, 440, 493, 500, 501, 505, 507
- American-style judicial review 17, 18, 20, 22, 24, 26, 28, 30, 32, 34, 35, 36
- evolution of judicial review 94, 95
- expansion of judicial review 7, 91
- increasing types of administrative action or omission under judicial review 124
- independent judicial review 60, 507
- system judicial review 17, 19, 23, 25, 32, 33, 36, 500
- timidity and deference in judicial review 106, 111
- weak-form of judicial review 6, 100, 111

judicial supervision 93, 101, 111

judicial system 18, 19, 20, 22, 23, 25, 26, 31, 32, 35, 36, 89, 476
- ideal judicial system 31, 36

judicialization 92, 93, 106, 111, 152, 157, 158, 164, 165, 171, 172, 175, 177, 178, 179, 180, 500

judicialization of administrative governance 152, 158, 164, 165, 171, 172, 175, 177, 178, 179

judiciary 26, 78, 111, 136, 140, 164, 174, 201, 386, 426, 491; (see also courts)

Jumin Weiyuanhui (居民委员会 [urban residents' committees]) 40, 61

jurisdiction(s) 6, 7, 8, 11, 18, 21, 26, 30, 31, 54, 65, 93, 95, 100, 108, 111, 117, 119, 137, 138, 139, 158, 160, 173, 183, 184, 187, 190, 191, 192, 193, 194, 195, 196, 197, 198, 200, 201, 202, 203, 204, 205, 207, 208, 209, 211, 212, 213, 214, 215, 216, 217, 219, 222, 276, 277, 278, 279, 288, 295, 299, 306, 311, 312, 317, 356, 370, 390, 396, 398, 465, 467, 486, 493, 494, 496, 497, 502, 507
- centralized jurisdiction 119, 138, 139, 493

jurisdictional boundaries 494, 502

jurisdictional conflicts 8, 30, 214, 497

justice (see administrative justice)
- substantive justice 505

K

Kaifa 306, 312, 313, 314, 315

knowledge 9, 28, 41, 75, 178, 222, 249, 261, 263, 271, 278, 280, 282, 291, 310, 333, 357, 366, 371, 372, 375, 404, 462, 472, 473, 474, 482, 487, 499, 503
- actual 472, 474, 487
- pharmacological 357, 366
- specialized 9, 375, 503

Kojima Iken 27, 28

L

LPAPS 412, 416, 437, 441, 443

labels, yellow 122, 123, 144, 145

labour 39, 41, 46, 53, 71, 225, 226, 228, 243, 253, 260, 277, 279, 281,

336, 366, 368, 370, 402, 415, 416, 444
division of 243, 402
inspectorate 277, 281
land 5, 7, 74, 75, 76, 77, 78, 79, 80, 81, 85, 87, 94, 100, 109, 110, 111, 114, 115, 116, 119, 122, 123, 124, 125, 133, 134, 154, 156, 160, 165, 166, 169, 170, 183, 192, 194, 195, 196, 198, 205, 206, 208, 224, 260, 269, 287, 289, 312, 313, 342, 398, 418, 420, 428, 431, 433, 441, 494
state-owned 77, 156, 160, 166
use 74, 76, 77, 78, 79, 80, 81, 114, 122, 123
Laodong Jiaoyang (劳动教养 [Re-education Through Labour]) 416, 444
law-and-order cases 411, 414, 422, 432, 435, 442, 444
law enforcement 70, 96, 201, 207, 225, 260, 276, 297, 310, 324, 331, 346, 367, 414, 480, 504
Law of Courts Organizations 19, 20, 23, 26, 28
Law on Penalties for Administration of Public Security (see LPAPS)
lawful rights 120, 123, 131, 154, 155, 244, 289
lawsuits 94, 101, 154, 299, 412, 422, 424, 425, 426, 427, 428, 430, 431, 432, 433, 434, 435, 438
legal certainty 195, 221, 376, 464, 487
legal development 6, 39, 40, 500
legal duties 242, 391
legal experiments 153, 156, 158, 170, 173, 175
legal frameworks 3, 5, 8, 43, 50, 52, 53, 55, 56, 58, 59, 92, 196, 205, 216, 224, 226, 227, 352, 355, 356, 365, 369, 370, 376, 485, 497, 498, 499
comprehensive 8, 55, 497
formal 224, 376
legal innovation 8, 153, 222
legal liability 135, 469, 475
legal persons 69, 84, 94, 99, 108, 120, 121, 123, 126, 134, 161, 359, 360, 464, 465
legal procedures 66, 74, 84, 126, 129, 142, 143, 474, 502
legal reforms 4, 46, 52, 215, 233, 265, 281
legal rights 94, 125, 394
legal rules 103, 117, 233, 289, 290, 388, 492, 501
legal standards 9, 59, 178, 473
legal standing 151, 153, 154, 155, 156, 166, 170, 173, 180
legal supervision 122, 153, 172, 181
legal systems 7, 8, 26, 31, 58, 65, 66, 91, 92, 94, 95, 100, 103, 104, 151, 155, 183, 184, 194, 198, 208, 212, 216, 220, 222, 228, 233, 234, 264, 271, 347, 352, 412, 413, 414, 495, 500
continental 31, 65
multiple 8, 222
socialist 66, 92
legal uncertainties 216, 221, 471, 473, 476, 486
legalisation 28, 265, 266, 291
legality 6, 28, 65, 68, 71, 79, 87, 97, 98, 99, 101, 102, 104, 105, 106, 107, 108, 109, 110, 142, 143, 144, 145, 151, 160, 162, 163, 166, 170, 178, 179, 180, 181, 472, 493, 505
of ANDs 99, 106, 108, 109, 110
formal 104, 151, 181

review 71, 101, 107, 142, 143, 145

substantive 71, 88, 151, 181

legally prescribed procedures 67, 71, 72, 75, 84

legislation 33, 35, 36, 38, 41, 42, 50, 52, 55, 66, 67, 69, 70, 72, 73, 74, 75, 82, 83, 86, 88, 91, 92, 93, 95, 96, 103, 104, 111, 120, 151, 162, 201, 206, 207, 220, 221, 228, 243, 260, 279, 281, 299, 301, 345, 347, 352, 353, 354, 369, 370, 374, 391, 395, 411, 412, 413, 415, 421, 443, 446, 452, 463, 464, 467, 470, 471, 472, 473, 474, 475, 476, 479, 491;

see also statutes

administrative 67, 74, 83, 345, 347

local 70, 369, 391

legislative reforms 119, 137, 147, 198, 220

legislature 28, 31, 66, 91, 101, 103, 151, 152, 153, 158, 386, 413

legitimacy 27, 32, 36, 57, 73, 75, 87, 184, 187, 204, 209, 211, 212, 216, 219, 221, 224, 225, 227, 228, 235, 253, 260, 262, 266, 297, 324, 340, 343, 376, 416, 456, 499

party 225, 260, 262

perceived 211, 219

legitimating functions 7, 496

leniency 317, 426

Letter and Visits and 'xinfang'')

levels of government 47, 103, 261, 266, 272, 345, 356, 369, 392, 399;

see also individual levels

leverage 180, 193, 196, 238, 246, 324, 371, 485

Li Huijuan 98

liability 135, 168, 242, 279, 281, 290, 415, 421, 461, 462, 463, 468, 469, 470, 471, 472, 474, 475, 486

legal 135, 469, 475

liberal democracies 385, 386, 387, 495

liberal democratic ideals 493, 495

licencees 360, 362, 373

licenses 9, 68, 69, 74, 84, 85, 117, 118, 120, 124, 125, 130, 131, 132, 144, 146, 191, 311, 312, 314, 317, 318, 340, 353, 356, 358, 359, 360, 361, 362, 363, 364, 365, 366, 371, 372, 373, 374, 375, 378, 494

administrative 68, 74, 85, 117, 118, 120, 124, 125, 129, 130, 131, 132, 146, 288

business 311, 312, 317, 318, 359, 360

overflow of 371, 373

lifetime responsibility 281, 282

lihai guanxi (利害关系[with interest in]) 120, 121, 130, 147

lihun lengjiqi zhidu (离婚冷静期制度 [divorce cooling-off system]) 451, 460

Limited Liability Companies (LLCs) 242

Linzhou City Court 133, 134

litigation 7, 12, 20, 34, 38, 42, 43, 51, 55, 56, 62, 65, 69, 71, 75, 77, 78, 85, 86, 87, 88, 89, 91, 93, 94, 95, 97, 98, 99, 100, 101, 105, 106, 107, 110, 111, 117, 118, 119, 120, 121, 122, 123, 127, 130, 133, 137, 139, 140, 141, 142

local level 40, 42, 103, 117, 135, 152, 157, 261, 266, 271, 272, 273, 274, 275, 278, 296, 303, 304, 319, 342, 345, 359, 373, 374, 494 local officials 40, 42, 54, 271, 275, 280, 283, 292, 296, 304, 376, 494, 497, 499

local police stations 417, 419, 420, 421, 428, 431, 440, 444

local procuratorates 154, 169, 175, 419

local protectionism 6, 9, 138, 139, 234, 345, 346, 357, 358, 371, 375, 496

local regulations 40, 41, 69, 72, 88, 96, 98, 129, 301, 329

local residents 27, 313, 318, 390, 392

lockdowns 383, 385, 386, 387, 402, 403, 404, 405, 406, 409, 410, 434, 437

logistics 183, 190, 217

losses 131, 132, 135, 290, 331, 339, 342, 343, 457

- economic 132, 134, 135
- job 341

low-visibility police oppression 10, 412, 421

lower courts 19, 23, 25, 26, 28, 35, 72, 76, 88, 106, 107, 109, 135, 136, 138

LPAPS (Law on Penalties for Administration of Public Security) 411, 412, 414, 415, 416, 418, 422, 423, 424, 425, 426, 430, 432, 433, 434, 437, 438, 439, 440, 441, 442, 443, 444, 504

- Articles 428, 430, 431, 432, 433, 434, 435, 438, 439, 441
- cases 422, 424, 437, 438, 442, 443
- enforcement 411, 412, 418, 422, 440, 443
- historical evolution 412
- lawsuits appealing penalty
- decisions 424, 425, 426
- misuse 412, 421, 443
- new safeguards and protection of human rights 411, 414, 438, 442
- offences 411, 414, 415, 419, 437, 438, 439
- offenders 411, 421, 424, 426, 437, 439, 442, 443
- penalties 411, 414, 415, 424, 426, 432, 433, 434, 437, 438, 439, 441, 442
- penalty decisions 424, 426, 432, 438, 439
- penalty records 433, 434
- police powers 411, 412, 415, 421
- and political oppression 412, 421, 441
- rationales for continuing existence 416
- revision 411, 442
- safeguards appeal mechanisms and efficiency 437

Luoyang City Intermediate Court 97, 98

lying flat 259, 261, 262, 263, 264, 265, 266, 269, 270, 271, 282, 283, 284, 285, 286, 287, 288, 291, 292, 293

leadership 266–7, 291

M

Ma Zhiyong 455, 456

Macao 183, 184, 186, 187, 189, 190, 192, 193, 194, 195, 196, 197, 198, 199, 200, 201, 203, 204, 205, 206, 208, 209, 212, 213, 214, 215, 216, 219, 220, 494

- law 195, 198
- Office for Personal Data Protection 194, 195, 198, 213

whitelist mechanism 195

mainland 3, 5, 25, 44, 87, 183, 184, 186, 187, 188, 189, 190, 191, 192, 193, 194, 195, 196, 197, 198, 199, 200, 201, 202, 204, 205, 206, 207, 208, 209, 210, 211, 212, 213, 214, 216, 218, 219, 273, 295, 388, 418, 494, 507

authorities 200, 210, 213

courts 200, 213, 214

regulators 194, 202

male heirs 38, 41, 42, 43

malpractices 415, 426, 428, 434, 435

police 415, 426, 428

management 9, 41, 42, 49, 50, 51, 53, 56, 82, 96, 100, 104, 110, 121, 124, 129, 130, 135, 146, 157, 167, 168, 169, 176, 199, 200, 210, 218, 226, 227, 231, 237, 239, 245, 246, 247, 253, 269, 270, 272, 273, 276, 277, 278, 285, 290, 296, 297, 303, 305, 309, 314, 326, 331, 332, 333, 334, 335, 336, 339, 341, 346, 348, 349, 351, 357, 358, 361, 362, 364, 374, 378, 385, 388, 389, 390, 391, 392, 393, 394, 397, 398, 399, 400, 401, 405, 406, 411, 414, 431, 462, 467, 475, 485, 496, 498, 502

crisis 388, 389, 405

environmental 296, 297, 303, 333, 335, 336, 339, 374

population 56, 390

senior 245, 246, 247

of society 411

urban 389, 394, 405

mass surveillance 389, 408

material resources 157, 372, 385

matrimonial home 451, 452

MDDL (Medical Devices Distribution License) 360, 363, 365

media 26, 27, 51, 55, 56, 57, 59, 72, 73, 74, 75, 79, 84, 85, 90, 97, 98, 117, 124, 127, 129, 130, 131, 132, 133, 134, 135, 136, 138, 139, 140, 141, 142, 146, 158, 160, 161, 166, 168, 169, 176, 177, 189, 192, 194, 213, 219, 228, 259, 268, 280, 296, 304, 305, 311, 313, 315, 318, 322, 328, 339, 340, 342, 344, 345, 368, 375, 388, 389, 394, 395, 397, 398, 399, 405, 406, 407, 417, 419, 425, 430, 431, 434, 436, 437, 448, 453, 455, 457, 458, 459, 461, 462, 467, 469, 471, 472, 474, 475, 476, 478, 485, 486, 492, 493, 495, 499

attention 177, 318

social see social media

state 56, 417, 419

mediation 55, 56, 57, 59, 140, 141, 169, 389, 397, 398, 419, 425, 430, 431, 437, 448, 455, 457, 459, 471

medical devices 348, 349, 354, 355, 357, 358, 360, 363, 365

Medical Devices Distribution License (MDDL) 360, 363, 365

Medical Insurance Designated Retail Pharmacy Agreement (MIDRPA) 360, 363, 365

medical treatment 355, 417, 432, 434

medicine 72, 168, 285, 286, 346, 348, 349, 355, 360, 361, 364, 366, 370, 377, 379, 383, 385, 403, 404, 436

Chinese herbal 360, 366

MEE (Ministry of Ecology Environment) 122, 145, 305, 327

MEM (Ministry of Emergency Management) 176, 276

Memoranda of Understanding (see MoUs)

Meta 474, 475, 478, 485

MIDRPA (Medical Insurance Designated Retail Pharmacy Agreement) 360, 363, 365

mining rights 132, 134, 135

Ministry of Ecology Environment (MEE) 122, 133, 145, 305, 327, 328, 335

Ministry of Emergency Management (MEM) 176, 276

Ministry of Health (MoH) 40, 347, 348, 349, 350, 351, 352, 356

Ministry of Human Resources Social Security (MOHRSS) 277

Ministry of Natural Resources (MNR) 145

Ministry of Public Security (MPS) 422, 437, 439, 440

minor offences 10, 416

minors' protection 170

misconduct 42, 46, 161, 230, 275, 369, 415, 438, 443, 449, 456, 495

police 415, 443

mistresses 430, 456

MNR (Ministry of Natural Resources) 145

mobilisation 262, 286, 305, 325, 327, 338, 339, 385, 388, 410

community 410

political 8, 12, 325, 338, 339, 501

mobility 185, 333, 387, 397, 403, 404, 407

social 333, 396, 407

model cases 76, 89, 117, 118, 122, 124, 126, 129, 130, 135, 136, 141, 144, 145

moderation tools AI-powered 461, 462, 463, 464, 473, 474, 475, 476, 486, 505

modernisation 18, 71, 73, 101, 262, 263, 268, 270

MoH (see Ministry of Health)

MOHRSS (Ministry of Human Resources and Social Security) 277

monitoring 117, 127, 133, 142, 146, 220, 225, 230, 242, 266, 296, 297, 300, 302, 304, 305, 309, 310, 311, 312, 315, 316, 317, 318, 319, 322, 323, 326, 331, 338, 343, 384, 389, 391, 396, 398, 399, 400, 407, 408, 468, 469, 473, 474, 486, 506

central 304, 305

environmental 127, 142

obligations 468, 469, 473, 474, 486

on-site 315, 316

real-time 146, 312

moral conservatism 448, 453

MoUs (Memoranda of Understanding) 186, 197, 199, 201, 219

MPS (see Ministry of Public Security)

multi-level governance 184, 218

N

Nanjing Intermediate People's Court 133, 139, 146

Nansha 306, 312, 313, 314, 315

narcotic drugs 349, 352, 353, 354, 361

National Copyright Administration of China (NCAC) 461, 477

nature reserves 124, 129, 135

negative media coverage 311, 318

negotiation 161, 162, 175, 176, 177, 178, 180, 181, 241, 336, 453, 502, 503, 504 neighbourhood police 390, 396

'New Era' 264, 268, 284, 285, 286, 291, 350

NGOs (see non-governmental organizations)

NHC (see National Health Commission)

Nicholas II tsar 27

'nine dragons taming a river' (*jiu long zhi shui* [九龙治水]) 350, 367, 377

Ningbo City 102, 109, 115, 116

NMPA (National Medical Products Administration) 176, 349, 350, 351, 352, 353, 354, 357, 358, 359, 367, 377

noise pollution 133, 298, 299, 302, 329, 330, 414

non-compliance 132, 199, 240, 310, 332, 339, 342, 343, 384, 386, 493

non-governmental organizations (NGOs) 119, 134, 154, 166, 296, 298, 402

non-personal datasets 217

non-prescription drugs 350, 354, 357, 360, 361, 362

nonfeasance 154, 155, 158, 160, 161, 163, 164, 165, 166, 168, 169, 174, 179, 181

administrative 160, 161, 163, 165, 169, 179, 181

normative documents 51, 79, 93, 96, 97, 98, 99, 100, 101, 102, 104, 111, 112, 122, 125, 144, 179, 352, 437, 440

normative frameworks 12, 495, 504

notice and takedown procedures 467, 469, 470, 471, 473, 474, 476, 478, 481, 486

notifications 68, 74, 78, 79, 87, 171, 198, 211, 212, 269, 284, 286, 290, 471, 473, 481

NPC (see National People's Congress)

NPCSC (see National People's Congress Standing Committee)

O

obnoxious odours 127

ODR (see online dispute resolution)

OECD (see Organisation for Economic Co-operation and Development)

offences 10, 27, 280, 291, 300, 411, 412, 414, 415, 416, 419, 421, 423, 425, 426, 427, 428, 432, 435, 437, 438, 439, 441, 443, 444

LPAPS 411, 414, 415, 419, 437, 438, 439

minor 10, 416

offenders 10, 278, 279, 398, 411, 414, 415, 416, 421, 424, 426, 427, 428, 429, 430, 431, 432, 433, 434, 435, 437, 438, 439, 440, 441, 442, 443

alleged 415

LPAPS 411, 421, 424, 426, 437, 439, 442, 443

Office of Administrative Supervision 157

officials 8, 9, 20, 25, 39, 40, 41, 42, 45, 49, 50, 53, 54, 56, 66, 67, 96, 105, 106, 155, 156, 161, 165, 174, 189, 192, 193, 200, 211, 213, 214, 215, 219, 239, 246, 249, 259, 260, 261, 262, 263, 264, 265, 266, 267, 268, 269, 270, 271, 272, 273, 274, 275, 276, 278, 279, 280, 281, 282, 283, 284, 285, 286, 287, 288, 289, 290, 291, 292, 293, 294, 295, 296, 297, 298, 300, 302, 304, 305, 306, 310, 311, 313, 314, 317, 318, 319, 323, 346, 349, 352, 357, 358, 367,

368, 369, 371, 372, 375, 376, 390, 392, 393, 395, 400, 401, 402, 405, 406, 407, 419, 422, 423, 425, 445, 446, 448, 449, 450, 453, 457, 475, 480, 491, 493, 494, 495, 497, 498, 499, 503, 507

governance of 263, 264

government 106, 249, 259, 261, 271, 281, 289, 300, 311, 390, 401, 405

local 40, 42, 54, 271, 275, 280, 283, 296, 304, 376, 494, 497, 499

lying flat 259, 261, 262, 264, 270, 283, 284, 285, 287, 288, 290, 291, 292

mediocre 261, 270, 294

party 238, 259, 262, 269, 288, 305

omissions 87, 101, 117, 118, 119, 120, 122, 124, 132, 141, 147, 161, 163, 259, 260, 261, 264, 265, 282, 288, 289, 483

administrative 117, 132

on-site inspection/monitoring 127, 304, 305, 316, 362, 363

one-child policy 39, 40, 44, 45, 48, 387, 409

'One Country Two Systems' 7, 183, 184, 186, 193

online content 461, 463, 468, 469, 474, 476, 478, 485

online dispute resolution (ODR) 461, 484

online platforms 133, 219, 474

original intention 29, 261, 262, 268, 270

overwork 261, 263, 265, 270, 271, 274, 282, 283, 287, 291, 292, 498

owners 74, 77, 80, 86, 121, 125, 130, 142, 145, 167, 230, 231, 232, 236, 237, 238, 239, 243, 249, 250, 314, 315, 317, 334, 343, 390, 393, 394, 395, 396, 403, 428, 434, 452, 461, 465, 467, 469, 471, 474, 475, 477, 485, 486

ownership 74, 77, 80, 125, 231, 232, 236, 237, 238, 239, 243, 249, 250, 334, 343, 394, 452, 467, 485, 486

reform 235

P

paichusuo (派出所 [police station]) 390, 410, 417, 419, 428, 435, 440, 444

PAL (see Pharmaceutical Administration Law)

pandemics 9, 11, 14, 265, 383, 384, 385, 386, 387, 388, 389, 390, 391, 392, 393, 394, 395, 396, 398, 400, 401, 402, 403, 404, 405, 406, 407, 408, 409, 410, 412, 426, 427, 434, 441, 496, 502

control 12, 383, 384, 385, 386, 387, 388, 390, 391, 392, 394, 395, 396, 398, 400, 401, 402, 403, 404, 405, 406, 408, 410, 502

Panyu 306, 316, 317, 318, 319

parastate organisations 390, 392

parents 45, 415, 452, 453

parliamentary sovereignty 35

participation 4, 60, 65, 68, 69, 73, 81, 117, 130, 132, 133, 146, 178, 191, 195, 207, 209, 212, 217, 220, 235, 245, 247, 385, 388, 391, 392, 394, 395, 403, 405, 409, 410, 505, 507, 508

citizen 4, 60, 505, 507, 508

public 117, 130, 132, 133

rights 69, 73, 212

party committees (CCP) 8, 110, 137, 174, 176, 223, 224, 226, 228, 229, 230, 231, 232, 234, 235, 236, 237, 238, 239, 240, 242, 244, 245, 246,

247, 248, 250, 252, 253, 254, 277, 289, 290, 304, 436, 437

involvement in SOEs 7, 223, 224, 226, 228, 230, 232, 234, 235, 236, 238, 239, 240, 242, 244, 245, 246, 247, 248, 250, 252, 254

local 137

members 238, 239, 240, 246, 253

party discipline 12, 270, 271, 280, 283, 287, 288, 291, 292

party leadership 264, 266, 270, 291

party legitimacy 260, 262

party members 231, 236, 237, 238, 245, 246, 247, 248, 253, 261, 264, 268, 284, 290, 291, 395, 401, 402

party officials 239, 259, 262, 269, 288, 305

party organizations 110, 111, 226, 235, 236, 237, 239, 244, 245, 247

party sanctions 284, 287, 290, 292

party secretaries 237, 255, 431, 436

party-state 3, 4, 5, 14, 55, 65, 88, 89, 105, 156, 157, 169, 191, 224, 232, 253, 254, 259, 387, 389, 390, 493, 495, 497, 503

Patriotic Health Campaign 327

PCPD (Privacy Commissioner Personal Data) 184, 189, 192, 193, 197, 200, 203, 212, 213, 214, 219

PDPO (Personal Data [Privacy] Ordinance) 183, 192, 197, 199

Pearl River Delta region 327, 335

peichang (赔偿 government compensation) 86, 134, 135, 136, 147, 168

penalties 6, 7, 10, 13, 39, 40, 42, 43, 50, 52, 67, 68, 69, 70, 71, 72, 73, 77, 78, 92, 117, 118, 124, 125, 126, 127, 128, 139, 142, 143, 209, 269, 279, 296, 297, 298, 300, 301, 302, 303, 310, 314, 317, 329, 330, 331, 332, 333, 339, 353, 355, 360, 372, 406, 411, 412, 413, 414, 415, 416, 422, 424, 425, 426, 427, 428, 429, 430, 431, 432, 433, 434, 435, 436, 437, 438, 439, 440, 441, 442, 444, 477, 480, 504; see also sanctions

administrative 10, 50, 67, 68, 69, 70, 71, 72, 73, 77, 78, 92, 117, 118, 124, 125, 126, 127, 128, 139, 142, 143, 302, 303, 329, 330, 360, 416, 425, 434, 438, 477

LPAPS 411, 414, 415, 416, 424, 426, 432, 433, 434, 437, 438, 439, 441, 442, 504

stricter 296, 300, 301, 310

penalty decisions 68, 124, 125, 126, 127, 128, 139, 142, 143, 302, 314, 317, 412, 414, 415, 422, 424, 426, 427, 428, 429, 432, 434, 435, 436, 437, 438, 439, 440, 442

police 414, 422, 424, 426, 428, 429, 440

People's Procuratorates (see procuratorates)

performance indicators 273, 274

permit-holders 129, 131, 355, 378

permits 24, 31, 40, 43, 50, 52, 54, 59, 62, 68, 77, 78, 121, 125, 126

pharmaceutical administration 346, 347, 348, 349, 350, 351, 352, 353, 355, 356, 357, 358, 359, 360, 361, 362, 365, 366, 367, 368, 369, 370, 371, 372, 373, 374, 375

law 346, 353, 354, 355, 356, 360, 361, 365, 369, 370, 371, 378

legal framework 352, 355, 369

recentralization and local implementers 347, 373, 375

regulating drug retailing 346, 354, 359, 365, 372, 373, 374, 375

pharmaceutical administrative laws 347

pharmaceutical administrative power 346, 351, 356, 375

pharmaceutical market 354, 362

pharmaceutical regulation 9, 367, 494, 507

pharmacies retail 346, 347, 359, 360, 361, 362, 363, 364, 365, 368, 370, 371, 373, 374

picking quarrels 10, 414, 420, 423, 432, 439, 444

PIL (see public interest litigation)

Pingzheng Yuan (平政院 [Administrative Appellate Court]) 20, 22, 30, 34, 37

PIPL (see Personal Information Protection Law)

plaintiffs 71, 74, 77, 78, 79, 85, 86, 97, 111, 117, 119, 120, 121, 122, 127, 128, 135, 136, 137, 138, 140, 141, 143, 144, 146, 173, 181, 425, 426, 436, 457

platform providers 462

platforms 10, 12, 66, 133, 156, 161, 171, 191, 196, 211, 216, 219, 264, 358, 394, 399, 400, 405, 408, 410, 461, 462, 467, 468, 469, 470, 471, 472, 474, 475, 476, 477, 478, 480, 484, 485, 486, 502

PLMI (Practicing License for Medical Institution) 360, 364, 365

PMCs (see property management companies)

police 6, 10, 13, 76, 105, 260, 275, 281, 297, 389, 390, 391, 396, 397, 398, 400, 401, 406, 407, 408, 410, 411, 412, 413, 414, 415, 416, 417, 418, 419, 420, 421, 422, 423, 424, 425, 426, 427, 428, 429, 430, 431, 432, 433, 434, 435, 436, 437, 438, 439, 440, 441, 442, 443, 444, 451, 504

abuses 415, 438, 440

discretion 412, 443

interrogation 436, 438

local stations 417, 419, 420, 421, 428, 431, 440, 444

low-visibility oppression 10, 412, 421

malpractices 415, 426, 428

misconduct 415, 443

neighbourhood 390, 396

officers 398, 411, 413, 415, 418, 419, 420, 421, 431, 437, 438, 439, 441

oppression 10, 412, 421, 443

penalties 6, 10, 414, 416, 422, 424, 426, 427, 428, 440, 441

penalty decisions 414, 422, 424, 426, 428, 429, 440

powers 10, 389, 411, 412, 414, 415, 416, 417, 418, 420, 421, 422, 424, 426, 428, 430, 432, 434, 436, 438, 440, 442, 443, 444, 504

LPAPS 411, 412, 415, 421

punishments 406, 408

stations 390, 396, 410, 417, 419, 420, 421, 428, 431, 440, 444

violence 421

policies 3, 4, 5, 6, 8, 9, 10, 11, 13, 14, 38, 39, 40, 41, 42, 43, 44, 45, 46, 47, 48, 49, 50, 51, 52, 53, 54, 55, 56, 57, 58, 59, 60, 61, 62, 66, 67, 70, 76, 89, 92, 93, 94, 104, 105, 106, 131, 136, 144, 145, 160, 164, 165, 168, 169, 170, 171, 175, 176, 180, 183, 185, 186, 187, 189, 191, 199, 200, 202, 204, 209, 210, 211, 212, 214, 215, 216, 218, 221, 222, 226, 227, 231, 240, 244, 251, 252,

260, 261, 264, 265, 267, 275, 277, 281, 282, 283, 284, 288, 296, 297, 302, 303, 304, 305, 325, 326, 327, 328, 330, 333, 335, 336, 337, 338, 341, 345, 346, 350, 355, 359, 367, 373, 384, 385, 386, 387, 388, 389, 390, 391, 392, 396, 397, 398, 399, 400, 401, 404, 406, 407, 408, 409, 410, 493, 495, 496, 497, 499, 504, 505, 507

administrative 42, 170, 171, 481, 483

drug 346, 350, 355

environmental 326, 327, 336, 341, 493, 505

population 38, 40, 42, 44, 46, 48, 50, 52, 54, 56, 57, 58, 59, 60, 62, 496

pronatalist 11, 38, 45, 46, 47, 48, 49, 56, 57, 60

proposals 209, 214, 215

reproductive 55, 57, 60

policing 260, 264, 265, 275, 284, 385, 390, 392, 396, 397, 398, 399, 410, 412, 442, 463, 474

community 264, 265, 284, 385, 397, 398, 410

policy goals 169, 170, 455, 495

political hierarchies 7, 88

population 5, 10, 11, 14, 38, 39, 40, 41, 42, 43, 44, 46, 47, 48, 49, 50, 51, 52, 53, 54, 55, 56, 57, 58, 59, 60, 61, 62, 183, 227, 361, 363, 383, 384, 389, 390, 396, 398, 402, 404, 421, 450, 496

ageing 10, 39, 43, 44, 48, 53, 56

control 10, 14, 38, 39, 40, 42, 43

policies 38, 40, 42, 44, 46, 48, 50, 52, 54, 56, 57, 58, 59, 60, 62, 496

quality 51, 61

Population and Birth Planning Law 38, 41, 48, 49, 55

population management 56, 390

power 3, 4, 5, 6, 7, 8, 9, 10, 11, 12, 13, 14, 17, 18, 19, 20, 21, 23, 24, 25, 26, 27, 28, 29, 30, 31, 32, 33, 35, 36, 40, 45, 49, 51, 54, 56, 57, 58, 59, 60, 63, 65, 66, 76, 88, 89, 91, 92, 93, 94, 97, 98, 99, 100, 102, 103, 104, 105, 106, 111, 117, 119, 122, 125, 126, 131, 136, 138, 141, 143, 144, 149, 151, 152, 153, 154, 155, 156, 160, 161, 163, 164, 165, 168, 170, 171, 172, 175, 177, 180, 181, 184, 195, 199, 202, 204, 205, 207, 209, 211, 212, 216, 219, 224, 225, 229, 230, 231, 232, 233, 234, 235, 238, 239, 240, 241, 242, 246, 247, 248, 249, 250, 254, 259, 260, 262, 263, 264, 265, 266, 268, 271, 273, 274, 276, 277, 278, 279, 281, 282, 285, 288, 291, 292, 298, 300, 302, 304, 305, 309, 310, 311, 313, 314, 315, 316, 317, 319, 322, 323, 324, 326, 327, 328, 329, 330, 332, 333, 334, 335, 336, 337, 338, 339, 340, 341, 342, 343, 344, 345, 346, 347, 348, 350, 351, 356, 358, 366, 367, 369, 371, 372, 373, 374, 375, 376, 377, 381, 383, 384, 386, 387, 388, 389, 390, 392, 401, 405, 406, 410, 411, 412, 413, 414, 415, 416, 417, 418, 420, 421, 422, 424, 426, 428, 430, 432, 434, 436, 438, 440, 442, 443, 444, 445, 448, 461, 462, 463, 464, 466, 467, 473, 474, 475, 476, 478, 479, 484, 485, 486, 487, 491, 492, 493, 494, 495, 496, 497, 499, 500, 501, 502, 504, 505, 507, 508

abuse of 143, 151, 181, 266, 305

administrative 4, 5, 7, 8, 9, 10, 13, 18, 21, 23, 28, 35, 60, 105, 164, 219, 224, 260, 263, 273, 276, 324, 345, 346, 347, 351, 356, 366, 375, 381, 413, 424, 491, 500, 501, 504, 505, 507

imbalances 57, 496, 507
judicial 7, 17, 18, 19, 20, 21, 28, 30, 31, 32, 63, 91, 92, 105, 125
public 35, 165, 492
redistribution 5, 6, 149, 495
relationships 143, 497, 499, 507, 508
state 4, 5, 9, 10, 11, 58, 59, 65, 66, 122, 250, 254, 259, 374, 390, 496, 499, 504, 508
unified 19, 23, 24, 36
power generation 333, 334, 335, 336, 337, 339, 340, 341, 343
power industry 326, 334, 335, 341
power plants 316, 324, 326, 327, 328, 334, 335, 336, 337, 338, 339, 340, 341, 342, 343, 344, 504
coal 324, 327, 334, 335, 336, 337, 338, 339, 340, 341, 342, 343, 344, 504
gas-fired 328, 340
self-supply 334, 335, 340
powers
discretionary 54, 76, 302, 329, 371
enforcement 117, 125, 276, 279, 282, 298, 300, 313, 315, 319, 322, 323, 485
police 10, 389, 411, 412, 414, 415, 416, 417, 418, 420, 421, 422, 424, 426, 428, 430, 432, 434, 436, 438, 440, 442, 443, 444, 504
separation of 19, 21, 152, 246
Practicing License for a Medical Institution (PLMI) 360, 364, 365
pre-litigation negotiation 161, 162, 164, 175, 176, 177, 178, 179, 180, 493
pressures economic 44, 48, 58, 228
prices 44, 45
housing 44, 45
prima facie evidence 218, 470, 473
privacy 84, 183, 184, 185, 189, 192, 193, 194, 197, 199, 200, 201, 203, 204, 205, 206, 207, 208, 209, 212, 214, 215, 216, 217, 218, 219, 220, 389, 408, 469, 473
Privacy Commissioner for Personal Data (PCPD) 184, 189, 192, 193, 197, 200, 202, 212, 213, 214, 219
Privacy Shield 205, 207, 208
private enterprises 249, 338
private parties 119, 122, 153, 157, 162, 163, 166
procuratorate-administration relationship 152, 153, 155, 162, 163, 171
procuratorate-initiated APIL 7, 151, 152, 153, 155, 157, 158, 159, 160, 164, 165, 170, 171, 172, 173, 174, 175, 176, 177, 179, 180, 501
influences regarding judicialization of administrative governance 180
practice 153, 154, 158, 165, 172, 174, 176
rise 152, 155, 157
system 7, 152, 153, 154, 155, 158, 165, 170, 171, 173, 175, 180, 493, 497
procuratorates 7, 11, 12, 26, 117, 118, 121, 122, 151, 152, 153, 154, 155, 156, 157, 158, 159, 160, 161, 162, 163, 164, 165, 166, 167, 168, 169, 170, 171, 172, 173, 174, 175, 176, 177, 178, 179, 180, 181, 408, 413, 415, 418, 419, 440, 443, 493, 495, 497, 501
local 154, 169, 175, 419
provincial 157, 169

procuratorial organs 153, 156, 157, 158, 159, 160, 161, 163, 164, 165, 171, 172, 173, 174, 175, 176, 177, 178, 179, 180

procuratorial suggestions 158, 161, 162, 166, 167, 168, 170, 171, 175, 176, 177, 178, 179, 180, 181

procurators chief 155, 162

professional expertise 9, 375, 503

pronatalist policies 11, 38, 44, 45, 46, 47, 48, 49, 50, 53, 54, 56, 57, 59, 60

property 10, 52, 73, 74, 77, 86, 102, 109, 124, 125, 126, 128, 154, 156, 160, 163, 166, 167, 169, 269, 288, 289, 355, 361, 390, 391, 393, 394, 395, 414, 435, 436, 437, 439, 446, 448, 449, 452, 457, 461, 462, 465, 467, 472, 474, 478, 480, 482, 487, 496

expropriation 102, 109

residential 449

rights 269, 289, 393, 394, 395, 465, 467

property management companies (PMCs) 10, 390, 391, 393, 394, 396, 398, 496

protection 8, 12, 13, 46, 49, 51, 52, 55, 58, 59, 60, 65, 88, 89, 119, 124, 131, 137, 154, 156, 160, 166, 169, 177, 183, 184, 192, 194, 195, 198, 204, 205, 206, 207, 213, 214, 219, 260, 263, 393, 394, 414, 445, 459, 461, 462, 465, 467, 472, 474, 476, 478, 480, 482, 486, 491, 495, 496

consumers 156, 445

copyright see copyright

environmental see

environmental protection

personal data 183, 192, 194, 195, 198, 204, 205, 206, 207, 213, 219

rights 8, 12, 13, 46, 52, 56, 59, 65, 88, 89, 119, 137, 160, 177, 184, 214, 260, 263, 393, 394, 414, 459, 465, 467, 476, 491, 495

of state-owned property 156, 160, 169

protectionism local 6, 9, 138, 139, 157, 169, 234, 345, 346, 357, 358, 371, 375, 493, 496

provinces 17, 31, 41, 43, 44, 46, 47, 48, 53, 58, 69, 70, 71, 73, 74, 78, 80, 84, 92, 93, 97, 98, 100, 101, 102, 108, 109, 110, 113, 114, 115, 116, 135, 137, 138, 139, 153, 156, 160, 166, 167, 168, 169, 170, 176, 197, 301, 303, 304, 305, 306, 326, 327, 329, 330, 335, 341, 347, 384, 387, 391, 400, 401, 402, 427, 428, 430, 431, 432, 433, 434, 435, 436, 437, 438, 439, 440, 441, 461; see also individual provinces

provincial capitals 19, 26, 347

provincial governments 102, 138, 174, 176, 301, 305, 367, 402

provincial level 9, 76, 157, 354, 356, 357, 358, 359, 367, 368, 370, 371, 378, 407

provincial-level agencies 358, 367

psychotropic drugs 353, 354, 361

public complaints 127, 128, 133, 134, 312, 316, 318, 333

public expectations 311, 315, 318

public health 10, 45, 123, 129, 131, 179, 359, 383, 385, 386, 387, 391, 404, 405, 406, 407

public interest 13, 70, 86, 117, 118, 121, 131, 134, 136, 140, 141, 151, 153, 154, 155, 156, 158, 159, 160, 161, 162, 163, 166, 167, 170, 171, 172, 173, 174, 175, 176, 177, 178,

179, 180, 181, 187, 188, 194, 211, 215, 243, 244, 493, 505

public interest litigation (PIL) 118, 121, 151, 152, 153, 154, 155, 156

Q

Qing dynasty 6, 18, 19, 22, 23, 25, 36, 243, 412

quality assurance 328, 350, 367

quarantine 277, 288, 290, 350, 383, 387, 392, 401, 403, 407

non-residential 403

quarrels, picking and provoking trouble (*xunxin zishi* [寻衅滋事]) 10, 414, 420, 423, 432, 439, 444

R

radioactive drugs 361

RCs (see Residential Committees)

real-time monitoring 146, 312

reasonableness 94, 99, 101, 105, 143, 151

recentralization 9, 346, 347, 365, 366, 367, 371, 373, 374, 375, 379, 503

reckless divorces 447, 454, 458, 459, 460

recognition 190, 196, 199, 218

mutual 190, 196, 199, 218

reconciliation 453, 455

reconsideration 51, 62, 65, 73, 74, 80, 81, 82, 83, 84, 85, 86, 87, 123, 129, 147, 164, 209, 210, 281, 414, 439

administrative 51, 65, 73, 74, 79, 81, 82, 83, 84, 85, 86, 123, 129, 164, 209, 210, 281, 414, 439

decisions 73, 80, 82, 85, 86

rectification 128, 129, 141, 144, 160, 260, 261, 264, 269, 283, 284, 285, 286, 287, 290, 291, 292, 305, 335

campaigns 260, 283, 284, 286, 287, 290, 291

special 283, 284, 285, 286, 287, 290, 292

specialist 269, 284, 286, 287, 292

redress 4, 13, 49, 54, 59, 61, 117, 119, 120, 130, 133, 138, 207, 209, 213, 215, 216, 221, 259, 282, 283, 287, 291, 462, 479, 492, 495, 499

judicial 117, 119, 120, 138, 209

mechanisms/systems 54, 61, 207, 209, 215, 479

reforms 3, 4, 5, 6, 7, 8, 9, 12, 13, 18, 19, 24, 25, 28, 37, 40, 44, 46, 47, 48, 52, 57, 58, 59, 60, 61, 66, 71, 88, 92, 105, 111, 118, 119, 125, 137, 139, 147, 152, 154, 156, 157, 169, 173, 174, 175, 177, 183, 192, 193, 194, 198, 209, 215, 220, 223, 224, 230, 231, 232, 233, 236, 241, 249, 250, 251, 254, 265, 271, 273, 274, 276, 281, 283, 284, 288, 291, 303, 310, 329, 330, 337, 345, 346, 347, 348, 349, 350, 352, 353, 354, 355, 356, 357, 358, 359, 362, 363, 367, 368, 369, 370, 371, 375, 376, 385, 396, 398, 399, 426, 439, 442, 446, 450, 457, 459, 471, 472, 496, 497, 499, 500, 502, 503, 506, 507, 508

administrative 9, 12, 58, 60, 224, 254, 347, 350, 367, 369, 370, 375, 507

environmental jurisdiction 496, 507

institutional 156, 157, 169, 174, 233, 249, 276, 303, 348, 349, 350, 358, 368, 370, 376, 503, 506, 507, 508

judicial 88, 118, 139

legal 4, 46, 52, 215, 233, 265, 281

legislative 119, 137, 147, 198, 220

procedural 6, 9, 496, 497, 498, 503, 507

SOE 236, 250

super-ministry 345, 349, 350

regions 7, 27, 31, 32, 41, 44, 47, 48, 50, 53, 54, 58, 69, 74, 84, 138, 139, 183, 185, 186, 187, 188, 189, 190, 194, 195, 196, 199, 200, 201, 202, 205, 206, 217, 218, 219, 221, 222, 295, 301, 327, 328, 335, 337, 339, 340, 344, 350, 356, 361, 363, 375, 391, 403, 467, 476, 480; see also individual region names

registered capital 170, 231

registration 38, 40, 43, 50, 52, 61, 73, 81, 145, 178, 352, 354, 360, 363, 365, 446, 447, 448, 449, 451, 452, 453, 454, 456, 457, 458, 459, 460, 465, 504

process 448, 451, 452, 453, 456

regular enforcement 309, 312, 324, 325, 330, 332, 342

regulated enterprises 310, 324, 333, 336, 343

regulated entities 211, 316, 325, 331, 332, 376, 501, 504

regulations 9, 10, 11, 22, 23, 24, 25, 26, 30, 38, 40, 41, 42, 43, 51, 55, 57, 58, 67, 69, 70, 71, 72, 77, 79, 88, 89, 95, 96, 97, 98, 100, 101, 104, 105, 108, 109, 110, 111, 112, 117, 119, 120, 122, 125, 126, 127, 129, 131, 132, 135, 136, 142, 143, 144, 145, 156, 164, 165, 171, 176, 179, 180, 188, 190, 192, 204, 205, 206, 207, 208, 209, 210, 211, 212, 221, 226, 227, 231, 232, 240, 241, 243, 247, 249, 250, 259, 260, 261, 266, 267, 268, 269, 271, 272, 275, 276, 277, 278, 279, 280, 282, 283, 287, 288, 289, 290, 293, 295, 296, 297, 298, 299, 300, 301, 302, 304, 306, 308, 310, 311, 312, 314, 316, 317, 318, 320, 322, 323, 325, 326, 329, 330, 331, 332, 333, 335, 336, 337, 338, 341, 342, 344, 346, 347, 348, 349, 350, 351, 352, 353, 354, 355, 357, 358, 359, 360, 361, 363, 364, 365, 366, 367, 368, 369, 370, 371, 372, 373, 374, 375, 376, 377, 383, 392, 401, 413, 414, 424, 428, 437, 439, 444, 446, 448, 454, 456, 459, 460, 462, 472, 473, 474, 475, 477, 478, 480, 483, 485, 486, 491, 493, 494, 503, 504, 507

regulatory documents 103, 143, 144, 145, 147, 151, 153

regulatory enforcement 13, 295, 296, 297, 298, 300, 302, 303, 304, 306, 308, 310, 311, 312, 314, 316, 318, 320, 322, 324, 325, 327, 358

contextual and institutional res

development [see chapter pp. 295–327]

Guangzhou 306

local 296, 303, 304, 306, 311, 315, 322, 365, 372

regulatory failures 260, 274, 275, 284, 292

regulatory frameworks 54, 302, 329, 331, 343, 376, 485

regulatory responsibilities 277, 278, 290, 303, 311

regulatory strategies 306, 309, 310, 312, 316

regulatory uncertainty 9, 376, 494

relocation 77, 82, 109, 113, 131, 141, 262, 285, 314, 317, 333, 336, 340, 342, 343

remedies 42, 56, 60, 69, 87, 184, 199, 208, 213, 263, 458

remuneration packages 310

renkou suzhi/suyang (人口素质/素养 [population quality]) 49, 51, 61, 62
repeal 78, 85, 87, 102, 111, 117, 145, 301, 302, 329, 413
reproduction 39, 41, 42, 45, 48, 55, 56, 450, 463, 464
reproductive autonomy 43, 57, 58, 59
reproductive policies 55, 57, 60
reproductive rights 43, 49, 52, 56
rescission 125, 134
residential areas 312, 313, 317, 337, 391
Residents' Committees (RCs; see also Jumin Weiyunhui 居民委员会)
residential communities 385, 389, 391, 393, 395, 410
residents 25, 27, 40, 42, 61, 115, 120, 121, 130, 146, 167, 169, 214, 219, 220, 309, 311, 312, 313, 315, 317, 318, 337, 338, 340, 341, 384, 385, 387, 389, 390, 391, 392, 393, 394, 395, 396, 397, 398, 399, 400, 401, 402, 403, 404, 405, 406, 407, 408, 409, 410, 418, 449
  local 27, 313, 318, 390, 392
resources 8, 9, 22, 38, 53, 56, 59, 77, 81, 87, 114, 118, 121, 122, 124, 125, 126, 127, 128, 130, 131, 133, 134, 135, 139, 145, 154, 157, 160, 161, 162, 166, 169, 170, 172, 174, 175, 176, 189, 192, 193, 197, 225, 235, 238, 239, 240, 252, 265, 273, 275, 277, 279, 281, 285, 286, 310, 311, 313, 315, 319, 322, 323, 325, 330, 334, 336, 340, 350, 363, 368, 370, 372, 373, 374, 375, 385, 388, 389, 392, 393, 394, 395, 397, 398, 399, 410, 416, 441, 443, 470, 471, 484, 494, 497, 499, 503
  allocation 235, 373
  allocation of 240
  cases 118, 122, 124, 126, 130, 131, 133, 135, 139
  human 77, 87, 273, 277
  limited 176, 310, 374, 388, 397, 503
  material 157, 372, 384
  natural 122, 125, 134, 145, 166, 285, 286
  protection 122, 160, 166, 169
responsibilities 8, 9, 39, 46, 47, 71, 85, 123, 173, 183, 223, 225, 226, 227, 228, 229, 236, 240, 241, 242, 243, 244, 245, 246, 247, 248, 252, 259, 260, 261, 262, 263, 266, 267, 268, 269, 270, 271, 272, 273, 274, 276, 277, 278, 281, 282, 283, 284, 287, 288, 289, 290, 291, 293, 294, 303, 305, 310, 311, 315, 323, 332, 338, 339, 342, 348, 354, 355, 357, 358, 359, 360, 367, 370, 376, 392, 395, 396, 399, 400, 405, 407, 411, 445, 455, 456, 477, 485, 491, 494, 497, 499
  joint 277, 289
  overlapping 278
  regulatory 277, 278, 290, 303, 311
  social 223, 225, 226, 227, 228, 229, 243, 244, 245, 248, 252, 338, 342
responsibility certificates 272, 283
restaurants 309, 312, 314, 318
restructuring institutional 9, 494
retail pharmacies 346, 347, 359, 360, 361, 362, 363, 364, 365, 368, 370, 371, 373, 374
retrials 103, 107, 111, 124, 130, 131, 135, 136
revenue 47, 169, 331, 336, 355, 357, 379, 474
  drug 355

tax 47, 169, 331

review 5, 6, 7, 12, 13, 17, 18, 20, 22, 24, 26, 28, 29, 30, 32, 34, 35, 36, 42, 45, 48, 54, 55, 56, 57, 59, 60, 63, 65, 67, 68, 70, 71, 72, 73, 75, 76, 80, 85, 86, 91, 92, 93, 94, 95, 96, 97, 98, 99, 100, 101, 102, 103, 104, 105, 106, 107, 108, 109, 110, 111, 112, 113, 114, 116, 117, 118, 119, 120, 121, 122, 123, 124, 125, 126, 128, 129, 130, 131, 132, 133, 134, 136, 137, 139, 140, 141, 142, 143, 144, 145, 146, 147, 151, 152

revocation 77, 123, 124, 125, 126, 130, 131, 137, 143, 360, 361, 362, 414, 428, 440

rhetoric 190, 270, 286, 400

rights 3, 4, 5, 8, 9, 10, 11, 12, 13, 19, 20, 25, 26, 32, 34, 35, 36, 40, 41, 42, 43, 46, 49, 51, 52, 54, 56, 57, 58, 59, 60, 65, 66, 67, 68, 69, 70, 71, 72, 73, 74, 75, 76, 77, 78, 79, 80, 81, 82, 83, 84, 85, 86, 87, 88, 89, 92, 94, 99, 100, 101, 108, 119, 120, 121, 123, 125, 130, 131, 132, 134, 135, 136, 137, 139, 142, 143, 145, 146, 154, 155, 156, 160, 163, 164, 166, 170, 173, 177, 183, 184, 185, 188, 203, 206, 208, 210, 212, 214, 215, 219, 220, 236, 239, 244, 250, 260, 263, 269, 275, 284, 289, 290, 313, 361, 371, 374, 381, 385, 387, 388, 390, 393, 394, 395, 399, 411, 414, 415, 416, 430, 434, 438, 442, 445, 448, 451, 453, 455, 456, 458, 459, 461, 462, 465, 466, 467, 468, 469, 470, 471, 472, 473, 474, 475, 476, 477, 478, 479, 480, 481, 484, 485, 486, 491, 492, 493, 494, 495, 496, 497, 498, 499, 500, 504, 505

citizen 3, 4, 5, 8, 9, 11, 60, 89, 381, 497, 500

data subjects 214, 219

due process 65, 67, 70, 71, 74, 75, 76, 77, 78, 81, 82, 88

environmental 145, 505

fundamental 66, 72, 84, 89, 92, 210, 469

hearing 68, 69, 73, 81, 83, 85, 86, 87, 146

holders 468, 486

individual 9, 10, 11, 12, 13, 58, 59, 60, 65, 89, 101, 188, 263, 458, 493, 494, 495, 496, 498, 499, 504

lawful 120, 123, 131, 154, 155, 163, 244, 289

legal 94, 125, 394

mining 132, 134, 135

property 125, 269, 288, 289, 361, 393, 394, 395, 465, 467

protection 8, 12, 13, 59, 65, 88, 89, 119, 184, 214, 263, 394, 459, 491, 495

reproductive 43, 49, 52, 56

women 46, 52, 455, 456, 459

risk aversion 384, 494, 498

risks 131, 140, 161, 167, 186, 187, 188, 189, 190, 191, 195, 196, 198, 199, 201, 211, 215, 217, 219, 220, 226, 227, 246, 249, 253, 262, 263, 265, 271, 273, 274, 275, 276, 279, 280, 281, 282, 284, 291, 311, 318, 332, 339, 341, 342, 363, 365, 384, 388, 401, 402, 406, 407, 416, 443, 474, 476, 483, 494, 498, 499, 502, 505

routine enforcement 330, 343

rule of law 8, 31, 32, 65, 66, 89, 92, 93, 102, 111, 119, 173, 222, 233, 246, 259, 260, 262, 267, 274, 275, 279, 284, 287, 353, 356, 376, 394, 425, 457, 476, 495, 499

rulemaking administrative 93, 94, 101, 111, 462, 480

rules 6, 8, 9, 12, 13, 23, 27, 31, 32, 35, 38, 43, 55, 65, 66, 69, 70, 71, 75, 79, 81, 84, 89, 91, 92, 93, 94,

95, 96, 97, 98, 99, 100, 101, 102, 103, 104, 105, 106, 107, 108, 109, 110, 111, 112, 114, 116, 117, 119, 125, 132, 139, 143, 144, 145, 158, 159, 160, 161, 162, 163, 164, 170, 173, 177, 179, 180, 184, 187, 190, 191, 192, 193, 195, 196, 203, 204, 206, 207, 209, 213, 214, 216, 220, 222, 224, 227, 233, 235, 239, 242, 246, 249, 254, 259, 260, 262, 263, 264, 266, 267, 268, 273, 274, 275, 279, 284, 287, 289, 290, 292, 302, 328, 329, 347, 352, 353, 356, 359, 364, 369, 372, 373, 375, 376, 384, 388, 391, 394, 395, 401, 403, 404, 407, 408, 414, 425, 428, 431, 434, 436, 442, 445, 452, 457, 462, 464, 465, 466, 468, 469, 471, 472, 475, 476, 480, 482, 491, 492, 493, 495, 499, 500, 501 administrative see administrative rules

legal 103, 117, 233, 289, 290, 388, 492, 501

rural areas 40, 41, 43, 44, 53, 58, 451

rural village committees 40, 61, 269, 272 (Cunmin Weiyuanhui [村民 委员会])

S

Saburo Ienaga 27, 28

safeguards 4, 7, 35, 36, 42, 66, 101, 111, 141, 146, 155, 159, 163, 173, 177, 184, 192, 193, 194, 198, 201, 205, 207, 208, 211, 212, 213, 217, 222, 243, 412, 414, 415, 421, 437, 438, 443, 469, 476, 491, 494, 504

procedural 7, 42, 184, 198, 222

safety 51, 120, 121, 123, 129, 131, 142, 154, 160, 167, 168, 169, 177, 179, 244, 248, 259, 260, 266, 271, 272, 276, 277, 278, 279, 282, 289, 290, 312, 314, 318, 348, 349, 350, 355, 364, 365, 374, 393, 398, 404, 406, 411, 414, 427, 428, 486, 494, 499

drinking water 123, 129, 131, 300

drug 121, 154, 160, 167, 177, 260, 348, 350, 355, 374

security 5, 10, 43, 44, 45, 46, 49, 51, 52, 71, 77, 87, 155, 171, 175, 183, 184, 185, 186, 187, 188, 189, 190, 191, 196, 197, 198, 200, 201, 202, 203, 205, 206, 207, 208, 209, 210, 211, 213, 215, 216, 218, 219, 220, 222, 227, 269, 277, 278, 289, 314, 318, 340, 355, 357, 363, 398, 408, 411, 413, 414, 415, 416, 422, 424, 425, 426, 427, 428, 430, 431, 432, 433, 434, 435, 436, 437, 438, 439, 440, 442, 443, 444, 476, 480, 483, 484, 494, 504

assessment 185, 188, 189, 198, 209, 210, 218

national 185, 186, 188, 189, 191, 202, 203, 205, 207, 208, 210, 211, 213, 222, 476

prior review 185, 188, 189, 198, 209, 210

segmented supervision 349, 350, 352, 376

seizure 128, 300

self-defence 430, 432, 440

self-examination 145, 284, 286

self-policing capacity 396, 398

self-regulation 70, 207, 208, 474, 475, 485

self-regulatory bodies 390

self-regulatory constraints 463, 474, 476, 485

senior management 245, 246, 247

sensitive personal data/information 186, 188, 189, 190

sentencing 426, 434, 437, 438

manuals 434, 437, 438

separation of powers 19, 21, 152, 246

servers 27, 49, 50, 52, 174, 193, 196, 198, 202, 203, 451, 452

service providers 207, 401, 461, 468, 469, 470, 471, 472, 473, 480, 486

services 18, 20, 37, 41, 45, 49, 50, 52, 61, 124, 134, 141, 146, 171, 183, 186, 188, 191, 198, 207, 227, 232, 237, 246, 259, 261, 273, 309, 324, 336, 350, 353, 355, 358, 362, 365, 376, 377, 390, 392, 393, 395, 397, 399, 400, 401, 403, 404, 405, 419, 437, 438, 442, 451, 461, 462, 468, 469, 470, 471, 472, 473, 476, 477, 478, 480, 483, 485, 486, 491

social 52, 227, 399, 400

settlement of disputes 142, 389

sex education 50

Shaanxi Province 167, 169, 170, 403, 438, 440

Shandong 69, 74, 82, 86, 346, 433, 434, 435, 436

Shanghai 50, 74, 75, 98, 121, 122, 123, 124, 126, 127, 130, 226, 227, 245, 385, 387, 395, 404, 406, 409, 410, 437, 465

Shanxi 156, 168, 346, 434, 435

shareholders 170, 224, 225, 228, 230, 231, 232, 237, 241, 242, 243, 244, 245, 250, 251, 253

activism 230

dominant 230, 245

meetings 230, 231, 241, 250

shehui fuyang fei (社会抚养费 [social maintenance fees]) 39, 40, 61

Shen Jiaben 18

Shen Xixian 120

shengli weisheng jiaoyu (生理卫 生教育 [physiological hygiene education, a term used for basic sex education]) 50, 61

shenpan ting (审判庭 [courts]) 37

Shenzhen 3, 175, 190, 191, 196, 198, 200, 202, 207, 213, 218, 226, 227, 245, 401, 418, 428, 445, 465, 482, 491

shequ (社区 [residential community]) 389, 390, 391, 393, 394, 397, 398, 399, 400, 401, 402, 403, 405, 409, 410

shequ jingwu (社区警务 [community policing]) 397, 410

shutdowns 131, 328, 331, 334, 342

Sichuan Province 43, 73, 111, 325, 430, 431

*sifa jianyi (*司法建议 [judicial proposal]) 102, 112

siji sanshen zhi (四级三审制 [fourinstance, three level system]) 37

Singapore model 230, 231, 251

'sinking' (xiachen 下沉) 398, 401, 402, 410

SMPA (State Medical and Pharmaceutical Administration) 349, 351, 353, 377

SMPGA (State Medical Pharmaceutical General Administration) 348, 349, 351, 353, 377

social attitudes 53

social conflict 168, 234, 397

social cost 225, 331

social development 227, 240, 374

social distancing 383, 384, 391, 396, 401, 402, 408, 428, 441

measures (SDMs) 383, 384, 385, 389, 391, 393, 395, 401, 404, 405, 406, 407, 408, 427, 441
social dynamics 341
social groups 59, 390, 392, 450
social instability 58, 168, 456
soft law 198, 201, 220, 253
SOMA (Social Order Maintenance Act) 442, 444
sources of enforcement pressure 306, 311, 314, 318
sovereignty 7, 35, 183, 184, 185, 186, 187, 191, 202, 213, 214, 215, 218, 221, 222
data 7, 184, 185, 191, 222
digital 187, 221
national 184, 187
parliamentary 35
Soviet model 65, 251
SPC (Supreme People's Court) 66, 67, 71, 72, 73, 76, 84, 88, 93, 94, 97, 98, 99, 100, 101, 102, 105, 106, 107, 108, 109, 110, 111, 113, 117, 118, 119, 120, 121, 122, 123, 124, 126, 127, 129, 130, 131, 132, 133, 134, 135, 136, 137, 138, 139, 141, 142, 144, 146, 158, 159, 162, 173, 424, 440, 447, 452, 458
Gazette 66, 71, 72, 73, 76, 84, 97, 105, 119, 120, 121, 132, 133
Interpretation of the ALL 97, 99, 101, 102, 120, 144
Special Administrative Regions (SARs) 186, 189, 190, 191, 194, 195, 199, 203, 206, 209, 295
special rectification 283, 284, 285, 286, 287, 290, 292
specialized courts 6, 7, 442, 496
spouses 10, 55, 448, 452, 453
SPP (Supreme People's Procuratorate) 153, 154, 155, 158, 159, 160, 167, 168, 169, 170, 171, 172, 173, 174, 175, 176
stability 3, 4, 10, 13, 22, 26, 44, 48, 53, 56, 58, 66, 78, 88, 89, 106, 137, 156, 168, 234, 240, 260, 261, 263, 264, 273, 274, 275, 284, 292, 340, 349, 359, 394, 399, 402, 410, 421, 441, 444, 450, 456, 466, 495, 499, 500, 504
maintenance 78, 88, 261, 399, 442, 444
social 10, 13, 48, 56, 66, 106, 137, 156, 168, 234, 274, 292, 410
staff establishment 310, 313, 315
stakeholder board 228, 229, 240, 243, 246, 253
stakeholder committee 228, 229, 232, 233, 234, 236, 237, 240, 241, 242, 244, 247, 248, 249, 252, 253, 503
members 228, 233, 247
stakeholders 190, 198, 201, 209, 212, 223, 224, 227, 228, 229, 232, 233, 234, 236, 237, 238, 239, 240, 241, 242, 243, 244, 246, 247, 248, 249, 250, 251, 252, 253, 254, 392, 394, 405, 462, 502, 503
interests 227, 229, 241, 242, 243, 244, 247, 248, 252, 254
representation 223, 224, 226, 238, 240, 242, 245, 246, 248, 249, 253, 254, 502
implementation in China 224, 227, 228, 229, 232, 234, 236, 238, 241, 242, 244, 245, 248, 250, 252, 254
within boards of directors 223, 228, 229, 232, 233, 234, 236, 237, 240, 241, 242, 243, 244, 246, 247, 248, 249, 252, 253, 503

within party committees 223, 224, 227, 228, 229, 232, 234, 236, 238, 240, 242, 244, 246, 248, 250, 252, 253, 254

standard contracts 186, 188, 189, 195, 197, 198, 199, 204, 208, 216, 217, 219, 221

standard contractual clauses (SCCs) 188, 197, 198, 199, 201, 204, 205

standards 9, 18, 31, 51, 54, 59, 65, 75, 80, 99, 108, 109, 114, 116, 117, 119, 127, 142, 145, 178, 184, 186, 187, 188, 189, 194, 195, 197, 198, 199, 201, 202, 203, 204, 205, 206, 208, 211, 213, 216, 217, 218, 219, 221, 222, 226, 227, 228, 232, 244, 245, 246, 250, 253, 278, 280, 288, 300, 309, 310, 313, 314, 315, 326, 327, 330, 331, 332, 333, 336, 337, 338, 339, 340, 342, 343, 354, 355, 362, 363, 365, 366, 369, 371, 387, 390, 405, 406, 407, 469, 472, 473, 480, 483, 485, 486, 487, 492

baseline 205, 208

emission 127, 327, 333, 337, 339, 340

enhanced 336, 342

environmental 252, 326, 330, 339, 342, 343

international 197, 407

legal 9, 59, 178, 473

of review 99, 108, 117, 119

standing 3, 4, 5, 6, 9, 12, 13, 14, 26, 30, 32, 33, 35, 42, 46, 49, 57, 67, 68, 89, 91, 96, 97, 117, 119, 120, 121, 151, 153, 154, 155, 156, 164, 166, 170, 173, 179, 180, 186, 199, 201, 216, 219, 220, 222, 224, 238, 254, 260, 261, 267, 269, 270, 271, 272, 274, 279, 281, 282, 283, 296

SOEs (State Owned Enterprises) 8, 170, 223, 224, 225, 226, 227, 228, 229, 230, 231, 232, 233, 234, 235, 236, 237, 238, 239, 240, 241, 242, 243, 244, 245, 246, 247, 248, 249, 250, 251, 252, 253, 254, 311, 314, 331, 334, 335, 338, 339, 340, 341, 342, 343, 344, 502

state-owned property protection 156, 160, 169

state policy 4, 45, 59, 499

state power 4, 5, 9, 10, 11, 58, 59, 65, 66, 122, 250, 254, 259, 374, 390, 496, 499, 504, 508

statistics 11, 210, 219, 304, 395, 422, 423, 424, 425, 449, 455, 506, 507

statutes 19, 22, 35, 38, 67, 72, 95, 96, 97, 98, 103, 105, 108, 109, 110, 112, 126, 128, 130, 187, 201, 203, 206, 221, 267, 366, 369, 370, 372 (see also legislation)

statutory duties/obligations 122, 132, 147, 166, 176, 289

street-level bureaucrats 8, 11, 296, 297, 501

street-level enforcement units 298, 317, 329

stress cumulative 333, 341, 342

structural problems 59, 263

subscribers 470, 471

subsidies 52, 53, 78, 234, 335, 336, 395

substandard drugs 355, 356

substantive legality 71, 88, 151, 181

suburban districts 312, 313, 315, 316

Sun Guihua 122, 123, 144

Sun Shihua 420

super-ministry reform 345, 349, 350, 376

supervision 26, 70, 71, 72, 86, 93, 96, 100, 104, 111, 116, 117, 122, 132, 133, 134, 144, 145, 147, 152, 153, 154, 156, 157, 164, 167, 168, 169, 172, 173, 175, 181, 190, 199,

224, 226, 230, 231, 235, 239, 243, 246, 254, 262, 264, 270, 274, 276, 277, 279, 280, 281, 284, 285, 286, 287, 290, 292, 304, 305, 309, 326, 335, 339, 346, 350, 352, 355, 356, 357, 358, 359, 363, 367, 370, 372, 376, 393, 398, 401, 415, 480, 483

administrative 86, 117, 157, 199

drug 346, 357, 367

environmental 133, 304, 305, 335

judicial 93, 100, 111

legal 122, 153, 172, 181

segmented 350, 352, 376

Supervision Commission 152, 156, 181, 262, 284, 290

supervisors 226, 242, 245, 246, 247, 253, 254

board of 226, 241, 245, 246, 247, 253, 254

supervisory institutions/bodies 103, 106, 123, 415

Supreme People's Court (see SPC) Supreme People's Procuratorate see (SPP)

surveillance 8, 9, 39, 54, 205, 207, 208, 217, 338, 343, 385, 389, 399, 405, 408, 420, 496

mass 389, 408

suspension 114, 124, 126, 128, 135, 141, 278, 290, 315, 360, 480, 497, 501

sustainable development 119, 147, 227, 228, 235, 246, 295, 299, 303, 304

synthesized market regulation 346, 351, 367

systemic constraints 8

T

Taiwan 25, 264, 313, 406, 442, 444

takedown procedures/process 461–2, 462, 467, 469–73, 474, 476, 478–80, 486

targets

selection 324, 342

veto 274, 283, 291, 293

tax revenues 47, 169, 331

TCM (see Traditional Chinese Medicine)

team leaders 306, 310–6, 318–9, 323

deputy 305–6, 312–3, 315–9

tensions 3–4, 6–7, 58–9, 183–4, 250, 252–3, 494, 497

social 4, 60, 77, 87, 88, 157, 499

theoretical frameworks 12, 333, 335, 505

three-child policy 39, 49–50, 55

Tiktok 467, 474, 478

'toilet revolution' (cesuo geming [厕所革命]) 269, 288, 293

top-down administrative reforms 369

torture 10, 415, 419, 421, 435

townships 124, 129, 160, 170, 317, 319, 323, 428

toxic drugs 353–4, 361

trade 204, 218, 349, 360

digital 183, 185, 191

global 249–50

international 189–90, 218

trade unions 46, 239

Traditional Chinese Medicine (TCM) 348, 361, 364, 385

transfers 135, 188–200, 202, 204–6, 210–5

data 188–9, 208–11

international/overseas 191

U

urban communities 385, 391–4
urban management 307, 389, 394, 405
US (see United States)
user-uploaded content 468, 471

V

vertical state-citizen relationships 7–8, 12, 497
veto targets 274, 283, 291, 293
videos 127, 171, 419, 431, 434, 439, 461–4, 467, 474, 478, 481
village committees 40, 61, 269, 272
villages 40, 55, 261, 269, 271–3, 283, 317, 431, 436–7
violence 311, 421, 438, 448, 451–2
  domestic 448, 451–2
  physical 421
  police 421, 438
volume-based exemptions 186, 189
voluntary compliance 42, 50, 323, 389, 396
volunteers 395, 401–4, 409
votes 21, 241, 242, 290, 391

W

warlords 5, 11, 17, 20–1, 26, 33, 35, 500
water 122–3, 125, 127, 129, 131, 135, 142, 166–7, 176, 277, 296, 298–301, 315, 318, 329–30, 338
  pollution 142, 298–301, 329–30
  resources 135, 166, 176, 277
Water Pollution Prevention Control Law see WPPCL
weak-form judicial review 6, 100, 103, 106, 111, 493, 500
WeChat 304, 313, 403, 435
Weibo 313, 474–5
weifa xingzheng xingwei (违法行政行为 [illegal administrative activity]) 160, 181
weiwen (维稳 [to maintain social stability)) 399, 410, 421, 441, 444
welfare 39, 43, 48, 51, 54, 191, 225, 244, 251–2, 254, 332, 340, 374, 404, 410, 445, 452, 497
  social 39, 43, 48, 54, 225, 307, 332, 340
Wenliang Li (Li Wenliang [李文亮] 12 October 1985 – 7 February 2020) 417, 428, 440
winning rates 136–7, 174, 176
Winning the Blue Sky Defense War 327, 338
WIPO (World Intellectual Property Organization), 479, 482
wives 456
World Intellectual Property Organization, see WIPO
women 10–1, 40–2, 45–7, 51–2, 54–6, 59, 445, 448–52, 454–6, 458–9, 504
  rights 46, 52, 455–6, 459
  rural 451
  urban 450
work health and safety 260, 276–7, 282, 289–90
Work Safety Law 276, 278–9, 289
workloads 8, 272, 280, 309, 317–8, 366–7
  excessive 272, 318
workplaces 40, 46, 49, 52, 59, 270, 276–7, 314
workstyles 271, 286, 291
World Intellectual Property Organization see WIPO

WPPCL (Water Pollution Prevention and Control Law) 142, 300

Wu Tingfang 18

Wuhan 387–8, 401–2, 405, 417, 428

Wuhe County Government 124, 141

X

Xi Jinping 92, 259, 262–8, 271, 278, 283–6, 291, 295, 299, 327, 338, 345, 350, 401

xiachen (下沉 [to sink]) 401, 410

*xian li hou bing (*先礼后兵 [courtesy before force]) 162, 181

Xiaoshan (萧山 [in Zhejiang Province]) 130, 146

xietiao (协调 [coordination]) 140, 147, 175

xieyi lihun (协议离婚 [divorce by mutual consent]) 445, 460

xinfang (信访 [letters and visits, petitions]) 120, 142, 280, 311

xinguan (新冠" [i.e., the Chinese abbreviated term for COVID-19]) 426–7, 444

xingwei (行为 [conduct or action as in *xingzheng xingwei* 行政行为, executive or administrative action]) 93, 112, 160

xingzheng buzuowei (行政不作为 [administrative nonfeasance] 160, 181

xingzheng fuyi (行政复议 [administrative reconsideration/review]) 42, 147, 414

xingzheng gongyi susong (行政公益诉讼 [administrative public interest litigation]) 153, 158–159, 163, 166–170, 172–176, 178

Y

yousheng youyu (优生优育 [eugenical childbearing]) 51, 62

YouTube 467, 474–5, 478

Yuan Shikai 20–21, 26, 30, 33

Yuexiu (越秀) 306–7, 309–11, 320

yufangxing gongyi susong (预防性公益诉讼 preventative public interest litigation]) 167, 181

Yunnan Higher People's Court 124, 131–2, 135

Z

Zengcheng 305–6, 308, 316–9, 321

Zhejiang 85, 100–2, 109, 115–6, 122–3, 144, 146, 156, 436, 439

Zhongguo Renmin Zhengzhi Xieshang Huiyi (中国人民政治协商会议 [Chinese People's Political Consultative Conference]) 161

Zhongguo Yiyao Gongsi 347–8

zhunsheng zheng (准生证 [birth permit] 40, 50, 62

www.ingramcontent.com/pod-product-compliance
Lightning Source LLC
LaVergne TN
LVHW092116300926
849161LV00002B/144
* 9 7 8 1 6 1 6 1 9 7 0 3 2 *